California Dreams and Realities

Readings for Critical Thinkers and Writers

THIRD EDITION

Sonia Maasik

University of California, Los Angeles

Jack Solomon

California State University, Northridge

Bedford/St. Martin's

Boston ◆ New York

For Bedford/St. Martin's

Developmental Editor: Genevieve Hamilton
Production Editor: Ara Salibian
Production Supervisor: Chris Gross
Senior Marketing Manager: Rachel Falk
Editorial Assistant: Jeffrey Voccola
Production Assistant: Amy Derjue
Copyeditor: Rosemary Winfield
Text Design: Claire Seng-Niemoeller
Cover Design: Billy Boardman
Cover Art: Redwood Trees, © Photonica/Dana Spaeth. *Traffic on Golden Gate Bridge,* ©
    Photonica/Bilderberg. *Harvesting Chardonnay Grapes,* © Jim Sugar/CORBIS.
    Mother Pushing Daughter on Swing, © Anne W. Krause/CORBIS. *Crowded Harbor
    Freeway,* © Bill Varie/CORBIS. *Che Guevera Wall Painting,* © Stephanie Maze/
    CORBIS. *Boy Lying on Skateboard,* © Photonica/Leland Bobbe.
Composition: Macmillan India
Printing and Binding: Haddon Craftsmen, Inc., an R.R. Donnelley & Sons Company

President: Joan E. Feinberg
Editorial Director: Denise B. Wydra
Editor in Chief: Karen S. Henry
Director of Marketing: Karen Melton Soeltz
Director of Editing, Design, and Production: Marcia Cohen
Managing Editor: Elizabeth M. Schaaf

Library of Congress Control Number: 2004107881

For information, write: Bedford/St. Martin's, 75 Arlington Street, Boston, MA 02116
(617-399-4000)

ISBN: 0–312–41289–4
EAN: 978–0–312–41289–0

Acknowledgments

Text

Blake Allmendinger, "All about Eden" from *Reading California: Art, Image, and Identity
    1900–2000.* Copyright © 2000 by Museum Associates, Los Angeles County
    Museum of Art and the Regents of the University of California. Reprinted by
    permission of the Los Angeles County Museum of Art.

*Acknowledgments and copyrights are continued at the back of the book on pages
441–44, which constitute an extension of the copyright page. It is a violation of the
law to reproduce these selections by any means whatsoever without the written
permission of the copyright holder.*

Preface for Instructors

The third edition of *California Dreams and Realities* appears at a peculiar time in California history. Hard upon the heels of a virtually unprecedented recall election that ousted one governor and replaced him with another—who, not so coincidentally, happened to be a Hollywood superstar—the Golden State finds itself in a somewhat ambiguous position. On the one hand, California's economy is in tolerable shape, with a booming real estate market and an improving employment picture, but on the other, its books are badly out of balance, budget cuts are slicing ever deeper into educational and social services, tax increases have been ruled out, and higher education is paying the price.

Because each edition of *California Dreams and Realities* seeks to reflect in a thematic way the overall state of the Golden State, choosing a theme for the third edition was a bit challenging. Things were much more clearcut when we prepared the first edition of this book (the state seemed to be falling apart) and the second (happy days were here again in the wake of the dot-com boom). Now, things aren't so certain. But one thing is clear: with the election of Arnold Schwarzenegger to the governorship, California has once again riveted the nation's attention, blazing a trail that has made the politics of the recall as enticing to other states as Proposition 13's tax revolt was in the 1970s, while continuing a California tradition of electing celebrities to public office—and tempting other states to do the same.

The theme for the third edition of *California Dreams and Realities* is, accordingly, "California: The Bellwether State." It's an old cliché that what happens in America happens in California first, but events suggest that this is more than a cliché. Whether we look at the electricity crisis of 2000–01, which served as a warning to other states of the perils of energy deregulation, or at California's demographic revolution, which, having produced a statewide population that has no racial majority, presages a similar national demographic transformation, we see that where California goes, so goes the nation.

To amplify this theme, we have added a new chapter to the third edition of *California Dreams and Realities*: "Exporting Culture: California and the Popular Imagination." The purpose of this chapter is to highlight the explicit ways in which California has been a shaper of the national consciousness through its leading role in the making of American popular culture. Readings on the Hollywood film industry, California car culture, and California commodity consumption all trace the starring role California has long played in American society, as well as the attitudes toward California that may be found in the rest of the country.

Another new chapter, "(Mis)Managing California: Politics, Environment, and the State of the State," contains two readings specifically devoted to the recall election of 2003, with a focus on the way that historic event looked to the rest of America. And the book's first two chapters— "California Dreaming: Myths of the Golden Land" and "The Great Migration: Immigrants in California History"—offer readings exploring the way that the "California dream" is both a heightened version of the American dream and a model for dreamers everywhere.

To guide students in their critical understanding of the Bellwether State, we include a general introduction, which sets out the theme of the book and situates California within the American imagination as a place where big things happen and often happen first. At the same time, the general introduction establishes the dual nature of the California experience: alongside all of the glamorous dreams stand gritty realities that Californians—and all Americans—are being challenged to address.

Individual chapter introductions provide background for the topics raised in the book's six chapters, along with frameworks for critical thinking and judgment. Some of the issues your students will confront in these chapters are controversial, so it is important to note that our chapter introductions are designed to stimulate lively classroom discussion and essay writing, not to dictate the terms or conclusions of those discussions and essays. The relative neutrality of our contextualizations does not mean that your students should be neutral: the point is for them to learn how to construct strong arguments to defend what may be passionately held positions.

The purpose of the readings, then, is to encourage students to think and write critically about issues that may strike close to home for them— issues like school testing, for example, or affirmative action in university admissions policies. Some of the readings are op-ed pieces that appear to provide solutions to the problems they address, but we do not intend them as ready-made answers to the dilemmas your students may be considering. Indeed, in some cases we have paired diametrically opposed opinion pieces to show how arguments can be constructed for different sides of a controversy. In other cases, the selections present striking arguments that invite rebuttal or further support.

There are no easy answers to the questions the readings raise—given the state's current problems, there hardly can be—and the exercises and assignments we provide in the editorial apparatus are not intended to supply such answers. Rather, they are designed to guide students in analytical thinking and argumentation, leading them to devise their own solutions to complex problems and, more important, reasoned justifications for those solutions. Some assignments call for in-class debates, others for formal essays, and still others for research. At the close of each chapter, we propose topics for more extensive research assignments.

What's New in the Third Edition

Like California itself, the third edition of *California Dreams and Realities* has evolved since the publication of its first edition. Of course, we have updated the readings to reflect the events of the twenty-first century, with two-thirds of the selections new to this edition. We have also brought a greater historical range to the readings, as well as a broader geographical diversity, especially represented in a new chapter on "The Geography of Desire: California and the Sense of Place." Responding to the increasing use of images to stimulate student thinking and writing, this edition also includes thematically related chapter-opening images and individual images within each chapter for student analysis and discussion. In the Introduction, a new section, "Developing Active Reading Strategies," provides guidance to student reading, focusing on one of the most popular selections in our last edition, Jack Lopez's "Of *Cholos* and Surfers."

We have preserved the second edition's concern with the environment and the politics of water in the Golden State, issues we have folded into "(Mis)Managing California: Politics, Environment, and the State of the State" in order to demonstrate to students how the popular discontent that led to the recall election of 2003 can be connected to broader political and environmental issues within the state. Our new chapter, "Exporting Culture: California and the Popular Imagination," looks outward to examine the effect of California on the rest of the nation.

Resources for Teaching

We have written a supplementary instructor's manual, *Editors' Notes to Accompany California Dreams and Realities*, to provide a context for the book's selections and to highlight what we believe to be the essential issues it raises. Because some of the readings in the book are controversial, calling for classroom debate and argumentation, we have not attempted in the manual to give the "right answers" to the suggested assignments. We do discuss each chapter and each selection, suggest ways of presenting readings to the class, and include assignments ranging from journal entries to in-class debates and extended research exercises.

New to *California Dreams and Realities* is a companion website at bedfordstmartins.com/californiadreams. Here students can find tools to help them extend their work with the book, including annotated research links for each chapter and interactive tutorials on the research process. The complete text of the instructor's manual is also available to instructors on this website.

Acknowledgments

We are grateful to our California colleagues who have chosen *California Dreams and Realities* for their classes, and are especially thankful to those who took the time and trouble to suggest improvements for the third edition. In many cases, these suggestions came in the form of actual articles for possible inclusion in the new edition—a kindness of which we are particularly appreciative. These reviewers include Melissa D. Aaron, California State Polytechnic University at Pomona; Dr. Randal Beeman, Bakersfield College; Jennifer Brezina, College of the Canyons; Kristin Brunnemer, University of California, Riverside; Sean Connelly, lecturer, University of California, Riverside; Mona Field, Glendale Community College; Mary G. Forte, California Polytechnic State University, San Luis Obispo; Marc J. Garcia-Martinez, Allan Hancock College; Ellen M. Gil-Gomez, California State University, San Bernardino; Cheryl Honeycutt, California State University, Fullerton; Ingrid Johnson, Modesto Junior College; Dimitri Keriotis, Modesto Junior College; Vincent T. Latino, California State University, Sacramento; and Diana Slampyak, University of California, Riverside.

The third edition of *California Dreams and Realities* constitutes our seventh Bedford/St. Martin's text, and we are, as always, indebted to many people there for making our new book a reality, from Joan Feinberg, who now carries on the visionary tradition that Chuck Christensen established with the founding of Bedford Books, to Genevieve Hamilton, our editor, who guided our project to completion. Thanks are due also to Ara Salibian for his handling of the production of our manuscript, to Claire Seng-Niemoller for her design of the text, to Joan Scafarello for securing permissions for the readings and the images in the book, and to Jeff Voccola and Judy Ashkenaz. These projects are never easy: our thanks to everyone who helped bring ours to a successful conclusion.

Brief Contents

Contents

2. The Great Migration
Immigrants in California History   81

4. The Geography of Desire
California and the Sense of Place   229

5. Exporting Culture
California and the Popular Imagination   315

6. (Mis)Managing California
Politics, Environment, and the State
of the State 379

Introduction

CALIFORNIA — THE BELLWETHER STATE

First there was the boom, then the bust. Then there was another boom, fueled principally by a high-tech economic explosion that went from "dot-com" to "dot-bomb" in less than five years. Meanwhile, a decade of immigration was working a demographic revolution, witnessing enormous growth in the state's Hispanic and Asian populations as the percentage of white residents declined. And with the new millennium came intractable budget crises and reductions in state spending on education even as property values, once again, soared.

Everything that we have summarized above happened within the state of California in the period between 1988 and the publication of this book. But it also happened in Massachusetts, where an economic "miracle" in the 1980s collapsed into an economic malaise in the early 1990s, which itself was reversed by a high-tech boom in the mid-1990s along Route 128, which, like California's Silicon Valley, lies in the north-central-coastal region of the state. Again, like California, Massachusetts has become home to a growing number of immigrant residents from Asia and Latin America, and it too is facing severe budgetary shortfalls that are being translated into cuts in education spending that are affecting students across the state.

Our point is that California, despite being the most populous and wealthy state in the union, is not unique. What happens here happens elsewhere. But while California is not unique, it is special, because what happens in the rest of the country so often happens first in California. After all, it is California's Silicon Valley that provided the prototype for high-tech development throughout America. It is California that has set all the trends for real estate booms and busts that are now common throughout the nation. It is California that has been on the cutting edge of immigration and consequent demographic change, and it is California that launched a wave of tax revolts throughout the country with the passage of Proposition 13. Indeed, California's influence on national politics has been profound, having produced some of the first show-biz politicians, including the election of George Murphy to the U.S. Senate, Sonny Bono to the U.S. Congress, Ronald Reagan to the presidency, and now Arnold Schwarzenegger to the governorship in an historic recall election that has prompted other celebrities, from Nick Clooney to Jerry Springer, to flirt with candidacies of their own.

More profoundly, thanks to its fundamental role in the development of the modern entertainment industry, it is California that has been shaping the dreams and desires of Americans ever since Hollywood was transformed from a quiet suburb of Los Angeles into the center of the culture industry. Indeed, from the days of the gold rush of 1849, California has stood as a special, gaudier, and more glamorous case of the American dream, holding a place in the American imagination that enables us to speak of the "California dream" in a way that no other state can boast. After all, The Mamas and the Papas didn't top the charts with a song called "Massachusetts Dreaming," and no one has ever crooned about the "Hotel Colorado."

California's special place in American history and consciousness can be attributed, in large part, to its geography. Lying at the far west of the West, California has represented the ultimate frontier to a nation built upon a frontier history and mythology. Of course, Washington and Oregon also stand at the terminus of the trails that led Americans west in the great migrations of the nineteenth century, but with its milder climate and richer geographical diversity, not to mention its gold, silver, and, a bit later on, oil reserves, California has stood out as the place where the American dream of upward social and economic mobility has combined with that frontier-induced restlessness, that itchy-footed desire to move forever onward, westward toward greener pastures, that has so characterized American history.

Which is why so many Californians have come from someplace else. In a state of over thirty-five million people, proportionately few can make the proud boast of having been born in California, and fewer still can trace their ancestors to California birthplaces. This makes California the ultimate immigrant state in a nation founded upon immigration. At first, this immigration came from the eastern and midwestern portions of the country—especially in southern California, where midwestern immigrants transformed the sleepy pueblo of Los Angeles into a sprawling metropolis of loosely linked communities, many of which, like Pomona and Santa Monica, were built to resemble the midwestern towns from which the bulk of their citizens came. More recently, this immigration has become international, with migrants from all over the world flocking to a California that still stands, in spite of so many blows to its image, as the Golden State, the place where the rainbow ends.

Thus, it is no surprise that the state with the Golden Gate should hold such a special place in the land of the Statue of Liberty. California could almost be called "America, concentrated," and so it is inevitable that so much that happens in America happens in California first. We cannot claim to be at the forefront of every development and trend in the nation, but a disproportionate share of the national destiny certainly seems to lie within our borders, making California a place worth paying special attention to, especially if one is a Californian.

And that is why we have written this book, because as Californians you are well situated to understand the many issues that are of interest within the state and beyond, and so are especially prepared to think and write critically about those issues. From the dream that has drawn so many to California, to the controversies over immigration, education, and the management of our natural resources, California offers a wealth of relevant topics to college students who are already participants in those controversies, as well as in the California culture that has proven to be such a model for the rest of America. To put this another way, if you are going to study critical thinking and writing in a California college or university, you might as well start with California itself as a subject to think and write about.

Writing California

Think for a moment about what California means to you. Is it just a place to live in and attend school, or is there more to it than that? Do you plan, or at least hope, to stay once you have completed your studies? Why or why not? What brought you, or your family, to this state in the first place? Did California keep its golden promise, or have you been disappointed somehow? Such questions, which can be asked of the residents of any state, are especially appropriate for California because it continues to be a place to which more people come annually than leave. For a brief time during the depths of the economic recession of the early to mid-1990s, it looked like the outflow of population would for the first time surpass the inflow, but that brief glitch in the history of the California dream has since disappeared, and California has reassumed its dizzying rise as the most populous state in the union.

But this testimony to the endurance of the dream also points to many a reality that is less than dreamlike. Overpopulation has brought environmental degradation and social strife, the specter of a water-deprived future, traffic jams, road rage, and racial division—not to mention sky-high real estate prices and rental rates. All of these realities, and many more which threaten to tarnish the dream, are issues that you are already confronting in your daily lives and will continue to confront as you pursue your own versions of the California dream.

With the dream so threatened by so many harsh realities, it is difficult to come up with simple remedies for California's current problems. Take the ever-rising cost of student fees in California's public colleges and universities. You may feel that the obvious solution is to raise taxes rather than to keep on raising fees, but how would you persuade a non-student who doesn't want taxes raised? To persuade someone who does not already agree with you, you need to be able to construct a cogent argument in favor of your position.

Learning how to construct cogently persuasive arguments is one of the goals of your first-year composition class. Another is to enhance your confidence in self-expression—in the articulation of your own thoughts and experiences. Your composition class is also designed to train you in the careful close reading and comprehension of texts, both expository and literary, as well as to prepare you to engage in collaborative learning and research. *California Dreams and Realities* will help you accomplish these goals. Each chapter focuses on a current California issue, presenting background information and conflicting views that can help you shape your own arguments, as well as literary selections that can help you explore the issues in more personal and poetic ways.

To start you on your project of writing California, the first chapter, "California Dreaming: Myths of the Golden Land," presents readings that invite you to explore the ways in which California has traditionally figured in our cultural imagination. Here you will find reflections on the California promise written from such diverse viewpoints as that of a fourth-generation Sacramento aristocrat and of an immigrant just crossing the border. The history of California, from its first appearance as a place name in literature, through the gold rush and into the traffic-congested present, is also sketched out in this chapter, offering an imaginative background for many of the issues that appear in the book's subsequent chapters.

Chapter 2, "The Great Migration: Immigrants in California History," focuses on the people whom the California dream has attracted through the years, including immigrants from Latin America, Asia, and the Near East. These readings explore not only the lives and the personal histories of California's immigrants but also the political and cultural controversies that immigration continues to raise in California discourse.

Next, Chapter 3, "The Best-Laid Plans: Education and the California Dream," extends the discussion of many of the issues explored in Chapter 2, with readings on affirmative action and the dilemmas of studying in a second language, while looking also at the impact of ever-higher public college costs and of the new testing regime that may soon determine whether or not California's high school students receive their diplomas.

Chapter 4, "The Geography of Desire: California and the Sense of Place," follows with a look at California's many regions and communities, from the suburban tracts of Irvine to the sprawling oil fields of Taft, and from the urban spaces of Los Angeles and San Francisco to the Sierra foothills. In each place you will find not only different landforms but different communities as well, peoples shaped, in part, by the spaces in which they live.

Chapter 5, "Exporting Culture: California and the Popular Imagination," investigates California's leading role in the shaping of popular culture through the Hollywood movie industry, its pioneering of American car culture, and its innovative patterns of consumer behavior. No other state has had the same impact on popular culture as California has had, which is one of the reasons so many people continue to come here in search of dreams that they may have first found in the movies.

Finally, Chapter 6, "(Mis)managing California: Politics, Environment, and the State of the State," explores the various ways in which things just keep going wrong in paradise, from freeway gridlock to political gridlock, water wars to water pollution. A state that recalled a newly reelected governor to put a Hollywood superstar in his place is bound to attract a lot of attention, and this chapter accordingly contains readings that analyze the Recall of 2003, an election whose repercussions, both locally and nationally, are still being felt and promise to continue to do so for years to come.

In each chapter you will find various viewpoints and arguments that are intended to stimulate the formation of your own arguments in both class discussions and new writing assignments. Each reading is accompanied by sets of questions designed to encourage careful close reading and to provide prompts for argumentative essays, journal essays, and in-class discussions and debates. Some questions encourage further individual or group research into the topics raised by a particular reading, and every chapter concludes with a special "researching the issues" section that suggests topics for expanded investigation of the issues raised by the chapter. Images are also included in each chapter, both as frontispieces and as illustrations within the readings themselves, to stimulate further discussion and analysis of the relevant issues that Californians face today.

We have written *California Dreams and Realities*, then, to serve two purposes: to help train you in college-level writing and critical thinking and to make you an informed citizen of our state, one who will be prepared to share in the leading role that California has long played in

American politics and culture. As you learn the techniques that you will need to succeed in your college coursework, you will also gain the understanding necessary to help California succeed in the future. California has always been a place of dreams: this book asks you to help keep it that way.

Developing Active Reading Strategies

Throughout this book, you'll find readings on California that you can use as models for your own writing, as evidence for your own arguments, and as texts that you can analyze and critique. It is likely that your instructor will ask you to base your own writing on a close reading of these selections, for much of college-level writing is *text-based*. That is, rather than asking you simply to describe your opinion about a topic, which is a common objective of high school writing assignments, college-level assignments more typically ask you to attend to the details of the texts that you read, to work with those texts at a greater level of specificity and critical attention. Thus one of the first steps in writing a strong essay is to read carefully and accurately the selections that your instructor has assigned.

By "read carefully," we suggest that you become an *active* reader: you want to do more than simply skim an essay and grasp the general idea. Many students are worried about being "slow" readers and believe that "good" readers are ones who can speed-read a text (advertisements for the many speed-reading audio tapes available appeal directly to this assumption). But while speed may seem to have its benefits, too often what is lost in the process is an understanding of the nuances of a text. And if you have only the general drift of a selection, it's unlikely that you'll be able to write about it with the detail and precision that your instructor expects. You should instead aim to go beyond gaining an overall sense of an author's message to determine *how* that author communicates that message and *why* it is important in the first place. Pondering the hows and whys behind an essay can make you engage with it more thoroughly and provide you with the deeper, more critical understanding of it that will enable you to write a stronger essay yourself.

To read actively, you want to do more than just go along with the "flow" of an essay; you should instead ask questions of it as you read to help you "see more" in the words before you. You can do this by stopping to check unfamiliar terminology, relating the text to other readings or to what you know already about the subject, and going back to compare the beginning of an essay with the end. You can also use more formal discovery techniques, or what are called *heuristics*. One of the most famous heuristics is the journalist's "Five W's and an H": Who, What, Where, When, Why, and How. By asking these questions, a reporter on the scene of a breaking story can more quickly unearth the essential details of the event and draft a clear account of it. In your writing class, your instructor may well provide you with questions you should ask of the selections you are assigned; indeed, those questions are likely intended to focus your attention on topics that you'll need to consider in an essay assignment. For argumentative essays, your instructor may ask you to consider questions, such as the ones that follow, that encourage you to evaluate how the essay forms an argument.

- What is the author's main argument? Try to summarize the thesis in your own words.

- What sort of evidence does the author advance to demonstrate that argument? And what is the quality of that evidence? Is it up-to-date and specific? Is the source reliable?

- What assumptions underlie the argument? In other words, are there unarticulated beliefs or biases that shape the author's opinion?

- Does the author consider counterarguments, and if so how does he or she treat them? Are they refuted with other evidence or with logic, or does the author concede them? Conversely, if no counterarguments are addressed, how does that affect the persuasiveness of the argument?

- What are the style and tone of the essay, and how do they contribute to its persuasiveness?

While questions such as these can help you actively read an argumentative essay, they may not be as effective with other sorts of readings that do not present a direct argument. In college courses across the curriculum, you may be asked to read, and integrate into your essays, texts that depart from the traditional academic argument. In a history course, for instance, you might read personal documents such as diaries, letters, personal narratives, or oral histories; in a political science class, you might read news stories, interviews, or documentaries as evidence of the prevailing political mood of a nation. In any number of courses, you might read literary works—poems, stories, novels, plays—to study them not as literature but as cultural artifacts. On the one hand, such texts are often enjoyable to read—you may simply have fun reading a novel, for instance—but on the other they require active reading just as academic arguments do. For they pose their own challenges: an oral history transcript may have a message, for instance, but it probably doesn't have a "thesis" or "evidence," and almost certainly not "outside sources."

To evaluate these sorts of texts, another set of questions can help you gain a richer understanding of what you're reading. These questions certainly are useful when you read argumentative essays as well, but you may find them particularly applicable for selections that do not present a traditional argument. To illustrate these questions, we'll ask them of the selection included in this section, Jack Lopez's "Of *Cholos* and Surfers." Because our goal is to encourage you to start thinking actively about Lopez's piece, we'll sketch out preliminary answers that you can take further, refine into your own, more specific reading.

- What is the *genre* of the selection?

Perhaps the most basic starting point is to understand the genre, or category of writing, as different genres have different conventions and intentions. "Of *Cholos* and Surfers" is a personal narrative in which Lopez reflects on his evolving sense of ethnic identity when he was a child in East Los Angeles. You can think of a personal narrative as operating somewhere between a diary entry and an argumentative essay. Like a diary, it focuses on an author's own experiences, but it is intended for public consumption and thus is crafted, both organizationally and rhetorically, in a way that diaries tend not to be. And like an essay, it usually has a message, some main idea, but it does not attempt to engage in direct, logical persuasion based on outside evidence. The potency of a personal narrative emerges instead from the cogency, vividness, and reliability of the author's personal vision, from its ability to allow the reader to visualize, and trust, the author's experiences.

Lopez organizes his narrative around two different but sequentially related episodes in his youth: his quest for a copy of *Surfer* magazine (and, more broadly, to belong to surfer culture) and a potentially dangerous confrontation with a *cholo* in his neighborhood. We, and our students, find a number of scenes particularly striking, such as the anecdote when Lopez visits the Food Giant with his father to buy the magazine. What does that anecdote reveal about Lopez's desire to "belong" to a group? What response does his father have to Lopez's purchase of the magazine, and why does Lopez include it? Then you might consider the anecdote of the fight with the *cholo* that did not occur. How does that build on your developing sense of Lopez's search for identity? And how do the two episodes combine to illustrate Lopez's assertion at the end that he had "the best of both worlds" (para. 34)?

- What is the *context* of the selection? What social, cultural, or political forces surround its topic?

In order to understand any text, a writer should be able to identify the larger historical context that surrounds it. To cite a case in point: several years ago, hundreds of cardboard "tombstones" bearing slogans like "R.I.P. Women's Studies" or "Farewell, Black Student Union" appeared mysteriously across the UCLA campus. Without knowing the context, a viewer might find these tombstones hard to interpret. Today, we might be tempted to see them as protests of the effects of budget cuts on public higher education. But in fact these tombstones appeared in October 1996, just before Proposition 209, which banned affirmative action from public hiring and education, was passed. Knowing that context can lead you to a different understanding of the tombstones' purpose: as a protest not of budget cuts but of Proposition 209.

In "Of *Cholos* and Surfers," Lopez clearly announces the historical time period that he is describing: it's the early 1960s. This was a period in American history when racial divisions were at once more acute (the civil rights movement fought overt and legalized discrimination) and more neatly defined (the American racial composition was less diverse and factionalized). In what ways do you see that context reflected in Lopez's narrative? And you might consider the make-up of Lopez's East Los Angeles neighborhood at the time. Rather than being predominantly Latino, as it is today, the names of some of his friends suggest that a wider range of ethnicities lived there in the 1960s (and Lopez alludes to this as well). What light does that shed on Lopez's comment that he was a "pioneer in the sociological sense that I had no distinct ethnic piece of geography on which my pride and honor depended" (para. 33)?

- What is the author's *persona*?

All writers have a persona or, more accurately, they have different personae depending on the circumstance. *Persona* is a Greek word that means "mask": it originates in Ancient Greek drama, where actors would reveal their state of mind by holding a mask in front of their faces (recall the familiar symbol of the theater, the pair of masks, one smiling and the other frowning). In writing, persona refers to the character we project. Whether intentionally or not, all writers have a persona. Think about it: when you write an essay for school, what sort of person do you want to "sound like"? Intelligent, prepared, and smart, maybe? Now think about what you prefer to sound like when you're e-mailing an old friend from back home. Laid-back? Intimate? Would you want to adopt your essay-writing persona when writing to your friend? Probably not, as your friend would be puzzled or irritated by your more formal, distant style, just as your instructor would find the persona you adopt for your pal to be inappropriate and cause for a grade reduction.

When we ask our students to characterize Lopez's persona, they typically use these adjectives: nice, friendly, honest, funny. Let's examine those words more closely. Lopez is funny, for instance, but what kind of humor does he use? In lines such as "We all wanted to be surfers, in fact called ourselves surfers even though we never made it to the beach," we see a mildly self-deprecating humor, one in which Lopez pokes gentle fun at his adolescent desires and obsessions. That humor is obviously very different from a Howard Stern, in-your-face taunt. So ask yourself: how does that gentle humor, and the overall niceness and openness of Lopez's demeanor, relate to the broader message he is conveying? How can broadly defined characteristics such as "niceness" and "honesty" also contribute to it?

- What is the selection's relation to its *readership*?

You can interpret this question in two ways. First it can mean "who is the intended audience for this selection?" Understanding who the audience is can help explain style, organization, and even content. Academic essays are written for other scholars in the field, for instance, so they tend to presume a prior knowledge of the research question they address and the specialized terminology they use. Diary entries are typically not written for other readers and thus may be more idiosyncratic in their style and organization. Lopez's personal narrative was published in a collection of essays titled *Cholos & Surfers: A Latino Family Album*, a volume that could be read by the generally educated public, both academic and nonacademic; the striking clarity of his writing style is well suited for such a readership.

But we can interpret the question another way: What relation does the author establish with the readers? Academic essays are typically written in an objective, third-person style, and their authors tend neither to address readers directly nor to refer to themselves personally. As a result, the relation between the selection and the reader is distant, impersonal. Lopez's selection is quite different in this regard: he freely uses the first person, and he uses conversational touches (for instance, "But I've got ahead of myself" [para. 32]) that, our students have told us, make it feel like he's in the room having a chat with his readers. You might then ask yourself: What connection does this more personal, friendly address to the reader have with Lopez's overall message?

As you develop active reading strategies, you'll see that, rather than being separate activities, reading and writing are interconnected. Becoming an active reader not only will help you engage the selections in this textbook more precisely, it will also help you become a better writer. The more aware you are of what makes for effective critical reading, the more effective you will be in both judging and responding to your own readers' needs.

Of *Cholos* and Surfers

JACK LOPEZ

On the West Side of L.A., where the population has traditionally been Anglo, lies the ocean. On the East Side, far from the beach but close to the original center of Mexican Los Angeles, dwell the descendants of the first Angelinos, as well as many new arrivals from Mexico. Born into the East L.A. community, **Jack Lopez** (b. 1950) writes here of the loyalties he feels for his birth community, even as he feels the lure of assimilation, of joining the world of surfing that has come to symbolize white culture and privilege. A fiction writer and essayist whose works include *Cholos & Surfers: A Latino Family Album* (1998), Lopez is a professor of English at California State University, Northridge.

The only store around that had this new magazine was a Food Giant on Vermont Avenue, just off Imperial. *Surfer Quarterly*, it was then called. Now it's *Surfer Magazine* and they've celebrated their thirtieth anniversary. Sheldon made the discovery by chance when he'd gone shopping with his mother, who needed something found only at Food Giant. Normally we didn't go that far east to shop; we went west toward Crenshaw, to the nicer part of town.

We all wanted to be surfers, in fact called ourselves surfers even though we never made it to the beach, though it was less than ten miles away. One of the ways you could become a surfer was to own an issue of *Surfer Quarterly*. Since there had been only one prior issue, I was hot to get the new one. To be a surfer you also had to wear baggy shorts, large Penney's Towncraft T-shirts, and go barefoot, no matter how much the hot sidewalks burned your soles.

That summer in the early sixties I was doing all sorts of odd jobs around the house for my parents: weeding, painting the eaves, babysitting during the daytime. I was earning money so that I could buy Lenny Muelich's surfboard, another way to be a surfer. It was a Velzy-Jacobs, ten feet six inches long, twenty-four inches wide, and it had the coolest red oval decal. Lenny was my across-the-street neighbor, two years older than I, the kid who'd taught me the facts of life, the kid who'd taught me how to wrestle, the kid who'd played army with me when we were children, still playing in the dirt.

Now we no longer saw much of each other, though he still looked out for me. A strange thing happened to Lenny the previous school year. He grew. Like the Green Giant or something. He was over six feet tall and the older guys would let him hang out with them. So Lenny had become sort of a hood, wearing huge Sir Guy wool shirts, baggy khaki pants with the cuffs rolled, and French-toed black shoes. He drank wine, even getting drunk in the daytime with his hoodlum friends. Lenny was now respected, feared, even, by some of the parents, and no longer needed or desired to own a surfboard—he was going in the opposite direction. There were two distinct paths in my neighborhood: hood or surfer.

I was entering junior high school in a month, and my best friends were Sheldon Cohen and Tom Gheridelli. They lived by Morningside Heights, and their fathers were the only ones to work, and their houses were more expensive than mine, and they'd both been surfers before I'd aspired toward such a life. Sheldon and Tom wore their hair long, constantly cranking their heads back to keep their bangs out of their eyes. They were thirteen years old. I was twelve. My parents wouldn't let hair grow over my ears no matter how much I argued with them. But I was the one buying a surfboard. Lenny was holding it for me. My parents would match any money I saved over the summer.

Yet *Surfer Quarterly* was more tangible since it only cost one dollar. Lenny's Velzy-Jacobs was forty-five dollars, quite a large sum for the time. The issue then became one of how to obtain the object of desire. The Food Giant on Vermont was reachable by bike, but I was no longer allowed to ride up there. Not since my older brother had gone to the Southside Theatre one Saturday and had seen a boy get knifed because he wasn't colored. Vermont was a tough area, though some of the kids I went to school with lived up there and they weren't any different from us. Yet none of them wished to be surfers, I don't think.

What was needed was for me to include my father in the negotiation. I wasn't allowed to ride my bike to Vermont, I reasoned with him. Therefore, he should drive me. He agreed with me and that was that. Except I had to wait until the following Friday when he didn't have to work.

My father was a printer by trade. He worked the graveyard shift. I watched my younger brother and sister during the day (my older brother, who was fifteen years old, was around in case anything of consequence should arise, but we mostly left him alone) until my mother returned from work—Reaganomics had hit my family decades before the rest of the country. Watching my younger sister and brother consisted of keeping them quiet so my father could sleep.

In the late afternoons I'd go to Sportsman's Park, where I'd virtually grown up. I made the all-stars in baseball, basketball, and football. Our first opponent on the path to the city championships was always Will Rogers Park in Watts. Sheldon and Tom and I had been on the same teams. Sometimes I'd see them in the afternoons before we'd all have to return home for dinner. We'd pore over Sheldon's issue of *Surfer* while sitting in the bleachers next to the baseball diamond. If it was too hot we'd go in the wading pool, though we were getting too old for that scene, since mostly women and kids used it.

When Friday afternoon arrived and my father had showered and my   10
mother had returned from work, I reminded my father of our agreement. We drove the neighborhood streets up to Vermont, passing Washington High School, Normandie Avenue, Woodcrest Elementary School, and so on. We spoke mostly of me. Was I looking forward to attending Henry Clay Junior High? Would I still be in accelerated classes? My teachers and the principal had talked with my parents about my skipping a grade but my parents said no.

Just as my father had exhausted his repertoire of school questions, we arrived at the Food Giant. After parking in the back lot, we entered the store and made for the liquor section, where the magazines were housed. I stood in front of the rack, butterflies of expectation overtaking my stomach while my father bought himself some beer. I knew immediately when I found the magazine. It looked like a square of water was floating in the air. An ocean-blue cover of a huge wave completely engulfing a surfer with the headline BANZAI PIPELINE. I held the magazine with great reverence, as if I were holding something of spiritual value, which it was.

"Is that it?" my father asked. He held a quart of Hamm's in each hand, his Friday night allotment.

"Yes." I beamed.

At the counter my father took the magazine from me, leafing through it much too casually, I thought. I could see the bulging veins in his powerful forearms, and saw too the solid bumps that were his biceps.

"Looks like a crazy thing to do," he said, finally placing the magazine   15
on the counter next to the beer. My father, the practical provider, the person whose closet was pristine for lack of clothes—although the ones he did own were stylish, yet not expensive. This was why he drank beer from quart bottles—it was cheaper that way. I know now how difficult it must have been raising four children on the hourly wages my parents made.

The man at the counter rang up the purchases, stopping for a moment to look at the *Surfer*. He smiled.

"*¿Eres mexicano?*" my father asked him.

"*Sí, ¿cómo no?*" the man answered.

Then my father and the store clerk began poking fun at my magazine in Spanish, nothing too mean, but ranking it as silly adolescent nonsense.

When we got back in the car I asked my father why he always asked   20
certain people if they were Mexican. He only asked men who obviously were, thus knowing in advance their answers. He shrugged his shoulders and said he didn't know. It was a way of initiating conversation, he said. Well, it was embarrassing for me, I told him. Because I held the magazine in my lap, I let my father off the hook. It was more important that I give it a quick thumb-through as we drove home. The *Surfer* was far more interesting for me as a twelve-year-old than larger issues of race.

I spent the entire Friday evening holed up in my room, poring over the magazine, not even interested in eating popcorn or watching *77 Sunset Strip*, our familial Friday-night ritual. By the next morning I had almost memorized every photo caption and their sequence. I spoke with Sheldon on the phone and he and Tom were meeting me later at Sportsman's Park. I did my chores in a self-absorbed trance, waiting for the time when I could share my treasure with my friends. My mother made me eat lunch before I was finally able to leave.

Walking the long walk along Western Avenue toward Century and glancing at the photos in the magazine, I didn't pay attention to the *cholo* whom I passed on the sidewalk. I should have been more aware, but was too preoccupied. So there I was, in a street confrontation before I knew what had happened.

"You a surfer?" he said with disdain. He said it the way you start to say *chocolate. Ch,* like in *choc—churfer.* But that didn't quite capture it, either.

I stopped and turned to face him. He wore a wool watch cap pulled down onto his eyebrows, a long Sir Guy wool shirt with the top button buttoned and all the rest unbuttoned, khaki pants so long they were frayed at the bottoms and so baggy I couldn't see his shoes. I wore Bermuda shorts and a large Towncraft T-shirt. I was barefoot. My parents wouldn't let hair grow over my ears. *Cholo* meets surfer. Not a good thing. As he clenched his fists I saw a black cross tattooed onto the fleshy part of his hand.

His question was *not* like my father's. My father, I now sensed,   25
wanted a common bond upon which to get closer to strangers. This guy was Mexican American, and he wanted to fight me because I wore the outfit of a surfer.

I rolled the magazine in a futile attempt to hide it, but the *cholo* viewed this action as an escalation with a perceived weapon. It wasn't that I was overly afraid of him, though fear can work to your advantage if used correctly. I was big for my age, athletic, and had been in many fights. The problem was this: I was hurrying off to see my friends, to share something important with them, walking on a summer day, and I didn't feel like rolling on the ground with some stranger because *he'd* decided we must do so. Why did he get to dictate when or where you would fight? There was another consideration, one more utilitarian: Who knew what sort of weapons he had under all that baggy clothing? A rattail comb, at the least. More likely a knife, because in those days guns weren't that common.

At Woodcrest Elementary School there was a recently arrived Dutch Indonesian immigrant population. One of the most vicious fights I had ever seen was the one when Victor VerHagen fought his own cousin. And the toughest fight I'd ever been in was against Julio, something during a baseball game. There must be some element of self-loathing that propels us to fight those of our own ethnicity with a particular ferocity.

Just before the *cholo* was going to initiate the fight, I said, "I'm Mexican." American of Mexican descent, actually.

He seemed unable to process this new information. How could someone be Mexican and dress like a surfer? He looked at me again, this time seeing beyond the clothes I wore. He nodded slightly.

This revelation, this recognition verbalized, molded me in the years 30 to come. A surfer with a peeled nose and a Karmann Ghia with surf racks driving down Whittier Boulevard in East L.A. to visit my grandparents. The charmed life of a surfer in the midst of *cholos*.

When I began attending junior high school, there was a boy nicknamed Niño, who limped around the school yard one day. I discovered the reason for his limp when I went to the bathroom and he had a rifle pointed at boys and was taking their money. I fell in love with a girl named Shirley Pelland, the younger sister of a local surfboard maker. I saw her in her brother's shop after school, but she had no idea I loved her. That fall the gang escalation in my neighborhood became so pronounced my parents decided to move. We sold our house very quickly and moved to Huntington Beach, and none of us could sleep at night for the quiet. We were surrounded by cornfields and strawberry fields and tomato fields. As a bribe for our sudden move my parents chipped in much more than matching funds so I could buy Lenny Muelich's surfboard. I almost drowned in the big waves of a late-autumn south swell, the first time I went out on the Velzy-Jacobs. But later, after I'd surfed for a few years, I expertly rode the waves next to the pier, surfing with new friends.

But I've got ahead of myself. I must return to the *cholo* who is about to attack. But there isn't any more to tell about the incident. We didn't fight that summer's day over thirty years ago. In fact, I never fought another of my own race and don't know if this was a conscious decision or if circumstances dictated it. As luck would have it, I fought only a few more times during my adolescence and did so only when attacked.

My father's question, which he'd asked numerous people so long ago, taught me these things: The reason he had to ask was because he and my mother had left the safe confines of their Boyle Heights upbringing. They had thrust themselves and their children into what was called at the time the melting pot of Los Angeles. They bought the post–World War II American dream of assimilation. I was a pioneer in the sociological sense that I had no distinct ethnic piece of geography on which my pride and honor depended. Cast adrift in the city streets. Something gained, something lost. I couldn't return to my ethnic neighborhood, but I could be a surfer. And I didn't have to fight for ethnic pride over my city street. The neighborhood kids did, however, stick together, though this was not based upon race. It was a necessity. The older guys would step forward to protect the younger ones. That was how it was done.

The most important thing I learned was that I could do just about anything I wished, within reason. I could be a surfer, if I chose, and even *cholos* would respect my decision. During my adolescence I went to my grandparents' house for all the holidays. They lived in East Los Angeles. When I was old enough to drive I went on my own, sometimes with a girlfriend. I was able to observe my Los Angeles Mexican heritage, taking a date to the *placita* for Easter service and then having lunch at Olvera Street. An Orange County girl who had no idea this part of Los Angeles existed. I was lucky; I got the best of both worlds.

UNDERSTANDING THE TEXT

1. What symbolic significance did being a surfer hold for Lopez and his friends?

2. How did Lopez's attitude toward his Mexican heritage compare with that of his father?

3. Why does the *cholo* object to Lopez's surfer clothing?

4. How did Lopez eventually reconcile his surfer and his Mexican American identities?

5. What did Lopez gain and lose through assimilation into mainstream California culture?

EXPLORING AND DEBATING THE ISSUES

1. In your journal, reflect on your own aspirations as they are shaped by California's open invitation to be whatever you want to be. If you do not see signs of that invitation, discuss instead the obstacles you believe you face.

2. In an essay, explain the extent to which Lopez's experiences demonstrate that California is a place where one can reinvent oneself.

3. A generational gap separated Lopez's and his father's attitudes toward assimilation. Compare that gap in attitude with that of the Vietnamese immigrants that Nancy Wride describes in "Vietnamese Youths No Longer Look Homeward" (p. 160). Be sure to keep in mind that Lopez is writing about the 1960s while Wride is discussing the 1990s.

4. Compare and contrast Lopez's search for ethnic identity with that of Mario Garcia, "My Latino Heart" (p. 166).

5. Read two or three additional personal experience essays in this text, and compile a list of the varying strategies the authors use to convey their messages. Use your list as a guide to writing your own personal experience essay. You might read Mario Garcia, "My Latino Heart" (p. 166), Jeanne Wakatsuki Houston and James D. Houston, "Manzanar, U.S.A." (p. 109), Ruben Navarrette Jr., "'Well, I Guess They Need Their Minority'" (p. 211), David Mas Masumoto, "As If the Farmer Died" (p. 248), or Judith Lewis, "Interesting Times" (p. 293).

1

California Dreaming
MYTHS OF THE GOLDEN LAND

It really all did begin with the glitter of gold in a pan. Before that, California was a sleepy, sparsely populated place, only recently acquired from Mexico in the wake of the Mexican-American War. But in 1848, John Marshall discovered gold in the depths of the American River at Sutter's Mill, and the rush was on. California would never be the same again.

These gold rush origins of modern California—and their original golden promise—have come to characterize the way that Californians and non-Californians alike think of this state. For the image of California is not simply one of a place where people can be prosperous and happy— after all, that is the promise of the American dream itself. The image is one where prosperity and happiness can be had effortlessly, without labor— an image of easy pleasure under endlessly sunny skies. New England, where a considerable part of the American dream originated, had too harsh a climate and too Puritanical a society to create such a soft, and ultimately hedonistic, vision of the good life. It would take the mild climate, richly beautiful land, and golden promise of easy wealth to make the California dream special, an intensified and more glamorous version of the larger promise of America.

The image of California has changed many times since the gold rush era. From the *Ramona* era of the late nineteenth and early twentieth centuries, when Helen Hunt Jackson's romantic novel featuring the sun-drenched lives of southern California ranchero and mission society lured thousands of Americans to California in search of easy living, to the

◄ California orange crate label, "California Dream" (c. 1920s).

present, when those who seek the California dream come from all over the world, the promise of California has been one of the easy life—easy climate, easy money, freedom under sunny skies, paradise. In between, the California dream has been shaped by Hollywood, which portrayed California as the epitome of modern glamour and pleasure, as well as by social changes in the years immediately following World War II, when California emerged as a model for a middle-class suburban lifestyle. In the 1950s and 1960s, surfing and the California beach culture emerged as a pop cultural craze with enduring influence, while the flower child era—headquarters, San Francisco—helped bring California to the forefront of the sexual revolution.

Those of us who actually live in California know there is quite a difference between the image and the reality. The reality is that the sun does not always shine (and when it does, it is often blocked by smog). The streets are not paved with gold, and paradise was marked with fault lines long before the great San Francisco earthquake of 1906 awakened us to the instability within the California earth. Even the orange groves, which were such a prominent feature of the state's image early in the twentieth century, have just about all been ripped up. Still, here we are. And native born and immigrant alike, we are still here and are still coming—because California offers us something special that no other state in the union seems to offer.

Perhaps your grandparents came to California to escape New England winters or Midwestern provinciality. Or perhaps your family came during World War II to work in the shipyards of Richmond or maybe afterward to take advantage of California's postwar economic expansion. Perhaps you yourself came because this is where the most exciting opportunities were or because you and your family arrived with the thousands who fled Vietnam in the aftermath of the war there. Perhaps you came fleeing civil war in Central America, poverty in Mexico, revolution in Iran, or persecution in the former Soviet Union. One way or another, most of us have arrived in California relatively recently, looking for a new beginning.

If you are descended from one of California's many Native American tribes, you may have a different point of view. The dream that has attracted so many immigrants—European, Asian, Latin American, and Near Eastern—may look to you like a nightmare: the long night of your people's dispossession. And for Chicanos, the California promise may look less like an offer than a seizure, for California was once a province of the Republic of Mexico before it was annexed by a victorious United States after the Mexican-American War.

But for the millions of other Californians who arrived after the Spanish and the American conquests, the myth of California has defined this place as a land of renewal and opportunity—an earthly paradise blessed with perpetual sunshine. To test the power of the myth of the golden land, think for a moment about leaving California. Where would you go? Would you seek one of those western states like Colorado, Arizona, or Nevada, where thousands of Californians have headed in recent years searching for what appear to be shinier, less tarnished versions of the California dream? If you would, you'll only find a paradox, for so frequently what happens in California eventually happens elsewhere. The western states are all now facing California-style problems: water shortages, suburban sprawl into fire-prone mountainsides, overcrowding, and drought. Perhaps, after all, there really is nowhere else to go.

Dream Visions

In this chapter, we look at the traditional vision of the California good life. This will be our touchstone—the standard against which we compare some contemporary versions of California life. The general rosiness of the traditional vision may strike you as being unrealistic, but it may also strike you with a shock of recognition—a feeling that, yes, this is what California has always meant to you.

Consider for a moment the images that spring to mind when you think of California. Do you see hot tubs on redwood decks suspended over steep canyons or Malibu villas overlooking the Pacific? Is it Hollywood that you see, with glamorous names inscribed along the Walk of Fame? Do you see Beverly Hills mansions and trendy crowds sauntering along Rodeo Drive or the Sunset Strip? Perhaps you see the redwoods along the Mendocino coast, the salt flats of Death Valley, or the razor edge of the Sierra Nevada's Range of Light. Or maybe you see the hills of San Francisco, the blue waters of the Bay, the Golden Gate Bridge, and Mount Tamalpais beyond. Perhaps you have a Valley view—not the San Fernando Valley but the seemingly endless plain of the Central Valley with its rows on rows of irrigated fields. And then again, perhaps no specific image comes to mind but only a feeling—an expectation that this is the place where desire is fulfilled, where freeways take you wherever you want to go, and where there are no limits to what you can do.

The Readings

James J. Rawls begins our survey of the California dream with an essay on the vision of the good life that California has long represented. Though fundamentally a glowing tribute to California, Rawls's essay still sounds a warning note as it explores the many paradoxes that California's inordinate promise presents whenever it fails. In the following excerpt from Garcí Rodriguez Ordóñez de Montalvo's fanciful novel *The Adventures of Esplandian*, the name of California first appears in history as the island home of a race of Amazons. The anonymous "Notes of a California Expedition" provides a much more realistic view of California in the throes of the gold rush of 1849, when greed and speculation were the orders of the day, while Denise S. Spooner's historical study of the Midwestern emigration to California in the years immediately after World War II analyzes California's twentieth-century attractions to Anglo Americans. Joan Didion's classic essay "Notes from a Native Daughter" proudly explores the California that non-Californians and coastal Californians tend to neglect: the Sacramento Valley, home to families like Didion's that descended from the pioneers who came to California in the mid-nineteenth century. Richard Rodriguez next offers a poetic meditation on the complex meaning of the California "promised land" for Mexican immigrants, a place of economic opportunity where "you can be anything you want to be" if you can get past *la migra*. Two poems conclude the chapter—Deborah Miranda's "Indian Cartography," an elegiac reflection on the vanished California of her native American ancestors, and Michael J. O'Brien's "Orange County Historian," a utopian, tongue-in-cheek imagining of what California could be like if only the cars would disappear.

California

A Place, a People, a Dream

JAMES J. RAWLS

"In the imagination of the twentieth century, California is the quintessential Promised Land," **James J. Rawls** (b. 1945) writes as he explores the California dream and its place in American mythology. But though the dream "is simply a vision of the good life," Rawls cautions, it also contains a paradox: With the high promise of its glittering reputation, can California always deliver? And if it can't, what disillusionment may follow? A long-time interpreter and chronicler of the California experience, Rawls teaches history at Diablo Valley College, is the author of several books, including *Indians of California: The Changing Image* (1984) and *California: An Interpretive History* (with Walter Bean, 1998), and is editor of *New Directions in California History* (1988) and *California: A Place, a People, a Dream* (with Claudia K. Jurmain, 1986), from which this essay is taken.

The California Dream—you can sense it in the crisp air of the High Sierra, taste it in the ocean spray at Malibu, feel it in the sun-drenched skies of the Central Valley, glimpse it in the mist and fog of Muir Woods. It surrounds and envelops you, engaging your senses, permeating your soul. The California Dream is a love affair with an idea, a marriage to a myth, a surrender to a collective fantasy. Unbounded by time or space, the California Dream is transcendent, creating a unity, a whole, a merging of past, present, and future in the total California experience. It's quite impossibly everything—and quite possibly nothing at all.

I suppose that there are as many versions of the California Dream as there are dreamers—or as there are essayists who try to capture its essence on paper. For most of us, the California Dream is simply a vision of the good life. It once was seen glittering in the California gold fields. Today it may be fashioned from images of California ranch houses, redwood decks and patios, outdoor barbecues and kidney-shaped swimming pools. The California Dream—whatever its present form—draws its power from universal human needs. Founded on expectation and hope, the California Dream promises to fulfill our deepest longings for opportunity and success, warmth, sunshine and beauty, health and long life, freedom, and even a foretaste of the future.

Opportunity and success—these promises are at the heart of the California Dream. When Stephen Wozniak and Steven Jobs launched Apple Computers a decade ago, they were acting in a long tradition of visionary California entrepreneurs. Forty years earlier, two young Stanford graduates named William Hewlett and David Packard founded in a Palo Alto garage a company destined soon to become one of the nation's premier electronics firms. The list of California successes is embarrassingly rich and endless. Before high technology and aerospace, there were motion pictures, oil fields, citrus groves, real estate, railroads, and, of course, gold. It's as though a special deity watches over California, for in each generation a new resource or new industry develops, reaffirming once again the identity of California with opportunity. California is America's own New World, a land of incredible enterprise, fortune, and good luck.

Warmth and sunshine—more glowing promises of the California Dream. The image of California as a land of perpetual sun—"It Never Rains in Southern California" so the song goes—has an obvious appeal to snowbound Easterners and Midwesterners. It's easy to identify with the sentiments of one Midwestern newcomer who wrote in the 1930s: "I'd get letters from friends that had settled here. . . . I'd hear about the orange groves and palms, . . . sunny days and cool nights, and how the only snow you saw was miles off in the mountains, and—well, I was sick of the prairie landscape and stoking the fire all winter and frying all summer, and first chance I got, I boarded a train to find out if this country came up to the brag." I've always suspected that the annual New Year's Day telecast of the Rose Parade in Pasadena—cameras panning healthy, tanned men and women sauntering in shirt sleeves under palm trees and clear skies—accounts for a sizeable share of the yearly migration to California. As if the seductive climate weren't enough, the mere mention of California conjures up images of stunning natural beauty. Endless blue skies and spectacular seacoasts, magnificent groves of giant sequoia, gentle hills and soaring mountains—all are part of the overwhelming vision of Beautiful California.

With such a salubrious climate, so it's said, California is also a partic-   5
ularly healthy place to live. Today's "fat farms," tanning booths, and longevity institutes are modern expressions of the same fitness impulse that was evident in the sanitoriums and health resorts of the nineteenth century. During the 1880s, southern California welcomed thousands of invalids who erroneously believed that the region's warm, clean air would cure their tuberculosis and ensure them a long and healthy life. Such healthfulness even brought on predictions that a new and superior "California race" was emerging here. As early as 1866, Charles Loring Brace claimed to have seen evidence of positive physical changes among those who had arrived in California. The superiority of *homo sapiens Californium* seemed to be confirmed by the 1984 Summer Olympics in Los Angeles. Under sunny blue skies, young Californians won the gold, silver, and bronze in vastly disproportionate numbers. A product of their own environment, how could they do less?

With visions of healthy, attractive, fit Californians in mind, it's easy to recall another suggestive promise of the California Dream—romance. "Sex and California," declared a recent *Los Angeles Times* article—"the two seem to go together." The identification of California and romance has taken many forms over the years. Malibu Barbie became, for a time, a popular icon for half the preteen population of America. Meanwhile, a line of cosmetics called California Girls offered the chance for older sisters to achieve at least the surface glow of a genuine Californian. And of course for everyone, there's Hollywood. Its glitter and allure have added an unmistakable glamour to the image of the Golden State. Romantic opportunity is the theme of countless Hollywood films, from *San Francisco* to the *Bikini Beach* series, where bronzed and nubile youths frolic to the music of Frankie Avalon. The lyrics and pulsating rhythms of the California Sound, pioneered by the Beach Boys in the early 1960s, capture the sensuous simplicity of life on the California beaches. And what did the Beach Boys write about? "They wrote about the beach and girls and cars, and that was it," remembers David Crosby. "All we really cared about was girls in the first place, and cars were a way to get from your parents and get the girls—and the beach was the place to go. And those were the main elements of our consciousness." Freedom, outdoor living, and romance—those are also the bright lights of the California Dream.

Freedom—in California it's a promise that allows unconventional political movements, personal eccentricities, and unusual fads and fashions to bloom unmolested. "Almost anything might work in California," Carey McWilliams once observed, "you never know." Free from the restraints of tradition and history, California seems uniquely able to shape the nature of things to come. A leader in adopting progressive reforms early in the century, California has altered the national political scene with such innovations as the use of professional campaign management firms, the techniques of image management, and the use of Hollywood celebrities as campaign fundraisers—or as candidates themselves. The idea of California as the harbinger of the American future—from campus turmoil and tax revolts to community colleges, freeways, and shopping malls—is by now a popular cliché.

Promising so much to so many, California is forever being described in superlatives. In the imagination of the twentieth century, California is the quintessential Promised Land. "Why *should* anybody die out here?" asked a character in Steward Edward White's 1920 novel, *The Rose Dawn.* "They'll never get any closer to heaven." And forty years later, Brian Wilson, one of the founding brothers of the Beach Boys, explained: "All good teenagers go to California when they die."

It's tempting to stop here, having neatly summarized and categorized the promises of the California Dream. But that would leave the great misimpression that the California Dream is somehow static and fixed. It would ignore the very essence, excitement, and energy of the dream. The California Dream can't be contained by neat categories. Like California and its people, the dream is alive, an ever-changing and turbulent dynamic. It's made not only of promises but also of paradoxes, the joining of seeming opposites. The paradoxes are what give the dream its dynamism, for in California there is an ongoing dialectic in which new syntheses are born from the paradoxes of the past.

We see this dialectic at work in what might be called the paradox of   10 expectations. The promises of the California Dream raise the expectations of the millions who come to California, hoping that their lives here will be better than what they leave behind. California is to them their best—or perhaps their last—chance for success. "There is no more new frontier," the Eagles have told us. "We have got to make it here." Many of those who come find what they are looking for. They become enthusiastic boosters of the Golden State, recruiting friends and relatives to join them. Yet California doesn't fulfill the expectations of all those who come. Many find that life here isn't at all what they had hoped or dreamed that it would be. Despair, isolation, and disillusionment arise out of the newcomers' experience, turning would-be dreamers into bitter antagonists who denounce the false promises of the California Dream.

Obviously there is a paradox here, for California is at once a land of great expectation and disappointment, lauded and damned with equal intensity. While the major chords in the California Dream have been affirmative and celebratory, audible too, usually in the background, are the minor chords of doubt and disillusionment. If only because California promises so much, its failure to live up to expectations has been especially vivid, conspicuous, and dramatic.

The gold rush experience itself was forged on this paradox of expectation. Hundreds of diaries and reminiscences extoll the charms of the golden land, but others speak of the painful contrast between California's vaunted promises and its actual conditions. "I really hope that no one will be deterred from coming here," wrote one disappointed argonaut in 1850. "The more fools the better—the fewer to laugh when we get home." And a popular gold rush ballad ended with the bitter refrain, "Oh land of gold you did me deceive, and I intend in thee my bones to leave."

California's writers have often provided a counterpoint to the myth of California as the land of boundless opportunity, success, and romance. The alleged failure of the myth became a major preoccupation for the writers of the 1930s, powerfully expressed in the works of Nathanael West, Aldous Huxley, and John Steinbeck. Today's California writers are still using the California Dream as a foil for their work. Much of the appeal of their work lies in the fact that the dream is always there, if only to be denied. In "Some Dreamers of the Golden Dream," Joan Didion tells the pathetic story of a desperate woman, living in the San Bernardino Valley, who is convicted of the murder of her husband. "Of course she came from somewhere else, came off the prairie in search of something she had seen in a movie or heard on the radio, for this is a Southern California story."

A new genre of anti-California literature—the minor chords now in concert—appeared in gloomy force in the late 1960s and 1970s. "California—Has Dream Gone Sour?" ran a headline in the *Los Angeles Times*, and the Pacific News Service syndicated an article captioned "Shades of the Sunbelt Shift: California Dream in a Body Bag." Books appeared with titles such as *Anti-California* and *California: The Vanishing Dream*. California seemed to be its own worst enemy as the impulse to debunk was powerfully stimulated by a bizarre set of "California events"—the Berkeley FSM,[1] the Watts riot, the flowering of Haight-Ashbury, the Manson cult murders, the Patty Hearst kidnapping, the People's Temple mass murder-suicide, and the assassinations of San Francisco mayor George Moscone and supervisor Harvey Milk.

[1] Free Speech Movement. [Eds.]

In this dire outpouring of pop commentary, the promises of the Cali- 15
fornia Dream are still present, but they have been turned inside out, frisked
for clues as to what went wrong. The image of California as the land of opportunity becomes a *cause* of California's multiple tragedies. The gold rush
syndrome—high hopes, soon dashed—makes California especially sus-
ceptible to the appeal of crackpot schemes of self-proclaimed messiahs.
Even California's climate is at fault—all that warmth and sunshine attracts
"emotionally unwrapped" people to the state. In these bleak analyses of the
1960s and 1970s, California is no longer seen as a land of health but as a
dark precinct of social pathology. Wide publicity is given to the state's rate
of alcoholism, drug abuse, and suicide—clear evidence that California is
now the land of failed dreams and broken promises. California, land of romance, becomes California, land of rampant immorality and sexual de-
viance. As for California's social freedom—by clear consensus—it is a case
of too much of a good thing. America take heed! Freedom from tradition
leads to disorientation and rootlessness, tolerance attracts the unbalanced
and antisocial.

The minor chords in the California Dream, always present, reached
a crescendo in the early 1970s. Then, just as this climax was passing,
we began to hear something new. California came to be the subject of a
remarkable new body of descriptive literature, what James D. Houston elsewhere calls the New Anatomy of California. Finally we began to see a clear-
sighted portrait of California, a balanced appraisal of the state's virtues and
accomplishments as well as its faults and failures. Kevin Starr's *Americans
and the California Dream* (1973) signaled the emergence of this new perception, identifying the "best possibilities" of the state's regional culture
rather than dwelling on the half-truths of contemporary cliché and stereotype. Five years later James D. Hart's *A Companion to California* was
published. This encyclopedic work neither boosts the California myth nor
belabors the state's excesses. It is a straightforward catalogue of California
people, places, and things, from Abalone to Zukor. . . .

Another paradox in the California Dream is the paradox of growth.
Here too we see the dynamic quality of the dream—the workings of a dialectic and the emergence of new forms. After more than a century of
phenomenal growth, California became the nation's most populous state
at the end of 1962. Today it leads New York, its closest rival, by more than
eight million people. Throughout California history, growth has been
thought of as the greatest good. We happily measure our success by it, for
it reassures us that faith in the California Dream remains strong, that its
promises are being fulfilled. Yet as the California Dream succeeds in at-
tracting ever greater numbers of people, the ability of California to fulfill
its promises diminishes.

This paradox of growth isn't just a phenomenon of our own times; it cuts across the state's history. With news of gold in California, "the world rushed in." By the end of 1848 some six thousand miners in California had wrested $10 million worth of gold from the foothills of the Sierra. By 1852, the peak year, the output was $80 million but the number of miners had risen to a hundred thousand. In just four years, the per capita yield of the California mines had been cut in half. Quick and easy wealth was the promise of California, yet as more and more hopeful miners arrived, the prospects for the promise being fulfilled dimmed accordingly. . . .

*

It's only been in recent years that Californians generally have come to appreciate the nature of this paradox. When California became the most populous state late in 1962, many residents joined in a statewide celebration of "Population Day," but it was apparent even then that growth had its price. In great rings around the state's cities, the geometry and monotony of tract development were replacing open space, green fields, and orchards. The state's parklands, hopelessly overcrowded, were in danger of being loved to death by vacationing Californians. Urban freeways, built as pathways for automobility, were becoming monuments to immobility.

Out of this paradox of growth—in which the ultimate success of the California Dream would mean its utter demise—there emerged a new synthesis. California, the most populous state, dedicated itself to the control of growth. Starting with a Petaluma ordinance in 1973, communities across the state began to take steps to limit further growth. Cities as diverse as Stockton and Belmont, Saratoga and Santa Cruz, passed ordinances controlling growth, and growth-control candidates were elected in such rapidly growing counties as Santa Clara, Orange, and San Diego. The growth-control movement represents a radical reversal of traditional values. California, once so proud of its phenomenal growth, is now home to the movement to limit growth. Apparently Californians have come at last to appreciate the wisdom of former governor Earl Warren. "Mere numbers," Warren remarked upon the occasion of California's emergence as the most populous state, "do not mean happiness."

Still there's another paradox in the California Dream—the paradox of plenty. From the gold rush to the present, fulfillment of the dream has most often meant getting rich. Money-making is a kind of fixed mania for many Californians, and the evidence of California's riches is plain enough. A stroll down Rodeo Drive in Beverly Hills should convince the most skeptical—stretch limousines at the curb, haberdashers offering their four-hundred-dollar cotton shirts, display windows adorned with bedspreads made from the fur of the Mongolian gray fox. Today California ranks third among the states in personal income, a full 13 percent

20

above the national average. If California were a separate nation, it would be one of the world's major economic powers, ranking twelfth in the value of international trade and eighth in gross national product.

Yet the pursuit of wealth in California has not been unopposed. California has long been a battleground between the forces of economic development and environmental protection. Here, where the environment is so magnificent and the drive to achieve economic success is so strong, the impulse to protect and defend the environment has been most powerfully aroused.

Whenever the state's environment has been threatened, from the days of John Muir to the present, Californians have risen in its defense. In 1969 an offshore well of the Union Oil Company sprang a leak and smeared the beaches of Santa Barbara with oil. Two years later, a pair of Standard Oil tankers collided in the fog just inside the Golden Gate, spilling their cargo of oil into San Francisco Bay. Both of these incidents, and countless others, provoked an impassioned and vigorous response from outraged Californians. The sight of beaches littered with the oil-soaked bodies of dead seagulls and dying marine mammals added tremendous emotional fuel to the environment movement.

Out of this intensely charged struggle between the forces of economic development and environmental protection has come the search for nonpolluting, renewable sources of energy. Solar, wind, and geothermal power represent ways in which economic development may proceed with a minimum of environmental damage. (They also are ways, of course, of reducing dependence on foreign oil.) Here again is evidence of the California dialectic at work. From opposing forces a new synthesis is being formed. Today California is *the* solar state in the union, containing more than 40 percent of the total United States solar collector capacity. San Diego, Santa Barbara, and Santa Clara counties are the first in the country to require solar water heating in new residential construction. California also leads the nation in the harnessing of wind and geothermal power. The world's largest wind energy project is being built by PG&E in the rolling hills of Solano County, while Sonoma County is the home of the nation's first commercial geothermal power plant. All are new solutions, born of the paradox of plenty. . . .

Promise and paradox are at the center of the California Dream. In spite   25 of the withering analyses of the past, the promises of California remain undiminished, bringing new generations of newcomers from around the world. The paradoxes find resolution through a dialectic in which new perceptions, relations, and ways of life are forever being created. The emerging syntheses are informed by the virtues of balance, control, restraint, and the willingness to experiment and seek innovation. It is through the pursuit of these virtues that we ensure the survival of California—a place, a people, a dream.

UNDERSTANDING THE TEXT

1. Summarize in your own words the classic "promises" of the California dream, as Rawls describes them, and then summarize his three paradoxes. Which do you find easier to summarize, and why?

2. What does Rawls see as popular culture's contribution to California's image?

3. List the specific details, anecdotes, and historical events that Rawls uses to illustrate his points, and then categorize them in related groups (such as business, music, and so forth). How does the range of references affect the persuasiveness of his discussion?

4. What does Rawls mean by asserting that "in California there is an ongoing dialectic in which new syntheses are born from the paradoxes of the past" (para. 9)?

EXPLORING AND DEBATING THE ISSUES

1. In your journal, brainstorm your own version of the California dream. Share your entry with your class, and discuss how students' versions compare with Rawls's description.

2. Rawls wrote this essay in 1986 and concludes by asserting that "the promises of California remain undiminished" (para. 25). Write an essay in which you argue whether his description of the California good life is still valid, supporting your position with current evidence. To develop your ideas, you might read or reread Victor Davis Hanson's "Paradise Lost" (p. 428).

3. Does Rawls's version of the California dream apply to all residents of this state? In class, discuss whether any groups of individuals may be excluded from this version. Drawing on this discussion, write an essay in which you argue the extent to which the California dream includes all its residents.

4. To what extent does Rawls's definition of the California dream apply to immigrants from other countries? To develop evidence for your position, consult any of the readings in Chapter 2 on immigration.

The Queen of California

GARCÍ RODRIGUEZ ORDÓÑEZ DE MONTALVO

It seems appropriate that California should have gotten its name from a popular fantasy novel that tells of a golden island that lies "very close to the side of the Terrestrial Paradise." Add to that geographical fact that the island was populated by black Amazons whose beautiful queen, Calafia, wished to plunder the world, and you have the makings of an episode of *Xena: Warrior Princess*. That novel— *The Adventures of Esplandian* written by the Spanish writer **Garcí Rodriguez Ordóñez de Montalvo** in 1510—is the best candidate for the source of the golden state's name. And why not? The story has it all: sex, violence, intrigue, and some really weird birds. If de Montalvo were alive today (and virtually nothing is known about his life, other than he made the first known written reference to "California"), he might make a great epic screen writer.

Now you are to hear the most extraordinary thing that ever was heard of in any chronicles or in the memory of man, by which the city would have been lost on the next day, but that where the danger came, there the safety came also. Know, then, that, on the right hand of the Indies, there is an island called California, very close to the side of the Terrestrial Paradise, and it was peopled by black women, without any man among them, for they lived in the fashion of Amazons. They were of strong and hardy bodies, of ardent courage and great force. Their island was the strongest in all the world, with its steep cliffs and rocky shores. Their arms were all of gold, and so was the harness of the wild beasts which they tamed and rode. For, in the whole island, there was no metal but gold. They lived in caves wrought out of the rock with much labor. They had many ships with which they sailed out to other countries to obtain booty.

In this island, called California, there were many griffins, on account of the great ruggedness of the country, and its infinite host of wild beasts, such as never were seen in any other part of the world. And when these griffins were yet small, the women went out with traps to take them. They covered themselves over with very thick hides, and when they had caught the little griffins they took them to their caves, and brought them up there. And being themselves quite a match for the griffins, they fed them with the men whom they took prisoners, and with the boys to whom they gave birth, and brought them up with such arts that they got much good from them, and no harm. Every man who landed on the island was immediately devoured by these griffins; and although they had had enough, none the less would they seize them, and carry them high

31

up in the air in their flight; and when they were tired of carrying them, would let them fall anywhere as soon as they died.

Now, at the time when those great men of the Pagans sailed with their great fleets, as the history has told you, there reigned in this island of California a Queen [Calafia], very large in person, the most beautiful of all of them, of blooming years, and in her thoughts desirous of achieving great things, strong of limb, and of great courage, more than any of those who had filled her throne before her. She heard tell that all the greater part of the world was moving in this onslaught against the Christians. She did not know what Christians were; for she had no knowledge of any parts of the world excepting those which were close to her. But she desired to see the world and its various people; and thinking that with the great strength of herself and of her women, she should have the greater part of their plunder, either from her rank or from her prowess, she began to talk with all of those who were most skilled in war, and told them that it would be well if, sailing in their great fleets, they also entered on this expedition, in which all these great princes and lords were embarking. She animated and excited them, showing them the great profits and honors which they would gain in the enterprise,—above all, the great fame which would be theirs in all the world; while, if they stayed in their island, doing nothing but what their grandmothers did, they were really buried alive,—they were dead while they lived, passing their days without fame and without glory, as did the very brutes.

UNDERSTANDING THE TEXT

1. Characterize the tone of this selection. How does it reveal de Montalvo's attitude toward the "island" of California?

2. List the details in "The Queen of California" that are realistic and those that are fantastic. What do your results suggest about the author's intentions in writing this selection?

3. Describe in your own words the gender relations depicted in this selection.

4. In what ways does the description of California suggest that "where the danger came, there the safety came also" (para. 1)?

5. What are the qualities that make the "queen" of California regal?

EXPLORING AND DEBATING THE ISSUES

1. In what ways does this selection reflect the typical "promises" of the California dream, as James J. Rawls ("California: A Place, a People, a Dream," p. 22) describes? In what ways does it depart from them?

2. In class, discuss your responses to de Montalvo's fantasy depiction of mythical Californians as powerful women who fed male prisoners to their pet griffins. How might your response differ if the gender roles were reversed?

3. Read Homer's *Iliad*, or check a website such as *Encyclopedia Mythica* (http://www.pantheon.org/mythica.html), and compare and contrast the depiction of mythical Greek Amazons with the women described in this selection.

4. In a paragraph, write a description of the "island" of California from the perspective of the male prisoners.

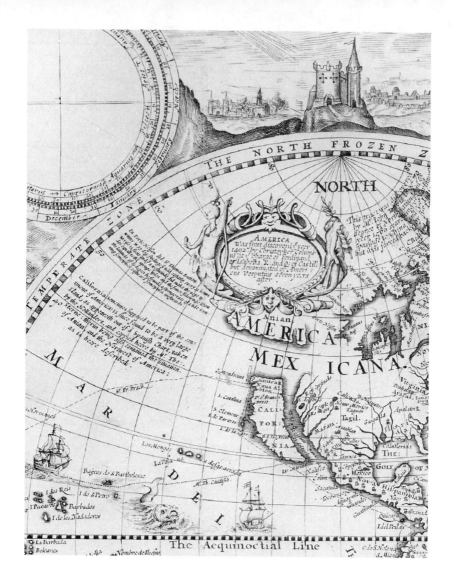

Map of North America Showing California as an Island (1625)

WILLIAM GRENT

1. Compare Grent's map of California with the description in Garcí Rodriguez Ordóñez de Montalvo's 1510 "The Queen of California" (p. 31). How do their fantasies about California compare?

2. What assumptions does Grent make about the political relations between California and other parts of what later would be the western United States? Between California and Mexico and Central America?

Notes of a California Expedition

ANONYMOUS

Gold brought an international stampede to California in 1849, but as these anonymous accounts from the gold rush era attest, the real money was probably in real estate, with grand land-speculation schemes driving San Francisco lot prices to "as high as twenty thousand dollars" (at a time when a few hundred dollars a year was considered a respectable annual income). Getting to the gold and getting the gold were actually very hard work and chancy stuff, as one poor "Tuwallamy" (Tuolemne) gold seeker relates here, while grabbing land and conning latecomers into buying it at grotesquely inflated prices were much surer bets. Has anything really changed? These contemporary accounts were first published in 1849 in the *Philadelphia Public Ledger and Daily Transcript*.

S AN FRANCISCO, California, July 9, 1849.

MESSRS. EDITORS: — After a passage of 49 days from Valparaiso and 174 days from New York, we are at length anchored in the Bay of San Francisco, where we arrived on the 6th inst. The Bay is a magnificent sheet of water, seventy miles in length, and varying in width from three to twelve miles, studded at intervals with beautiful islands, and is capable of affording an excellent harbor for as much shipping as ever can be sent to it. At the present time there are now here about one hundred vessels, (and among them the *Grey Eagle*, of Philadelphia, which made the passage in 103 days, and was the *first* vessel from the United States,) the crews of all of which deserted shortly after their arrival, and they lay here dismantled of sails and upper spars, looking the picture of desolation. It will be some time before they can be got away, as sailors are offered and refuse $200 a month!

The *city* contains about one thousand houses, the greater portion of which are nothing more than muslin stretched over a light frame; and hundreds of tents belonging to those preparing to go to the mines are stuck along the shore. There is nothing like comfort to be found here. Every thing — houses, manners of the people, and the courtesies that render civilized life desirable — all, all are in the rudest possible state; added to which, the presence of persons of all nations, the Indian, Chinese, Mexican and Chilian, decked out in the gaudy variety of colors, and almost every man armed to the teeth, reminds one of some of the rude scenes in the dark ages, and inclines us to think it rather of the character of one of the romances of *Arabian Nights* than the sober reality. Common laborers receive $1 an hour, and carpenters are in demand from $15 to $20 a day! Every thing else is in proportion, and the California value of money would not be believed if I were to write you the sober truth. Enormous schemes of land speculations, and the building of splendid cities — on paper — is

35

carried on with a rivalry exceeding those in the United States several years since. As high as twenty thousand dollars have been paid for a lot here, and the prices are advancing every day.

So far as relates to the wonderful mineral wealth of California, the most exaggerated stories that have been told of it do not over-color the reality. The whole country is full of gold, which can be had for the digging of it. But those who come here, as many do, and imagine that it is easily to be picked up, will be wonderfully disappointed. The digging of gold, so far as regards labor, requires far more *excessive* work than the digging of canals. The ore is unequally distributed through the earth, of a very tough nature, which is compelled to be penetrated from the depth of one to eight feet before the stratum of alluvial is reached, that contains the gold. Then the trouble has but just commenced, for oftentimes the dirt has to be conveyed on the back in pails full, some distance to the water, to be washed. Machinery is of no use, and cannot be transported at present over the hard roads necessary to be travelled before the mines are reached; though those whose bodies are capable of enduring excessive fatigue, the rays of a burning sun 90 degrees in the shade, and who are willing to work steadily, may amass considerable though not the average immense fortunes so often related in the newspapers as having been obtained at one successful stroke.

Some difficulties between the Indians and whites have taken place, and several fights occurred in April and May, in which a number were killed on both sides, and a number of Indians taken prisoners. Everything is quiet now, except that the Americans have determined to drive from the mines every foreigner speaking the Spanish tongue. They are required to leave the mines in a certain time; failing in which, the "*Hounds,*" a self-constituted tribunal of Judge Lynch, arrest, try, and hang them, or cut their throats! The consequence is that this gentle hint is generally taken, and hundreds of them are leaving the mines. One hundred Chilians sailed from here for Valparaiso on Monday last. We are preparing to go to the mines; so you must excuse the brevity of this.

Adieu, D. N.

Mushroom Cities

The annals of '49, in California, says a correspondent of the *Tribune*, will   5
so eclipse the records of the '36 land speculation in the States as to render the latter hardly worthy of note as an epoch. Gigantic schemes are being planned by scientific wire-workers from the States, and immense paper cities adorn the counting-houses of most of the leading merchants at San Francisco and the various towns on the river. Certain interests are

at work to make this or that locality of *immense* worth to those who may be so fortunate as to secure lots *before they are all taken up*, and men have that over-sanguine, half-deranged air about them that characterized the '36 victims. Some fourteen new cities have been laid out on paper and put into market. Few of them will ever be of any account, except for speculative purposes.

The Labor at the Mines

A gold seeker at the Tuwallamy diggings, July 30th, says:—The labor of gold digging and washing is exhausting in the extreme. Thousands who come out here brimfull of hope and courage are bringing their exuberant stock to a poor market—for, after divesting their white hands of their white kid gloves, and working *a la mode* for one week, your amateur dealers in gold dust find themselves bankrupt of mental "pluck" and physical strength, and leave in disgust, some (grown already way-wise) for home, but many to hunt down the *ignis fatuus*. These unfortunate sportsmen will only be "in at the death" of their own unreasonable expectations. Any body can make from five dollars to an ounce per day, but he must work faithfully and intelligently, or he is as likely to make nothing as a buyer of lottery tickets is to purchase a blank.

The Celebration of the Fourth of July in the Mines

The 4th day of July was celebrated throughout the placers by an entire cessation of labor, and the usual discharge of fire-arms, squibs, crackers, and other patriotic combustifiers. Thousands of "Liberty poles" arose, and mountains of blazing pines lent their rude fire-works to the occasion. All became drunken with enthusiasm, and I own I am sorry to say it, upon bad rum at $1 a glass.

The Character of the Country

Gentlemen, do not advise a dog to come to California. Why have Col. Fremont, Farnham, and others so studiously misrepresented this parched, barren, mountainous country? The entire Northern portion of Upper California is inferior to New England in every respect, while the Southern half of the same territory is baked and burned by a scathing, scorching sun for nine months of the year, without rain or dews, and deluged during the other three. The timber is sparse and almost valueless. It is so dry that a tree of one-and-a-half or two feet diameter will become thoroughly seasoned in forty-eight hours after cutting. Ought intelligent, forehanded farmers to be induced to leave comfortable homes, and to bring their families to a land, however rich in mineral wealth, where Indians positively cannot live? The harvest of gold will be gathered in two years, and the gleanings will be poor indeed. After that, woe unto him whose cupidity or stupidity brings him hither.

Prosperity of the Country

I am happy to add that the country is prospering physically as well as morally, or rather commercially as well as politically. Prices of most articles are improving, particularly those of suitable clothing and of certain kinds of provisions. The absorbent capacities of the interior are so marvellous as to astonish every one. Many goods that were not worth landing when I wrote you six weeks since, are now in lively demand. Of this you will have some proof in the amount of specie carried out by this steamer, which is double that shipped in either of its predecessors.

Population of the Country

The present population of the country is set down at 45,000. Some 10 12,000 more are yet to arrive from the States via Cape Horn, and I know not how many over the prairies and through Mexico and Texas. To this, which the American papers will furnish, add what you can learn of European emigration, and you will form a tolerably correct idea of the population six months hence. The emigration from this coast may be said to have ceased. Our countrymen are like pikes, who drive out all other fish from a pond. Encouraged by General Smith's Continental Proclamation from Panama, they have expelled most unjustly, and, as the picture will show, most injudiciously, all foreigners from the mines. Vessels bound down the coast are filled with Mexican, Peruvian, and Chilian emigrants, returning home. The country is thus deprived of the only available cheap labor within reach until the yield of the mines shall have fallen off 50 per cent. I am happy to hear that General Riley, with equal good sense and humanity, has gone to the southern mines with a view to protect such foreigners still there as may decide to apply for letters of naturalization.

Sickness at the Mines

Sickness has already shown itself in the mines, and the next two months will, I fear, terminate the earthly hopes of many miners. A good many cases of diarrhœa had occurred in a form very like the Cholera. Unless checked within a day or two it proved fatal.

Miscellaneous

A Yankee Trick—We were accidentally listeners, and not a little amused, at a colloquy held by a long, green Yankee with a machine similar to a common New England churn, which he was examining minutely: "I bought you for a gold washer, and you are *one* of the washers. Here I've lugged and backed and packed you all through Mexico, and now you ain't worth a continental darn—you've turned out only a churn; ain't I a sweet-scented darn fool, ain't I?" Here wrought into a passion and over-come by his feelings, he seized an axe and entirely demolished the churn, casting the cog-wheel and crank nearly into the middle of the Sacramento.

—*Sacramento Times.*

A duel was fought on Friday morning last, in the west part of the town. Both parties are said to have behaved "handsomely," and one of them went off the ground with a severe graze on the side of his face and head. This was considered a sufficient salve for "wounded honor," and we believe the matter has since been amicably arranged. The quarrel is said to have grown out of some misunderstanding at a faro table.

—*Alta California,* July 26.

UNDERSTANDING THE TEXT

1. Why are the boats that transport the prospective gold miners "the pic-ture of desolation" (para. 1)?
2. How does the author depict social relations in gold rush California?
3. What attitudes toward Native Americans and foreign workers are ex-pressed? Why do you think these attitudes developed?
4. What is the point of the tale about the man with the New England churn?

EXPLORING AND DEBATING THE ISSUES

1. To what extent do these anonymous accounts of the gold rush illustrate James J. Rawls's concept of the paradox of expectations? To develop your ideas, consult Rawls's "California: A Place, a People, a Dream" (p. 22).
2. Compare the forty-niners' expectations for their future with those of Mexican immigrants to California a hundred fifty years later. How does each group understand the California dream? How do you account for any differences in their views? You might consult Richard Rodriguez's "Proofs" (p. 64), Pierrette Hondagneu-Sotelo's "Maid in L.A." (p. 116), or William Langewiesche's "Invisible Men" (p. 130).
3. This selection describes the ways in which land speculation distorted the value of money in California. In an essay, argue whether you think

that a similar distortion exists today. To develop your ideas, consult Chapter 6 on politics.

4. Some historians have claimed that the gold rush was an instance of mass hysteria (hence the term *gold fever*), with a resulting breakdown in the social fabric. Analyze both the individual and group behaviors described in this selection, and write an essay in which you argue the extent to which "Notes of a California Expedition" demonstrates that mass hysteria did indeed occur.

A New Perspective on the Dream

DENISE S. SPOONER

When we think of today's newcomers to the Golden State, we usually imagine immigrants from Latin America, Asia, the Near East, and even post-Soviet Russia. But as **Denise S. Spooner** shows in this essay, originally published in *California History*, an enormous number of migrants from the Midwest flocked to California in the years following World War II seeking not only opportunity and glamour but also freedom from the rigid social conventions of the Midwestern towns and villages they were fleeing. Spooner is coeditor of *H-California* and teaches California and U.S. history at California State University, Northridge.

California. For over a century it has been a name that has evoked vivid images in the minds of Americans. Sunshine, oranges, beaches, Hollywood—the pursuit of a life defined by these images has long been thought to have been the primary motivation for the migration of millions of Americans to southern California from the late 1880s through the twentieth century. Indeed, as a number of California historians have noted, in the late nineteenth and early twentieth centuries a series of promotional campaigns sponsored by corporations and institutions with an economic stake in the region's growth used many of these symbols as a means of generating migration to southern California.[1]

---

[1] Carey McWilliams was first to write on this subject in *Southern California Country: An Island on the Land* (New York: Duell, Sloan & Pierce, 1946; reprint Santa Barbara, Calif.: Peregrine Smith, Inc., 1979), chaps. 6 and 7. See also John Bauer, *Health Seekers of Southern California* (San Marino, Calif.: Huntington Library Publications, 1959), chaps. 1 and 2; John L. Phillips, "Crating Up the California Dream," *American Heritage* (April 1977): 88–93; Alfred Runte, "Promoting the Golden West: Advertising and the Railroad," *California History* 70 (Spring 1991): 62–75; Kevin Starr, *Inventing the Dream: California through the Progressive Era* (New York: Oxford University Press, 1985); Richard S. Street, "Marketing California Crops at the Turn of the Century,"

The Midwest was specially targeted by turn-of-the-century promoters, a marketing scheme that provided returns certainly beyond the grandest projections of the sponsors. Recorded as the largest stream by early 1900, the flow of migrants from the Midwest to California continued as such until it was interrupted by the Great Depression and World War II. In the postwar decades it resumed. The 1960 census recorded the West North Central and East North Central census divisions, which make up the Midwest, as the numbers one and three contributors to California's population.[2]

Considering that change is the one constant in life, it would be quite peculiar to find that the dream that inspired post–World War II Midwestern migrants was the same as that that motivated those who came earlier in the century. As Robert Fogelson pointed out almost thirty years ago, southern California was sold to late-nineteenth- and early-twentieth-century Midwesterners, and initially developed, as a place like the Midwest, but better. The citrus groves, sunshine, and ocean were to serve as a more congenial backdrop for the same type of community as the one they had left, one Fogelson described as "embodied in single-family houses, located on large lots, surrounded by landscaped lawns, and isolated from business activities."[3] Today when you visit many of the cities in the region that developed between approximately 1870 and 1920, especially in Orange County and the San Gabriel Valley of Los Angeles County, you find many townscapes that appear to be realizations of the Midwesterners' desire for a new setting for their former communities.[4]

In the post–World War II years, however, some migrants had a different vision of what life in southern California promised. While many still imagined it as a place of exceptional physical beauty, some also envisioned it as an opportunity to escape from a type of community common

---

Southern California Quarterly 61 (1979): 239–53; T. H. Watkins, "The Social History of a Singular Fruit," *American Heritage* (April 1977): 94–95; Oscar O. Winther, "The Use of Climate as a Means of Promoting Migration to Southern California," *Mississippi Valley Historical Review* 33 (1946): 411–24; Tom Zimmerman, "Paradise Promoted: Boosterism and the Los Angeles Chamber of Commerce," *California History* 64 (Winter 1985): 22–23.

[2] Margaret S. Gordon, *Employment Expansion and Population Growth: The California Experience,* 1900–1950 (Berkeley: University of California Press, 1954), table A-2, p. 162; U.S. Bureau of the Census, *U.S. Census of Population: 1960, Subject Reports, State of Birth,* Final Report PC (2) 2-A (Washington, D.C.: U.S. Government Printing Office, 1963), table 18.

[3] Robert Fogelson, *The Fragmented Metropolis: Los Angeles, 1850–1930* (Cambridge, Mass.: Harvard University Press, 1967), 144–45.

[4] Here I am thinking of cities such as Orange and Tustin in Orange County and Claremont and Monrovia in the San Gabriel Valley.

throughout the Midwest, one that judged people on the basis of the degree to which they adhered to various locally determined norms. For these people, southern California in the postwar years represented a place where their lives could be different, where they would be free to express their individuality as openly or privately as they wished.[5] Examining the images migrants held prior to leaving the Midwest, and investigating the conditions that produced them, deepens our understanding of the culture of post–World War II southern California.

From the start of the boosters' program in the late nineteenth century   5
through much of this one, a special relationship grew between southern California and one Midwestern state in particular, Iowa. The creators of the marketing plan recognized early that the profitability of Iowa's agriculture made for a relatively well-off, retirement-age population ready to remove themselves to a place with a far more temperate climate. Such was partly the motivation behind the California Fruit Growers' special promotional trains to Iowa between 1907 and 1911, which used some of the symbols noted above, especially those related to citrus and sunshine, to encourage people to settle in southern California. The seeds of that effort took root, grew beautifully, and continued to bear fruit throughout much of the next fifty years. In every census taken between 1910 and 1930, Iowa ranked among the top ten state contributors to California's population, along with far more populous states such as New York, Illinois, and Pennsylvania. Mirroring the trend of Midwestern migration in general, the flow of migrants from Iowa to southern California slowed considerably during the Depression and war years, and then resumed its pre-Depression course during the great population boom of the post–World War II decades. For example, in 1960, when the West North Central census division was recorded as the number one contributor to California's population at the division level, among the states in that division, only Iowa and Missouri were also on the list of the top ten states contributing to California's population.[6] It is no wonder that one of the myths popular in southern California for years was that the region was

[5] These conclusions are based on responses to questionnaires I sent to, and interviews I conducted with, migrants whose names, addresses, and places of birth I took from records maintained by the registrars of voters for Los Angeles and Orange counties. The sample I compiled consisted of 982 respondents, 407 from Los Angeles County and 574 from Orange County. Of the 982 questionnaires sent out, 277, or approximately 28 percent were returned. Of those 277, I netted 106 who had migrated within the time frame of my study, 1946–1964.

[6] McWilliams, *Southern California Country*, 129, 161, 163–64; Gordon, *Employment Expansion and Population Growth*, table A-3, 163; U.S. Bureau of the Census, *U.S. Census of Population: 1960, State of Birth*, table 18.

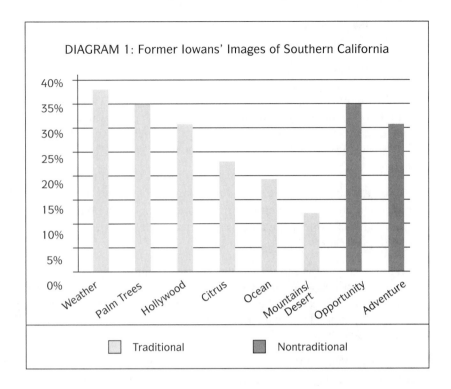

DIAGRAM 1: Former Iowans' Images of Southern California

largely made up of former Iowans. That exaggeration aside, the census figures suggest that by using Iowans as a case study group we might extend our understanding of the California Dream as it was envisioned by Midwestern migrants in the post–World War II years.

The premigration images of California held by the migrants I surveyed and interviewed are depicted in Diagram 1.[7] Images I have labeled "traditional" were reported by 81 percent of my subjects. Those symbols, many of which were devised by the early promoters, portrayed the region as a physically wondrous place. Visions of sunshine, palm trees, citrus, mountains, and ocean contrasted sharply with many migrants' experience of Iowa as a climate of extremes, in a landscape of sameness: sweltering summers and long, cold, gray winters, across gently, but relentless, rolling hills. Nancy Rutherford was one who envisioned southern California as a place fantastically different from Iowa. As a youngster, bed-ridden with

---

[7] Together the percentages equal more than 100 percent because most people reported more than one image that they associated with southern California. The percentages depicted in the diagram are as follows: weather = 38 percent; palm trees = 35 percent; Hollywood = 31 percent; citrus = 23 percent; ocean = 19 percent; mountains/desert = 12 percent.

rheumatic fever, she began writing to an uncle in southern California who was recovering from a heart attack:

> He would talk about those huge palm trees and I had this wonderful vision. It wasn't really Beverly Hills, but a beautiful place with palm trees and swimming pools and blue sky all year 'round. When I was younger I used to do a lot of day dreaming in the midst of the snowstorms in January and February, and I would hear from my uncle. Just think! He was getting to look out at the sun and trees and green grass and all that.[8]

To this list of images that depicted southern California as a place with a balmy climate and a more varied landscape, some postwar migrants added images of the entertainment industry, which I have labeled "Hollywood."[9] Of course, the movies played a central role in creating this image for many, including Don Fromknecht:

> We used to go down to the Capitol Theater in Sioux City, Iowa, and sit there and watch Bing Crosby movies, and I said, "Man, is that what it's like out there? I got to get out there!" See how naive we were. Why, hey. They could paint those palm trees in the back of those movie sets as fast as you could leave.[10]

With the establishment of the television and pop music industries in southern California in the postwar decades, younger migrants such as Priscilla Eckert, who was in her early twenties when she left Iowa, were influenced by the impressions of the region they received through those media:

> That's when the Beach Boys were a large part of the teenage life, as far as music went; and [they] had a connotation of the beach and the bikinied girls and the tans, the blonds, the water. . . . I did figure that California looked like that.[11]

And then there were migrants like William Powell, who imagined southern California as the entertainment capital of the world, as well as the balmy paradise captured in images the industry produced:

[8] Nancy Rutherford, interview with the author, 21 September 1988, Carlsbad, California, tape recording and transcript, California State University, Fullerton: Oral History Collection, 21–22 (hereinafter OHC).

[9] Carey McWilliams mentions the addition of entertainment to the images of the California Dream in *Southern California Country*, 135–36. Kevin Starr gives the topic a thorough examination in the final two chapters of *Inventing the Dream: California through the Progressive Era*.

[10] Don Fromknecht, interview with the author, 8 October 1988, Fullerton, California, tape recording and transcipt, OHC, 11–12.

[11] Priscilla Eckert, interview with the author, 29 October 1988, Irvine, California, tape recording and transcript, OHC, 9–10.

[Southern California was] all glamorous: the palm trees and the movie stars and everything. Back in those days [the 1950s], it was the place to go.[12]

In addition to these traditional images, 58 percent of the migrants had a somewhat different view of southern California, one I have labeled "nontraditional" on the diagram. They still imagined it as a place, but rather than emphasizing the environmental characteristics that distinguished it from the places where they had grown up, their vision of southern California was as a place of adventure and opportunity, a place where their lives could be different.[13]

Associating California with adventure and opportunity was not a new phenomenon. The Spanish settlers of the eighteenth century, as well as the American infiltrators and gold rushers of the mid-nineteenth century, identified California with risk, danger, excitement, and the chance of acquiring a fortune. This was exactly what some of the migrants had in mind when they imagined southern California as a land of adventure and opportunity. For example, when Dee Ann Shaw dreamed of southern California, she thought of the many exciting things there would be to do for fun, and all the different sorts of businesses there would be in which a person could find a job.[14] Don Cameron equated southern California with opportunity, which he described strictly in terms of the chance to make more money. In Iowa, where he was born and raised, he worked as a salesman for a wholesale produce company, but his goal was to get into the origination end of that business. As garden to so much of the United States, California was the best place to live in order to achieve that goal, he decided.[15]

But there were other migrants who give a unique twist to the south-   10
ern California-as-adventure-and-opportunity image. Seventy-three percent of those who identified the region in this way used *adventure* and *opportunity* as code words for "escape from community." In the towns and rural neighborhoods of Iowa in which they lived, community was created through cooperation and judgment. In essence, both were used to measure who was a part of the group and who was not. Some migrants found this aspect of community repressive. Martha Celmer was one.

---

[12] William Powell, interview with the author, 10 October 1988, Anaheim, California, tape recording and transcript, OHC, 7.

[13] Thirty-five percent identified California with opportunity; 31 percent associated it with adventure.

[14] Dee Ann Shaw, interview with the author, 10 December 1988, Laguna Beach, California, tape recording and transcript, OHC, 10.

[15] Don Cameron, interview with the author, 27 September 1988, Anaheim, California, tape recording and transcript, OHC, 26.

Throughout her life she held a variety of images of southern California, but the one that motivated her migration was envisioning southern California as a chance for a different, freer life:

> As a young teenage girl, it was just all Hollywood at its best; but I never got out here when I was a young girl. So I never got to see if that was really true. By the time I finally got out here, I was already maybe twenty-six, twenty-five. I had matured a little. My perception of things wasn't quite the same as it had been as a teenager. I came out with my sister-in-law and brother-in-law the first time and I guess while I was here, I developed an idea that I could make it out here and I went from there. I don't want to say that it was land of milk and honey, because I wasn't that far off in my perception of things past at that point, but I also realized that it was an opportunity to live a different kind of lifestyle, and maybe one that I thought might be a little better for me than living in the Midwest.[16]

The lifestyle Martha Celmer and some of the other migrants wanted was one where they were free to be whomever and whatever they wanted to be, without limitations on individuality imposed by community in the cities, towns, and rural neighborhoods they lived in through cooperation and judgment.

As Kenneth Jackson has written, "the term *community* implies cooperation," and in much of the Midwest from the time of settlement through the first half of the twentieth century, cooperation between neighbors in work and social life was essential to success, if not survival.[17] For instance, Collins Roe's father got his start as an independent farmer through the money he made one season when he and a neighbor worked together to try to harvest more corn than anyone else in Iowa.[18] Moreover, the financial health of businesses in many Iowa communities was directly tied to the profitability of farming.

In addition, the isolation of farm families and lack of entertainment opportunities in small towns made neighbors dependent on one another for their social life. Typically, Saturday nights brought farm families to town. During those visits farmers purchased supplies and talked prices and politics with other men while women gathered in automobiles to visit with one another.[19] Other factors that brought country and town

[16] Martha Ann Celmer, interview with the author, 14 November 1988, Rancho Palos Verdes, California, tape recording and transcript, OHC, 13–14.

[17] Kenneth T. Jackson, *Crabgrass Frontier: The Suburbanization of the United States* (New York: Oxford University Press, 1985), 272.

[18] Collins Roe, interview with the author, 22 September 1988, Garden Grove, California, tape recording and transcript, OHC, 4.

[19] Kenneth Bauermeister, interview with the author, 6 October 1988, Newport Beach, California, tape recording and transcript, OHC, 3–5; Robert Littschwager, interview

people together were those that maintained shared institutions, such as churches, schools, the local chapters of the Farm Bureau, various fraternal organizations, including the Masons and Odd-fellows, and the community memory of important events, like the Civil War and World War I.[20]

For those who grew up and lived in larger cities and towns, the presence of movie houses, amusement parks, and such made neighbors somewhat less reliant on one another for a social life. Still, people from cities recalled their neighborhoods as warm, open, nurturing places. For example, Lynn Achak described her Davenport neighborhood as a place without fences, where neighbors roasted hot dogs and marshmallows together in the autumn over bonfires built from fallen leaves they had all raked out to the curb. Robert Allison explained the widespread participation in community by saying that "back in Des Moines, or in small towns in Iowa, you knew everybody in town. It took everybody in town to make it a town."[21]

Together, the interaction between people in spheres of work and leisure created cohesiveness and interdependence. But there was that other activity that helped create community: judgment. The Midwestern tendency to judge people, a theme prevalent in the writings of Hamlin Garland, Sherwood Anderson, and Sinclair Lewis, and inferred in Grant Wood's famous painting, *American Gothic*, was reflective of many aspects of Midwestern culture, including the predominance of small towns throughout the region and its heritage from the mid-nineteenth century, when nativism was a force throughout the nation. Viewing anyone or anything different as a threat to the prevailing order was characteristic of both. Thus, judging people across a wide spectrum of characteristics and according to a restrictive moral code was common in Iowa communities. In this way, judging emphasized likeness as a basis for community. It isolated those who did not conform to various criteria, including the community norms of class, ethnicity, and religion.

---

with the author, 23 September 1988, Newport Beach, California, tape recording and transcript, OHC, 5; Collins Roe, interview with the author, 22 September 1988, Garden Grove, California, OHC, 5–6.

[20] All of the interviewees, except two, recalled that they and/or their family participated in these sorts of groups. Church was the most often mentioned, followed by the Farm Bureau or coop; social groups such as square dance, card club, or lodge; and a variety of other groups. Memorial Day was remembered by Margaret Pille as a special celebration that brought town and rural folks together. Lynn Achak and Margaret Pille, interview with the author, 22 October 1988, El Toro, California, tape recording and transcript, OHC, 23–24.

[21] Lynn Achak and Margaret Pille, interview with the author, 22 October 1988, El Toro, California, OHC, 7–9; Robert Allison, interview with the author, 17 October 1988, Redondo Beach, California, tape recording and transcript, OHC, 30.

Class divisions within communities were drawn along two nonexclu-   15
sive lines: farm versus town, and the more usual manner, according to social group based largely on income. According to Irene Molloy, farm kids
such as herself were one step down from "the kids on the other side of the
track," at least in the eyes of people who lived in town.[22] Growing up in
the 1940s and 1950s in Burlington, Iowa, Priscilla Eckert, the daughter of
an electrical engineer and a school teacher, recalled her awareness of the
existence and importance of class:

> I think I was [aware of it] in high school. I wasn't before that, but I think I
> was in high school because, when I started dating, there were boys who
> couldn't come to the golf club for things that were going on there. I
> couldn't understand that, because everyone went there, I thought. But,
> in fact, everyone didn't go there.[23]

Ethnicity was also a characteristic by which individuals were judged
within and between communities. Dee Ann Shaw explained that, in the
area of Iowa where she grew up, communities were organized based on
where in Scandinavia a family had originated. Norwegians and Swedes
populated her hometown, Callendar, while fifteen miles away was a
town that was primarily Danish. Tension between the towns was so intense that when the Lutheran church burned down in the Danish community, some people in Callendar balked at the idea of Danes coming to
Callendar to go to their Lutheran church.[24]

People were also judged by their religious identification. Discrimination against those not belonging to the dominant Protestant churches was
common, especially in the form of anti-Catholicism. Not only did religious
discrimination divide even people with the same national heritage, it also
denied participation in social life to those not belonging to the dominant
religion, and it helped determine who shared work with whom.[25]

[22] Irene Molloy, interview with the author, 12 September 1988, Los Angeles, California,
tape recording and transcript, OHC, 9–10.

[23] Priscilla Eckert, interview with the author, 29 September 1988, Irvine, California,
OHC, 42.

[24] Dee Ann Shaw, interview with the author, 10 December 1988, Laguna Beach, California, OHC, 27–28. Deborah Fink reported the existence of geographically consolidated, or isolated, depending on how you choose to look at it, ethnic groups in Iowa
as late as the 1980s in her study *Open Country, Iowa: Rural Women, Tradition, and
Change* (Albany: State University of New York Press, 1986), 91. Carl Hamilton also
noted its presence in his reminiscences of farm life in Iowa, 1914–1940, in *No Time at
All* (Ames: Iowa State University Press, 1974), 28–29.

[25] Kenneth Bauermeister, interview with the author, 6 October 1988, Newport Beach,
California, OHC, 23; Joseph Conway, interview with the author, 5 December 1988,
Tustin, California, tape recording and transcript, OHC, 20–21; Doris Headrick, in-
terview with the author, 20 October 1988, La Habra, California, tape recording and

In addition to classification according to class and culture, a second type of judging also was prevalent: the judging of conduct. The tendency to judge conduct, rather than adherence to specific moral rules, has seemed to sociologist Robin Williams to be the basis of Americans' moral orientation.[26] This sort of moral orientation did not go unnoticed by the former Iowans I studied. Eighty-four percent reported it as an aspect of life in Iowa that they remembered most vividly. However, contrary to Williams's belief, it is evident throughout my conversations with the Iowa migrants that there was a moral code against which conduct was appraised. The degree to which a person could be judged a hard worker, and adherence to traditional morals such as honesty, were central elements of that code.

That many Iowans were not far removed from a farming past where survival, not to mention prosperity, depended on everyone doing their part probably accounts for much of the emphasis on being a good, hard worker. Of those I studied, 62 percent were either the children or grandchildren of farmers. But respect for hard work was a value held by city people too. In talking about which Iowa qualities he tried to impart to his children, Don Fromknecht, who was born and raised in Sioux City and Des Moines, noted that one of the values he took from his upbringing was the idea that people get paid what their labor warrants. "I'm still carrying that [motto] the old man [his father] taught us. I still believe that value earned is value received."[27]

Adherence to traditional morals was another standard against which 20 conduct was judged in Iowa. Honesty was cited most frequently as an eminent value. Kenneth Bauermeister explained its importance:

> [There was a] tremendous belief that all people had that they should be as fair and honest with their neighbors as they possibly could because everybody knew everybody. If you started telling a little white lie or whatever it was, it was soon to catch up with you, no matter what it was. It wasn't like the big city where you could hide in an atmosphere of anonymity.[28]

transcript, OHC, 32; Irene Molloy, interview with the author, 12 September 1988, Los Angeles, California, OHC, 26; Helen Perez, interview with the author, 11 October 1988, Burbank, California, tape recording and transcript, OHC, 10; Dee Ann Shaw, interview with the author, 10 December 1988, Laguna Beach, California, OHC, 27–28.

[26] Robin M. Williams, *American Society: A Sociological Interpretation* (New York: Knopf, 1961), 424, quoted by Scott G. McNall and Sally Allen McNall in *Plains Families: Exploring Sociology through Social History* (New York: St. Martin's Press, 1983), 71–72.

[27] Don Fromknecht, interview with the author, 8 October 1988, Fullerton, California, OHC, 63–65.

[28] Kenneth Bauermeister, interview with the author, 6 October 1988, Newport Beach, California, OHC, 13.

In essence, honesty and being a hard worker were essential components of a good reputation in Iowa's small towns. In larger cities, the size of the population made it difficult to make those sorts of assessments about everyone. Instead, other methods were used. For example, Don Fromknecht reported that, in the section of Des Moines where he lived, those who tried to win respect by displaying all that their money could buy were considered not quite trustworthy.[29]

The migrants had mixed feelings about the dynamic of community that I have just described. Generally, all had fond memories of sharing work and social life, but their feelings about judgment varied. Fifty-four percent had decidedly negative feelings on the subject, while the rest were neutral. Common throughout the statements of those in the first group was the sense that judging limited self-expression. It determined the sort of work individuals could pursue, the friendships and marriage bonds that were formed, and even what people did for fun and relaxation. As a result, community proved too restrictive for many.

The consequences for these individuals and for California were significant. Sixty-seven percent of those who were dissatisfied with the judging that went on in Iowa communities held images of southern California as a place of adventure and opportunity. Not coincidentally, the reasons many of them gave for moving to southern California also reflect the adventure and opportunity theme. . . . Of those who stated that they moved in search of greater economic opportunity and/or the desire for more autonomy, anonymity, and adventure than existed in Iowa, 50 percent held images of southern California as a place where life could be different. In short, many of these were the people who defined the California Dream, in part, as an escape from community.

Several questions remain. First, how did the migrants come to associate southern California with escape from community? Second, after they moved to the region, did they like it? Were they satisfied with the level and kind of community that existed in southern California? The first question is difficult to answer definitively because I did not collect any information on how migrants came by their vision of the dream. Still, it is possible to speculate. Many of the migrants who held images of southern California as an escape from community were people looking for something different from what they had in Iowa. And the traditional images portrayed a place not just different, but wonderfully so. The sun, palm trees, citrus, and ocean all depicted a climate where there was greater freedom of movement and dress than was found in Iowa. In addition, the

---

[29] Don Fromknecht, interview with the author, 8 October 1988, Fullerton, California, OHC, 65.

never-ending stories of music, film, and television personalities rising from obscurity to stardom, plus the likewise incessant tales of celebrities' marital peccadillos might have communicated the message that in southern California there was more social freedom as well. To people yearning for greater freedom of self-expression, these traditional images might have conveyed the idea that southern California was just the place for them.

Another way people might have come to associate southern California with escape from the limitations of community is suggested in comments made by Lois Smith. When she was a child in Iowa, her family was desperately poor. During those years, she had an uncle who had moved to California and who occasionally brought his family back to Iowa to visit. It seemed to Smith that her uncle and his family had far more money than her family *because* they had moved to California. She believed that her uncle, who had grown up in the same circumstances in Iowa as her mother, where community imposed restrictions on upward mobility, had been able to escape those conditions in California.[30] So perhaps some migrants came to imagine southern California as an escape from the limitations imposed by community, based on contact with friends and relatives who seemed to have made that escape themselves. Indeed, 65 percent of the migrants had networks of family and friends who had made the trek to California before them.

The migration of Americans who defined the California Dream in part as an escape from community must have had some influence on the nature of that institution in southern California in the post–World War II era. At this time, it is not possible to say when the weak state of community evident today in many suburban neighborhoods of southern California became prevalent. The history of community in southern California has yet to be written. But there is little doubt that the migration of people whose experiences caused them to flee close-knit communities must have had some role in the development of the kind of community that exists today. When asked if they missed the closeness of community they had experienced in Iowa, not surprisingly, some of those who had envisioned southern California as an escape from community replied that they did not. What is surprising, however, is that others, who did not leave Iowa because they were dissatisfied with community life there, also said that they did not long for a more closely knit community life once they settled in the region. For example, Richard Mongar says:

25

---

[30] Lois Smith, interview with the author, 10 September 1988, Lakewood, California, tape recording and transcript, OHC, 14–16.

> Out here in California people have a lot of things going on in their own [lives.] They don't really pay too much attention to other people. I kind of like that though. I like neighbors, but I don't like to have them come in and have a drink in the afternoon, or coffee in the morning. I like to live an independent [life].[31]

Perhaps Mongar's preference for the greater autonomy that life in southern California provided was a result of his adaption to the culture of the region. Or perhaps the cause was his feelings about the closeness of community in Iowa, which he did not reveal. . . .

Throughout the immediate post–World War II decades, the California Dream continued to lure Midwesterners to the Golden State. Portraits of a land of movie stars, palm trees, the ocean, oranges, and a place for a sun-kissed life continued to be central images of the dream. But this examination of the lives of a group of postwar migrants from one state suggests that there was another set of images attached to southern California; that, in fact, the dream was more complex than most of us realize. Images of southern California as an escape from community in the Midwest, where judgments made about people on the basis of class, ethnicity, religion, and adherence to traditional morals seemed to limit individuality, also were a part of the dream, for some.

By understanding these images, and the conditions that created them, we achieve two things. First, we have identified one piece of the puzzle of community in postwar suburban southern California. Through the attitudes and lives of people such as those I studied, we find that the weak sense of community that prevails in many suburban areas of the region is not a fluke. It is the result of probably a number of factors, including the one I have explored here, the new residents' negative experiences of more intimate community elsewhere. And second, for people interested in studying California, these images lend a new perspective to the California Dream, a feature unique to the state, as it was envisioned by some in the postwar decades.

UNDERSTANDING THE TEXT

1. What traditional images and industries attracted Midwesterners to California, according to Spooner?
2. In addition to the traditional images of California, Spooner claims that the state offered a special, unusual attraction. What was it, and why did it appeal particularly to Midwesterners?

---

[31] Richard Mongar, interview with the author, 19 October 1988, Seal Beach, California, tape recording and transcript, OHC. Overall, 31 percent said they did not miss the closeness of the neighborhoods they had left in Iowa.

3. Why, in Spooner's view, did California promotional campaigns target Iowans?

4. What are the positive and negative connotations that Spooner believes the Midwestern migrants attached to the word *community*? How did their attitudes toward community influence their interest in California?

5. According to Spooner, in what ways did Midwesterners judge each other?

EXPLORING AND DEBATING THE ISSUES

1. Spooner claims that because some migrants to California sought an "escape from community" (para. 10), there is "the weak state of community evident today in many suburban neighborhoods of southern California" (para. 25). Write an essay in which you support, challenge, or modify this claim, being sure to focus your discussion on specific neighborhoods or towns. To develop your ideas, you might consult Chapter 4 on California places, particularly the selections by J. A. English-Lueck ("Identified by Technology," p. 236) and Joel Garreau ("Edge City: Irvine," p. 298).

2. Spooner writes that southern California attracted many Midwesterners because they saw it "as a place like the Midwest, but better" (para. 3). Write an essay in which you test her assertion on a city that she mentions, such as Orange, Tustin, or Claremont. If you are unfamiliar with those locations, you could analyze the ways in which the Sacramento community that Joan Didion describes in "Notes from a Native Daughter" (p. 54) resembles a Midwestern community.

3. Interview several friends or relatives who migrated to California from another region in the United States during the post–World War II decades. What were their reasons for moving to this state, and what were their expectations? Did their experiences live up to their expectations? Use your findings to write your own analysis of the images and values that attracted people to California.

4. In class, debate whether the ability to reinvent oneself (which Spooner describes as a motivation for Midwesterners to move to California) is a reality for today's immigrants (from another state or country) to California.

5. Compare and contrast the attitudes toward community held by the Midwesterners whom Spooner describes and those held by the foreign immigrants whom Donald E. Miller, Jon Miller, and Grace Dyrness describe in "Religious Dimensions of the Immigrant Experience" (p. 141).

Notes from a Native Daughter

JOAN DIDION

Few Californians have distinguished themselves as such prominent interpreters of the California scene as **Joan Didion** (b. 1934). The author of numerous essays, short stories, and novels—many of them set in her home state—Didion here presents her perspective as a descendant of Sacramento Valley pioneers, for whom the California dream has a special, even rather exclusive, resonance. In this selection excerpted from her renowned collection of essays *Slouching towards Bethlehem* (1968), Didion admonishes those for whom California ends a few miles east of the coastline not to forget the interior valleys and their place in the California vision. Didion's many books include *Play It As It Lays* (1970), *The White Album* (1979), *Salvador* (1983), *Democracy* (1984), *After Henry* (1992), *The Last Thing He Wanted* (1996), *Political Fictions* (2001), and *Where I Was From* (2003).

It is very easy to sit at the bar in, say, La Scala in Beverly Hills, or Ernie's in San Francisco, and to share in the pervasive delusion that California is only five hours from New York by air. The truth is that La Scala and Ernie's are only five hours from New York by air. California is somewhere else.

Many people in the East (or "back East," as they say in California, although not in La Scala or Ernie's) do not believe this. They have been to Los Angeles or to San Francisco, have driven through a giant redwood and have seen the Pacific glazed by the afternoon sun off Big Sur, and they naturally tend to believe that they have in fact been to California. They have not been, and they probably never will be, for it is a longer and in many ways a more difficult trip than they might want to undertake, one of those trips on which the destination flickers chimerically on the horizon, ever receding, ever diminishing. I happen to know about that trip because I come from California, come from a family, or a congeries of families, that has always been in the Sacramento Valley.

You might protest that no family has been in the Sacramento Valley for anything approaching "always." But it is characteristic of Californians to speak grandly of the past as if it had simultaneously begun, *tabula rasa*, and reached a happy ending on the day the wagons started west. *Eureka*—"I Have Found It"—as the state motto has it. Such a view of history casts a certain melancholia over those who participate in it; my own childhood was suffused with the conviction that we had long outlived our finest hour. In fact that is what I want to tell you about: what it is like to come from a place like Sacramento. If I could make you understand that, I could make you understand California and perhaps something else besides, for Sacramento *is* California, and California is a place in which a boom mentality and a sense of

Chekhovian loss meet in uneasy suspension; in which the mind is troubled by some buried but ineradicable suspicion that things had better work here, because here, beneath that immense bleached sky, is where we run out of continent.

In 1847 Sacramento was no more than an adobe enclosure, Sutter's Fort, standing alone on the prairie; cut off from San Francisco and the sea by the Coast Range and from the rest of the continent by the Sierra Nevada, the Sacramento Valley was then a true sea of grass, grass so high a man riding into it could tie it across his saddle. A year later gold was discovered in the Sierra foothills, and abruptly Sacramento was a town, a town any moviegoer could map tonight in his dreams—a dusty collage of assay offices and wagonmakers and saloons. Call that Phase Two. Then the settlers came—the farmers, the people who for two hundred years had been moving west on the frontier, the peculiar flawed strain who had cleared Virginia, Kentucky, Missouri; they made Sacramento a farm town. Because the land was rich, Sacramento became eventually a rich farm town, which meant houses in town, Cadillac dealers, a country club. In that gentle sleep Sacramento dreamed until perhaps 1950, when something happened. What happened was that Sacramento woke to the fact that the outside world was moving in, fast and hard. At the moment of its waking Sacramento lost, for better or for worse, its character, and that is part of what I want to tell you about.

But the change is not what I remember first. First I remember running a boxer dog of my brother's over the same flat fields that our great-great-grandfather had found virgin and had planted; I remember swimming (albeit nervously, for I was a nervous child, afraid of sinkholes and afraid of snakes, and perhaps that was the beginning of my error) the same rivers we had swum for a century: the Sacramento, so rich with silt that we could barely see our hands a few inches beneath the surface; the American, running clean and fast with melted Sierra snow until July, when it would slow down, and rattlesnakes would sun themselves on its newly exposed rocks. The Sacramento, the American, sometimes the Cosumnes, occasionally the Feather. Incautious children died every day in those rivers; we read about it in the paper, how they had miscalculated a current or stepped into a hole down where the American runs into the Sacramento, how the Berry Brothers had been called in from Yolo County to drag the river but how the bodies remained unrecovered. "They were from away," my grandmother would extrapolate from the newspaper stories. "Their parents had no *business* letting them in the river. They were visitors from Omaha." It was not a bad lesson, although a less than reliable one; children we knew died in the rivers too.

When summer ended—when the State Fair closed and the heat broke, when the last green hop vines had been torn down along the H Street road and the tule fog began rising off the low ground at night—we would go back to memorizing the Products of Our Latin American Neighbors and to visiting the great-aunts on Sunday, dozens of great-aunts, year after year of Sundays. When I think now of those winters I think of yellow elm leaves wadded in the gutters outside the Trinity Episcopal Pro-Cathedral on M Street. There are actually people in Sacramento now who call M Street Capitol Avenue, and Trinity has one of those featureless new buildings, but perhaps children still learn the same things there on Sunday mornings:

Q. In what way does the Holy Land resemble the Sacramento Valley?
A. In the type and diversity of its agricultural products.

And I think of the rivers rising, of listening to the radio to hear at what height they would crest and wondering if and when and where the levees would go. We did not have as many dams in those years. The bypasses would be full, and men would sandbag all night. Sometimes a levee would go in the night, somewhere upriver; in the morning the rumor would spread that the Army Engineers had dynamited it to relieve the pressure on the city.

After the rains came spring, for ten days or so; the drenched fields would dissolve into a brilliant ephemeral green (it would be yellow and dry as fire in two or three weeks) and the real estate business would pick up. It was the time of year when people's grandmothers went to Carmel; it was the time of year when girls who could not even get into Stephens or Arizona or Oregon, let alone Stanford or Berkeley, would be sent to Honolulu, on the *Lurline*. I have no recollection of anyone going to New York, with the exception of a cousin who visited there (I cannot imagine why) and reported that the shoe salesmen at Lord & Taylor were "intolerably rude." What happened in New York and Washington and abroad seemed to impinge not at all upon the Sacramento mind. I remember being taken to call upon a very old woman, a rancher's widow, who was reminiscing (the favored conversational mode in Sacramento) about the son of some contemporaries of hers. "That Johnston boy never did amount to much," she said. Desultorily, my mother protested: Alva Johnston, she said, had won the Pulitzer Prize, when he was working for the *New York Times*. Our hostess looked at us impassively. "He never amounted to anything in Sacramento," she said.

Hers was the true Sacramento voice, and, although I did not realize it then, one not long to be heard, for the war was over and the boom was on and the voice of the aerospace engineer would be heard in the land. Vets no down! Executive living on low FHA!

Later, when I was living in New York, I would make the trip back to Sacramento four and five times a year (the more comfortable the flight, the more obscurely miserable I would be, for it weighs heavily upon my kind that we could perhaps not make it by wagon), trying to prove that I had not meant to leave it all, because in at least one respect California—the California we are talking about—resembles Eden: It is assumed that those who absent themselves from its blessings have been banished, exiled by some perversity of heart. Did not the Donner-Reed Party,[1] after all, eat its own dead to reach Sacramento?

I have said that the trip back is difficult, and it is—difficult in a way   10 that magnifies the ordinary ambiguities of sentimental journeys. Going back to California is not like going back to Vermont, or Chicago; Vermont and Chicago are relative constants, against which one measures one's own change. All that is constant about the California of my childhood is the rate at which it disappears. An instance: On Saint Patrick's Day of 1948 I was taken to see the legislature "in action," a dismal experience; a handful of florid assemblymen, wearing green hats, were reading Pat-and-Mike jokes into the record. I still think of the legislators that way—wearing green hats, or sitting around on the veranda of the Senator Hotel fanning themselves and being entertained by Artie Samish's emissaries. (Samish was the lobbyist who said, "Earl Warren may be the governor of the state, but I'm the governor of the legislature.") In fact there is no longer a veranda at the Senator Hotel—it was turned into an airline ticket office, if you want to embroider the point—and in any case the legislature has largely deserted the Senator for the flashy motels north of town, where the tiki torches flame and the steam rises off the heated swimming pools in the cold Valley night.

It is hard to *find* California now, unsettling to wonder how much of it was merely imagined or improvised; melancholy to realize how much of anyone's memory is no true memory at all but only the traces of someone else's memory, stories handed down on the family network. I have an indelibly vivid "memory," for example, of how Prohibition affected the hop growers around Sacramento: The sister of a grower my family knew brought home a mink coat from San Francisco, and was told to take it back, and sat on the floor of the parlor cradling that coat and crying. Although I was not born until a year after Repeal, that scene is more "real" to me than many I have played myself.

---

[1] California pioneers who practiced cannibalism while trapped in the snow of the High Sierras during the winter of 1846. [Eds.]

I remember one trip home, when I sat alone on a night jet from New York and read over and over some lines from a W. S. Merwin poem I had come across in a magazine, a poem about a man who had been a long time in another country and knew that he must go home:

> . . . But it should be
> Soon. Already I defend hotly
> Certain of our indefensible faults,
> Resent being reminded; already in my mind
> Our language becomes freighted with a richness
> No common tongue could offer, while the mountains
> Are like nowhere on earth, and the wide rivers.

You see the point. I want to tell you the truth, and already I have told you about the wide rivers.

It should be clear by now that the truth about the place is elusive, and must be tracked with caution. You might go to Sacramento tomorrow and someone (although no one I know) might take you out to Aerojet-General, which has, in the Sacramento phrase, "something to do with rockets." Fifteen thousand people work for Aerojet, almost all of them imported; a Sacramento lawyer's wife told me, as evidence of how Sacramento was opening up, that she believed she had met one of them, at an open house two Decembers ago. ("Couldn't have been nicer, actually," she added enthusiastically. "I think he and his wife bought the house next *door* to Mary and Al, something like that, which of course was how *they* met him.") So you might go to Aerojet and stand in the big vendors' lobby where a couple of thousand components salesmen try every week to sell their wares and you might look up at the electrical wallboard that lists Aerojet personnel, their projects and their location at any given time, and you might wonder if I have been in Sacramento lately. MINUTE-MAN, POLARIS, TITAN, the lights flash, and all the coffee tables are littered with airline schedules, very now, very much in touch.

But I could take you a few miles from there into towns where the banks still bear names like The Bank of Alex Brown, into towns where the one hotel still has an octagonal-tile floor in the dining room and dusty potted palms and big ceiling fans; into towns where everything—the seed business, the Harvester franchise, the hotel, the department store and the main street—carries a single name, the name of the man who built the town. A few Sundays ago I was in a town like that, a town smaller than that, really, no hotel, no Harvester franchise, the bank turned out, a river town. It was the golden anniversary of some of my relatives and it was 110 degrees and the guests of honor sat on straight-backed chairs in front of a sheaf of gladioluses in the Rebekah Hall. I mentioned visiting Aerojet-General to a cousin I saw there, who listened to me with interested disbelief. Which is the true California? That is what we all wonder.

Let us try out a few irrefutable statements, on subjects not open to inter-   15
pretation. Although Sacramento is in many ways the least typical of the Valley towns, it *is* a Valley town, and must be viewed in that context. When you say "the Valley" in Los Angeles, most people assume that you mean the San Fernando Valley (some people in fact assume that you mean Warner Brothers), but make no mistake: We are talking not about the valley of the sound stages and the ranchettes but about the real Valley, the Central Valley, the fifty thousand square miles drained by the Sacramento and the San Joaquin Rivers and further irrigated by a complex network of sloughs, cutoffs, ditches, and the Delta-Mendota and Friant-Kern Canals.

A hundred miles north of Los Angeles, at the moment when you drop from the Tehachapi Mountains into the outskirts of Bakersfield, you leave Southern California and enter the Valley. "You look up the highway and it is straight for miles, coming at you, with the black line down the center coming at you and at you . . . and the heat dazzles up from the white slab so that only the black line is clear, coming at you with the whine of the tires, and if you don't quit staring at that line and don't take a few deep breaths and slap yourself hard on the back of the neck you'll hypnotize yourself."

Robert Penn Warren wrote that about another road, but he might have been writing about the Valley road, U.S. 99, three hundred miles from Bakersfield to Sacramento, a highway so straight that when one flies on the most direct pattern from Los Angeles to Sacramento one never loses sight of U.S. 99. The landscape it runs through never, to the untrained eye, varies. The Valley eye can discern the point where miles of cotton seedlings fade into miles of tomato seedlings, or where the great corporation ranches— Kern County Land, what is left of DiGiorgio—give way to private operations (somewhere on the horizon, if the place is private, one sees a house and a stand of scrub oaks), but such distinctions are in the long view irrelevant. All day long, all that moves is the sun, and the big Rainbird sprinklers.

Every so often along 99 between Bakersfield and Sacramento there is a town: Delano, Tulare, Fresno, Madera, Merced, Modesto, Stockton. Some of these towns are pretty big now, but they are all the same at heart, one- and two- and three-story buildings artlessly arranged, so that what appears to be the good dress shop stands beside a W. T. Grant store, so that the big Bank of America faces a Mexican movie house. *Dos Peliculas, Bingo Bingo Bingo.* Beyond the downtown (pronounced *down*town, with the Okie accent that now pervades Valley speech patterns) lie blocks of old frame houses—paint peeling, sidewalks cracking, their occasional leaded amber windows overlooking a Foster's Freeze or a five-minute car wash or a State Farm Insurance office; beyond those spread the shopping centers and the miles of tract houses, pastel with redwood siding, the unmistakable signs of cheap building already blossoming on those houses which have survived the first rain. To a stranger driving 99 in an air-conditioned car (he would be on business, I suppose, any stranger driving 99, for 99 would never get a tourist to Big Sur or San Simeon, never get him to the California he came to see), these towns must seem so flat, so impoverished, as to drain the imagination. They hint at evenings spent hanging around gas stations, and suicide pacts sealed in drive-ins.

But remember:

Q. In what way does the Holy Land resemble the Sacramento Valley?
A. In the type and diversity of its agricultural products.

U.S. 99 in fact passes through the richest and most intensely culti-   20
vated agricultural region in the world, a giant outdoor hothouse with a billion-dollar crop. It is when you remember the Valley's wealth that the monochromatic flatness of its towns takes on a curious meaning, suggests a habit of mind some would consider perverse. There is something in the Valley mind that reflects a real indifference to the stranger in his air-conditioned car, a failure to perceive even his presence, let alone his thoughts or wants. An implacable insularity is the seal of these towns. I once met a woman in Dallas, a most charming and attractive woman accustomed to the hospitality and social hypersensitivity of Texas, who told me that during the four war years her husband had been stationed in Modesto, she had never once been invited inside anyone's house. No one in Sacramento would find this story remarkable ("She probably had no *relatives* there," said someone to whom I told it), for the Valley towns understand one another, share a peculiar spirit. They think alike and they look alike. *I* can tell Modesto from Merced, but I have visited there, gone to dances there; besides, there is over the main street of Modesto an arched sign which reads:

WATER — WEALTH
CONTENTMENT — HEALTH

There is no such sign in Merced.

I said that Sacramento was the least typical of the Valley towns, and it is—but only because it is bigger and more diverse, only because it has had the rivers and the legislature; its true character remains the Valley character, its virtues the Valley virtues, its sadness the Valley sadness. It is just as hot in the summertime, so hot that the air shimmers and the grass bleaches white and the blinds stay drawn all day, so hot that August comes on not like a month but like an affliction; it is just as flat, so flat that a ranch of my family's with a slight rise on it, perhaps a foot, was known for the hundred-some years which preceded this year as "the hill ranch." (It is known this year as a subdivision in the making, but that is another part of the story.) Above all, in spite of its infusions from outside, Sacramento retains the Valley insularity.

To sense that insularity a visitor need do no more than pick up a copy of either of the two newspapers, the morning *Union* or the afternoon *Bee*. The *Union* happens to be Republican and impoverished and the *Bee* Democratic and powerful ("The Valley of the Bees!" as the McClatchys, who own the Fresno, Modesto, and Sacramento *Bees*, used to headline their advertisements in the trade press. "Isolated from All Other Media Influence!"), but they read a good deal alike, and the tone of their chief editorial concerns is strange and wonderful and instructive. The *Union*, in a county heavily and reliably Democratic, frets mainly about the possibility of a local takeover by the John Birch Society; the *Bee*, faithful to the letter of its founder's will, carries on overwrought crusades against phantoms it still calls "the power trusts." Shades of Hiram Johnson, whom the *Bee* helped elect governor in 1910. Shades of Robert La Follette, to whom the *Bee* delivered the Valley in 1924. There is something about the Sacramento papers that does not quite connect with the way Sacramento lives now, something pronouncedly beside the point. The aerospace engineers, one learns, read the San Francisco *Chronicle*.

The Sacramento papers, however, simply mirror the Sacramento peculiarity, the Valley fate, which is to be paralyzed by a past no longer relevant. Sacramento is a town which grew up on farming and discovered to its shock that land has more profitable uses. (The chamber of commerce will give you crop figures, but pay them no mind—what matters is the feeling, the knowledge that where the green hops once grew is now Larchmont Riviera, that what used to be the Whitney ranch is now Sunset City, thirty-three thousand houses and a country-club complex.) It is a town in which defense industry and its absentee owners are suddenly the most important facts; a town which has never had more people or more money, but has lost its *raison d'être*. It is a town many of whose most solid citizens sense about themselves a kind of functional obsolescence. The old families still see only one another, but they do not see even one another as much as they once did; they are closing ranks, preparing for the long night, selling their rights-of-way and living on the proceeds. Their children still marry one another, still play bridge and go into the real-estate business together. (There is no other business in Sacramento, no reality other than land—even I, when I was living and working in New York, felt impelled to take a University of California correspondence course in Urban Land Economics.) But late at night when the ice has melted there is always somebody now, some Julian English, whose heart is not quite in it. For out there on the outskirts of town are marshaled the legions of aerospace engineers, who talk their peculiar condescending language and tend their dichondra and plan to stay in the promised land; who are raising a new generation of native Sacramentans and who do not care, really do not care, that they are not asked to join the Sutter Club. It makes one wonder, late at night when the ice is gone; introduces some air into the womb, suggests that the Sutter Club is perhaps not, after all, the Pacific Union or the Bohemian; that Sacramento is not *the city*. In just such self-doubts do small towns lose their character.

I want to tell you a Sacramento story. A few miles out of town is a place, six or seven thousand acres, which belonged in the beginning to a rancher with one daughter. That daughter went abroad and married a title, and when she brought the title home to live on the ranch, her father built them a vast house—music rooms, conservatories, a ballroom. They needed a ballroom because they entertained: people from abroad, people from San Francisco, house parties that lasted weeks and involved special trains. They are long dead, of course, but their only son, aging and unmarried, still lives on the place. He does not live in the house, for the house is no longer there. Over the years it burned, room by room, wing by wing. Only the chimneys of the great house are still standing, and its heir lives in their shadow, lives by himself on the charred site, in a house trailer.

That is a story my generation knows; I doubt that the next will know it, the children of the aerospace engineers. Who would tell it to them? Their grandmothers live in Scarsdale, and they have never met a great-aunt. "Old" Sacramento to them will be something colorful, something they read about in *Sunset*. They will probably think that the Redevelopment has always been there, that the Embarcadero, down along the river, with its amusing places to shop and its picturesque fire houses turned into bars, has about it the true flavor of the way it was. There will be no reason for them to know that in homelier days it was called Front Street (the town was not, after all, settled by the Spanish) and was a place of derelicts and missions and itinerant pickers in town for a Saturday-night drunk: VICTORIOUS LIFE MISSION, JESUS SAVES, BEDS 25¢ A NIGHT, CROP INFORMATION HERE. They will have lost the real past and gained a manufactured one, and there will be no way for them to know, no way at all, why a house trailer should stand alone on seven thousand acres outside town.

But perhaps it is presumptuous of me to assume that they will be missing something. Perhaps in retrospect this has been a story not about Sacramento at all, but about the things we lose and the promises we break as we grow older; perhaps I have been playing out unawares the Margaret in the poem:

> Margaret, are you grieving
> Over Goldengrove unleaving? . . .
> It is the blight man was born for,
> It is Margaret you mourn for.

UNDERSTANDING THE TEXT

1. Explain in your own words why Didion feels that "Sacramento *is* California" (para. 3).

2. How has Didion's Sacramento changed since her childhood, and what is her response to that change?

3. What tone does Didion adopt in this essay, and how does it affect your response to it?

4. List the occasions where Didion describes the interactions of Sacramento natives with outsiders. What do those events reveal about the "peculiar spirit" (para. 20) she ascribes to the natives?

5. What is the significance of the "Sacramento story" about a man who lives in a trailer on his family's former ranch (para. 25)?

EXPLORING AND DEBATING THE ISSUES

1. Considering that coastal California is home to the majority of the state's population, write an argument in which you support, challenge, or complicate Didion's contention that the Central Valley is the true California.

2. To what extent do you agree with Didion's vision of U.S. 99 as symbolic of the Central Valley and thus of California? If you share her view, write an essay in which you advance your own evidence to support this position. If you disagree, explain why, and propose an alternative freeway or road as a symbol of the state, being sure to explain how its features are characteristically Californian.

3. Didion provides a wealth of details that allow the reader to visualize life in the Central Valley. Using her essay as a model, write an account of your personal experiences in your own hometown. Select details that show your reader the character of the place.

4. In class, discuss the social-class implications of Didion's celebration of Sacramento's "old families" (para. 24). How might someone who worked at Aerojet-General or on a farm respond to her essay?

5. Write an essay in which you support, refute, or modify Didion's belief that the Central Valley has "a peculiar spirit" (para. 20) that is predominantly insular and stagnant.

Proofs

RICHARD RODRIGUEZ

California, like America, is a land of immigrants, but getting here isn't always easy. As **Richard Rodriguez** (b. 1944) describes in this selection, for many Mexican immigrants "you trip, you fall" on the way to *el norte*. You try to avoid *la migra*, or U.S. Border Patrol officers, who seek to thwart your journey to San Diego, San Joaquin, or Sacramento. And "you run." Born to an immigrant family in the San Francisco Bay Area, Rodriguez is an editor for the Pacific News Service who has written for the *Los Angeles Times, Harper's*, the *Saturday Review, Nuestro*, and the *New York Times*, among other publications. He is the author of *Hunger of Memory: The Education of Richard Rodriguez* (1982), an autobiography; *Days of Obligation: An Argument with My Mexican Father* (1992); and *Brown: The Last Discovery of America* (2003).

You stand around. You smoke. You spit. You are wearing your two shirts, two pants, two underpants. Jesús says if they chase you, throw that bag down. Your plastic bag is your mama, all you have left: the yellow cheese she wrapped has formed a translucent rind; the laminated scapular of the Sacred Heart nestles, flame in its cleft. Put it in your pocket. Inside. Put it in your underneath pants' pocket. The last hour of Mexico is twilight, the shuffling of feet. Jesús says they are able to see in the dark. They have X rays and helicopters and searchlights. Jesús says wait, just wait, till he says. Though most of the men have started to move. You feel the hand of Jesús clamp your shoulder, fingers cold as ice. *Venga, corre.* You run. All the rest happens without words. Your feet are tearing dry grass, your heart is lashed like a mare. You trip, you fall. You are now in the United States of America. You are a boy from a Mexican village. You have come into the country on your knees with your head down. You are a man.

Papa, what was it like?

I am his second son, his favorite child, his confidant. After we have polished the DeSoto, we sit in the car and talk. I am sixteen years old. I fiddle with the knobs of the radio. He is fifty.

He will never say. He was an orphan there. He had no mother, he remembered none. He lived in a village by the ocean. He wanted books and he had none.

You are lucky, boy.   5

In the nineteenth century, American contractors reached down into Mexico for cheap labor. Men were needed to build America: to lay track, to mine, to dredge, to harvest. It was a man's journey. And, as a year's contract was extended, as economic dependence was established, sons followed their fathers north. When American jobs turned scarce—during the Depression, as today—Mexicans were rounded up and thrown back over the border. But for generations it has been the rite of passage for the poor Mexican male.

I will send for you or I will come home rich.

In the fifties, Mexican men were contracted to work in America as *braceros*, farm workers. I saw them downtown in Sacramento. I saw men my age drunk in Plaza Park on Sundays, on their backs on the grass. I was a boy at sixteen, but I was an American. At sixteen, I wrote a gossip column, "The Watchful Eye," for my school paper.

Or they would come into town on Monday nights for the wrestling matches or on Tuesdays for boxing. They worked over in Yolo county. They were men without women. They were Mexicans without Mexico.

On Saturdays, they came into town to the Western Union office where   10 they sent money—money turned into humming wire and then turned back into money—all the way down into Mexico. They were husbands, fathers, sons. They kept themselves poor for Mexico.

Much that I would come to think, the best I would think about male Mexico, came as much from those chaste, lonely men as from my own father who made false teeth and who—after thirty years in America—owned a yellow stucco house on the east side of town.

The male is responsible. The male is serious. A man remembers.

Fidel, the janitor at church, lived over the garage at the rectory. Fidel spoke Spanish and was Mexican. He had a wife down there, people said; some said he had grown children. But too many years had passed and he didn't go back. Fidel had to do for himself. Fidel had a clean piece of linoleum on the floor, he had an iron bed, he had a table and a chair. He had a coffee pot and a frying pan and a knife and a fork and spoon, I guess. And everything else Fidel sent back to Mexico. Sometimes, on summer nights, I would see his head through the bars of the little window over the garage at the rectory.

The migration of Mexico is not only international, south to north. The epic migration of Mexico, and throughout Latin America, is from the village to the city. And throughout Latin America, the city has ripened, swollen with the century. Lima. Caracas. Mexico City. So the journey to Los Angeles is much more than a journey from Spanish to English. It is the journey from *tu*—the familiar, the erotic, the intimate pronoun—to the repellent *usted* of strangers' eyes.

Most immigrants to America came from villages. The America that   15
Mexicans find today, at the decline of the century, is a closed-circuit city of ramps and dark towers, a city without God.

It is 1986 and I am a journalist. I am asking questions of a Mexican woman in her East L.A. house. She is watchful and pretty, in her thirties, she wears an apron. Her two boys—Roy and Danny—are playing next door. Her husband is a tailor. He is sewing in a bright bedroom at the back of the house. His feet work the humming treadle of an old Singer machine as he croons Mexican love songs by an open window.

For attribution, mama says she is grateful for America. This country has been so good to her family. They have been here ten years and look, already they have this nice house. Outside the door is Mexican Los Angeles; in the distance, the perpetual orbit of traffic. Here old women walk slowly under lace parasols. The Vietnam vet pushes his tinkling ice cream cart past little green lawns. Teenagers in this neighborhood have scorpions tattooed onto their biceps.

The city is evil. Turn. Turn.

At 16th and Mission in San Francisco, young Mexican Americans in dark suits preach to the passing city from Perfectbound Bibles. They pass leaflets for Victory Outreach—"the junkie church."

In Latin America, Catholicism remains the religion of the village. But   20
in the city now, in Lima as in Los Angeles, more and more souls rap upon the skin of the tambourine for the promise of evangelical Protestantism: You can be cleansed of the city, you can become a new man, you can be born again.

The raven-haired preacher with a slash on his neck tells me his grandmother is from Jalisco, Mexico. His mother understood Spanish but she couldn't speak it. She couldn't do anything right. She was a junkie. She had him when she was seventeen. She disappeared.

"I lived out on the streets. Didn't go past seventh grade. Grass, crack, dust—I've had it all; messed up with gangs, rolled queers. I've stabbed people, man, I've stuck the blade all the way in and felt a heart flutter like a pigeon.

"I was a sinner, I was alone in the city. Until I found Jesus Christ. . . ."

The U.S. Border Patrol station at Chula Vista has a P.R. officer who handles journalists; he says he is glad to have us—"helps in Washington if the public can get a sense of the scope of the problem."

Right now he is occupied with a West German film crew. They were   25
promised a helicopter. Where is the helicopter? Two journalists from a Tokyo daily—with five canvas bags of camera equipment between them—lean against the wall, arms folded. One of them brings up his wrist to look at his watch. A reporter from Chicago catches my sleeve, says, Did I hear about the other night? What? There was a carload of Yugoslavians caught coming over.

The Japanese reporter who is not looking at his watch is popping Cheezits into his mouth. The Border Patrol secretary has made some kind of mistake. She has me down as a reporter for *American Farmer*. Fat red steer in clover. Apologies. White-out. "I . . . agree to abide by any oral directions given to me during the operation by the officer in charge of the unit. . . ." Having signed the form, I am soon assigned a patrolman with whom I will spend the night.

We stop for coffee at a donut shop along the freeway. The patrolman tells me about growing up Tex-Mex in Dallas. After City College, he worked with an antipoverty agency. Then he was a probation officer. He got married, needed money, moved to California, and took this job with the *migra.*

Once into the dark, I cannot separate myself from the patrolman's intention. We ride through the dark in a Ram Charger, both intent upon finding people who do not want to be found.

We come upon a posse of Border Patrolmen preparing to ride into the canyon on horseback. I get out of the truck; ask the questions; pet the horses in the dark, prickly, moist, moving in my hand. The officers call me sir. It is as though I am being romanced at some sort of cowboy cotillion. "Here," says one, "have a look." He invites me so close to his chin I can smell cologne as I peer through his night-vision scope.

Mexico is on the phone—long distance.   30

A crow alights upon a humming wire, bobs up and down, needles the lice within his vest, surveys with clicking eyes the field, the cloud of mites, then dips into the milky air and flies away.

Juanito killed! My mother shrieks, drops the phone in the dark. She cries for my father. For light.

The earth quakes. The peso flies like chaff in the wind. The police chief purchases his mistress a mansion on the hill.

The doorbell rings. I split the blinds to see three nuns standing on our front porch.

Mama. Mama.   35

Monsignor Lyons has sent three Mexican nuns over to meet my parents. The nuns have come to Sacramento to beg for Mexico at the eleven o'clock Mass. We are the one family in the parish that speaks Spanish. As they file into our living room, the nuns smell pure, not sweet, pure like candles or like laundry.

The nun with a black mustache sighs at the end of each story the other two tell. Orphan. Leper. Crutch. Dry land. One eye. Casket.

¡Que lastima!

But the Mexican poor are not bent. They are proof of a refining fire.

The Mexican nuns smile with dignity as they stand after Mass with   40
their baskets extended, begging for Mexico.

A dusty black car pulls up in front of our house. My uncle has brought his family all the way from Ciudad Juarez. During their visit, my mother keeps trying to give them things to take back. There is a pair of lamps in the living room with porcelain roses. My aunt's eyes demur with pleasure to my uncle. My uncle says no. My uncle says his sister's children (I am the only one watching) would get the wrong impression of Mexico.

Mexico is poor. But my mama says there are no love songs like the love songs of Mexico. She hums a song she can't remember. The ice cream there is creamier than here. Someday we will see. The people are kinder — poor, but kinder to each other.

My mother's favorite record is *"Mariachis de Mexico y Pepe Villa con Orchestra."* Every Sunday she plays her record *("Rosas de Plata"; "Madrecita Linda")* while she makes us our pot roast dinner.

Men sing in Mexico. Men are strong and silent. But in song the Mexican male is granted license he is otherwise denied. The male can admit longing, pain, desire.

HAIII — EEEE — a cry like a comet rises over the song. A cry like   45
mock weeping tickles the refrain of Mexican love songs. The cry is meant to encourage the balladeer — it is the raw edge of his sentiment. HAIII-EEEE. It is the man's sound. A ticklish arching of semen, a node wrung up a guitar string, until it bursts in a descending cascade of mockery. HAI. HAI. HAI. The cry of a jackal under the moon, the whistle of the phallus, the maniacal song of the skull.

Tell me, Papa.

What?

About Mexico.

I lived with the family of my uncle. I was the orphan in the village. I used to ring the church bells in the morning, many steps up in the dark. When I'd get up to the tower I could see the ocean.

The village, Papa, the houses too. . . . 50

The ocean. He studies the polished hood of our beautiful blue DeSoto.

Mexico was not the past. People went back and forth. People came up for work. People went back home, to mama or wife or village. The poor had mobility. Men who were too poor to take a bus walked from Sonora to Sacramento.

Relatives invited relatives. Entire Mexican villages got recreated in three stories of a single house. In the fall, after the harvest in the Valley, families of Mexican adults and their American children would load up their cars and head back to Mexico in caravans, for weeks, for months. The school teacher said to my mother what a shame it was the Mexicans did that—took their children out of school.

Like wandering Jews. They carried their home with them, back and forth; they had no true home but the tabernacle of memory.

Each year the American kitchen takes on a new appliance. 55

The children are fed and grow tall. They go off to school with children from Vietnam, from Kansas, from Hong Kong. They get into fights. They come home and they say dirty words.

The city will win. The city will give the children all the village could not—VCRs, hairstyles, drum beat. The city sings mean songs, dirty songs. But the city will sing the children a great Protestant hymn.

You can be anything you want to be.

We are parked. The patrolman turns off the lights of the truck—"back in a minute"—a branch scrapes the door as he rolls out of the van to take a piss. The brush crackles beneath his receding steps. It is dark. Who? Who is out there? The faces I have seen in San Diego—dishwashers, janitors, gardeners. They come all the time, no big deal. There are other Mexicans who tell me the crossing is dangerous.

The patrolman returns. We drive again. I am thinking of epic migra- 60 tions in history books—pan shots of orderly columns of paleolithic peoples, determined as ants, heeding some trumpet of history, traversing miles and miles . . . of paragraph.

The patrolman has turned off the headlights. He can't have to piss again? Suddenly the truck accelerates, pitches off the rutted road, banging, slamming a rock, faster, ignition is off, the truck is soft-pedaled to a stop in the dust; the patrolman is out like a shot. The cab light is on. I sit exposed for a minute. I can't hear anything. Cautiously, I decide to follow—I leave my door open as the patrolman has done. There is a boulder in the field. Is that it? The patrolman is barking in Spanish. His flashlight is trained on the boulder like a laser, he weaves it along the grain as though he is untying a knot. He is: Three men and a woman stand up. The men are young— sixteen, seventeen. The youngest is shivering. He makes a fist. He looks down. The woman is young too. Or she could be the mother? Her legs are very thin. She wears a man's digital wristwatch. They come from some- where. And somewhere—San Diego, Sacramento—somebody is waiting for them.

The patrolman tells them to take off their coats and their shoes, throw them in a pile. Another truck rolls up.

As a journalist, I am allowed to come close. I can even ask questions. There are no questions.

You can take pictures, the patrolman tells me.   65

I stare at the faces. They stare at me. To them I am not bearing wit- ness; I am part of the process of being arrested. I hold up my camera. Their eyes swallow the flash, a long tunnel, leading back.

Your coming of age. It is early. From your bed you watch your mama moving back and forth under the light. The bells of the church ring in the dark. Mama crosses herself. From your bed you watch her back as she wraps the things you will take.

You are sixteen. Your father has sent for you. That's what it means: He has sent an address in Nevada. He is there with your uncle. You re- member your uncle remembering snow with his beer.

You dress in the shadows. You move toward the table, the circle of light. You sit down. You force yourself to eat. Mama stands over you to make the sign of the cross on your forehead with her thumb. You are a man. You smile. She puts the bag of food in your hands. She says she has told *La Virgin*.

Then you are gone. It is gray. You hear a little breeze. It is the rustle of   70 your old black *Dueña*, the dog, taking her short-cuts through the weeds, crazy *Dueña*, her pads on the dust. She is following you.

You pass the houses of the village, each window is a proper name. You pass the store. The bar. The lighted window of the clinic where the pale medical student from Monterrey lives alone and reads his book full of sores late into the night.

You want to be a man. You have the directions in your pocket: an ad- dress in Tijuana, and a map with a yellow line that leads from the highway to an "X" on a street in Reno. You are afraid, but you have never seen snow.

You are just beyond the cemetery. The breeze has died. You turn and throw a rock back at *La Dueña*, where you know she is—where you will always know where she is. She will not go past the cemetery. She will turn in circles like a *loca* and bite herself.

The dust takes on gravel, the path becomes a rutted road which leads to the highway. You walk north. The sky has turned white overhead. Insects click in the fields. In time, there will be a bus.

I will send for you or I will come home rich.   75

UNDERSTANDING THE TEXT

1. Rodriguez combines first-, second-, and third-person points of view in this selection. Write an outline that charts the shifts in narrative perspective. What effect does his strategy have on the reader?

2. What is the effect of starting the selection with "you" (para. 1)?

3. What does Rodriguez mean by saying that the journey from Mexico or Latin America to Los Angeles "is the journey from *tu* . . . to the repellent *usted*" (para. 14)?

4. What are the connotations of the word *proofs*, and how do those connotations shed light on Rodriguez's purpose in writing this selection? Be sure to consider the meaning of *proofs* in photography.

EXPLORING AND DEBATING THE ISSUES

1. Write a letter to a prospective Mexican immigrant in which you attempt to prepare him or her for life in your region of California. As you compose your letter, take into account Rodriguez's characterizations of the goals and interests of Mexican immigrants.

2. Write an essay in which you support, refute, or modify Rodriguez's assertion that the Mexicans he discusses "had no true home but the tabernacle of memory" (para. 54).

3. Rodriguez focuses almost as much on Mexico as he does on the destination of the immigrants he describes. In class, discuss what is significant about that focus and what it suggests about the immigrants' attitudes toward the California dream.

4. Assume the role of the U.S. Border Patrol officer whom Rodriguez describes, and compose a letter to Rodriguez in which you respond to his characterization of you and your professional activities. To develop your ideas, consult William Langewiesche's discussion of the Border Patrol agents in "Invisible Men" (p. 130).

5. Read or reread William Langewiesche's "Invisible Men" (p. 130) and Pierrette Hondagneu-Sotelo's "Maid in L.A." (p. 116), and write an essay in which you analyze the meaning of the California dream for Mexican immigrants. Be sure to note not only similarities in the views of the immigrants described in these selections but also the different attitudes and varying legal, family, and employment conditions that may have shaped those attitudes.

Indian Cartography

DEBORAH MIRANDA

Before the Spanish and before the Americans, there were the Indians; and before the Indians there were the land and the animals, like the salmon that once swam up the Santa Ynez River to spawn. As **Deborah Miranda** writes in this elegaic poem about a place haunted by people, animals, and rivers that are no longer there, almost everything in that river valley is gone except the names that time leaves behind. Dams erase history, geography, and species, this poem tells us, but they can't erase memory, so long as there are those to remember. Miranda is an assistant professor of English at Pacific Lutheran University and is the author of a book of poems, *Indian Cartography* (1999), which received the North American Native Authors First Book Award.

My father opens a map of California—
traces mountain ranges, rivers, county borders
like family bloodlines. Tuolomne,
Salinas, Los Angeles, Paso Robles,
Ventura, Santa Barbara, Saticoy,   5
Tehachapi. Places he was happy,
or where tragedy greeted him
like an old unpleasant relative.
A small blue spot marks
Lake Cachuma, created when they   10
dammed the Santa Ynez, flooded
a valley, divided
my father's boyhood: days
he learned to swim the hard way,
and days he walked across the silver scales,   15
swollen bellies of salmon coming back
to a river that wasn't there.
The government paid those Indians to move away,
he says; I don't know where they went.
In my father's dreams   20
after the solace of a six-pack,
he follows a longing, a deepness.
When he comes to the valley
drowned by a displaced river
he swims out, floats on his face   25
with eyes open, looks down into lands not drawn
on any map. Maybe he sees shadows

72

of a people who are fluid,
fluent in dark water, bodies
long and glinting with sharp-edged jewelry,   30
and mouths still opening, closing
on the stories of our home.

UNDERSTANDING THE TEXT

1. In your own words, summarize the sequence of events in the life of Miranda's father. What message does Miranda convey in describing her father's youth and his current dreams?

2. Check a map of California, and identify the places Miranda mentions in the poem. What does the location of those places suggest about her father's familiarity with the state? How does that degree of familiarity affect your response to the poem?

3. What are the connotations suggested in the title "Indian Cartography"? What different connotations would be conveyed by a title such as "Indian Maps"?

4. In reflecting on the past, Miranda's father "looks down into lands not drawn / on any map" (ll. 26–27). What is Miranda suggesting in these words?

EXPLORING AND DEBATING THE ISSUES

1. In one or two prose paragraphs, rewrite Miranda's poem, trying to convey the same message. What is lost or gained in using poetry to communicate this message? In using prose?

2. Write an essay in which you analyze what the promises of the California dream mean to Miranda's father (consult James J. Rawls's "California: A Place, a People, a Dream," p. 22).

3. Study Judith Lowry's "Roadkill Warrior: Last of His Tribe" (p. 74). Write an essay in which you argue whether this painting can serve as a visual analog to "Indian Cartography."

4. Compare and contrast "Indian Cartography" with Michael J. O'Brien's "Orange County Historian" (p. 75), considering both poems' messages, characters, and imagery. What different or similar goals do "cartographers" and "historians" have, and how does each label affect your understanding of the poems?

Roadkill Warrior: Last of His Tribe (2001)

JUDITH LOWRY

1. This painting tells a story. What is it? You might start with the significance of the title.
2. To what extent might the story described in this painting differ depending on the viewer's perspective—for instance, the perspective of the boy or of an outsider observer?
3. Analyze the inclusion of specific details, such as the lumber truck and real estate signs. How do they contribute to the painting's message?

Orange County Historian

MICHAEL J. O'BRIEN

California is the true home of American car culture, the place where freeways replaced the toll roads of the East in a grand vision of free automobility for all. But
what would happen to the peculiarly Californian song of the open road if the
mother of all traffic tie-ups were to hit, say, Orange County? **Michael J. O'Brien**
explores the possibility in this at once sardonic and utopian 1990 poem in which a
commuter's apocalypse leads to a triumphant return to a saner and more organic
relationship to the California earth. It might be something to consider the next time
you're stuck in traffic.

At 7:30 that Monday morning
all Orange County freeways were congested
terminally
due to three jack-knifed trucks
(a Peterbilt, a Kenworth, and a Mack)   5
which restructured twelve cars
(two Subarus, one Honda, two Hyundais
three Nissans, two Toyotas, one Buick and a
Peugeot),
one trash-truck tipping over   10
(spreading its privates for all to see),
stalled Cadillacs and Pontiacs (about seventeen,
all in the number one and two lanes)
several spinouts on the Garden Grove due to Harry
Tubbs (a high school dropout) who overnight   15
had turned sprinklers away from the ivy
and onto the pavement,
causing the aforementioned vehicles to do
perilous doughnuts on the 22.
Like bathroom drains, on-ramps and off-ramps got   20
plugged up tight, so the thousands who sought
to get to work or school slowed to a crawl,
then to a stop. Airborne traffic reporters
got so excited they ran into each other
or out of gas, gliding down   25
to join the mess congealing on the ground.
After an hour of sitting anxiously,
desperate commuters self-consciously
crawled out of the safety of their steel shells

to look ahead, only to see lines of the disabled. 30
They turned off their engines
began to venture conversations
with their competitors in the race to work,
those who'd sideswiped, tailgated, driven like
jerks, 35
and found them human, decent, companionable,
and, really, just like themselves.
Some commuters fell in love.
Some of those who did not fall in love,
abandoned their cars, began to walk. Others 40
tried phoning, to explain to employers
why they were late, only to find that
no one was there. The circuits cooked,
causing Pac Tel's conduits to explode.
Most lived too far from work to bike or walk. 45
Schools could not open. Mothers lost control,
sent their children outside where they formed
entrepreneurial gangs, hawking sandwiches and
Cokes
they had stolen from refrigerators at home 50
to BMW and Mercedes drivers fearful
of abandoning their machines.
Truckers opened up their trailers right there
sold cantaloupes, Cuisinarts, books by Flaubert.
By Wednesday stores and markets ran empty. 55
Mormons sold provisions from their emergency
supplies,
making profits, (but faithfully tithing)
keeping many people from dying.
Of course, if you've read its history 60
you know that Orange County became again mostly
agrarian, families tearing up dichondra lawns
to plant subsistence crops, working from dawn
to tend potatoes, turnips, brown onions;
those near the sea foraging for mollusks, 65
casting out for bonita, wading in the surf
to spread nets for the barred perch.

UNDERSTANDING THE TEXT

1. What is O'Brien's attitude toward the "agrarian" Orange County at the end of the poem?
2. How does the traffic accident alter human relations in the poem?
3. How does O'Brien use hyperbole and humor to make his point?
4. List the images and metaphors that O'Brien includes in this poem. How do they contribute to the poem's message?
5. What is the effect of including specific car and truck names early in the poem?

EXPLORING AND DEBATING THE ISSUES

1. In your journal, write your own narrative about your experiences with traffic, using O'Brien's details as a model. Your narrative can be poetry or prose, and it can depict either a positive or negative experience.
2. O'Brien's poem narrates a fantasy traffic accident, not a real one. In class, discuss the significance of the poem's title and the poem's presumed description of an "historical" event.
3. In an essay, discuss whether O'Brien's fantasy scenario of how Orange County is transformed by a traffic accident reflects human nature. Do you recognize, even if in exaggerated form, the reactions of the motorists caught in the accident? You might read or reread David Carle, "Sprawling Gridlock" (p. 403).
4. In class, form teams, and debate whether the poem depicts the California dream or, alternately, a paradise lost. To develop your ideas, consult James J. Rawls's "California: A Place, a People, a Dream" (p. 22) and Victor Davis Hanson's "Paradise Lost" (p. 428).

Researching the Issues

1. To what extent do students at your school believe in the traditional California dream? Interview at least half a dozen students about their aspirations and expectations for the future. Write a report detailing and evaluating your findings.

2. Research the California gold rush of 1849. In an essay, explain how it contributed to the formation of the California dream. Be sure to consider the costs as well as the rewards of the gold rush in your analysis.

3. Use the Internet to research the ways in which other states have enacted laws or encouraged public policies that originated in California (some examples include the elimination of affirmative action in public hiring and education, the three strikes law, the use of the recall process

to remove unpopular elected officials). Use your findings as the basis for an argumentative essay that assesses the extent to which California is indeed a bellwether state.

4. Brainstorm in class a list of television programs or movies that feature California as a setting for the action (e.g., *Falling Down, Blade Runner, Beverly Hills 90210, American Graffiti, L.A. Story, Boyz N the Hood, L.A. Confidential,* and *San Francisco*) and then pick one to analyze, showing the ways in which it reflects California mythology.

5. Interview some recent immigrants to California, either from other states or from other nations, and then use your findings to write an essay on why people still come to the Golden State.

6. Interview some members of a California Indian tribe, and ask them what they think of the California dream. Report your findings to the class. You may want to consult *The Earth Is Our Mother: A Guide to the Indians of California, Their Locales, and Historic Sites* by Dolan H. Eargle Jr. (San Francisco: Tress Company Press, 1986).

7. Research the history of Spanish exploration in California, and write a report on the views of such explorers as Gaspar de Portolá and Juan Rodriguez Cabrillo. Consider how the Spanish vision of California differed from, or agreed with, the American vision.

8. Read Joan Didion's novel *Play It As It Lays* (1970), and write an analysis of its interpretation of the southern California dream.

9. Visit the Oakland Museum's online exhibition of gold rush art (http://www.museumca.org/goldrush/art.html), and study the images of gold rush life. To what extent are the images realistic, romanticized, or distorted? Use your observations to support an argument about the likely effect such art had on the nation's perceptions of California in the mid-nineteenth century.

MARVELOUS
DRIVE IN

TUXEDOS

15 AÑERAS
BODAS·PROMS

손금 봅니다   Conselera
                ESPIRITUAL
213 - 387 - 3100   213 - 387 - 3100

- 4 HR. SPECIAL -

15 ANERAS - DAS
TUXEDOS -   OMS
COMUNIO
381 - 25

2

The Great Migration

IMMIGRANTS IN CALIFORNIA HISTORY

On September 10, 2001, all signs were pointing to an epochal event in American immigration history. Two newly elected presidents, George W. Bush of the United States and Vincente Fox of the Republic of Mexico, were poised to conclude a deal that would grant amnesty to millions of undocumented immigrants living in the United States, establish a massive guest-worker program, and, many Mexicans hoped, virtually open the border between the United States and Mexico.

On the next day, all of this changed. With the attacks on the Pentagon and the World Trade Center on September 11, more came crashing down than the twin towers. Suddenly, America's focus shifted from opening its borders to finding ways to police them more effectively. This post-9/11 shift has had particular resonance in California, which, with its long border with Mexico and nation-leading number of Mexican immigrants, documented and undocumented, holds America's greatest stake in immigration policy. As this book is published, three years after the September 11 attacks, negotiations on the future of immigration have resumed, with President Bush proposing, in effect, a guest-worker program that would provide temporary legality to illegal immigrants. But his proposals are already provoking controversies on both sides of the immigration debate, and it is safe to assume that the politics of immigration at both the national and state levels will continue to be contentious issues in the years to come.

In this chapter, you will read and write about immigration, a topic of perennial interest and political controversy in California. This topic never

---

◀ Dennis Keeley, *Strip Mall, Los Angeles, 1996.*

fails to elicit powerful emotions from both supporters and opponents of immigration, and it especially convulsed California politics in the 1990s as ballot initiatives with direct and indirect consequences for immigrants were put to the vote and passed—Proposition 187 (1994), which sought to restrict social services for illegal immigrants; Proposition 209 (1996), which ended affirmative action in state contracting and education; and Proposition 227 (1998), which restricted bilingual education in public schools. After an apparent cooling-off period as California's economy boomed, the issue heated up again in 2003 when then governor Grey Davis signed a bill that granted illegal immigrants the right to obtain California driver's licenses. A major issue in the campaign to recall Governor Davis, the driver's license bill was hastily repealed by Arnold Schwarzenegger in one of his first moves as governor.

The More Things Change, the More They Remain the Same

The politics of immigration demonstrates once again that what happens in America seems to happen in California first. Californians have long debated the pros and cons of immigration, especially non-European immigration, from the late nineteenth century when nativist hostility in California toward Chinese immigrants prompted the nation's first anti-immigrant legislation, the Chinese Exclusion Act of 1882. And although Japanese Americans were interned in detention camps throughout the West during World War II, Manzanar, the most notorious of those camps, was erected in the Owens Valley.

But California's often uneasy immigration history has not been restricted to newcomers from other countries. Indeed, when in the 1930s thousands of Dust Bowl refugees—the Okies immortalized in John Steinbeck's *Grapes of Wrath*—fled to California during the Great Depression, they were met with hostility and suspicion. African Americans came to California after the Civil War, arriving in especially large numbers in the 1940s to work in California's shipyards and munitions factories, flocking to such cities as Richmond and Los Angeles in search of work. (Walter Mosley's detective novel *Devil in a Blue Dress* provides an entertaining fictional portrait of an African American employee in the aerospace industry that flourished in post–World War II L.A.)

Today, as the country experiences demographic changes driven by the arrival of large numbers of Latin American and Asian immigrants, how California resolves its immigration-related conflicts may well serve as a model for the rest of the nation. How we will resolve those conflicts is hard to predict. If you are like most residents of this state, you probably have some strong feelings about the matter—and those feelings might often be diametrically opposed to each other. But no matter what your opinions are, you are likelier than most Americans to have attended a school where both the student body and the curriculum have been affected by immigration. Perhaps you attended a high school where English was not the first language of a majority of the students—indeed, where you and most of your classmates spoke English as a second language. And if you happen to be from Los Angeles, the number of languages that students speak at home make the city's campuses a veritable linguistic United Nations. Such experiences will serve you well as a citizen of a state that will have to resolve its immigration problems harmoniously if it is to survive and, in doing so, may once again lead the nation into the future.

The Readings

Jewelle Taylor Gibbs and Teiahsha Bankhead begin this chapter with an historical overview of California's immigrant saga, a multicultural story filled both with hope and disappointment, opportunity and oppression. A pair of opinion pieces follows, with Yeh Ling-Ling arguing that California cannot solve its educational and budgetary problems as long as immigration remains unchecked, and the editors of the *Contra Costa Times* following with a call for a guest-worker program to stem the tide of immigrant deaths that has accompanied the tightening of America's borders in the wake of 9/11. The next two readings focus on the experience of Asian immigrants to California: Connie Young Yu's family saga documents the lives of Chinese immigrants, especially women, to California in the early twentieth century, and Jeanne Wakatsuki Houston and James D. Houston's classic memoir recounts the internment of Wakatsuki Houston's family at Manzanar following Executive Order 9066, the measure that enabled the detention of virtually the entire Japanese American population during World War II. Pierrette Hondagneu-Sotelo's "Maid in L.A." takes a close look at the often invisible Latin American women who take care of the children and clean the houses of affluent Californians, revealing their often striking opinions about the people who employ them, while William Langewiesche explores the hidden canyons of San Diego County, where undocumented laborers live bleak lives in cardboard shanties. Donald E. Miller, Jon Miller, and Grace Dyrness next study the role that religion plays in California's immigrant communities, especially among those immigrants whose religious traditions are not Judeo-Christian, and Nayereh Tohidi analyzes the experiences of Iranian immigrants to Los Angeles, focusing on immigration's effects on Iranian American gender relations. Nancy Wride's newspaper feature on the children of Vietnamese immigrants to Southern California reveals their mixed emotions when they contemplate their parents' homeland and the new world in which they live, while Mario Garcia concludes the chapter with a personal reflection on what his Latino identity means to him.

Coming to California

Chasing the Dream

JEWELLE TAYLOR GIBBS AND TEIAHSHA BANKHEAD

As Ellis Island and the Statue of Liberty were to early twentieth-century European im-migrants to America, San Francisco and the Golden Gate Bridge have been to late twentieth-century and early twenty-first-century immigrants from Asia and the Pacific Islands. But the place that Asian immigrants called Gold Mountain has also been a magnet for immigrants from all over the earth, the setting for an epic immigrant saga whose outlines are sketched in this historical overview by Jewelle Taylor Gibbs and Teiahsha Bankhead. This saga has not been without conflict, setbacks, and bigotry, and with immigration once again on the front burner of California political contro-versy, it is far from over. But it has also made California the place it is today, a "benchmark," in the authors' words, "for the rest of the country, the initiator of trends, the cradle of creativity, and the bellwether for change." **Jewelle Taylor Gibbs** (b. 1933) is the Zellerbach Family Fund Chair in Social Policy, Community Change, and Practice (Emerita) at the School of Social Welfare, University of California at Berkeley. She is the author of numerous books, including *Race and Justice: Rodney King and O. J. Simpson in a House Divided* (1996), and is a coeditor of *Young, Black and Male in America: An Endangered Species* (1988). **Teiahsha Bankhead** is an as-sistant professor of social work at California State University, Sacramento.

[My mother] told me California was a special place where people judged you on what you did and nothing else. So I worked hard and studied hard. I've always believed California is a very special place. . . . It's a place where if you work hard . . . you can set your goals high and not only dream dreams, but you and your children can then go out and realize them.

— Tom Bradley, Mayor of Los Angeles (qtd. in Rieff, 1991, 62)

San Francisco: Gateway to Asia

If one visits the International Terminal at the San Francisco Airport (per-petually under construction since the 1960s to accommodate the ever in-creasing flow of immigrants, refugees, businessmen, and tourists), one can see the hundreds of Asians and Pacific Islanders arriving daily, tired but excited, speaking rapidly in a cacophony of musical languages, with children, aging parents, and precious possessions in tow. As they fly in low over the Pacific Ocean, the pilot will graciously point out the Golden Gate Bridge, as much a symbol of freedom and opportunity to them as the Statue of Liberty was for the millions of European immigrants who streamed through the turnstiles of Ellis Island in the early years of the twentieth century.

As the hub of the second largest metropolitan area in California, San Francisco epitomizes the tolerance, sophistication, and optimism of Northern California with its proximity to two world-class universities, Silicon Valley, and expensive suburban satellite communities. From the early days of the Gold Rush and the transcontinental railroad, San Francisco has attracted Asian immigrants as laborers, skilled craftspersons, and small entrepreneurs. After the Vietnam War, the San Francisco Bay Area was one of the major ports of disembarkation for thousands of Southeast Asian refugees, who added more spice and style to the city's ethnic salad bowl. In more recent years, the growth of the corporations and the telecommunications industry has spurred a new wave of immigrants from East and South Asia, spawning a new breed of entrepreneurs and the upscale services to cater to their cultural preferences.

Although the heterogeneous Asian population has become the largest ethnic minority group in San Francisco, the City-by-the-Bay has also witnessed the influx of sizable groups of immigrants and refugees from Central America, East Africa, Eastern Europe, and the Middle East, testing both its ability to absorb so many ethnic groups and its flexibility in adapting to such diverse cultures.

In 1997, non-Hispanic whites were only 39 percent of the city of San Francisco's population, compared to 35 percent of Asians, 17 percent of Latinos, 11 percent of African Americans, and less than 1 percent of "others" (Johnson, 1999). While Los Angeles reflects a distinctive Latino culture, San Francisco owes its predominant international flavor to Asia. In just over 25 years, the population of the San Francisco Bay Area (including the six counties surrounding San Francisco to the north, south, and east) shifted from a non-Hispanic white majority population of 77 percent in 1970 to a bare majority of 54 percent in 1997. In 1997, Asians and Latinos in the Bay Area metropolitan region each constituted 19 percent, African Americans 9 percent, and American Indians only 1 percent of the people of color, but nonwhites are predicted to become the majority of the Bay Area's population by 2008.

> It is a dramatic change, but what is happening today is much more in keeping with the state's history than that brief period in the mid-century when it seemed like the only people who came here were whites from other states. (Hans Johnson, cited in McLeod, 1998, 22)

The Lure of Gold Mountain

California, with its lure of gold, its abundant land, and its balmy climate,   5
has attracted immigrants, adventurers, and visionaries ever since it was explored by Spanish missionaries in the eighteenth century. The Golden State
has been a magnet for many looking for a new opportunity, a changed
lifestyle, a new start. Successive waves of migrants and immigrants have
arrived to seek their fortune in the gently rolling hills, the verdant valleys,
the pristine lakes, and the sun-baked desert of California. The latter-day
migrants came as pioneers in movie making, computers, television, and
communications with their theme song "California Dreamin'" and their
inchoate yearnings to find their own places in the sun—dreams of land,
wealth, power, success, and fame.

From its earliest days as part of the northward expansion of the
Spanish conquest of Mexico, California has cultivated close ties with
Mexico and reflected the Spanish-Indian culture in its language, its land
grants, its religion, and its architecture. The missions founded by Father
Junipero Serra in his travels from Baja, California, north along the Pacific
Coast bore the Spanish names of San Diego, Los Angeles, Santa Barbara,
San Jose, and San Francisco, all destined to become major centers of
commerce, industry, and culture in the new state of California (Starr,
1985).

European immigrants and native-born discontents, searching for
adventure and opportunity, many eager to escape the social conventions
and economic constraints of the East and South, flocked to California
during the gold rush fever of the 1850s. Soon joined by imported Chinese
laborers, these whites and Asians provided the sweat and sacrifice that
fueled the growth of the gold country, created the prosperity of San Francisco, and spread the image of Northern California as "Gold Mountain"
to beckon countless generations of Asian immigrants.

While Northern California was developing into a center of commerce, banking, and industry, Southern and Central California welcomed white Southern migrants and immigrants from China, Japan, and
the Philippines to develop their vast agricultural lands. The expansion of
the railroads created another incentive for imported labor to Northern
and Southern California. Mexican laborers found year-round opportunities as they moved from the fertile fields of central California to the vineyards of Napa and Sonoma Counties in Northern California, where Italian
farmers were developing a domestic wine industry (McWilliams, 1946;
Starr, 1985).

As each wave of immigrants and migrants settled into its own economic and cultural niche in California, the state developed its own

map of ethnic heterogeneity. Northern California, especially the San Francisco Bay Area, was a welcoming beacon for Asians, Europeans, and Mediterranean immigrants. Los Angeles, with its proximity to Baja California and the Southwest, was a convenient magnet for Mexicans, Southern whites, and African Americans, while the Central Valley was a haven for Middle Eastern immigrants, Midwestern farmers escaping the "Dust Bowl," and cowboys searching for the last frontier. As communities were confronted with streams of nonwhite immigrants in escalating numbers, the early arriving white immigrants and migrants became increasingly restive and resentful about the minority groups who, in their view, were encroaching upon their land, competing for their jobs, and straining their public schools and social services (Davis, 1992; Schrag, 1998).

Scapegoating "Strangers and Outsiders"

Politicians, always seeking issues to exploit, were quick to sense the ambivalence and anxieties of the white farmers, small businessmen, and blue-collar workers who were concerned about depressed wages, rising land prices, and inflated consumer products. Whenever these anxieties surfaced in California communities, the politicians all too quickly and eagerly found a new immigrant group (nearly always ethnic minorities) who could be blamed for the community's problems. During periods of severe economic depression and wartime hysteria in California, the scapegoating of "strangers and outsiders" was reinforced and legitimized by state and national legislation and further justified and endorsed by the mass media (Daniels & Olin, 1972).

"Strangers and outsiders" were code terms, all too often affixed as pejorative labels to people of color, people who came from non-European countries, people who spoke English with an accent, if at all. These people did not look like the golden-haired models and the tanned lifeguards smiling seductively from the magazine ads and billboards welcoming newcomers to California. No, they looked foreign, spoke foreign languages, and belonged to foreign cultures, thus they could not possibly be mistaken for "real Americans" or treated as equals (Perea, 1997).

Against this backdrop we can understand the motives underlying the Chinese Exclusion Act of 1904, the deportation of thousands of Mexican nationals in the 1930s and 1950s, the restricted entry of Japanese laborers and the alien land laws in the early twentieth century, and the internment of Japanese Americans in relocation camps during World War II (Takaki, 1994). During the Korean War years (1950–1953), the Koreans, who had been imported to fill the agricultural and manufacturing jobs left vacant by the exclusion of the Chinese and Japanese, found themselves targeted as the new "Yellow Peril" by the American public (Kim, 1993).

African Americans, who first migrated to California in small numbers as freed slaves after the Civil War, flocked in groups during the depression years and the Great Migration from the South between the 1920s and 1950s. Most blacks headed straight across Route 66 from Texas and Louisiana to Bakersfield, Los Angeles, and the Central Valley, where they sometimes competed with Mexican migrants for menial service and agricultural jobs. But the majority of blacks preferred urban communities where opportunities for blue-collar jobs and higher wages were available. However, after the Great Depression in 1929 when thousands of Southern whites also fled from the ravages of the dust bowl in Oklahoma, Arkansas, and Texas, demographic changes altered the dynamics of race relations, particularly in Southern and Central California (McWilliams, 1946). The Southern white migrants, socially displaced and economically impoverished, found some measure of misplaced pride and fragile dignity in asserting their Southern norms of racial superiority and separation to distinguish themselves from their black fellow migrants, thereby signaling to prospective employers, realtors, and entrepreneurs that they expected and deserved preferential treatment in employment, housing, and consumer services (Horne, 1995). Skin color superseded all other salient characteristics as a ticket to claim a share of the California pot of gold.

Race, Work, and Politics

There were a series of racial incidents in Southern and Northern California that epitomized the conflicts between whites and nonwhites in the decade between 1940 and 1950. These included:

1. the boycott of white-owned Los Angeles businesses in the 1940s by African Americans who protested racial discrimination in hiring;
2. the "Zoot Suit" riots in June 1943 when angry young Mexican American *pachucos* brawled in the streets of East Los Angeles with Anglo-American sailors who had verbally abused them with racial epithets;
3. the mutiny of black sailors at the Port Chicago naval depot in 1944 after an explosion killed 202 of their comrades who were engaged in loading ammunition onto ships;
4. the protests over segregated housing and restrictive covenants; and
5. the chronic complaints about racial incidents in restaurants, hotels, and public accommodations throughout the decade (Davis, 1992; Horne, 1995).

These protests, demonstrations, and riots were dramatic and divi-   15
sive, but they probably represented the tip of the iceberg of deepening
despair and frustration among people of color toward equally frustrated
and angry whites who perceived some threat to their way of life, their
economic security, and their cultural dominance.

Before and after World War II, successive waves of Chinese, Japanese,
and Filipino laborers had experienced racial discrimination, economic exploitation, and social exclusion as their numbers grew and their needs for
housing, schools, and social services increased. The leaders of the emerging
labor union movement, who viewed them as a threat to white workers' job
security, launched a campaign of racist propaganda against them, joined
forces with nativist politicians, and succeeded in removing the majority of
them as competition for jobs in the expanding economy (Daniels & Olin,
1972). It was the first time, but not the last, when organized labor would
team up with conservative politicians in California to keep a minority group
in its place or, more to the point, to challenge its right to have a place at all.

Meanwhile, other European groups were arriving in California, themselves looking for a chance to win the brass ring. Italians settled in San
Francisco, attracted first by the potential of the commercial fishing industry and later moving into construction, the restaurant industry, and small
businesses. Portuguese fisherman established a niche in the east side of
San Francisco Bay, settling in small towns near Oakland where they could
replicate the cottages and gardens of their native Portugal. Armenians and
Greeks gravitated to the Central Valley, where they brought small farms
and small businesses to rural areas that reminded them of home. When
these newcomers from the southern Mediterranean and middle-Eastern
countries arrived, most were olive-skinned and dark-haired, with prominent features unlike the fair-skinned Irish, English, and Germans who had
preceded them. In recent discussions of the evolution of white ethnic
identity, several writers have asserted that these darker immigrants were
hardly considered "white" in America and were rarely treated as social or
cultural equals by those from Northern and Western Europe (Alba, 1990).
In fact, they were viewed as socially inferior, treated as foreigners or "white
ethnic groups" before that term was in vogue, and tolerated as long as they
did not compete directly with the ruling elite of Anglo-Americans who had
formed the vanguard of the white settlers in California.

However, unlike Asians, Hispanics, Indians, and African Americans,
these European ethnic groups were generally allowed to buy property, establish businesses, and engage in commercial and professional activities
without fear of exclusion, deportation, or overt discrimination. There was
an unwritten and unspoken gentleman's agreement that these newer
immigrants, at the very least, were still Europeans and thus should be

treated with greater respect and dignity than people of color, no matter how many generations they had been in America.

By the beginning of World War II, industries in Southern and Northern California had begun to recruit blacks in order to replace the white workers who were joining the armed services. For the first time in their lives, many of these blacks had the opportunity to move into high-paying skilled and semi-skilled manufacturing jobs in the shipbuilding, airplane manufacturing, and other defense-related industries, creating a solid working-class group among urban African Americans in California (Davis, 1992; Horne, 1995).

At the end of World War II, returning black veterans whose families   20
had bought small homes and created a thriving African American community during the war, found that they were no longer valued workers as defense industries in Northern and Southern California downsized or were transformed into peacetime manufacturing plants (Glasgow, 1980; Horne, 1995). African Americans were not part of the postwar prosperity in California, but part of the postwar surplus. Once again, in an all-too-familiar cycle, blacks were the first fired and the last hired when the economy slowed down and the privilege resurfaced.

The California Multicultural Mosaic

After the Korean War and the Hungarian uprising, two new groups of immigrants arrived in California to compete for their place in the sun. Prior to World War II, the Koreans had a small community in Los Angeles, but this community rapidly expanded from the 1960s to the 1980s (Kim, 1993). Korean shopkeepers soon saw opportunities to expand as middle-man entrepreneurs to other areas around the state, creating a series of small Korea-towns in San Francisco, San Jose, and other cities. During the 1960s and 1970s, Hungarians and other immigrants from Eastern Europe fled repressive Communist regimes to seek political asylum and economic security in the United States, with California as one of their favored destinations.

In the mid- to late 1970s, after the end of the Vietnam War, California welcomed yet another group of refugees from Vietnam, Cambodia, and Laos, introducing a new culture from Southeast Asia to cities like San Jose, Stockton, Sacramento, and Long Beach (Reimers, 1985). As a reward for their military assistance to the United States during World War II, these Southeast Asian refugees, many of whom were illiterate and unskilled from traditional peasant cultures, were afforded an array of economic benefits and social services such as low-cost loans for housing and small businesses, employment training programs, and classes in the English language and American culture. The government's efforts to acculturate and incorporate these refugees into American society stood in striking contrast to their benign neglect of previous immigrants from Asia, Mexico, and Latin America. Within a decade, with the active assistance of government aid, these Southeast Asian refugees had established thriving communities with a commercial infrastructure, social institutions, and political organizations. They, too, had bought into the "California Dream," but would they see their dream turn into a nightmare?

In the 1980s and 1990s the California Dream continued to beckon to still newer groups of immigrants and refugees from El Salvador and Guatemala, fleeing political violence in Central America; from Eritrea and Ethiopia, seeking refuge from three decades of war and revolution in the Horn of Africa; from the chaos of revolution and the trauma of famine in West and Central Africa; from the fall of Communism in Russia and Eastern Europe; and from the poverty and corruption of the Caribbean Islands and South American dictatorships (Maharidge, 1996; Reimers, 1985; Rieff, 1991). Along with those escaping from intolerable social, political, and economic conditions are those immigrants from countries such as India, Pakistan, and South Asia seeking to parlay their technological and scientific skills into material success and professional achievement in California's preeminent high-technology industries and those from the Middle East, searching for freedom from religious and social fundamentalism.

In less than two decades, California has become the home of one of the largest groups of Muslims in the United States with about 150,000 in the San Francisco Bay Area alone. Often dressed distinctively with women in their *hijabs* (head scarves) and modest long dresses and men in their robes and sandals, groups of Muslims have established mosques in several communities, along with successful businesses, restaurants, and farms. Perhaps more than any other group of recent immigrants, Muslims have been the targets of religious prejudice, ethnic discrimination, and various forms of verbal and physical abuse. Viewed by some Americans as "outside the box" due to their traditional dress and unfamiliar religious practices, they are often lumped by association with Middle Eastern terrorists who have been accused of several devastating attacks on American embassies and tourists, airplanes, military installations, and private businesses (e.g., the World Trade Center bombing in New York). This "guilt by association" is frequently used as an excuse to justify the prejudice and discrimination against them by "real Americans," without exposing the underlying anxiety evoked by their "otherness" and the threat of being engulfed by their "exotic" culture and "alien" religion.

Since the end of World War II, in just 50 years, California has become   25
the most racially and culturally diverse state in the nation, home to over 100 ethnic groups who speak even more languages and dialects, are

affiliated with dozens of religious denominations and cults, practice a bewildering array of culturally diverse behaviors, and enjoy a variety of ethnic foods, music, dress, and leisure activities (Maharidge, 1996; Rieff, 1991; Schrag, 1998). California can no longer be characterized in simple stereotypes as the home of the Valley Girl, the Surfer, the Movie Starlet, or the Hippie. While all these images remain a part of the California gestalt, the state's current reality reflects a multicultural and multiracial mosaic of people of color and white ethnic migrants, immigrants, and refugees from around the world, alongside native-born sons and daughters, speakers of many languages, rural, urban, and suburban, rich and poor, skilled and unskilled, traditional and nontraditional.

This California mosaic of racially diverse people, ethnic cultures, and polyglot languages generates the energy that drives the expanding economy, creates the excitement that nurtures the creative arts, and provides the vision that fosters innovation in fields as discrete as fashion design and computer software. California is the benchmark for the rest of the country, the initiator of trends, the cradle of creativity, and the bellwether for change.

References

Alba, R. D. (1990). *Ethnic identity: The transformation of white America.* New Haven: Yale University Press.

Daniels, R., & Olin, S. C., Jr. (1972). *Racism in California: A reader in the history of oppression.* New York: Macmillan.

Davis, M. (1992). *City of Quartz.* New York: Vintage Books.

Glasgow, D. G. (1980). *The black underclass: Poverty, unemployment, and entrapment of ghetto youth.* San Francisco: Jossey-Bass.

Horne, G. (1995). *Fire this time.* Charlottesville: University Press of Virginia.

Johnson, H. (1999). How many Californians? A review of population projections for the state. *California Counts: Profiles and Trends, 1*(1), 10–15.

Kim, E. (1993). Home is where the Han is: A Korean-American perspective on the Los Angeles upheavals. In R. Gooding-Williams (Ed.), *Reading Rodney King/Reading urban uprising* (pp. 215–235). New York: Routledge.

Maharidge, D. (1996). *The coming white minority: California, multiculturalism and America's future.* New York: Vintage Books.

McLeod, R. G. (1998). Minority majority well on its way in state. *San Francisco Chronicle,* September 4, p. 22.

McWilliams, C. (1946). *Southern California country: Island on the land.* New York: Duell, Sloan & Pierce.

Perea, J. F. (Ed.). (1997). *Immigrants out! The new nativism and the anti-immigrant impulse in the United States.* New York: New York University Press.

Reimers, D. (1985). *Still the golden door: The third world comes to America.* New York: Columbia University Press.

Rieff, D. (1991). *Los Angeles: Capital of the third world.* New York: Simon & Schuster.

Schrag, P. (1998). *Paradise lost: California's experiences, America's future.* Berkeley: University of California Press.

Starr, K. (1985). *Inventing the dream: California through the Progressive Era.* New York: Oxford University Press.

Takaki, R. (Ed.). (1994). *From different shores: Perspectives on race and ethnicity in America* (2nd ed.). New York: Oxford University Press.

UNDERSTANDING THE TEXT

1. Summarize in your own words the reasons that California, according to Gibbs and Bankhead, "has been a magnet for many looking for a new opportunity, a changed lifestyle, a new start" (para. 5).

2. The authors describe a number of successive periods in which immigrants from different nations arrived in California. Create a chart of these periods in which you identify the predominant nationalities that came to California. In class, draw on your knowledge of political and economic history, and try to account for the patterns of immigration that your chart reflects.

3. What social and economic factors have some Californians tended to use to distinguish between insiders and "strangers and outsiders" (para. 10)? To what extent has the tendency changed during the time period discussed in this selection?

4. How were the lives of African Americans affected by waves of immigration in the historical periods described in this essay?

5. While most laypersons consider historians to be "objective" recorders of fact, current academic historiography acknowledges the role that personal and theoretical perspectives may play in an historian's rendition of the past. Examine Gibbs and Bankhead's tone and style. To what extent do you find this selection either to be objective or to reveal an implicit argument about the past?

EXPLORING AND DEBATING THE ISSUES

1. Before reading this selection, write a journal entry in which you compile a list of the primary historical events or details related to immigration to California that you have previously learned. After reading the essay, list the information that you had not been aware of, and compare your two lists. Did the essay describe events or experiences of ethnic groups that you had not known of previously? Discuss the results of your experiment with your class.

2. To what extent does the immigrant experience in California, as detailed by Gibbs and Bankhead, reflect the desire to achieve the California dream as James J. Rawls describes it (see "California: A People, a Place, a Dream," p. 22)? To develop your essay, consult the other selections in this chapter.

3. Gibbs and Bankhead assert that "As each wave of immigrants and migrants settled into its own economic and cultural niche in California, the

state developed its own map of ethnic heterogeneity" (para. 9). Consult Mark Baldassare's "Regional Diversity" (p. 387), and develop an essay in which you assess the extent to which the authors of this selection are accurate in their assertion.

4. The authors describe the way immigrants often have been considered "strangers and outsiders" (para. 10). Read or reread William Lange-wiesche's "Invisible Men" (p. 130) and Pierrette Hondagneu-Sotelo's "Maid in L.A." (p. 116). To what extent are the immigrants in these selections considered "strangers and outsiders" by native Californians? To what extent would the immigrants prefer to have a different status?

State Needs a "Time-Out" from Mass Immigration

YEH LING-LING

With annual population increases of over half a million people a year, much of it from immigration, California is having trouble making ends meet. In 2003, California voters recalled a governor whom they blamed for the state budgetary mess, but **Yeh Ling-Ling** (b. 1953) has a different opinion: in her view, unchecked immigration and the drain on social services, including education, that is caused by immigrant-driven population increases are to blame. Weighing in on the perennial controversy over immigration in no uncertain terms, in this September 5, 2002, *Mercury News* article she calls for a moratorium "on most categories of legal immigration" until California's many problems have been resolved. A first-generation immigrant from Vietnam, Yeh is executive director of the Diversity Alliance for a Sustainable America.

Californians feel pessimistic about the direction of the state. That's according to a new poll conducted by the Public Policy Institute of California. Education, jobs and the economy, electricity, and the state budget rank as the top four concerns for California voters. But can any state leader effectively address those concerns without simultaneously advocating a "time-out" from mass immigration?

In the 1950s, California's educational system was one of the finest in this country. Sadly, California's 2000 education achievement ranked near the bottom in the nation in math, although the state's overall budget for education, $49 billion in 2000–2001, far exceeds that of the other states. Many of our schools are struggling to cope with exploding immigration-related enrollment. Many teachers without proper credentials have been hired to deal with English-deficient kids. According to a 2000 news report, a California Department of Education study found that 25 percent of California's 5.6 million schoolchildren could not speak English well enough to understand what goes on in the classroom.

Immigration advocates argue that California's Proposition 13 has curbed property revenues to fund education. But has high immigrant enrollment in our schools improved or exacerbated the problem of overcrowding?

Not surprisingly, according to a Zogby poll released last year, 62 percent of voters in California, including 66 percent of Hispanics, believed that continued immigration made state education reform more difficult. Presently, more than half of Californians surveyed in the new poll are convinced that the area where they live is in a recession. Many Californians indeed cannot make ends meet. Is raising property tax or passing additional billion-dollar bonds the real solution to our problems?

Due to current economic woes, hundreds of thousands of workers in California, professional and low-skilled, are unemployed or underemployed. In addition, according to a study released in 1997 by the National Academy of Sciences, each native household paid an additional $1,200 a year due to services provided to immigrant families.

The state Legislature struggled to close a budget deficit of $24 billion. Painful spending cuts will have to be implemented. Why continue an immigration policy that adds large numbers of workers, students, drivers, and electricity and service users to the state and exacerbates the budgetary problems?

Immigration advocates argue that immigrant workers pay taxes and therefore contribute to the economy. However, a third of immigrants have no high school diplomas. <u>Most low-skilled workers do not pay enough taxes to offset even the costs of educating their children</u>, around $7,000 per child per year, let alone other infrastructure. In fact, low-income people, especially those with many children, qualify for the Earned Income Tax Credit and actually receive as much as $3,500 per family when they file their federal income tax return.

California cannot expect long-term prosperity if we continue to import poverty. The 2000 Census showed a statewide 30 percent increase in people living in poverty in California in the 1990s. A recent news article reported that "legions of working-poor immigrants contribute mightily to inflated poverty levels and declining per capita incomes." Ruth Milkman, director of the UCLA Institute for Labor and Employment, was quoted earlier this year as saying: "We're beginning to resemble much more a Third World society where a class of people are stuck at the bottom."

We all are immigrants or descendants of immigrants, and many foreign-born are good workers and have contributed to California in many ways. However, recent yearly increases of nearly 600,000 people,

(margin annotations: "Overcrowded with students who need extra help", "5", "※")

mostly immigrants, have added a tremendous burden to our infrastructure and government budgets.

Deteriorating quality of life affects natives as well as immigrants. 10 Therefore, if Governor Gray Davis is serious about addressing Californians' concerns, he should urge President Bush and Congress to adopt a moratorium on most categories of legal immigration and fund measures to curb illegal immigration. He should also veto any legislation granting benefits to illegal immigrants.

✳ California needs this time-out to solve many problems that are heightened by exploding population.

UNDERSTANDING THE TEXT

1. What impact has immigration had on education in California, according to Yeh?
2. What strategies does Yeh use to respond to opposing viewpoints?
3. What sort of evidence does Yeh advance to demonstrate her position, and how persuasive do you find it?
4. What are Yeh's solutions to the problems she believes that immigration causes?

EXPLORING AND DEBATING THE ISSUES

1. Yeh uses statistics and rhetorical questions in her essay. In class, discuss the effect of these strategies on the persuasiveness of her argument. What sorts of evidence would you need to gather to refute her position?
2. Write an essay in which you support or refute the proposition that Yeh's status as a first-generation immigrant disqualifies her from arguing for immigration restrictions.
3. Assuming the validity of Yeh's information, what immigration policy would you recommend for California? Write an essay arguing for your recommended policy. To develop your ideas, consult any of the other selections in this chapter.
4. Assume the role of a recent immigrant to California, and write an essay in response to Yeh's argument. You might consult Richard Rodriguez's "Proofs" (p. 64), Nancy Wride's "Vietnamese Youths No Longer Look Homeward" (p. 160), or Pierrette Hondagneu-Sotelo's "Maid in L.A." (p. 116).
5. What are the implications of Yeh's argument for the future of the California dream? To support your position, draw on any of the selections in this chapter or in Chapter 1, "California Dreaming: Myths of the Golden Land."

The New Order

RICARDO DUFFY

1. Catalog the many iconic images in this picture. What is their social and political significance, and how do they illustrate the designer's message?
2. Focus on the figure of George Washington, including the specific details of his clothing. What are they meant to signify?
3. Describe in your own words what "the new order" means, according to this picture.

Revamp Immigration

EDITORS, *CONTRA COSTA TIMES*

Tightened U.S. Border Patrol policies have led, in recent years, to more desperate attempts by undocumented immigrants to enter California, attempts that have in turn led to increased mortality rates among the immigrants themselves. Early in his presidency, George W. Bush began to address the problem of illegal immigration in negotiations with Mexican president Vincente Fox, but the terrorist attacks of September 11, 2001, ended that diplomatic effort. But as the editors of the *Contra Costa Times* argue in this June 4, 2003, editorial, 9/11 didn't put an end to the problem, and steps should be taken to end the suffering and death. "What is needed," they argue, "is a 'guest-worker' system that allows hard-working people to legally cross the border without becoming permanent residents." One wonders if either side in the bitter debate over illegal immigration would concur.

The horrific deaths in Texas of 19 illegal immigrants who suffocated while being transported in locked big rigs, puts an exclamation mark on the urgency for change in the United States' immigration policy. Their deaths were tacked on to the nearly 2,000 people who have died crossing the border while eluding border patrols.

Mexican President Vicente Fox and President Bush got off to a fine start when both were inaugurated within months of each other. The top issue on both their agendas was the issue of illegal immigration.

All that changed after 9/11. The terrorist attacks changed the way the United States viewed all foreigners as potential terrorists; talks between Mexico and the United States were put on the back burner behind Afghanistan and Iraq; and the Immigration and Naturalization Service became part of the Department of Homeland Security. Relations between the two countries cooled even further when Fox spoke out against the United States' war against Saddam Hussein's Iraq.

If the big-rig victims had reached their destinations safely, they would have found jobs in the United States in a variety of industries that depend on undocumented workers. We see them every day and we benefit from their labor. They harvest our food, clean our offices at night, fix our hotel beds, and work in the kitchens of some of our fanciest restaurants.

Mexico's economy still hasn't recovered from the decades of government neglect and abuse under the PRI ruling party. Fox realizes that Mexico's economy cannot create—in the foreseeable future—the millions of jobs it needs to lift his people out of poverty.

On this side of the border, there are jobs that go begging because no one else will do them. And already Mexican workers sent up to $10 billion back to their families, according to a 2002 report.

What is needed is a "guest-worker" system that allows hard-working people to legally cross the border without becoming permanent residents. Both countries would benefit from this arrangement. While here, the guest workers would be protected by labor laws and pay U.S. taxes.

Secretary of State Colin Powell specifically mentioned this proposal last week when trying to assure Mexican Foreign Affairs Secretary Luis Ernesto Derbez that a new immigration policy is still a priority, but a short meeting between Fox and Bush last weekend at the G-8 meeting failed to produce any results. We have tightened our border security with more guards and high-tech detection devices, but as the Texas tragedy shows us, illegal crossings with their accompanying risks are still occurring.

With the increased emphasis on security, it is better to know who is crossing the border, on what day, and where they're working than to continue to force them to come in the dark of night in suffocating truck trailers.

UNDERSTANDING THE TEXT

1. What effect did the September 11, 2001, terrorist attacks have on America's immigration policy, according to the editors?
2. What view do the writers have of immigrants' role in our economy?
3. What solutions to the dilemmas surrounding immigration do the editors suggest?

EXPLORING AND DEBATING THE ISSUES

1. This brief editorial does not elaborate on the suggestion that a "guest-worker" (para. 7) program be instituted to allow the immigration that California needs for certain categories of labor. Review the history of such programs that existed in the past in Jewelle Taylor Gibbs and Teiahsha Bankhead's "Coming to California: Chasing the Dream" (p. 84), and write an essay in which you propose your own version of a guest-worker program. To develop your ideas, you might explore the employment status of workers as described in Pierrette Hondagneu-Sotelo's "Maid in L.A." (p. 116), William Langewiesche's "Invisible Men" (p. 130), or Richard Rodriguez's "Proofs" (p. 64).
2. Adopt the perspective of Yeh Ling-Ling ("State Needs a 'Time-Out' from Mass Immigration," p. 94), and write a response to this editorial.
3. The editorial notes that in California "there are jobs that go begging because no one else will do them" (para. 6). In class, discuss the likely reasons for this employment shortage. Use your class discussion as a prewriting brainstorming session for your own argumentative essay about whether immigration should be further restricted or, as this editorial

suggests, encouraged in a controlled fashion. To develop your ideas, consult any of the articles in this chapter.

4. Two politically sensitive issues that the editorial raises are the facts that many immigrants from Mexico send money out of the country and do not plan to become American citizens. To what extent should this behavioral pattern be taken into account in devising immigration policy? As you develop your argument, you might consult Pierrette Hondagneu-Sotelo's "Maid in L.A." (p. 116), William Langewiesche's "Invisible Men" (p. 130), or Richard Rodriguez's "Proofs" (p. 64).

The World of Our Grandmothers

CONNIE YOUNG YU

Chinese women immigrating to California at the turn of the century often had to overcome both the restrictive traditions of Old World Chinese culture and the nativist hostility of the New World to which they came. **Connie Young Yu** tells the moving story of such women here, focusing on the experiences of her own grandmother, whose struggles to establish herself and her family in California were eventually rewarded. An historian and biographer of Chinese Americans, Yu has published *Profiles in Excellence* (1986) and *Chinatown, San Jose USA* (1993).

In Asian America there are two kinds of history. The first is what is written about us in various old volumes on immigrants and echoed in textbooks, and the second is our own oral history, what we learn in the family chain of generations. We are writing this oral history ourselves. But as we research the factual background of our story, we face the dilemma of finding sources. Worse than burning the books is not being included in the record at all, and in American history—traditionally viewed from the white male perspective—minority women have been virtually ignored. Certainly the accomplishments and struggles of early Chinese immigrants, men as well as women, have been obscured.

Yet for a period in the development of the West, Chinese immigration was a focus of prolonged political and social debate and a subject of daily news. When I first began searching into the background of my people, I read this nineteenth-century material with curious excitement, grateful for any information on Chinese immigration.

Looking for the history of Chinese pioneer women, I began with the first glimpses of Chinese in America— newspaper accounts found in bound volumes of the *Alta California* in the basement of a university library. For Chinese workers, survival in the hostile and chaotic world of Gum San, or Gold Mountain, as California was called by Chinese immigrants, was perilous and a constant struggle, leaving little time or inclination for reflection or diary writing. So for a look into the everyday life of early arrivals from China, we have only the impressions of white reporters on which to depend.

The newspapers told of the comings and goings of "Chinamen," their mining activities, new Chinese settlements, their murders by claim-jumpers, and assaults by whites in the city. An item from 17 August, 1855, reported a "disgraceful outrage": Mr. Ho Alum setting his watch under a street clock when a man called Thomas Field walked up and deliberately dashed the time-piece to the pavement. "Such unprovoked assaults upon unoffending Chinamen are not of rare occurrence. . . ." On the same day the paper also reported the suicide of a Chinese prostitute. In this item no name, details, or commentary were given, only a stark announcement. We can imagine the tragic story behind it: the short miserable life of a young girl sold into slavery by her impoverished parents and taken to Gum San to be a prostitute in a society of single men.

An early history of this period, *Lights and Shades in San Francisco* by B. E. Lloyd (1878), devoted ten chapters to the life of California Chinese, describing in detail "the subjects of the Celestial Kingdom." Chinese women, however, are relegated to a single paragraph:

> Females are little better than slaves. They are looked upon as merchantable property, and are bought and sold like any other article of traffic, though their value is not generally great. A Chinese woman never gains any distinction until after death. . . . Considering the humble position the women occupy in China, and the hard life they therefore lead, it would perhaps be better (certainly more merciful) were they all slain in infancy, and better still, were they never born.[1]

Public opinion, inflamed by lurid stories of Chinese slave girls, agreed with this odious commentary. The only Chinese women whose existence American society acknowledged were the prostitutes who lived miserable and usually short lives. Senate hearings on Chinese immigration in 1876 resounded with harangues about prostitutes and slave girls corrupting the morals of young white boys. "The Chinese race is debauched," claimed one lawyer arguing for the passage of the Chinese Exclusion Law: "They bring no decent women with them." This stigma on the Chinese immigrant woman remained for many decades, causing unnecessary hardship for countless wives, daughters, and slave girls.

Chinese American society finally established itself as families appeared, just as they did in the white society of the forty-niners who

---

[1] B. E. Lloyd, *Lights and Shades in San Francisco* (San Francisco: San Francisco Press, 1878).

arrived from the East Coast without bringing "decent women" with them. Despite American laws intended to prevent the "settlement" of Chinese, Chinese women did make the journey and endured the isolation and hostility, braving it for future generations here.

Even though Chinese working men were excluded from most facets of American society and their lives were left unrecorded, their labors bespoke their existence—completed railroads, reclaimed lands, and a myriad of new industries. The evidence of women's lives seems less tangible. Perhaps the record of their struggles to immigrate and overcome discriminatory barriers is their greatest legacy. Tracing that record therefore becomes a means of recovering our history.

Our grandmothers are our historical links. As a fourth-generation Chinese American on my mother's side, and a third-generation on my father's, I grew up hearing stories about ancestors coming from China and going back and returning again. Both of my grandmothers, like so many others, spent a lot of time waiting in China.

My father's parents lived with us when I was growing up, and through them I absorbed a village culture and the heritage of my pioneer Chinese family. In the kitchen my grandmother told repeated stories of coming to America after waiting for her husband to send for her. (It took sixteen years before Grandfather could attain the status of merchant and only then arrange for her passage to this country.)[2] She also told stories from the village about bandits, festivals, and incidents showing the tyranny of tradition. For example, Grandma was forbidden by her mother-in-law to return to her own village to visit her mother: A married woman belonged solely within the boundaries of her husband's world.

Sometimes I was too young to understand or didn't listen, so my mother—who knew all the stories by heart—told me those stories again later. We heard over and over how lucky Grandpa was to have come to America when he was eleven—just one year before the gate was shut by the exclusion law banning Chinese laborers. Grandpa told of his many jobs washing dishes, making bricks, and working on a strawberry farm. Once, while walking outside Chinatown, he was stoned by a group of whites and ran so fast he lost his cap. Grandma had this story to tell of her anger and frustration: "While I was waiting in the immigration shed,[3]

10

---

[2] Under the Chinese Exclusion Act of 1882, Chinese laborers could no longer immigrate to America. Until the act was repealed in 1943, only merchants, diplomats, students, and visitors were allowed to enter.

[3] Between 1910 and 1940 Chinese immigrants arriving in the port of San Francisco were detained at the Angel Island Immigration Station to await physical examinations and interrogation to determine their right to enter this country. Prior to 1910 immigrants were detained in a building on the wharf known as "the shed."

Grandpa sent in a box of *dim sum*.[4] I was still waiting to be released. I would have jumped in the ocean if they decided to deport me." A woman in her position was quite helpless, but she still had her pride and was not easily pacified. "I threw the box of *dim sum* out the window."

Such was the kind of history I absorbed. I regret deeply that I was too young to have asked the questions about the past that I now want answered; all my grandparents are now gone. But I have another chance to recover some history from my mother's side. Family papers, photographs, old trunks that have traveled across the ocean several times filled with clothes, letters, and mementos provide a documentary on our immigration. My mother—and some of my grandmother's younger contemporaries—fill in the narrative.

A year before the Joint Special Committee of Congress to investigate Chinese immigration met in San Francisco in 1876, my great-grandmother, Chin Shee, arrived to join her husband, Lee Wong Sang, who had come to America a decade earlier to work on the transcontinental railroad. Chin Shee arrived with two brides who had never seen their husbands. Like her own, their marriages had been arranged by their families. The voyage on the clipper ship was rough and long. Seasick for weeks, rolling back and forth as she lay in the bunk, Chin Shee lost most of her hair. The two other women laughed, "Some newlywed you'll make!" But the joke was on them as they mistakenly set off with the wrong husbands, the situation realized only when one man looked at his bride's normal-sized feet and exclaimed, "But the letter described my bride as having bound feet!" Chin Shee did not have her feet bound because she came from a peasant family. But her husband did not seem to care about that nor that the back of her head was practically bald. He felt himself fortunate just to be able to bring his wife to Gum San.

Chin Shee bore six children in San Francisco, where her husband assisted in the deliveries. They all lived in the rear of their grocery store, which also exported dried shrimp and seaweed to China. Great-Grandma seldom left home; she could count the number of times she went out. She and other Chinese wives did not appear in the streets even for holidays, lest they be looked upon as prostitutes. She took care of the children, made special cakes to sell on feast days, and helped with her husband's work. A photograph of her shows a middle-aged woman with a kindly, but careworn face, wearing a very regal brocade gown and a long, beaded necklace. As a respectable, well-to-do Chinese wife in America, married to a successful Chinatown merchant, with children who were by birthright American citizens, she was a rarity in her day. (In contrast, in 1884 Mrs. Jew Lim, the wife of a laborer, sued in federal court to be allowed to join her husband but was denied and deported.)

---

[4] Chinese pastries.

In 1890 there were only 3,868 Chinese women among 103,620 Chinese males in America. Men such as Lee Yoke Suey, my mother's father, went to China to marry. He was one of Chin Shee's sons born in the rear of the grocery store, and he grew up learning the import and export trade. As a Gum San merchant, he had money and status and was able to build a fine house in Toishan. Not only did he acquire a wife but also two concubines. When his wife became very ill after giving birth to an infant who soon died, Yoke Suey was warned by his father that she was too weak to return to America with him. Reminding Yoke Suey of the harsh life in Gum San, he advised his son to get a new wife.

In the town of Foshan, not far from my grandfather's village, lived a girl who was recommended to him by his father's friend. Extremely capable, bright, and with some education, she was from a once prosperous family that had fallen on hard times. A plague had killed her two older brothers, and her heartbroken mother died soon afterwards. She was an excellent cook and took good care of her father, an herb doctor. Her name was Jeong Hing Tong, and she was pretty, with bound feet only three and a half inches long. Her father rejected the offer of the Lee family at first; he did not want his daughter to be a concubine, even to a wealthy Gum San merchant. But the elder Lee assured him this girl would be the wife, the one who would go to America with her husband.

So my maternal grandmother, bride of sixteen, went with my grandfather, then twenty-six, to live in America. Once in San Francisco, Grandmother lived a life of confinement, as did her mother-in-law before her. When she went out, even in Chinatown, she was ridiculed for her bound feet. People called out mockingly to her, *"Jhat!"* meaning bound. She tried to unbind her feet by soaking them every night and putting a heavy weight on each foot. But she was already a grown woman, and her feet were permanently stunted, the arches bent and the toes crippled. It was hard for her to stand for long periods of time, and she frequently had to sit on the floor to do her chores. My mother comments: "Tradition makes life so hard. My father traveled all over the world. There were stamps all over his passport—London, Paris—and stickers all over his suitcases, but his wife could not go into the street by herself."

Their first child was a girl, and on the morning of her month-old "red eggs and ginger party" the earth shook 8.3 on the Richter scale. Everyone in San Francisco, even Chinese women, poured out into the streets. My grandmother, babe in arms, managed to get a ride to Golden Gate Park on a horse-drawn wagon. Two other Chinese women who survived the earthquake recall the shock of suddenly being out in the street milling with thousands of people. The elderly goldsmith in a dimly lit Chinatown store had a twinkle in his eye when I asked him about the scene after the quake. "We all stared at the women because we so seldom saw them in the streets." The city was soon in flames. "We could feel the fire on our faces," recalls Lily Sung, who was seven at the time, "but my sister and I couldn't walk very fast because we had to escort this lady, our neighbor, who had bound feet." The poor woman kept stumbling and falling on the rubble and debris during their long walk to the Oakland-bound ferry.

That devastating natural disaster forced some modernity on the San Francisco Chinese community. Women had to adjust to the emergency and makeshift living conditions and had to work right alongside the men. Life in America, my grandmother found, was indeed rugged and unpredictable.

As the city began to rebuild itself, she proceeded to raise a large family, 20 bearing four more children. The only school in San Francisco admitting Chinese was the Oriental school in Chinatown. But her husband felt, as did most men of his class, that the only way his children could get a good education was for the family to return to China. So they lived in China and my grandfather traveled back and forth to the United States for his trade business. Then suddenly, at the age of forty-three, he died of an illness on board a ship returning to China. After a long and painful mourning, Grandmother decided to return to America with her brood of now seven children. That decision eventually affected immigration history.

At the Angel Island immigration station in San Francisco Bay, Grandmother went through a physical examination so thorough that even her teeth were checked to determine whether she was the age stated on her passport. The health inspector said she had filariasis, liver fluke, a common ailment of Asian immigrants which caused their deportation by countless numbers. The authorities thereby ordered Grandmother to be deported as well.

While her distraught children had to fend for themselves in San Francisco (my mother, then fifteen, and her older sister had found work in a sewing factory), a lawyer was hired to fight for Grandmother's release from the detention barracks. A letter addressed to her on Angel Island from her attorney, C. M. Fickert, dated 24 March 1924, reads: "Everything I can legitimately do will be done on your behalf. As you say, it seems most inhuman for you to be separated from your children who need your care. I am sorry that the immigration officers will not look at the human side of your case."

Times were tough for Chinese immigrants in 1924. Two years before, the federal government had passed the Cable Act, which provided that any woman born in the United States who married a man "ineligible for citizenship" (including the Chinese, whose naturalization rights had been eliminated by the Chinese Exclusion Act) would lose her own citizenship.

So, for example, when American-born Lily Sung, whom I also interviewed, married a Chinese citizen she forfeited her birthright. When she and her four daughters tried to reenter the United States after a stay in China, they were denied permission. The immigration inspector accused her of "smuggling little girls to sell." The Cable Act was not repealed until 1930.

The year my grandmother was detained on Angel Island, a law had just taken effect that forbade all aliens ineligible for citizenship from landing in America.[5] This constituted a virtual ban on the immigration of all Chinese, including Chinese wives of U.S. citizens.

Waiting month after month in the bleak barracks, Grandmother   25
heard many heart-rending stories from women awaiting deportation. They spoke of the suicides of several despondent women who hanged themselves in the shower stalls. Grandmother could see the calligraphy carved on the walls by other detained immigrants, eloquent poems expressing homesickness, sorrow, and a sense of injustice.

Meanwhile, Fickert was sending telegrams to Washington (a total of ten the bill stated) and building up a case for the circuit court. Mrs. Lee, after all, was the wife of a citizen who was a respected San Francisco merchant, and her children were American citizens. He also consulted a medical authority to see about a cure for liver fluke.

My mother took the ferry from San Francisco twice a week to visit Grandmother and take her Chinese dishes such as salted eggs and steamed pork because Grandmother could not eat the beef stew served in the mess hall. Mother and daughter could not help crying frequently during their short visits in the administration building. They were under close watch of both a guard and an interpreter.

After fifteen months the case was finally won. Grandmother was easily cured of filariasis and was allowed—with nine months probation—to join her children in San Francisco. The legal fees amounted to $782.50, a fortune in those days.

In 1927 Dr. Frederick Lam in Hawaii, moved by the plight of Chinese families deported from the islands because of the liver fluke disease, worked to convince federal health officials that the disease was noncommunicable. He used the case of Mrs. Lee Yoke Suey, my grandmother, as a precedent for allowing an immigrant to land with such an ailment and thus succeeded in breaking down a major barrier to Asian immigration.

My most vivid memory of Grandmother Lee is when she was in her   30
seventies and studying for her citizenship. She had asked me to test her

---

[5] The Immigration Act of 1924 affected all Asians who sought to immigrate to the United States. Congress repealed the law as to Chinese in 1943, and then in 1952 through the McCarran-Walter Act as to other Asian ethnic groups.

on the three branches of government and how to pronounce them correctly. I was a sophomore in high school and had entered the "What American Democracy Means to Me" speech contest of the Chinese American Citizens Alliance. When I said the words "judicial, executive, and legislative," I looked directly at my grandmother in the audience. She didn't smile, and afterwards, didn't comment much on my patriotic words. She had never told me about being on Angel Island or about her friends losing their citizenship. It wasn't in my textbooks either. I may have thought she wanted to be a citizen because her sons and sons-in-law had fought for this country, and we lived in a land of freedom and opportunity, but my guess now is that she wanted to avoid any possible confrontation—even at her age—with immigration authorities. The bad laws had been repealed, but she wasn't taking any chances.

I think a lot about my grandmother now and can understand why, despite her quiet, elegant dignity, an aura of sadness always surrounded her. She suffered from racism in the new country, as well as from traditional cruelties in the old. We, her grandchildren, remember walking very slowly with her, escorting her to a family banquet in Chinatown, hating the stares of tourists at her tiny feet. Did she, I wonder, ever feel like the victim of a terrible hoax, told as a small weeping girl that if she tried to untie the bandages tightly binding her feet she would grow up ugly, unwanted, and without the comforts and privileges of the wife of a wealthy man?

We seemed so huge and clumsy around her—a small, slim figure always dressed in black. She exclaimed once that the size of my growing feet were "like boats." But she lived to see some of her granddaughters graduate from college and pursue careers and feel that the world she once knew with its feudal customs had begun to crumble. I wonder what she would have said of my own daughter who is now attending a university on an athletic scholarship. Feet like boats travel far?

I keep looking at the artifacts of the past: the photograph of my grandmother when she was an innocent young bride and the sad face in the news photo taken on Angel Island. I visit the immigration barracks from time to time, a weather-beaten wooden building with its walls marked by calligraphy bespeaking the struggles of our history. I see the view of sky and water from the window out of which my grandmother gazed. My mother told me how, after visiting hours, she would walk to the ferry and turn back to see her mother waving to her from this window. This image has been passed on to me like an heirloom of pain and of love. When I leave the building, emerging from the darkness into the glaring sunlight of the island, I too turn back to look at my grandmother's window.

UNDERSTANDING THE TEXT

1. According to Yu, what are the differences between oral history and written history?

2. How did nineteenth-century American writers depict the Chinese immigrants, in Yu's view?

3. Why does Yu choose to concentrate on her grandmother's stories rather than on her grandfather's tales?

4. What dual predicament did Chinese women face as immigrants to California?

5. Yu's grandmother never told her about her experiences on Angel Island, nor did she celebrate Yu's high school speech about the values of democracy. In your own words, explain the grandmother's response.

EXPLORING AND DEBATING THE ISSUES

1. If your family immigrated to the United States within the last century, write your own family's immigration narrative. Using Yu's essay as a model, you can base your narrative on interviews with relatives, on your memories of family stories, and on other documents or photographs. Alternately, interview a friend whose family emigrated during this period, and ask about his or her family's experiences.

2. Chinese women not only faced racism in America but also encountered new opportunities that are implicit in Yu's account. In an essay, evaluate the drawbacks and benefits that immigration offered to women such as Yu's grandmother.

3. Compare Yu's response to her grandmother's immigration experiences with the responses that the students interviewed by Nancy Wride have to their immigration tales ("Vietnamese Youths No Longer Look Homeward," p. 160). How do you account for any differences you observe?

4. Jewelle Taylor Gibbs and Teiahsha Bankhead ("Coming to California: Chasing the Dream," p. 84) describe the experience of many early-twentieth-century immigrants as being "strangers and outsiders." In an essay, analyze the extent to which this characterization applies to the immigrants mentioned in Yu's selection, considering both the attitudes of mainstream society toward the "outsiders" and the attitudes of the immigrants toward living in a new culture.

Manzanar, U.S.A.

JEANNE WAKATSUKI HOUSTON
and JAMES D. HOUSTON

In 1942, most of the Japanese Americans who were living in the United States (around 120,000 people), native born and immigrant alike, were rounded up and sent to detention camps for the duration of World War II. The camp at Manzanar in the Owens Valley, just east of Mt. Whitney and the Sierra Nevadas, is the most famous of the camps, briefly becoming the largest "city" between Reno and Los Angeles, as **Jeanne Wakatsuki Houston** (b. 1934) and **James D. Houston** (b. 1921) observe in the classic memoir *Farewell to Manzanar* (1973), from which this selection is taken. It is difficult to imagine today how the U.S. government could have ordered members of virtually the entire Japanese American community (many of whom lived in California) to leave their homes and report for forced detention (the U.S. Supreme Court ruled in 1944 that loyal citizens could not be detained against their will), but that is what happened. In this selection, the authors summarize Wakatsuki Houston's family's years in Manzanar, years endured through the spirit conveyed in the Japanese phrase *Shikata ga nai*: "It cannot be helped." "It must be done." As the authors describe here, the inmates at Manzanar transformed the camp into a miniature image of the America that had rejected them, "complete with schools, churches, Boy Scouts, beauty parlors . . . softball leagues," and dance bands. On their release in 1945, many of the detainees found that the property that they had been forced to abandon had been taken by others. It wasn't until the passage of the Civil Liberties Act of 1988 that the U.S. government offered an official apology and reparations of $20,000 to the survivors. Wakatsuki Houston is a Nisei, or second-generation Japanese American, who was born in Inglewood and graduated from San Jose State College (now San Jose State University). Houston, her coauthor and husband, is one of California's most prominent writers, whose many books include *Continental Drift* (1978), *Californians: Searching for the Golden State* (1982), and *The Last Paradise* (2003).

In Spanish, Manzanar means "apple orchard." Great stretches of Owens Valley were once green with orchards and alfalfa fields. It has been a desert ever since its water started flowing south into Los Angeles, sometime during the twenties. But a few rows of untended pear and apple trees were still growing there when the camp opened, where a shallow water table had kept them alive. In the spring of 1943 we moved to Block 28, right up next to one of the old pear orchards. That's where we stayed until the end of the war, and those trees stand in my memory for the turning of our life in camp, from the outrageous to the tolerable.

Papa pruned and cared for the nearest trees. Late that summer we picked the fruit green and stored it in a root cellar he had dug under our new barracks. At night the wind through the leaves would sound like the surf had sounded in Ocean Park, and while drifting off to sleep I could almost imagine we were still living by the beach.

Mama had set up this move. Block 28 was also close to the camp hospital. For the most part, people lived there who had to have easy access to it. Mama's connection was her job as dietician. A whole half of one barracks had fallen empty when another family relocated. Mama hustled us in there almost before they'd snapped their suitcases shut.

For all the pain it caused, the loyalty oath finally did speed up the relocation program. One result was a gradual easing of the congestion in the barracks. A shrewd house-hunter like Mama could set things up fairly comfortably—by Manzanar standards—if she kept her eyes open. But you had to move fast. As soon as the word got around that so-and-so had been cleared to leave, there would be a kind of tribal restlessness, a nervous rise in the level of neighborhood gossip as wives jockeyed for position to see who would get the empty cubicles.

In Block 28 we doubled our living space—four rooms for the twelve of us. Ray and Woody walled them with sheetrock. We had ceilings this time, and linoleum floors of solid maroon. You had three colors to choose from—maroon, black, and forest green—and there was plenty of it around by this time. Some families would vie with one another for the most elegant floor designs, obtaining a roll of each color from the supply shed, cutting it into diamonds, squares, or triangles, shining it with heating oil, then leaving their doors open so that passers-by could admire the handiwork.

Papa brought his still with him when we moved. He set it up behind the door, where he continued to brew his own sake and brandy. He wasn't drinking as much now, though. He spent a lot of time outdoors. Like many of the older Issei men, he didn't take a regular job in camp. He puttered. He had been working hard for thirty years and, bad as it was for him in some ways, camp did allow him time to dabble with hobbies he would never have found time for otherwise.

Once the first year's turmoil cooled down, the authorities started letting us outside the wire for recreation. Papa used to hike along the creeks that channeled down from the base of the Sierras. He brought back chunks of driftwood, and he would pass long hours sitting on the steps carving myrtle limbs into benches, table legs, and lamps, filling our rooms with bits of gnarled, polished furniture.

He hauled stones in off the desert and built a small rock garden outside our doorway, with succulents and a patch of moss. Near it he laid flat steppingstones leading to the stairs.

He also painted watercolors. Until this time I had not known he could paint. He loved to sketch the mountains. If anything made that country habitable it was the mountains themselves, purple when the sun dropped and so sharply etched in the morning light the granite dazzled almost more than the bright snow lacing it. The nearest peaks rose ten thousand feet higher than the valley floor, with Whitney, the highest, just off to the south. They were important for all of us, but especially for the Issei. Whitney reminded Papa of Fujiyama, that is, it gave him the same kind of spiritual sustenance. The tremendous beauty of those peaks was inspirational, as so many natural forms are to the Japanese (the rocks outside our doorway could be those mountains in miniature). They also represented those forces in nature, those powerful and inevitable forces that cannot be resisted, reminding a man that sometimes he must simply endure that which cannot be changed.

Subdued, resigned, Papa's life—all our lives—took on a pattern that   10
would hold for the duration of the war. Public shows of resentment pretty much spent themselves over the loyalty oath crises. *Shikata ga nai* again became the motto, but under altered circumstances. What had to be endured was the climate, the confinement, the steady crumbling away of family life. But the camp itself had been made livable. The government provided for our physical needs. My parents and older brothers and sisters, like most of the internees, accepted their lot and did what they could to make the best of a bad situation. "We're here," Woody would say. "We're here, and there's no use moaning about it forever."

Gardens had sprung up everywhere, in the firebreaks, between the rows of barracks—rock gardens, vegetable gardens, cactus and flower gardens. People who lived in Owens Valley during the war still remember the flowers and lush greenery they could see from the highway as they drove past the main gate. The soil around Manzanar is alluvial and very rich. With water siphoned off from the Los Angeles–bound aqueduct, a large farm was under cultivation just outside the camp, providing the mess halls with lettuce, corn, tomatoes, eggplant, string beans, horseradish, and cucumbers. Near Block 28 some of the men who had been professional gardeners built a small park, with mossy nooks, ponds, waterfalls and curved wooden bridges. Sometimes in the evenings we could walk down the raked gravel paths. You could face away from the barracks, look past a tiny rapids toward the darkening mountains, and for a while not be a prisoner at all. You could hang suspended in some odd, almost lovely land you could not escape from yet almost didn't want to leave.

As the months at Manzanar turned to years, it became a world unto itself, with its own logic and familiar ways. In time, staying there seemed far simpler than moving once again to another, unknown place. It was as if the war were forgotten, our reason for being there forgotten. The present, the little bit of busywork you had right in front of you, became the most urgent thing. In such a narrowed world, in order to survive, you learn to contain your rage and your despair, and you try to re-create, as well as you can, your normality, some sense of things continuing. The fact that America had accused us, or excluded us, or imprisoned us, or whatever it might be called, did not change the kind of world we wanted. Most of us were born in this country; we had no other models. Those parks and gardens lent it an oriental character, but in most ways it was a totally equipped American small town, complete with schools, churches, Boy Scouts, beauty parlors, neighborhood gossip, fire and police departments, glee clubs, softball leagues, Abbott and Costello movies, tennis courts, and traveling shows. (I still remember an Indian who turned up one Saturday billing himself as a Sioux chief, wearing bear claws and head feathers. In the firebreak he sang songs and danced his tribal dances while hundreds of us watched.)

In our family, while Papa puttered, Mama made her daily rounds to the mess halls, helping young mothers with their feeding, planning diets for the various ailments people suffered from. She wore a bright yellow, long-billed sun hat she had made herself and always kept stiffly starched. Afternoons I would see her coming from blocks away, heading home, her tiny figure warped by heat waves and that bonnet a yellow flower wavering in the glare.

In their disagreement over serving the country, Woody and Papa had struck a kind of compromise. Papa talked him out of volunteering; Woody waited for the army to induct him. Meanwhile he clerked in the co-op general store. Kiyo, nearly thirteen by this time, looked forward to the heavy winds. They moved the sand around and uncovered obsidian arrowheads he could sell to old men in camp for fifty cents apiece. Ray, a few years older, played in the six-man touch football league, sometimes against Caucasian teams who would come in from Lone Pine or Independence. My sister Lillian was in high school and singing with a hillbilly band called The Sierra Stars—jeans, cowboy hats, two guitars, and a tub bass. And my oldest brother, Bill, led a dance band called The Jive Bombers—brass and rhythm, with cardboard fold-out music stands lettered J. B. Dances were held every weekend in one of the recreation halls. Bill played trumpet and took vocals on Glenn Miller arrangements of such tunes as "In the Mood," "String of Pearls," and "Don't Fence Me In." He didn't sing "Don't Fence Me In" out of protest, as if trying quietly to mock the authorities. It just happened to be a hit song one year, and they all wanted to be an up-to-date American swing band. They would blast it out into recreation barracks full of bobby-soxed, jitter-bugging couples:

> Oh, give me land, lots of land
> Under starry skies above,
> Don't fence me in.
> Let me ride through the wide
> Open country that I love . . .

Pictures of the band, in their bow ties and jackets, appeared in the   15
high school yearbook for 1943–1944, along with pictures of just about
everything else in camp that year. It was called *Our World*. In its pages
you see school kids with armloads of books, wearing cardigan sweaters
and walking past rows of tarpapered shacks. You see chubby girl yell
leaders, pompons flying as they leap with glee. You read about the school
play, called *Growing Pains* ". . . the story of a typical American home, in
this case that of the McIntyres. They see their boy and girl tossed into the
normal awkward growing up stage, but can offer little assistance or direction in their turbulent course . . ." with Shoji Katayama as George
McIntyre, Takudo Ando as Terry McIntyre, and Mrs. McIntyre played by
Kazuko Nagai.

All the class pictures are in there, from the seventh grade through
twelfth, with individual head shots of seniors, their names followed by
the names of the high schools they would have graduated from on the
outside: Theodore Roosevelt, Thomas Jefferson, Herbert Hoover, Sacred
Heart. You see pretty girls on bicycles, chicken yards full of fat pullets,
patients back-tilted in dental chairs, lines of laundry, and finally, two
large blowups, the first of a high tower with a searchlight, against a Sierra
backdrop, the next a two-page endsheet showing a wide path that curves
among rows of elm trees. White stones border the path. Two dogs are following an old woman in gardening clothes as she strolls along. She is in
the middle distance, small beneath the trees, beneath the snowy peaks. It
is winter. All the elms are bare. The scene is both stark and comforting.
This path leads toward one edge of camp, but the wire is out of sight, or
out of focus. The tiny woman seems very much at ease. She and her tiny
dogs seem almost swallowed by the landscape, or floating in it.

UNDERSTANDING THE TEXT

1. What is the significance of the title of this selection?
2. What did the natural environment, particularly the mountains that surround the Owens Valley, mean to the Japanese Americans interned at
   Manzanar?
3. Describe in your own words what *"shikata ga nai"* (para. 10) means.
   What evidence in this selection demonstrates that the Manzanar internees lived by this precept?
4. Chart the ways in which the different generations living at Manzanar
   adapted to their captivity. What differences and similarities do you see?
5. Describe Wakatsuki Houston and Houston's tone in this selection. What
   does that tone reveal about Wakatsuki Houston's reflections on her
   childhood experiences at Manzanar?

EXPLORING AND DEBATING THE ISSUES

1. Write an essay in which you analyze how the Japanese Americans interned at Manzanar coped with their imprisonment. In what ways did they attempt to recreate a life of normalcy, and to what extent did they succeed or fail in doing so?

2. In class, discuss the responses of Wakatsuki Houston's mother and father to being forced to live at Manzanar. How do you account for any differences you may observe?

3. In an essay, compare the detention of Japanese Americans during World War II to the treatment of Chinese Americans and immigrants in the early twentieth century (see Connie Young Yu, "The World of Our Grandmothers," p. 100, and Jewelle Taylor Gibbs and Teiahsha Bankhead, "Coming to California: Chasing the Dream," p. 84). What do the forced isolation and immigration policies suggest about American attitudes toward Asians?

4. The forced detention of American citizens such as Wakatsuki Houston is a case where the dream of opportunity offered by California disappeared. In an essay, assess the accuracy of James J. Rawls's picture of the promises California can offer its citizens ("California: A People, a Place, a Dream," p. 22). Keep in mind that California was not responsible for the U.S. government's decision to establish internment camps during World War II.

Group of Young Japanese Girls Arriving at Long Beach Railroad Station (1942)

1. Describe this photograph. What is taking place? What seems to be the girls' mood? What do you think the girls' parents told them about their future destination?

2. In what ways do the girls resemble—or differ from—the children described in Jeanne Wakatsuki Houston and James D. Houston's "Manzanar, U.S.A." (p. 109)?

Maid in L.A.

PIERRETTE HONDAGNEU-SOTELO

In Guatemala City, Maribel Centeno had learned the music of classical composers like Ludwig van Beethoven and pianists like Richard Clayderman, but in America, where she took a live-in position as nanny and housekeeper in a twenty-three-room house, such knowledge didn't count for much. Soraya Sanchez, a nanny/housekeeper as well, believes that the women who hire her and her compatriots do so because they just don't "like being with their own kids." True or not, thousands of middle-class and upper-middle-class California families who hire Latina immigrants to take care of their children and houses (at usually below minimum-wage pay rates) don't realize that their quiet and almost invisible servants have lively opinions of their own about the affluent world that their labor helps keep running smoothly. **Pierrette Hondagneu-Sotelo** sets out in this selection to learn about those opinions and about the lives of the women who allow many of California's middle-class and upper-middle-class families to function. An associate professor in the department of sociology at the University of Southern California, Hondagneu-Sotelo is the author of *Doméstica: Immigrant Workers Cleaning and Caring in the Shadows of Affluence* (2001), from which this selection is taken.

Live-In Nanny/Housekeeper Jobs

For Maribel Centeno, newly arrived from Guatemala City in 1989 at age twenty-two and without supportive family and friends with whom to stay, taking a live-in job made a lot of sense. She knew that she wouldn't have to spend money on room and board, and that she could soon begin saving to pay off her debts. Getting a live-in job through an agency was easy. The *señora*, in her rudimentary Spanish, only asked where she was from, and if she had a husband and children. Chuckling, Maribel recalled her initial misunderstanding when the *señora*, using her index finger, had drawn an imaginary "2" and "3" in the palm of her hand. "I thought to myself, well, she must have two or three bedrooms, so I said, fine. 'No,' she said. 'Really, really big.' She started counting, 'One, two, three, four . . . two-three rooms.' It was twenty-three rooms! I thought, *huy!* On a piece of paper, she wrote '$80 a week,' and she said, 'You, child, and entire house.' So I thought, well, I have to do what I have to do, and I happily said, 'Yes.'"

"I arrived on Monday at dawn," she recalled, "and I went to the job on Wednesday evening." When the *señora* and the child spoke to her, Maribel remembered "just laughing and feeling useless. I couldn't understand anything." On that first evening, the *señora* put on classical music, which Maribel quickly identified. "I said, 'Beethoven.' She said, 'Yeah,' and began asking me in English, 'You like it?' I said 'Yes,' or perhaps I said, '*Sí*,' and she began playing other cassettes, CDs. They had Richard

116

Clayderman and I recognized it, and when I said that, she stopped in her tracks, her jaw fell open, and she just stared at me. She must have been thinking, 'No schooling, no preparation, no English, how does she know this music?'" But the *señora*, perhaps because of the language difficulty, or perhaps because she felt upstaged by her live-in's knowledge of classical music, never did ask. Maribel desperately wanted the *señora* to respect her, to recognize that she was smart, educated, and cultivated in the arts. In spite of her best status-signaling efforts, "They treated me," she said, "the same as any other girl from the countryside." She never got the verbal recognition that she desired from the *señora*.

Maribel summed up her experiences with her first live-in job this way: "The pay was bad. The treatment was, how shall I say? It was cordial, a little, uh, not racist, but with very little consideration, very little respect." She liked caring for the little seven-year-old boy, but keeping after the cleaning of the twenty-three-room house, filled with marble floors and glass tables, proved physically impossible. She eventually quit not because of the polishing and scrubbing, but because being ignored devastated her socially.

Compared to many other Latina immigrants' first live-in jobs, Maribel Centeno's was relatively good. She was not on call during all her waking hours and throughout the night, the parents were engaged with the child, and she was not required to sleep in a child's bedroom or on a cot tucked away in the laundry room. But having a private room filled with amenities did not mean she had privacy or the ability to do simple things one might take for granted. "I had my own room, with my own television, VCR, my private bath, and closet, and a kind of sitting room—but everything in miniature, Thumbelina style," she said. "I had privacy in that respect. But I couldn't do many things. If I wanted to walk around in a T-shirt, or just feel like I was home, I couldn't do that. If I was hungry in the evening, I wouldn't come out to grab a banana because I'd have to walk through the family room, and then everybody's watching and having to smell the banana. I could never feel at home, never. Never, never, never! There's always something invisible that tells you this is not your house, you just work here."

It is the rare California home that offers separate maid's quarters, but that doesn't stop families from hiring live-ins; nor does it stop newly arrived Latina migrant workers from taking jobs they urgently need. When live-ins cannot even retreat to their own rooms, work seeps into their sleep and their dreams. There is no time off from the job, and they say they feel confined, trapped, imprisoned. 5

"I lose a lot of sleep," said Margarita Gutiérrez, a twenty-four-year-old Mexicana who worked as a live-in nanny/housekeeper. At her job in a modest-sized condominium in Pasadena, she slept in a corner of a three-year-old child's bedroom. Consequently, she found herself on call day and night with the child, who sometimes went several days without seeing her mother because of the latter's schedule at an insurance company. Margarita was obliged to be on her job twenty-four hours a day; and like other live-in nanny/housekeepers I interviewed, she claimed that she could scarcely find time to shower or brush her teeth. "I go to bed fine," she reported, "and then I wake up at two or three in the morning with the girl asking for water, or food." After the child went back to sleep, Margarita would lie awake, thinking about how to leave her job but finding it hard to even walk out into the kitchen. Live-in employees like Margarita literally have no space and no time they can claim as their own.

Working in a larger home or staying in plush, private quarters is no guarantee of privacy or refuge from the job. Forty-four-year-old Elvia Lucero worked as a live-in at a sprawling, canyon-side residence, where she was in charge of looking after twins, two five-year-old girls. On numerous occasions when I visited her there, I saw that she occupied her own bedroom, a beautifully decorated one outfitted with delicate antiques, plush white carpet, and a stenciled border of pink roses painstakingly painted on the wall by the employer. It looked serene and inviting, but it was only three steps away from the twins' room. Every night one of the twins crawled into bed with Elvia. Elvia disliked this, but said she couldn't break the girl of the habit. And the parents' room lay tucked away at the opposite end of the large (more than 3,000 square feet), L-shaped house.

Regardless of the size of the home and the splendor of the accommodations, the boundaries that we might normally take for granted disappear in live-in jobs. They have, as Evelyn Nakano Glenn has noted, "no clear line between work and nonwork time," and the line between job space and private space is similarly blurred.[1] Live-in nanny/housekeepers are at once socially isolated and surrounded by other people's territory; during the hours they remain on the employers' premises, their space, like their time, belongs to another. The sensation of being among others while remaining invisible, unknown and apart, of never being able to leave the margins, makes many live-in employees sad, lonely, and depressed. Melancholy sets in and doesn't necessarily lift on the weekends.

Rules and regulations may extend around the clock. Some employers restrict the ability of their live-in employees to receive telephone calls, entertain friends, attend evening ESL classes, or see boyfriends during the workweek. Other employers do not impose these sorts of restrictions, but because their homes are located on remote hillsides, in suburban enclaves, or in gated communities, their live-in nanny/housekeepers are effectively kept away from anything resembling social life or public culture. A Spanish-language radio station, or maybe a *telenovela*, may serve as their only link to the outside world.

[1] Glenn 1986:141.

Food—the way some employers hoard it, waste it, deny it, or just   10
simply do not even have any of it in their kitchens—is a frequent topic of
discussion among Latina live-in nanny/housekeepers. These women are
talking not about counting calories but about the social meaning of food
on the job. Almost no one works with a written contract, but anyone taking a live-in job that includes "room and board" would assume that adequate meals will be included. But what constitutes an adequate meal?
Everyone has a different idea, and using the subject like a secret hand-
shake, Latina domestic workers often greet one another by talking about
the problems of managing food and meals on the job. Inevitably, food
enters their conversations.

No one feels the indignities of food more deeply than do live-in employees, who may not leave the job for up to six days at a time. For
them, the workplace necessarily becomes the place of daily sustenance.
In some of the homes where they work, the employers are out all day.
When these adults return home, they may only snack, keeping on hand
little besides hot dogs, packets of macaroni and cheese, cereal, and
peanut butter for the children. Such foods are considered neither nutri-
tious nor appetizing by Latina immigrants, many of whom are accustomed to sitting down to meals prepared with fresh vegetables, rice,
beans, and meat. In some employers' homes, the cupboards are literally
bare. Gladys Villedas recalled that at one of her live-in jobs, the *señora*
had graciously said, " 'Go ahead, help yourself to anything in the kitchen.'
But at times," she recalled, "there was nothing, nothing in the refrigerator!
There was nothing to eat!" Even in lavish kitchens outfitted with Sub-
zero refrigerators and imported cabinetry, food may be scarce. A
celebrity photographer of luxury homes that appear in posh magazines
described to a reporter what he sees when he opens the doors of some
of Beverly Hills' refrigerators: "Rows of cans of Diet Coke, and maybe a
few remains of pizza."[2]

Further down the class ladder, some employers go to great lengths to
economize on food bills. Margarita Gutiérrez claimed that at her live-in
job, the husband did the weekly grocery shopping, but he bought things
in small quantities—say, two potatoes that would be served in half portions, or a quarter of a watermelon to last a household of five all week. He
rationed out the bottled water and warned her that milk would make her
fat. Lately, she said, he was taking both her and the children to an upscale
grocery market where they gave free samples of gourmet cheeses, breads,
and dips, urging them all to fill up on the freebies. "I never thought," exclaimed Margarita, formerly a secretary in Mexico City, "that I would
come to this country to experience hunger!"

[2] Lacher 1997:E1.

Many women who work as live-ins are keenly aware of how food and meals underline the boundaries between them and the families for whom they work. "I never ate with them," recalled Maribel Centeno of her first live-in job. "First of all, she never said, 'Come and join us,' and secondly, I just avoided being around when they were about to eat." Why did she avoid mealtime? "I didn't feel I was part of that family. I knew they liked me, but only because of the good work I did, and because of the affection I showered on the boy; but apart from that, I was just like the gardener, like the pool man, just one more of their staff." Sitting down to share a meal symbolizes membership in a family, and Latina employees, for the most part, know they are not just like one of the family.

Food scarcity is not endemic to all of the households where these women work. In some homes, ample quantities of fresh fruits, cheeses, and chicken stock the kitchens. Some employer families readily share all of their food, but in other households, certain higher-quality, expensive food items may remain off-limits to the live-in employees, who are instructed to eat hot dogs with the children. One Latina live-in nanny/housekeeper told me that in her employers' substantial pantry, little "DO NOT TOUCH" signs signaled which food items were not available to her; and another said that her employer was always defrosting freezer-burned leftovers for her to eat, some of it dating back nearly a decade.

Other women felt subtle pressure to remain unobtrusive, humble, 15 and self-effacing, so they held back from eating even when they were hungry. They talked a lot about how these unspoken rules apply to fruit. "Look, if they [the employers] buy fruit, they buy three bananas, two apples, two pears. So if I eat one, who took it? It's me," one woman said, "they'll know it's me." Another nanny/housekeeper recalled: "They would bring home fruit, but without them having to say it, you just knew these were not intended for you. You understand this right away, you get it." Or as another put it, "*Las Americanas* have their apples counted out, one for each day of the week." Even fruits growing in the garden are sometimes contested. In Southern California's agriculture-friendly climate, many a residential home boasts fruit trees that hang heavy with oranges, plums, and peaches, and when the Latina women who work in these homes pick the fruit, they sometimes get in trouble.[3] Eventually, many of the women solve the food problem by buying and bringing in their own food; early on Monday mornings, you see them walking with

---

[3] One nanny/housekeeper told me that a *señora* had admonished her for picking a bag of fruit, and wanted to charge her for it; another claimed that her employer had said she would rather watch the fruit fall off the branches and rot than see her eat it.

their plastic grocery bags, carting, say, a sack of apples, some chicken, and maybe some prepared food in plastic containers.

The issue of food captures the essence of how Latina live-in domestic workers feel about their jobs. It symbolizes the extent to which the families they work for draw the boundaries of exclusion or inclusion, and it marks the degree to which those families recognize the live-in nanny/housekeepers as human beings who have basic human needs. When they first take their jobs, most live-in nanny/housekeepers do not anticipate spending any of their meager wages on food to eat while on the job, but in the end, most do—and sometimes the food they buy is eaten by members of the family for whom they work.

Although there is a wide range of pay, many Latina domestic workers in live-in jobs earn less than minimum wage for marathon hours: 93 percent of the live-in workers I surveyed in the mid-1990s were earning less than $5 an hour (79 percent of them below minimum wage, which was then $4.25), and they reported working an average of sixty-four hours a week.[4] Some of the most astoundingly low rates were paid for live-in jobs in the households of other working-class Latino immigrants, which provide some women their first job when they arrive in Los Angeles. Carmen Vasquez, for example, had spent several years working as a live-in for two Mexican families, earning only $50 a week. By comparison, her current salary of $170 a week, which she was earning as a live-in nanny/housekeeper in the hillside home of an attorney and a teacher, seemed a princely sum.

Many people assume that the rich pay more than do families of modest means, but working as a live-in in an exclusive, wealthy neighborhood, or in a twenty-three-room house, provides no guarantee of a high salary.

---

[4] Many Latina domestic workers do not know the amount of their hourly wages; and because the lines between their work and nonwork tend to blur, live-in nanny/housekeepers have particular difficulty calculating them. In the survey questionnaire I asked live-in nanny/housekeepers how many days a week they worked, what time they began their job, and what time they ended, and I asked them to estimate how many hours off they had during an average workday (39 percent said they had no time off, but 32 percent said they had a break of between one and three hours). Forty-seven percent of the women said they began their workday at 7 a.m. or earlier, with 62 percent ending their workday at 7 p.m. or later. With the majority of them (71 percent) working five days a week, their average workweek was sixty-four hours. This estimate may at first glance appear inflated; but consider a prototypical live-in nanny/housekeeper who works, say, five days a week, from 7 a.m. until 9 p.m., with one and a half hours off during the children's nap time (when she might take a break to lie down or watch television). Her on-duty work hours would total sixty-four and a half hours per week. The weekly pay of live-in nanny/housekeepers surveyed ranged from $130 to $400, averaging $242. Dividing this figure by sixty-four yields an hourly wage of $3.80. None of the live-in nanny/housekeepers were charged for room and board—and . . . this practice is regulated by law—but 86 percent said they brought food with them to their jobs. The majority reported being paid in cash.

Early one Monday morning in the fall of 1995, I was standing with a group of live-in nanny/housekeepers on a corner across the street from the Beverly Hills Hotel. As they were waiting to be picked up by their employers, a large Mercedes sedan with two women (a daughter and mother or mother-in-law?) approached, rolled down the windows, and asked if anyone was interested in a $150-a-week live-in job. A few women jotted down the phone number, and no one was shocked by the offer. Gore Vidal once commented that no one is allowed to fail within a two-mile radius of the Beverly Hills Hotel, but it turns out that plenty of women in that vicinity are failing in the salary department. In some of the most affluent Westside areas of Los Angeles—in Malibu, Pacific Palisades, and Bel Air—there are live-in nanny/housekeepers earning $150 a week. And in 1999, the *Los Angeles Times* Sunday classified ads still listed live-in nanny/housekeeper jobs with pay as low as $100 and $125.[5] Salaries for live-in jobs, however, do go considerably higher. The best-paid live-in employee whom I interviewed was Patricia Paredes, a Mexicana who spoke impeccable English and who had legal status, substantial experience, and references. She told me that she currently earned $450 a week at her live-in job. She had been promised a raise to $550, after a room remodel was finished, when she would assume weekend housecleaning in that same home. With such a relatively high weekly salary she felt compelled to stay in a live-in job during the week, away from her husband and three young daughters who remained on the east side of Los Angeles. The salary level required that sacrifice.

But once they experience it, most women are repelled by live-in jobs. The lack of privacy, the mandated separation from family and friends, the round-the-clock hours, the food issues, the low pay, and especially the constant loneliness prompt most Latina immigrants to seek other job arrangements. Some young, single women who learn to speak English fluently try to move up the ranks into higher-paying live-in jobs. As soon as they can, however, the majority attempt to leave live-in work altogether. Most live-in nanny/housekeepers have been in the United States for five years or less; among the live-in nanny/housekeepers I interviewed, only two (Carmen Vasquez and the relatively high-earning Patricia Paredes) had been in the United States for longer than that. Like African American women earlier in the century, who tired of what the historian Elizabeth Clark-Lewis has called "the soul-destroying hollowness of live-in domestic work,"[6] most Latina immigrants try to find other options.

---

[5] See, e.g., Employment Classified Section 2, *Los Angeles Times*, June 6, 1999, G9.

[6] Clark-Lewis 1994:123. "After an average of seven years," she notes in her analysis of African American women who had migrated from the South to Washington, D.C., in the early twentieth century, "all of the migrant women grew to dread their live-in situation.

Until the early 1900s, live-in jobs were the most common form of paid   20
domestic work in the United States, but through the first half of the twentieth century they were gradually supplanted by domestic "day work."[7] Live-
in work never completely disappeared, however, and in the last decades of
the twentieth century, it revived with vigor, given new life by the needs of
American families with working parents and young children—and, as we
have seen, by the needs of newly arrived Latina immigrants, many of them
unmarried and unattached to families. When these women try to move up
from live-in domestic work, they see few job alternatives. Often, the best
they can do is switch to another form of paid domestic work, either as a
live-out nanny/housekeeper or as a weekly housecleaner. When they do
such day work, they are better able to circumscribe their work hours, and
they earn more money in less time.[8]

Live-Out Nanny/Housekeepers

When I first met twenty-four-year-old Ronalda Saavedra, she was peeling
a hard-boiled egg for a dog in the kitchen of a very large home where I
was interviewing the employer. At this particular domestic job, the fifth
she had held since migrating from El Salvador in 1991, she arrived daily
around one in the afternoon and left after the children went to bed. On a
typical day, she assisted the housekeeper, a middle-aged woman, with

---

They saw their occupation as harming all aspects of their life" (124). Nearly all of these
women transitioned into day work in private homes. This pattern is being repeated by
Latina immigrants in Los Angeles today, and it reflects local labor market opportunities
and constraints. In Houston, Texas, where many Mayan Guatemalan immigrant
women today work as live-ins, research by Jacqueline Maria Hagan (1998) points to the
tremendous obstacles they face in leaving live-in work. In Houston, housecleaning is
dominated by better-established immigrant women, by Chicanas and, more recently,
by the commercial cleaning companies—so it is hard for the Maya to secure those
jobs. Moreover, Hagan finds that over time, the Mayan women who take live-in jobs see
their own social networks contract, further reducing their internal job mobility.

[7] As noted in chapter 1, several factors explain the shift to day work, including urbanization, interurban transportation systems, and smaller private residences. Historians
have also credited the job preferences of African American domestic workers, who rejected the constraints of live-in work and chose to live with their own families and
communities, with helping to promote this shift in the urban North after 1900 (Katzman 1981; Clark-Lewis 1994:129–35). In many urban regions of the United States, the
shift to day work accelerated during World War I, so that live-out arrangements eventually became more prevalent (Katzman 1981; Palmer 1989). Elsewhere, and for different groups of domestic workers, these transitions happened later in the twentieth
century. Evelyn Nakano Glenn (1986:143) notes that Japanese immigrant and Japanese
American women employed in domestic work in the San Francisco Bay Area moved
out of live-in jobs and into modernized day work in the years after World War II.

[8] Katzman 1981; Glenn 1986.

cleaning, laundry, and errands, and at three o'clock she drove off in her own car to pick up the children—a nine-year-old boy, whom she claimed was always angry, and his hyperactive six-year-old brother.

Once the children were put to bed, Ronalda Saavedra drove home to a cozy apartment that she shared with her brother in the San Fernando Valley. When I visited her, I saw that it was a tiny place, about half the size of the kitchen where we had first met; but it was pleasantly outfitted with new bleached oak furniture, and the morning sunshine that streamed in through a large window gave it a cheerful, almost spacious feel. Ronalda kept a well-stocked refrigerator, and during our interview she served me *pan dulce*, coffee, and honeydew melon.

Like many other women, Ronalda had begun her work stint in the United States with a live-in job, but she vastly preferred living out. She slept through the night in peace, attended ESL classes in the morning, ate what she wanted when she wanted it, and talked daily on the phone with her fiancé. All this was possible because live-out jobs are firmly circumscribed. Even when women find it difficult to say no to their employers when they are asked, at the last minute, to stay and work another hour or two, they know they will eventually retreat to their own places. So while the workday tasks and rhythms are similar to those of live-ins, the job demands on live-outs stop when they exit the houses where they work and return to their own homes, usually small and sometimes crowded apartments located in one of Los Angeles' many Latino neighborhoods. For such women with husbands or with children of their own, live-out jobs allow them to actually live with their family members and see them daily.

Live-out nanny/housekeepers also earn more money than live-ins. Most of them work eight or nine hours a day, and of those I surveyed, 60 percent worked five days a week or fewer. Their mean hourly wages were $5.90—not an exorbitant wage by any means, but above the legal minimum, unlike the wages of their peers in live-in jobs. Ronalda earned $350 for her forty-hour workweek, making her hourly wage $8.75. On top of this, her employer gave her an additional $50 to cover gasoline expenses, as Ronalda spent a portion of each afternoon driving on errands, such as going to the dry cleaners, and ferrying the children home from school and then to and from soccer practices, music lessons, and so on. In the suburban landscape of Los Angeles, employers pay an extra premium for nanny/housekeepers who can provide this shuttling service. Only Latina nanny/housekeepers with experience, strong references, English skills, and an impressive array of certificates and licenses enjoy earnings that reach Ronalda's level.

Today, most Americans who hire a domestic worker to come into   25
their homes on a daily basis do so in order to meet their needs for *both*

housecleaning and child care. Most Latina nanny/housekeepers work in households where they are solely responsible for these tasks, and they work hard to fit in the cleaning and laundry (most of them don't cook) while the children are napping or at school. Some of them feel, as one woman said, that they need to be "octopuses," with busy arms extended simultaneously in all directions. A big part of their job requires taking care of the children; and various issues with the children present nanny/housekeepers with their greatest frustrations. Paradoxically, they also experience some of their deepest job satisfaction with these children with whom they spend so much time.

After what may be years of watching, feeding, playing with, and reprimanding the same child from birth to elementary school, day in and day out, some nanny/housekeepers grow very fond of their charges and look back nostalgically, remembering, say, when a child took her first steps or first learned nursery rhymes in Spanish. Ronalda, an articulate, highly animated woman who told stories using a lot of gestures and facial expressions, talked a great deal about the children she had cared for in her various jobs. She imitated the voices of children she had taken care of, describing longingly little girls who were, she said, "*muy* nice" or "*tan* sweet," and recalled the imaginary games they would play. Like many other nanny/housekeepers, she wept freely when she remembered some of the intimate and amusing moments she had spent with children she no longer saw. She also described other children who, she said, were dour, disrespectful, and disobedient.

Many live-out nanny/housekeepers made care work—the work of keeping the children clean, happy, well nourished, and above all safe—a priority over housecleaning duties. This sometimes created conflicts with their employers, who despite saying that their children should come first still expected a spotless house. "The truth is," explained Teresa Portillo, who looked after a child only on the weekends, "when you are taking care of children, you can't neglect anything, absolutely nothing! Because the moment you do, they do whatever little *travesura*, and they scrape their knees, cut themselves or whatever." Nanny/housekeepers fear they will be sent to jail if anything happens to the children.

Feeding the children is a big part of the job. Unlike their live-in peers, when live-out nanny/housekeepers talk about food, they're usually concerned with what the children eat or don't eat. Some of them derive tremendous pleasure and satisfaction from bringing the children special treats prepared at their own homes—maybe homemade flan or *pan con crema*, or simply a mango. Some nanny/housekeepers are also in charge, to their dismay, of feeding and cleaning the children's menagerie of pets. Many feel disgusted when they have to bathe and give eyedrops to old, sick dogs, or clean the cages of iguanas, snakes, lizards, and various rodents. But these tasks are trivial in comparison to the difficulties they encounter with hard-to-manage children. Mostly, though, they complain about permissive, neglectful parents.

Not all nanny/housekeepers bond tightly with their employers' children, but most are critical of what they perceive as their employers' careless parenting—or, more accurately, mothering, for their female employers typically receive the blame. They see mothers who may spend, they say, only a few minutes a day with their babies and toddlers, or who return home from work after the children are asleep. Soraya Sanchez said she could understand mothers who work "out of necessity," but all other mothers, she believed, hired nanny/housekeepers because they just didn't like being with their own kids. "*La Americana* is very selfish, she only thinks about herself," she said. "They prefer not to be with their children, as they find it's much easier to pay someone to do that." Her critique was shared by many nanny/housekeepers; and those with children of their own, even if they didn't live with them, saw their own mothering as far superior. "I love my kids, they don't. It's just like, excuse the word, 'shitting kids,'" said Patricia Paredes. "What they prefer is to go to the salon, get their nails done, you know, go shopping, things like that. Even if they're home all day, they don't want to spend time with the kids because they're paying somebody to do that for them." For many Latina nanny/ housekeepers, seething class resentments find expression in the rhetoric of comparative mothering.

When Latina immigrant women enter the homes of middle-class and upper-middle-class Americans, they encounter ways of raising children very different from those with which they are familiar. As Julia Wrigley's research has shown, the child-rearing values of many Latina and Caribbean nannies differ from those of their employers, but most are eager to do what middle-class parents want—to adopt "time out" discipline measures instead of swatting, or to impose limits on television viewing and Nintendo.[9] Some of them not only adapt but come to genuinely admire and appreciate such methods of child rearing. Yet they, too, criticize the parenting styles they witness close up in the homes where they work.

Some nanny/housekeepers encounter belligerent young children, who yell at them, call them names, and throw violent temper tantrums; and when they do, they blame the parents. They are aghast when parents, after witnessing a child scratch or bite or spit at them, simply shrug their shoulders and ignore such behavior. Parents' reactions to these incidents were a litmus test of sorts. Gladys Villedas, for example, told me

[9] Wrigley 1995.

that at her job, a five-year-old "grabbed my hair and pulled it really hard. Ay! It hurt so much I started crying! It really hurt my feelings because never in my own country, when I was raising my children, had this happened to me. Why should this happen to me here?" When she complained to her employer, she said the employer had simply consulted a child-rearing manual and explained that it was "a stage." Not all nanny/housekeepers encounter physically abusive children, but when they do, they prefer parents who allow them the authority to impose discipline, or who back them up by firmly instructing their children that it is not okay to kick or slap the nanny. Nanny/housekeepers spoke glowingly about these sorts of employers.

When nanny/housekeepers see parent-child interactions in the homes where they work, they are often put off and puzzled by what they observe. In these moments, the huge cultural gulf between Latina nanny/housekeepers and their employers seems even wider than they had initially imagined. In the home where Maribel Centeno was working as a live-out nanny/housekeeper, she spent the first few hours of her shift doing laundry and housecleaning, but when a thirteen-year-old boy, of whom she was actually very fond, arrived home from school, her real work began. It was his pranks, which were neither malicious nor directed at her, and parental tolerance of these, that drove her crazy. These adolescent pranks usually involved items like water balloons, firecrackers, and baking soda made to look like cocaine. Recently the boy had tacked up on his parents' bedroom door a condom filled with a small amount of milk and a little sign that read, "Mom and Dad, this could have been my life." Maribel thought this was inappropriate behavior; but more bewildering and disturbing than the boy's prank was his mother's reaction—laughter. Another nanny/housekeeper had reacted with similar astonishment when, after a toddler tore apart a loaf of French bread and threw the pieces, balled like cotton, onto the floor, the father came forward not to reprimand but to record the incident with a camcorder. The regularity with which their employers waste food astounds them, and drug use also raises their eyebrows. Some nanny/housekeepers are instructed to give Ritalin and Prozac to children as young as five or six, and others tell of parents and teens locked in their separate bedrooms, each smoking marijuana.

Nanny/housekeepers blame permissive and neglectful parents, who they feel don't spend enough time with their own children, for the children's unruly behavior and for teen drug use. "The parents, they say 'yes' to everything the child asks," complained one woman. "Naturally," she added, "the children are going to act spoiled." Another nanny/housekeeper analyzed the situation this way: "They [the parents] feel guilty because they don't spend that much time with the kids, and they want to replace that missed time, that love, with toys."

Other nanny/housekeepers prided themselves on taming and teaching the children to act properly. "I really had to battle with these children just to get them to pay attention to me! When I started with them, they had no limits, they didn't pick up their toys, and they couldn't control their tempers. The eldest—oof! He used to kick and hit me, and in public! I was mortified," recalled Ronalda Saavedra. Another woman remarked of children she had looked after, "These kids listened to me. After all, they spent most of the time with me, and not with them [the parents]. They would arrive at night, maybe spend a few moments with the kids, or maybe the kids were already asleep." Elvia Areola highlighted the injustice of rearing children whom one will never see again. Discussing her previous job, she said, "I was the one who taught that boy to talk, to walk, to read, to sit! Everything! She [the child's mother] almost never picked him up! She only picked him up when he was happy." Another nanny/housekeeper concluded, "These parents don't really know their own children. Just playing with them, or taking them to the park, well, that's not raising children. I'm the one who is with them every day."

Nanny/housekeepers must also maneuver around jealous parents, who may come to feel that their children's affections have been displaced. "The kids fall in love with you and they [the parents] wonder, why? Some parents are jealous of what the kids feel toward you," said Ronalda Saavedra, "I'm not going to be lying, 'I'm your mommy,' but in a way, children go to the person who takes care of them, you know? That's just the way it is." For many nanny/housekeepers, it is these ties of affection that make it possible for them to do their job by making it rewarding. Some of them say they can't properly care for the children without feeling a special fondness for them; others say it just happens naturally. "I fall in love with all of these children. How can I not? That's just the way I am," one nanny/housekeeper told me. "I'm with them all day, and when I go home, my husband complains that that's all I talk about, what they did, the funny things they said." The nanny/housekeepers, as much as they felt burdened by disobedient children, sometimes felt that these children were also a gift of sorts, one that parents—again, the mothers—did not fully appreciate. "The babies are so beautiful!" gushed Soraya Sanchez. "How is it that a mother can lose those best years, when their kids are babies. I mean, I remember going down for a nap with these little babies, how we'd cuddle. How is it that a person who has the option of enjoying that would prefer to give that experience to a stranger?" Precisely because of such feelings, many Latina immigrants who have children try to find a job that is compatible with their own family lives. Housecleaning is one of those jobs.

35

References

Clark-Lewis, Elizabeth. 1994. *Living In, Living Out: African American Domestics in Washington, D.C., 1910–1940*. Washington, D.C.: Smithsonian Institution Press.

Glenn, Evelyn Nakano. 1986. *Issei, Nisei, Warbride*. Philadelphia: Temple University Press.

Hagan, Jacqueline Maria. 1998. "Social Networks, Gender, and Immigrant Incorporation." *American Sociological Review* 63:55–67.

Katzman, David M. 1981. *Seven Days a Week: Women and Domestic Service in Industrializing America*. Urbana: University of Illinois Press.

Lacher, Irene. 1997. "An Interior Mind." *Los Angeles Times*, March 16, E1, E3.

Palmer, Phyllis. 1989. *Domesticity and Dirt: Housewives and Domestic Servants in the United States, 1920–1945*. Philadelphia: Temple University Press.

Wrigley, Julia. 1995. *Other People's Children*. New York: Basic Books.

UNDERSTANDING THE TEXT

1. Why, according to Hondagneu-Sotelo, do "the boundaries that we might normally take for granted disappear in live-in jobs" (para. 8)?

2. Why is food "a frequent topic of discussion among Latina live-in nanny/housekeepers" (para. 10)?

3. Characterize in your own words the relationships that live-in nannies have with the children they supervise and with the women who employ them.

4. What are the advantages of working as a live-out nanny?

5. What are the typical attitudes that nannies have toward their employers' parenting skills?

EXPLORING AND DEBATING THE ISSUES

1. Compare and contrast the living conditions of live-in and live-out nannies, being sure to account for any differences you may observe.

2. Assume the role of Maribel Centeno, and write a letter to her employer in which you express your attitudes toward your job and the way your employer treats you.

3. This selection describes a range of immigrant women who work for low wages. What are the implications of their employment status for America's immigration policy? To develop your argument, read or reread Yeh Ling-Ling, "State Needs a 'Time-Out' from Mass Immigration" (p. 94), and the editorial from the *Contra Costa Times*, "Revamp Immigration" (p. 98).

4. Write an analysis of the class relations described in this selection. What attitudes do the nannies have toward their employers, and why? How do the employers regard the women whom they hire?

5. What does the California dream mean to the live-in and live-out nannies whom Hondagneu-Sotelo describes? To develop your ideas, read or reread James J. Rawls's "California: A Place, a People, a Dream" (p. 22).

Invisible Men

WILLIAM LANGEWIESCHE

Living twilight lives camped out beneath freeway underpasses and deep inside barely accessible canyons, a few thousand undocumented laborers hide out from the U.S. Border Patrol by night while seeking minimum-wage work by day. In this selection, **William Langewiesche** (b. 1955) goes in search of an encampment of such workers, men and women who, in his words, "occupy the lowest place in the entire United States." Telling the story of one Jesús Ruíz, Langewiesche paints an unusual portrait of hope and despair, as Ruíz and his family find in America a life that is only marginally better than the one they left behind in Mexico. A writer and journalist, Langewiesche is a correspondent for the *Atlantic Monthly*; his work, including this essay, has also appeared in *The New Yorker*. His books include *Cutting for Sign* (1993), *Sahara Unveiled* (1996), and *American Ground* (2002).

Five million people live illegally in the United States. Two million live in California alone. More than half of those are Mexican, and by the standards they left behind almost all are doing well. Many now inhabit apartments in the barrios of Los Angeles and other cities, where they can blend with the large populations of legal immigrants and walk the streets openly, without worrying about arrest and deportation. Even for those who have settled outside the safety of the barrios, it is not a bad life, warmed as it is by hard work. But there are gradations to the experience, and they are severe. At one extreme are a few thousand squatters who have scattered into the construction-torn hills of northern San Diego County. They scavenge jobs and hide in furtive groups, inhabiting cracks in the affluent suburbs and enduring ferocious new pressures from the United States Border Patrol.

There have been Mexican squatters in San Diego for at least a hundred years, and at times they have been hunted but never before so intently. Three years ago, the local authorities razed the last of the old established camps—regular shantytowns, some with shanty bars and shanty churches. And the squatters who remain in the hills today are the ones who cannot be bulldozed away. Estimates of the numbers out there range from five thousand to forty thousand. Lacking contacts and knowledge that would allow them to reach safer ground, they crouch instead in farm sheds and camouflaged scrap-wood shacks, and bear the weight of California's displeasure. There are too few of them to form an underclass, but they are the people who now occupy the lowest place in the entire United States.

They are not easy to find. I spent days in January looking for them among the colliding coastal towns—Del Mar, Encinitas, Carlsbad,

Oceanside—and east across twenty miles of fractured landscape to Escondido and the craggy mountains, which rise like a wall, imposing an end to the helter-skelter of the county's development. The search was a spiral descent through the rankings of illegal immigrants. Beyond the easily found apartment dwellers, beyond the well-housed crews on big vegetable and flower farms, I was led eventually to smaller farms, where the owners were not to know of my presence, and where the workers sometimes ran from my approach. Those workers were squatters, and felt hounded and insecure, but on private farmland they enjoyed some protection from the Border Patrol, so they lived one step above the bottom.

The bottom was a place I finally found fifty miles north of the border and just inland from the coast, in a brushy ravine known loosely as Los Olvidados, which means "the forgotten ones," although the people there were living like ghosts, unseen rather than out of mind. This ravine lay like a scar through an area of expensive residential developments with more uplifting names—La Costa, Marea, Serenata—which had spread in advancing patterns of half-million-dollar houses across the hilltops overlooking it. The houses had been painted in pastels, and given cathedral ceilings and high arched windows, and seemed so light and airy that they might have been inflated. The streets were clean. Some were protected by electric gates. The ravine, by contrast, seemed merely ugly—a steep-sided gulch about half a mile long, bisected by a high-tension power line and littered with piles of illegally dumped trash—the sort of place that San Diegans pass by and hardly see. But I had been told to stop and to notice that some of those trash piles had roofs and walls, and that the wind might carry the sound of men's soft whistles, and that on gray winter days smoke rose from campfires hidden among the stunted trees.

A rain had fallen. I clambered up an embankment and started down   5
into the ravine, moving carefully along foot trails through the brush because I was concerned that I might be mistaken for the Border Patrol. The ravine's population was said to have been about a hundred last summer but to be fewer now. About halfway down, I heard voices and spotted a patch of tin roofing through the trees below. I was cut off by a gully and forced onto another trail, which eventually led to a windowless hut with a padlocked door. The hut seemed to have been abandoned, if only temporarily. But just down the trail beyond it I came to a larger shack that I now know as the home of Jesús Ruíz.

I called *"Buenas tardes"* from a distance and was answered quietly from the inside. The shack perched on a narrow terrace dug into the hillside fifty feet above the floor of the ravine. It was built of plywood and corrugated plastic, patched with black plastic sheeting, and held together with nails, branches, and the frame of a wheelbarrow, which had been wedged into the dirt. Trash spilled down a steep slope below it. The bushes smelled of urine. The center of the shack was a roofed but open-sided living area, which looked out over the ravine below; it was joined at one end to a three-walled kitchen, with rough shelving and a gas burner on a plywood table, and at the other end to a windowless sleeping room about the size of a big mattress. The sleeping room had a door that could be locked with a bicycle cable.

Jesús Ruíz sat in the living area on a plastic garden chair. He was twenty-two years old—a short, Indian-looking man dressed in a windbreaker, jeans, and untied basketball shoes. He had high cheekbones, clear eyes, and a musical voice, which imparted a peculiar quizzicality to his speech. He spoke no English. His Spanish was better than mine, but crude nonetheless: he confused *he* and *she*, and had problems with the use of the past and future tenses. This was because he was a Zapotec, from the Mexican state of Oaxaca, and he spoke primarily Zapoteco. But he was not given to conversation in any language. After he invited me in, we sat mostly in silence. He did not understand my interest in his life. He said that, like the other squatters at Los Olvidados, he was a day laborer. He found jobs by knocking on doors or standing on the streets. Usually, he worked as a gardener.

During that first visit, he did not mention the Border Patrol or deportations or his long experience with coming back across the line. All that may have seemed too obvious to him. He told me that he had moved north in 1991 and had returned to Oaxaca four times since. He might have been talking about vacation travel. He said he preferred to fly from Tijuana rather than to take the bus. When I expressed surprise, he explained impatiently that the flying was faster than the driving—five hours instead of eight days. He meant that his time was worth money. Otherwise he would have stayed in Mexico.

I was more interested in why he stayed here, under siege in Los Olvidados, instead of moving on, at least to the relative safety of a farm. He would say only that he did not like hard labor. But, as I later learned, there was more to his immobility. Like other Zapotecs in the ravine, he came from a parched mountain village called Santa Ana Yareni, five hours from the city of Oaxaca in a four-wheel drive—a place so isolated and Indian that for years it had lacked any connection to the labor market of the United States. But, beginning in 1984, many of the men there were recruited by a California flower grower who needed workers for his farm, in Somis, an hour north of Los Angeles. The Zapotecs were taken by train to Tijuana and smuggled to Somis, and there they were enslaved: held in a compound in perpetual debt, frightened into submission by warnings about the Border Patrol, and forced to work sixteen hours a day. Some of the men eventually sought help. In 1990, a federal grand jury in Los Angeles indicted the grower on charges of slavery. The slavery charges were dropped in a plea bargain, but he pleaded guilty to corporate racketeering, as well as to labor and immigration violations, after a complex prosecution that navigated the difficult distinctions between safety and captivity, hard labor and servitude.

The Zapotec slaves had meanwhile fled south to the ravine at Los   10 Olvidados, where a few villagers had already established themselves, because of the presence nearby of an aging hippyish couple who liked to drink and party with them. The couple had visited Santa Ana Yareni and had once taken a village elder to Marine World to "blow his mind." This was the closest thing the Zapotecs now had to a useful immigrant network in California, and it wasn't much. The trauma of the Somis slave camp had set them back at just the wrong time in American history— four years after the great immigration amnesty of 1986, and at a time when political sentiment had turned strongly against immigration. The attraction of Olvidados was at first the freedom it offered, the day-to-day choices to work at one job or another, or simply to rest in the ravine. But within a few years that freedom meant little.

Jesús Ruíz was too young to have been a slave, but he was affected by the Somis experience just the same. In 1991, his father fell to his death while planting corn on the precipitous mountain above Santa Ana Yareni. Jesús was sixteen. After the funeral, he decided to head north, and he knew of nowhere to go but Los Olvidados. In January, when I first met him, he faced the same lack of choice.

Outside his shack, a little stuffed elephant hung by its trunk on a string from a tree. Jesús said that he had three children. The first—a girl now four years old—was born in Mexico. After spending nearly a year alone with the baby, his young wife, Juana, had insisted on coming north to unite the family. "She wanted to see California," Jesús told me. "She thought everything would be easy."

In 1993, Juana took the baby on the bus to Tijuana and, after sneaking across the border, moved into the shack. Everything was not easy. Then, as now, water had to be hauled in yoked buckets down the steep slope from a ridge-top hydrant. But, aside from the threat of sudden deportation, the living conditions in the ravine were no worse than they had been within her memory in Oaxaca. Jesús wanted Juana to be realistic about coming north. "I told her, 'You have to work if you want to live here. That's the way it is in California.'" He got her a cleaning job three days a week. There were other women living in the ravine, and they helped with the baby.

But then she got pregnant with their second daughter and had to stop working. When she went into labor, Jesús took her to an emergency room and naively signed her in for a two-day stay at the hospital. The hospital did not ask about the couple's immigration status. The baby was born an American citizen, and Jesús was presented with a staggering bill for four thousand dollars. Slowly, he managed to pay it. By then, the family had moved into a two-bedroom apartment in Carlsbad with seven other Oaxacans and were beginning to live the urban lives of more typical illegal immigrants. At a vegetable-packing operation near the ravine, I met an old Oaxacan peasant with a pencil mustache and a straw hat, who described the horror not of such overcrowding but of the unnatural vertical stacking that is part of apartment life—the footsteps above and the quarrelling below, the distance from the sweet soil. Jesús and Juana were less attached to the land, but they realized that they were saving no money. In 1996, they returned to Los Olvidados. Jesús assured me that Juana did not mind. When she got pregnant again, she enrolled in a prenatal program, which cut the medical bill in half. The family's third child and its second American citizen, a boy, was born last September.

One rainy afternoon in November, 1997, when the new baby was two   15
months old, the Border Patrol raided the ravine. Jesús was returning on his bicycle when he spotted the vans parked on the nearby streets. He could do nothing to help his family, and he slipped away. The Border Patrol agents closed in on the ravine, moving heavily down the trails with their radios squawking. They were preceded by a chorus of whistles and warning cries: *"La Migra!,"* short for *Inmigración*. The agents were slowed by the slickness of the ground, and, as a result, almost everyone in the lowland escaped. Juana, up on the steep hillside, had her babies to think of and could not run. A cousin who also lived in the ravine was visiting her. The two women shut themselves into the darkness of the sleeping room and tried to soothe the children.

The United States Border Patrol is not a timid organization. In San Diego County, where a third of its sixty-eight hundred agents are deployed, there were more than a quarter of a million apprehensions and arrests in fiscal 1997 alone. That number is about half of what it was just two years earlier—a reduction that now seems to be undeniably the result of a tough new defensive effort initiated in October, 1994, throughout San Diego County, and especially along the critical fourteen miles of border facing Tijuana. The effort, dubbed Operation Gatekeeper, is based on an increase in fences, surveillance, and front-line patrols, and also on a new commitment to patrolling north of the border. Within the confines of San Diego County, the operation has been a success. Its national significance is harder to judge. Critics say that illegal immigrants are simply bypassing the operation by moving a few miles to the east or that, more ominously, apprehensions are down because the new defenses have forced a professionalization of the border crossing, which, in turn, means that the flow has become smarter and more difficult to stop. But Border Patrol agents are not prone to indulge in such doubts. San Diego is their sacred ground, and the success of Gatekeeper, however narrow, has at last given them a scent of victory.

In Los Olvidados, the squatters imitate the heavily burdened agents yelling "Stop running, you Mexican motherfuckers!," and they boast about their own taunting responses of *"Chinga tu madre!"* It is not just a word game. The agents do sometimes club people, and they separate families during deportation and deliver terrified peasants by the thousand to the predators who inhabit the filthy streets of the Mexican border cities. Nevertheless, the Border Patrol is not, as its critics claim, an inherently abusive organization. Its arrests are routinely softened by a grudging respect between the pursuers and the pursued. In rare cases, this may lead agents simply to let people go. I'm guessing here because no one will admit to such acts of grace. But when two rain-soaked agents finally got to Jesús' shack they found a frightened family inside, and after hearing that the babies were Americans they turned and went away. Still, Jesús had to assume that next time the outcome would be different. He had been captured twice already in 1997 and deported to Tijuana. This was not how he wanted to rear his children.

In the end, it was the talk of El Niño as much as the increasing pressure from the Border Patrol that drove the family apart. Even before the seasonal rains started, many of the women and children in the lowland had gone scurrying for shelter—some to local apartments but most back home to Mexico. After the November raid, the last of them left. The rain kept falling. Jesús reinforced the shack, but by early December the solitary living had become too hard for Juana. Jesús bought airline tickets for Mexico City and sent the family off to live there with a cousin. The departure left only two women in Los Olvidados—a toothless Chihuahuan, who slept in a tree house with a vicious little dog, and a peroxided hooker who frequented a colony of heavy drinkers on the far hillside. From Mexico City, Juana sent Jesús a note in Spanish, which he taped to the sleeping-room door: "Specially for you my love. I always want to be close to your side, but it is not easy. Night and day I think of you because I feel a coldness in my heart that you are not in my arms in order to hold you and to kiss your sweet lips. I love you and I miss you, but destiny has made us be apart from one another. The end."

I asked Jesús why Juana had not moved back to Santa Ana Yareni. He said that there was nothing for them there. I asked about their future. He said that it lay on the outskirts of Mexico City, where, with the money he would save now, he might eventually buy a piece of land and build a one-room house. It was something permanent to work toward. But I am not sure he really believed in it. He would be lucky to make three dollars a day in Mexico. His retirement plan was simply to grow old so he wouldn't have to eat much. He told me that he would visit his family in the summer of 1999, and that he would stay for two months before leaving again for California.

I said, "It's hard."   20

He said, "It's life."

Still, I wondered why he did not acknowledge his troubles. Was it politeness? Naiveté? A sense of privacy? For nearly two weeks, I kept coming back to talk to him. Only with time could I get him even to admit that within the ravine there is crime, that hard drugs are used, that men get crazy drunk and fight and set their shacks on fire, that men get sick and babies die, that the shacks are burglarized, that skinheads threaten Zapotecs on the street, that Chicano gangs attack and rob them within the ravine, that a man must be ready to run at all times, that capture by the Border Patrol is a serious setback. All this I had to learn first from other men. But Jesús had made a commitment to endure here illegally, and he insisted that it was the right commitment, and I came to realize that he described his life to himself as he described it to me. Only once, at night, over a beer that had slurred his speech, did he come close to expressing regret. He showed me a guitar, and said he was learning to play it. I asked him why, and he said, "So I'm not just hanging around crying." And even then he was not maudlin. He told me, too, that he enjoyed listening to music, especially *norteño* ballads—stories in song about love and violence and life underground in the United States. I noticed that Jesús had taken Juana's note off the door. We were not friends, but we could talk if I did not insult him with pity.

One step higher in the underground life, I found my way to a different group of squatters, who, because they had a little something to lose, were concerned that I not identify them by name. The group consisted of a dozen farmworkers who were mestizos from Michoacán. I spent several cold nights with them, huddled around a smoky wood-burning heater built of two fifty-gallon drums stacked horizontally and welded together. The men lived in a derelict chicken shed on a family farm that nestled against the steep slopes of the eastern mountains, about an hour from the coast.

The farm grew avocados. Most of the remaining farms in San Diego County are just such family operations, unable to survive without illegal workers. There are big farms, too, but, like those elsewhere in California, they tend by now to hire legal workers, often unionized, and to house them more or less correctly. The small farmers are not necessarily bad people, but they lack the economies of scale. Rather than comply with burdensome regulations pertaining to the living conditions of farmworkers (whether illegal immigrants or not), they have simply dropped out of the system. For them, the beauty of the arrangement is its deniability. Near Escondido, a flower grower said to me of his own foreman, "Manuel? Manuel? No, I don't know no Manuel. If you mean one of those wetbacks who come walking through here, I've got nothing to do with them." We understood each other perfectly. It was early evening, and he had studiously turned his back on the men who were settling into the shell of a wrecked greenhouse. Many other farmers similarly turn their backs. Their men become "trespassers," for whom they cannot be held responsible. And then, of course, every morning the farmers turn around and hire the same "trespassers," having at some point gone through the motions of checking their immigration documents.

The avocado grower who employed the workers in the chicken shed   25 did not know that I had been talking to them. I asked his permission only afterward, and he found a way to deny it. But I liked him. He was a hard, flat-bellied man of nearly seventy, a classic California grower — silver-haired, tanned, handsome, a Ronald Reagan type. He called his softer friends "puss guts." And he had a sense of humor. He said, "Fifteen pickers show up one morning, but only one's got papers, so I have to tell the others I'm real sorry but I can't use them. What happens? Two hours later, they show up again, and this time they've all got papers. There's only one problem — every one of these fellas was born on the same day, and every one of them crossed the border at the exact same time." He shrugged. The law did not require him to be an expert.

He thought of himself as a good employer. He told me he would never ask his workers to do something that he himself couldn't do. That was not necessarily a reassuring thought. He had hired college students on summer break, but they couldn't keep his pace for more than a morning. He had hired high-school athletes, but they didn't know how to dig or hammer. And that was in the past — the situation was worse today, of course. Finding Americans of any description had become practically impossible. He thanked God for the Mexicans, who came begging for the jobs and were strong pickers and knew how to dig and hammer and didn't whine or complain. He described what they went through, hour after hour, climbing the steep slopes of the groves carrying hundred-pound bags of easily bruised avocados. "You ought to try it," he said, eyeing me skeptically.

He said he got good work from the Mexicans by staying on them all the time. He liked Rush Limbaugh. He disliked the ACLU. But he also disapproved of the way some of the local farmers treated their men, and he included his own brother in that category. He pointed out that the chicken shed was a chicken shed no longer, and that he provided the workers there with power and running water and that when they remembered to remind him he replenished their gas, so they could have hot showers as well. He thought he treated them fairly.

The men in the chicken shed didn't exactly disagree. They said the farmer was tough and explosive, but if they went about their work correctly, he left them alone. They knew about living conditions at neighboring places, which were dark and brutishly cold. They had found this farm through their friends and had been coming here for years. The advantage of the job was the relative security it offered—an approximate assurance that there would be work on most days and that without a warrant or the farmer's permission the Border Patrol could not come onto the property and take the workers away. This farmer had mixed emotions about illegal immigrants and wanted those in the cities to be rounded up, but he did not like the Border Patrol, and for thirty years he had kept its agents off his land. So the chicken shed, however leaky its roof, was in the most important sense a good shelter.

I asked the men about the financial details of the job. They said that they made the minimum wage, but that after deductions for taxes and Social Security it amounted to less than five dollars an hour. They used phony Social Security numbers and knew they would never see that money again. They were paid by check every two weeks, and if they did well they earned about nine thousand dollars a year, of which they might mail six thousand dollars in money orders to their families in Mexico. Sometimes they carried cash when they returned to Mexico, but hemmed into their clothes because of shakedowns by the Mexican customs officials and the police. Within Mexico, they preferred to travel by air not merely for speed but for altitude: it allowed them to fly over all such risks of the road. I told them that I was familiar with the habit from traveling in Africa. They asked me if life in Africa was truly harder than in Mexico, and I answered that, yes, in general it seemed to be.

We got back to life in San Diego. The chicken shed had a Coke machine outside and a television somewhere. The men slept on wooden bunks in tangles of coats and blankets, and did their cooking on two old gas stoves. Every day, a *lonchero* drove up in an aluminum-sided catering truck to sell hot drinks and groceries and a few clothes—and also, quietly,

30

perhaps beer, penicillin, and marijuana. *Loncheros* gain exclusive rights to farm encampments. The term, which derives from *lunch,* understates their importance to the besieged workers: by delivering the necessities (which include check-cashing and loans) to places like the chicken shed, they allow the squatters the choice of remaining within the boundaries of their refuge for weeks at a time. Later, when I talked to the farmer's wife, she expressed confusion at the men's allegiance to their *lonchero.* She had offered to do their grocery shopping for them at a store called Smart & Final, and they had refused. But, of course, grocery shopping was all she would have done for them, and they knew it.

To the men in the shed, the Border Patrol's Gatekeeper operation felt like a storm outside. One night during my stay, a man arrived after five days of crossing the border on foot. He had joined a guided group that intended to skirt the defenses by taking a bus thirty miles east from Tijuana. The group crossed the border, but within a few miles it was surprised by a roving team of Border Patrol agents. The man ran, and during the following nights he made his way north, navigating by the lights of airline flights. It hadn't always been so hard. One of his friends in the shed said, "You can tell they're looking for different ways to keep people down." I disagreed, saying, "I think they're looking for ways to keep people out." But that was an argument about intent.

The fear outside the farm was palpable. One night, I went up a dirt road into a canyon where prostitutes gather every Monday to provide the workers with sex. Because the farmers don't want prostitutes on their land, the men are forced to emerge into the open. That night, about thirty men had taken the risk. The prostitutes were Mexicans and worked in shifts arranged by age, starting with the oldest, who were perhaps in their midtwenties. The women carried cardboard to lie on and transacted their business quickly in the darkness — fifteen dollars for the basic, twenty-five without a condom. A *lonchero* had arrived to sell beer and music tapes, but it was a bad party. The canyon had been raided the night before, and the men were extremely nervous, startled by every flicker of light or unexpected footstep on gravel. *"Aguas!"* they kept hissing, which means "Look out!"

Back at the chicken shed, the squatters acknowledged the relief they felt upon returning to their refuge. I told them about Jesús Ruíz and the day laborers of Los Olvidados — people who had found no such shelter. They knew all about that kind of life. They told me about migrants who had lived nearby in a clay cave beside the Pala River until one rainy day the cave collapsed and killed them. The story was about gradations. There are two kinds of squatters in San Diego. The farmworkers did not feel privileged to live in a chicken shed, but they were glad not to have been buried alive.

UNDERSTANDING THE TEXT

1. Why does Jesús Ruíz prefer to live a squatters' camp in Los Olvidados rather than live on one of the farms that employs laborers like him?

2. Why, according to Langewiesche, do the avocado farmers continue to hire undocumented workers? How do they justify breaking the law?

3. For Jesús Ruíz and his family, how does life in Los Olvidados compare to life in their homeland, Oaxaca, Mexico?

4. Study Langewiesche's tone and selection of details. What do they reveal about his attitude toward the Mexican immigrants, their employers, and the U.S. Border Patrol?

EXPLORING AND DEBATING THE ISSUES

1. The farmer whom Langewiesche interviews points to his chicken shed as a sign of how good an employer he is. In an essay, evaluate the farmer's self-assessment.

2. Both Langewiesche and Richard Rodriguez ("Proofs," p. 64) describe the experiences and attitudes of Mexican immigrants who have just crossed the border. Compare and contrast their depictions. How do you account for any differences you may observe?

3. In class, form teams, and debate whether the California dream applies to immigrants such as the Ruíz family.

4. In an essay, defend or argue against the strategies used by the U.S. Border Patrol to control illegal immigration from Mexico to California. You might consult Richard Rodriguez's "Proofs" (p. 64) to develop your ideas.

5. Read or reread Pierrette Hondagneu-Sotelo's "Maid in L.A." (p. 116) and Richard Rodriguez's "Proofs" (p. 64), studying the patterns of experiences that men and women immigrants have. Write an essay in which you analyze the gendered nature of the immigrant experience in California. How do you explain any differences that you might discern?

Religious Dimensions of the Immigrant Experience

DONALD E. MILLER, JON MILLER, and GRACE DYRNESS

Culture shock is one of the most common effects of immigration, especially for recent non-European immigrants who "often see a stark contrast between the values they have been raised with and the values of American mainstream culture," according to this overview of the religious dimensions of the immigrant experience. For many Hindu, Muslim, Buddhist, and Sikh immigrants, the differences between their religious traditions and the Judeo-Christian heritage of their newly adopted country are disorienting. When the particular temptations offered by a place like Los Angeles are added, it is easy to understand why many immigrants choose "to embrace their religion more firmly . . . rather than to float along with what they [perceive] to be the permissive values of American culture." This religious diversity is just as striking as the racial and linguistic diversity that now characterizes California life. **Donald E. Miller** is the executive director of the Center for Religion and Civic Culture at the University of Southern California. **Jon Miller** is a professor in the sociology department at USC and the director of Research at the Center for Religion and Civic Culture. **Grace Dyrness** is the associate director of the Center for Religion and Civic Culture at USC.

Religious Practice and Living in Los Angeles

That there is considerable freedom and many options from which to choose is for many part of the cultural shock of living in Los Angeles. There is no longer the certainty of one assumed religious identity. In this area of life alone, people face literally dozens of options. Moreover, even for a person surrounded by a kinship group, the cultural restraints on making choices are rarely as limiting as they were in the home country. Although immigrants interviewed for this project often remarked on the dangers of such pluralism, they also tended to like the freedom they experienced. They felt that they could "be themselves" in this new homeland. With some frequency, immigrants from Hindu and Muslim countries said that they felt they could live "more honestly" in America, by which they meant they were free from bribes, corruption, and other practices that sometimes are a way of life in their home country. Having said this, however, they also indicated there were temptations in Los Angeles that they did not face at home—especially temptations associated with drugs, alcohol, and promiscuous sex. Women sometimes commented with approval that here, they could practice their religion in public ways that were proscribed in the homeland, where they had to confine their worship to the home. Finally, those we interviewed rarely mentioned religious discrimination once they moved to Los Angeles. In fact, some individuals, especially college students, said that being an "ethnic" practicing an "exotic" religion brought them a certain envious regard among their peers.

Indeed, a Hindu we interviewed said, "In India it was much easier to preserve and practice Hinduism because it is all over the place," whereas here, she said, it takes a conscious effort to drive "all the way to Malibu to keep track of auspicious days and festivals." But on the other side of the balance, it was not at all uncommon among those who shared their experiences with us to say that their faith had grown stronger since moving to the United States. They offered several explanations for this increased commitment and energy. Some said that at home their religion was taken for granted. Several times a year they might go to the temple to offer oblations, but religion was so pervasive and so unquestioned that it never felt like a conscious choice. Even prayer, some said (including Muslims who pray five times a day), was something done routinely, without thinking.

On this same theme, in the American context and particularly in Los Angeles, immigrants often see a stark contrast between the values they have been raised with and the values of American mainstream culture. Hence, they find themselves faced with a clear if sometimes painful choice. Those we interviewed often *elected* to embrace their religion more firmly—now making a clear, conscious *choice*—rather than to float along with what they perceived to be the permissive values of American culture. A Muslim from Lebanon, asked whether his faith had changed upon coming to the United States, replied, "Actually, it has improved, to be frank with you. I think we devote more time to the religion [here] even though it should have been more over there, back home." And several second-generation Sikh boys told us that, at first, they wanted to abandon the turban worn by their fathers, but now see it as an important element of their Sikh identity. In spite of adolescent peer pressure to conform (backward baseball caps?), they have chosen to be different. . . .

Finally, for many immigrants religion continues to exercise a strong attraction because it provides a setting and a reason to be in contact with their fellow immigrants. Religion, in other words, is a source of community, a place to speak one's native tongue, eat one's native food, and, not unimportant, find a husband or wife who shares one's cultural background. A group of Hindu women told us that they didn't mind doing the cooking for the temple's activities on the weekends because it provided a welcome time for them to see their friends and talk in Gujarati. And young people in the same temple, one of our research assistants noted, seemed to quite enjoy being at the temple, wearing *gaghras* and saris and the latest chic Indian fashions, especially for important religious occasions.

But a complete picture requires us to note that there are also nega- 5 tive factors related to religious practice and life in Los Angeles. Immigrants often mentioned that they are so busy trying to make a living that it leaves little time for religion. Muslims in particular said that it sometimes feels awkward in their workplace to observe the daily routine of prayer, even if there is no objection from their employer. Immigrants from Asia said that, without temples being omnipresent in society, religious practice demands a different rhythm than the occasional formal observance that they followed in their home country, and this cultural difference, uncomfortable for many, is not easily addressed. A Vietnamese priest noted a different problem: namely, that it is difficult to recruit clergy in this country, since so many other alternatives are open to young men.

On the other hand, for every objection to life in Los Angeles a counterbenefit was cited. Women from Latin American countries indicated, for example, that they appreciated the view toward domestic violence that they experienced in this country. Pastors and priests teach against it, they said, whereas in their home country "machismo" practices were tolerated, if not actively accepted. Women from the Philippines said that they like the fact that religion is not as likely to be labeled "women's work" in this country, and their husbands are also expected to be active in the church. There were also expressions of appreciation with the fact that interfaith dialogue is respected in this country, at the same time there is acceptance of firmly held beliefs. In the home country, strict beliefs were often viewed as antithetical to tolerance and appreciation of others' rights to hold deep convictions. The advanced technology available in Los Angeles is also having an impact. At risk of overstatement, there seems to be a positive correlation between the marginality of a religion and the size of its Web site. Religious groups that do not command a large number of adherents have put up some of the most sophisticated Web pages. The Internet, in other words, represents an entirely new equalizing medium for achieving visibility and expanding the boundaries of communication.

The Practical Role of Religion in the Lives of New Immigrants

While much of the discussion of immigrant religion appropriately concentrates on matters of belief and worship, it is also important to catalog the very mundane, though nevertheless crucial, ways in which religion affects the daily lives of immigrants. Perhaps foremost in this connection is the role it plays as a "conduit" for people who are considering emigrating. Because of the thousands who have preceded them, those considering the move to Los Angeles know that there will be a ready-made community waiting for them when they arrive here. Leaving home is always a process fraught with considerable anxiety, an emotion that photographer Sebastiao Salgado has brilliantly captured in his documentary collection of photographs called *Migrations*.[1] But to know that there is a community at the far end of the road that shares one's values and understands the challenges one is confronting eases some of the tension associated with being uprooted and facing the challenge of starting a new life. Other institutions often develop alongside and in close association with churches, temples, synagogues, or mosques, and before long an area becomes known as "Little Saigon" or "Koreatown"—often with religious congregations as the anchor institutions. Religion addresses the problem of loneliness, in other words, by providing entry to a familiar community with familiar beliefs and practices that give structure and meaning to life—all elements of stability that are especially important in a new environment where expectations about what to believe or think are unclear. Indeed, worship and ritual have the potential to bind people together in ways that other institutions are not equipped to do.

To put it succinctly, religious institutions are a safety net for immigrants, spiritually, psychologically, and culturally. Some of the large "megachurches" approach this task by dividing their congregations into cell groups that meet in people's homes. Young Nak (Korean) Presbyterian Church, for example, has thousands of worshippers but relies on 127 such groups of twelve to twenty people, each to provide a more intimate religious experience. In addition to studying the Bible, there are times of sharing in these informal settings, followed by prayer for each other's needs. If someone is out of work, this is made known within the cell group which functions, in many ways, like an extended family. Even if someone in the group cannot supply a connection for a job, at least the person in need feels the warmth and compassion of a caring group of friends. Small storefront churches also often operate like extended family networks. Congregations are voluntary associations and even if they have paid staff they always provide multiple outlets for sharing talents and abilities—whether it be singing in a choir, directing a children's program, or cooking and serving food. Congregations of all sizes provide opportunities for expressing leadership, something that may not be possible for immigrants within their workplace or the larger society.

[1] Sebastiao Salgado, *Migrations: Humanity in Transition*, concept and design by Lelia Wanick Salgado, 1st English language ed. (New York: Aperture, 2000).

Religion also serves as a mediating institution, functioning as a bridge between immigrants and a culture that they fear and have not learned to navigate. Sometimes this is as simple as offering translation services for the newly arrived. At other times the mediation is more practical: connecting newcomers to various social services, advising them on a good doctor, or telling them where they can buy food cheaply. Congregations with professionals among them often set up legal clinics for immigrant members or offer health screening and referral. Young Nak employs a parish nurse; other groups have prison ministries directed to fellow immigrants who have had trouble with the law and need support as well as an advocate on their behalf. Churches and interfaith coalitions of clergy and laity have taken an active role in the defense of the rights of immigrants when police, schools, the INS, or other public agencies engage in practices that cause concern.

Advocacy, in fact, is a major role played by religious institutions. At a political level, it is to counter the nativist impulse that always arises when population shifts dramatically and individuals feel threatened that newcomers will take their jobs, work at a lower wage rate, or displace them from housing. Immigrant congregations across Los Angeles were strongly opposed to California's Proposition 187, which was intended to strip undocumented immigrants of many social services. The congregation-based Industrial Areas Foundation (IAF) went on the offensive with public demonstrations and, through its Active Citizenship Campaign, registered thousands of immigrants to vote. The IAF actively petitioned the INS to speed up the processing of applications for citizenship, so that these individuals could be turned into voters and thereby defend their rights on their own.

Cardinal Roger Mahony of the Archdiocese of Los Angeles has been a strong advocate for immigrants. In an important pastoral letter in 1993, he captured the thinking of many religious leaders when he said:

> Today we are witnessing a distressing and growing trend among political leaders, segments of the media, and the public at-large, which capitalizes on prevailing fears and insecurity about the growing number of immigrants in our communities. In today's social climate, we have special reasons to study and ponder the Bible's positive view of strangers, sojourners and aliens [quoting from the New Testament book of Hebrews]. Our biblical tradition encourages us to encounter the "strangers in our midst" — not with fear and negativity — but with compassion and hopeful expectation. Our social teaching challenges us to embody this sentiment in our personal actions, in our response as a community, and in public policy.[2]

[2] Cardinal Roger Mahony, "You Have Entertained Angels — Without Knowing It," *The Tidings*, weekly newspaper of the Archdiocese of Los Angeles, 10 October 1993, pp. 10–12.

Specifically attacking the sentiment that was to later be focused in Proposition 187, he said:

> We know that nothing is gained by denying citizenship and access to education to the children of undocumented workers. On the contrary, the human potential of these dynamic new Americans will be lost. Our society will not be improved by creating an even larger under-class deprived of education.

Citing papal encyclicals and appealing to scripture as well as personal empathy, Cardinal Mahony has used his bully pulpit effectively. The *Los Angeles Times* frequently publishes his opinion articles, and the press turns to him when they want a proimmigrant statement.

At a local congregational level, religious rhetoric is matched by actions, even in small Pentecostal churches such as Templo Calvario, with its "Adopt a Family" program in which church members target specific families in their community that need a helping hand. While (or because) many individuals who adopt a family were themselves immigrants only a few years previously, they believe they have an obligation to help others. One individual from this church put it this way, "We are not volunteers. We are servants doing God's work." As another member of this church explained, this dedication is fueled by the fact that the members are repaying the kindness that was offered to them by strangers when they were new to the city.

It is important to note that churches and other religious organizations do not, typically, provide services only to those within their congregation or even to those who affirm their same faith. Rather, food, clothing, citizenship, and other programs are offered, without stipulation, to everyone in the community. Informal assistance, on the other hand, often occurs because a new immigrant is a member of a cell group or participates in other church-related programs and consequently their needs are known because of the close friendships that have developed. But because of the sheer volume of requests for help, some churches have made a policy of referring individuals to Catholic Charities, the Salvation Army, or other professional charities that are capable of dealing with the complex needs of individuals and their families.

Other faith-based groups resist the idea of "charity" and instead work hard at helping individuals to be self-sufficient. For example, an Episcopal priest with an immigrant congregation decided to start a janitorial service. Father Philip Lance said that this small "capitalistic enterprise," along with a thrift store he started, is employing forty-one people. And an enterprising Jesuit priest, Fr. George Schultz, organized day laborers, creating an employment center associated with St. Joseph Center so that men and women will not be exploited simply because they are poor and not legal residents of the City of Los Angeles. With the welfare reform legislation of 1996, the Charitable Choice provision is encouraging congregations to partner with government in creating job readiness programs, which should further buttress the role that religion is playing in the areas of employment and self-sufficiency.

Because they are so consumed with problems of their own members, one might assume that immigrant congregations would be unable to think far beyond their own community, but that is not the case. During the period of our study, the Hsi Lai Temple, whose members are predominantly Buddhists from Taiwan, not surprisingly gave generously to victims of an earthquake that wreaked havoc in their homeland, but also came forward to help those affected by a devastating hurricane in Honduras and an earthquake in Colombia.

15

Armenian congregations have a long history of sponsoring orphans, sending money to build schools in the Republic of Armenia, and helping the elderly to cope after the collapse of the Soviet Union (and with it, the pension system), not to speak of the millions of dollars that they sent to Armenia after an earthquake in 1988 that killed 25,000 people and left a half million homeless. An Armenian priest in Pasadena told us that he recently had intervened with youth from his church who were upset that a photo in the school yearbook linked Armenian youth with gang activity, which they resented.

Islamic groups in Los Angeles have expressed their humanitarian views by encouraging discussion of State Department policy, such as the ongoing embargo of Iraq, which has claimed the lives of thousands of children because of the lack of medicine and basic nutrition. At the same time, Muslims were very pointed in their support of U.S. actions and NATO[3] troops in Kosovo. The Muslim Public Affairs Council has been very proactive in countering stereotypes about Muslims—especially those that portray them as terrorists.

Korean Buddhist temples and Korean churches have sent tens of thousands of dollars worth of aid to help counter the food shortages in North Korea, and when a destructive earthquake struck El Salvador in January 2001, a Korean church called Oriental Mission quickly raised an astonishing $3 million for medical and other supplies for the victims.[4]

---

[3] North Atlantic Treaty Organization. — [Eds.]

[4] Antonio Olivo, "Digging Deep for Quake Aid," *Los Angeles Times*, 23 January 2001, sec. B.

UNDERSTANDING THE TEXT

1. List the advantages and disadvantages that coming to the United States poses for immigrants who wish to maintain their religious identity.
2. How are religious experiences different for male and female immigrants, according to Miller, Miller, and Dyrness?
3. According to the article, why do many immigrants "embrace their religion more firmly" (para. 3) in the United States than in their native land?
4. In what ways does religion bind an immigrant community?
5. What political roles are played by religious institutions in immigrant communities?

EXPLORING AND DEBATING THE ISSUES

1. If you are an immigrant, write a personal essay in which you examine your family's experiences in light of this article. To what extent has your family "*elected* to embrace their religion more firmly" (para. 3) or, conversely, faced any negative consequences for practicing their religion? If you are not an immigrant, you might interview an acquaintance who is an immigrant about his or her family's religious practices.
2. In an argumentative essay, analyze the extent to which religious institutions — Christian, Jewish, Muslim, Buddhist, Hindu, Sikh, and others — enable immigrants to assimilate within mainstream culture.
3. Interview several immigrants who have a Judeo-Christian background and several who do not. As you select your interviewees, remember that racial background is not necessarily equated with religion (while many South Asians are Hindu, for example, others may be Christian). In an essay, compare and contrast their experiences of practicing their religion in California. How has their religion affected their daily lives? Have they found practical difficulties in preserving their faith?
4. The authors assert that "there seems to be a positive correlation between the marginality of a religion and the size of its Web site" (para. 6). In class, brainstorm a list of less common religions. Then form teams, and assign each team one religion. Using a search engine such as Google.com or Askjeeves.com, test the authors' claim. Share your results with the class. How do you account for your findings?
5. Read or reread the essays in this chapter that illustrate gender patterns in immigrants' experiences. See, for instance, the selections by Connie Young Yu (p. 100), Nayereh Tohidi (p. 149), Pierrette Hondagneu-Sotelo (p. 116), and William Langewiesche (p. 130). Drawing on these selections for evidence, write an essay that supports, refutes, or modifies the authors' suggestion that women may benefit more than men from the cultural changes they experience when they immigrate to California.

Iranian Women and Gender Relations in Los Angeles

NAYEREH TOHIDI

In California, the popular face of immigration tends to be either Latin American or Asian, but large numbers of immigrants who come from other regions in the world, especially the Near East, have been quietly reshaping California demography. In this study, **Nayereh Tohidi** focuses on the Iranians who have come to Los Angeles in the wake of the 1979 Iranian revolution, largely middle- and upper-middle-class Tehranians who have fled the repressive policies of the current post-Shah, fundamentalist regime. But American freedoms have offered particular challenges to Iranian immigrants, especially women, who tend to have "more egalitarian views of marital roles than Iranian men," in Tohidi's words, a "discrepancy" that has led to "new conflicts between the sexes." Thus, Iranian women immigrants are at once freer than their sisters in Iran, more conflicted, and more in need of a "new identity acceptable to their ethnic community and appropriate to the realities of their host country." Tohidi is an associate professor of women's studies at California State University, Northridge. She directs a new program in Islamic Community Studies at CSUN and is also a research associate at the Center for Near Eastern Studies at the University of California, Los Angeles. Tohidi's publications include *Feminism, Democracy, and Islamism in Iran* (1996), *Women in Muslim Societies: Diversity within Unity* (1998), and *Globalization, Gender, and Religion: The Politics of Women's Rights in Catholic and Muslim Contexts* (2001).

Immigration is a major life change, and the process of adapting to a new society can be extremely stressful, especially when the new environment is drastically different from the old. There is evidence that the impact of migration on women and their roles differs from the impact of the same process on men (Espin 1987; Salgado de Snyder 1987). The migration literature is not conclusive, however, about whether the overall effect is positive or negative. Despite all the trauma and stress associated with migration, some people perceive it as emancipatory, especially for women coming from environments where adherence to traditional gender roles is of primary importance. As [one researcher] said, "When the traditional organization of society breaks down as a result of contact and collision . . . the effect is, so to speak, to emancipate the individual man. Energies that were formerly controlled by custom and tradition are released" (Furio 1979, 18).

My own observations of Iranians in Los Angeles over the past eight years, as well as survey research I carried out in 1990,[1] reveal that Iranian

[1] This article draws on a survey of a sample of 134 Iranian immigrants in Los Angeles, 83 females and 51 males, and on interviews with a smaller sample of women and men.

women immigrants in Los Angeles are a homogeneous group, despite ethnic diversity. Most of them come from Tehran and represent an urban cosmopolitan subculture. And most are educated members of the upper-middle and middle classes who oppose the present regime in Iran and its repressive policies against women.

Migration has had both costs and benefits for women. Positive experiences include the sense of freedom, new opportunities and options, increased access to education and gainful employment, and a move toward egalitarian conjugal roles in many Iranian families. On the negative side is grief over the loss of the homeland, loved ones, and the social and emotional support of the kinship network. Many also feel marginal and, at least initially, experience a decline in their own socioeconomic status or that of their husbands. Moreover, conflicts between parents and their children and between women and men have heightened tension and led to an increasing divorce rate.

Migration involves culture shock. Immigrants' experiences of migration and the process of adaptation are influenced by a number of variables (Dane 1980; Melville 1978; Taft 1977; Salgado de Snyder 1987; Espin 1987; and Shirley 1981). Personal characteristics, such as age, language proficiency, educational level, and job skills, influence the migrants' ability to adapt. Immigrants are also affected by attitudinal factors, such as their own perceptions of the decision to emigrate, their sense of responsibility for those left behind, and their perceptions of the conditions in both home and host countries. Economic factors also play a role, especially the immigrants' ability to find a job, their financial resources, and their losses or gains in social status or class. Another set of influential conditions includes the attitudes of the citizens of the host country toward the migrant group and the degree of similarity between the two cultures. Finally, some personal factors, such as ego strength, decision-making skills, resolution of feelings of loss, and the ability to tolerate ambiguity (including ambiguity about gender roles), also influence the intensity of the culture shock experienced by the immigrants and their ability to adapt.

All these factors vary substantially for men and women, with the result   5
that the processes of acculturation and adaptation differ for them as well.

The survey questionnaire consists of a demographic section and five scales measuring acculturation, national/ethnic identity, perceived prejudice, acculturative stress items, and attitudes toward gender roles. To measure the respondents' attitudes toward gender roles, a Persian adaptation of the Spence-Helmreich scale (1978) has been employed. This scale consists of twenty-five declarative statements about proper roles and behavioral patterns for women and men. For each statement there are four response alternatives: agree strongly, agree mildly, disagree mildly, and disagree strongly.

Acculturation and Changes in Gender Roles

All immigrants experience acculturation, a process involving changes in values, beliefs, attitudes, and behaviors. The inevitable collision of home and host cultures ensures that some acculturation will take place. This does not mean that all values, customs, and behaviors originating in the home culture will disappear. In fact, the healthiest experiences of acculturation result in biculturalism or multiculturalism. Not every individual immigrant, however, manages to attain a bicultural balance. Many never cease feeling alienated in the new society, while others experience complete assimilation.

As part of the process of acculturation, all immigrants develop a "new identity" that integrates elements from the host and home cultures (Garza-Guerrero 1974). A psychologist who experienced the challenging and often painful process of migration firsthand writes:

> Immigrants in accepting a new identity (or a new version of the old one) at the price of instant identification and intense work must leave behind not only old countries but also unlived futures, and not only enemies to be disavowed but also friends to be left behind — maybe to perish. What right, then, does the immigrant have to usurp a new identity? (Erickson 1974, 77)

For Iranian women, the process of developing a new identity is perhaps the most psychologically challenging and delicate aspect of immigration. . . .

Iranian women and girls are entering North American society at a time when the role of women is changing, both here and in their homeland. During the peak of the Iranian influx into the United States, the progressive forces of revolution, on the one hand, and the subsequent character of the Islamic government, on the other, fostered a transformation in the role of women. The Islamization of the last decade, however, has enforced a uniform identity for Iranian women, based on traditional and restricted roles. The difference between appropriate behavior for women in Iran and in the United States is much greater than that for men in the two societies. The differing demands on men and women can either facilitate acculturation or create confusion and conflicts for women.

My survey indicates that changes in traditional conceptions of womanhood, manhood, and marriage — from an autocratic male-dominated model to a more egalitarian one — are taking place faster among Iranian women than among Iranian men. Studies of Latina immigrants reveal similar patterns. Even though the pace of acculturation tended to be slower for Latinas in other respects, the women exhibited more egalitarian attitudes toward gender roles than men (Vazquez-Nuttall, Romero-Garcia, and DeLeon 1987; Espin 1987).

In studies of the acculturation of Iranians in the United States, Ghaf-   10
farian (1989) found the same patterns; that is, that Iranian male immigrants were more acculturated than females and that despite their lower
level of overall acculturation, Iranian women migrants had more egalitarian views of marital roles than Iranian men. Such a discrepancy would
naturally lead to new conflicts between the sexes.

This is not to say that changes in sexual attitudes and family roles are
the result of migration and acculturation into American society. Actually,
the cultural collision between modernism and traditionalism, between
liberalism and conservatism, and between male chauvinism and feminism had begun in Iran long before the major waves of Iranian immigration to the United States. By the turn of the century, growing urbanization
and the introduction of new industries, new modes of production, and
new ideas had wrought major changes and raised questions concerning
the proper role and place of women in the new society, and their access
both to education and to work outside the home. Long-standing cultural
and religious traditions, such as the segregation of women's space from
men's and veiling requirements, were called into question. During the
1978–1979 revolution, special emphasis was placed on discovering the
authentic (*aseel*) identity of Iranian women, especially in comparison to
"West-struck" or "Westoxicated" (*gharb zadeh*) women. All these issues
have remained unresolved since the . . . first decade of the twentieth
century.

Women and the Family in Iran

During the years preceding the 1978–1979 revolution, the "woman question" became part of the Iranian intelligentsia's debate about national
identity, development, modernization, and cultural and moral integrity.
Those participating in the discussion included Iranian nationalists, Islamists, Marxists, and those influenced by the West.

Islam undergirds the patriarchy in Iran, just as Judeo-Christian
ethics justify the same system in the United States. The family, with its
patrilineal and patriarchal structure, is the basic social unit. Male and female roles are organized in a hierarchy based on sex, age, and experience. A traditional Iranian woman's place is in the home. Because her
role and activities are limited to familial and domestic spheres, she has
no identity outside the family. She is identified only by her connections
to her male kin—she has status only as the daughter, sister, wife, and
mother of male family members. As a wife, her status is determined by
her fertility, especially her ability to give birth to sons. The wife is always
under her husband's tutelage or, in his absence, that of her eldest son.

Her honor (*namus*) requires that she never be left unprotected by her father, husband, or other male kin (Nassehi-Behnam 1985, 558).

An old Persian expression illustrates the traditional conception of women in Iran: "Woman is a sweetheart when a girl and a mother when married." Such a view reduces women to their sexual and reproductive capacities.

The gender-based discrimination and double standards that pervade   15
Iranian social life restrict women's movements, the physical spaces they may enter, their work and economic autonomy, their access to education, their personal power and authority, their sexual behavior, and their ability to express themselves artistically. From childhood, the members of each sex are socialized to prescribed roles. Boys are taught to command, to protect, and to make a good living for themselves and their families. Girls learn to be chaste and beautiful and to find a good husband. . . .

The Impact of Migration

The impact of migration on Iranian women in Los Angeles depends on the reasons for their migration and the conditions under which it took place. . . .

Some women left Iran (with or without their husbands) to provide their children with better education and broader opportunities. They found the Islamization of the educational system and the political indoctrination of their children unacceptable. Other women accompanied their adolescent sons into exile to ensure that the youths would not be drafted during the Iran-Iraq war. Still others came to the United States alone, leaving their husbands and other family members behind because of economic considerations or to increase the likelihood of their getting a U.S. visa. These motivations are reflected in the immigrants' sense of marginality, their development of a new identity, and other aspects of acculturation.

Individual and Political Freedom

In comparison with women living in Iran, migrant and refugee women have gained considerable personal and political freedom. Their basic human rights are no longer violated by such institutions of control as the mandatory veil, strict dress code, and sexual apartheid. Many middle-class and professional women who found these repressive measures intolerable appreciate their new freedom. The sense of relief is even more profound for those women who escaped persecution and imprisonment in Iran.

Women who migrated alone may feel free of familial control, of constant surveillance by the kinship network. They may feel free to experiment with new patterns of behavior and to search for a more autonomous personal identity. The opportunity to become self-reliant and to develop a personal identity is often considered the most positive consequence of migration for women. Many Iranian women who immigrated alone, however, feel shame and guilt for developing an American-influenced identity. Other Iranian immigrants or family members back home may criticize them for not conforming to traditional roles. Although they may have left their families behind, the success or failure of individual family members reflects on the family as a whole. A woman's misbehavior, especially sexual misbehavior, brings shame not only on her, but on all members of her family (Barakat 1985).

Iranian women who successfully adapt to American society are often rejected by the home culture. Iranian immigrants in Los Angeles, especially the women, have a reputation for conspicuous consumption among other Iranian immigrants in this country and in Europe, as well as back home. They are stereotyped as *taghooti*, a term rooted in idolatry that in this context implies decadence, narcissism, immorality, and hedonism. The Iranian community in Los Angeles is known in Iran as the source of contraband music videos—vulgar and commercial, these represent the worst elements of westernization.

Because of love-hate sentiments toward the West in general and Americans in particular, immigrants in Los Angeles, particularly the females, must prove that such stereotypes do not apply to them. To be westernized or Americanized has strong negative connotations, politically, culturally, and sexually.

Even before the revolution, westernized members of the urban upper-middle and middle classes were regarded as a fifth column, promoting imperialism, family disintegration, moral degeneration, and cultural erosion. In the campaign against westernization waged by the Iranian intelligentsia, particularly the Islamists, westernized women were held to epitomize all social ills (Najmabadi 1989; Tohidi 1993). The clergy cleverly pointed to a few highly visible upper-middle- and middle-class women preoccupied with Western fads and fashions in condemning all unveiled, nontraditional, and progressive women as "Westoxicated." In the Islamic clergy's political discourse, modern women were stereotyped as frivolous and westernized and condemned as *fitna*, the erotic agents of social and moral disorder (Mernissi 1975). The clergy demanded a return to the veiled Islamic model of womanhood. During the Islamic revolution, the Iranian women's rights movement, which opposed the discriminatory and retrogressive policies of the new government, was crushed as an accomplice to imperialism.

With such a political history, Iranian immigrant women have had to search for a new identity acceptable to their ethnic community and appropriate to the realities of their host country. To avoid becoming marginal members of both societies, these women are trying to find their way along a painful and tangled route between tradition and modernity. The quest for personal as well as national and cultural identity has become a major concern of educated and politically conscious Iranian women, immigrant or otherwise. A very difficult challenge for a migrant woman is to balance her individuality and personal aspirations with a positive ethnic identity.[2]

Migration studies show that "light-skinned, young, and educated migrants usually encounter a more favorable reception in the United States than dark-skinned, older, and uneducated newcomers" (Espin 1987, 493). Even though the majority of Iranian women immigrants in Los Angeles possess these helpful attributes, hostile political relations between Iran and the United States have kept them from being accepted. The American bias against Arabs and other Middle Easterners was compounded by the "hostage crisis," making Iranians one of the least liked minority groups in American society.

Nevertheless, Iranian women migrants perceive less ethnic and racial discrimination against them in American society than do Latinas, for example. They are less worried about having an Iranian surname than Latinas are about having a Spanish surname (Blair 1991). No significant differences were found in the perceived prejudice against Iranians in Los Angeles based on gender.

The marginality of Iranian immigrants and the other difficulties they encounter in the United States are not without rewards for women. Women can wield power from their position as mediators between the two cultures. But the positive potential of marginality can be realized only by women of the right age, class, and educational status, with the right reasons for migrating. For others the cost of being marginal to both societies is overwhelming. Isolation from one's family, especially if the separation from parents and loved ones is premature and traumatic, exacerbates the sense of belonging nowhere.

Intergenerational Conflicts   Immigrant parents tend to be distressed by the rapid pace of their children's acculturation, brought about by the media, American schools, and American peers. Whereas parental authority in the traditional Iranian family is based on the parents' passing

---

[2] See N. Tohidi, "Identity Politics and the Woman Question in Iran: Retrospect and Prospects," in *Identity Politics and Feminism: Cross-National Perspectives,* ed. V. Mogadam (Oxford University Press: forthcoming).

on to their children their own knowledge of life, children in immigrant families cannot readily apply their parents' knowledge to their own new lives. Instead, roles become somewhat reversed. The children are the ones passing on important information to their parents, correcting their English, and helping them in their daily interactions with Americans.

Such role reversals threaten traditional relations in the family and create tension. The children's development of an identity culturally different from that of their parents intensifies intergenerational conflicts. The gap is especially wide in families whose children grow up in American society.

One particular area of conflict concerns children's rights to privacy and personal boundaries. For example, reading mail addressed to an adolescent son or daughter is considered part of an Iranian parent's responsibility rather than an invasion of privacy. Iranian parents often resist their children's wishes to become financially independent or to move into their own apartments once they turn eighteen. While the children complain about their parents' interference in their lives, the parents complain about their children's lack of respect.

Adolescent girls and young women, especially those who immigrated 30 with their families, must decide how to "become American" without losing their own cultural heritage, if they decide to "become American" at all. Role models of successful and respected bicultural Iranian American women are scarce, and for young women the negative cultural and political connotations of being westernized or Americanized are particularly problematic. Given the myth prevalent among Iranians that American women are sexually loose, being Americanized may be equated with sexual promiscuity. Conflicts between female adolescents and their parents frequently focus on appropriate sexual behavior. Hanassab's 1991 study of dating and sexual attitudes among younger Iranian immigrants shows that the women are torn between two norms: behavior acceptable to their American peers, on the one hand, and their parents' expectations and their own obligations to their native culture, on the other. Some young women rebel against parental pressure by turning their back on Iranian culture and customs—changing their Iranian names to American ones (Blair 1991), for example, or refusing to speak Persian at home.

Gender Role Conflicts   Commentators who cite cultural collision, economic pressures, and sexual freedom as the causes of familial instability among Iranian immigrants also blame women for the current crisis because of their failure to fulfill their proper role. Women who have become "Americanized" are criticized for their loss of originality (*esalat*) and Iranian "female virtues," including obedience (*etaat*), chastity (*nejabat*), patience (*saburi*), and self-denial (*fadakari*). Americanization, which is equated with individualism and selfishness, undermines the commitment to family and the endurance needed to withstand the hardships of immigration.

In response, some immigrant women, particularly feminists, criticize Iranian men for failing to adjust their attitudes and expectations in the face of new realities. Women criticize their resistance to egalitarian relationships and their conscious or unconscious adherence to traditional values and patriarchal norms.

Some men actually cling to traditional norms for gender relations as a reaction to the perceived threat of women's new independence. A similar reaction is also seen among parents who perceive their children's faster pace of acculturation and parent-child role reversals as intolerable challenges to parental power and authority. When adult immigrants are uncertain and confused about what is right and wrong, many hold on to the "old ways," which they idealize in defending against a loss of identity. This refusal to accept change may intensify both intergenerational and gender-role conflicts in the immigrant families (Espin 1987, 493).

Ethnic Variations   Such defensive loyalties to the traditional gender norms of the home culture seem to be less common among Muslim immigrant families than among the religious and ethnic minorities. In my survey, for example, Jewish and Armenian Iranians exhibited more conservative attitudes toward sexual norms and gender roles than their Muslim counterparts,[3] perhaps in part because Iranian Jews and Armenians tended to migrate to the United States as families and kinship groups rather than as isolated individuals. Therefore, from the beginning of the acculturation process, ethnic pressure and the surveillance of the kinship network have reinforced conformity to traditional norms. The very presence of the kinship network may protect young women so that they need not develop self-reliance and autonomy.

Muslim Iranians tend to be more secularized than other Iranian ethnic groups. Perhaps they developed an antipathy to Islam and Islamic tradition out of their own political and cultural opposition to the Islamic theocratic government in Iran and found that it was reinforced in the United States by the pervasively negative image of Muslims in the media and public opinion. For most Muslim Iranians in Los Angeles, male and female alike, language and national culture, rather than religion, seem to constitute the primary components of identity (Ansari 1990).

[3] The number of other Iranian ethnic or religious groups in the research sample was too small to allow any meaningful comparisons.

References

Ansari, M. 1990. "Nasli Dowwm Iranian dar Amrica: Bohrane Howwiyat meli va mazhabi" (The second generation of Iranians in America: National and religious identity crisis). *Iran Times*, March 23, 9–12.

Barakat, H. 1985. "The Arab Family and the Challenge of Social Transformation." In *Women and the Family in the Middle East*, edited by E. W. Fernea. Austin: University of Texas Press.

Blair, B. A. 1991. "Personal Name Change among Iranian Immigrants in the U.S.A." In *Iranian Refugees and Exiles since Khomeini*, edited by A. Fathi. Costa Mesa, Calif.: Mazda Publishers.

Dane, N. 1980. "Social Environment and Psychological Stress in Latin American Immigrant Women." Ph.D. diss., California School of Professional Psychology, Berkeley.

Erikson, E. H. 1974. *Dimensions of a New Identity*. New York: Norton.

Espin, O. 1987. "Psychological Impact of Migration on Latinas." *Psychology of Women Quarterly* 11: 489–503.

Furio, Colomba Marie. 1979. "Immigrant Women and Industry: A Case Study, the Italian Immigrant Women and the Garment Industry, 1880–1950." Ph.D. diss., New York University.

Garza-Guerrero, C. 1974. "Culture Shock: Its Mourning and the Vicissitudes of Identity." *Journal of the American Psychoanalytic Association* 22: 408–429.

Ghaffarian, S. 1989. "The Acculturation of Iranian Immigrants in the United States and the Implications for Mental Health." Ph.D. diss., California School of Professional Psychology, Los Angeles.

Hanassab, S. 1991. "Acculturation and Young Iranian Women: Attitudes toward Sex Roles and Intimate Relationships." *The Journal of Multicultural Counseling and Development* 19: 11–21.

Melville, M. B. 1978. "Mexican Women Adapt to Migration." *International Migration Review* 12: 225–235.

Mernissi, F. 1975. *Beyond the Veil: Male-Female Dynamics in a Modern Muslim Society.* Cambridge, Mass.: Schenkman Publishing.

Najmabadi, A. 1989. "Power, Morality, and the New Muslim Womanhood." Paper presented at a workshop on Women and the State in Afghanistan, Iran, and Pakistan, Massachusetts Institute of Technology, Center for International Studies.

Nassehi-Behnam, V. 1985. "Change and the Iranian Family." *Current Anthropology* 26, no. 5 (December): 557–562.

Salgado de Snyder, V. N. 1987. "Factors Associated with Acculturative Stress and Depressive Symptomatology among Married Mexican Immigrant Women." *Psychology of Women Quarterly* 11: 475–488.

Shirley, B. 1981. "A Study of Ego Strength: The Case of the Latina Immigrant Woman in the United States." Ph.D. diss., Boston University.

Taft, R. 1977. "Coping with Unfamiliar Cultures." In *Studies in Cross-Cultural Psychology*, edited by N. Warren. New York: Academic Press.

Tohidi, N. 1993. "Gender, Modernization, and Identity Politics in Iran." In *Gender and National Identity: The Woman Question in Algeria, Iran, Afghanistan, and Palestine*, edited by V. Moghadam. London: Zed Books.

Vazquez-Nuttall, E. V., L. Romero-Garcia, and B. DeLeon. 1987. "Sex Roles and Perceptions of Femininity and Masculinity of Hispanic Women: A Review of the Literature," *Psychology of Women Quarterly* 11: 409–425.

UNDERSTANDING THE TEXT

1. According to Tohidi, why can immigration be "emancipatory" (para. 1) for women?

2. Summarize in your own words the male and female gender roles that are predominant in Iranian social life. How did the 1978–1979 revolution affect Iranian attitudes toward gender roles?

3. What have been the typical affects of immigration on Iranian women?

4. What does the term "Westoxicated" (para. 11) mean?

5. What generational conflicts do Iranian families often experience when they immigrate to California?

EXPLORING AND DEBATING THE ISSUES

1. In an essay, compare and contrast the ways in which Iranian men and women acculturate to American society. Who has an easier time assimilating, and why?

2. Compare and contrast the generational conflicts that Tohidi describes with those that Nancy Wride discusses in "Vietnamese Youths No Longer Look Homeward" (p. 160). Do you see cultural differences? What impact did the Iranian revolution and the Vietnam War have on each group? How do you account for any differences you might observe?

3. Both Iranian and Mexican immigrants come from traditional, largely patriarchal societies. In an essay, analyze the extent to which the women from these two cultures find immigration to California to be "emancipatory" (para. 1). How might cultural and class distinctions affect the experiences of each group of women? In addition to Tohidi's article, consult Pierrette Hondagneu-Sotelo's "Maid in L.A." (p. 116).

4. To what extent is the California dream available to the Iranian women immigrants whom Tohidi discusses? To develop your analysis, consult James J. Rawls's "California: A Place, a People, a Dream" (p. 22), paying attention to the different components of the dream that he outlines.

Vietnamese Youths No Longer Look Homeward

NANCY WRIDE

Following the Vietnam War, thousands of Vietnamese took to the high seas to escape the Communist regime that seized power in 1975. Many of these "boat people," and others who escaped by other routes, eventually made their way to California, where they continued a long tradition of immigrant assimilation into American society. In this selection, **Nancy Wride** (b. 1959) interviews a group of California high school and college students—the so-called 1.5 generation, who were born in Vietnam but raised in America—who share their thoughts about the American dream (California style), their Vietnamese ancestry, and assimilation. Wride is a staff writer for the *Los Angeles Times* who specializes in writing about people who are ordinarily ignored by the media.

Trouble seeped into Huy Tran's tranquil childhood in Vietnam like blood on sand. Coming home after a day of chasing crickets, he would overhear his parents whisper urgently in the hallway. Dispatches from the war front would flash across the TV at the town church. Then came the jailings of his father, a teacher, by the Communist regime.

Finally, when he was twelve, Tran and his father pushed off to sea and a new life in America. The boat trip was some kind of hell, he says. During the trek, a woman crazed by dehydration tried to kill herself with her fingernails. Tran finally made it to California, but it was six years before he saw his mother and siblings again.

Tran, twenty-two, will never forget his family's ordeal, yet he favors America's recent restoration of trade with the government that tormented them. He believes that doing business with Vietnam will be good for refugees in the United States and those struggling in his homeland.

"I'm still sorry our lives were disrupted by the Vietnam War. But you cannot compare my anguish or anger toward the Vietnam War to my parents'," said Tran, a computer consultant in Irvine. "They expect me to feel the same, but they also understand that, because of my age, I might not be able to remember the persecution they had to go through, and the corruption, the hardship the South had to endure once the North took over."

Vietnam-born but American-bred, Tran belongs to a generation that 5 seems detached from the war that tore apart their birthplace, forced the exodus of 1.5 million people and left up to 2 million dead.

Most are under thirty, coming of age as the twentieth anniversary of the fall of Saigon nears next year. By the end of this century, they will make up a great part of the Vietnamese American community's Establishment, from business to political leadership.

Generally, they have not inherited their parents' hatred of Communism or qualms about trading with a former enemy.

American schools do not teach them Vietnamese history. And most immigrant parents are so busy working to support their families that there is little time to review the past together—presuming they and their children can still speak the same language.

As for the children, they are trying to be a part of a society that wants to forget the Vietnam War.

"They are totally socialized into American society. I find that because   10 there is nothing in the curriculum, even in the UC system, [about] their background, they are generally ignorant to the circumstances that brought them to the United States," said Eric Crystal, coordinator of the Center for Southeast Asia Studies at UC Berkeley.

"For these kids, first of all, their whole lives are not oriented toward what happened in South Vietnam. They've never really lived there. And then there's something vaguely negative about Vietnam to an American— it means war, soldiers, prostitutes."

It is hard to find a voice of authority about the Vietnamese American experience, Crystal said, because it has been largely ignored by U.S. universities, perhaps because it is a relatively new immigrant experience. And those who are just now approaching adulthood, Crystal said, "have been studied even less."

"But the story of this group is that their fundamental preoccupation is with the country that they know, not their parents'," Crystal said.

First-generation immigrants generally retain most of their homeland's customs and values. Their children are expected to adopt the culture of their own native country. Generational conflicts are predictable.

Straddling these worlds are young Vietnamese Americans who, like   15 other children born in the old country but raised in the new, have been dubbed "the 1.5 generation" by academics.

Born in a country where parental authority goes unquestioned, this in-between generation is growing up in a freedom-loving society whose aggressive anthem often is "Just Do It." They are "really torn between two worlds," said a counselor at Westminster High School, home to the nation's largest Vietnamese student population.

In California, where nearly half of America's Vietnamese refugees live, many children of former political prisoners and war veterans say necessity forces them to focus not on past horrors but on their future: entering the mainstream and seeking decent jobs and the good life for their families.

"We as the younger generation expect a little bit more out of this country, and from ourself," said Helen Nguyen, twenty-one, a UC Irvine biology major who was born in Saigon and fled with her family when she was seven.

Her father was a soldier in the Vietnam War and was a prisoner for a year in the brainwashing "re-education" camps of the Communist North Vietnamese, Nguyen said. After a year of processing at a Malaysian camp, her family made its way to Ventura, where her parents live. This painful family history, she added, is seldom discussed at home.

"The first level [of immigrants], where our parents came in, were just grateful [to be here]," she said. "I can see how the younger people are just struggling to work and have a solid career. I think if you give the 1.5 generation more time, after they've established careers and families, then they later will come around to activism."   20

For now, though, such interest seems secondary. "My parents don't speak much about the war. My dad did serve a year in a re-education camp; he took it as natural. [In the war], men fought, we suffered, it is past now, and we move on."

"I think the generational conflict is both universal and unique," said Yong Chen, a UC Irvine Asian American studies professor specializing in U.S. immigration history. "If you look to earlier immigrants from Europe, you will find a similar generational conflict."

More recently, new appreciation of ethnic differences and cultural diversity have reversed past patterns of abandoning heritage for the mainstream, Chen said. Those of the 1.5 generation can select what they deem the best of past and present cultures.

Dr. Duong Cao Pham has a front-row seat to the 1.5 generation. He is a visiting professor of Vietnamese history and culture at UC Irvine and UCLA and teaches high school full time. His four children were born in Vietnam. The eldest was eight when the family fled just before Saigon fell in 1975.

The Vietnamese only began immigrating en masse nineteen years ago, he said. For these immigrants, technology—including radio, television, and faxes—has built unprecedented bridges between the old and new worlds. "It's easier to maintain ties and knowledge about what's going on in each country," Pham said. "We are now in another age, compared to the Chinese in the nineteenth century or the Filipinos after World War II, or the Koreans in the 1960s."   25

Despite the technology, Pham's twenty-one-year-old son, Vu Pham, sees greater differences between the generations. Moving from Saigon to the United States when he was three, Vu grew up in Fountain Valley and is a graduate student in UC Irvine's humanities honors program. He is writing his senior thesis on members of the 1.5 generation—particularly their lack of community involvement compared to their parents.

"In my research, I've found that there are very, very few people in the 1.5 generation who are community activists," Vu said. "Many are concentrating only on mainstreaming."

In his interviews, Vu said he found that his peers are emotionally and intellectually removed from such issues as restored trade ties because they have only considered the financial benefits and not the political reality. If many Americans seemed resigned about renewed ties with a former enemy, he noted, why wouldn't Vietnamese Americans be as well?

"More personal is that there is this alienation from Vietnam, aside from faint memories," Vu Pham said. "A lot of the 1.5 . . . don't plan to return to Vietnam, they don't have any relatives in Vietnam, or if they do, they are usually relatives of their parents."

Finally, he said, there is the handicap of ignorance. "One of the major   30
reasons you don't deal with issues about Vietnam at my age is that it's not taught in school. I had nothing taught to me in high school about the Vietnam War. We reached the late twentieth century, and it wasn't ever mentioned."

To help fellow refugees, Vietnamese student organizations have formed at numerous southern California colleges. One is Project Ngoc (pearl), which was organized in 1989 to help a new wave of refugees and asylum seekers. The groups are less political than service and social and cultural clubs such as the Vietnamese Student Association, which has chapters throughout the Southland, and the Vietnamese American Coalition, formed by four UC Irvine students, including Tran.

Out of respect, Vietnamese American students often preface their own horror stories by stressing that others have suffered much more when their country was ruined by war. "It was very hard for me, the first few years without my mom," Tran said. "I've known families that didn't reunite for ten or twelve years later."

From Vietnam, he and his father traveled to Indonesia, Texas, and finally to Los Angeles, where they were later reunited with Tran's mother and brothers. He graduated from John Marshall High School in Los Angeles, and enrolled as a biology major at UC Irvine. After one quarter he switched to political science. His parents virulently opposed the move, believing hard sciences to be a better-paying field and less discriminating against the foreign-born.

Tran had to pay his own tuition, although he was allowed to live at home. He has never regretted the decision, but he has not found work in social services and remains a full-time computer consultant. Despite all the torment, he said, coming to America "has meant I have a better life than I would have had, a better education."

At La Quinta High School in Westminster, about 60 percent of the   35
1,283 students are Vietnamese, the highest percentage in the country.
Last year's homecoming court was Vietnamese, as was this year's queen.
And all but one of the candidates for La Quinta's highest honor—Aztec
boy and girl student of the year—are Vietnamese, too. The Vietnamese
Club, with two hundred members, is the biggest on campus. But all meetings are in English, and it is a service group that does not focus on culture
or ethnicity. Copresident Lynn Phu is Cambodian but was born after her
family fled to Vietnam.

It is a sign, some experts say, of the cultural crossroads that define
Generation 1.5-ers.

In the days after President Clinton announced the renewal of trade
ties with Vietnam, Rita Corpin's world history honors class discussed
what it all meant. A twenty-year-old bumper sticker on Corpin's lectern
read "MIAs—Only Hanoi Knows." The class was celebrating the arrival of
the Tet New Year. Of the thirty-six students, twelve were born in Vietnam.
A show of hands revealed that the students were in agreement: they
thought lifting the embargo was good. Why? Because it would make it
easier to fly into Ho Chi Minh City, formerly Saigon.

Nobody mentioned the war, boat people, or concerns about doing
business with a former enemy. Nobody mentioned prisoners of war.

"It will be better for two-way travel and to visit relatives now," said
one student, although he added that his family had already done this. "It
will be easier for us to send money there," another said.

At La Quinta, it is not just dating and curfew and report card hassles that   40
Vietnamese-born children bring to school with them each day. There are
twenty-seven English as a second language classes taught here, and the
school common is visibly divided between Americanized Vietnamese and
the newcomers, who speak their native language and squat Asian-style
through lunch.

"We had a girl commit suicide the month before I came here," said
principal Mitch Thomas, "and it was over one thing: assimilation. . . . She
was a bright, beautiful, capable kid. And those kids—who say what are
you talking about, what embargo?—they are interested in the here and
now. Their parents know all the politics, but the kids, all of their energy is
striving for assimilation."

One thing about kids is universal, say Thomas and other educators
working with Vietnamese students. No matter what their nationality,
they all want to fit in.

Senior Thanh Tang, seventeen, vice president of the student body and
honor roll student, is something of an exception. He is among the students

who seem to hold an educated opinion about the reopening of trade: He opposes it—perhaps, he says, more strongly than his parents do.

In Vietnam, his parents imported produce—mostly grapes and oranges. Before that, his father was a police officer. Here, they rise at five and work seven days a week at their Santa Ana restaurant. They lost so much to come here, he said, and Americans will lose plenty now, too.

"I think with the embargo gone we'll be losing more of the workers. 45 Soon we'll see Sony in Vietnam; the labor is cheaper. And the environmental concerns . . . people building factories without standards and destroying the rain forest there. Someone's killing your people [prisoners of war and soldiers listed as missing in action], and you're *opening trade with them?*" he said, his face turning incredulous.

Of those like him, born in Vietnam but raised here, he said: "Some people are too young to see or feel any of that: Why did you lift the embargo on people who hurt my parents and made me go through that?

"When I first came here, my parents talked about Communists! Communists! But they don't talk about it anymore," said Tang, who works weekends at the restaurant and has dreams of attending Harvard Business School. "When I have time to sit down and talk, it's not about Vietnam; it's more [about] what I'm doing after high school, where I'm going to school.

"I think parents don't tell them about it," Tang added. Like his family and those of his friends, "everybody is too busy trying to work to support their family."

UNDERSTANDING THE TEXT

1. Why have academics called young Vietnamese Americans "the 1.5 generation" (para. 15)?

2. Why, according to Wride, are the attitudes of young Vietnamese Americans toward their cultural background different than their parents' attitudes?

3. What view do young Vietnamese Americans tend to have of the Vietnam War, according to Wride?

4. According to the selection, what is the attitude most young Vietnamese Americans have toward restoring trade ties between the United States and Vietnam, and why do they feel that way?

5. Why does La Quinta High School principal Mitch Thomas say "all of [Vietnamese American students'] energy is striving for assimilation" (para. 41)?

EXPLORING AND DEBATING THE ISSUES

1. Write an essay that supports, refutes, or modifies the proposition that California colleges and universities should include in their curricula courses on the Vietnamese American experience and on the experiences of other major immigrant groups.

2. If you are an immigrant, write a journal entry in which you describe your life in your native country and the circumstances surrounding your immigration. If you are not an immigrant, write an entry in which you reflect on the experiences of the Vietnamese immigrants described in Wride's essay.

3. Interview at least five students on your campus who are immigrants (from any nation), asking them about their desires to assimilate and also to preserve their native culture. Then compare your findings with the experiences of young Vietnamese Americans as described by Wride. How can you account for the similarities or differences in attitude you may find?

4. Assuming the perspective of Huy Tran, Vu Pham, or one of the other students mentioned in Wride's essay, write a response to Yeh Ling-Ling's ("State Needs a 'Time-Out' from Mass Immigration," p. 94) argument for restricting immigration.

5. Assuming the role of a Vietnamese parent, write a letter to your "child" about the family's need to preserve its cultural heritage. Alternately, write a letter from the perspective of a 1.5 generation student to your Vietnamese "parent" in which you discuss your desire to assimilate.

My Latino Heart

MARIO GARCIA

"What am I, Dad?" **Mario Garcia** once asked his father. "You're a Mexican," he replied, brusquely. "You're a Mexican American," his mother replied, more gently. But these answers seemed meaningless because he did not speak Spanish and his friends were Anglos. Later, Garcia preferred to think of himself as an Aztec or a Toltec, but his physical features didn't fit the mold. And so, as Garcia tells us in this autobiographical self-exploration, his search for an identity continued. Now he can call himself many things — "Mexican, Mexican American, Chicano, Latin American, Hispanic, Latino" — but concludes that in the end, "Perhaps names do not matter," only the love that "transcends nationality, race, and religion." Garcia is an English teacher for the Los Angeles Unified School District and an adjunct professor for the Ventura County Community College District. His work on Latino issues has been read on National Public Radio and published in *Kaleidoscope*.

One could say ethnic identity has been an "issue" for me since elementary school. At that time, our family of six moved from an impoverished Latino neighborhood in Los Angeles to a small, mostly white community beyond the San Fernando Valley.

What I remember most about moving is my first day at the new school. The boys and girls played games I did not understand. An expanse of freshly mown grass met a smooth blacktop with brightly painted lines. The school I'd come from had little grass. The faded coarse asphalt there was cracked and raised where the weeds had pushed through.

"How do you like it here?" my father asked when he came home late that evening. He had completed enough college to secure his first job in the aerospace industry. The money was good, but the company was in Anaheim, a two-hour commute from where we lived.

"I like it fine," I said, listening. In the old house, I had grown accustomed to the rustling of rodents within the walls. The week before we moved, the rodents had been especially bad, and my mother had used poison. The house reeked from their decaying bodies and the Pine-Sol she had used to mask the stench. The new house was quiet except for the low hum of a new refrigerator. The kitchen was bright and smelled pleasantly of new plaster.

But everything now began to change. My older sister studied modeling and dutifully walked the house with a beauty pageant smile. My younger sister and I began piano lessons. Soon, my mother gave birth to another child. She returned from the hospital looking exhausted, yet beautiful and happy. My father bought a new car, a blue Chevrolet Impala that roared when he revved the engine. There were new clothes and a set of encyclopedias. There was new furniture and a television we weren't allowed to watch. We never talked about the old house or our old friends. One could say we never had it better, but I was uneasy with our abrupt split from the old neighborhood and the people we had known. I lay awake some nights with a hollow pain that grew as something I could not name burrowed inside me.

By the time I was in junior high, I noticed a few other students with Spanish surnames. There was a boy with the last name Gonzalez. He was my size but stronger and quicker. In PE class we were matched for wrestling. Although I had made the school team, I could not pin him. One day I saw him outside the locker room.

"Where you from?" he demanded.

"Nowhere," I shrugged. Wanting no trouble for us, my mother had instructed me not to mention the old neighborhood or its gangs. He gave me an impatient glance.

"What *are* you?" he insisted.

"Like you," I said awkwardly. He shook his head and drew away from   10
me. We weren't anything alike. We had different classes and different
friends. We liked different girls. He was dark-skinned, a medium shade of
burnt sienna. During the winter months, my skin was a pasty white.

"What am I, Dad?" I asked my father that evening. Timing was a
tricky proposition with him. He was a cold-war engineer working sixty-
and seventy-hour work weeks on the Minuteman Missile. What little
time he had at home was necessarily divided between five kids, a wife,
and a house.

"You're a Mexican," he replied with what I understood to be surprise
and anger. I had picked a bad time. I let the subject drop but later asked
my Mother.

"You're a Mexican American," she answered.

"But what does that mean?"

"It means you'd better clean up that filthy room of yours."   15

Growing up in a family of seven left little time for philosophical issues.

By the time I was in my teens, I'd resolved to canvass my extended family. Two or three times a year, relatives visited from all parts of Los Angeles. My siblings and I would assume ordered positions on the stairs
where we endured our family's peculiar affection. Aunts carelessly kissed
us, smearing our faces with lipstick. Uncles with work-hardened hands
patted our heads with brain-jostling force.

The early part of the evening was usually not a good time for conversation. An oppressive air clouded the room, like the cigarette smoke that
hung midway between the floor and ceiling. But as the liquor began to
flow, hostility gave way to civility. Later, civility would blossom into love.
They would sing *corridos* and *rancheras* and laugh wildly. Much later,
after we children were sent to bed, there would be vicious arguments.

One evening, I spoke with an aunt who drank in a room separate
from the others. Beside her was an ashtray full of butts marked with her
lipstick.

"Auntie," I asked, "are you Chicano?"   20

"I think you mean, Chicana," she said laughing in a way that did not
embarrass me. "I'm Mexican," she finally said.

"Are you from Mexico?" I asked.

"No. But my mother and father are. That makes me Mexican."

"So what am I?"

"Come here. I'll tell you what you are." She pulled my head forward   25
and kissed me. "You're you," she said. "Now, please get your auntie some
ice."

She was a thin woman with red hair, finely chiseled features, and eyes that glimmered with silent laughter. I could smell her perfume on me that night as I went to bed. I wondered if she'd understood the question. "You're you." What kind of answer was that?

I never got the chance to ask what her statement meant. Months later a phone call came late in the night. Something had happened. My mother cried and my father pounded the living room table with his fists. Nobody would mention her after that. When I asked about my aunt, my parents would only say she was sick.

Her sickness was alcoholism. By the time she died, her abdomen had bloated horribly, and her face was puffy and ashen. Someone said the funeral parlor had done the best they could. When they buried her, I recalled my aunt's perfume and laughter and wondered if this was somehow part of being Mexican.

The family gatherings continued, though smaller. I shied away from my cousins, favoring the company of adults and the stories they told. My uncles talked longingly of old cars and of feats they'd accomplished as younger men. From the kitchen, my aunts recalled hazy lyrics to old ballads. Sometimes they would talk quietly about the war and lost family. After dinner the adults assembled in the living room to sing, smoke, and drink. One could say I felt their longings and unfulfilled dreams. It seemed they inhabited an empty and meaningless present, irretrievably alienated from the persons they'd been in the past, much like the wrinkled black and white photographs they carried of lost loves and dead children.

"What are you?" The question dogged me in high school, a monstrous abstraction, daring my intellect to grapple with it. For years, the challenge had arisen, but I had avoided the confrontation, walking away from the barrier of labels and slogans twisted around each other like pernicious vines, each trying to deprive the others of light and life.

Mexican American is what I called myself in high school, but it was a label without meaning. I didn't speak Spanish, and the few friends I had were Anglos. "We don't think of you as a Mexican," they would assure me, and I took a perverse comfort in that.

By the time I reached my twenties, I had set aside the mystery of my identity along with my piano studies. I attended to my new engineering career, and my marriage to a white girl who'd read Octavio Paz and Garcia-Lorca in translation. On the weekends, I restored a vintage Porsche. One could say certain matters had been decided.

Our family gatherings continued, but the old records stayed in their sleeves, and there was no singing. Grandmother would sit in matronly silence in a wooden chair and drink deeply from the goblets of wine my father brought her. I was captivated by her piercing eyes. Like dark murky pools, they seemed to hold knowledge commensurate with her years. Perhaps she knew the answer to my question, but I was too embarrassed to reveal my ignorance. I would sit nearby to help her to the bathroom. My father would give me an approving nod.

After my own marriage collapsed, I wondered why my family still continued to brood together. Even the booze didn't make them happy. My mother would complain bitterly about the mess grandmother made in the bathroom. After everyone was gone, my father would sit in the dark and smoke.

"Next time, why don't you play piano for your grandmother," he said   35
to me before I left for my apartment. It was an October evening. The Santa Ana winds mourned through the trees. I hadn't played piano for many years. I saw something of my grandmother in his piercing eyes. "An easy piece." Something stirred, gnawed, and scratched at my insides. I agreed.

I practiced for several months at my apartment on a hastily bought console. A Chopin Nocturne. By Thanksgiving, I was ready. When my grandmother arrived, I calmed myself to play, but my fingers fumbled. The trills were uneven, and the sweet pathos of the melody seemed drowned in the clanging of dishes from the kitchen. I apologized when I finished. Then I saw tears streaming down her face as she peered into space, a place where I could not see.

"Thank you," she said. They were among the few words she ever spoke to me in English.

By the time I was in my midtwenties, I was calling myself a Mexican. I studied that country's history. I was proud of the indigenous Indians but despised the Spaniards and their colonialism that brought destruction and death to so many. I would look at my face in the mirror and search for some sign of the Aztec, the Olmec, the Toltec. I could find none. I hated my light skin, round eyes, and sharp European nose. My search for a label was becoming a twisted joke. I fit nowhere, had no "people" I could claim and, perhaps worse, none that would claim me.

My family moved again, this time to an even larger house with a study dominated by my father's grand piano. Whenever she visited, my grandmother would wait there for me. We had an unspoken understanding. I played for her: Scarlatti, Schubert, Ravel, and her favorite, Chopin. Every now and then I'd catch that stare of hers, piercing into an unknown realm.

At her funeral, one of two surviving daughters draped herself over   40
my grandmother's body, kissing her face and hands. The funeral director stood at the door checking his watch.

"Let's go, Auntie."

"My mother," was all she could say between sobs.

"She's gone now. Can't you feel it?" I said, taking my aunt's hand. I placed it where my grandmother's heart had once beaten.

"Yes, I can," she said and let go.

What am I? What is any person? A legion of footsore labels plod behind   45
the front lines of any dialectic that seeks to define a people. Mexican, Mexican American, Chicano, Latin American, Hispanic, Latino. Haven't they all gained and lost ground, engaged in a banal and predictable competition for hegemony? Perhaps names do not matter, so long as they challenge and set us on a path to discovery.

Today, I have a beautiful wife who could have been an Olmec princess. She has given me a daughter. I watch her grow with a sense of humility and awe. The school where I teach has children from all over the world, including sons and daughters from the neighborhood I left behind. Love transcends nationality, race, and religion. I look at my family, my students, and understand we are here for each other. I can see this truth and others in the beautiful depths of their eyes.

UNDERSTANDING THE TEXT

1. Summarize the differences between Garcia's old and new neighborhoods. How do his attitudes toward each neighborhood compare?

2. Why do you think Garcia's aunt replies "You're you" (para. 25) when he asks her "what am I"?

3. Why do you think Garcia says "It seemed they [his adult relatives] inhabited an empty and meaningless present, irretrievably alienated from the persons they'd been in the past" (para. 29)?

4. List the various attempts Garcia makes to discern his ethnic identity.

EXPLORING AND DEBATING THE ISSUES

1. In class, discuss the reasons that Garcia found ethnic identity so confusing as he was growing up, being sure to address his family's move to a new home and community, his physical appearance, and his status as a child of immigrants.

2. Write a personal essay in which you address the question of ethnic identity that obsessed Garcia: "What am I?" (para. 11).

3. To what extent could Garcia's family be said to have achieved the California dream? You might focus particular attention on his parents and his grandmother. To develop your ideas, consult James J. Rawls's "California: A Place, a People, a Dream" (p. 22).

4. Write an essay in which you support, refute, or complicate Garcia's conclusion that ethnic labels have "all gained and lost ground, engaged in a banal and predictable competition for hegemony" (para. 45). As you develop your ideas, consider the various meanings that ethnic identity may have for native Californians (of whatever ethnic origins) and also for recent immigrants from other nations. Consult any of the readings in this chapter for specific evidence.

Researching the Issues

1. Visit your college library, and locate a copy of the Treaty of Guadalupe Hidalgo, which ended the Mexican-American War in 1848 and required Mexico to cede California to the United States. Write a report detailing the treaty's disposition of the Mexican population in California at the time.

2. Some Chicano activists do not accept the Treaty of Guadalupe Hidalgo (see question 1), claiming that California is in fact still Mexican territory. Research this position, and then write an essay arguing for or against it. You may wish to consult Rudolfo Acuña's *Occupied America* (New York: HarperCollins, 1988) as part of your research.

3. Immigrants to California have often faced restrictive legislation. Research the Chinese Exclusion Act of 1882 and the Alien Laws of 1913 and 1924, and write a report in which you explain how these laws affected Asian immigrants.

4. Research the demographic composition of your college or university campus. To gather data, consult your admissions office or student affairs office. Share your data with your class.

5. In a research project, study the history of the Japanese detention camps during World War II. What were the social and political circumstances leading to their creation?

6. Pick an ethnic group (anything from African Americans to Cambodian refugees to Soviet Jews), and trace the history of their immigration to California. Choose from the groups discussed in this chapter, or think of a different group not included here. Why did they leave their state or land of origin, and why did they settle where they did? What did the California dream mean to this group? In addition to library research, you may want to interview some immigrants to obtain their perspective.

7. Research the history of the civil wars in Central America during the 1970s and 1980s and their effect on immigration to California. Then

write an essay in which you argue for or against the proposition that U.S. support for the governments in power makes the United States morally responsible for the refugees.

8. Should the United States "seal its borders," particularly in California? Form groups, and work together to research the role of the U.S. Border Patrol, and the effects of Operation Gatekeeper, in preventing illegal immigration to California. Then stage a debate in class, supporting your group's position with research data.

9. Rent a videotape of Edward R. Murrow's *Harvest of Shame*, an exposé of conditions suffered by migrant farmworkers in the 1960s, and show it in class. Then write an essay in which you sketch what a version of the movie updated for the early twenty-first century would look like. Base your new version on research you conduct in your college library and, if you live in an agricultural region, on visits to farms in your area.

10. Form groups to volunteer some time for a local social-services agency that specializes in immigrants' needs. Then prepare a report in which you assess the problems that immigrants face in adjusting to life in California, making specific recommendations for change. Share your project with both your class and the agency for which you have worked.

11. Research the contributions of Chinese laborers, particularly those who were required to work on railroad construction, during the nineteenth century.

12. Rent a videotape of *The Grapes of Wrath* or read the novel, and write an analysis of why it became a classic depiction of the California dream.

3

The Best-Laid Plans

EDUCATION AND THE CALIFORNIA DREAM

"Testing one, two, three. Testing, Testing. Testing one, two, three."

That's practically all you hear about these days when California's education system is discussed—that and "budget cuts and college fee increases," of course. But testing now affects the content and curriculum of education in the Golden State, and if you have taken California's high school exit exam, it has affected you in a particularly potent way. And so you may well wonder what all the fuss over testing is about.

We should first note that this new emphasis on testing—and also on what is called "accountability"—reflects the unusual level of politicization in California's system of public education. In the 1990s, electoral politics entered the educational arena in a big way with such high-profile ballot initiatives as Propositions 187 (which sought to exclude the children of undocumented immigrants from California public schools), 209 (which ended affirmative action programs in California's colleges and universities), and 227 (which dramatically limited bilingual instruction in the public schools). In each case, public education was subjected to direct political intervention due to social controversies—especially regarding immigration—that were not pedagogical in origin. Thus, these initiatives could be said to reflect concerns over the profound social and demographic changes of the last decade or so rather than concerns over education.

The focus on testing in the schools also arises from a concern about education, of course, but the job of solving the perceived problem has

◀ Paul Fell, "Time for Another Tuition Increase, Sir?"

been taken away from educators by legislators and those who elect them. In a nutshell, the political perception is that California's public-education system is failing to do its job and is graduating students (this means you, so you have an enormous stake in the matter) who are not prepared for college-level study or for the workforce. Many teachers and students agree that California's public-education system could be improved, and some may have their own ideas about how to accomplish this. But in the governor's office, the legislature, and the editorial pages of many California newspapers, the opinion seems to be that teachers cannot be trusted to do their own jobs and that outside agencies (which have a business interest in designing standardized tests) are better prepared to solve the problem. And so, from your early grade-school years on, you have taken a lot of standardized tests, while your teachers—whose jobs may be on the line if you don't perform well on those tests—have been compelled (or at least felt compelled) to teach a curriculum designed to prepare you for testing and more testing.

The need to teach to the test has been driving both the curriculum and the pedagogy of public education in California for several years. Those who endorse testing believe that such a regime will ensure accountability in the schools and will make certain that California's students are well prepared for further study or for employment. Those who disagree (and their ranks are dominated by the teachers who actually teach students) worry that teaching to the test will produce students who know how to take a certain kind of test but who have not really been educated—that is, cannot think critically or creatively. It's too early to say which side is right. But in the summer of 2003, the California Board of Education postponed for another two years the enforcement of the high school exit exam—an indicator that testing might well be yet another politically driven solution to educational problems that creates more problems than it solves.

Getting In

Access to California's public colleges and universities also continues to create political controversy over forty years after the 1960 California Master Plan for Higher Education first promised a tuition-free college education to every citizen of California. California's public college and university system hasn't been tuition-free for years, but with the gargantuan state budget deficits of 2003–2004, fees rose so dramatically in the University of California, California State University, and Community College systems that many students feared being excluded on financial grounds alone. And even with the fee increases, California's colleges and universities have had to curtail enrollments to adjust to the massive budget cuts being imposed in Sacramento—at the same time that the college-age population has burgeoned (commonly known as Tidal Wave II).

Simultaneously, controversy over Proposition 209, the ballot initiative that effectively ended affirmative action in the state's admissions policies, continued to fester as reports circulated that some students with lower Scholastic Aptitude Test scores had been admitted to the UC system over those with higher SAT scores. On the other side of the debate, claims of plunging minority enrollments at UC Berkeley and UCLA, the two most sought-after UC destinations, continued to be made, putting pressure on administrators to find ways to increase minority enrollments without violating the terms of Prop. 209. As we write these words, it is not at all difficult to predict that such controversies will continue to roil the waters of California education for years to come.

In such a climate, you—the major stakeholders in California education—need to be as well informed as you can be. Crucial decisions affecting your educational future and beyond are being made every day. What do you think about testing? About college and university fees? About admissions? Do you have any thoughts about the never-say-die voucher movement, which, after several defeats at the ballot box, continues to press for the privatization of public education? The readings in this chapter are designed to help you think about such matters, for if you don't think about them yourselves, you can be sure that somebody else will do it for you.

The Readings

Frank Norris's sardonic view of the English department at Berkeley in the late nineteenth century opens our chapter on California education, followed by Mike Rose's visit to a modern middle school in Watts, a reading in which he presents a vision of how things can be done right in California's inner-city schools. Carol Jago follows with a personal account of her role in compiling the California Department of Education's "Recommended Literature: Kindergarten through Grade Twelve" reading list. Next are two selections that explore the current emphasis on testing in our public schools: Sylvia S. Fox first analyzes the politics of testing and "accountability" that currently dominates the state's educational policy, and Sandra Nichols's opinion piece on the high school exit exam offers an alternative to the do-or-die testing regime that determines whether a student will receive a high school diploma. Lesli A. Maxwell follows by looking at the budget cuts that are threatening the California Master Plan for Higher Education's promise of a college or university education to all qualified California students. Two pieces related to the controversy over affirmative action follow, with Ruben Navarrette Jr. telling the story of what it was like to be a Central Valley Chicano admitted to Harvard University and John McWhorter arguing that "hardship," as long as it is a euphemism for race, should not be a factor in UC admissions. Concluding the chapter, Chitra Banerjee Divakaruni's poem on the language difficulties that South Asian immigrants face in California schools offers a personal insight into the challenges of educating a multilingual population.

The "English Courses" at the University of California

FRANK NORRIS

What would happen if a prominent California novelist were asked to "assess" the quality of literary education at, say, the University of California, Berkeley? Well, it actually happened, and the results aren't pretty, as you can see in this satiric essay by **Frank Norris** (1870–1902). As far as Norris is concerned, the literature faculty there was systematically destroying any creative initiative or imagination their students may have had and was driving them to elaborate schemes of plagiarism. In short, everyone flunks Norris's test, except the good folks at Harvard, who receive high marks for simply reading literature aloud to their students. A product himself of the UC Berkeley English department, Norris would go on to write two classic novels, *McTeague* (1899) and *The Octopus* (1901), in spite of the damage he insists was inflicted on him by his professors.

In the "announcement of courses" published annually by the faculty of the University of California the reader cannot fail to be impressed with the number and scope of the hours devoted by the students to recitations and lectures upon the subject of "literature." At the head of this department is Professor Gayley (the same gentleman who is to edit the volumes of Shakespeare for Macmillan at the expense of the State of California). Be pleased for a moment to consider these "literary" courses. They comprise "themes" written by the student, the subject chosen by the instructor and the matter found in text books and encyclopedias. They further include lectures, delivered by associate professors, who, in their turn have taken their information from text books and "manuals" written by other professors in other colleges. The student is taught to "classify." "Classification" is the one thing desirable in the eyes of the professors of "literature" of the University of California. The young Sophomore, with his new, fresh mind, his active brain and vivid imagination, with ideas of his own, crude, perhaps, but first hand, not cribbed from text books. This type of young fellow, I say, is taught to "classify," is set to work counting the "metaphors" in a given passage. This is actually true—tabulating them, separating them from the "similes," comparing the results. He is told to study sentence structure. He classifies certain types of sentences in De Quincey and compares them with certain other types of sentences in Carlyle. He makes the wonderful discovery—on suggestion from the instructor—that De Quincey excelled in those metaphors and similes relating to rapidity of movement. Sensation!

In his Junior and Senior years he takes up the study of Milton, of Browning, of the drama of the seventeenth and eighteenth centuries, English comedy, of advanced rhetoric, and of aesthetics. "Aesthetics," think of that! Here, the "classification" goes on as before. He learns to read Chaucer as it was read in the fourteenth century, sounding the final e; he paraphrases Milton's sonnets, he makes out "skeletons" and "schemes" of certain prose passages. His enthusiasm is about dead now; he is ashamed of his original thoughts and of those ideas of his own that he entertained as a Freshman and Sophomore. He has learned to write "themes" and "papers" in the true academic style, which is to read some dozen text books and encyclopedia articles on the subject, and to make over the results in his own language. He has reduced the writing of "themes" to a system. He knows what the instructor wants, he writes accordingly, and is rewarded by first and second sections. The "co-eds" take to the "classification" method even better than the young men. They thrive and fatten intellectually on the regime. They consider themselves literary. They write articles on the "Philosophy of Dante" for the college weekly, and after graduation they "read papers" to literary "circles" composed of post-graduate "co-eds," the professors' wives and daughters and a very few pale young men in spectacles and black cutaway coats. After the reading of the "paper" follows the "discussion," aided and abetted by cake and lemonade. This is literature! Isn't it admirable!

The young man, the whilom Sophomore, affected with original ideas, does rather different. As said, by the time he is a Junior or Senior, he has lost all interest in the "literary" courses. The "themes" must be written, however, and the best way is the easiest. This is how he oft-times goes about it: He knows just where he can lay his hands upon some fifty to a hundred "themes" written by the members of past classes, that have been carefully collected and preserved by enterprising students. It will go hard if he cannot in the pile find one upon the subject in hand. He does not necessarily copy it. He rewrites it in his own language. Do you blame him very much? Is his method so very different from that in which he is encouraged by his professor; viz., the cribbing—for it is cribbing—from text books? The "theme" which he rewrites has been cribbed in the first place.

The method of English instruction of the University of California often develops capital ingenuity in the student upon whom it is practiced. We know of one young man—a Senior—who found himself called upon to write four "themes," yet managed to make one—re-written four times—do for the four. This was the manner of it. The four "themes" called for were in the English, chemical, German and military courses respectively. The young fellow found a German treatise on the manufacture of gunpowder, translated it, made four copies, and by a little ingenuity passed it off in the four above named departments. Of course the thing is deplorable, yet how much of the blame is to be laid at the door of the English faculty?

The conclusion of the whole matter is that the literary courses at the University of California do not develop literary instincts among the students who attend them. The best way to study literature is to try to produce literature. It is original work that counts, not the everlasting compiling of facts, not the tabulating of metaphors, nor the rehashing of text books and encyclopedia articles.

They order this matter better at Harvard. The literary student at Cambridge has but little to do with lectures, almost nothing at all with text books. He is sent away from the lecture room and told to look about him and think a little. Each day he writes a theme, a page if necessary, a single line of a dozen words if he likes; anything, so it is original, something he has seen or thought, not read of, not picked up at second hand. He may choose any subject under the blue heavens from a pun to a philosophical reflection, only let it be his own. Once every two weeks he writes a longer theme, and during the last six weeks of the year, a still longer one, in six weekly installments. Not a single suggestion is offered as to subject. The result of this system is a keenness of interest that draws three hundred men to the course and that fills the benches at every session of the class. The class room work consists merely in the reading by the instructor of the best work done, together with his few critical comments upon it by the instructor in charge. The character of the themes produced under this system is of such high order that it is not rare to come across one of them in the pages of the first-class magazines of the day. There is no sufficient reason to suppose that the California collegians are intellectually inferior to those of the Eastern States. It is only a question of the means adopted to develop the material.

UNDERSTANDING THE TEXT

1. Characterize in your own words how Norris claims that students are taught in literature classes at the turn-of-the-century University of California. What cognitive skills do the courses teach? What kinds of literature? What is the effect of these English classes on a student's desire to learn?

2. What is Norris's tone in this selection? Note both his language and his use of punctuation, such as quotation marks and exclamation points.

3. According to Norris, how do female students respond differently than male students to their education?

4. What is the sample student's approach to writing a "theme" essay?

5. How does Harvard's approach to education compare to that of the University of California?

EXPLORING AND DEBATING THE ISSUES

1. Write your own assessment of your experiences in high school English courses, being sure to make clear to your reader the particular assignments and texts that have led you to your overall argument.

2. Compare and contrast the methods of teaching that Norris describes with those that dominate the writing course that you are now taking. Pay attention not simply to the assignments and themes but also to the course conduct (for instance, do you engage in small-group work?). How do you account for any differences?

3. In class, study the "announcement of courses" (para. 1) published by your college or university, focusing on the English courses. How do they compare to the courses Norris describes? Use your observations to discuss the ways in which college-level literature courses may have changed since the late nineteenth century.

4. Read or reread Mike Rose's "A Visit to Edwin Markham Intermediate School" (p. 182). Adopting the perspective of teacher Yvonne Divans Hutchinson, write an analysis of the approach to education that Norris describes. To what extent do you think Hutchinson would approve of these literature courses?

5. Consult a writing handbook on the use of references and the definition of plagiarism. To what extent would the upper-division student's approach to writing "themes" be considered appropriate or inappropriate?

A Visit to Edwin Markham
Intermediate School

MIKE ROSE

Inner-city schools, especially in communities like Watts, don't get much respect these days, so **Mike Rose** (b. 1944) decided to visit one to see what was really going on. Rose found an educational environment that was neither dysfunctional nor hopeless, encountering instead dedicated teachers who were offering their students a vibrant multicultural education as well as hope for the future. Part of an ambitious project to defend public education at a time when it is coming under fire in California and America, Rose's visit to the Edwin Markham Intermediate School is documented in his book *Possible Lives: The Promise of Public Education in America* (1995). One of America's leading voices in educational circles, Rose is a professor in the Graduate School of Education at UCLA and the author of such acclaimed books as *Writer's Block: The Cognitive Dimension* (1984), *Lives on the Boundary* (1990), and *The Mind at Work: Physical Work and the Thought It Takes to Do It* (2004).

We'll start south of downtown Los Angeles, close to the geographical center of the Basin, in Watts. During the first decades of this century, Watts was a semirural junction for the Pacific Electric Railway, Henry Huntington's "Red Car," the largest urban electric railroad system in the nation. Every Red Car traveler from agricultural and beach cities to the west and south rode through Watts en route to Los Angeles. The area became a mixed-race community of Germans, Blacks, Jews, Japanese, Mexicans, and Italians. Simon Rodia, who in 1921 began his ornate and airy construction of steel, mortar, tile, glass, and shell known as the Watts Towers, was an Italian immigrant. In the late 1930s and the 1940s burgeoning manufacturing industries generated a sizable migration of blacks from the South and from Texas. Because most real estate in Los Angeles was barred to them by race-restrictive covenants, they settled in the Central and South-Central regions of the city, a settlement that was further concentrated in Watts by the building of public housing. L.A.'s heavy industries—aircraft and defense, automotive (for a time, L.A.'s auto production was second only to Detroit's), steel, rubber, metal plating—provided steady, if dirty and dangerous, work for the rapidly growing population of Watts and for a range of blue-collar communities that surrounded the industrial corridor. I remember riding buses full of workmen in oil- and soot-stained denim.

Though Watts began to feel the social effects of overcrowding and inadequate infrastructure, it became a center of African American life and culture. But as the factories began closing in the 1960s and 1970s, the community, and others like it in the corridor, lost its economic base,

experienced a devastating rise in unemployment and crime, and under-
went dramatic shifts in demographics. (In the last fifteen years, through
immigration from Mexico and Central America, Watts has become a
community that is 43 percent Latino.) There has been little reinvestment
in Watts and similar communities—they are very poor now, palm tree
ghettoes—and the few jobs that remain tend to be low skilled and low
paying. In the last twenty years, unemployment has risen by 50 percent;
in 1990, the average household income in Watts was $12,700.

Watts. Since the summer of 1965, the name conjures up images of fire
and violence. Given what Angelenos read in the paper or see on television,
it is hard to imagine Watts as anything other than a site of drive-by shoot-
ings, street crime, squalid projects. Few people other than residents would
think of going through there. To get to Watts, you would take the Harbor
Freeway, heading south out of downtown L.A. toward the harbors in San
Pedro, and exit to the east at Century Boulevard. You would pass Cathy's
Nails and Red's Mini-mart and Pete's Burgers, a gas station, a coin laundry,
a liquor store, a place to cash checks, some apartment buildings, and a lot
of people on the street. At the corner of Century and Success Avenue, a
green metal sign announces WATTS. Some of the side streets you might
take would reveal abandoned houses, bars on windows, old couches rot-
ting in vacant lots. But other streets have well-kept single-family homes,
trimmed lawns, flower beds. If you got back onto Century Boulevard, continued east to Compton Avenue, and took a right turn, you'd soon find
Edwin Markham Intermediate School, a good school sustained by the co-
hesive forces in the community, by those people who, as one resident said,
"try to do the right thing, are ordinary, decent folks."

There are graffiti on several of Markham's bungalows and on the
windows of the snack bar. Classrooms sometimes get vandalized. But
when you walk into the main courtyard, you'll find a wide stretch of deep
green grass, palm and pine trees, azaleas. In the principal's office are a
number of trophies for "school beautification" and for academic pen-
tathlon victories. (In 1990, Markham was one of two L.A. schools desig-
nated a California Distinguished School.) Outside the office is a bulletin
board that displays certificates for achievement. "Laureates of the Week"
it announces. Each certificate bears a student's name "for attendance
and academic performance at Markham Middle School." Two girls coast
by on their bikes. "Hey," one says to the other, "did you see? Latisha made
the honor roll."

It was three in the afternoon in Room 56, and Yvonne Divans Hutchinson   5
had just kicked off her shoes and was stretching out, spent, releasing the
day. She began reflecting on her long local history.

"I grew up here, over in the projects, and went to school in the neighborhood, went to this school, in fact. And I can remember some teachers saying awful things to us. I remember one in particular who told us that we should be glad he came to Watts because no one wanted to teach here. We were always confronted with attitudes like that. Well, I took umbrage at that comment. I had wanted to be a teacher for as long as I could remember, and on that day, I decided that not only was I going to be a teacher, but I was going to teach at *this* school because we needed teachers who *believed* in us."

She was about eight when her parents moved to Los Angeles from Arkansas and settled in Exposition Park, an area close to the L.A. Coliseum. She remembers a rooming house, her sister and brother and her sleeping in one bed. And she remembers her mother's excitement when they were finally able to move into the projects called Imperial Courts: "We're going to have a house all our own!" That was in 1954. Yvonne remembers roller-skating around the neighborhood, over to the library on Grandee. She recalls walking to school along the tracks of the Red Car, playing in the courtyard of the Watts Towers, going to the Largo Theater for thirty-five cents. She entered Edwin Markham Junior High School when it opened and was in the first graduating class, in 1958. She returned to teach in 1966 and has been there ever since.

"I've been a mentor teacher and the department chair, and I've had teachers tell me, 'This class can't think; they can't do the work; I can't find anything they can do.' And I'm astounded. You can look at a child and see that brightness, that eagerness. People who come to the classroom with preconceived notions about the kids don't give them a chance. It angers me and saddens me."

Room 56 was brick and dry wall, painted light mustard, some water stains along the baseboards. A long sign over one of the blackboards reads: NOTHING IS MORE IMPORTANT THAN YOUR EDUCATION. A life-sized cut-out of Bill Cosby on the back door said the same thing. A table in the back of the class was filled with autobiographies, stood upright on display: Ernesto Galarza's *Barrio Boy*, Dick Gregory's *Nigger*, *The Autobiography of Malcolm X*, Elie Wiesel's *Night*, Russell Baker's *Growing Up*. Along the chalk tray of the blackboard was a range of novels and stories, many of them autobiographical in content: Amy Tan's *The Kitchen God's Wife*, Maya Angelou's *I Know Why the Caged Bird Sings*, John Knowles's *A Separate Peace*, Sandra Cisnero's *The House on Mango Street*. One of the themes in the district guidelines for ninth grade is "understanding ourselves," and Yvonne had selected books that, for the most part, reflected the backgrounds of her students.

"I had a young Hispanic man tell me last year that he couldn't carry   10
books because he was a homeboy—he didn't want to be a schoolboy. A lot
of boys want to be cool, so they'll put their books in their lockers when they
go to class. A lot of African American boys will carry Pee-Chee folders because they can roll them up and put them in their coat pockets or jam them
down the back of their pants. So I give notice on the first day of school that
for my class you have to have a notebook that can't be folded up. A lot of
our kids, the boys especially, identify with the streets; they want to be cool.
They don't want to look like nerds. But I like to tell them [laughs], 'The
nerds shall inherit the Earth!' [pause] It *is* serious, though. The whole idea
of being identified as a tough guy yet also doing well in school is a real
dilemma for young black men—in this neighborhood especially. We have
people who are scholarly types, and when they leave the school, they go to
the projects and have to prove themselves. It's really difficult."

All around the classroom, student writing and student art was on
display. To the right of Yvonne's desk was Mariah Legans's drawing of four
very different women, sort of middle-school Cubist in style, colorful,
striking: an oblong face, a full, round face, blue spiked hair, tight black
hair, tiny eyes, big eyes, a smile, a frown, a nose ring. "We are all individuals," she had written under it. "We don't look alike, we don't dress the
same way, but we are all humans living on the same earth. So we need to
learn to get along and respect each other."

On the bulletin board by the door was a cluster of four-by-six index
cards, arrayed against orange, yellow, and blue art paper. These were
done in class, responses to the books the students were reading. Yvonne
had asked them to select a passage that grabbed them, draw it as best
they could in pencil or pen, and comment on it.

Yardenna Aaron rendered a moment from the early pages of Malcolm X's autobiography:

> The scene depicted is when the police took Mrs. Little to the hospital to
> see and identify her dead husband. She was very hysterical. My drawing
> represents my idea and Malcolm's about her. The atmosphere when she
> entered the room containing the dead bodies. I think the policemen were
> laughing when she saw her husband. I believe that having no compassion
> in a case like this is a sin. The police were probably happy that he was
> killed because he was a strong man and taught Negroes about themselves.

Evonne Santiago had this to say about page 45 of *The House on
Mango Street*:

> This nun has made Esperanza embarrassed of where she lived. This re-
> minds me of myself. I always hated where I lived (in New Jersey) because
> everyone in my Catholic school had beautiful houses and my house was
> in a bad neighborhood and had rats and roaches.

Alejandra Mendoza, who was still mastering written English, wrote   15
about a scene in Elie Wiesel's *Night*:

> My drawing represents the German throwing the kids up in the air and
> killing them with a machine gun. The reason the German killed them is
> because the kids are Jewish. It reminds me of L.A. because every day
> there's a kid dying by violence.

Yvonne continued. "Teachers will say either 'We can't lower our standards' or 'This poor child is reading below grade level, so I'll need a third-
or fourth-grade book.' But what you need to do is find a way to make that
eighth-grade book *accessible*. You have to respect the child. . . . I used to
give a speech to new teachers in which I began by enumerating all the
adjectives used to describe our kids: *slow, poor, impoverished, deprived,
oppressed*. We get so busy looking at children in terms of labels that we
fail to look for the *potential*—and to demand that kids live up to that potential. I tell these teachers, 'Do not think that because a child cannot
read a text, he cannot read *you*.' Children can tell right off those people
who believe in them and those who patronize them. They can tell once
they come into the room—as if there's a smell in the air—they can tell
right away if this teacher means business or if this teacher is, as they say,
jive. They rise to whatever expectations are set. They rise or fail to rise.
And when they rise, they can sometimes rise to great heights."

And so it was in this room on that day that Michallene Hooper read a
draft of a profile of her friend Jennifer:

> "Nothing is more important than my education," declared Jennifer Rene
> McKnight, ninth-grader of Markham Intermediate School, who thinks
> very highly of her education. She plans on getting a scholarship for college
> and becoming a worker in the medical field. . . . This tall, slim, dark-
> skinned fourteen-year-old was born and raised in Los Angeles and has al-
> ways been for helping her fellow Los Angelenos and influencing them to
> do the same. . . . Once while she was [stranded in the rain] a boy of her age
> with an umbrella offered to walk her home. "And after that," explained
> Jennifer, "I have never doubted the abilities of my neighbors. There's no
> telling what these good people are capable of or are going to do."

And it was in this room that the class held what Yvonne called a Quaker
reading of Maya Angelou's inaugural poem, "On the Pulse of Morning."
Each student selected some lines that spoke to him or her and read them,
in sequence, into a tape recorder, creating a class reading, a new rendering:

> Across the wall of the world,
> A River sings a beautiful song. It says
> Come, rest here by my side . . .

So say the Asian, the Hispanic, the Jew
The African, the Native American, the Sioux . . .

I, the Rock, I, the River, I, the Tree
I am yours — your passages have been paid.

And it was in this room that Evonne Santiago — the girl who, in reading *The House on Mango Street*, recalled her old house in New Jersey — it
was Evonne who explained to the class what she thought Maya Angelou's
poem meant:

> She tells us our faults so we can see what to do with our country, she's
> telling us how to make it a better country. . . .
>   The rock means strength. And the river — you know how a river goes
> through the land and picks up different water, well, that's like different
> cultures. And the tree is America — that can grow big and strong. . . .
>   She's asking all these people — the Asian, the Hispanic, the African
> American — she's asking them to come under the tree, to let their dream
> grow. And she writes it for the inauguration because the president, he
> has to lead the country, he has great influence. If we grow today, we will
> be strong tomorrow. . . .

And all day long in this room, in every class — just as she did every day   20
here in this room — Yvonne Divans Hutchinson demonstrated, encouraged, celebrated, and guided students through an active and critical
reading process that undercut the common perception that reading simply
involved the decoding of words, that print had single, basic meanings that
students had to decipher quietly and store away. She had students write in
a "Reading Journal" a dialogue between themselves and the author of
whatever book they were currently reading, "agreeing, disagreeing, sympa-
thizing, questioning — engaging the *ideas* in the pages." Before distributing
an essay on courage, she asked her students to talk about a movie or television show in which people acted courageously, and from those examples
try to explain what courage meant — all this to raise to critical
consciousness their own definitions of courage. She had been involved in
the development of a new statewide proficiency exam — one that encour-
ages students to offer interpretations of texts — and she handed out a draft
of the scoring guide and urged her students to analyze it. And Mariah
Legans, whose Cubist plea for tolerance decorated the wall behind
Yvonne's desk, said that "when they say *literal* they mean that you just
write down what you got from the reading, but when they say *thoughtful*
they mean you put some interpretation in it." And Michallene Hooper, the
author of the personality profile, explained that when they ask for *implications*, they're referring to those times "when you read something, and it

won't just come right out and say what it meant, but kind of suggests it."
And from there the class began to discuss what it meant to read critically.

And in this room, at the end of the day, Rahsaan Thorpe took a moment to look at his paper that Yvonne had on yet another display, a response to a quotation about the value of interracial friendships. It began:

> I recall from ages eight to twelve, I was in close relation to other races. I grew up in a house-apartment, and during my time living there many neighbors came and went. Until one Christmas Eve a family moved in next door to me. The next morning I looked outside, and there was a [Salvadoran] boy sitting alone playing. I saw him and decided to make conversation, and ever since that day, we have been friends. . . .

And from there, Rahsaan and the others went out to 104 Street or to Compton Avenue, some leaving for surrounding communities, some walking home, holding their words clean and tight.

UNDERSTANDING THE TEXT

1. In your own words, explain how Watts came to be a largely African American community. What, according to Rose, were the causes of economic decline in Watts?

2. What presuppositions do some teachers at Edwin Markham Intermediate School have about their students?

3. Describe Yvonne Divans Hutchinson's teaching techniques. How does she attempt to reach students who prefer the streets to the school?

4. Describe Rose's tone and how it shapes a reader's response to the teacher and students at this middle school.

EXPLORING AND DEBATING THE ISSUES

1. In your journal, reflect on the encouragement — or lack of it — that you received as a child in school. How did your teachers' and parents' assumptions about your learning ability and about the value of education influence your academic success?

2. Yvonne Divans Hutchinson criticizes the practice, common among her colleagues, of labeling students according to background or ability. Write an essay in which you evaluate the validity of Hutchinson's criticism. To develop your ideas, feel free to draw on your own educational experiences and your observations of other students.

3. According to Rose, Hutchinson selects her literary texts to reflect her students' backgrounds. In an argumentative essay, support, challenge, or complicate the assumption that students learn best when they can personally identify with reading materials. To support your position, you may draw on your own experiences or those of friends.

4. Hutchinson is trying to teach her students to read and think critically. In class, discuss what critical reading and thinking are. How would a college-level definition compare to one for high school students?

5. Hutchinson explains that some students who are affected by peer pressure don't want to appear to be nerds. In an essay, analyze both the positive and negative effects that peer pressure can have on teenagers. To develop your ideas, draw on your own experiences and the observations of others, and consult Ruben Navarrette Jr., " 'Well, I Guess They Need Their Minority' " (p. 211).

Something There Is That Doesn't Love a List

CAROL JAGO

Carol Jago likes book lists, even though she recognizes that they are often highly controversial and arbitrary in their composition. So when the California Department of Education published its recommended book list for K–12 students in 2001 (a list that Jago helped compile), she was not surprised when, as she puts it, "criticism began pouring in." How could the list leave out Emerson, Swift, Yeats, Dante, and Lincoln, critics asked? Balancing her desire to include multicultural texts that reflect the actual experiences of contemporary California students with her own love of the classics, Jago concedes that the new K–12 book list could be improved, concluding that reading lists are good things to have, should never be final, and should be allowed to evolve as literary history evolves. Jago is an English teacher at Santa Monica High School and is the director of the California Reading and Literature Project at UCLA. She is also the author of *With Rigor for All: Teaching Classics to Contemporary Students* (2000).

In his poem "Mending Wall," Robert Frost explores our love/hate relationship with walls. On the one hand, we believe that "good fences make good neighbors." At the same time, we worry about who is being walled in and walled out. Book lists inspire a similar ambivalence. No sooner is one constructed than forces on every side begin marshalling arguments either to augment or bring it down. Personally, I think book lists make good reading.

However authoritative a book list pretends to be, most are actually quite arbitrary. Lists include and exclude texts based upon criteria that are sometimes unclear even to the list makers. When the Modern Library released its selection of the hundred best novels written in English in the twentieth century, the list was met with outrage. How could James

Dickey's *Deliverance* be better than anything Joseph Conrad ever wrote? How is it possible that not a single book by Doris Lessing, Nadine Gordimer, Patrick White, Toni Morrison, or John Updike appears? Is *Ulysses* really the best novel written in the 20th century? So make your own list, said the publishers of the Modern Library, and then proceeded to provide a Web site where readers could create alternative lists. I like that response. Readers enjoy making lists of "best" books almost as much as they like poking holes in other people's lists. Besides, lists are fair game. The fact that they inspire challenges is part of their value. Criticizing someone else's list helps us refine our own criteria for what makes a book worthwhile.

California's Department of Education recently created a new book list, *Recommended Literature: Kindergarten through Grade Twelve* (http:// goldmine.cde.ca.gov/ci/literature). The list is descriptive rather than restrictive. It is designed to provide guidance for teachers, parents, and publishers about the kinds of books children should be reading. But no sooner was the site containing the new list up and running than criticism began pouring in. As one of the contributors responsible for creating the list, I feel compelled to defend our choices, but the teacher in me longs to scrawl across the top of the page in red ink, "Needs more work!" Though the list was intended to be a living document and a work in progress, without funding to support revision, it is likely to remain in its present state for some time to come. What is needed is a clear plan, with dollars attached, to provide for an annual review of the list, not only to delete out-of-print books and add new titles but also to take advantage of criticisms and suggestions about what should be on the list.

The California recommended reading list was designed to replace an outdated 1987 list. It was compiled, over the course of a year, by a group of approximately twenty-five teachers, librarians, and consultants from the Department of Education, who met every six to eight weeks in Sacramento. Members of the committee were nominated by professional organizations like the California Association of Teachers of English and the California Reading Association and were sorted into subcommittees by grade level: K–2, 3–5, 6–8, and 9–12. Noticeably missing from our group were university literature professors. They should have been among us.

It does not impugn the expertise of the five people sitting around the   5
table in my working group for grades 9–12 to say that we were bound to make mistakes. Most embarrassingly, authors like Ralph Waldo Emerson, James Fenimore Cooper, and Jonathan Swift are nowhere to be found. How can any list be considered authoritative without William Butler Yeats, Dante Alighieri, or Aristophanes? I don't remember ever making the decision not to include Eugene O'Neill or Abraham Lincoln, yet they don't appear either. And how could we forget Nobel Prize–winners Isaac Bashevis Singer, Saul

Bellow, and Joseph Brodsky? While Asian American titles are well represented, Asian writers are not. The trouble was, so much depended upon so few readers. Early in the process, I suggested that we include the whole of the Penguin paperback classics catalogue. However, we only felt able to include books that someone at the table had read, which eliminated many great books. Then, too, every title submitted needed to be annotated by someone from the committee. How could we find the time to fill in the unfortunate gaps in our reading of the classics *and* write 2,700 short plot summaries? The practical problems involved in compiling a list to be published by California's Department of Education and carry the authoritative title "Recommended Literature" were sometimes overwhelming.

Tough Choices

One of the greatest challenges the group faced was determining the criteria for choosing books. The mandate that the list should be a "collection of outstanding literature for children and adolescents and reflect the quality and the complexity of the types of material students should be reading both at school and outside of class" left a great deal of room for individual judgment. What makes a book "outstanding"? The committee very much wanted to include contemporary and multicultural titles, particularly those of literary worth and likely to become tomorrow's "classics." Some teachers wished to weight the list heavily in favor of the kinds of books that their students loved—science fiction, romance, young adult titles. Others were adamant that the list needed to include a broad selection of classic literature. There was widespread agreement about the need for books with multicultural themes. But when we talked about including picture books at every grade level, discussions sometimes became heated. So did discussions about books in languages other than English. We listened to one another. We compromised.

We knew that many teachers were unfamiliar with literary classics and hoped that the list would offer ideas for their own reading as well as for classroom instruction.

There was strong support for the inclusion of young adult titles, books with teenage protagonists facing teenage dilemmas. My position was that any list for young people should include two very different kinds of books, serving different purposes in a reading program. One kind acts as a mirror—it reflects students' own experiences with peers, parents, sex, drugs, and school. Young people need stories in which someone who looks and thinks as they do handles the problems they face, for better and for worse. Apart from a lively book talk to interest them in picking up the volume, teenagers shouldn't need a teacher's help with "mirror" books. In fact, our penchant for discussions about foreshadowing, symbolism, and themes tends to ruin such stories for kids.

Students also need books that act as windows. These stories offer readers access to other worlds, other times, other cultures. Few young people think they have much in common with Odysseus until an artful teacher helps them see how we are all on a journey toward self-discovery. Few relate to Pip until they walk for a while in Dickens' fictional world and begin to understand their own great expectations. It's not a matter of either/or. Students need both kinds of books. Of course, teenagers need help looking through the window of most classic texts. At first glance a classic seems opaque, full of incomprehensible references and unfamiliar language. It is the teacher's job to clear the windowpane so that students can peer through—helping them learn to unpack inverted sentences, approach unfamiliar vocabulary, and pronounce characters' names. Often students need background information about foreign customs and cultures.

Many well-intentioned teachers have abandoned the classics for   10
what they think will be more user-friendly titles. This is a mistake. Just because students can't read a book on their own doesn't mean they can't and shouldn't read it with help. Instead of choosing more seemingly "relevant" stories, we should be showing all our students how classic heroes struggled with the very same monsters we face today.

A Window Worth Opening

If I were in charge of the world, I would mandate that every ninth-grader read Robert Louis Stevenson's *The Strange Case of Dr. Jekyll and Mr. Hyde*. How better to help young people consider the dark side that lurks within us all? The short novel is rich and layered, unfolding like a mystery story. Teachers shouldn't be put off by the fact that many students would find the text difficult. I have stopped telling students, as I hand out books, that they are going to love this text and instead tell them that what they are about to read may at first seem quite hard. I even warn them that, at first, they may hate it. I promise to help them through and also assure them that in my professional opinion, they will ultimately feel that the struggle was worthwhile. Stevenson's first sentence describes the story's narrator, the dour Mr. Utterson:

> Mr. Utterson the lawyer was a man of rugged countenance, that was never lighted by a smile; cold, scanty, and embarrassed in discourse; backward in sentiment; lean, long, dusty, dreary, and yet somehow lovable.

I invite students to think about why it makes good sense that this tale of extraordinary horror should be told by such an utterly reliable narrator. I also help them negotiate Stevenson's complex sentences. We talk about his word choice and define unfamiliar vocabulary. Together we picture Victorian London in our minds' eyes. I call this teaching.

It seems wrong to me that schools should reserve the classics for honor students. Ignoring the elitism that such a curricular decision betrays, teachers defend a watered-down reading list for "regular" students by explaining to themselves and others that most teenagers simply can't understand the difficult vocabulary. Besides, they argue, today's kids won't read anything that is old. I worry that in our determination to provide students with literature they "relate to," we end up teaching works that students actually don't need much help with. And I worry that we do this at the expense of teaching classics that students most certainly do need assistance negotiating. This is not to suggest that we stop putting contemporary literature into students' hands, but only to urge that we teach in what Lev Vgotsky calls the "zone of proximal development." He wrote that, "The only good kind of instruction is that which marches ahead of development and leads it." If students can read a book on their own, if it is a mirror book, it probably isn't the best choice for classroom study. Classroom texts should pose intellectual challenges to young readers. These texts should be books that will make students stronger readers, stronger people for having studied.

When an excerpt from Jack London's *White Fang* appeared on California's 2001 exit exam, many teachers argued that their urban students didn't have the background information to read the passage with comprehension. I would argue that few of us have been out in the Alaskan wild or had much experience with wolves. We acquired our "background knowledge" from books. If the only stories students are reading are ones set in their own time and their own milieu, how will they ever know the rest of the world? How will they know history? If we only hand students books containing words they already know, how will they learn new ones? Any recommended list of books worth its salt should include titles that challenge students and encourage teachers to help young people stretch.

Sins of Omission

It seems to me that a list succeeds or fails not on the basis of a book that's on or is missing but because of the range it suggests. Tim Rutten, the *Los Angeles Times* culture correspondent, is evenhanded with his praise and blame. He describes the California recommended literature list as

> an imperfect but serious 2,700-book blueprint for "peace with honor" in the cultural conflict. . . . Earnest and obviously well-intentioned, the state's

list is nonetheless diffident and so self-evidently tentative in insisting on where quality resides, that it is difficult to deduce the standards applied.

The committee paid careful attention to offering a balance of male and female authors, contemporary and classic texts, and to ensuring ethnic diversity. The list includes titles in five languages other than English: Spanish, Hmong, Vietnamese, Chinese, and Filipino. The selection committee's sins were of omission rather than commission.

In a provocative editorial for the *Sacramento Bee*, Peter Schrag decries the "omission of almost any of the great affirmative themes of American or Western history." Schrag points out the omission, other than books about the Japanese internment camps or the Holocaust, of stories about the main figures and events of World War II. He continues:

> Look under independence, and there's a biography of Gandhi, but nothing about Thomas Jefferson; look under American Revolution or liberty and the only notable work is Esther Forbes' novel *Johnny Tremain*; Magna Carta and Churchill get you nothing. . . . The only view of Columbus is through the eyes of an Indian boy trying to warn his people about the white man.

I took Schrag's criticism to heart and came to a couple of tentative conclusions. The committee did not start out with any themes in mind. We thought in terms of books and genres—and this probably contributed to the limitation Schrag describes. Also, there was only one man on the selection committee, Armin Schultz, and his specialty was children's literature. Without stereotyping male and female readers unduly, it is my experience that women tend to read fiction more than nonfiction, and novelists tend to prefer social and psychological themes to the heroic themes Schrag may be thinking about. Once again, the committee members omitted books they had not read.

California's recommended literature list could be an awesome document. But to be so, it will need constant revision by teachers, scholars, librarians, parents, and students. Like the wall in Robert Frost's poem, a list needs constant attention. "The gaps I mean, / No one has seen them made or heard them made, / But at spring mending-time we find them there." A Web-based list should be easy to mend.

Good lists make good readers.

References

Rutten, Tim. "Weighing the Classics," *Los Angeles Times,* July 15, 2001.

Schrag, Peter. "What Kids Should Read That the State Left Off Its List," *Sacramento Bee,* Aug. 22, 2001.

Vgotsky, L. S. *Thought and Language,* ed. E. Hanfmann and G. Vakar, Cambridge, Mass.: MIT Press, 1962.

UNDERSTANDING THE TEXT

1. Summarize in your own words the process that was used by the California Department of Education to create the current recommended reading list.

2. What sort of imbalances does Jago admit the reading list has, and why did they occur?

3. What is Jago's attitude toward the reading list that she helped to create?

4. What assumptions were made by the creators of the reading list about what students "need" to read?

5. What were some of the reactions to the reading list?

EXPLORING AND DEBATING THE ISSUES

1. Divide the class into four teams, and assign to each team one of the four grade levels of the California recommended reading list. Visit the California Department of Education's website (see para. 3 for the URL), and study your section of the reading list. Compare your results in class. Does the list seem imbalanced, as Jago suggests, or do you find it to be a good list?

2. In class, compile your own list of books that would be appropriate for high school students. Then compare your list to the California Department of Education's list. What patterns of overlap or difference do you observe, and how do you account for your results?

3. Jago asserts that "It seems wrong to me that schools should reserve the classics for honor students" (para. 12). In an essay, argue whether you believe that the reading list should include more classic texts or whether it should concentrate on contemporary books to which students can "relate." To develop your ideas, consider the approach to selecting texts described in Mike Rose's "A Visit to Edwin Markham Intermediate School" (p. 182).

4. Jago describes the committee that compiled the list as "approximately twenty-five teachers, librarians, and consultants from the Department of Education" (para. 4) and notes that committee members included only books that they had previously read. In an essay, assess the composition of this committee. Based on the list that the committee produced, do you agree with Jago that university literature professors should have been included? Because any such list is politically controversial, do you think the committee membership should have been broadened to include authors, parents, or members of the general public?

Testing, Anyone?

SYLVIA S. FOX

In 1999, the California legislature authorized the development of the California High School Exit Examination, an exam that, if and when it is fully implemented, will decide who receives a public high school diploma in California and who does not. For high school students, this exam just might constitute "the mother of all tests." In this essay from the pages of the *California Journal* (September 2001), **Sylvia S. Fox** explains how things got this way, analyzing the two sides in the larger debate over standardized testing in California schools. It all boils down to "accountability"—a word that, as Fox writes, "isn't an academic term. It is a political term" that expresses the opinion of those who feel that California's public schools are not teaching students the skills they need to thrive in college and the workplace beyond. Opponents of standardized testing respond that "a single test can never work in a state as diverse as California," and so the debate continues. Fox is a professor of journalism at California State University, Sacramento.

Scratch nearly anyone connected with education these days and you'll likely get an opinion on "testing." Teachers, parents, administrators, students, politicians — most folks have a definite view.

Testing in this case doesn't mean a snap quiz thrown at students to see who bothered to read a history assignment. It isn't an academic term. It is a political term — the preferred buzzword for "accountability." Hence, the current battle over testing — whether it is good or bad, helpful or hurtful — is intensely political. Caught in the middle are students and their parents, many of whom fear that testing programs have skewed the way children are taught and that statewide test results play too *prominent* a role in evaluating overall student performance.

Few argue that measuring student proficiency is a bad idea, or that educators ought not to be held accountable. Rather, the controversy over testing centers on California's methods of measuring student proficiency and whether a single exam ought to determine academic fate. There also are broad concerns among educators — both here and nationally — that how well students test now defines the quality of the education they receive.

Advocates of statewide testing programs argue that schools must be able to demonstrate — in measurable ways — that students understand the basics. They also argue that critics have been too quick to judge the results and that not enough time has elapsed to adequately evaluate the findings. Opponents counter that testing has warped school culture by corrupting what takes place in the classroom and that test proficiency is emphasized at the expense of learning. They also charge that it is heavily skewed against non-English-speaking students.

At the heart of this quarrel are two statewide tests: the SAT-9, admin-   5
istered through the Standardized Testing and Reporting (STAR) Program,
and a high school "exit exam" required for graduation.

STAR Bright?

Introduced in 1997, the STAR program is part of an education-reform pack-
age and costs the state $65.6 million annually to administer. Its centerpiece
is the Stanford-9 basic skills test (SAT-9) given in English to all California
public-school students in grades 2 through 11 and designed to compare
California students with their peers nationally. SAT-9 is a stopgap, however,
while the state develops a more parochial California Standards Test to align
with state academic standards. The California Standards Test currently is
being given as a trial run and is scheduled to "go live" in 2003.

The STAR program involves more than a test, however. It also has a
carrot attached in the form of cash payments designed to reward schools
and teachers whose students do well on the tests. In this vein, STAR distributes $677 million in three categories. First, schools themselves win
cash awards by increasing SAT-9 scores, based on an Academic Performance Index, or API, ranking of all public schools. Second, teachers and
all full-time staff at eligible schools, including secretaries and custodi-
ans, receive bonuses that this year totaled $591.32 per employee. To be
eligible, at least 95 percent of the students in an elementary school must
have taken the test, 90 percent in a high school. Schools that fall short
are disqualified and lose their ranking for two years. Finally, a more substantial award is targeted exclusively at schools in the bottom half of API
rankings. Teachers at these schools can earn from $5,000 to $25,000
if their school shows the greatest gains in test scores over a two-year
period.

The second test is a statewide high school "exit exam" added in 1999.
It was given to ninth graders for the first time this year, with results to be
released in mid-September. Still another high school test, the Golden
State Examination, is given to honor students in various subject areas in
order to establish eligibility for scholarship awards from the governor.

Each test has been the subject of controversy.

Defenders and Critics

The current testing program, supporters contend, is a necessity born of   10
circumstance and, as such, it has full-faith backing from Democratic
Governor Gray Davis and his administration — as it did from Davis' pre-
decessor, Republican Pete Wilson. Administration officials contend the

current testing program arose because the state had to find a way to measure progress.

Standardized testing—the foundation for "accountability"—came after years of evidence that high school graduates did not possess appropriate skills or education, said Kerry Mazzoni, Davis' secretary for education. "Students were being tested, but they weren't taking the same tests, and districts weren't required to give the same data," she said. According to Mazzoni, the best way to get a baseline of information was to start with a test that conformed to national norms. Hence, SAT-9.

It was critical, Mazzoni said, to move away from the accepted notion that if input (teaching, resources and dollars) is good then the output will be good. But, she argued, that concept didn't work. In addition, the former Bay Area legislator said, large numbers of children were not being served, and excuses were made for various groups (such as those for whom English is a second language) who then weren't held to a high standard.

"They were robbed of their futures," Mazzoni said. "We let our teachers teach the way they wanted. It didn't work. It's tragic and it's inexcusable. Now we have to keep focused."

Critics answer with a laundry list of complaints and warnings, chief among them the notion that a single test can never work in a state as diverse as California. They also see the STAR program as a political rather than academic solution, and they view as troublesome the financial incentives given to teachers and schools based on test scores generated from a single source. They complain that the tests themselves are flawed, take up too much instructional time, pit teachers against one another, and hurt students—especially bilingual students. Finally, they argue that the Golden State scholarship exam reflects nothing more than family wealth, placing a majority of scholarships in the hands of students from high-income zip codes.

Bob Schaeffer, public education director for FairTest, a national coalition to fight standardized testing, says California is the nation's flagship of testing overkill. That assessment is shared by Bob Raines, who runs the testing unit for San Diego Unified School District. "We're testing kids to death in this state right now," said Raines.

Some critics argue that a backlash against testing is growing among parents and students, but evidence to back this claim is scanty. The primary mode of protest—opting out of the test altogether—is an option granted under state law and has cropped up in various places over the past two years, notably in San Diego County. But the message is mixed, and it is unclear whether these protests mark the beginning of a backlash against testing in general or are isolated revolts based on problems that can be fixed.

15

Another measure of discontent is found among the debris left by various national polls, but those results, too, deliver a mixed message. For instance, a poll taken in October 2000 by Public Agenda showed that parents strongly support higher academic standards and don't believe standardized tests are too difficult or dominate classroom instruction. But the poll also revealed that a majority of parents feel that schools place too much emphasis on test scores, and they object to a single test being used to determine promotion or graduation. Along those same lines, a poll last year by the American Association of School Administrators found that 63 percent of parents disagreed with the notion that a year's worth of academic progress can be summarized by a single test.

The English Problem

The most immediate form of protest is to "opt out" — a decision made by parents who refuse to have their children tested. In San Diego County, this tactic has been used mostly by parents whose children are not proficient in English.

Part of the criticism in California has focused on the fact that the SAT-9 is administered in English, even to students who lack English proficiency. In San Diego during the 2000 school year, this caused something of an open revolt among Spanish-speaking or bilingual parents once they learned that their children did not have to take the test.

"It's a no-brainer," said Susan Harmon, a special education teacher   20
in Contra Costa County and co-founder of CalCARE, which is affiliated with FairTest. "How can kids test well in a language they can't speak?"

As a result, many San Diego schools with high numbers of Latino students had low numbers of test-takers. Balboa Elementary, bordering National City, had 85 percent Latino students, about 62 percent of whom are limited in English. In 2000, nearly 46 percent of Balboa parents refused to have their children tested. Neighboring Emerson/Bandini Elementary, with equally high numbers of Latino students, had 38 percent opt out. In fact, almost all San Diego South Bay elementary schools experienced high numbers of "opt outs" in 2000, ranging from 13 percent to Balboa's 46 percent. As a result, thirteen San Diego schools were declared ineligible for incentive awards this year because "excessive" numbers of parents would not let their children be tested.

But the "opt out" revolt lost much of its steam in the 2000–2001 school year. According to Sally Bennett, San Diego Unified's assistant director for standards assessment and accountability, the district worked with schools to encourage testing, explaining to parents how opting out hurts individual schools. "They explained to parents that it was not high stakes for individual students, that this kind of test would not make their children be retained," Bennett said.

The turnaround was dramatic. In 1999–2000, 3,555 San Diego students opted out of testing. This year 1,201 declined to take the test, a drop of nearly two-thirds. At Balboa, where nearly half of the parents opted out in 2000, no parents chose to keep their children out in 2001. Only two students at nearby Emerson-Bandini declined the test, compared with 370 the previous year.

Part of the solution was a second assessment test in Spanish, instituted in 1999 — the SABE 2, required for students who have been in the district for less than 12 months, speak Spanish as a primary language and have limited English proficiency. Although these test results are not used for API school rankings, they do measure achievement in a language more suited to the student.

Although opting out gained some notoriety in San Diego, the tactic   25
hardly caused a ripple elsewhere. In 1999–2000, only 56,000 parents statewide — or a little more than 1 percent — refused to have their children tested. The number of exemptions for 2000–2001 will be released in October.

Exit Exam or Drop-Out Exam?

The high school exit exam has caused its own set of controversies. Expected to be in place for the class of 2004, the exam was given for the first time this year to the ninth graders who will make up that graduating class. It is designed to measure the minimum set of academic skills needed to graduate from high school, and students have several chances to pass both its verbal and math portions during their high school careers. Still, a high failure rate for this first test is predicted when scores are released in mid-September, a result that won't surprise one test critic — California Federation of Teachers President Mary Bergan.

"It never should have been given to them," Bergan said. "It's an exit exam [for high school]. They are being tested on a curriculum standard that wasn't in place for them until now."

California Teachers Association President Wayne Johnson agreed. The exit exam is "poorly designed, not fully tested, and maybe 60 percent will fail," he said. Johnson said the CTA is not opposed to the concept of an exit exam, but "this exam was a disaster." Again, the students most harmed by the test, according to Johnson, were that those with limited proficiency in English. Teachers worry those students will be so discouraged they will decide to drop out of school. Johnson said 1.2 million students will not pass the math portion this year because it tested math that isn't required of ninth graders.

Administration officials concede that the test procedure was flawed this year and have taken steps to correct the problem. Ninth graders took the exam on a voluntary basis, as prescribed by law. But testing experts have argued that testing only part of a statewide class (75 percent of ninth graders did so in 2001) skews test data.

"We need to administer the test to all of the kids at the same time," said Bob Spurlock, assistant education secretary for assessment and accountability. To correct this problem, Spurlock said, the administration has sponsored a bill (AB 1609) to eliminate ninth graders from the exam.

Although many critics don't like the notion of standardized testing, FairTest's Bob Schaeffer said his group is not asking that all tests be repealed, just not relied upon as the sole judge of student success. "One standards test can't portray the difference in school quality between Beverly Hills and . . . the Central Valley or Watts or L.A.," he said. "It doesn't factor in types and amount of resources, or teacher quality."

Meanwhile, the California Teachers Association won't support any testing legislation until high school exit exam and standardized testing issues are resolved. In July, the National Education Association voted to support laws allowing parents to opt out of standardized testing. They also approved a resolution to encourage a variety of assessments. Supporters of FairTest are hoping for a national boycott against standardized testing next spring, said CalCare's Harmon, who called it "a mass refusal."

Teacher Protests

In addition to the activity of their union, individual teachers have shown their disapproval by rejecting the $591 incentive checks, calling them "blood money" and "bribery." Other teachers and staff reportedly donated the money to various scholarships and charities. Some students voiced displeasure as well by creating bubble-dot artwork with their answer sheets, organizing boycotts or drawing a line through one column of answers.

Even the big-buck incentive program hit a snag. Roughly $100 million was budgeted for bonuses of up to $25,000 for individual teachers at low-performing schools, but distribution of those checks was delayed for months by a lawsuit filed by teachers at a Sacramento elementary school who challenged the two-year requirement for improvement in test scores. The state won the case, but the teachers have appealed.

Education Secretary Mazzoni was quick to note that while the STAR program isn't perfect, it provides a starting point. She pointed to changes such as streamlining the tests, eliminating redundant tests and reducing awards. The Legislature, too, she said, is working on incremental fixes. Among them is a bill (SB 233) to extend the STAR program to

2005, mandate a math test for eighth and ninth graders who haven't taken algebra, reduce teaching time, require the test to align with school curriculum, and consolidate or merge some tests; and a bill (AB 1609) to review the high-school exit exam, allow the State Board of Education to postpone consequences for students who fail it and eliminate ninth graders from taking the exam.

Mazzoni argued for time, saying that scores have improved and that most critics will be satisfied after about three years of sustained higher scores.

"It may take six years to get there," she said, "but that's when the naysayers may be silenced. We truly are trying to have a smart system."

Yet unresolved in the debate over testing is a question posed by some educators and parents: What is the relationship between testing and a quality education?

Virtually none, said Edna Mitchell, a professor of education at Mills College in Oakland and director of the Women's Leadership Institute at Mills.

"Testing is the lowest level of measurement," said Mitchell, who does   40 not oppose testing but questions its prominence. "It does not evaluate how children approach thinking. And it does not measure or have any respect for the skills of problem-solving and inquiry. It teaches a child to look for a reward by getting the right answer, and by feeling that achievement and success come from turning in a paper where you fill in bubbles."

The fact that a test doesn't measure everything, responded the administration's Spurlock, "doesn't devalue what it does measure. We need to know what schools are doing."

Yes, said Mitchell, but testing puts too much pressure on teachers. "When you reward [teachers] with bonuses or punish them by publishing test scores," she said, "we deprive children of teachers who are responsive and interactive, and who know how to turn a classroom into a place of learning rather than a place of drill. It narrows the achievement process."

UNDERSTANDING THE TEXT

1. Describe in your own words the positions held by supporters and opponents of testing programs.
2. What do educators mean by "accountability" (para. 2), and how is testing supposed to determine it?
3. Why do some parents ask that their children "opt out" (para. 18) of testing, and what are the consequences of this action?

4. What are some of the problems associated with the high school exit exam?

5. What sort of incentives do the testing programs provide for teachers, and why are these incentives controversial?

EXPLORING AND DEBATING THE ISSUES

1. You probably went to a school that participated in the testing programs that Fox describes. In your journal, reflect on whether you felt that your education was at least in part designed to help you do well on the tests or whether your instruction was not influenced by the tests. How test-conscious were you in school, and did your attitude enhance or damage your ability to learn?

2. Fox outlines the various positions in support of and in opposition to the SAT-9 and the high school exit exams. In an essay, argue whether you support or oppose such programs, taking into account Fox's discussion and responding to the counterarguments.

3. Critics of testing argue that the testing programs are unfair for the many California schoolchildren who are not proficient in English. Write an essay that supports, opposes, or modifies this position.

4. Fox quotes Edna Mitchell, a Mills College education professor, who argues that "When you reward [teachers] with bonuses or punish them by publishing test scores, we deprive children of teachers . . . who know how to turn a classroom into a place of learning rather than a place of drill" (para. 42). In an essay, support, refute, or modify Mitchell's claim. To develop evidence for your position, you might interview several former or current teachers about their attitudes toward testing and how it affects their teaching.

5. The tests that Fox describes are designed not by California teachers but by national education consulting companies. Supporters claim that it is cost-effective to have such companies produce the exams. Critics have charged that the testing does not accurately reflect what students learn in the classroom. In an essay, argue whether using these nationally designed tests is an appropriate way to assess California students' performance.

A Win-Win for the High School Exit Exam

SANDRA NICHOLS

In 2003, the California Board of Education decided to postpone for two years any enforcement of the California High School Exit Examination (CAHSEE or HSEE). This delay removed some of the pressure from a growing controversy. As **Sandra Nichols** reports here, "Only 60 percent of the class of 2004 have passed the math section of the HSEE," with greater difficulties reported among "English-language learners, minorities, and children in special education." So what should be done: Continue to ignore the HSEE and disappoint those who have worked hard to pass it? Or let nearly half of California's public-education students fail to receive high school diplomas? Nichols offers a compromise: reward the students who have passed the HSEE with a special acknowledgment printed on their diplomas, and let those who have failed the test receive diplomas without the acknowledgment. President of the Pajaro Valley Unified School District Governing Board, Nichols is a speech and language specialist in the Santa Cruz City school system. The opinions expressed here are her own and do not necessarily represent those of any school district, print publication, or website.

The California High School Exit Examination (HSEE) has been long in coming, and it seems to be having a difficult birth.

Yes, the test is now in existence. Yes, several versions have been taken by throngs of students, many having spent sleepless nights worrying about the outcome. HSEE preparation courses have sprung up. Teachers have developed new techniques to assist students specifically to pass this test.

Fact: Current high school juniors are slated to be the first ones who will have to pass the HSEE to earn their diplomas. These students are on the leading edge of a plan to make a diploma more meaningful and for some more elusive.

Dilemma: Only 60 percent of the class of 2004 have passed the math section of the HSEE. English-language learners, minorities, and children in special education are having even more difficulty with the test.

Recently, high school students have been expressing their reactions 5 and concerns about this high-stakes test. We have learned that there is as wide a variety of reactions to the test as the variety seen in the test scores.

Students who have passed both the language-arts and math sections want the test to count. They were prepared and feel they should be rewarded. If the test doesn't count, they will feel cheated. Students scoring only points away from passing have their fingers crossed and are trying hard to raise their scores. One can only imagine how those students feel whose scores fall far below the passing level.

Teachers are trying to stimulate students' "can-do" attitudes. It's that silly old ant in the song, trying to move a rubber tree plant. It's "Si se puede" repeated as a confidence-building experience. Without the student-confidence factor, what will happen to the student who just cannot pass that test or those who think they can't?

Now, I was a California girl, raised and educated in the public schools. I graduated from high school during those golden years when California public schools were held in high esteem, being one of the best school systems in the country, if not top of the class. There was no high school exit exam other than the Real Life Test: Did the students love learning so much that they continued their education after high school? Did the students secure good employment? Did the students' education serve them well in terms of developing intellectual potential?

So here we are facing another case of the haves—those that have been prepared for the HSEE—and the have nots—the other ones.

An idea is brewing. It is an idea that recognizes the value of a HSEE   10
as the test that proves one has met the state's standard. It is an idea that does not demoralize the students who have little chance of passing. It is fair. It is wise. And it can work.

Definition: a diploma represents that a person has successfully completed a particular course of study. A diploma is recognition for taking and passing the coursework defined by the State of California and the local school district. A diploma means you have the stamina to work persistently toward the goal of graduating.

We all know that some students do more than just take and pass classes. Some students master the subject matter. Some students excel and exceed the teacher's wildest expectations. The HSEE can be a tool that indicates their level of achievement. Passing both language-arts and math sections of the HSEE should result in a reward. Why not make that reward be a special statement of recognition on the diploma? THIS STUDENT HAS DEMONSTRATED COMPETENCE ON THE CALIFORNIA HIGH SCHOOL EXIT EXAMINATION.

Now, I don't care whether the recognition is a gold diploma or contains an affixed special seal of approval. However, it should be standard and recognizable to all and at least as difficult to duplicate as a dollar bill. In this manner, the student who passes gets the reward. Potential employers will learn to use the HSEE if general-education skills and the state standards are relevant to the line of work. Universities and colleges will recognize the difference between a graduate and a student who not only graduated but also demonstrated competency on the test.

Far wiser than dumbing down the test and far more fair to students who have passed the test, this proposal would be a win-win for all. I would think that the legislators would be pleased to have a meaningful test in place. Students who pass get the recognition they deserve. Students who do not pass the test are not kept from earning a diploma that recognizes success at that level. No student would be faced with denial of a diploma because of poor test-taking skills.

I like it. I think we can do this. I think everyone can be happy about   15
this one.

UNDERSTANDING THE TEXT

1. What are the effects of Nichols's juxtaposition of the labels "Fact" and "Dilemma" in the early part of her article (paras. 3–4) and her inclusion of "Definition" toward the end (para. 11)?
2. What has been the typical response of teachers to the high school exit exam?
3. What problems are created by the high school exit exam, according to Nichols?
4. In your own words, what is Nichols's solution to those problems?
5. Why do you think that Nichols relates her own experience as a student in California public schools?

EXPLORING AND DEBATING THE ISSUES

1. It is likely that you were among the first students to take the California High School Exit Examination "for real." In class, list on the board the various ways that your high schools prepared you for the exam, and then assess those strategies. Which techniques does the class feel were most beneficial, and why?
2. In arguing against making the exit exam a pass-fail test that denies some students their diplomas, Nichols claims that college admissions officers and potential employers will recognize the value of a special acknowledgment for students who pass the exam. In an essay, support, refute, or complicate her claim. To develop support for your essay, you might interview admissions officers at your school or local employers of young adults.
3. In an essay, argue whether testing programs, such as a state high school exit exam, can harm some students' access to higher educational opportunities (or as Nichols puts it, whether "we are facing another case of the haves—those that have been prepared for the HSEE—and the have nots—the other ones" [para. 9]). Develop your ideas by consulting Sylvia S. Fox, "Testing, Anyone?" (p. 196).
4. In class, discuss the various political controversies surrounding public-school testing as described in Sylvia S. Fox's "Testing, Anyone?" (p. 196). Then write an essay in which you propose a plan for implementing Nichols's suggested revision of the status of the high school exit exam. Be sure to articulate and respond to the likely objections from both the proponents and opponents of testing.

Cuts Crush College Promise

LESLI A. MAXWELL

Lesli A. Maxwell's 2003 title almost sounds like a promotional teaser for a television news program, but it's no joke. With California's system of higher education suffering from severe budgetary cuts stemming from the state's ongoing fiscal crisis, the promise of the 1960 California Master Plan for Higher Education to provide access to a college education to every state citizen is being compromised. As Tidal Wave II brings an unprecedented number of students into their college years, the state is reducing its funding for public higher education. The result has been that the state's public colleges and universities are being forced to limit their growth in order to balance their budgets with insufficient funds. Those who will be left out because of higher fees, Maxwell suggests, will be those who are most in need of an affordable system of higher education. Maxwell is a staff writer for the *Sacramento Bee*.

It was a bold promise that became a model for the rest of the nation: Any Californian who wanted a college education could have one. Money, social background, and geography were not to be barriers.

With that mission, California built its vast, tiered system of public higher education with a door that opened for high school graduates with the right grades. Three distinct institutions—the University of California, California State University, and California Community Colleges—grew into 140 campuses statewide, where students could buy a first-rate education for little money.

Now, California's record budget crisis has state leaders backing off that pledge. Their decision to halt money for enrollment growth—at least for next year and possibly beyond—means that for the first time since the Master Plan took shape forty-three years ago, California will not provide a slot for all students eligible for one of its four-year colleges. Enrollment will be capped, and students will be turned away—by the thousands. At the same time, fees will rise at all three institutions, a move also expected to keep some high school graduates from going on to college.

"The promise of the Master Plan was so generous. Everybody could go," said Jane Wellman, senior associate with the Washington, D.C.–based Institute for Higher Education Policy. "Now, you have an explicit, outfront decision that wholesale revisions to the California promise are going to have to be made. I would say now that California is the anti-model."

As California's public treasury began to dry up and the gap between 5
spending and revenue ballooned to $38.2 billion this year, lawmakers looked for cuts in almost every public sector. Higher education took a heavy hit, with more than $700 million cut from the UC and CSU systems.

207

University officials say the cuts left them with little or no money to add new faculty and classes to accommodate the growing numbers of potential students.

For the first time in its history, CSU has made a formal decision to turn away qualified students this spring—a move expected to keep out as many as thirty thousand students across the twenty-three-campus system, the nation's largest.

UC leaders likely will follow in the fall of 2004 with plans to freeze enrollment growth for freshmen, transfer students, and graduate students. That decision would block entry for an estimated five thousand eligible students.

Higher-education experts say the decisions mark the first major retreat from the state's decades-old Master Plan for Higher Education, a heralded public policy that made California a pioneer in bringing higher education to the masses.

"California has not rationed its higher education before," CSU Chancellor Charles Reed said. "Students who have not done as well in high school could suffer the most. We have given them a chance to work on their English and math here, but now we may have to tell them to do that at the community colleges and transfer to us later."

The timing couldn't be worse.   10

As the economy languishes, California high schools are churning out record numbers of graduates, prompting an enrollment boom at public colleges that educators call Tidal Wave II. Both CSU and UC grew 5 percent to 7 percent a year in the past several years and expect growth demands to remain at that level through 2010. The Legislature, however, said the state would provide no money for growth next year. If California's economic fortunes don't turn around in two years, the enrollment freezes could persist.

"This is a serious mismatch of needs for students and the economic times," said Patrick Callan, president of the San Jose–based National Center for Public Policy and Higher Education. "If you get several years of this in a row, students are going to stop believing in the promise. They will think it doesn't matter how hard you work; you could still be frozen out."

Under the Master Plan, the top 12.5 percent of California's high school graduates are promised a seat at one of the nine UC campuses. The top third are guaranteed the same at CSU. For every other high school graduate, there would be a slot in the 108 community colleges, where students could spend two years, beef up their academic résumés, and transfer to UC or CSU.

But these are tough times for higher education across the country, and leaders say they've been forced to make grim choices.

Budget shortfalls set records this year in many states, prompting law-   15
makers to carve deeply into public university budgets that had expanded
rapidly during the technology-driven boom of the late 1990s and 2000.

One of the chief areas taking a hit is tuition. After several years of
steady or decreasing fees, university leaders nationwide are asking students to pay a larger share of the tab, and California has led the way. UC
and CSU fees have risen 40 percent since December. The price tag for
community college fees is to increase this fall from $11 per unit to $18.

Still, higher-education officials note that students have endured tuition increases and program cuts during other lean times. They cite the
state's last budget crisis ten years ago, when fees took a similar jump, and
people adapted.

But this year is different for California because of what CSU's Reed
calls the "double whammy." "At the very time that California's economy
and budget are shrinking, its need for higher education and demand for
access is accelerating," Reed said. "It's a scary thing."

Some experts point to signs of shrinking access long before the latest
budget crisis.

One measure of California's success in keeping college accessible to a   20
range of students has been its participation rates, said David Longanecker,
executive director of the Western Interstate Commission for Higher Education. In 1996, 61 percent of recent California high school graduates became
first-time freshmen at a state college or university, according to commission figures. By 2000, California's number dropped to 43 percent, though it
remained ahead of other Western states, where the same figure averaged 40
percent.

In a different evaluation of college-going rates done last year, the National Center found that 34 percent of California students enrolled in
college right after high school—above average nationwide but fewer
than in North Dakota, Massachusetts, and New Jersey.

"What had been a state that led the nation became quite average,"
Longanecker said.

When it comes to college graduation rates, the story gets worse. In 1999,
according to the National Center, California ranked thirty-fifth in the nation
for producing college students who completed baccalaureate degrees.

Where California kept an edge was affordability—but only when
cost-of-living expenses aren't included. "For the quality of education you
get in California, particularly at the UC, no one can beat that combination," Wellman said.

Experts agree that California's tradition of higher education is facing   25
an important test. What's murky is whether the choices being made during the economic crunch will become permanent.

"The pattern in California has been that we spend lavishly on higher education when times are good, and in bad times, we cut it ruthlessly," Callan said. "It's all about timing. . . . Students who finish high school in good economic times are the lucky ones."

For students such as Guadalupe Alvarado, the eighteen-year-old daughter of immigrant farm workers, timing matters a lot.

"I'm the first in my family to go to college, and it's important for me to set that example for my brothers and sister," said Alvarado, who will be a freshman at CSU, Sacramento, this fall. "When I first decided I could get in and afford to go, it cost 40 percent less. Now, it's going to be much more, but I will do everything I can to make sure that the money doesn't keep me out."

UNDERSTANDING THE TEXT

1. Explain in your own words what the California Master Plan for Higher Education is and how it is being subverted by budget problems.

2. Why does Maxwell say that "The timing couldn't be worse" (para. 10) for the current budget problems that are afflicting California's public college and university systems?

3. What are the implications of the current budget crisis for equal access to higher education, according to this article?

4. How does California's public higher-education system compare to other such systems nationally?

5. Why does the author say that "timing matters a lot" (para. 27) to California State University, Sacramento, student Guadalupe Alvarado?

EXPLORING AND DEBATING THE ISSUES

1. Higher-education costs at both public and private institutions have been escalating. In your journal, explore the effects of these cost increases on your life as a student. If you are facing financial difficulties, how are you attempting to resolve the problems? If you're not, what suggestions would you offer students who are?

2. California's Master Plan promises access to higher education to all qualified high school graduates in the state. In class, discuss the impact of recent fee increases and political initiatives, such as Proposition 209, on students' access to a public college or university education. Use your class discussion as a basis for an essay in which you argue whether the Master Plan should be continued or eliminated as public policy.

3. Write a letter to the state legislator for your district or to the governor in which you argue your view on fee increases in higher education. Be sure to consider how revenue should be generated if you argue that fees should be stabilized or cut.

4. To what extent is preserving the Master Plan for Higher Education essential to achieving the California dream? To develop your ideas, you might interview some students about their goals and the role that they believe a higher education plays in achieving them. In addition, you might read or reread James J. Rawls's "California: A Place, a People, a Dream" (p. 22).

"Well, I Guess They Need Their Minority"

RUBEN NAVARRETTE JR.

How would you feel if you were admitted to a prestigious university and none of your friends thought you deserved to get in? That is the dilemma that **Ruben Navarrette Jr.** (b. 1968) describes in this excerpt from *A Darker Shade of Crimson: Odyssey of a Harvard Chicano* (1993). Reflecting on affirmative action college admissions policies and their effects on minority applicants, Navarrette declares his desire to be viewed as an individual whose grades and performance have gotten him where he wants to go. A writer and lecturer, Navarrette has contributed to *Hispanic* and *Change* magazines as well as to the *Los Angeles Times*, the *San Francisco Chronicle*, and the *Fresno Bee*. He currently is a columnist and editorial board member of the *Dallas Morning News*.

Affirmative action tantrums, although often unfair, are understandable. We start with the presumption that all parents deem their offspring immensely qualified to attend any college they choose. Inevitably, there are some who are confronted by the unpleasant April reality that — after years of compassionate child rearing, private tutorials, family reading time, and expensive SAT prep courses — their child is simply not able to pull that off.

For them, minority students perform an invaluable service. Disappointed parents loyally reject the very real possibility that Johnny and Jessica were, in the sterile file room of some admissions office littered with empty coffee cups, simply outgunned by another more qualified, more interesting candidate of the same color. Instead, they trumpet to golf partners that their children are the victims of a chic, new kind of discrimination. Reverse discrimination. It seems to them particularly insidious because it affects those who are not accustomed to being hampered by the color of their skin.

So messy is the issue of affirmative action that it blurs the usual lines separating those who label themselves "liberal" or "conservative." Even those teachers who were usually supportive of Latino students, in this case, only compounded our discomfort.

One day a teacher, a self-professed liberal and voting Democrat with whom I had agreed on numerous political issues during the recent election, approached me in his European history class. He had heard through the gossip that permeated the teachers' lounge that I had been accepted to high-caliber schools. He intended to support my achievements. He chose entirely the wrong words. Instead of reminding me, as he could have, that I had earned one of the highest grades in his class and that I had consistently impressed him and my classmates with my work in it, he said only one thing.

"You know, I'm in favor of affirmative action. . . ."   5

As he returned to his desk, as proud of himself as if he had just sent a check to the American Civil Liberties Union, I realized that I had not mentioned affirmative action. It was he who had invoked the term and he who had instinctively, even if approvingly, linked the concept to my admission to these various colleges. . . . I knew that any congratulatory remarks to my white classmates would conspicuously lack any reference to affirmative action.

The teachers' lounge gossip persisted, and my ears burned. "Did you hear about Ruben Navarrette? Well, I guess they need their minority." At one point, a teacher of mine came to my defense. Fed up with innuendo from his colleagues — ironically people paid to build kids up and not tear them down — he lost his temper one morning and snapped back.

"Look, you wanna compare Ruben with your favorites . . . let's do it. Let's go to the registrar, get the transcripts and scores, and lay it all out. Then we'll see who's qualified!"

His colleagues relented and shifted their gossip back to local affairs and divorces and the like.

A man is embarrassed to admit the petty torments of a boy. Still, those   10
were lonely and hurtful days for me. Especially lonely and extra hurtful for one simple reason: those white students doing the accusing were my friends. We were close. We had grown up together, met each other's parents, confided in one another our schoolyard crushes on pretty girls. We trusted one another, in the kind of fragile trust that exists between children and adolescents. That trust was shattered in the spring of our senior year in high school by a wave of innuendo and slander. Children parroting adults. My friends' affirmative action tantrums left me with an acute sense of isolation, even betrayal. I was alone. Not knowing in whom to confide. To trust.

April became May, and the days were longer. I remember that at that crucial window in time, the one thing that I wanted was for someone, anyone, to put their hand on my shoulder, to hug me and tell me what I already knew: I was qualified, more than qualified, to be accepted by a school like Harvard. Each morning, as I reluctantly pulled my tired young body from its resting place, I hoped that this would be the day without innuendo, accusation, or insults disguised as compliments. I hoped that this would be the day that teachers, principals, and classmates would swallow their prejudice and own up to the truth: I had excelled according to their own standards of excellence and had done my modest part to bankrupt their sacred myth that Mexican Americans were somehow not as good as whites. But that day would not come for me. And even as I write this, I know that it has not come for hundreds of thousands of bright Latino students across the country.

There was a harsh irony to all this. If I found myself alone in those few months, it was because for many years before that I had painted myself into such a corner through my academic achievement. Since elementary school, I had done my homework, obeyed my teachers, strived for As instead of Bs, and through it all, distanced myself from my fellow Mexican American classmates. It was no accident, then, that as I sat in calculus class or physics or a variety of advanced placement courses, I was surrounded by white faces.

There were other Latinos, of course, but Latinos like me—smart, ambitious, with no trace of an accent. We were presumably immune to discrimination; low expectation was a foreign concept. We dated white girls. We considered ourselves acceptable to white America, and so we expected to be accepted by white America. Imagine our profound disillusionment after April's accusations.

Not so privileged were the others. Young men with dark skin, dark hair sprayed stiff and motionless, dark eyes. Hollow eyes devoid of hope. Knowing things that a valedictorian did not. I knew them, once. We played kickball during recess in a dusty elementary school. Five or six of us gathered routinely in the bathroom in sixth grade and gawked at pictures from forbidden magazines, played poker, talked about girls' developing anatomy, and gingerly toyed with tools of vice. There was intimacy. We felt at ease with one another. Each of us, Mexican. Each of us, headed down a different road.

In junior high school—a crucial point for students labeled "at risk" by   15
educators—we lost one. One day, he dressed differently. Acted differently. He cut class, then classes, then the school day, then the school week. A thirteen-year-old was getting tougher, harder before my eyes. He cared about sex, alcohol, intimidation, money, and most of all being *cool*. We acknowledged each other with a wave, then a nod, then not at all. He gave up on education; education reciprocated. His vices became more serious. Later, it was juvenile hall and then county jail, maybe prison. I don't know.

The others remained in school, struggling to graduate. School was to be endured, not enjoyed. In our senior year, they leaned neatly against the wall of a high school corridor in between classes, single file, side by side. Dressed impeccably in clean white T-shirts, khaki pants, and patent leather shoes. Hard bodies, hard faces. Hollow eyes. The *pachucos*[1] of the 1940s, immortalized in Luis Valdez's play *Zoot Suit*, had gracefully evolved into the *cholos*[2] of the 1980s. Hands in pockets, perhaps caressing a switchblade or even a gun. Certainly not a pencil. I didn't know. Because I didn't know them anymore. I walked their gauntlet on my way to some stuffy, high-browed class where I would study abstraction with people like me. Unlike me. I smiled to an old friend from kindergarten. We didn't talk. What would we talk about? What would my five acceptance letters mean to him? Nothing. Absolutely nothing.

Still, there was a respect between us, and perhaps mutual admiration. Maybe they liked that I was engaged daily in academic battle with the *gringos*, the sons and daughters of those who had treated our parents so badly. And, unnerving to some, in the competition for grades, I was winning. Taking the same tests, reading the same books, *Good with your hands*. . . . Hands full of acceptance letters to places that have rejected you.

In return, I admired my old friends' strength, their strong sense of self. They would not later write editorials in national newspapers with headlines like: "How Mexican Am I?" They knew. They also knew discrimination. They might have snickered at my disillusionment and said that, of course, white people think themselves superior. Of course. "Where have you been for seventeen years?" they might have said to me, shaking their heads mockingly that someone who knew so much could know so little.

The intimacy of our youth was gone. It had been sacrificed years before at the altar of academic success. We were no longer close. The American educational system's first and most thorough lesson is one of division. Remedial students. Honors students. Gifted students. *Better* students.

And so, when I was beseiged by the insults of white classmates, my   20
old friends were not there for me. Could not be there for me. I was in another world. What would they have done to defend me, anyway? They likely would not have been able to debate reflectively citing newspaper articles defending affirmative action.

I dreamed of a confrontation. An old friend would come to my rescue against the pack. He would enter the high-browed classroom for better

---

[1] Mexican youths of the 1930s and 1940s who developed their own style and language living in American barrios. [Eds.]

[2] Gang members. [Eds.]

students. He would approach the student body president and tell him that his homeboy had beaten him out not because of some improper system but because he was simply smarter than him. He would point the finger at the end of his muscular, brown arm at the terrified young white man turning paler each second and expose him as a child of privilege. He would mock the young man's contention that things should be "equal" in the admissions process by reminding him that the two of them lead lives that are anything but equal. He would invite him home to see the squalor and the neglect and the hardworking parents who had been told by guidance counselors to work in the canneries. And so they had, providing for their children an existence that compared more closely to those in Third World countries than it did to that of the privileged young man who trembled before him. He would argue finally that for Latinos, the ticket out of the American underclass was in the hands of ambitious and successful Latinos like his old friend, and how dare he or anyone else get in the way of that progress with their snide, childish, self-centered remarks.

In my splendid fantasy, the *cholo* would win the debate with the student body president because the victor knew something that the loser did not. He knew what it was like to be considered less intelligent, less capable, less, less, less by a system that was grooming others to succeed in his place. He knew what it was like to be Mexican American in public school. But the student body president, surrounded by friends, would not concede. My old friend would lose his temper and strike out in a more primitive, though more effective, way. Like our fathers had done at the same school three decades before, he would resort to knocking the shit out of his opponent before being hauled away to face punishment.

But reality was not so comforting. There was no rescue. The *cholos* stayed in their world. I was alone in mine. In that tiny school, as in life, they were separated from me (and from those whom the educational system expected more of than a life of dropping out, pregnancy, and crime) by a wall much higher, much more formidable than the one that they leaned on in between classes. This was my fight, and mine alone. At stake, I realized for the first time, was not only my own pride and self-image but also the dignity and progress of a whole race of people.

Should the reader tire of my complaining or see it as mere whining, I offer here a true story of an academic casualty in this battle for respect. As a college student and recruiter for Harvard, I spoke one day to a high school class in the San Joaquin Valley about the admissions process at Ivy League schools. A young man confronted me about what he considered to be the impropriety of race-conscious admissions. He spoke with passion and anger. Surprising to me at the time, he was Mexican American.

He was angry because he claimed that, no matter what his accomplishments, he would never be taken seriously by his white classmates. We argued. We resolved nothing.

Three months later, I received a phone call from a friend in the admissions office. Had I heard? The same young man, an outstanding student, had been accepted into both our incoming class and that of Yale. He had decided, the caller continued, to reject both offers of admission and instead attend a small, less assuming college in New England. My friend was baffled. For the young man to stay in California was one thing. Yet to be willing to travel 3,000 miles but not to accept what were clearly more highly coveted spots in schools like Harvard or Yale seemed not to make much sense. For me, given the frustration, and perhaps embarrassment, that I saw in the young man's eyes during our heated exchange months earlier, I understood at once his desire to pick a less conspicuous apple from the tree.

"Tell me," I asked my friend. "If you're invited to a party, but don't feel that you deserve the invitation, would you go?"

"You don't mean . . ." the voice fell off to a whisper. "Shit!"

Ultimately, the young man in question was not spared, as he had hoped he would be, the ribbing of his high school classmates even though he had chosen to attend the small, less assuming college in New England at which he never felt comfortable and from which he eventually withdrew. A statistic in a government study, he and his nearly 1400 SATs now went on to attend a community college in Fresno. There, he was no longer subjected to ribbing by classmates and instructors, who finally considered him to be exactly where he was "qualified" to be. He became one of the hundreds of thousands of Mexican American students who attend community college in California, and not one of the just over one hundred such students who at any given time attend Harvard, apparently those who constitute a more controversial and threatening entity.

UNDERSTANDING THE TEXT

1. Why does Navarrette say that "minority students perform an invaluable service" (para. 2) for white parents who are disappointed in their children's college admissions?

2. When Navarrette was admitted to Harvard University, what reactions did he face from his teachers and fellow students (both white and Mexican American)?

3. Summarize in your own words Navarrette's attitudes toward whites and toward Mexican Americans.

4. Why did the Mexican American student from the San Joaquin Valley refuse to accept admission to Harvard or Yale?

5. What does Navarrette mean when he says to his friend, "If you're invited to a party, but don't feel that you deserve the invitation, would you go?" (para. 26). How does that question relate to the larger issue of college admissions?

EXPLORING AND DEBATING THE ISSUES

1. In your journal, reflect on how attending college has shaped your sense of personal identity. Has your status as a college student affected your relationship with high school friends?

2. Write a letter to the San Joaquin Valley student whom Navarrette describes, advising him on how to respond to the ridicule he received from his peers. Or write a letter to Navarrette in which you defend the student's choices. Share your letter with your classmates.

3. In 1996, Proposition 209 prohibited the use of affirmative action in accepting students to California's public colleges and universities. It does not affect private California institutions or public or private schools in other states. In class, form teams, and debate whether affirmative action in college admissions does more harm than good.

4. According to Navarrette, "So messy is the issue of affirmative action that it blurs the usual lines separating those who label themselves 'liberal' or 'conservative' " (para. 3). Interview at least ten students and teachers on their political positions and views on affirmative action, and use your findings as the basis for an essay in which you evaluate the validity of Navarrette's claim.

It Shouldn't Be Good
to Have It Bad

JOHN MCWHORTER

Faced with declining minority enrollments at Berkeley and UCLA in the wake of Proposition 209 — the 1996 ballot initiative that effectively ended affirmative action in California public college and university admissions — the UC system adopted a new policy that granted extra points to candidates who had endured certain lifetime "hardships." This policy stirred up a good deal of controversy in the fall of 2003 when it was reported that the hardship points were allowing students with low test scores and grade-point averages to be admitted at campuses like Berkeley over applicants with higher scores. **John McWhorter**, an associate professor of linguistics at UC Berkeley, could well have said "I told you so" at that time because he had written in this August 4, 2002, opinion piece for the *Washington Post* that "hardship" was a euphemism for "race" and that the new policy was essentially an "end run around . . . Proposition 209." Why not "simply base a preference system on socioeconomic class," McWhorter asks, and thus achieve a truly race-neutral admissions policy? McWhorter is the author of numerous books, including *Losing the Race: Self-Sabotage in Black America* (2001) and *Authentically Black: Essays for the Black Silent Majority* (2003).

At UC Berkeley, where I teach, we are awaiting the arrival of the first freshman class selected under a revised admissions policy for the University of California schools. All applicants are being evaluated according to whether they have survived "hardships," with those who have done so netting extra points.

Under this policy, the student submitting a top-level dossier who has led a lucky life will often be less likely to get in than one whose dossier is just as good but also attests to suffering from family strife, the care of younger siblings, certified emotional problems, or the like. This is technically a "race-neutral" policy, but it's really just old wine in a new bottle. The UC "suits" have crafted a canny end run around 1996's Proposition 209, which outlawed racial preferences in college admissions. The new policy is designed to bolster the presence of "brown" minorities — blacks and Latinos — without explicitly targeting race. (The Asian minority, who submit top applications out of proportion to their numbers, are considered something to work around.) In fact, this new policy enhances the culture of victimization, teaching students of any color a lesson history will consider curious and misguided.

After Proposition 209 took effect beginning with the entering class of 1998, the numbers of brown students admitted to Berkeley and UCLA dropped sharply. The usual coalition of pundits and faculty radicals shouted "resegregation," and Berkeley erupted with endless rallies. Among the faculty, it quickly became a required gesture to shake one's head ruefully and look off into the distance whenever the demise of racial preferences came up (although after a glass of wine many would privately admit that it had been long overdue).

In reality, the outlawing of racial preferences did not so much bar black and Latino students from the UC system as reshuffle them. While the numbers of these students fell at the flagships Berkeley and UCLA, which have the very highest admissions standards, they rose at several other UC schools, all solid institutions and many prestigious, such as UC Santa Barbara and UC San Diego.

Nevertheless, the idea of a brown student of any background being held to the same standards as others remained alarming to scattered committees and student groups. I will never forget how blithely such people assumed that a black professor like me would share their opinion, and their screaming indignation deeply unsettled the UC top brass.

They were in truth concerned as much for UC's public reputation as for the moral principles involved: I had one conversation with a very highly placed Berkeley official who said he agreed with me but could never say it in public. With the futility of reversing the new law clear, the "hardship" factor has been added as a palliative.

Of course, the official line is that administrators are deeply concerned about hardship across race lines, but it doesn't wash. How seriously can we take this sudden concern for the coal miner's daughter when we heard not a peep of such class-based indignation during three decades of racial preferences? In any case, here we are.

And in a constructive vein, sniffing out hardship among all students looks great on paper. But the seams show in practice. It must be remembered that hardship has always factored into student assessments across America at almost all schools, as you would expect. Who would not give a break to a student with cerebral palsy or one who speaks English as a second language? But focusing on "hardship" in evaluating all students sends us drifting into murkier waters.

Because I once sat on a committee that distributes scholarship money, I have already seen at close hand how this kind of evaluation operates. After Proposition 209 passed — even before the new universally applied hardship policy — scholarship awards were rechanneled according to such life trials, with packages once earmarked for "diversity" newly labeled as "hardship" bonuses. During the committee's decision-making process, one part of me felt that the new policy was an advance over the old, where too often extra funding went to "diverse" students of affluent circumstances who were essentially "white" culturally. But another part of

me could not help sensing that before the new regime, the types of life experiences we were acknowledging would not have struck any of us as de-
manding a thumb on the scale. And as so often happens, social policies
that seem noble in theory have a way of drifting into farce on the individual level.

A *Wall Street Journal* piece some weeks ago described a student with   10
a 1410 SAT score who, having failed to describe any hardships she had
suffered, was denied admission to Berkeley and UCLA, while another student with an 1120 SAT, stressing her humble origins and her help with
supporting the family as her mother fought breast cancer, was admitted
to both. In other words, a superficially well-intentioned policy penalized
the first young woman for feeling that her concrete accomplishments
made a sufficient case for her admission. And this despite the fact that as
the child of a struggling Korean-immigrant pastor, the first young woman
had actually survived hardships —just as, well, most of us have. Most
people's lives are far from perfect.

Those who have known neither parental divorce, severe illness, social ostracization, or extended emotional trauma are exceptions, whom
many of us privately dismiss as "boring" or "too perfect." We often think
that a little hard-core misery would do these people some good! Indeed,
most of us would worry that the child who has known no suffering is at
risk in later life.

In my eight years teaching here, I can attest that among students of
all classes and races, those who cannot refer to at least one unfortunate
stain upon their life trajectories are rare. They tend to refer to themselves
almost guiltily as "just lucky" and often seek out experiences with the
less fortunate, such as tutoring underprivileged students in bad Oakland
neighborhoods, to make themselves "better rounded."

Making do despite obstacles, then, is a matter of ordinary human re-
silience. As such, the new policy at UC is ranking students according to
how vibrantly human they are. And this is a sharp departure from assessing
how well a student is likely to perform academically. Wangling grace and
dignity out of this vale of tears is hardly limited to the academically gifted.

Certainly, hardship of obvious significance must be taken into account
when evaluating an applicant. But when a black high schooler tells a newspaper interviewer, "I hope Berkeley can understand that I had to babysit
after school," we see the results of a culture of excuse-making. And no one
would argue that performance is enhanced by focusing on obstacles.

For decades now, students entering college have imbibed a "victimol-   15
ogist" perspective; now UC's "hardship" policy serves as a kind of college
prep course on the subject. In the end, one must ask why UC administrators could not simply base a preference system on socioeconomic class.

Various studies have shown that class crucially affects the correlation between students' grades and scores and their actual abilities. Of course, income alone would be too coarse a measure. A point system could be established also taking into account parental occupation, quality of high school, and whether or not a student's parents had gone to college. This would address the indisputable obstacles to success in American society, without scanning every single applicant's life span for "handicaps" that the students and their parents often — rightly — never thought of as such. A class-based policy would also bring in brown students of humbler circumstances without catching in the net brown children of affluent parents (who today are as much a norm as disadvantaged ones).

This would fulfill the original goal of affirmative action, to give opportunities to those unfairly barred from advancement, rather than making do with crude color-coded headcounts. The reason class alone does not move the UC administrators is no mystery. As Shelby Steele has argued, racial preference policies have always been less about giving a race the skills to succeed than assuaging white guilt.

To all but the diehard Marxist, class difference is a deep-seated and permanent reality — and thus few are guilty about it. Advocates of the new policy openly sniff that a class-based preference system would net more working-class whites and Asians than brown students. This is true — particularly for whites, whose large numbers mean that numerically there are more of them living on the other side of the tracks than blacks.

But if the true goal of the policy were to address societal injustice, then those so troubled by "hardship" would have no problem with an influx of working-class whites. After all, it surprises no one that there are more whites than blacks or Asians in California.

Instead, the new admissions system does look to high school quality and parents' education level — but these are not seen as sufficient without the "hardship" measure appended. This might seem redundant, until we see that it is being utilized as a way to revive precisely the racial bean-counting that Proposition 209 outlawed. [20]

It's no accident, then, that the rejected student above is Korean while the admitted one is Latino — nor even that a Korean student with a 1500 SAT who, just like the Latino one, helped support his family when his mother got breast cancer, was rejected.

A while ago, an older white professor who had read my book *Losing the Race* genially informed me that whatever the value of my arguments against race-based preferences, "I insist on my right to be guilty." He's not alone, and life will go on — we had a nice chuckle of truce. But on the subject of students of any color or background, I will continue to insist that the person we pity is a person we do not respect — "hardships" or not.

UNDERSTANDING THE TEXT

1. Summarize in your own words the post–Proposition 209 changes in admissions policies at the University of California.
2. What does McWhorter mean by the term "culture of victimization" (para. 2)?
3. Characterize McWhorter's tone here. How does it affect your response to his argument?
4. McWhorter self-identifies as an African American. What affect does this item of information have on your response to his writing?
5. According to McWhorter, what problems arise when hardship is considered in university admission? What are the advantages to making socioeconomic class an admissions criterion?

EXPLORING AND DEBATING THE ISSUES

1. In your journal, reflect on McWhorter's comment that "the person we pity is a person we do not respect — 'hardships' or not" (para. 22).
2. In class, form teams, and debate McWhorter's proposal to make socioeconomic class an important factor in university admissions. To develop your ideas, you might interview students from a variety of backgrounds about their family and educational experiences. Use the debate as a group brainstorming session to prepare for your own argumentative essay on whether class or race should be considered during the college admissions process.
3. Adopting the perspective of Ruben Navarrette Jr. in "'Well, I Guess They Need Their Minority'" (p. 211), write a response to McWhorter's proposal. Do you think that Navarrette would support or oppose the distinction that McWhorter makes between academic achievement and success in handling personal adversities? Alternately, adopt the perspective of teacher Yvonne Divans Hutchinson (see Mike Rose, "A Visit to Edwin Markham Intermediate School," p. 182). Do you think Hutchinson would imagine that factors other than socioeconomic ones affect students' academic performance?
4. Opponents of testing in public schools often claim that it can harm underprivileged students, particularly minorities and those whose native language is not English. Read or reread Sylvia S. Fox's "Testing, Anyone?" (p. 196) and Sandra Nichols's "A Win-Win for the High School Exit Exam" (p. 204), and write an assessment of McWhorter's proposal. How might the various testing programs contribute to the likely success or failure of his suggested policy?

Yuba City School

CHITRA BANERJEE DIVAKARUNI

Chitra Banerjee Divakaruni (b. 1956), who was born in India, is the author of six books of stories and poetry in English, but she can remember the days when her tongue felt "stiff and swollen" when speaking English to her child's schoolteacher. Reflecting on the feelings of her son, whose native language is Punjabi but who attends a school where everyone else speaks English and Spanish, Divakaruni dramatizes the experiences of California's many South Asian immigrants, whose own bilingual needs have gone largely unnoticed in the controversy over bilingual education. A poet and short-story writer whose works include *Arranged Marriage* (1995), *The Mistress of Spices* (1997), *Leaving Yuba City* (1997), *Sister of My Heart* (1999), *The Unknown Error of Our Lives: Stories* (2001), and *Vine of Desire: A Novel* (2002), Divakaruni teaches creative writing at the University of Houston.

From the black trunk I shake out
my one American skirt, blue serge
that smells of mothballs. Again today
Neeraj came crying from school. All week
the teacher has made him sit   5
in the last row, next to the fat boy
who drools and mumbles,
picks at the spotted milk-blue
skin of his face, but knows
to pinch, sudden-sharp,   10
when she is not looking.

The books are full of black curves,
dots like the eggs the boll-weevil lays
each monsoon in furniture-cracks
in Ludhiana. Far up in front   15
the teacher makes word-sounds
Neeraj does not know. They float
from her mouth-cave, he says,
in discs, each a different color.

Candy-pink for the girls   20
in their lace dresses, marching
shiny shoes. Silk-yellow
for the boys beside them,
crisp blond hair, hands raised
in all the right answers. Behind them   25
the Mexicans, whose older brothers,

he tells me, carry knives,
whose catcalls and whizzing rubber bands
clash, mid-air, with the teacher's
voice, its sharp purple edge.　　　　　　　　　30
For him, the words are
a muddy red, flying low and heavy,
and always the one he has learned to understand:
idiot, idiot, idiot.

I heat the iron over the stove. Outside　　　35
evening blurs the shivering
in the eucalyptus. Neeraj's shadow
disappears into the hole
he is hollowing all afternoon.
The earth, he knows, is round, and if　　　40
one can tunnel all the way through,
he will end up in Punjab,
in his grandfather's mango orchard,
his grandmother's songs lighting
on his head, the old words　　　　　　　　45
glowing like summer fireflies.

In the playground, Neeraj says,
invisible hands snatch at his uncut hair,
unseen feet trip him from behind,
and when he turns, ghost laughter　　　　50
all around his bleeding knees.
He bites down on his lip
to keep in the crying. They are
waiting for him to open his mouth,
so they can steal his voice.　　　　　　　　55

I test the iron with little drops of water
that sizzle and die. Press down
on the wrinkled cloth. The room fills
with a smell like singed flesh.
Tomorrow in my blue skirt I will go　　　60
to see the teacher, my tongue
stiff and swollen
in my unwilling mouth, my few
English phrases. She will pluck them
from me, nail shut my lips. My son　　　65
will keep sitting in the last row
among the red words that drink his voice.

UNDERSTANDING THE TEXT

1. Why does Neeraj cry after school (l. 4)?

2. Read the poem aloud in class. How does reading it aloud affect your response to it?

3. Why does Divakaruni say that Neeraj's mother's tongue will be "stiff and swollen" (l. 62) when she speaks with her son's teacher?

4. Catalog the images that Divakaruni uses to describe language and speech.

EXPLORING AND DEBATING THE ISSUES

1. Divakaruni comes from the Punjab region of India, and although Neeraj's birthplace is not specified, we may presume he comes from the same region. How do his difficulties in school, as a student from a relatively small immigrant population, complicate the issues surrounding bilingual education?

2. If you are not a native English speaker, write a journal entry (it could be a poem) reflecting on your own experiences in school.

3. Most of the bilingual-education debate focuses on students, but educators agree that much of the success of English-language instruction depends on a student's home life. In class, brainstorm ways to help immigrant parents who do not speak English to become more involved in their children's education.

4. Consider the poem aesthetically, and analyze the ways that it uses imagery and achieves its effects. Alternately, rewrite the poem as a prose narrative. What differences do you observe between the poetic and the prose forms?

5. In an essay, analyze the implications of Neeraj's experiences for the appropriateness of the various testing programs used in California public schools. To what extent do his experiences validate these programs or demonstrate deficiencies in them? To develop your ideas, consult Sylvia S. Fox, "Testing, Anyone?" (p. 196) and Sandra Nichols, "A Win-Win for the High School Exit Exam" (p. 204).

Researching the Issues

1. Visit your college library, and research the provisions of the 1960 California Master Plan for Higher Education. Then use your findings as the basis for an essay that argues whether the vision of the Master Plan still holds for California college students today.

2. Interview at least five students on your college campus about their goals and aspirations. Then use the results of your interviews to formulate an argument about whether higher education can help students achieve the California dream in the twenty-first century.

3. As a class project, form teams and arrange to offer tutoring services to needy students, whether on your own campus or at a local public school. Keep a journal or log of your tutoring experiences; use these entries as the basis of an essay in which you explain the educational needs of the students with whom you worked.

4. Rent a videotape of a film that features an educational setting, such as *To Sir with Love, Dead Poets' Society, Stand and Deliver, Higher Learning, Election,* and *School of Rock.* Then write a critique of the film: How realistic is its depiction of educational issues such as the school environment, teacher-student relationships, the learning process, and student motivation?

5. Interview at least five students who have immigrated to America (whether legally or not) about their experiences in U.S. schools. Then use your findings as the basis of an essay in which you explain the obstacles facing nonnative students — and what strategies for success your interviewees devised.

6. Research the costs of other state university systems such as New York's and Michigan's, and construct a table comparing them to the costs of the UC and CSU systems.

7. If you attend a public college or university, investigate the ways your school has responded to Proposition 209, as well as the effects the proposition has had on student enrollment. If you attend a private university, investigate the affirmative action policies of your campus. Use your findings to formulate a report in which you either defend the admissions procedures or recommend changes to them.

8. Investigate the controversy triggered in 1998 when the San Francisco Board of Education proposed using racial quotas for the authors on its list of approved texts for its schools.

9. Research the Oakland Board of Education's 1996 proposal to consider speakers of ebonics, or Black English Vernacular, as ESL students.

10. Investigate the debate about a "core curriculum" that raged at Stanford University, among other universities, in the early 1990s. Then study your own school's curriculum. To what extent do you see your school's curriculum as influenced by the intellectual debate that occurred then?

4

The Geography of Desire
CALIFORNIA AND THE SENSE OF PLACE

It somehow seems ironic that Robert Frost, the poetic voice of New England, was born in San Francisco. Or that Jack London, raised in Oakland, is best known for his stories of the Alaska gold rush. Indeed, when we try to come up with the name of a writer who most reflects the spirit, indeed the soul, of California, it isn't at all easy. The American South has William Faulkner and Flannery O'Conner, and the Midwest Sinclair Lewis and Sherwood Anderson, but who speaks for California? Johnny Carson?

Our point is not that California is lacking in literary giants. Many writers have been produced in the Golden State whose work is distinctly Californian—like John Steinbeck and Joan Didion—and many more have come here to create some of their most distinguished works—like Eugene O'Neill, who wrote such plays as *The Iceman Cometh* while living in Danville. Our point is that California is at once too new and too diverse a place, too mutable and too reinventing, to be summed up by any single figure or voice.

California is less a place than a dynamic mosaic of places where tradition counts for relatively little and change and innovation are ever the orders of the day. In this sense, California, once again, stands as an intensified version of a particularly American trait. For from its colonial inception, America has always been a place that people escape to, where they forget the places of their past, where change has been more highly valued than tradition, and where the future seems brighter than days gone by. Thus, it is no accident that when Disneyland opened in the

◀ *California quarter.*

229

1950s, Tomorrow Land was one of its most popular attractions. When California does look at the past, it does so mostly by way of imitations or, as postmodern analysts would put it, of simulacra, like Riverside's Mission Inn, which simulates a Spanish mission while throwing in a Roman catacombs for good measure, or Disneyland's own Main Street entrance, which simulates an early twentieth-century Midwestern town. The few remnants of California's authentic past, like Los Angeles's Olvera Street or the surviving missions themselves, are essentially tourist attractions rather than living parts of the present.

To put this another way, in California the past is regarded as a source of entertainment. Rather than revering historical tradition, Californians tend to approach history as a pleasant diversion, something to be amused by. Nathanael West, another California writer, noted this more than a half century ago in his novel *The Day of the Locust*, which lampooned the ways in which Hollywood uses history as a prop for the creation of cinematic fantasies rather than as a reality to be studied and cherished. West's satiric depiction of a Hollywood version of the Battle of Waterloo is an especially striking and funny parody of what happens when the movie industry takes on classic historic events. (In the movie version, the battle ends in a draw as a crucial portion of the set collapses on the "combatants.") And West also satirizes the essentially placeless place that Los Angeles has become in his representation of the architectural styles of L.A.: styles that are borrowed from all over the earth, like Mexican ranch houses, Samoan huts, Mediterranean villas, Egyptian and Japanese temples, Swiss chalets, Tudor cottages, and so forth, which he found dotted on the hillsides of Hollywood. Visitors from the East Coast (and West's often caustic vision of L.A. was very much a product of his New York upbringing) and Europe often deem this relative lack of an authentic sense of place either amusing or contemptible, but most Californians—with the exception of the descendants of the few surviving pioneer families—don't really seem to mind or even notice.

A Profound Diversity

When Californians think of their state as a place, they think geographically rather than historically. The many regions of California are a part of the Golden State's luster. From the north woods of the Eureka coast to the Mojave Desert, and from the lava beds of the northeast corner of the state to the Central Valley and beyond to the coastal megalopolis that now stretches almost continuously from San Francisco to San Diego, California offers a bewildering variety of landscapes. We have our own "alps" (from Siskayu to the Sierra), our own "dead sea" (in the Salton basin), our own Sahara (in the dunes of Death Valley), our own Riviera (in the gold coast of Malibu), and our own redwood forests that are unexampled anywhere else on earth. Such a scenic diversity makes California something of a global microcosm and a magnet for tourists from all over the world.

California's geographic diversity is reflected in a certain cultural diversity as well. When most Americans think of California, they think of the coast, a cosmopolitan region whose cultural references are often directed, in a generally competitive way, to New York. But there is also the California of the north Central Valley, where, as Joan Didion has written, the descendants of the original Anglo-Saxon pioneers still recall their heyday in the nineteenth century, as well as the California of the southern San Joaquin Valley, where the descendants of Dust Bowl–era refugees, especially those involved in the oil industry, maintain a culture that is distinctly Texan and Oklahoman in origin. North Coastal Californians, for their part, have a lot in common with their timber-industry-dependent neighbors just to the north in Oregon, while the suburban neighborhoods of Pomona and San Bernardino still retain a Midwestern, Bible Belt flavor. Through much of the Central Valley, a distinctively Mexican American culture characterizes the communities formed around an agricultural economy, while in such cities as Los Angeles an urban variant identifies communities within a community like East L.A. and Pacoima.

This diversity prevents us from identifying any single trait that can be called truly Californian. There is no single or distinct California "accent," no distinct California landscape, ethnicity, culture, or even economic activity. But perhaps it is precisely California's diversity that most distinguishes the Golden State as a specific place, and here, once again, California stands as a bellwether to the rest of the nation, a harbinger of things to come. For bit by bit, the regional specificities of America, along with regional linguistic accents and cultural codes, are disappearing. As more and more Americans begin to speak a standard American speech, an unaccented accent, everyone is beginning to sound more and more Californian. And as California cultural practices (explored in Chapter 5 of this book) come to be adopted throughout the rest of the country, largely due to the influence of California-based media, the once highly differentiated regions of America are increasingly coming to resemble California. Add to that the demographic changes that have been long noted in California but are now beginning to be felt throughout America, and the place that we call California holds an important place indeed in the national identity.

The Readings

The chapter opens with a poem by Dana Gioia that celebrates one of California's most distinctive natural terrains: the oak-studded hillside savannahs that dry to a golden hue every summer. Looking to the Bay Area, J. A. English-Lueck offers an anthropological analysis of the culture of Silicon Valley, where high-tech success is virtually a religion, while "The Castro Q&A" takes a look at San Francisco's famous Castro District, which has become a center for gay culture in America. David Mas Masumoto takes us to the Central Valley, where he reflects on his own experiences as an organic farmer and offers a vision for a less toxic future for California agriculture, while Gary Snyder next reports on the ways in which he and his neighbors in the foothills of the Sierra Nevadas are striving to manage their lands in an ecologically sustainable manner. Ernesto Galarza's "Barrio Boy" follows with a portrait of the immigrant community in early twentieth-century Sacramento. James D. Houston then goes in search of "Oildorado," which he finds in the southern San Joaquin Valley, and Ramon Garcia offers a poetic look at Modesto, where Mormons and homeboys cover the same turf. Judith Lewis's "Interesting Times" provides a personal view on the perennial sense of crisis that seems to grip Angelenos, while Joel Garreau shows how urban planners and developers, in effect, sought to eliminate the word *crisis* from the vocabulary of Irvine's suburbanites. Gary Paul Nabhan concludes the chapter with a vision of Palm Springs, where Anglo and Indian attitudes toward the environment contrast dramatically in the patchy shade of the palm trees.

California Hills in August

DANA GIOIA

Perhaps some Californians in the northwest coastal regions of California, where the rain breeds redwoods and ferns, do not know well the scene that **Dana Gioia** (b. 1950) paints here: the dry, chaparral-covered hills of August, where the foxtails stick to your socks and everything cries out for water. But being from California—where water is often scarce and, more often than not, "the skyline of a hill . . . [may] be broken by no more / trees than one can count,"—Gioia loves the arid California summer in a way that those who are accustomed to wetter climates may not and celebrates that love in this poetic landscape. The author of numerous books, including *Interrogations at Noon* (2001), a collection of poems that won the 2002 American Book Award, and coeditor, with X. J. Kennedy, of *Literature: An Introduction to Fiction, Poetry, and Drama* (8th ed., 2001), Gioia is also chair of the National Endowment for the Arts.

I can imagine someone who found
these fields unbearable, who climbed
the hillside in the heat, cursing the dust,
cracking the brittle weeds underfoot,
wishing a few more trees for shade. 5

An Easterner especially, who would scorn
the meagerness of summer, the dry
twisted shapes of black elm,
scrub oak, and chaparral, a landscape
August has already drained of green. 10

One who would hurry over the clinging
thistle, foxtail, golden poppy,
knowing everything was just a weed,
unable to conceive that these trees
and sparse brown bushes were alive. 15

And hate the bright stillness of the noon
without wind, without motion,
the only other living thing,
a hawk, hungry for prey, suspended
in the blinding, sunlit blue. 20

And yet how gentle it seems to someone
raised in a landscape short of rain—
the skyline of a hill broken by no more
trees than one can count, the grass,
the empty sky, the wish for water. 25

UNDERSTANDING THE TEXT

1. In your own words, why would an Easterner find California hillsides "unbearable" (l. 2), and how does that view contrast with the native Californian's view of local hillsides?

2. How does Gioia's selection of natural details contribute to his message?

3. Study the degree of intolerance toward California hillsides expressed in each of the first four stanzas. What pattern of development do you see? How does that pattern prepare you for the last stanza?

4. Characterize the speaker's mood in this poem. How does it shape your response?

EXPLORING AND DEBATING THE ISSUES

1. Read aloud the poem in class. How does the oral rendition affect your response to it? What message do you think Gioia is communicating?

2. Compare and contrast the attitudes toward nature expressed in this poem and in Gary Soto's "The First" (p. 426). Which of the two perspectives that Gioia presents is more aligned with that of the Native Americans in Soto's poem?

3. Write your own description of a different natural feature of the California landscape—such as the High Sierras, a particular section of the coastline, or the Mojave Desert—from the perspectives of both a native Californian and someone from out of state. Your description can be either poetry or prose. Then write an analysis of your description that examines how the two perspectives compare and the logic that underlies any differences.

4. Write a paragraph in which you adopt Gioia's perspective and analyze the landscape of Palm Springs (see Gary Paul Nabhan's "The Palms in Our Hands," p. 308). What response do you think Gioia would have to the palm trees?

Petaluma Fields (1987)

WILLARD DIXON

1. In what ways could the landscape in Willard Dixon's painting be called "gentle," as Dana Gioia uses the term (p. 233, l. 21)?

2. Assuming the perspective of the Easterner in Gioia's poem, write a prose paragraph describing your response to the scene in this painting. Then, assuming the perspective of David Mas Masumoto ("As If the Farmer Died," p. 248), write a response to the Easterner's paragraph.

Identified by Technology

J. A. ENGLISH-LUECK

Silicon Valley is not simply a geographical region where more high-tech firms are clustered than anywhere else on earth. It is, in **J. A. English-Lueck**'s view, an ethnogenetic vortex, a place where a hothouse climate of technological research and development is forging a new culture that, in turn, may one day transform the culture of America. Like the monastic movement of the early middle ages, Silicon Valley is generating its own "religion" of work and corporate prosperity, English-Lueck suggests, whose "saints" are the great technological innovators, like Marc Andreessen and David Packard, who made it all possible. A professor and chair in the anthropology department at San Jose State University, English-Lueck is the author of *Chinese Intellectuals on the World Frontier* (1997), *Health in the New Age: A Study in California Holistic Practices* (1990), and *Cultures@Silicon Valley* (2002), from which this selection is taken.

Life is not just lived in Silicon Valley; it is, at least in part, designed. While people experience their daily lives at the individual level, as in the stories you have already read, there are social institutions that operate beyond the individual. Technology saturation of Silicon Valley infiltrates personal choices and actions, but it also acts at a broader level. How does the culture of Silicon Valley affect social entities beyond the individual level? How do networks, work organizations, and civic organizations support and shape the region? The civic fabric of the community at large reflects conscious group efforts, not only the sum of random individual actions. The area is not a mere collection of individuals with their established separate identities but is a composite of multiple shifting communities, networks, and alliances. New identities are forged around the compound identities and distinctive work that brought people to the region. Symbols are used by individuals to shape meaning, but they are also used by groups to define the whole region. Technology thus has implications not only for individuals but also for the whole community, as Silicon Valley people learn to live in a culture of their own creation.

The process of creating new culture is called ethnogenesis. Innovative economic patterns, technologies, and social organizations are invented to replace or augment the old ways. A distinctive ethos comes first to be associated with that way of living, and then to actually define the new society. As I cast about for cross-cultural examples, I found historical frontiers to be rife with instances of ethnogenesis.

When a population moves into a new territory, it lacks the resources and often the desire to duplicate the parent society. Economic specializations are impossible to duplicate in the new sparse setting, or are wildly inappropriate. The old social order is insufficiently reproduced, and new relationships and values are instituted. There are many historical examples of this process. In the post-Roman frontier society that divided early medieval Europe, extending the social order of "civilized" Europe was no longer simply a military exercise to extend the political economy of Rome. The infrastructure for such a wholesale conversion was lacking. Instead the agents of cultural conversion were linked to the Holy Roman Church.

In the fifth, sixth, and seventh centuries monasticism provided the incubator for a number of cultural inventions that transformed Western Europe. The "outposters" of monastic life did not simply duplicate the social order of the societies from which they were drawn; they created new structures. The monastics established the Benedictine rule to create islands of industry and cultural reproduction. The new monastic social orders marked "milestones in economic history," radically reorganizing the patterns of work practices (Sullivan 1979: 33). The new orders mandated manual labor for people from all classes—even the nobles—some of whom would never have known such labor before. They also introduced a civilian lifestyle regulated by schedules, heretofore a military concept.

The religious orders invented new managerial techniques to govern the monks. Hagiographies, the stories of saints' lives, created a lore of leadership stories that defined what it meant to be "good." The ideals of denial of "human nature" and submission to God reshaped the qualities expected not only of holy men but also of kings, warriors, and workers. The medieval ethos, a pessimism that mistrusted human frailty and advocated utter dependence on God, flowed from monastic ideology. That ideology underlay a religious epistemology, an explanation of the universe, and a religious problem-solving perspective that dominated both medieval intellectual endeavor and the actions of people in everyday life. God, not the chemical properties of willow bark, relieved pain and healed the sick. God dominated discourse, from political pronouncements to the profanities that invoked God's body parts. Monks were "Christ's athletes," an image that suggested action and sanctity as models for community. Born of frontier innovations, the social organizations and beliefs of the monasteries thus transformed historic Europe.

In Silicon Valley, ethnogenesis takes a different form. Corporate entities and transorganizational networks dominate the social order. The heroes are technological innovators, whose admirable qualities are creativity, efficiency, and entrepreneurship. Elliot's[1] account of Silicon Valley's success reflects this admiration:

> We're optimistic here in Silicon Valley because we have no reason not to be. I mean a little company called Fairchild Semiconductor started messing around with these integrated circuits, and boom, Silicon Valley happened! And then some researcher in Stanford started messing around with the DNA molecule and splicing it, and boom, we have the biotechnology revolution! . . . The ground zero is right around Stanford, the epicenter, and . . . the boom can be heard around the world. So sure, we're optimistic about technology. The internet . . . that basically started here with Marc Andreessen [creator of the Mosaic browser and cofounder of Netscape], and what he did for providing the graphic user interface. I mean the ARPANET had been around for decades. But who used it? You know, a couple of researchers? Then you provide a graphical user interface, and boom, [he laughs] the world is using it!

The accounts of heroes foster an optimistic worldview, dramatic and successful. The engineering skills that underpin that heroism are dominated by planning, design, and other future-oriented activities. These qualities are imbued in the models of leadership that extend beyond industry into education, governance, and even religion. They create a distinct problem-solving perspective in which innovation is favored over following the tried-and-true. Technological solutions are promoted for a variety of social ills, from poor health to illiteracy. Silicon Valley is particularly vulnerable to the " 'dazzle' effect—presuming that the best solutions are the most technological" (Hakken 1993: 118). Technology is "cool," and to be a part of it, even tangentially, is "exciting." Engineering thinking processes link function with structure, what things do with what they are. This framework is applied in turn to human relationships, instrumentally linking what people do and who they are, making efficiency, networking, and innovation inherently admirable.

The chief agent for the penetration of these notions into the culture is the workplace, Silicon Valley's counterpart to a medieval monastery. Silicon Valley has an array of corporate cultures—each with its own mission, structure, and "culture of values"—that are shared, if only temporarily, by its regular workforce. Temporary workers may partake of the culture, hoping to use their participation in it as a vehicle for promotion. Immersion in the corporate culture, not always possible for telecommuters or outside contractors, is viewed as the instrument for enculturation and

[1] The author's research is based on extensive interviews with employees of Silicon Valley high-tech firms who are identified only by a first name.

success. Some companies, like Apple, view their culture as a key commodity. While the new monochrome logo makes it no longer necessary to "bleed six colors"—a term borrowed from the old rainbow-colored logo that was once used to describe corporate loyalty—work at Apple is viewed in missionary hues. Beth, a researcher, comments:

> Being in Silicon Valley, it's part of a culture of people who put their heart and soul into their jobs. . . . [It] seems to be more socially conscious. . . . [Y]ou think about how the place you work affects the community or affects the world. . . . When I first [worked at] Apple, we felt we were changing the world. At Apple you definitely have the feeling that you impact people's lives.

David Packard's book, *The H-P Way* (1995), recites the history of two men working out of a garage as the origin-myth of a philosophy of democratic and inclusive management that continues to guide the organization. Such companies define a work style, a mission, and an ethos that tries to transcend mere employment, taking it to the level of social transformation. As I noted in the previous chapter, people are changed through the process of management training sessions and by the process of management itself—setting goals, meeting objectives, and anticipating market changes.

Jerome, a veteran electrical engineer turned executive, predicts that   10
work will increasingly demand that individuals manage themselves or risk being completely consumed:

> We'll get up, shower, brush our teeth, have breakfast [and start working]. There would be a lot of information sources available. There is a very . . . compelling scenario that work could become a twenty-four-[hour] experience, which, I think, would be horrible. But the information technology will allow you to do that. So, I think it will be dependent on you and your own self-discipline to separate the church and the state. [Each one of us will] have to separate what I'm going to spend on work and what I'm going to spend on my personal life because lines will blur.

Workers in Silicon Valley are viewed as mobile "bundles of skills," and they must constantly work on themselves to meet changing demands. This "work" includes self-marketing, keeping one's résumé updated and one's social network intact, and accurately anticipating the changes in future products and the skills they will require. Jeff, a survivor of many project closures, notes:

> So, you know, the companies are always looking for the next product or the right technology or the right way to market what they've got and to fight down their competitors and keep their niche. And their employees

are doing exactly the same thing from a different angle. They're trying to find the right job within the company to keep their job security and to keep their career nicely burnished and looking good. You make a wrong decision, a wrong prediction, about the market, and suddenly you're in a backwater product—[the] project that gets canceled and becomes unimportant. And the skills you spent two years investing in it are not interesting anymore. A bad guess can leave you kind of stranded, and it can be a real hunt to find a project that will . . . energize your career again. Which way am I gonna jump? What's the market going to look like in two years? Is this the hot project, or [is] this going to be the one they suddenly realize was a total waste of fifteen million dollars and gets canceled next summer?

The prediction of the future job market and upgrading of skills become the leading passion of workers in the Valley. It also makes it clear that the burden for maintaining the social contract between worker and company is placed on the individual worker.

The ambivalence inherent in the relationship between worker and company is seen vividly in their discourse on loyalty. Job mobility drives a social contract that is increasingly one of mutual instrumentality. Turnover in Silicon Valley is twice that of the national average (Joint Venture: Silicon Valley Network 1999: 10). Loyalty is not viewed as a lifelong contract between workers and companies, but a temporary arrangement. Workers have learned the hard way about the realities of the social contract. Jeff again notes wisely:

> Being laid off feels like being back-stabbed, but you have to keep the company afloat, so—I tend to be forgiving about that. There's a little cynicism worked in there. You go to work for a company and they come at you all "rah-rah" and they talk about "team spirit" and the "company loyalty." . . . There is such a thing as company loyalty, and it can work both ways. But you have to remember that you're working for a business that's responsible to its shareholders. And loyalty stops there. If they stop the money, loyalty goes. And that's . . . fair. If [my old company] was loyal to all the people it had laid off and not laid them off, it would probably be gone now. And we'd still be out of a job. That's tough; that's the realities of life. [The company] was loyal in a different way and gave us nice severance packages. I worked for a company once that tried intensely hard to be loyal to its people and did go out of business.

The need for workers, who may return as contract workers after being laid off, has led to a climate in which layoffs must be handled gingerly. "Most companies are now trying to keep their cool in the exit process. Ex-employees don't want to burn any bridges either. And employee recycling has become an ecological business necessity" (Ewell 1997: 1A, 8A).

References

Ewell, Miranda. 1997. "Sweet Sorrow Tech-Style." *San Jose Mercury News*, June 17, 1A, 8A.

Hakken, David. 1993. "Computing and Social Change: New Technology and Workplace Transformation, 1980–1990." *Annual Review of Anthropology* 22: 107–32.

Joint Venture: Silicon Valley Network. 1999. *Workforce Study: An Analysis of the Workforce Gap in Silicon Valley.* San Jose: Joint Venture: Silicon Valley Network.

Packard, David. 1995. *The H-P Way: How Bill Hewlett and I Built Our Company.* Edited by David Kirby and Karen Lewis. New York: HarperBusiness.

Sullivan, Richard. 1979. "The Medieval Monk as Frontiersman." In *The Frontier: Comparative Studies.* Vol. 2, ed. William Savage and Stephen Thompson, pp. 25–49. Norman: University of Oklahoma Press.

UNDERSTANDING THE TEXT

1. Define in your own words the sociological term "ethnogenesis" (para. 2).

2. Catalogue the ways in which Silicon Valley culture resembles a religious community, according to English-Lueck.

3. How, in the author's view, do "engineering thinking processes" (para. 7) affect human relationships?

4. How are Silicon Valley workers viewed, both by themselves and by their employers?

5. How would you characterize English-Lueck's tone here, and what attitude toward the Silicon Valley ethos does it convey?

EXPLORING AND DEBATING THE ISSUES

1. Write an essay in which you assess English-Lueck's comparison of Silicon Valley culture with monastic culture. To what extent do you share her sense that high-tech communities operate in a way similar to religious communities?

2. This selection was written during the peak of the Silicon Valley boom, when unemployment fell below 2 percent. Since then, the dot-com frenzy has fallen victim to a severe economic slowdown. To what extent has the Silicon Valley ethos that English-Lueck describes remained the dominant Californian mentality? To develop evidence for your position, you might analyze local newspapers or business magazines or visit an online source such as http://www.siliconvalley.com. You might consult as well Andrew Murr and Jennifer Ordonez, "Tarnished Gold" (p. 383).

3. Write an essay in which you analyze the meaning of work for the high-tech employees whom English-Lueck describes. Has work transcended the ordinary need to earn a living? You might develop your discussion by interviewing acquaintances who work in the high-tech industry or, alternately, students who are aspiring to work in that field.

4. English-Lueck claims that various Silicon Valley companies have their own "corporate culture." Visit the websites of several big high-tech firms, such as Apple or Hewlett-Packard, and analyze the image the sites create for their companies. Are the sites designed to "dazzle" visitors?

5. How does the Silicon Valley ethos that English-Lueck describes relate to the California dream defined by James J. Rawls ("California: A Place, a People, a Dream," p. 22)? Be sure to note similarities as well as differences.

The Castro Q&A

KQED

Like many neighborhoods in California, the Castro District of San Francisco has been transformed by immigration, but you will not find the immigrants who have redefined the identity of the Castro on any conventional census form because they are gay men and lesbians who began coming to the neighborhood in large numbers in the 1970s. As a result, the Castro has become something of a "signature" ethnic neighborhood—as Peter L. Stein, a filmmaker whose film *The Castro* charts the history of a community that is now a symbol of gay liberation, puts it. But like other such neighborhoods, including San Francisco's Chinatown, the Castro may be in danger of becoming a "Disneyland version" of itself—that is, commercialized to the point of political irrelevance. In this interview with **KQED**, Northern California's flagship Public Broadcasting radio station, Stein describes both the history of the Castro and his own experience of growing up there before the change, when it was still an ethnic working-class neighborhood.

It was an unlikely setting for a revolution. A modest San Francisco neighborhood became, virtually overnight, an icon for a social and political movement. Filmmaker Peter L. Stein reflects on the making of the Castro, which traces the dramatic transformation of a quiet, working-class neighborhood of European immigrants into an international symbol of gay liberation.

Q: Why is this documentary about a neighborhood in San Francisco important to a national audience?

A: I think that the story of San Francisco's Castro District is one of the great immigrant stories of our country. The twist is, though, that these immigrants weren't fleeing distant tyrants or famines but intolerant communities and families in their own country. Once they

found each other in the streets of the Castro, they built a culture together, found political strength, and became part of a movement that
was sweeping the nation. More than any other place, this one neighborhood came to symbolize, for better or for worse, the growing
visibility of a group of people whose invisibility would have been preferred by much of the country.

Q: You're seeming to claim the Castro is the first gay neighborhood. How
can that be?

A: Oh, even as far back as the 1920s there were certainly neighborhoods 5
where homosexuals knew they could find each other, not only in San
Francisco but notably in Greenwich Village in New York. But before
the era of the Castro, so-called gay neighborhoods were associated
strictly with nightlife, or vice and prostitution, or at best a kind of
Bohemian attitude that tolerated everybody, not just gays and lesbians. The Castro was really the first place where gay people set out
to plant a rainbow flag in a neighborhood and stake a claim to it as
their turf, where they could own businesses, buy property, elect their
own officials, and walk down the street as a gay or lesbian person
twenty-four hours a day. This was new. It was a new way of thinking
about being a gay person in America. Not only could you be visible;
you could have a home base. And your strength could be counted at
the polls, at the cash register, in the property tax rolls. That's a powerful shift for a group of people who never felt they could be "at
home" anywhere.

Nowadays you have neighborhoods in many cities—West Hollywood, Chicago's North Halsted Street, and Miami's South Beach, for
example—that are proudly gay-identified. But the Castro, because it
sprang up so fast and with such notoriety, became a kind of archetype of gay America. It also became a lightning rod for America's discomfort with so-called gay power.

Q: It seems that gay life was not very well recorded until the explosion of
the 1970s. Did that hamper your efforts to tell the story?

A: Gay history is mainly a hidden history until very recently. We are fortunate in having a local repository, the Gay and Lesbian Historical
Society of Northern California, that has tried to preserve the images
and the ephemera of gay life in this area. But it took a lot of hunting.
My associate producer David Condon and I spoke with some two
hundred people before ever rolling a foot of tape. Sometimes we were
fortunate in our discoveries: a visiting out-of-towner happened to find
out about our project and supplied us with exquisite and poignant

home movies of gay life in San Francisco in the forties and fifties. And sometimes we lost out: many of the important storytellers of the Castro, who should by all rights be around to share their tale, have died in the last fifteen years. AIDS casts such an enormous shadow over the neighborhood.

Q: Were you ever concerned that the tragedy of AIDS would overwhelm your documentary?

A: AIDS is overwhelming, and it had to be dealt with in the story. But 10 here again, time and history are funny things. I don't think I could have made this documentary even three years ago. The neighborhood was still in the depths of a kind of psychic trauma that couldn't allow for any perspective on the momentous drama that happened there in the seventies. But when we began shooting in 1996, it seems that gay men of the generation who had lived through the nightmare were just beginning to turn the corner on AIDS—not simply from a health standpoint but in a larger sense. It seems people were beginning to try to make sense of the big picture—and to remember with fondness the roller-coaster ride they had been on. And I think that joy of reminiscence is so important.

Q: A surprising bit of trivia from the documentary is that one of Tony Bennett's signature songs, "I Left My Heart in San Francisco," was written by two gay men. What are some other gems that you uncovered?

A: Yes, "I Left My Heart in San Francisco" was written by George Cory and Douglas Cross, two songwriters from New York who visited the city in the 1950s and were obviously taken with what they found here. It turns out that San Francisco in the 1950s was pretty well known as a friendly town for gays, despite the routine entrapments, harassment, and police raids they suffered. Another surprise I found—and this is not really trivia at all, but pretty important—was regarding San Francisco's well-developed gay political community long before the Castro and Harvey Milk. You know, "gay liberation" is often seen as being born in June 1969 with the riots at New York's Stonewall Bar. And certainly that uprising was nationally significant. But four years earlier in San Francisco, an incident took place on New Year's Day that put this city's gay and lesbian community on the map. There was a raid on a gay fundraising event that angered a lot of progressive heterosexuals (because some of them had been arrested too!), and eventually a judge threw out all the charges. It didn't have the national impact that Stonewall did, but it helped develop a public awareness in San Francisco that gays and lesbians should be, to some degree, left unharassed.

And then, of course, there is the Twin Peaks Bar. In the early 1970s, a couple of lesbians bought one of the old Irish bars at the corner of Castro and Market Streets. It was pretty decrepit, dark and quiet. At the time, the trend in the swinging straight taverns was the "fern bar" look—big windows, lots of plants, and a big wooden bar. Well, the women decided to open a gay men's bar with a similar look, and they installed enormous plate-glass windows fronting Castro Street. It's hard to believe, but it was the first time that a gay bar had opened itself up so the world could look inside. That was only twenty-five years ago. And the bar is still there.

Q: What drew you to the story of the Castro District?

A: I have a rather unusual connection to it because I am one of those rare people who didn't immigrate to San Francisco to begin a new life but instead was actually born and raised here—as was my father. We watched the neighborhood change before our eyes. So as a native, I could sympathize with the sense of loss that many of the old-timers felt in seeing their tight-knit community break apart. But just as important, I'm keenly aware of how transforming the experience of the Castro was to a whole generation of gay men and women—the sense of finding their "people" for the first time. So I had a unique perspective on the history.

Interestingly, though, when I first moved back to San Francisco as an adult in the early eighties, I didn't really like the Castro. I found it claustrophobic, too homogeneous, and relentlessly sexualized. My women friends felt invisible there. But after getting to know so many men and women whose lives were changed by the experience of the neighborhood, I really came to have a sense of wonder about the history that happened there. Even with its problems, the Castro is really an extraordinary chapter in a larger struggle that virtually every American minority has undergone—the struggle for identity, survival, and ultimately, acceptance. And that was a story I wanted to tell.

Q: The documentary brings up some of the problems the neighborhood has experienced—not just from neighbors but from within the gay community. Is there a lot of criticism about the Castro?

A: Well at first, the very fact that a lot of open homosexuals were claiming a neighborhood as their "turf" was problematic for many of the old-timers. But it's important to point out that on the whole, Eureka Valleyites have been extremely tolerant of the earth-shaking changes that swept the neighborhood. Of course, many of them benefited, as they watched their property values skyrocket in the 1970s and 1980s. But there were wonderful changes that happened, too. Places like Most Holy Redeemer Church, which at the outset was very critical of the gay "influx," turns out now to be a very progressive, gay-friendly congregation that turned their old convent into an AIDS hospice.

Within the gay community, women and people of color have always felt marginalized by the very white, very mainstream, very male world that the Castro became in the 1970s. And only in the last ten years has the gay community begun to address these issues. To this day, there are still no women's bars or hangouts in the Castro.

Q: Where is the neighborhood headed now?   20

A: There is a lot of trepidation over the growing commercialization of the Castro. And it's a fascinating parallel with some of the other "signature" ethnic neighborhoods in the United States, like San Francisco's Chinatown or Boston's [Italian] North End. Parts of those neighborhoods have become Disneyland versions of themselves, with no relation to the communities they once served. And as gays and lesbians find that they can live in lots of different places without fear, the very need for a "gay neighborhood" may in fact be obsolete. So what's to keep the Castro from becoming just another yuppie enclave?

But you know, one of the people I interviewed for the show, Sharon Johnson, told me a wonderful story. She grew up in the neighborhood when it was Eureka Valley, and she's seen it change a lot. She met a gay taxi driver in the Castro a little while ago who said, "I've only been here a couple of months, but somehow, this place feels like home." And Sharon said, "Well, welcome home." And that's really the spirit of the place. It has always opened its arms to newcomers who needed a place to call home. I hope it never loses that.

UNDERSTANDING THE TEXT

1. Summarize in your own words the ways in which the Castro District resembles an immigrant community, according to filmmaker Peter L. Stein, who is interviewed in this selection.

2. How has the AIDS epidemic affected the Castro District?

3. How is the Castro District an "archetype of gay America" (para. 6), according to Stein?

4. What internal tensions exist in the Castro's gay community, according to Stein?

5. Why, in Stein's view, was the opening of the Twin Peaks Bar a watershed moment in gay history?

EXPLORING AND DEBATING THE ISSUES

1. Write an essay in which you evaluate the validity of Peter L. Stein's analogy between the Castro District and immigrant communities. To develop your ideas, consult Jewelle Taylor Gibbs and Teiahsha Bankhead, "Coming to California: Chasing the Dream" (p. 84).

2. Stein claims that, as with many ethnic neighborhoods, "[t]here is a lot of trepidation over the growing commercialization of the Castro" (para. 21). Visit a gay or ethnic community in your city, and interview residents and shopkeepers about future development plans for their neighborhood. Use the results of your interviews as the basis for an argument for or against the proposition that commercialization harms the character of such communities.

3. Write an argument that supports, refutes, or modifies Stein's suggestion that "the very need for a 'gay neighborhood' may in fact be obsolete" (para. 21). As you develop your ideas, you might consider the various debates, both in California and nationally, over the legality of same-sex marriage and the attitudes toward homosexuality that are expressed in those debates.

4. Rent a videotape of *The Castro*, and write an essay in which you define the "spirit of the place" (para. 22).

As If the Farmer Died

DAVID MAS MASUMOTO

Today the Central Valley is better known for its gigantic agribusinesses than for individual farmers, but the breed has not entirely disappeared. One such farmer is
David Mas Masumoto (b. 1954), a third-generation Japanese American who,
while not tending his family's eighty acres of peach trees and grapevines in Del
Rey, writes the stories and essays that are making him one of California's newest
literary voices. In this selection from *Epitaph for a Peach: Four Seasons on My
Family Farm* (1995), Masumoto reflects on his decision to abandon his war against
the "weeds" that infest his fields, regarding them instead as "native grasses" that
belong there. By foregoing the costly and toxic use of chemical pesticides, Masumoto thus offers a model for other Central Valley farmers. Winner of the 1986
James Clavell National Japanese American Literary Contest, Masumoto is also the
author of *Silent Strength* (1985), *Country Voices* (1987), *Harvest Sun: Planting
Roots in American Soil* (1998), and *Four Seasons in Five Senses: Things Worth Sa-
voring* (2003).

Allowing Nature to Take Over

I used to have armies of weeds on my farm. They launch their annual assault with the first warm weather of spring, parachuting seeds behind
enemy lines and poking up in scattered clumps around the fields.

They work underground first, incognito to a passing farmer like me.
By the end of winter, dulled by the holidays and cold fog, I have my
guard down. The weeds take advantage of my carelessness.

The timing of their assault is crucial. They anticipate the subtle
lengthening of each day. With exact calculation they germinate and push
upward toward the sunlight, silently rooting themselves and establishing
a foothold. The unsuspecting farmer rarely notices any change for days.

Then, with the first good spring rain, the invasion begins. With
beachheads established, the first wave of sprouting creatures rises to
boldly expose their green leaves. Some taunt the farmer and don't even
try to camouflage themselves. Defiantly they thrust their new stalks as
high as possible, leaves peeling open as the plant claims more vertical
territory. Soon the concealed army of seeds explodes, and within a week
what had been a secure, clear territory is claimed by weeds. They seem to
be everywhere, no farm is spared the invasion.

Then I hear farmers launching their counterattack. Tractors roar from   5
their winter hibernation, gunbarrel-gray exhaust smoke shoots into the
air, and cold engines churn. Oil and diesel flow through dormant lines as
the machines awaken. Hungry for work, they will do well when let loose in
the fields. The disks and cultivators sitting stationary throughout winter

248

rains await the tractor hitch. The blades are brown with rust stains, bearings and gears cold and still since last fall. But I sense they too may be anxious to cleanse themselves in the earth and regain their sleek steel shimmer.

Even the farmers seem to wear peculiar smiles. Through the cold winter season, they were confined to maintenance, repairing equipment, fixing broken cement irrigation gates, replanting lost trees and vines. Their hibernation culminates with a desk assignment at the kitchen table, where they sit surrounded by piles of papers, laboring on taxes (farmers are required to file by March first). After restless hours of poring through shoe boxes of receipts and trying to make sense of instructions written by IRS sadists eager to punish all of us who are self-employed, farmers long for a simple task outside. We are anxious to walk our fields, to be productive, to work our land. A full winter's worth of pent-up energy is unleashed on the tiny population of weeds.

Within a day or two, the genocide is complete. Fields become "clean," void of all life except vines and trees. Farmers take no prisoners. I can sometimes count the number of weeds missed by their disks. "Can't let any go to seed," a neighbor rationalizes. Each seed becomes a symbol of evil destruction and an admission of failure.

Farmers also enlist science to create a legion of new weapons against the weeds. They spray preemergent herbicides, killing latent seed pods before they germinate. Others use contact or systemic killers, burning the delicate early growth of weeds and injecting the plants with toxins that reach down to the roots. As spring weeds flourish between rows, a strip of barren earth beneath each vine or tree magically materializes from a spray applied a month or two before. At times I wonder what else is killed in order to secure the area.

A weed might be defined as any undesirable plant. On my farm, I used to call anything that wasn't a peach tree or a grapevine a weed. I too considered a field clean if it contained nothing but dirt, barren of anything green except what I had planted. All my neighbors did likewise. We'd compete to see whose field would be the cleanest. But our fields weren't clean. They were sterile.

We pay a high price for sterility, not only in herbicide bills and hours   10
of disking but also in hidden costs like groundwater contamination. Some farmers can no longer use a certain herbicide because the California Department of Agriculture tested and discovered trace residues contaminating the water tables beneath their farms. It had been widely used because it kills effectively and is relatively cheap; for about $10 per acre it would sterilize an entire field.

But signatures of a clean field can stay with the farm for years. Behind my house, I planted some landscape pines, hardy, cheap, grow-anywhere black pines—that kept dying. They died a slow death, the needle tips burning before turning completely brown, the top limbs succumbing first, the degeneration marching down toward the heartwood like a deadly cancer. Uncertain of the cause of death, I gave up trying to grow the pines after the third cremation. Staring at the barren area I at last discovered the reason: nothing grew on that strip of earth. The preemergent herbicide I once used remains effective and has left a long-term brand on the land.

But I now have very few weeds on my farm. I removed them in a single day using a very simple method. I didn't even break into a sweat. I simply redefined what I call a weed.

It began with an uncomfortable feeling, like a muse whispering in my ear, which led to an observation about barren landscapes. It doesn't make sense to try and grow juicy grapes and luscious peaches in sterile ground. The terms *juicy* and *luscious* connote land that's alive, green most of the year with plants that celebrate the coming of spring.

A turning point came when a friend started calling his weeds by a new name. He referred to them as "natural grasses." I liked that term. It didn't sound as evil as "weeds," it had a soft and gentle tone about it. So I came to think of my weeds as part of the natural system at work on my land, part of allowing nature to take over my farm.

And nature did take over. Once I let my guard down and allowed a generation of seeds to germinate, they exploded everywhere. For years I had deceived myself into thinking I had destroyed every weed seed. I was wrong, they were just waiting for an opportunity.

The first weed of spring is the pineapple weed, covering the vine berms. But it quickly wilts with the first heat of May. Chickweed hugs every tree, growing into a lush mat before dying with the first eighty-degree days. This grass may be allelopathic, producing toxins that kill competing weeds. Because few other plants grow through the mat, the yellowed and dry chickweed works like a protective mulch guarding the tree trunks.

By the middle of spring, the grasses flourish and a sea of weeds fills all but the sandiest and weakest earth. I try to keep my vine and orchard berms clear, a lesson gleaned from an earlier confrontation with a weed named mare's tail. This tall and slender creature can grow straight up into a vine leaf canopy and out the top. Mare's tail doesn't hurt vines, but at harvest the workers must battle the pollen and fight through a wall of stalks and leaves to reach the precious grapes. So I try and keep my new natural grasses away from the vine berms and tree trunks.

As nature takes over my farm, everything grows voraciously. New insect life swarms in my fields. Aphids coat sow thistle like pulsating black paint. Normally aphids aren't a problem for grapevines and peach trees, they would rather suck on sow thistle. But they are denied that meal because of the thousands of lady beetles that invade my fields for spring feasting. I wonder what other invisible life thrives in the natural grasses, what pathogens and parasites join my farm. I can't measure their presence but I feel secure, and the grapes and peaches still look fine.

I walk my fields and feel life and energy. In the evening a chorus of voices calls out, legions of insects venturing out to feed. On family bike rides we have to keep our mouths closed or bugs will fly in.

I often think, There's something going on out here, and smile to myself.   20

I was a fool to try to control weeds. I fooled myself by keeping fields sterile without knowing the long-term prices I was paying. Allowing nature to take over proved easier than I imagined. Most grasses will naturally die back without my intervention, and I've learned to recognize those few that I should not ignore. Most natural grasses are not as bad as farmers fear.

In the eyes of some farmers, my farm looks like a disaster, with weeds gone wild. Even my father grows uncomfortable. He farmed most of his life during an era of control, and to him the farm certainly now appears completely chaotic. He keeps a few rows next to his house weed-free as if to maintain a buffer between him and a lifetime of nightmares from fighting weeds.

I still have bad dreams about some obnoxious grasses like Bermuda, but my nightmares ended once I stopped thinking of them as weeds.

Lizard Dance

While weeding, I feel something tickle my calf. Without stopping my shovel, I brush the back of my leg. It happens again and I assume the clumps of johnsongrass I dug out are rolling off their pile, the thick stalks and stems attacking their killer in a vain attempt at revenge. Finally, I shake my right leg, and the thing bolts upward.

Immediately I throw down my shovel and stamp my feet. The adrenaline shoots into my system and my heart races. I initiate my lizard dance, shaking my leg, pounding my feet, patting my pants as the poor creature runs wild up my leg. The faster I spin and whirl, the more confused the lizard becomes and the more frantically he scrambles up and down the dark caverns of my pant leg.   25

In the middle of my dance, I begin laughing, recalling the familiar feel of a lizard running up my pants, through my shirt, and down my sleeves. My body dances uncontrollably to the feel of its tiny feet and little claws grabbing my skin. I try to slow down, knowing the lizard will too if we both relax.

But as the creature scampers up higher and higher my imagination runs wild. Vulnerable body parts flash in my mind.

If other workers were around, they would laugh, watching me tug at my belt, frantically trying to drop my pants. With luck, I won't open a crevice in my shorts, inviting the lizard into another dark hiding place. Instead he'll be attracted to daylight, leap out of my crotch, and tumble to the ground, dazed for a moment before scampering into the safety of weeds and undergrowth.

I enjoy the return of lizards to my farm. They were plentiful in my youth, soaking up the rays of the sun, eating bugs and insects, living happily in the patches of grasses and weeds. Then we disked and plowed their homes and sprayed to kill most of their food. The lizards left.

I didn't plan on raising lizards, but they're part of a natural farm landscape. Besides, their presence reminds me of my childhood. I can't return to those days but I can try and foster new life on the farm, along with laughter and the lizard dance.

Farming with Chaos

Chaos defines my farm. I allow natural grasses to go wild. I see new six-legged creatures migrating into my fields, which now look like green pastures. I watch with paranoid panic, wanting to believe all will be fine while terrified I may lose the crop and even the farm. I need a lesson on managing chaos.

The small town of Del Rey is two and a half miles from my farm. When Japanese immigrants first settled there in the early 1900s, one of the first structures erected was a community hall, a place for meetings, gatherings, dinners, and festivals, a refuge from the tough life in the fields. The grounds around the hall were never truly landscaped. The sparse collection of trees and shrubs was lost in droughts and freezes, taken out for a basketball court, or neglected during World War II, when all Japanese were forced to evacuate the West Coast, leaving the trees without a caretaker. But there are still a few trees and bushes at the old hall, sporadically cared for during community gatherings. At one of these meetings I was taught my first lesson on chaos.

Two old-timers were pruning one of the Japanese black pines. They were retired farmers and gardeners, a common dual profession for struggling farmers who found that they could supplement their income by tending other people's gardens. The two old men worked in silence as they clipped away, pulling off needles and shaping the tree. The pine was not an eighty-year-old bonsai masterpiece. It was probably something left over from one of their gardening jobs, an extra pine donated to the hall perhaps fifteen years ago and gradually shaped and pruned.

I asked if I could help. They both nodded without looking up and kept working. I waited for some direction but they kept probing the bottom of each limb, stopping at a small outgrowth and quickly snapping it off. Their fingers gently raked the branches, tugging and separating unwanted growth. Their glassy old eyes wandered across the needles, stopping and guiding clippers, then moving on, scanning and studying the tree.

"How do you know what to cut?" I asked. One glanced up and smiled   35
softly. His entire face seemed to mold around the grin as if all the wrinkles worked in unison to accommodate the gesture. A smile was familiar to that face.

I repeated my question and he whispered something in Japanese I could not hear or understand. They both returned to their clipping and snipping. The next time, just as he cut a small branch, I pointed and asked, "Why did you cut that one?"

He looked up as if wakened from a trance and blinked. "*Saa* . . . I don't know." He returned to his work.

I was relegated to watching their movements, trying to guess why they cut or passed on a branch, why some needles were pulled and thinned and others weren't. Their hands massaged the pine, their eyes wandering up and down a scaffold as fingers stroked and probed the interior of the tree. I tried with my hands but was quickly entangled in decisions. When do you leave a new branch and for how long? What was the rule when pruning? What are the criteria for cutting? I was overlooking something very basic, something I couldn't see in front of me.

The pine was only maintained once or twice a year. It had a wild quality about it, unlike the meticulously tended backyard Japanese garden variety. It was a living chaos, a reflection of the natural ebbs and flows of erratic irrigations, unprotected frosts and heat waves, and inconsistent care from an aging ethnic farm community. Yet out of this uncontrolled growth, these two old-timers were sculpting a beautiful tree, simple and innocent.

I never did grasp the art of pruning that pine tree. Later, during a   40
summer heat wave, when the farmers were all out desperately trying to get water to thirsty grapes and trees, one of the hall's pine trees

died. (I also learned that both old men had acute hearing problems and probably hadn't heard any of my questions.) But as I try to farm more naturally, I keep thinking of those two farmers and their dancing hands. They had no secret pruning method. Perhaps there is no secret to farming and managing chaos—you blend tradition and science with some common sense and trust you'll have a crop. In fact, most good farmers I know are like those two old men, tending to their trees and vines as best they can, comfortable with their work, and confident that the final product will be fine. Whether they know it or not, seasoned farmers are already experts at chaos.

As If the Farmer Died

This year I've abandoned my old farmwork schedules, which were often set by the calendar. I have no set mowing program or irrigation timeline. I devote more hours to monitoring my fields, and I curb my impulse to find quick fixes. Not only can I identify the pests that are munching on my fruits, I also recognize when they don't seem to be doing any more damage than usual. I'm learning to live with them, realizing that I've probably always had these pests but never scrutinized the farm so closely. I monitor the weeds as they creep up to new heights and discover some I have never seen before. I watch for new lush growth and wonder if the compost I added last fall is working. Each day I accumulate impressions more than lessons, as I develop the instincts of those two old farmers.

I used to farm with a strategy of un-chaos. I was looking for regularity, less variability, ignoring the uniqueness of each farm year. But now my farm resembles the old pine at the Del Rey Hall; wildness is tolerated, even promoted. The farm becomes a test of the unconventional, a continuous experiment, a journey of adaptation and living with change. I've even had to change my ways of counting. It's no longer important how *many* pests I have, what matters is the ratio between good bugs and bad bugs. I try to rely less and less on controlling nature. Instead I am learning to live with its chaos.

UNDERSTANDING THE TEXT

1. Explain in your own words what Masumoto means by the farming "strategy of un-chaos" (para. 42).
2. According to Masumoto, what are the different connotations of the words "weeds" and "natural grasses" (para. 14), and how do they affect our attitudes toward the land?

3. Why does Masumoto call this essay "As If the Farmer Died"?

4. Chart Masumoto's use of metaphors in the section entitled "Allowing Nature to Take Over" (para. 1). How do they shape your response to his message?

5. Characterize Masumoto's persona in this selection. What sort of person does he sound like, and how does his style affect your response to this selection?

EXPLORING AND DEBATING THE ISSUES

1. In your journal, reflect on any gardening practices that you or your family may engage in. Have you shared the desire for a "clean" (para. 7) garden, or do you prefer a "chaotic" (para. 22) garden environment? Which does more to enhance your sense of personal space? Alternately, reflect on the sort of park that you prefer to visit: an urban park with benches, walkways, and playing fields or a wilderness park with trails and little else added? Why do you prefer one over the other?

2. In class, analyze the ways in which Masumoto creates a sense of place in this selection. What message is he communicating about his farm? Which details do you find most effective in conveying that message?

3. Compare and contrast Masumoto's and Gary Snyder's ("Cultivating Wildness," p. 256) attitudes toward their land. How are their visions similar and different? How might their uses of their land affect their visions?

4. When discussing the pruning techniques of the two Japanese farmers at the community center, Masumoto is deliberately general in his description of their secret to wise plant nurturing. In class, discuss Masumoto's purpose in relating this anecdote.

5. In an essay, argue for or against the proposition that Masumoto's chaotic farming method should be applied to large-scale farming as well as to his small family farm.

Cultivating Wildness

GARY SNYDER

One of the best-known of the Beat generation poets, **Gary Snyder** (b. 1930) has long been a leading figure in American literary history and culture. But his credentials as an environmentalist are equally as impressive, and as Snyder shows here, his vision for a sustainable future in California land-use policy reveals a level of practical know-how that is anything but naive idealism. Through the management of his own land in the foothills of the Sierra Nevadas, Snyder accordingly offers a proposal for public-private land-use cooperation that could serve as a model for the rest of the nation. The author of numerous volumes of poetry and essays, Snyder's more recent works include *Right in the Trail* (1990), *No Nature: New and Selected Poems* (1992), *A Place in Space: New and Selected Prose* (1995), *Mountains and Rivers without End* (1996), and *The High Sierra of California* (2002). Snyder is Professor of English at the University of California, Davis.

Jets heading west on the Denver-to-Sacramento run start losing altitude east of Reno, and the engines cool as they cross the snowy Sierra crest. They glide low over the west-tending mountain slopes, passing above the canyon of the North Fork of the American River. If you look north out the window, you can see the Yuba River country, and if it's really clear you can see the old "diggings"—large areas of white gravel laid bare by nineteenth-century gold mining. On the edge of one of those is a little hill where my family and I live. It's on a forested stretch between the South Yuba canyon and 2,000 treeless acres of old mining gravel, all on a forty-mile ridge that runs from the High Sierra to the valley floor near Marysville, California.

From the air, you can look out over the northern quarter of the Greater Sierra ecosystem: a vast summer-dry hardwood-conifer forest, with drought-resistant shrubs and bushes in the canyons, clearcuts, and burns.

In ten minutes the jet is skimming over the levees of the Sacramento River and wheeling down the airstrip. It then takes two and a half hours to drive out of the valley and up to my place. The last three miles always seem to take the longest: we like to joke that it's still the bumpiest road we've found, go where we will.

Back in the mid-1960s I was studying in Japan. Once, while I was on a visit to California, some friends suggested that I join them in buying mountain land. In those days land and gas were both still cheap. We drove into the ridge and canyon country, out to the end of a road. We pushed through manzanita thickets and strolled in open stretches of healthy ponderosa pine. Using a handheld compass, I found a couple of the brass caps that mark corners. It was a new part of the Sierra for me. But I knew the assembly of plants—ponderosa pine, black oak, and associates—well enough to know what the rainfall and climate would be, and I knew that I liked their company. There was a wild meadow full of native bunchgrass. No regular creek, but a slope with sedges that promised subsurface water. I told my friends to count me in. I put down the money for a twenty-five acre share of the one hundred acres and then returned to Japan.

In 1969, back for good in California, we drove out to the land and   5 made a family decision to put our life there. At that time there were virtually no neighbors, and the roads were even worse than now. No power lines, no phones, and twenty-five miles—across a canyon—to town. But we had the will and some of the skills as well. I had grown up on a small farm in the Northwest and had spent time in the forests and mountains since childhood. I had worked at carpentry and been a Forest Service seasonal worker, so mountain life (at 3,000 feet) seemed doable. We weren't "in the wilderness" but rather in a zone of ecological recovery. In the hills beyond us, the Tahoe National Forest stretched for hundreds of square miles.

I had been a logger on an Indian reservation in the ponderosa pine forests of eastern Oregon, where many trees were more than two hundred feet tall and five feet through. Up north it was drier and a bit higher, so the understory was different, but it was the same adaptable cinnamon-colored pines. The trees down here topped out at about one hundred feet—getting toward being a mature stand but a long way from old growth. I talked with a ninety-year-old neighbor who had been born in the area. He told me that when he was young he had run cattle over my way and had logged here and there and that a big fire had gone through about 1920. I trimmed the stump on a black oak that had fallen and counted the rings: more than three hundred years. There were still lots of standing oaks that big around, so it was clear that the fires had not been total.

Besides the pine stands (mixed with incense cedar, madrone, a few Douglas firs) our place was a mosaic of postfire manzanita fields with small pines coming through; stable climax manzanita; an eight-acre stand of pure black oak; and some areas of blue oak, gray pine, and grasses. Also lots of the low ground-cover bush called kitkitdizze in the language of the Wintun, a nearby valley people. It was clear from the very old and scattered stumps that the land had been selectively logged once. A neighbor with an increment borer figured that some trees had been cut about 1940. The surrounding lands and the place I was making my home flowed together with unmarked boundaries—to the eye and to the creatures, it was all one.

We had our hands full the first ten years just getting up walls and roofs, bathhouse, small barn, washhouse. A lot of it was done the old way: we dropped all the trees to be used in the frame of the house with a two-man falling saw and peeled them with drawknives. Light was from kerosene lamps; we heated with wood and cooked with wood and propane. Wood-burning ranges, wood-burning sauna stoves, treadle-operated sewing machines, and propane-using Servel refrigerators from the 1950s were the targets of highly selective shopping runs. Many other young settlers found their place in northern California back in the early 1970s, so eventually there was a whole reinhabitory culture living this way in what we like to call Shasta Nation.

I set up my library and wrote poems and essays by lantern light, then went out periodically, lecturing and teaching around the country. I thought of my home as a well-concealed base camp from which I raided university treasuries. We named our place Kitkitdizze, after the aromatic little shrub.

The scattered neighbors and I started meeting once a month to talk   10
about local affairs. We were all nature lovers, and everyone wanted to cause as little impact as possible. Those with well-watered sites, with springs and meadows, put in small gardens and planted fruit trees. I tried fruit trees, a chicken flock, a kitchen garden, and beehives. The bees went first. They were totally destroyed in one night by a black bear. The kitchen garden did fairly well until the run of dry winters that started in the 1980s and may finally be over. And of course, no matter how you fence a garden, deer find a way to get in. The chickens were constant targets of northern goshawks, red-tailed hawks, raccoons, feral dogs, and bobcats. A bobcat once killed twenty-five in one month. The fruit trees are still with us, especially the apples. They, of all the cultivars, have best made themselves at home. (The grosbeaks and finches seem to always beat us to the cherries.)

But in my heart I was never into gardening. I couldn't see myself as a logger again either. Except for cutting downed oak and pine for firewood, felling an occasional pole for framing, and clearing the low limbs and underbrush well back from the homestead to reduce fire hazard, I hadn't done much with the forest. I wanted to go lightly, to get a deep sense of it, and I thought it was enough to leave it wild and to let it be the wildlife habitat it was.

Living in a place like this is absolutely delicious. Coyote-howl fugues, owl exchanges in the treetops, the almost daily sighting of deer (and hearing the rattle of antlers at rutting season), the frisson of seeing a poky rattlesnake, tracking critters in the snowfall, seeing cougar twice, running onto humongous bear scats—sharing all this with the children—is more than worth the inconveniences.

My original land partners were increasingly busy elsewhere. It took a number of years, but we bought out our old partners and ended up with the whole one hundred acres. That was sobering. Now Kitkitdizze was entirely in our hands. We were cash-poor and land-rich, and who needed more second-growth pine and manzanita? We needed to rethink our relation to this place, with its busy—almost downtown—rush of plants and creatures. Should we leave it alone? Use it, but how? And what responsibility came with it all?

Now it is two grown sons, two stepdaughters, three cars, two trucks, four buildings, one pond, two well pumps, close to one hundred chickens, seventeen fruit trees, two cats, about ninety cords of firewood, and three chainsaws later. The kerosene lights have been replaced by a photovoltaic array powering a mixed AC/DC system. The phone company put in an underground line to our whole area at its own expense. My wife, Carole, and I are now using computers, which are the writer's equivalent of a nice little chainsaw. (Chainsaws and computers both increase macho productivity and nerdy stress.) My part-time teaching job at the University of California, Davis, provides me with an Internet account. We have finally entered the late twentieth century and are tapping into political and environmental information with a vengeance.

The whole Sierra is a mosaic of ownership—various national forests, Bureau of Land Management (BLM) land, Sierra Pacific Industries land, state parks, and private holdings—but to the eye of a hawk it is one great sweep of rocks and woodland. We, along with most of our neighbors, were involved in the forestry controversies of the past decade, particularly in regard to the long-range plans for the Tahoe National Forest. We were part of a nationwide campaign to reform forest practices. The upshot was a real and positive upheaval on a national scale in the U.S. Forest Service and the promise of "ecosystem management" on our public lands—something that is not yet clearly defined.

We turned our focus next to nearby public lands managed by the BLM. It wasn't hard to see that they were a key middle-elevation part of a passageway for deer and other wildlife from high country to the valleys below, with our own holdings part of the same corridor. Soon we were catapulted into a whole new game: the BLM area manager for central California, Deane Swickard, became aware of our interest, drove up, and walked the woods with us, talked with us, consulted with the community, and then said, "Let's cooperate in the long-range planning for these lands. We can share information." We agreed to work with him and launched a biological inventory, first with older volunteers and soon with our own wild teenagers jumping in. We studied close to 3,000 forested acres. We crawled on hands and knees, belly-slid on snow, bushwhacked up and down canyons in order to find out just what was there, in what combinations, in what quantity, in what diversity.

Some of it was tallied and mapped (one local youth just back from college had learned GIS—Geographic Information System—and put the data into a borrowed Sun Sparc workstation), and the rest of our observations were put into bundles of notes. We had found some very large trees, located a California spotted owl pair, noted a little wetland with carnivorous sticky sundew, described a unique barren dome with plants found only in serpentine soils, identified large stands of vivid growing forest, and been struck by the tremendous buildup of fuel. The well-intended but ecologically ignorant fire-exclusion policies of the government agencies over the past century have made the forests of California an incredible tinderbox.

The droughty forests of California have been shaped for millennia by fire. A fire used to sweep through any given area, we are now told, roughly every twenty-five years and in doing so kept the undergrowth down and left the big trees standing. The native people also deliberately started fires, so that the California forests of two hundred years ago were structured of huge trees in parks that were fire-safe. Of course there were always some manzanita fields and recovering burns, but overall there was far less fuel. To "leave it be wild" in its present state would be risking a fire that might set the land back to first-phase brush again. The tens of thousands of homes and ranches mixed among the wooded foothills down the whole Sierra front could burn.

These studies and explorations resulted in the formation of the Yuba Watershed Institute, a nonprofit group made up of local people, which is sponsoring projects and research on forestry, biodiversity, and economic sustainability with an eye to the larger region. One of the main joint-management-plan conclusions was to try to reduce fuel load by every available means. We saw that a certain amount of smart selective logging would not be out of place, could help reduce fuel load, and might pay some of the cost of thinning and prescriptive burning. We named our lands, with the BLM's blessing, the Inimim Forest, from the Nisenan word for pine, in recognition of the first people here.

The work with fire, wildlife, and people extends through public lands and private parcels (with willing owners) alike. Realizing that our area plays a critical biological role, we are trying to learn ground rules by which humans might live together with animals in an "inhabited wildlife corridor." A San Francisco State University project for netting and banding migrant songbirds during nesting season (information for a Western Hemisphere database) is located on some Kitkitdizze brush-lands, rather than public land, simply because it's an excellent location.

Our cooperative efforts here can be seen as part of the rapidly changing outlook on land management in the West, where public-private partnership is being talked about in a big way. Joint-management agreements between local communities, other local and committed interests, and neighboring blocks of public lands are a new and potent possibility in the project of responsibly "recovering the commons" region by region. The need for ecological literacy, the sense of the home watershed, and a better understanding of our stake in public lands are beginning to permeate the consciousness of the larger society.

Lessons learned in the landscape apply to our own lands too. So this is what my family and I are borrowing from the watershed work as our own three hundred-year Kitkitdizze Plan: we'll do much more understory thinning and then a series of prescribed burns. Some patches will be left untouched by fire, to provide a control. We'll plant a few sugar pines where they fit, burn the ground under some of the oaks to see what it does for the acorn crop, burn some bunchgrass patches to see if they produce better basketry materials (an idea from the native basket-weaving revival in California). We'll have a percentage of dead oak in the forest rather than take it all for firewood. In the time of our seventh-generation granddaughter there will be a large area of fire-safe pine stands that will provide the possibility of the sale of an occasional valuable, huge, clear, old-growth sawlog.

We assume something of the same will be true on surrounding land. The wildlife will still pass through. Visitors from the highly crowded lowlands will come to walk, study, and reflect. A few people will be resident on this land, getting some part of their income from forestry work. The rest will come from the information economy of three centuries hence. There might even be a civilization with a culture of cultivating wildness.

You can say that this is outrageously optimistic. It truly is. But the possibility of saving, restoring, and wisely (yes!) using the bounty of wild nature is still with us in North America. My home base, here at Kitkitdizze, is but one tiny node in an evolving net of bioregional workers.

Beyond all this studying and managing and calculating, there's another level of knowing nature. You can go about learning the names of things and doing inventories of trees, bushes, and flowers. But nature often just flits by and is not easily seen in a hard, clear light. Our actual experience of many birds and wildlife is chancy and quick. Wildlife is known as a call, a cough in the dark, a shadow in the shrubs. You can watch a cougar on a wildlife video for hours, but the real cougar shows herself only once or twice in a lifetime. One must be tuned to hints and nuances.

After twenty years of walking right past it on my way to chores in the meadow, I actually paid attention to a certain gnarly canyon live oak one   25 day. Or maybe it was ready to show itself to me. I felt its oldness, suchness, inwardness, oakness, as if it were my own. Such intimacy makes you totally at home in life and in yourself. But the years spent working around that oak in that meadow and not really noticing it were not wasted. Knowing names and habits, cutting some brush here, getting firewood there, watching for when the fall mushrooms bulge out are skills that are of themselves delightful and essential. They also prepare one for suddenly meeting the oak.

UNDERSTANDING THE TEXT

1. In your own words, trace the evolution of Snyder's attitudes toward the land from the 1960s to the present.

2. Why does Snyder consider life at Kitkitdizze "absolutely delicious" (para. 12)?

3. What assumptions underlie Snyder's "optimistic" (para. 23) vision of a public-private management of the land?

4. Why have forest-service fire-suppression practices made wilderness areas more vulnerable to fire, according to Snyder?

EXPLORING AND DEBATING THE ISSUES

1. In your journal, reflect on the effect that being in a natural or wild area had on you during a day trip or vacation.

2. Write an analysis of the strategies that Snyder uses to create a sense of place, paying close attention to details and images that he includes.

3. Snyder lives in a near-wilderness area. Discuss in class the extent to which his visions of living harmoniously with the land can be applied to urban or suburban life.

4. Write an essay in which you support, challenge, or modify Snyder's contention that "the possibility of saving, restoring, and wisely . . . using the bounty of wild nature is still with us in North America" (para. 23).

5. Snyder is best known as a poet. Read some of his poetry (in collections such as *The Back Country* and *Turtle Island*), and write an essay in which you discuss his poetic treatment of the environment.

6. Assume Snyder's perspective, and write a response to the Chapter 6 frontispiece, "Monarch, California's last wild grizzly and symbol for state flag" (p. 378).

Barrio Boy

ERNESTO GALARZA

Joan Didion's Sacramento is a place where her pioneer ancestors established a kind of Anglo aristocracy. **Ernesto Galarza**'s Sacramento is a very different place entirely. In a reminiscence of a time just before World War I, Galarza (1905–1984) shows us the immigrants' Sacramento—a place where Mexicans, Japanese, Chinese, Filipinos, Hindus, Portuguese, Italians, Poles, Yugoslavs, and Koreans came together to make a home. Related by their common difference from the "Americans," who mostly lived in the "upper" part of town, they were distinguished by the myriad lands from which they had come. A barrio chicano fresh from Mexico, Galarza soon learned the ways of his new home, helping his fellow immigrants even as he himself developed into a *pocho*—that is, a Mexican growing up in California. The author of *Barrio Boy* (1971), from which this selection is taken, Galarza was the author of many works of fiction and nonfiction, including *Tragedy at Chualar* (1977) and *Farm Workers and Agribusinesses in California* (1977), that have established him as one of California's most prominent Latino writers.

It was late in the afternoon after countless hours from Tucson that the conductor stopped by our seat, picked up our stubs and, pointing to us, said "Sacramento." With the greatest of ease I said "tanks yoo" and felt again the excitement of arriving somewhere. We looked out at the countryside to be sure we didn't miss the first sights of the city with the Mexican name where we were going to live. As far as I could see there were rows on rows of bushes, some standing by themselves, some leaning on wires and posts, all of them without leaves. "Vineyards," my mother said. I always wanted to know the number or quantity of things. "How many?" I asked. "A heap," she answered, not just *un montón*, but *un montonal*, which meant more than you could count, nobody really knows, sky-high, infinity, millions.

We left the vineyards behind, passing by orchards and pastures with cattle. At the crossroads, our locomotive hooted a salute to droves of cattle, automobiles, and horse-drawn buggies with school children waiting to cross.

Our train began to make a great circle, slowing down. The roadbed carried the train higher than the rooftops, giving us a panorama of the city. Track crews standing by with the familiar brown faces of Mexicans waved to us. I looked hard for Gustavo and José, for the last we had heard they were working on the Southern Pacific, making tracks or locomotives. Through the window we could see long buildings with stacks belching smoke like a dozen Casas Redondas, boxcars, flatcars, coaches, gondolas, cabooses, and locomotives dismantled or waiting for repairs.

A brakeman opened the door at the front of the coach and called, "Sack-men-ah," by which we knew he meant Sa-cra-men-to, for we had passed a large sign with the name in black and white at the entrance to the corporation yard.

Unlike the Mexicans, the Americans were not in a great hurry to leave the coach. We were the last, carrying our luggage.   5

We stepped down into a frightening scene, a huge barn filled with smoke and noise and the smell of burnt oil. This was the station, nearly as long as the train and with a sooty roof twice as high as the *mercado* in Mazatlán. Our locomotive was still belching black clouds from the stack. Men were hurrying along, pulling four-wheeled carts loaded with baggage, jerking hoses close to the train and thrusting the nozzles into holes here and there, washing windows with brushes on long sticks, opening the axle boxes with hammers and banging them shut.

We dashed through the confusion over the tracks and into the waiting room, myself dragging one of the shopping bags. The depot was a gloomy, dangerous place. We sat watching the crowd thin out. Our train departed, headed in the same direction, and I felt that we were being left behind.

Out of the bag my mother pulled the small envelope with the address of the Hotel Español. She handed me the paper. Holding it I watched the men in uniforms and green visors who passed by us and the clerks behind the ticket counters. Taking a chance I stopped one and thrust the paper at him. I said "plees" and waited, pinching one corner of the envelope while he read it. Like the conductor, the man guessed our problem. He smiled and held up a forefinger, crooking and straightening it while he looked at us. I had no idea what he meant, for in Mexico you signaled people to follow you by holding up your hand and closing all the fingers over the palm with a snap a few times. But Doña Henriqueta knew instantly, and he guided us under an arch and out of the station. Handing back the envelope, he pointed down the street and smiled us on.

One more stop to ask our way with another "plees" and we were at the Hotel Español. . . .

Once the routine of the family was well started, my mother and I began   10 to take short walks to get our bearings. It was half a block in one direction to the lumberyard and the grocery store; half a block in the other to the saloon and the Japanese motion picture theater. In between were the tent and awning shop, a Chinese restaurant, a secondhand store, and several houses like our own. We noted by the numbers on the posts at the corners that we lived between 4th and 5th Streets on L.

Once we could fix a course from these signs up and down and across town we explored farther. On 6th near K there was the Lyric Theater with a sign that we easily translated into Lírico. It was next to a handsome red stone house with high turrets, like a castle. Navigating by these key points and following the rows of towering elms along L Street, one by one we found the post office on 7th and K; the cathedral, four blocks farther east; and the state capitol with its golden dome.

It wasn't long before we ventured on walks around Capitol Park, which reminded me of the charm and the serenity of the Alameda in Tepic. In some fashion Mrs. Dodson had got over to us that the capitol was the house of the government. To us it became El Capitolio or, more formally, the Palacio de Gobierno. Through the park we walked into the building itself, staring spellbound at the marble statue of Queen Isabel and Christopher Columbus. It was awesome, standing in the presence of that gigantic admiral, the one who had discovered America and Mexico and Jalcocotán, as Doña Henriqueta assured me.

After we had thoroughly learned our way around in the daytime, we found signs that did not fail us at night. From the window of the projection room of the Lyric Theater a brilliant purple light shone after dark. A snake of electric lights kept whipping round and round a sign over the Albert Elkus store. K Street on both sides was a double row of bright show windows that led up to the Land Hotel and back to Breuner's, thence down one block to the lumberyard, the grocery store, and our house. We had no fear of getting lost.

These were the boundaries of the lower part of town, for that was what everyone called the section of the city between 5th Street and the river and from the railway yards to the Y-Street levee. Nobody ever mentioned an upper part of town; at least, no one could see the difference because the whole city was built on level land. We were not lower topographically, but in other ways that distinguished between Them, the uppers, and Us, the lowers. Lower Sacramento was the quarter that people who made money moved away from. Those of us who lived in it stayed there because our problem was to make a living and not to make money. A long while back, Mr. Howard, the business agent of the union, told me there had been stores and shops, fancy residences, and smart hotels in this neighborhood. The crippled old gentleman who lived in the next room down the hall from us explained to me that our house, like the others in the neighborhood, had been the home of rich people who had stables in the backyards, with back entrances by way of the alleys. Mr. Hansen, the Dutch carpenter, had helped build such residences. When the owners moved uptown, the backyards had been fenced off and sub-divided, and small rental cottages had been built in the alleys in place of the stables. Handsome private homes were turned into flophouses for men who stayed one night, hotels for working people, and rooming houses, like ours.

Among the saloons, pool halls, lunch counters, pawnshops, and   15
poker parlors was skid row, where drunk men with black eyes and un-shaven faces lay down in the alleys to sleep.

The lower quarter was not exclusively a Mexican barrio but a mix of many nationalities. Between L and N Streets two blocks from us, the Japanese had taken over. Their homes were in the alleys behind shops, which they advertised with signs covered with black scribbles. The women walked on the street in kimonos, wooden sandals, and white stockings, carrying neat black bundles on their backs and wearing their hair in puffs with long ivory needles stuck through them. When they met they bowed, walked a couple of steps, and turned and bowed again, re-peating this several times. They carried babies on their backs, not in their arms, never laughed or went into the saloons. On Sundays the men sat in front of their shops, dressed in gowns, like priests.

Chinatown was on the other side of K Street, toward the Southern Pacific shops. Our houses were old, but those in which the Chinese kept stores, laundries, and restaurants were older still. In black jackets and skullcaps the older merchants smoked long pipes with a tiny brass cup on the end. In their dusty store windows there was always the same as-sortment of tea packages, rice bowls, saucers, and pots decorated with blue temples and dragons.

In the hotels and rooming houses scattered about the barrio the Fil-ipino farmworkers, riverboat stewards, and houseboys made their homes. Like the Mexicans, they had their own pool halls, which they called clubs. Hindus from the rice and fruit country north of the city stayed in the rooming houses when they were in town, keeping to them-selves. The Portuguese and Italian families gathered in their own neigh-borhoods along 4th and 5th Streets southward toward the Y-Street levee. The Poles, Yugo-Slavs, and Koreans, too few to take over any particular part of it, were scattered throughout the barrio. Black men drifted in and out of town, working the waterfront. It was a kaleidoscope of colors and languages and customs that surprised and absorbed me at every turn.

Although we, the foreigners, made up the majority of the population of that quarter of Sacramento, the Americans had by no means given it up to us. Not all of them had moved above 5th Street as the barrio became more crowded. The bartenders, the rent collectors, the insurance sales-men, the mates on the riverboats, the landladies, and most importantly,

the police—these were all gringos. So were the craftsmen, like the bar-
bers and printers, who did not move their shops uptown as the city grew.
The teachers of our one public school were all Americans. On skid row we
rarely saw a drunk wino who was not a gringo. The operators of the pawnshops and secondhand stores were white and mostly Jewish.

For the Mexicans the barrio was a colony of refugees. We came to   20
know families from Chihuahua, Sonora, Jalisco, and Durango. Some had
come to the United States even before the revolution, living in Texas before migrating to California. Like ourselves, our Mexican neighbors had
come this far moving step by step, working and waiting, as if they were
feeling their way up a ladder. They talked of relatives who had been left
behind in Mexico, or in some far-off city like Los Angeles or San Diego.
From whatever place they had come, and however short or long the time
they had lived in the United States, together they formed the *colonia
mexicana*. In the years between our arrival and the First World War, the
colonia grew and spilled out from the lower part of town. Some families
moved into the alley shacks east of the Southern Pacific tracks, close to
the canneries and warehouses, and across the river among the orchards
and rice mills.

The *colonia* was like a sponge that was beginning to leak along the
edges, squeezed between the levee, the railroad tracks, and the river-
front. But it wasn't squeezed dry, because it kept filling with newcomers
who found families who took in boarders, in basements, alleys, shanties,
rundown rooming houses, and flop joints where they could live.

Crowded as it was, the *colonia* found a place for these *chicanos*, the
name by which we called an unskilled worker born in Mexico and just
arrived in the United States. The *chicanos* were fond of identifying
themselves by saying they had just arrived from *el macizo*, by which they
meant the solid Mexican homeland, the good native earth. Although
they spoke of *el macizo* like homesick persons, they didn't go back. They
remained, as they said of themselves, *pura raza*. So it happened that
José and Gustavo would bring home for a meal and for conversation
workingmen who were *chicanos* fresh from *el macizo* and like ourselves,
pura raza. Like us, they had come straight to the barrio where they
could order a meal, buy a pair of overalls, and look for work in Spanish.
They brought us vague news about the revolution, in which many of
them had fought as *villistas*, *huertistas*, *maderistas*, or *zapatistas*. As an
old *maderista*, I imagined our *chicano* guests as battle-tested revolu-
tionaries, like myself.

As poor refugees, their first concern was to find a place to sleep, then to
eat and find work. In the barrio they were most likely to find all three, for
not knowing English they needed something that was even more urgent

than a room, a meal, or a job, and that was information in a language they could understand. This information had to be picked up in bits and pieces—from families like ours, from the conversation groups in the pool-rooms and the saloons.

Beds and meals, if the newcomers had no money at all, were pro-vided—in one way or another—on trust, until the new *chicano* found a job. On trust and not on credit, for trust was something between people who had plenty of nothing, and credit was between people who had something of plenty. It was not charity or social welfare but something my mother called *asistencia*, a helping given and received on trust, to be repaid because those who had given it were themselves in need of what they had given. *Chicanos* who had found work on farms or in railroad camps came back to pay us a few dollars for *asistencia* we had provided weeks or months before.

Because the barrio was a grapevine of job information, the transient   25
chicanos were able to find work and repay their obligations. The pass-word of the barrio was *trabajo* and the community was divided in two—the many who were looking for it and the few who had it to offer. Pickers, foremen, contractors, drivers, field hands, pick and shovel men on the railroad and in construction came back to the barrio when work was slack, to tell one another of the places they had been, the kind of *patrón* they had, the wages paid, the food, the living quarters, and other impor-tant details. Along 2nd Street, labor recruiters hung blackboards on their shop fronts, scrawling in chalk offers of work. The grapevine was a mesh of rumors and gossip, and men often walked long distances or paid bus fares or a contractor's fee only to find that the work was over or all the jobs were filled. Even the chalked signs could not always be relied on. Yet the search for *trabajo*, or the *chanza*, as we also called it, went on be-cause it had to.

We in the barrio considered that there were two kinds of *trabajo*. There were the seasonal jobs, some of them a hundred miles or more from Sacramento. And there were the closer *chanzas* to which you could walk or ride on a bicycle. These were the best ones, in the railway shops, the canneries, the waterfront warehouses, the lumberyards, the produce markets, the brick kilns, and the rice mills. To be able to move from the seasonal jobs to the close-in work was a step up the ladder. Men who had made it passed the word along to their relatives or their friends when there was a *chanza* of this kind.

It was all done by word of mouth, this delicate wiring of the grapevine. The exchange points of the network were the places where men gathered in small groups, apparently to loaf and chat to no purpose. One of these points was our kitchen, where my uncles and their friends sat and talked of *el macizo* and of the revolution but above all of the *chanzas* they had heard of.

There was not only the everlasting talk about *trabajo*, but also the never-ending action of the barrio itself. If work was action the barrio was where the action was. Every morning a parade of men in oily work clothes and carrying lunch buckets went up Fourth Street toward the railroad shops, and every evening they walked back, grimy and silent. Horse-drawn drays with low platforms rumbled up and down our street carrying the goods the city traded in, from kegs of beer to sacks of grain. Within a few blocks of our house there were smithies, hand laundries, a macaroni factory, and all manner of places where wagons and buggies were repaired, horses stabled, bicycles fixed, chickens dressed, clothes washed and ironed, furniture repaired, candy mixed, tents sewed, wine grapes pressed, bottles washed, lumber sawed, suits fitted and tailored, watches and clocks taken apart and put together again, vegetables sorted, railroad cars unloaded, boxcars iced, barges freighted, ice cream cones molded, soda pop bottled, fish scaled, salami stuffed, corn ground for *masa*, and bread ovened. To those who knew where these were located in the alleys, as I did, the whole barrio was an open workshop. The people who worked there came to know you, let you look in at the door, made jokes, and occasionally gave you an odd job.

This was the business district of the barrio. Around it and through it moved a constant traffic of drays, carts, bicycles, pushcarts, trucks, and high-wheeled automobiles with black canvas tops and honking horns. On the tailgates of drays and wagons, I nipped rides when I was going home with a gunnysack full of empty beer bottles or my gleanings around the packing sheds.

Once we had work, the next most important thing was to find a   30
place to live we could afford. Ours was a neighborhood of leftover houses. The cheapest rents were in the back quarters of the rooming houses, the basements, and the run-down clapboard rentals in the alleys. Clammy and dank as they were, they were nevertheless one level up from the barns and tents where many of our *chicano* friends lived, or the shanties and lean-tos of the migrants who squatted in the "jungles" along the levees of the Sacramento and American Rivers.

Barrio people, when they first came to town, had no furniture of their own. They rented it with their quarters or bought a piece at a time from the secondhand stores, the *segundas,* where we traded. We cut out the ends of tin cans to make collars and plates for the pipes and floor moldings where the rats had gnawed holes. Stoops and porches that sagged we propped with bricks and fat stones. To plug the drafts around the windows in winter, we cut strips of corrugated cardboard and wedged them into the frames. With squares of cheesecloth neatly cut and sewed to screen doors, holes were covered and rents in the wire mesh mended. Such repairs, which landlords never paid any attention to, were made *por mientras*, for the time being or temporarily. It would have been a word equally suitable for the house itself, or for the barrio. We lived in run-down places furnished with seconds in a hand-me-down neighborhood, all of which were *por mientras*.

We found the Americans as strange in their customs as they probably found us. Immediately we discovered that there were no *mercados* and that when shopping you did not put the groceries in a *chiquihuite*. Instead everything was in cans or in cardboard boxes or each item was put in a brown paper bag. There were neighborhood grocery stores at the corners and some big ones uptown, but no *mercado*. The grocers did not give children a *pilón*, they did not stand at the door and coax you to come in and buy, as they did in Mazatlán. The fruits and vegetables were displayed on counters instead of being piled up on the floor. The stores smelled of fly spray and oiled floors, not of fresh pineapple and limes.

Neither was there a plaza, only parks which had no bandstands, no concerts every Thursday, no Judases exploding on Holy Week, and no promenades of boys going one way and girls the other. There were no parks in the barrio, and the ones uptown were cold and rainy in winter, and in summer there was no place to sit except on the grass. When there were celebrations nobody set off rockets in the parks, much less on the street in front of your house to announce to the neighborhood that a wedding or a baptism was taking place. Sacramento did not have a *mercado* and a plaza with the cathedral to one side and the Palacio de Gobierno on another to make it obvious that there and nowhere else was the center of the town.

It was just as puzzling that the Americans did not live in *vecindades*, like our block on Leandro Valle. Even in the alleys, where people knew one another better, the houses were fenced apart, without central courts to wash clothes, talk, and play with the other children. Like the city, the Sacramento barrio did not have a place which was the middle of things for everyone.

In more personal ways we had to get used to the Americans. They 35 did not listen if you did not speak loudly, as they always did. In the Mexican style, people would know that you were enjoying their jokes tremendously if you merely smiled and shook a little, as if you were trying to swallow your mirth. In the American style there was little difference between a laugh and a roar, and until you got used to them you could hardly tell whether the boisterous Americans were roaring mad or roaring happy.

It was Doña Henriqueta more than Gustavo or José who talked of these oddities and classified them as agreeable or deplorable. It was she also who pointed out the pleasant surprises of the American way. When a box of rolled oats with a picture of red carnations on the side was emptied, there was a plate or a bowl or a cup with blue designs. We ate the strange stuff regularly for breakfast and we soon had a set of the beautiful dishes. Rice and beans we bought in cotton bags of colored prints. The bags were unsewed, washed, ironed, and made into gaily designed towels, napkins, and handkerchiefs. The American stores also gave small green stamps which were pasted in a book to exchange for prizes. We didn't have to run to the corner with the garbage; a collector came for it.

With remarkable fairness and never-ending wonder we kept adding to our list the pleasant and the repulsive in the ways of the Americans. It was my second acculturation.

The older people of the barrio, except in those things which they had to do like the Americans because they had no choice, remained Mexican. Their language at home was Spanish. They were continuously taking up collections to pay somebody's funeral expenses or to help someone who had had a serious accident. Cards were sent to you to attend a burial where you would throw a handful of dirt on top of the coffin and listen to tearful speeches at the graveside. At every baptism a new *compadre* and a new *comadre* joined the family circle. New Year greeting cards were exchanged, showing angels and cherubs in bright colors sprinkled with grains of mica so that they glistened like gold dust. At the family parties the huge pot of steaming tamales was still the center of attention, the *atole* served on the side with chunks of brown sugar for sucking and crunching. If the party lasted long enough, someone produced a guitar, the men took over, and the singing of *corridos* began.

In the barrio there were no individuals who had official titles or who were otherwise recognized by everybody as important people. The reason must have been that there was no place in the public business of the city of Sacramento for the Mexican immigrants. We only rented a corner of the city and as long as we paid the rent on time everything else was decided at City Hall or the county courthouse, where Mexicans went only when they were in trouble. Nobody from the barrio ever ran for mayor or city councilman. For us the most important public officials were the policemen who walked their beats, stopped fights, and hauled drunks to jail in a paddy wagon we called La Julia.

The one institution we had that gave the *colonia* some kind of image 40 was the Comisión Honorífica, a committee picked by the Mexican consul in San Francisco to organize the celebration of the Cinco de Mayo and the Sixteenth of September, the anniversaries of the battle of Puebla and the beginning of our War of Independence. These were the two events which stirred everyone in the barrio, for what we were celebrating was not only the heroes of Mexico but also the feeling that we were still Mexicans ourselves. On these occasions there was a dance preceded by speeches and a concert. For both the Cinco and the Sixteenth, queens were elected to preside over the ceremonies.

Between celebrations neither the politicians uptown nor the Comisión Honorífica attended to the daily needs of the barrio. This was done by volunteers—the ones who knew enough English to interpret in court, on a visit to the doctor, on a call at the county hospital, and who could help make out a postal money order. By the time I had finished the third grade at the Lincoln School I was one of these volunteers. My services were not professional but they were free, except for the IOUs I accumulated from families who always thanked me with "God will pay you for it."

My clients were not *pochos*—Mexicans who had grown up in California, who probably had even been born in the United States. They had learned to speak English of sorts and could still speak Spanish, also of sorts. They knew much more about the Americans than we did, and much less about us. The *chicanos* and the *pochos* had certain feelings about one another. Concerning the *pochos*, the *chicanos* suspected that they considered themselves too good for the barrio but were not, for some reason, good enough for the Americans. Toward the *chicanos*, the *pochos* acted superior, amused at our confusions but not especially interested in explaining them to us. In our family when I forgot my manners, my mother would ask me if I was turning *pochito*.

Turning *pocho* was a half step toward turning American. And America was all around us, in and out of the barrio. Abruptly we had to forget the ways of shopping in a *mercado* and learn those of shopping in a corner grocery or in a department store. The Americans paid no attention to the Sixteenth of September, but they made a great commotion about the Fourth of July. In Mazatlán Don Salvador had told us, saluting and marching as he talked to our class, that the Cinco de Mayo was the most glorious date in human history. The Americans had not even heard about it.

UNDERSTANDING THE TEXT

1. Describe in your own words the initial impression of Sacramento that the young Galarza had when he first arrived in the city.
2. What, according to Galarza, was the difference between lower and upper Sacramento?

3. How did the various nationalities in lower Sacramento interact?

4. Why does Galarza say that "[t]he *colonia* was like a sponge that was beginning to leak along the edges" (para. 21)?

5. How did different groups in the barrio create symbiotic relationships that helped form a community?

6. What were the contradictory attitudes that barrio residents had toward Americans?

EXPLORING AND DEBATING THE ISSUES

1. Both Galarza and Joan Didion ("Notes from a Native Daughter," p. 54) write about Sacramento's past. In an essay, compare and contrast their depictions of this city. How do they identify Sacramento as a place, as a community? Keep in mind that Galarza is writing about the early part of the twentieth century and Didion refers to the middle part of the century.

2. Galarza and Richard Rodriguez ("Proofs," p. 64) describe how Mexican immigrants adapt when they arrive in California. Compare and contrast their accounts of such immigrants' arrival here. Do you notice behavioral patterns that may be considered traditional for Mexican immigrants? How do you account for any differences you might observe?

3. The title suggests that the community Galarza describes is racially homogeneous, but in fact it comprises many nationalities. In an essay, analyze the relationship among these nationalities. To what extent is the barrio a successful "multicultural mosaic," in the words of Jewelle Taylor Gibbs and Teiahsha Bankhead ("Coming to California: Chasing the Dream," p. 84)?

In Search of Oildorado

JAMES D. HOUSTON

It's not easy living in the Central Valley if you have to put up with coastal California's almost complete neglect of you and your region. **James D. Houston** (b. 1933), a long-time writer and novelist on the California scene, went out to try to correct the problem by visiting Kern County, the fourth-largest oil-producing region in America and the eighteenth largest in the world. Making his way to Taft, California, home to the Oildorado festival and its court, the Maids of Petroleum, Houston found a place much more like Texas and Oklahoma than the California the rest of world imagines. In fact, many of the Central Valley's residents can trace their family lines back to the Okies who emigrated in the 1930s. A writer, editor, and novelist, Houston has published many books, including *Continental Drift* (1978), *Californians: Searching for the Golden State* (1982), from which this selection is taken, *Farewell to Manzanar* (with Jeanne Wakatsuki Houston, 1973), and *Snow Mountain Passage* (2002).

California's best-known exports nowadays are not things. They are images, composed of such unnatural resources as lifestyle frontiers and the shapes of leisure—not the bottled wine itself but the chilled chardonnay in the hot tub; the kid on the trail bike, on the rim of the bluff, at sunset. The images depict all varieties of the West Coast adventure in Life with a capital L, the Living and Exploring and Spending and Expanding and Exploding. They are exported on film, on record and tape, via the covers and inside pages of the *National Enquirer, Road and Track, TV Guide, People, Self,* and *Us.* Meanwhile, more traditional resources, such as timber, cotton, cattle, hogs and poultry, crude oil and natural gas, come to the public's attention when some feature of the environment has been violated or is about to be swamped. But for the most part, though they fuel and finance the rest of it, these tend to exist in the shadow of The Great Postindustrial Experiment, which dazzles us with such a blinding light.

To see this other part of California, the resource-full part, it helps to get away from the coast from time to time, and head inland, which is why I found myself on the road to Bakersfield again, over there in Kern County. About 7 percent of the cotton grown in the United States comes out of Kern County. According to Bill Rintoul, it is also the nation's fourth-largest oil-producing region.

"If Kern seceded from the rest of California," says Bill, "which of course it is not planning to do, at least not right away, but if it were separated off, this county all by itself would be running fourth in oil, after Texas, Alaska, and Louisiana. For that matter, it is the eighteenth-largest oil producer in the world."

Bill is a Kern County patriot. I do not mean he would defend his county's honor with guns and knives. But he likes the place, he has spent most of his life there, and takes its flaws along with its virtues. He actually prefers the unrelieved flatness of the landscape. We were talking once about the heavy groves and wooded canyons characteristic of the northern coast, and he said, "You know, it's funny, but there is something about that kind of country that just doesn't feel right. Those trees all around you. And the rain it takes for that kind of growth, the way it drips down through the trees. The way the mountains rise up. Half the time you can't see the sun. I suppose it's just what a person gets used to. You get used to a certain idea of what the world is supposed to look like. I'd just rather see the sun and know where I'm going."

Bill makes his living as a petroleum journalist. He writes columns for the *Bakersfield Californian* and the *Tulsa Daily World*. When I called and told him I might be heading his way, there was a pause. He is not a fast talker. He thinks things over. After a moment he said, "Well, if you time it for next weekend, you could be here for some of Oildorado. I am going to be the Grand Marshal in the parade this year. Maybe you could ride along with me in the limousine."

I had heard of Oildorado but didn't know much about it. The fact is, on the day I called him, everything I knew about oil in California could fit easily into the spare can I carry around in the back of my Mercedes, which has a diesel engine, by the way, an old 1960 190D. It will give me thirty-five miles to the gallon on a trip like this, where the roads are straight and flat.

Naively I asked, "Does the parade run through the oil fields?"

"No, it runs right through downtown Taft. On second thought, maybe you'd be better off watching from the sidewalk. That way you'll be sure to see all the floats and the Oildorado Queen and the Maids of Petroleum. If you want to see the fields themselves, my suggestion is to drive down Highway 33. There is no other road quite like it in the eleven western states."

In literature, Kern's finest moment comes in that scene midway through *The Grapes of Wrath*, when the Joad family stops at Tehachapi Pass to take a first long and thirsty look at this land they have struggled so hard to reach. Ruthie and Winfield, the youngest, are awestruck by the sight, "embarrassed before the great valley," is the way Steinbeck described it:

> The distance was thinned with haze, and the land grew softer and softer in the distance. A windmill flashed in the sun, and its turning blades were like a little heliograph, far away. Ruthie and Winfield looked at it, and Ruthie whispered, "It's California."

The vista Steinbeck chose, in 1939, to flesh out the dream these immigrants carried with them from Dust-Bowl Oklahoma is a long way from the world most Californians inhabit now. The largest cities, the densest networks of subdivisions, mobile home parks and retirement towns are found along a coastal strip, some forty miles wide, between Sonoma County and San Diego. By and large, this is where The Big Experiment is going on. It is also a zone of intense tourism. People living in or near the coastal communities often find themselves caught in that mind-boggle between how a place once looked and felt and how its packaging looks once it has become merchandise on the international travel circuit.

In Kern County you do not have to put up with much of this. In the   10
1979 *Atlas of California,* on the page where "Major Tourist Attractions" are marked with circles and dots of various colors, Kern is blank. Gray Line buses do not linger in Bakersfield or Oildale or Taft. Movie stars and sports celebrities seldom buy homes there, though they might well invest in the land. People don't visit, as a rule, unless they have business there, or relatives, or have come searching for Oildorado.

Heading east out of Paso Robles, I cross the county line halfway through a lonesome dip in the Coast Range called Antelope Valley. The hills along here are so dry and brown they shine in the sunlight as if ready to burst into flame. Just as the county sign flashes past, I hear Conway Twitty on the radio, station KUZZ out of Bakersfield coming in clear now. His voice rich with stoic remorse, Conway tells some lost sweetheart she is standing on a bridge that just won't burn. It seems perfect. This land could torment you for years without ever quite killing you. And the road signs for what lies up ahead don't seem to promise much relief: Bitterwater Valley, Devils Den, Lost Hills.

The first blur of color is startling, almost uncanny, when this narrow passage opens out into cotton fields, hundreds, perhaps thousands of acres, with bolls white and ready for picking. A couple of miles go by, and one side of the road turns from cotton into a long orchard of dusty almond trees. As the last slopes level out, where Antelope Valley joins the broad San Joaquin, the first grapevines appear, their leaves half green, half rusty brown after harvest. To the south the rows look about a mile long, stretching across to the base of the Temblor Range. To the north there is no telling how far the rows extend, no limits visible up that way. Vines merge toward the horizon.

A few more miles go by, and the vines give way to another stand of almond trees, older and thicker, bearing well, and then a peach orchard, and now, across this highway, facing the orchards you can see what all this land looked like once, and would look like now without the aqueduct. The contrast is spectacular. In this landscape almost nothing grows naturally. No shrubs, no trees, no houses. No people. Out this way there aren't even any beer cans. Without the aqueduct that intersects this highway a few miles up ahead, there would be nothing here but tumbleweed and sagebrush and the diesel rigs powering past on their way to Interstate 5.

Water is one of three resources that have shaped Kern County. Oil and country music are the other two. The water is imported from rivers farther north. The music is what you might call a hybrid product, transplanted southwestern and Okie energy finding new roots here, giving Bakersfield its nickname, Nashville West. The oil, however, is indigenous. While the guitars and the fiddles and the gospel quartets float through the airways a few feet above the ground, and while the piped-in water taps the riches in the first foot of earth, thousands and thousands of wells suck up the riches farther down, planted there fifty or sixty million years ago when uncountable generations of plankton sifted downward through the fathoms of this one-time inland sea and left tiny skeletons behind to be transformed into crude.

When we talked on the phone Bill told me Kern County is now producing more oil than some of the OPEC nations. He said this with such genuine pride in his home region, I felt obliged to ask him which OPEC nations he was referring to.   15

Again there was a pause, as if he had forgotten. He had not forgotten. Bill is a living encyclopedia of petroleum lore, but he will hesitate like this, as if the facts are elusive and hard to pin down. "Oh, I think Qatar is one," he said. "Gabon is another. Ecuador is in there somewhere."

On the radio Willie Nelson is singing, "Whiskey River, don't run dry." Out here on Highway 46 the crops have disappeared for a while. Sand and sagebrush stretch away on both sides of the road. It's odd to be comparing this alkaline wasteland with Ecuador.

Standing all alone in the sand and the wind, where Highway 46 meets 33, there is a cafe with a couple of gas pumps called Blackwells Corner. I swing right, as Bill instructed me to do, heading south. Within a few miles I am surrounded by walking beams, steam generators, derricks, and fields of grimy pipe. No crops at all grow along this side of the San Joaquin. The soil is parched. Animals are scarce. The only movement in this moon-like realm comes from the pumps, their metal beams nodding with the motion and profile that has stirred several dozen writers to compare them to praying mantises. I now see why. This type of field pump resembles nothing in the world as much as a mantis on a string. What you see from the road are hundreds of praying heads, painted orange or yellow or black and connected by cable to something underground that seems to pull each one by the nose, so that they are all, on their various cycles, silently, ceaselessly bowing.

I will soon learn from Bill that if there was a Guinness book of financial records, this oil field would be in it. Late in 1979 Shell bought it for what was said at the time to be the largest sum ever to change hands in a corporate transaction. The field, called Kernridge, which now produces fifty thousand barrels each day, was sold for $3,653,272,000. Shell's geologists estimate 364 billion cubic feet of natural gas are waiting underground here, along with five to six hundred million barrels of oil, most of which had long been considered too expensive to get at or too viscous to pump. Soaring prices changed that view.

South of this field, and near the village of McKittrick, I enter a much   20 larger and more valuable oil field, a legendary field that has created five towns and numerous fortunes. It is called the Midway-Sunset. It is over twenty miles long. As Bill is soon to tell me, it is among the twelve largest fields in the United States. It was the fourth in the history of the country to deliver a billion barrels—as of 1967—and they are still a long way from the bottom.

I have some trouble with figures like a billion barrels, or 364 billion cubic feet. I have some trouble with the scale of this whole business. It is almost too much to grasp. These fields and Bill's almanac memory are filled with numbers that simply bring the imagination to a standstill. Standard Oil of California grossed $42 billion in fiscal 1980. Kern County produces nearly four million barrels of oil per week. The United States still imports about five million barrels per day. A typical reason, or symptom: there are 5.1 million automobiles in Los Angeles. These cars alone burn fifteen million gallons of gasoline every day. There are forty-two gallons in a barrel. By 1967 this field I'm driving through produced a billion barrels. In other words, 42 billion gallons, 168 billion quarts. But where are they now? And how big a cavity does that leave below? Is it bigger or smaller than Carlsbad Caverns? And how much bigger can it get before the roof caves in?

I am beginning to wonder if it helps to drive out through these oil fields. Even here, right in the middle of it, along Highway 33, which displays the most elaborate collection of field equipment west of Oklahoma, there is not much to see, not much to hold to, nothing nearly as immediate as that vast field of cotton with its bolls like a field of white eyes along the roadside watching you pass.

I think it was easier in the old days, when they had gushers that would blow the tops off the derricks, puddle the earth with lakes of oil and fill the air for miles around here with an oily haze that would stain the laundry and cloud the sun. The most dramatic of these, Lakeview Number One, blew in on March 14, 1910, with such force and volume it could not be brought under control, and it was never brought under control. People still talk about the soaring column of oil and sand and rock. Unable to cap or channel it, they used timbers and sandbags to construct great dikes and holding sumps. Of the nine million barrels said to have come pouring forth during the year and a half it gushed and gey-sered, some four million were trapped and processed. The rest just ran free and seeped back into the earth from whence it came. This went on for 544 days without restraint. Then one day it stopped as suddenly as it had begun. The bottom fell in, due to some shift of underground pres-sure, and that was the end of the Lakeview Gusher, but the beginning of flush times in the Midway-Sunset, as well as the true launching of Taft, the largest town among these west-side fields. (The sign at the edge of town listing weekly luncheon times for Kiwanis, Lions, Optimists, and Rotary, claims a population of 18,500, but a plumbing contractor Bill in-troduced me to confessed that the true population is closer to twelve thousand. "People will throw these numbers around," he said. "They will try to rope in Fellows and Tupman and some of the outlying areas, but as long as I've been here, which is forty-four years, the population of the town itself hasn't changed that much one way or the other.")

Taft happened to incorporate in the same year Lakeview Number One burst forth, and it looks back upon that event as a grand and almost supernatural announcement of the town's arrival. Emblazoned across the 1980 souvenir T-shirts being sold in Taft, where Oildorado originated, is the phrase SEVENTY YEARS OF BLACK GOLD.

Seventy years. Even in the foreshortened history of California this place is very, very young. My house in Santa Cruz is older than any two-by-four in Taft. In this part of the world the coastal mission towns, like Santa Cruz, go back as far as towns go. The central valley had to wait until after statehood. And Taft's side of the valley had to wait even longer. As late as 1900 there was still nothing here but sagebrush. In 1902 South-ern Pacific ran a spur line out this far, to service the new wells. The end of that spur line gathered a dusty collection of shacks and tents and con-verted boxcars. The town is still built close to the ground, in a hollow be-tween hills studded with producing wells. The view in all directions is of dry, oil-bearing hillsides, their bare slopes defined by a few wooden der-ricks that survive from the early days—the same kind of definition trees provide.

Hills like these are uncommon in the San Joaquin, which by nature is as flat as a football field and about the same shape. Geologists call them anticlines. Where they rise from the plain, oil from sand and shale layers farther down has been gathered upward, within easy reach of the surface. Just out of sight, a few miles east, there lies another low range called Elk Hills, an unassuming cluster of tawny ridges that offer almost nothing to the passing eye, yet Elk Hills happens to be California's number-one producing field. Since 1912 it has belonged to the federal government, as a naval petroleum reserve. For a while in the 1920s, it was famous for its role in the most notorious oil scandal of all time though never quite as famous as Wyoming's Teapot Dome field—another naval reserve—which gave the scandal its name.

In 1921 Albert Fall, then Secretary of the Interior, brought the control of these fields into his department and promptly leased them out to high-rolling cronies. Elk Hills went to Edward Doheny, the original California oil baron and L.A. entrepreneur, in exchange for "a personal loan" of $100,000. After the dealings were exposed, Fall became the first cabinet officer in American history to be convicted of a felony and sent to prison. Doheny was acquitted. Elk Hills spent the next fifty years rather quietly, as a low-production reserve administered by the navy. It was not until the Arab oil embargo of 1973, and the new pressure to develop domestic fuel supplies, that the idea of reopening Elk Hills for commercial use was seriously considered. Bill Rintoul says a hundred sixty thousand barrels a day come out of there now, and two hundred million cubic feet of gas.

At a small shop called Oildorado Headquarters, on the main street in downtown Taft, I pick up a couple of the black and gold T-shirts, an official program, and the special issue of the Taft *Daily Midway Driller*. In a back room, beyond the cash register, bright lights are shining. Life-size costume boards have been set up, with notches at the top for neck and chin. The costumes are old-time and turn-of-the-century Western. People are waiting in line to have their pictures taken standing behind these boards, as souvenirs of this festival which is already three days along. It started Wednesday with the queen contest and the official opening of the Westside Oil Museum. Things will begin to peak tomorrow with the big parade and hopefully climax with the World Championship Welding and Backhoe Races at Franklin Field.

Outside this shop, where I am meeting Rintoul, numerous sheriffs are passing by, numerous vests and cowboy hats, bonnets and gingham dresses. Bill is easy to spot. He is not in costume. A man of simple tastes, he never overplays his hand. As Grand Marshal of tomorrow's parade he could get away with almost anything, but he shows up in checkered slacks and a short-sleeved sport shirt. No string tie. No turquoise. He has a brand-new cowboy hat, which he has left in the car. He pretends to be worried that the parade committee might get the wrong idea.

"If they see that hat they might start talking about horses. Then I might   30
have to tell them to forget the whole thing." He grins a weathery grin, as if

he is turning into a heavy wind to look at me. "I think the Grand Marshal deserves a limousine, don't you?"

Whatever they give him to ride, Bill is going to do well as Oildorado Marshal. His heart is in exactly the right place. He is an oil fields aficionado, a man fascinated with every feature of the way this business works. He grew up here in Taft, joined the army during World War II, came back for a few years in the fields before going off to Stanford for a degree in journalism. Secretly I suspect he writes his daily columns and his feature pieces for *Pacific Oil World*, *Well Servicing*, and *The Drilling Contractor* so he can continue to roam among these anticlines at will. He loves all of it, the mathematics, the geology, the look of a drilling rig, the lore of the roughneck, the gusher legends, the way a late sun tints steam plumes rising from the generators. He jumped at the chance to meander once again through his own home territory, to take me on a little tour, which now begins, in the Veterans Hall, where the Oildorado Civic Luncheon is being served, and where the Grand Marshal's attendance is expected.

We walk in moments before the invocation. Bill moves directly to the head table, while I find a spot, a vacant folding chair, at one of the long tables lined up in rows across the hall. Maybe two hundred people are here, merchants and their wives, the civic leaders of Taft, dressed as cowhands, schoolmarms, desperadoes. The brightest outfits are black and gold, worn by a dozen young girls dressed as saloon dancers, 1890s style, with high fringed skirts and high-heeled shoes. These are the girls who ran for queen, sponsored by such groups as the Taft Rotary, the Desk and Derrick Club, the Moose Lodge. The winner, sponsored by Veterans of World War I, Barracks 305, is a slim and pretty senior from Taft High. She wears a glossy beauty-contest banner that says OILDORADO QUEEN. The others each wear a banner saying MAID OF PETROLEUM. Later, two hours from now, after speeches by Oildorado presidents, mayors, and council members past and present, after all the testimonials to the community of Taft and the Oildorado tradition, these fourteen girls will dance a cancan routine to taped music, a high-stepping, side-kicking, skirt-lifting dance that will end with their backsides first to the speakers' table and then to the crowd. They are giddy with anticipation, jumping up and sitting down and hurrying out to the lobby. Now they all come to a temporary halt as the M.C. calms the room and asks us to stand while a portly minister intones the blessing.

Still standing, we put our hands over our hearts, face the flag, and say the pledge of allegiance. Then we sing "God Bless America." It has been a long time since I sang "God Bless America" before lunch. It feels good. One thing I will say about the people of Taft: they are not cynical.

They do not intend the phrase "Maid of Petroleum" to have more than one meaning. They genuinely want America to be blessed by someone. And though relatively little of the profits from these mammoth oil reserves trickles into town, they are thankful when the fields come back to life, as they have in these past few years, because then Taft comes back to life. The mood on this particular afternoon in Veterans Hall is one of carefully nurtured prosperity.

During lunch—paper plates of fried chicken, potato salad, carrot-and-raisin salad, coffee or iced tea from pitchers—I talk to the plumbing contractor who moved here forty-four years ago. He wears a rodeo shirt and cowboy hat and has let his beard grow out for the whiskerino contest. Business has been good, but it is a mixed blessing. He complains about the hard time he has finding qualified help. "They all want to go work in the oil fields now. Out there they start at seven-fifty, and move up to nine, nine-fifty right away. Your best workers are going to head for the fields. So I've always got a new man to break in."

After lunch we drive out to the site of the Lakeview Gusher, south of town, on Petroleum Club Road. The distance is ten kilometers, a figure I remember from the program. Early Saturday morning there is to be a footrace, an event called "The Lakeview Gusher 10K" starting where the original derrick stood before the gush of oil and gas reduced it to splinters, and ending downtown.

The race is another tribute to that great explosion. The place where those racers will assemble, "The Site," is a built-up pit perhaps forty yards across. Its walls were originally made of timbers, sandbags, and dirt. A wetter climate would long ago have flattened these walls, but seventy years from now it will probably look pretty much the same. Sandbags can still be seen, tattered strips of burlap show through the dirt and the grimy boards. In the special edition of the *Midway Driller* there is a photo of two grinning, oil-stained men standing on an oil-encrusted wooden raft floating in a shiny lake of oil. They are poling from one side to the other. This caked and sandy pit Bill and I are standing in used to be that lake.

While we wander to the far side he is telling me the story, one he heard firsthand from an uncle who worked this field in the earliest years. Eventually both of us fall silent, kicking at the shards of oily sand. Something eerie hovers here, something reverent in the breeze across these scarred dunes, in the near-absence of motion or life where once there had been such a swarm, such frenzy.

Between the pit and roads stands a monument, with a plaque affixed, which says AMERICA'S MOST SPECTACULAR GUSHER. It's a California

Registered Historical Landmark. If you squint, it could be a gravestone. Around here they talk about this gusher as if it had a life and an identity, the great creature who sprang forth, lived its wild existence for a year and a half, and suddenly died, of subterranean causes. Seventy years later there are photos everywhere—in the Oildorado program, in the special issue of the *Driller*, in shop windows downtown, and on permanent display in the new Westside Oil Museum—the lakes and rivers of oil, the oily workers rafting through it, the shattered derrick, the black spurting geyser of oil. They commemorate the early time, which was also the time of wildness, before this piece of earth had been quite tamed, and the sky-high gusher who could not be contained burst forth, made a huge and glorious mess, then disappeared or perhaps just retreated back into its cave.

I don't know why, but when you're driving around in the central valley, the songs from these country and western stations always seem to be providing some ironic comment on the landscape or the general situation. As we pull away from the gusher site, Bill switches on KUZZ, and it's an old Buck Owens arrangement called "Today I Started Loving You Again."

Buck is singing it. Merle Haggard wrote it. They both happen to be   40 Kern County heroes. As we near the oil field village of Maricopa, Bill says in passing that he knows someone who went to high school with Merle in the days before he married Bonnie Owens. Everyone in Kern County seems to know someone who knows Buck Owens or Bonnie or Merle or all three. "She was married to both of 'em, you know. Of course, not at the same time."

By pure coincidence the one thriving business in Maricopa is called Buck's Steakhouse. No connection. "Best place to eat, for as long as I can remember," says Bill. From the look of things, it is the only place to eat. Taft and Maricopa started even, back in 1910, when they both incorporated. By 1911 Maricopa had its own opera house. In the mid-1970s, when they were filming *Bound for Glory*, Woody Guthrie's life story, Maricopa was chosen as the location for some early scenes set in the wind-blown west Texas town of Pampa during the 1930s. Very little had to be changed. It still has that sanded, worn-down Western patina. Only the cars are new, and some of the pickups outside Buck's.

Maricopa sits near Midway-Sunset's southern edge. We head due east now, along the base of the Temblor Range, running almost parallel to the California Aqueduct, which also swings eastward here, with its long flow from the Delta passing through these lowlands before making the salmon's leap over the Tehachapis and down again, to water Southern California. Along here the aqueduct waters more cotton fields. A few miles out of Maricopa we are driving through one of those tracts so vast your eyes burn trying to see the end of it. And right out in the middle of this small continent of cotton, about half a mile off the road, stands the drilling rig we have come looking for. With no pumps or derricks in view, the rig looks like some intergalactic vehicle that has landed in the wrong place.

It's part of Bill's beat to see how they are doing, how deep the hole is, and whether they've had any show. This is a wildcat well, he says, in a part of the valley that hasn't been drilled before. "There's probably some oil down there, but ten years ago you wouldn't have found anybody drilling that deep."

He takes a side road, looking for access, finds it, and we are easing along a dirt track between cotton rows toward a clearing where maybe half an acre has been opened up to make room for the platform, the caravan of trailers.

Bill has two hard hats in the trunk. We don these and climb the metal ladder. Everything is made of metal and painted battleship gray. The steel platform is thirty feet above the cotton, and rising a hundred thirty feet above the platform is the bolted network of struts and pulleys they call the mast. Climbing aboard you have the feeling of boarding a great vessel, anchored in the invisible waters of the inland sea.

Five men are working, the standard crew, all wearing hard hats and T-shirts, and smeared with grease and oil. Bill introduces me to Terry the tool pusher, the crew leader, who grins when I offer to shake his hand and shows me the palm thick with grease. Something about the way he stands would tell you he is in command, even if you hadn't been told in advance. His face is lean, his hair black and straight. He could be part Cherokee. Early thirties. He wears cowboy boots and jeans, no shirt. Without being muscular, his body looks powerful, whip-like. He stands with one foot forward, like a sailor on a rolling deck.

Bill mentions a man who died a couple of days ago, on another rig in some other part of the county. "I read in the paper that the cable crushed his chest."

Terry laughs and shakes his head, nods toward the draw works, the broad metal drum that winds and unwinds the cable that feeds up to the top of the mast, then down toward the center of the platform where the lengths of pipe are lowered or raised.

"I read that story," Terry says. "There is no way this cable is gonna crush your chest. If it breaks and comes whipping out of that drum it might knock you around some. It got me once. But it's not gonna crush your chest. What I figure is, they were pulling on the pipe, and it was the pipe broke loose and come free and swung out and got him. That pipe is what can crush you."

Any of this stuff could crush you. This is what Terry is ready to roll   50
with, not an ocean, but the great chunks of moving metal that surround him. The drilling pipe comes in thirty-foot sections. They are slung from the cable on a lobster-shaped hook the size of a VW bus, which hangs directly overhead. Next to us, another large piece of thick steel is hanging loose, about the size of a Harley-Davidson. When I ask Terry about it he says, "All this is here is a great big pipe wrench. We just clamp it onto the pipe there to tighten the fit."

He shrugs it off, makes it simple. And it is simple. You put a bit on the end of a pipe, and you start cutting a hole in the ground. After a while you screw on another length of pipe, and you cut a little deeper. It isn't the act that's impressive. Like everything else in the oil business, it's the magnitude. This rig down here at the absolute bottom edge of the San Joaquin Valley is running a pipe that is now twelve thousand feet into the ground, chipping and grinding through the next inch or foot of sand or shale or ancient fossil layer. What we have here is a brace and bit over two miles long, which is deep, Bill says. An average well in Kern County runs four to five thousand feet. Lakeview Number One came in at 2,225 in 1910.

Retracing our route through the rows of cotton we head back toward Taft, where I left my car. From there I follow Bill to Bakersfield and our final stop, a Basque place downtown called The Pyrenees, established in the days when Basque shepherds roamed the foothills east of here. The food is served family style, and the folks who run the place pile it on the table as if everyone who walks in is a shepherd just back from a month in the mountains or a roughneck coming off a seventy-two-hour shift.

This is Bill's favorite restaurant. The house beverage, Picon Punch, warms his county patriotism, stirs to life an epilogue for today, a prologue for tomorrow's parade.

"Kern is a kind of headquarters, you see. This is the biggest drilling year in the history of the state of California, and two-thirds of the new wells are here in this county—over two thousand wells. Meanwhile, oil people fan out from here in all directions. The contractor Terry works for has twenty-one rigs like that one we climbed. His main yard is outside town, but his rigs are trucked to Nevada, Wyoming, and into the Rockies where all the new exploration is going on. You take Terry himself. He grew up here in Bakersfield, started out as a roughneck, worked his way up to tool pusher. He just got back from Evanston, Wyoming. Couple of years ago he was working in Alaska. It's typical. Some of those fellows over in Taft, you would never know it to see them walking along the street, but they have been to Peru, to Arabia, Iran, and Venezuela, and they wind up right back home again."

The next morning we start out in separate cars, planning to meet at the   55
reviewing stand. I am ten miles south of Bakersfield, whizzing along to Loretta Lynn's version of "I've Never Been This Far Before," and near the village of Pumpkin Center, when I smell the smell of warm rust, glance down and see my temperature needle heading off the gauge.

I pull over, pop the hood open, and gingerly ease the cap loose. Steam pours out but no water. There isn't much left. The top seam on my radiator has split. I make it to a phone and call the first place listed in the Yellow Pages that claims to be open on weekends. I cadge some water from a Freddy Fast-Gas and limp back to this radiator shop on the outskirts of Bakersfield, in the middle of a district that seems coated with rubber dust and filmed with oil, not from wells but from the generations of cars that have moved through its grimy jungle of transmission shops, upholstery parlors, abandoned service stations, warehouses, and wrecking yards.

I pull in with steam billowing around my hood and a trail of what could be diluted blood. The radiator man is sympathetic, a fellow in dark coveralls whose eyes cannot quite open, as if the lashes have been coated with honey. He says that since it is Saturday and he plans to close at 1:00 p.m. he will do the repairs only if I pull the radiator myself and install it again. I agree, making it clear that I am truly in a rush since my friend is going to be the Grand Marshal in the Oildorado parade. I emphasize this, figuring the local reference might enhance our relationship. He stops me right there.

"The what parade?"

"Oildorado."

"What the hell is that?"   60

Well, I think, this is curious. Here is a fellow whose entire livelihood depends on the internal-combustion engine, the heat it generates while burning gasoline, heat that must be cooled with water, which must circulate and sooner or later spring a leak, which he then is qualified to repair. And this fellow has never heard of the event I have driven halfway across the state to attend, the celebration of an industry that keeps not only this radiator man but a good part of California, if you will pardon the expression, solvent.

"You mean to tell me," I say, "that you work on cars all day long, every day, and you have never heard of Oildorado over there in Taft?"

Something in my tone unnerves him. We are both on edge. For a moment his eyelashes pull apart. I see indignation in there. "Hey," he says, "you want this goddamn radiator fixed?" Before I can reply he says, "Taft is thirty-five miles away. How the hell am I for Christ sake supposed to know what's going on over in Taft!"

I don't argue. It is important for the two of us to get along, at least for the next hour, which we do, working side by side, sometimes eyelash to eyelash, above and below the fittings.

By the time I reach Taft it is midafternoon. I have missed the parade.   65
I have missed the Lakeview Gusher 10K Run. I have missed the Fly-in at Taft Airport and the barbecue at The Petroleum Club. Searching for Bill, I stop at Franklin Field, where the World's Championship Backhoe Contest is scheduled. It hasn't started yet. I happen to catch the most intense tug-of-war I have ever witnessed. These are not college kids pulling each other across a mudhole at the Spring Fling. These are some of the largest men in the state — truckers, hay-buckers, roustabouts, and derrick-men — thick men bursting through their T-shirts and playing for keeps.

One team is fully outfitted with matching blue and white jump suits, paratrooper boots for sure footing, and ball caps that say "Duval Sporting Goods." They have a coach, also in uniform, who paces back and forth in a half-crouch, muttering instructions before the match begins. They have some moves worked out, some hand and voice signals. They have prepared for this moment, and it is sad to watch those thick boot soles sliding through the sand as they are dragged across the line in less than thirty seconds by some ragtag group who have evidently organized at the last moment, who wear Adidas running shoes, whose T-shirts do not even match, but whose pecs and biceps would bring tears to the eyes of many regulars at Santa Monica's Muscle Beach. After a few rebel yells the winners swagger off toward the Budweiser truck, while the team from Duval Sporting Goods stand there frowning at each other, gazing at their shoes in bewilderment.

In the middle of the bare acreage called Franklin Field, sixty backhoes are lined up, their earth-scraping bulldozer blades drawn in low at the back, their crane-arms crooked high in front, scoops at the ready, waiting for the championship to begin. The cabs are empty. On one windshield a sticker says "Iran Sucks." In a half-circle a thousand fans wearing cowboy hats stand around sipping Budweiser and waiting too. This is where I finally find Bill. I recognize him by his bare head. He is carrying his hat. I still have not seen him wearing it.

He doesn't take my absence personally. When I explain what happened he laughs and says it reminds him of the old Merle Haggard tune

"Radiator Man from Wasco," which is set in a Kern County town north of Bakersfield, up Highway 43.

"Sounds like you've been reliving Merle's song," he says.

I ask him if the parade committee had made him ride a horse.   70

"Nope, a fellow here in town provided a Cadillac, which would have been real comfortable if the top was down. It wasn't a convertible, though. The roof was so low I couldn't get my cowboy hat on. In that respect I guess I lucked out. My wife, Frankie Jo, was with me, so we all three sat hunched in the front. The fact is, I am weary. Waving to so many people, trying to keep a smile on for an hour and a half, and then not sure anybody can even see you, under a low roof like that."

Bill grins all through this account, amused by the parade, and narrows his eyes as if faced with heavy weather, which at the moment happens to be true. It is clouding up. Warm heavy clouds have filled the sky.

"I'm glad I don't have to do this again," he says. "Five years from now, it'll be somebody else's turn. They only have Oildorado every five years, you know. For a while it was annual. But people were running out of time for anything else."

I have a couple of beers and wait for the backhoe drivers to mount their rigs. I can only guzzle so much Bud, since I plan to start north this afternoon, sooner or later, and there are mountains to climb. I decide on sooner. It is looking more and more like rain, and the backhoes are still sitting like tanks on D day waiting for the signal from Eisenhower. Something has delayed the contest. No one is certain what, and no one much cares as long as the Bud holds out.

I say good-bye to Bill and start out 33 through the Midway-Sunset,   75
making one last quick stop at Fellows, another oil-field village five miles away. Fellows reminds me of the pueblos in New Mexico, the ones you pass driving out of Albuquerque—no roadside billboards in any direction, no pitch to the motorist, no hotels or motels or fast-food neon, no Rotary lunch. It's just a village, a cluster of low buildings a mile or so off the road, out there all by itself in the high desert. Pumping wells dot the slopes beyond town, where the Temblor Range begins to rise. More wells decorate the plains spreading south. There is no main street in Fellows, no grocery store. Where the houses stop, I find what I have left the highway for, another gusher site Bill has recommended, another monument stone, another plaque:

THE FIRST GUSHER

Midway Field 2-6, which made the Midway Oil Field famous. Blew in over the derrick top, November 27, 1909, and started the Great California Oil Boom. At its peak it produced 2000 barrels a day.

Lakeview was the biggest and wildest. Midway 2-6, coming four months sooner, gets credit for being first. The granite block stands by itself inside a low fence. The air and land nearby is strangely quiet under the lowering sky, punctuated by a faint creaking from the nearest well, where the cable rubs once in every cycle. No wind this day, no dogs, no cars. Perhaps everyone who lives in Fellows went off to Franklin Field. In the hills and plains around the monument where the first gusher blew in, nothing moves but the bowing pumps, the silent praying of a thousand mantises near and far across the western San Joaquin.

UNDERSTANDING THE TEXT

1. How, in Houston's descriptions, does Kern County differ from the traditional images of coastal California?

2. Houston is a visitor to Oildorado. How do his attitudes toward the Kern County oil fields evolve throughout his selection?

3. How does Houston use humor to convey his descriptions of Kern County?

4. What role does Bill play in Houston's narrative?

EXPLORING AND DEBATING THE ISSUES

1. Both Houston and Joan Didion ("Notes from a Native Daughter," p. 54) begin their selections by dismissing the popular images of coastal California. Compare and contrast the tone and purpose of the two writers' essays on the Central Valley. Do they share the same sense of the Valley as a "place"?

2. Write an essay arguing either that Kern County residents are typically Californian or that they more resemble American Southerners or Midwesterners. To what extent does Kern County's population reflect the Okie migration depicted in John Steinbeck's *The Grapes of Wrath*?

3. In an essay, define the sense of community that emerges in Houston's essay. What are the social, economic, and cultural markers that give this part of Kern County a special identity, at least as presented by Houston?

4. Judith Lewis ("Interesting Times," p. 293) comes to California with two images in mind: the glamour of Hollywood and Beverly Hills and the poverty and violence of South Central L.A. Assume her perspective, and write a response to the Kern County that Houston describes. In what ways would her prior expectations have prepared her for visiting Kern County and perhaps for attending the Oildorado parade?

Oildorado Days (1965)

1. To what extent does this photograph reflect James D. Houston's assertion that "One thing I will say about the people of Taft: they are not cynical" (para. 33)?

2. This photograph depicts women who are wearing costumes in the style of the nineteenth century, when the oil industry was established in California, and men who are wearing modern clothes and have just won an Oildorado Days competition. What gender roles are implied by this photograph?

Suburbia

RAMON GARCIA

In **Ramon Garcia**'s Modesto, Mormon missionaries and zootsuited homeboys compete for converts, while the Salvation Army and an X-rated book shop vie for customers. Such are the contradictions in this Central Valley town, which has few trees but a lot of churches, video stores, and fast-food restaurants. A hot, sleepy sort of place that never sleeps, with an unending stream of truck traffic and all-night bars, Modesto stands as the California that the rest of the world (and much of California, too) never sees, hidden behind the gaudy mask of the coast. Garcia is a professor in the department of modern and classical languages and literatures at California State University, Northridge.

The Baptist church buildings
occupy four blocks of downtown.
Suited-up Mormons and zootsuited-up homeboys
ride religiously—
the holy bikes and lowrider Chevy's   5
cruise for conversion
in good and bad neighborhoods
alike.

The missionary jingle of the ice cream truck
has its regular following   10
of afternoon children.
Morning Mormons knock on anonymous doors.
Supermarkets and fast food restaurants
grow faster than trees.
A video store and a church may be found   15
on everyone's neighborhood.

On the street corner of 1st and 10th St
near the Pacific Railroad tracks
the taco van is open all night.
Down the street is the Estrella Azul bar   20
wailing rancheras until morning.
Further down is the X rated bookshop
and the Salvation Army store.
The KKK has its headquarters on the
outskirts of town.   25

Cheap motels glow their neon advertisements
beckoning the fast lanes of the highway.

Semi-trucks scream their hoots in the streets
twenty four hours a day.
The smoke of the factories possesses   30
the air with odorous ghosts.

UNDERSTANDING THE TEXT

1. What expectations did you have when you read the title of the poem, and did the poem fulfill those expectations? Why do you think Garcia chose this title?

2. Trace the comparison that Garcia makes between the Mormons and the homeboys. What imagery does he use to establish a connection between the two groups?

3. The poem moves from "downtown" (l. 2) to other neighborhoods. What is the progression of this movement, and how does it affect your response to the poem?

4. Garcia is describing Modesto in this poem, but he doesn't mention the city's name. Why do you think he omits that name?

EXPLORING AND DEBATING THE ISSUES

1. In class, discuss the effect of Garcia's connection between Mormons and homeboys. How does that connection influence your sense of Modesto as a place?

2. In an essay, compare Garcia's depiction of a Central Valley city with Joan Didion's discussion of the Central Valley in "Notes from a Native Daughter" (p. 54).

3. Analyze the contradictions between groups of people, locations, business, and churches in this poem. How do the contradictions contribute to Garcia's message about "Suburbia"?

4. Read or reread Joan Didion, "Notes from a Native Daughter" (p. 54) and James D. Houston, "In Search of Oildorado" (p. 274). In class, discuss the varying images of the Central Valley that these selections present. Then, write your own synthesis of the selections, expressing your sense of the sort of place the Valley is.

Interesting Times

JUDITH LEWIS

Like many non-Californians, **Judith Lewis**'s mental image of Los Angeles was split between a glittering montage of surfer/celebrity glamour and a gritty mug shot of gang warfare—or as she puts it, between "fairie dust" and "ashes." Then she actually moved to L.A. in 1991, and at first, it was all ashes: car breakdowns on the freeway, a string of natural disasters, and the riots following the Rodney King beating acquittals. But she got used to it, deciding that "the belief that adversity gives depth to life, that we are better for having suffered together, sets the people I know in Los Angeles apart." The strains of Los Angeles life, as Lewis sees it, have created a community of the proudly ambivalent that is utterly invisible to those non-Angelenos who see only the glittering and gritty clichés. Lewis is a staff writer for the *LA Weekly* whose work has appeared in such magazines as *Elle*, *Wired*, and *American Theatre*.

I live in Hollywood. It's a strange thing to me, this fact, as strange as if someone were to tell me that, twenty years from now, I will sit in on the French parliament. At the Mayfair supermarket a block from my house I spot celebrities: Lily Tomlin dresses up in a hat and sunglasses everyone recognizes as uniquely hers; Joanna Gleason walks the aisles with a look on her face that says *don't ask*. Up the street exactly eight-tenths of a mile, I exercise my dogs in a part of Griffith Park we call the "Bat Caves," not because they're home to so many bats, but because they served as the exterior shot of Batman's lair in the 1960s television series. On many mornings I have wandered through those caves in the silent company of so many movie people that I've been assumed to be one. A woman I know named Carol called me Jessica for years and I never thought to correct her, until one rainy day I let it slip that my last name was not Harper.

This, I think sometimes, is not the life for which I was destined. I did not expect to live among the moguls and demiurges of commercial entertainment; I harbored lust for neither beach culture nor the landmarks of noir fiction. And while I cannot pinpoint the moment I started bragging about my latest tumble in a robust wave, or when I took the first of many neighborhood walks to ogle Neutra homes, or stopped worrying about whether my doors were locked when I drove down Florence past Normandie, I know for certain when I survey my Self that I have become an Angeleno. I have grown into this scene; absorbed its perverse aesthetic by osmosis, along with its polluted air, impossible beauty standards, and bad driving habits. Cell phone caught between shoulder and chin, I drive wildly in the passing lane, dashing to appointments, always late, huffing about traffic as I breeze through the door. I jog, eat granola for breakfast, guzzle Chardonnay, practice yoga, attend premieres. I am a walking cliché.

On the other hand, I am not always sure this character is me. Like Estelle in Sartre's *No Exit*, I have the urge to pat my body to confirm my existence. When I catch myself wondering, as I stare at my furrowed brow, whether a little shot of botulism toxin, or "botox"—the cosmetic procedure that's all the rage in Beverly Hills—might be just the thing to smooth those lines out, I have to consider whether the crazy man I met nine years ago in Venice—the one who insisted I get a lead bracelet because aliens were about to bombard the West Coast with brainwashing radiation—might have been telling the truth. I didn't get like this without provocation. Something extraordinary must have happened.

I drove out from Minnesota to Los Angeles in 1991 carrying a copy of Mike Davis's *City of Quartz* and a bad attitude. I was emigrating for a job, not out of any particular infatuation with the city. I took Davis at his word: L.A., he argued, had been built on greed and was verging on apocalypse, and what emerged from his prose managed to dislodge any dim hope I had of fun in the sun and impending fame. In Pocatello, Idaho, I stopped in a cheap motel that had little but CNN to recommend it, turned on the TV for company, and happened upon a series of interviews with disgruntled Angelenos, all of them fixed on flight. The crime, the smog, the earthquakes, they complained—it's a wonder anyone settled here in the first place. My thoughts, as I crept toward the Pacific, turned from whether I should learn to surf to how to best dodge a gang shootout should I take the wrong exit off the freeway.

Like so many newcomers, I wanted a sprinkle of the city's faerie dust   5 but none of its ashes, and as I wound my reluctant way west, dallying among the glorious red rocks of southern Utah and getting waylaid by blackjack in Las Vegas, ashes were all I could imagine. I would like to say that once I arrived the dread abated, but instead it lingered like a chronic illness exacerbated by a toxic environment. Within the first six months, my car—a nondescript foreign economy model in an apparently ill-fated red—was stolen twice, once from my driveway, again from outside my office in broad daylight. The second time it happened, Davis himself offered me a replacement, a VW Dasher he'd been planning to sell. He asked for no money right away; he insisted only that I register it quickly. I didn't. Instead, I drove the car for exactly nine days before it exploded in a rush of steam on the Glendale Freeway (an ending that seemed to me almost poetically Davisian). A series of other cars followed—a diesel Mercedes, an old Volvo station wagon, a ratty little Honda. Each of them at one time or another left me stranded mid-lane at night on some crowded freeway, and each of them, in the end, died painful, grisly deaths.

To be sure, those were difficult years for the whole city: On more evenings than I can now remember, I hunkered down in my nondescript Westside house watching some television station's Emergency Live Action Cam track bodies being swept down the Sepulveda Dam in a sudden rainstorm, or homes imploding in Malibu fires, or a fevered businessman on the roof of a La Brea Avenue stereo store defending his business from looters with a gun. In the five days following the verdict that acquitted the police officers accused of beating Rodney King, my neighbors and I sat on our lawns in the pink-hued air of dusk watching plumes of smoke rise to the south, wondering how it could be possible that, in this modern American city, we could be required by law to stay indoors after sundown.

But civil strife, like personal crises, has strange side effects. During those 1992 riots, I went to a wedding. It was held in a small church near the beach in Santa Monica; the reception was at a nearby hotel. After dinner, as expected, all of us who had attended were stuck in that hotel; to leave would have meant breaking the curfew. We were journalists, and could have traveled home with impunity by declaring ourselves on duty, but truth be told we all wanted an excuse to live life for a night as if during wartime. People broke off into small groups to secure rooms for the night and returned to party like the world was ending. Antisocial brooders drank too much champagne and told strangers their troubles; snobs gave up pretense to dance as flamboyantly as they would in their living rooms; ex-lovers made out in the corners, less for their own satisfaction than for the opportunity they had to create tedium-alleviating scandal. It was, at that time, the finest night of my life in Los Angeles; it remains one of my happiest memories. It was the night I learned that the saying "May you live in interesting times" is not entirely a curse.

It was then that my transformation began. At my neighborhood Vons supermarket—which was suddenly flooded with residents of Inglewood and South L.A. whose own grocery stores were closed, looted, or on fire—I would stare into the eyes of black women as bewildered as I was. We would shake our heads and roll our eyes like co-conspirators, as if we were assuring each other that this war was not between us. On the Venice boardwalk, I exchanged sympathetic glances with fellow joggers who had donned protective masks against the smoke—our faces half-covered, we still managed to telegraph camaraderie. As Parker Center's trees lit up with fire and Payless Shoes got ransacked, I felt myself increasingly ensconced in a community of reasonable people, black and white, who held in equal contempt then–police chief Daryl Gates's lawless hooligans, the exurban jury that exonerated them, and the opportunistic looters who rioted recklessly on blameless stores. Some new version of the city began to come into focus, some collective identity that had to do not with greed or artifice, but a tenacious insistence on remaining civilized even when bombarded by stupidity and turpitude. During those riots, I observed close up what riches adversity dredges up in people's spirits.

On the morning of January 18, 1994, I drove east on the 10 freeway, detouring with the masses around the segment near La Cienega Boulevard that had collapsed in the Northridge earthquake. Stunned and dizzy and guzzling coffee, I was struck by a comforting thought: Every driver on every side of me was in much the same shape. We were united by shock and sleep deprivation. A few nights later, over dinner at an Italian restaurant that had remained sturdy enough to stay open, I confessed to a friend that I would not for all the world have wanted to have been away when the quake hit. If this city were to be shaken down to rubble, I wanted to be here to feel it.

The belief that adversity gives depth to life, that we are better for   10
having suffered together, sets the people I know in Los Angeles apart. What our counterparts in other American cities can only imagine, we have tasted and touched; we have proved to ourselves how intrepid we are, carried that knowledge with us into less eventful days. Angelenos get bad press—we are assumed to be shallow and apolitical; vain and fickle. When the British punk folksinger Billy Bragg visited the city during the combined strikes of the janitors, screen actors, and bus drivers in the year 2000, he expressed amazement that Los Angeles had become a hotbed of political action. But Bragg and others like him settle for surface appraisals—screenwriters, swimming pools, and movie stars; the infamous blond gargoyles of Bel Air, the followers of Fabio who crowd Gold's Gym, and those all-important People Who Don't Read. They miss the solidarity of small neighborhoods, the social activism television actors practice to compensate for work they fear is insipid, the steadfast friendships—even among Hollywood's elite—that survive widening gaps in income and notoriety, because even movie stars know that in a city so mercurial and sprawled, they run the risk of unbearable loneliness. Yes, Angelenos are isolated from one another. All the more reason, when you find one you like, to make yourself known as a true and trusted friend.

Los Angeles has always inspired ambivalence. But mixed feelings hold some allure. Bertolt Brecht derided this land of exile but wrote *Galileo* while living within its boundaries; Chester Himes wrote that the city's racism left him "shattered," but at the height of his distress, he began his startling novel *If He Hollers Let Him Go*. People who say they hate New

York City generally avoid New York City, but people who say they hate Los Angeles take up defiant residence in its hardest neighborhoods to chronicle their resistance to its empty and awful culture, and sometimes, for their pains, find themselves honored with grant money. Ambivalence is not an incidental feature of this city's citizens. We do not stay here in spite of our mixed feelings. We stay here because of them. Ambivalence defines us.

Long after I had acclimated to the pitch and yaw of Los Angeles life, after I had learned to swim in the big waves (both literally and figuratively), feared no freeway exit, and accepted the inevitability of collapsing bookshelves and broken dishes once in a while, I reflected, as the helicopters circled over O.J.'s house, that all this artifice outsiders insist on associating with Los Angeles serves merely to distract them from the city's true cultural muscle. Los Angeles is where life is being lived most vigorously in this country, be it over movie-deal lunches, or on crowded Saturday sidewalks in Koreatown, or at the beach in Malibu. Life here is not simple, and many of this city's rewards have emerged from events that initially seemed like doom. But after a decade, I have finally come to realize that Los Angeles has treated me well—not by allowing me an undramatic, luxurious existence, but by giving me a world to battle as much as I revel in it. It has given me a life in interesting times.

UNDERSTANDING THE TEXT

1. Summarize in your own words how Lewis's attitude toward Los Angeles evolved from before 1991 to the time she wrote this essay.
2. In paragraph 2, Lewis declares "I am a walking cliché." Does this self-characterization seem accurate? Why or why not?
3. What was the significance of the L.A. riots for Lewis?
4. Characterize Lewis's use of humor in this essay. How does it affect your response to her essay? Is she trying only to amuse, or does she have a serious message as well?

EXPLORING AND DEBATING THE ISSUES

1. In class, form teams, and debate the accuracy of Lewis's claim that "The belief that adversity gives depth to life, that we are better for having suffered together, sets the people I know in Los Angeles apart" (para. 10). Use the debate as a group brainstorming exercise for your own essay that supports, challenges, or complicates Lewis's sense of Los Angeles as a place.
2. Both Lewis and Alice Kahn ("Berkeley Explained," p. 359) focus largely on the stereotypes of the city that each describes. In an essay, compare and contrast their essays: Do they use stereotypes to communicate the

same or different messages about their city? How does their use of humor compare?

3. Lewis says that non-Angelenos "settle for surface appraisals" of Los Angeles (para. 10). Visit the library or do an Internet search, looking for news coverage of L.A. events from media across the nation. Analyze the coverage, looking for evidence of exaggeration, clichés, or stereotypes. To what extent is Lewis's assertion valid?

4. Lewis mentions that before she moved to California, her view of Los Angeles was shaped by Mike Davis's *City of Quartz*. Read this book, and then write an essay in which you consider the extent to which one author's view is more accurate—either Davis's vision of the city or Lewis's conclusion that "Los Angeles is where life is being lived most vigorously in this country" (para. 12).

5. In an essay, analyze the extent to which Lewis's selection mirrors the image of California as described in James J. Rawls's "California: A Place, a People, a Dream" (p. 22). Be sure to consider whether Lewis sees any paradoxes in addition to the idealized image.

Edge City: Irvine

JOEL GARREAU

To their detractors, they might be "compared with the Stepford Wives," but what **Joel Garreau** calls the new "Edge Cities"—places like Orange County's Irvine that combine residential neighborhoods, industrial parks, and shopping centers all in one vast master-planned community—are providing a blueprint for the future of both California and America. Here everything is clean, prosperous, well organized, and identical. But if Irvine is, in Garreau's words, "the latest version of the Southern California dream," like all paradises it has its limits. Its uniform blandness can give people "the creeps" and make them wonder who they are and where their roots lie. Garreau is a staff writer for the *Washington Post*, a senior fellow at George Mason University's Institute of Public Policy, and the author of *Edge City: Life on the New Frontier* (1991), from which this selection is taken.

M y brother Peter has a wife and three children and he lives in a group of identical houses and I used to think it was very eerie. But then I remember going over there on Halloween," says John Nielsen.

Nielsen, thirty-four, is talking about community and identity in the new American world built by developers like his father. The elder Nielsen,

Tom, is a leading light behind a place in Southern California called Irvine. It is by far the largest Edge City landscape ever developed by a single company.

"Every place I've lived since I got out of college, Halloween is known as the nightmare movie. It's not known as a holiday. Except here. Here were all these people who had just moved into this suburb at the same time, brand new. And no one knew what was going to happen—whether there was going to be a tradition in this place.

"Here were my nieces Emily and Sara; one was dressed up as a crayon. They kind of poked their heads out the door. It was just at dusk and here comes a crayon looking out this door. They gathered in their cul-de-sac, this herd of kids, and they had a herd of parents behind them. It was the first time I realized that everybody was the same age and there was that kind of community, I guess. They came out not knowing what's going to happen and they turned the corner and there was this army of children. They all just went back and forth, door to door, and I thought, That's neat. That's a tradition that has died elsewhere that's being sustained here. I remember my mother following me with a staple gun because I was a mummy. I would unravel, she'd come up and snip me back together while I was collecting Sugar Babies. There is something historical about that.

"Then Emily and Sara came home. I was helping one trade with her   5
sister for the right kind of treats. You want the Milk Duds, and you want the red Life Savers. You don't want the green ones.

"I just felt I was passing on some sort of higher knowledge."

John Nielsen grew up in a family where the food was put on the table by his father's converting thousands of acres of orange groves and pastureland into the Southern California that exists today. John wound up an environmental writer for National Public Radio. He is the kind of person who, no matter in what region he finds himself, lives in the most Dickensian neighborhood available. He has thus spent much of his life considering where his world intersects with that of his father's, and where both connect to personality and character.

"People ask me where I'm from and I don't know what to say. 'I'm from the suburbs,' is what I usually say. And they say, 'Oh, me too.' It doesn't matter where they're from, we'll exchange some stories about *Gilligan's Island* and then we're friends." He pounded on his chest: "Tarzan of the 'Burbs. Raised by developers." He gave a soft, ironic version of a jungle yell: "Aiiieyaeyaeyaea."

Flashing back twenty years, he recalls, "Me and my brother, we had this Allan Sherman record: 'My Son the Nut.' Ever hear that record?" John sings:

Here's to the crabgrass
Here's to the mortgage,
And here's to sah-BURR-bee-yah.
Lay down your briefcase,
Far from the rat race,
For nothing can dis-TURR-bee yah.

"My brother and I had that memorized. They'd bring us out and we'd   10
sing it."

Nielsen loves neighborhoods that "seethe." He loves places where
you can walk to work and if you regularly stop at a little joint on the way
to pick up a carton of coffee, soon everybody in the neighborhood knows
you. He likes to talk to people in different strata of society. He likes urban
areas that are full of surprises. He thinks the whole point of cities is to
bring diverse people together.

That is why it troubles him that he feels personally excluded from
Edge Cities like the one built by his father, vice chairman of the Irvine
Company. His dilemma is sharpened because each such development
emphasizes the idea of community. As in "master-planned community."

"I feel locked out in the financial sense," says Nielsen of the Irvine
that has been such a market success that the median home prices in its
region are the third highest in America.[1]

"But I don't mean to imply that if I had enough money that is where
I'd go. The things I am interested in are not part of a place like Irvine.
There's that whole notion: We're going to build this thing that is perfect
for you. We haven't met you but we know what you're like and we know
you're going to like it here. That is a repulsive idea, and I wouldn't trust
the person who tried to tell me that. You're in the artist's conception. You
wake up and you're one of those lanky people walking around evenly
spaced. I can't see that. My experience has been that in places like that
you have a lot of people who think they have it figured out. You just have
the coffee-bean machine here and . . ." Nielsen's voice descends to a
whisper. He is almost talking to himself. Then he hurtles back.

"That kind of ordered circumstance is scary to me. Maybe the world   15
is divided into people who love to hum 'Is that all there is?' and take random walks and people who don't. It's a hard thing for me."

What Nielsen is struggling with is the extent to which Edge Cities
weave or unravel the American social fabric. For this reason, his conflicts are historic. Ever since the rise of what used to be called "bedroom

[1] Median home prices, second quarter of 1990: Honolulu, $345,000; San Francisco,
$263,000; Anaheim–Santa Ana, $248,900; Los Angeles, $216,000; Bergen-Passaic,
$193,000. National Association of Realtors.

communities"—that is, classic residential suburbs—scholars have been trying to define where these places fit into a larger social scheme. Especially in the 1950s, when the floodtide of homes moved out past our old conception of city, the outpouring of journalism, fiction, and sociology on these issues was prodigious.[2] It had a distinct tone. Herbert J. Gans, in his landmark 1967 work, *The Levittowners*, pungently described the shots that were taken.[3] If you believed the critics, he wrote, the "myth of suburbia"[4] would have you surmise:

"The suburbs were breeding a new set of Americans, as mass-produced as the houses they lived in . . . incapable of real friendships; they were bored and lonely, alienated, atomized, and depersonalized. . . .

"In unison," Gans wrote of that time, "the authors chanted that individualism was dying, suburbanites were miserable, and the fault lay with the homogeneous suburban landscape and its population." Gans described John Keats, author of *The Crack in the Picture Window*, as "perhaps the most hysterical of the mythmakers."

Keats's book began: "*For literally nothing down* . . . you too can find a box of your own in one of the fresh-air slums we're building around the edges of American cities . . . inhabited by people whose age, income, number of children, problems, habits, conversation, dress, possessions, and perhaps even blood type are also precisely like yours." They were, Keats claimed, "developments conceived in error, nurtured by greed, corroding everything they touch. They . . . actually drive mad myriads of housewives shut up in them."[5]

Subsequently, Gans observed, "literary and social critics chimed in. . . . Suburbia was intellectually debilitating, culturally oppressive, and politically dangerous, breeding bland mass men without respect for the arts or democracy." 20

Gans bought a house and *lived* in New Jersey's Levittown for two years to study what processes turned a group of strangers into a true community in the waning days of the Eisenhower era. Of course, the sociologist and city planner could uncover little evidence that there was much change in people when they moved to the suburbs, or that the change that took place could be traced to the new environment: "If

---

[2] I am indebted to Nicholas Lemann, "Stressed Out in Suburbia: A Generation after the Postwar Boom, Life in the Suburbs Has Changed, Even If Our Picture of It Hasn't," *Atlantic*, November 1989, 34, for many of the literary citations here.

[3] Herbert J. Gans, *The Levittowners: Ways of Life and Politics in a New Suburban Community* (New York: Pantheon, 1967), xv.

[4] Phrase coined by Bennett Berger. Gans, *Levittowners*.

[5] John Keats, *The Crack in the Picture Window* (Boston: Houghton Mifflin, 1956).

suburban life was as undesirable and unhealthy as the critics charged, the suburbanites themselves were blissfully unaware of it. They were happy in their new homes and communities, much happier than they had been in the city."[6]

This has not, however, prevented Edge City from giving people the creeps. When I first started reporting on these places, an art critic of my acquaintance pulled up a chair, pushed his face toward mine closer than was really comfortable, and proceeded to get agitated about my project. "Those are not cities!" he exploded.

When I systematically questioned him as to why he felt this way, given all the job numbers and market numbers and population numbers, what I found was intriguing. His real beef was that he refused to believe these places brought people together in any larger social sense. He was saying these were not "cities," but what he really meant was that he could not believe they were "communities." It was very specific. To him, Edge Cities were hollow because, among other things, there were not, as in the neighborhoods he loved, front stoops for people to sit on to watch the human drama.

Here we were, more than thirty years after David Riesman's *The Lonely Crowd*, William H. Whyte's *The Organization Man*, Sloan Wilson's *The Man in the Gray Flannel Suit*, and the stories of John Cheever.[7] And he was still proclaiming the landscape out past the old downtowns as having no ties that bind, no sense of identity, no way of making people believe they were part of something larger than themselves. He felt people had no personal stake in these places. Nobody cared about them. Therefore, these places could not be regarded as cities.

I had come to believe that it was not particularly useful to insist that a place was not urban merely because it contained few front stoops or political boundaries. But that didn't mean my friend the art critic had it all wrong. After all, for a place to have an identity, people really must feel they are stakeholders in it. They must feel that it is, at gut level, theirs; that they are willing to fight over it and for it. They must see it as having an importance relative to their personal interests. They must see it, at some level, as community.

Yet the forces that bring about Edge City pull strongly in different directions. Edge City arose as a result of individuals seeking out the best combinations of how and where to live, work, and play. Maybe Edge City isn't the puddle of atomization and anomie that 1950s critics of American

25

---

[6] Gans, *Levittowners*, xvi.

[7] *The Lonely Crowd* was published in 1950, *The Organization Man* in 1956.

society wished to believe. But it is less than clear where it connects with ideas like community—the hunger for human contact and the yearning to belong to a larger whole.

This is why Irvine is interesting. It is part of the Los Angeles Basin, the birthplace of the American landscapes and life styles that are the models for Edge Cities worldwide. Moreover, Irvine, thirty-five miles southeast of downtown Los Angeles, is at the center of a development of staggering proportions. Originally a Spanish land-grant ranch, the hundred-square-mile holdings of the Irvine Company span Orange County, that vast jurisdiction between San Diego and Los Angeles that in the 1980s was the fastest-growing part of Southern California. The Irvine Company controls sixty-four thousand acres of land, much of which stretches past the incorporated city of Irvine. Some of those acres sell for $1 million apiece. Irvine is not just another Levittown, a suburb from which people can find work only by commuting some-where else. The stages of Edge City growth that took two generations elsewhere was collapsed into a third of a lifetime here. The Irvine area is now so big that it can be described as encompassing all or part of three job-rich Edge Cities.

The two middle-sized ones are known as Irvine Spectrum and New-port Center–Fashion Island. But the third, the size of downtown Seattle, is named after—it had to happen—John Wayne.[8] Actually, the area's continental-connection airport is named after John Wayne. And the Edge City, which includes the Costa Mesa–South Coast Plaza complex, has be-come known after the name of the airport. But it was only a matter of time before it came to something like this. Orange County, the birth-place of Richard Nixon, has such a reputation for conservatism that a politician once only half kidded about joining the John Birch Society in order to capture the middle-of-the-road vote. The Irvine area's rapidly growing population, meanwhile, already approaches 200,000, with a high-technology job base of 150,000. The Irvine Company's spread is so big—stretching from the Pacific Ocean to as much as twenty miles inland—that its tentacles ensnare an entire University of California campus and two Marine bases.

Irvine, moreover, is the latest version of the Southern California dream. This makes it a prototype of great importance. Irvine is only ten miles from Disneyland in Anaheim. Disney produced such resonant dreams that people carry them around in their heads all over the globe.

[8] Downtown Seattle was at 21.9 million square feet (Office Network) when the John Wayne Airport area, including Newport Beach–Fashion Island, was at 25.6 million (Grubb & Ellis, Newport Beach).

His Main Street is a more real crystallization of idealized community for more people than any actual nineteenth-century small American town. And Irvine is deep kin to this ideal. It is full of newcomers who are still reaching out to find why they came, what they lost, and who they are.

In fact, a travel guide called *The Californias*, published by the California Office of Tourism, describes Orange County this way: 30

> It's a theme park—a seven hundred and eighty-six square mile theme park—and the theme is "you can have anything you want."
>
> It's the most California-looking of all the Californias: the most like the movies, the most like the stories, the most like the dream.
>
> Orange County is Tomorrowland and Frontierland, merged and inseparable . . .
>
> The temperature today will be in the low 80s. There is a slight offshore breeze. Another just-like-yesterday day in paradise.
>
> Come to Orange County. It's no place like home.[9]

The danger of a dream, however, is that a place that reminds people of Eden can also taunt them. People's fears and anxieties may be heightened when the dream does not turn out to be as boundless as it first seems; when it quickly hits limits. In fact, Irvine has been compared with the Stepford Wives—perfect, in a horrifying sort of way. The development's newest residential section, Westpark, is an unbroken field of identical Mediterranean red-clay roof tile, covering homes of indistinguishable earth-tone stucco. Homes in Irvine are far more repetitive than those in the old Levittowns. The old Levittowns are now interesting to look at; people have made additions to their houses and planted their grounds with variety and imagination. Unlike these older subdivisions, Irvine has deed restrictions that forbid people from customizing their places with so much as a skylight. This is a place that is enforced, not just planned. Owners of expensive homes in Irvine commonly volunteer stories of not realizing that they had pulled into the driveway of the wrong house until their garage-door opener failed to work. Driving around, what one mainly sees is high blank walls. The shopping center near the University of California at Irvine struggled for years, unsuccessfully, to support a bookstore. And this is the place that bills itself as America's premiere master-planned community. It underlines the "community" symbolism with a ten-minute sound-and-light show called *Roots and Wings*.

Roots and Wings is a singular production. It is a twenty-thousand-slide, sixteen-projector extravaganza housed in its own little theater, and

[9] Quoted by Edward W. Soja, "The Orange County Exopolis: A Contemporary Screenplay," unpublished.

it culminates with the rotation of a hydraulically controlled model of some 150 square miles of the area. The model weighs half a ton. It is so exactly detailed, with 385,000 separate structures, that people living in Irvine can identify their own houses. This show is so lavish that the Irvine Company refuses to divulge its cost.

Intriguingly, this hymn to community is not used to sell homes. People who are in the market merely for quarter-million-dollar residences never get the red-carpet treatment that includes *Roots and Wings*. The people who see this pageant are those thinking of moving their companies to Irvine. *Roots and Wings* is reserved for customers looking for massive amounts of Edge City research-and-development or office space. Yet in this pitch, the customers never hear a word about dollars per square foot. The Irvine Company believes that the following approach is what sells commercial real estate in their Edge City.

The lights go down, the sea gulls start flashing on the screens, the music comes up, and the deep male voiceover booms from multiple concealed speakers:

> How long since you watched the new day lean down upon the shore? No one about but you and your thoughts. And time, sliding by on its spiral glide.
>
> Here, along the sea, far from the crowds, one can see how perfectly Nature casts her characters and places them upon her stage. Each living thing is drawn to that habitat most ideally suited to the development of its full potential. It is a law of Nature. Instinct, we are told.
>
> But, we wonder, what of that wandering species called man? Called woman? Called child? Are we not also embraced by Nature's laws? Shaped by our habitat, just as the sea bird's flight is shaped by the wind for that special place on earth to hold and nourish our lives?
>
> It is said there are only two lasting things we can give our children; one is roots, the other is wings. This then is the dream. To find a place where we can put down roots; to find a place where our lives can take wing.

The Irvine show proceeds to extol the development's "beauty," "work style," "life style," and its "critical mass of finance, knowledge, and re-source to rival any major city in America." But then it swings right back and starts hammering at that community theme some more:

> If the human community is to work, there must be a lively interplay between the commerce and the arts, between nature and technology, between work and leisure, between private interest and the public good. In a sense it's like planning and creating a living mosaic. . . . The design of this living mosaic is especially refreshing because of the rare relationship between where one works and where one lives, in communities

where planning brings the workplace closer. It is a gift of time. More time to enjoy another gift. The gift of family. . . .

Then the wind-up:

Here is a place where life is lived with a grand and glorious sense of quality and style. Here is a place providing opportunities for the full range of human experience. . . . Here is a place where individuals are free to shape their own future, as a sculptor shapes clay.

A daddy is shown lifting his child. Freeze frame. He lifts the child higher. Freeze frame. The child is lifted all the way up. Freeze frame.
Then the pitch:

We have the dream. We have the plan. We have the people. We have the patterns of a vision firmly in our minds and in our hearts.

The child's image melds into that of a sea gull, which, in multiple-image long-lens slow-mo, explodes into flight.

We have the place where we can put down roots.
And our lives can take wing.

Music swells, image fades, screen lifts, gauze curtain rises, dramatic　40 lights flare, and the half-ton model of Irvine, turning on its gimbles, rotates into view, beckoning.
One is left in awe, speechless.
Heavy freight being loaded here. Loaded on ideas and values that are elemental: Roots. Wings. Community. This is the place that Tom Nielsen built, that John Nielsen can't handle. Irvine thus demands that these words—and what they mean to us in the late twentieth century—be probed.

UNDERSTANDING THE TEXT

1. Summarize in your own words John and Tom Nielsen's attitudes toward suburbia.

2. How do "Edge Cities" differ from the bedroom communities of the 1950s, according to Garreau?

3. What are the typical criticisms of suburbia, and how does Garreau respond to those accusations?

4. Why does Garreau find Irvine to be particularly "interesting" (para. 27), and why does he say that Irvine "is the latest version of the Southern California dream" (para. 29)?

5. Why do you think that Garreau quotes the narration from the *Roots and Wings* production (paras. 31–42)?

EXPLORING AND DEBATING THE ISSUES

1. Write a journal entry in which you discuss the sort of community that you prefer (whether you live there or not). Like John Nielsen, do you prefer "neighborhoods that 'seethe'" (para. 11)? Or do you feel more comfortable in planned developments such as Irvine? How do you account for your preferences?

2. Compare and contrast John and Tom Nielsen's attitudes toward community. To develop your ideas, you might visit neighborhoods similar to those that each man advocates.

3. Write an essay in which you analyze the *Roots and Wings* production (paras. 31–42). What images and language does it use to create a sense of place? To what extent do you see this production as a positive depiction of community or as a dangerous example of corporate propaganda?

4. In class, heed Garreau's concluding advice, and probe values such as "roots," "wings," and "community" (para. 42). To what extent do these words suggest values that the class shares? And in what sorts of neighborhoods do class members believe these values can thrive? Use the class discussion as a springboard for writing your own definition of a healthy community. Be sure to ground your definition in specific references to the physical design of the place.

5. Garreau mentions that "Irvine has been compared with the Stepford Wives" (para. 31). In other words, the city and others like it are criticized for being too perfect, overplanned, and essentially sterile and conformist. In an essay, argue whether you think this sort of development is "dangerous" (para. 20), as some critics assert, or whether such planning enhances residents' lifestyles, as developers claim.

The Palms in Our Hands

GARY PAUL NABHAN

Palm Springs is aptly named: palm trees really are all over the place. Most of those trees were planted by real estate developers and speculators to ornament the subdivisions whose inhabitants, mostly retirees, survive the blistering summer temperatures by the grace of air conditioning and Southern California Edison. But **Gary Paul Nabhan** (b. 1952) wants us to know that there is another way to live in the desert, the traditional ways of the Sonoran Indians whose dwellings (or hukis) are dug into the earth to provide a natural air conditioning and who use fibers from the native palmetto trees to weave into useful desert items such as "petaca" baskets and sombreros. Such a stark juxtaposition, which reflects two profoundly different cultural visions, could be instructive, especially in this era of electricity shortages and thousand-dollar monthly electricity bills. A MacArthur fellow, Nabhan is the author of numerous books, including *The Desert Smells Like Rain* (1982) and *Gathering the Desert* (1985), which won the John Burroughs Medal for nature writing.

Around Palm Springs, California, half of the sixty thousand residents are over sixty years old. In August, the asphalt running in to the various retirement subdivisions drives the thermometer up over 170 degrees. The pavement is so hot, you can fry a snowbird's egg on it—if you can find one. Most of the old birds who stay year-round stay inside during the summer. They may take a couple of showers a day to stay fresh. Many of them pay Southern California Edison a thousand dollars a month or more to keep their air conditioners running straight through the summer.

Outside, there is little shade you can sit under. Carports or porches, if those can be considered "outside." A eucalyptus in the backyard, perhaps. A couple of lollipop-shaped citrus trees or an African sumac, though they are seldom manicured so that you can fit a warm body beneath their canopies. The Hollywood junipers in the front may throw a shadow on the wall, but they don't shade a soul.

Then there are the palms. All the planned adult communities have broad streets lined with widely spaced palms. They are lucrative commodities in the landscape-nursery industry of southern California, sold by the foot, hauled by truck, and propped up in yards as if a motion picture studio were making an instant oasis movie right there in the new neighborhood. Introduced date palms are placed in strategic locations, but they usually have a big puddle of irrigation water at their bases which keeps folks from sitting beneath them. And there are the lines of native palms, the shorter "California fan palms" with petticoats of dead fronds trimmed halfway down their stout trunks, interspersed every sixty feet with tall, slender "Mexican skydusters." Landscape architects love how these two variants of *Washingtonia filifera* "rise out of the bare earth" on the curbs of urban boulevards, either in monotonous rows "for cadence" or singly, "like an exclamation point." They are planted in these subdivisions to make each landowner feel that he is living within his very own "oasis paradise." Yet these palms are stuck out on the side of the street where hardly anyone walks. Separated from one another by irrigated lawns of empty space, each throws a tiny oval shadow down on the ground. Torn from their evolutionary history of being densely clustered with other palms of various ages, each is as lonesome as a fish out of school.

When the more speculative subdivisions dry up economically, the faucets close, and the flow of water from some subterranean aquifer slows. The billboard showing a life of leisure played out beneath a palm grove cracks in the wind, then blows over. On one abandoned boulevard near Palm Springs, a starved *Washingtonia* finally curls down, fronds gone, dead growth tip touching the dust. The whole plant makes a big, sad U. It looks like a lean-legged ostrich hiding its head in the ground.

Nearby, a speculator leaves his office—a mobile trailer—and heads into town for a noonday drink. Parking his air-conditioned Oldsmobile, he locks the doors and walks, sweating, across the superheated paved lot. A palm silhouette shaped of menthol-green neon lights the window of the entrance to the Oasis Tap, promising paradise and lunch inside. His arms quiver and he makes a quiet grunt while pulling open the heavy door. Coldness rushes out. He enters. He can hardly see anything except for the flashing lights of the electric Coors ski-slope sign on the far wall. He takes off his sunglasses and his eyes adjust to the dimly lit tavern. He is glad to have taken refuge in this little electrically simulated oasis, away from business, bright lights, and the blazing sun. He finds a stool. Perspiration cools quickly on his arm.

"Whatchou guys been up to, huh? Hey," he pants, "gimme a cold one. Hey, what they got on the tube today? Are the Padres gonna let the Goose pitch today? Is that game on? What time is it anyway?"

He reaches for the icy Coors in front of him and takes the first gulp. A chill hits his chest. He gasps. Staring at the TV, still sweating, he can't see a single Padre.

He never walks out of the Oasis Tap.

Three women ascend from a hole in a mound near their house as the shade begins to slide up the Sonoran barranca slope. It is after four on a June afternoon. They have been in the shelter of their *huki* since eleven or so. The two younger women joke while casually stripping palm fiber for the rectangular-shaped *petaca* baskets that they will begin the next day. The older woman, plaiting a new palm sombrero for her husband, is quiet, thoughtful. The last double-weave sombrero like this one lasted her husband for four years; his newer, store-bought plastic fiber hat hardly weathered seven months of his constant use. So she starts twilling its roundish crown, working down toward the pliant brim, and tomorrow will weave back to the top and tie it in. It will take several days of work for something that most people now buy at the store. But then again, having a durable hat is important. It is all that stands between her husband and the scorching sun on these June days when he has to work long hours to prepare his fields for the rainclouds that will soon cross central Sonora.

By noon on most days since early May, she has been retreating with   10
the other women into the huki, a semi-subterranean shelter where a roof of logs, palm fronds, dirt, and brush covers a shallow excavation into a hillside. There, with her bare feet on the earthen floor, she hums quietly to herself while weaving, or giggles at the jokes the other two make about the men. There, in the musky dark, the frond fibers of the Sonoran palmetto, *Sabal uresana*, remain moist and workable. There, too, she has a break after helping her husband do the milking, after making breakfast and cheese, after sweeping the house and the ramada. Her thoughts are her own in the huki. Although she continues to work, the shadowy solitude somehow restores her freshness.

UNDERSTANDING THE TEXT

1. What is Nabhan's attitude toward the two groups who reside in Palm Springs: the retirees and speculators and the Native Americans?
2. How do the landscape palms capture the spirit of the developed Palm Springs?
3. What is the huki, and why is it important to Native Americans?

EXPLORING AND DEBATING THE ISSUES

1. In class, compare the attitudes of the Palm Springs retirees and speculators with those of the Native Americans. What sense of place does each group have, and how are their attitudes toward palm trees symbolic of their belief systems?
2. Nabhan's own attitude toward nature is implied in this selection. Write an essay in which you compare Nabhan's attitude with that of David Mas Masumoto ("As If the Farmer Died," p. 248). How do you account for any differences you might observe?

3. Analyze the figurative language and descriptive language in this selection, and write an essay in which you argue how the language conveys Nabhan's implicit attitude toward the two groups of people in his essay.

4. Adopt the perspective of the real estate speculator, and write a response to Nabhan's essay. Alternately, take the view of the Native Americans, and write a critique of the way in which Palm Springs has been developed.

Researching the Issues

1. Divide the class into teams, and conduct an intensive study of campus life and places. Explore different areas such as housing, athletic facilities, classroom buildings, the student union building, and eateries. Be sure to note who uses these places, why they use them, and how they respond to them. Do patrons of a campus restaurant, for instance, linger and study, or do they eat and run? What is it about the place that stimulates patrons' behavior? Use your findings as the basis of an essay in which you define the sort of community that exists on your campus.

2. Interview students and other people who live in the area surrounding your campus, asking them about the sense of place created by your college or university. Do residents see your school as enhancing their quality of life or as being a nuisance? Do students feel like they are part of the surrounding community, or is their sense of place limited to campus? Use your interview results to compare and contrast the "town" and the "gown" views of how your school fits into the neighborhood.

3. Visit a town or city council meeting. Try to interview council members and citizens before or after the session on how well they believe that community concerns are addressed in this forum. You might additionally locate in a local newspaper an article covering the session. Write an essay in which you evaluate the session. To what extent do you believe it served community needs and interests?

4. Research the history of the settlement of your hometown or region. Who were the first non-Native settlers? Are their descendants still prominent in the community, or have other inhabitants changed the demographic profile of the area? What were the causes of any changes you may observe? Use your findings as the basis of an essay in which you explain the evolution of your town or region. To develop evidence, you might consult a local library or the Los Angeles Public Library's "Regional History Resources" site located at http://www.lapl.org/elec_neigh/index.html.

5. Since the 1960s, California, and especially San Francisco, has been the center of gay politics in the United States. Research the history

of the gay political movement in California, and write an essay in which you outline the ways that gay activists became involved in the political system, both locally and statewide, to further their causes. You might begin by consulting the late Randy Shilts's *The Mayor of Castro Street: The Life and Times of Harvey Milk* (1982).

6. Research the history of California's national parks, especially Yosemite National Park. How did such lands come to be preserved? What obstacles were faced in the process of their preservation?

7. Tourism is one of California's leading industries. Conduct a research project in which you determine the most popular tourist sites in the state, and then write an analysis of how these places have come to represent California to the rest of the country. What places are emphasized, and what places are left out of the picture? How can you account for your findings?

8. Visit an established ethnic neighborhood and interview shopkeepers or patrons who would count as old-timers, asking them about any changes they may have observed. Have they observed demographic or economic shifts? If so, how have these affected business? If there have been few changes, how do the locals account for such community stability? Use your interview results to support an argument about the extent to which this neighborhood has been influenced by social change.

9. Use the Internet to research a region in California that tends not to receive much attention from either the media or even state politicians (counties such as Del Norte or Modoc, mining towns such as Trona near the Panamint Mountains, ecologically devastated regions such as the Salton Sea). Study the region's economy, demography, political leanings, and prevailing way of life. Has the region faced changes in the last decade or so, or has the status quo prevailed? Use your research to formulate an essay that explores the region's sense of place, and present your conclusions to the class.

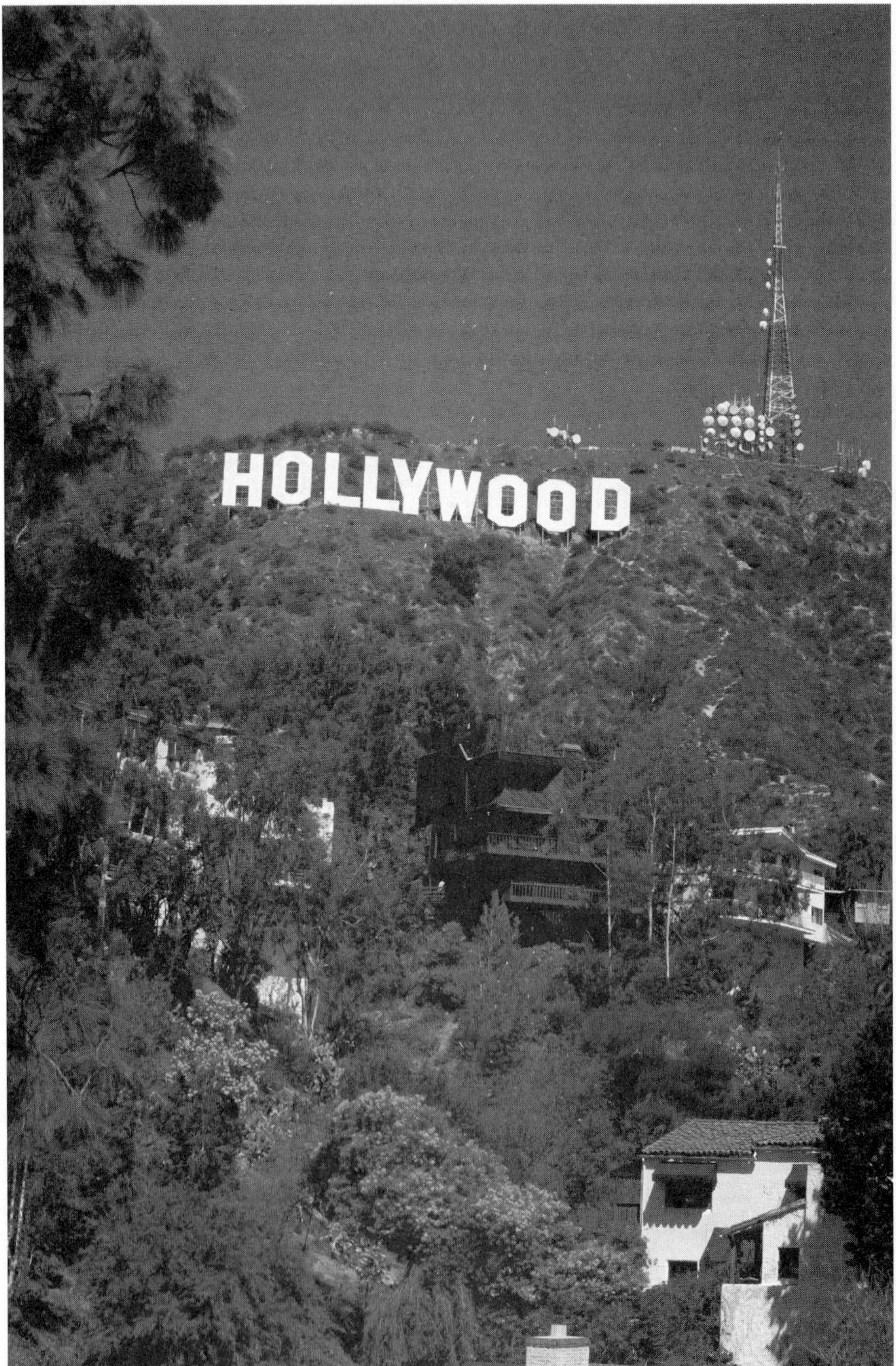
HOLLYWOOD

5

Exporting Culture
CALIFORNIA AND THE POPULAR IMAGINATION

"Carolina Dreaming." "The Little Old Lady from Tuscaloosa." "PA Woman." "It Never Rains in Arizona." "I Wish They All Could Be Louisiana Girls." *Forest Hills 11375*. "Do You Know the Way to Santa Fe?" "I Left My Heart in San Antonio." *Straight Outta Brooklyn.*

These titles don't sound right, do they? Sure, other states have had songs and albums written about them and TV shows and movies set in them, but California has inspired American culture, particularly popular culture, ever since the movie industry first set down its roots in the once quiet village of Hollywood. It isn't simply that California has become a center of popular media and thus a broadcaster and exporter of culture. California has become a center of desire and thus a place whose lifestyle is envied and emulated around the country. New York may still rule the roost when it comes to high culture and the arts, but you can't beat California for seizing the national imagination when it comes to just about anything else.

Indeed, it isn't just economic opportunity that brings so many people here. Something about the California lifestyle has lured Americans and non-Americans alike to the golden state since the late nineteenth century, when Helen Hunt Jackson's *Ramona* set off a mission furniture craze and a stampede to Southern California. By the 1930s, Nathanael West was satirizing, in his novel *The Day of the Locust*, the hordes of Midwesterners who

---

◄ *Hollywood sign.*

315

had come to L.A. in the hopes of having some of the Hollywood mystique rub off on them, and in the 1950s and early 1960s, the long summer of California surf culture, as celebrated by the Beach Boys and any number of *Beach Blanket Bingo*–style movies, became a youth cultural icon. And don't forget that the Summer of Love was launched in San Francisco in 1967 or that the hippie subculture that grew out of it made the intersection of two streets, Haight and Ashbury, internationally famous. And while rap was invented in New York City, it was a California outfit, N.W.A., that established one of its most long-lived and most influential genres.

It is also worth noting that while the East Coast's Howard Johnson's restaurants can lay a better claim to having invented the modern fast-food chain, it is San Diego's McDonald's that has turned fast food into an international symbol of American consumer culture. Similarly, while thousands of carnival grounds throughout America, including New York City's Coney Island, long predated Anaheim's Disneyland, it is Disneyland that looms as the grandiose symbol of the modern American-style theme park. Finally, though the computer was no California invention, it was a couple of guys from the Bay Area who made personal computing a national pastime, compelling the East Coast's computing colossus, IBM, to come up with the PC to compete with their innovative little Apple.

So, while it does tend to get on the nerves of non-Californians, we Californians do get a lot of attention. This might be one reason why the rest of the country can seem so fascinated with the darker side of the California lifestyle, as happened when Charles Manson, Jim Jones, O. J. Simpson, and the Hillside Strangler seized the national headlines. Every silly California-based fad is sure to receive more than its fair share of disdain (for instance, hot tubs, which are now a national lifestyle fixture, were sneered at as typically "Californian" when they first appeared in the 1960s and 1970s), while news teams from across the nation are ready to converge on the Golden State at the first rumbling of an earthquake or when the first beach house slides into the sea. Let's face it: glamour breeds envy, and plenty of non-Californians seem eager for the Big One to open up oceanfront real estate opportunities in Nevada.

Putting the Pop in Popular Culture

California's place in the popular imagination did not come by accident. Though its climate has played a significant role in the construction of the California mystique, the most important contribution that California has made to American culture stems from its dominance of the entertainment industry. For ever since the locus for the movie industry shifted from the Northeast to Hollywood and its environs, California has stood as the central pillar of what cultural critics Theodore Adorno and Max

Horkheimer have called the "culture industry." Beginning with the movies and the recording industry, the culture industry has branched out in innumerable directions, which now include radio, television, and the Internet, media that disseminate the films, music, television programs, and Web-based entertainments and commentaries that have become such key elements in contemporary American life. And California has not only produced a major share of the content of these entertainments; it has also produced, through its dominance in high-tech research and development, many of the means for creating that content. Just think of the computer-generated special effects that are so essential to movies these days: someone had to invent the technologies that make them possible, and often those inventors have been Californians.

In a society in which entertainment is not only a key economic industry but also a central component of our consciousness and the major shaper of our desires, California's historic domination of the culture industry has dramatically magnified the image of California in the rest of the country and world. Where once Paris, London, and New York defined global cultural horizons, L.A. (whose initials virtually anyone can recognize) now lays claim to being the most influential center of cultural development. Los Angeles also has high cultural contributions to make—for example, an internationally honored symphonic orchestra now housed in a glamorous new concert hall designed by Frank Gehry and sponsored by the Disney Corporation, as well as vibrant artistic, literary, and dramatic communities—but somehow those contributions aren't what most people seem to care about. What really gets attention is Academy Awards night, which, even when broadcast from New York, is a quintessentially Californian phenomenon.

Star Maps and Red Bandannas

Thus Hollywood is no longer simply a place. It is a symbol, a metaphor for a galaxy of entertainments that, even when they are not actually produced in California (and a great deal of such production has been moved out of state in recent years), project an image of California that persists even as multinational corporations swallow up the old Hollywood studios. For California is not only where it all began, it is also the place where many, if not most, of the most popular stars within the culture industry actually dwell. Whether it is Santa Barbara, Malibu, Beverly Hills, or the Hollywood Hills—and many less well known posh communities—Southern California is the place where the stars go (or at least maintain one of their many residences). This was the case with silent-era stars who built extravagant mansions (Mary Pickford and Douglas Fairbanks called their palace "Pickfair") in the Southern California hills to dramatize their stardom and wealth and who created a new aristocracy of entertainers whose often humble origins would make them especially gaudy exemplars of the American dream. Gazing on the mansions raised by Hollywood-generated wealth, generations of star seekers who course through the hills of L.A. with star maps clutched in their hands can find reflections of their own dreams and desires.

This is why the image of California, especially Southern California, is so skewed in the national imagination. When other Americans think of California, they tend to see the images that Hollywood has sent them: images of seaside or hilltop palaces with dramatic vistas of the sea. But there is a flip side to the image. California has projected an image of extreme wealth to America, creating desires, if only in fantasy, to live extravagantly, but its culture industry has also projected a much grittier image of the urban streets. Ever since N.W.A. helped establish the "gangsta" genre of hip hop and movies like *Boyz N the Hood* and *Colors* transmogrified the violent realities of urban poverty into middle-class teen fashions, the other image of California has been framed through the vision of an urban street gang. In fact, Californians are probably the most diversely domiciled of Americans, living on farms and in forests, in deserts and middle-class tracts, and in penthouses and apartment blocks. When non-Californians think of California, however, they see either Beverly Hills or Compton, a drastic distortion of a complex reality that has been made possible by television and the movies.

California is not all celebrities and street gangs, surfers and gangsters. There isn't a Disneyland on every street corner. But thanks to a popular culture that Californians have been instrumental in creating, these images are what the rest of the world sees and is either attracted or repelled. This cartoon vision manages to glamorize poverty and urban violence and make them a source for entertainment. And in an entertainment-obsessed society where fantasy trumps reality almost every time, California's place in the dream-weaving machinery of the culture industry (remember that Steven Spielberg calls his studio Dreamworks) virtually assures that it will remain a locus of American and global desire, as well as an exporter of those desires.

The Readings

Helen Hunt Jackson's popular novel *Ramona* probably did more to establish California as a lifestyle exporter than anything else prior to the establishment of the Hollywood movie industry, and Blake Allmendinger's literary analysis of the novel, which opens this chapter, traces varying ways in which the California dream works as a defining motif for this and other literary works. David Fine's "Endings and Beginnings: Surviving Apocalypse" analyzes the way that California, especially Southern California, has been a favorite site for the apocalyptic imaginations of filmmakers who, all in all, seem to believe that the Golden State is where everything is destined to come to an end. Nathanael West's satirical look at the way Californians, particularly the residents of Hollywood, express their fantasies through elaborate fashion and architectural charades exposes California's leading role in the dissemination of desire, while Dana Polan analyzes the ways in which the image of California is constructed in the popular imagination through Hollywood filmmaking. James J. Flink next surveys the leading role that California has played in the mass motorization of America. Alice Kahn and Patricia Leigh Brown follow with a pair of readings—one humorous, the other journalistic—focusing on California-style consumption, a style that is by no means limited to Californians. And William McClung concludes the chapter with a study on Arcadian and Utopian images that shaped early-twentieth-century America's imaginings of California and that were expressed in California's famous orange-crate art.

All about Eden

BLAKE ALLMENDINGER

The dream is of success, pleasure, glamour, and fame. The reality, as **Blake All-mendinger** writes here, is all too often a matter of "oppression, disappointment, and failure that contradicts the success stories." The reception of Helen Hunt Jackson's best-selling novel *Ramona* (1884) is a striking case in point. On the surface, a romantic tale of gracious living on a vast Californo-Mexican rancho, *Ramona* helped launch an architectural and domestic design fad that made mission-style architecture and furniture coveted luxuries throughout America and helped lure thousands of American immigrants to sunny Southern California. But in reality, *Ramona* is about feudal-style repression, racism, and the dispossession of the California Indians from their land. Indeed, sometimes California seems to be an optical illusion. A professor in the English department at UCLA, Allmendinger's books include *The Cowboy: Representations of Labor in an American Work Culture* (1992), *Ten Most Wanted: The New Western Literature* (1998), and *Over the Edge: Remapping the American West* (1998).

Throughout time, California has been objectified by artists and writers, politicians and kings, missionaries and military explorers, and dream-seeking settlers and immigrants. In the year 1500, the Spanish novelist Garcí Ordóñez de Montalvo envisioned California as an "island of Amazons," mythically located "near to the terrestrial paradise."[1] Subsequent

---

[1] Howard R. Lamar, ed., *The Reader's Encyclopedia of the American West* (New York: Harper and Row, 1977), 149.

Spanish missionaries, in the seventeenth and eighteenth centuries, attempted to transform California into a divine earthly outpost where men of God rescued the souls of "savage" Native Americans. In the early nineteenth century, when Mexico secured its independence from Spain, the missions were secularized and transformed into ranchos run by the wealthy elite. The commercial exploitation of California continued in the mid-nineteenth century, when gold miners rushed into the new U.S. territory in the late 1840s. Ever since then, California has beckoned to millions of hopeful new citizens, who come to the state looking for job opportunities, sunshine and surf, safe refuge, or stardom.

Versions of the California Dream are as various as the people who come here in search of fulfillment. Yet every dream, it seems, has a similar sequel, one that spells disillusion. For every invader who conquers the land, there is a native or previous occupant who must be displaced. For every gold miner, movie star, or high-tech entrepreneur who succeeds, there are many more who don't strike it rich. While California has been depicted as an Edenic utopia, as an exotic tropical paradise, as the ultimate cash prize and end point of Manifest Destiny, and as a glamorous celebrity haven, it has also witnessed a history of oppression, disappointment, and failure that contradicts the success stories. The enslavement of Native Americans, the ridicule of Chinese, the persecution of Okies, the exploitation of migrant farmworkers, and the tensions that led to race riots in Watts and greater Los Angeles are reminders that the California Dream often mocks the reality.

Nowhere is this more true than in literature. In the late nineteenth century, two landmark novels, written by women from dissimilar backgrounds, both indicted the dream. *Ramona* (1884), by Helen Hunt Jackson, addressed the removal and persecution of an Indian peasantry, while *The Squatter and the Don* (1885), by María Amparo Ruiz de Burton, dealt with the subsequent sufferings of the Mexican gentry, who were displaced in their turn by white U.S. settlers. Published within a year of each other, both novels depicted a bucolic world that had been invaded by foraging outsiders who sought to deprive the region's previous inhabitants of their land and their lives.

As time passed and the region developed, California remained a contested terrain whose symbolic landscape changed only superficially. *The Big Sleep* (1939), by Raymond Chandler, and *If He Hollers Let Him Go* (1945), by Chester Himes, take place in a modern metropolitan locale very different, it seems, from the rustic scenes described by Helen Hunt Jackson and María Amparo Ruiz de Burton. Philip Marlowe, Chandler's detective, spends most of his time traversing the mean streets of Los Angeles; like Bob Jones, Himes's protagonist, Marlowe finds no redemption in the

City of Angels, but instead becomes part of its nastiness. All four novels portray California as a post-lapsarian world tainted by racism, interclass warfare, and greed. But whereas Jackson and Ruiz de Burton are earnestly outraged by the wrongs done to impoverished Native Americans and wealthy rancheros alike, Chandler and Himes, as literary exponents of white and African American noir, seem cynically resigned to the defeat of their white and black characters.

The California Dream—deferred or defeated—is a trope that recurs   5
not just in fiction but in fact-based writings as well. *Epitaph for a Peach* (1995), by David Mas Masumoto, and *Fields without Dreams* (1996), by Victor Davis Hanson, recount real-life struggles to keep the region's family farms going, in spite of threats posed by surrounding cities and the presence of corporate competitors. Like the pastoral elegies by Jackson and Ruiz de Burton, and the urban pulp fiction by Chandler and Himes, the autobiographies by Masumoto and Hanson are dystopic narratives. Although they vary in tone—Masumoto's calm meditation reads like a eulogy, while Hanson's work draws inspiration from ancient Greek tragedy—the books share the same depressed outlook, as their titles suggest. Whether a white man or woman, a member of the Mexican upper class, an African American blue-collar worker, or a Japanese immigrant, the writers assembled here all face the same challenge: to reconcile some version of the California Dream with the actual or imagined reality.

The Garden

Helen Hunt Jackson's novel tells the story of Ramona, a half-breed, who falls in love with Alessandro, a native boy. Ramona is disowned by her Mexican stepmother for choosing to marry an Indian. She and her husband, along with their children, are forced from Indian lands and chased by Anglo invaders until Alessandro and their oldest child eventually die. The picturesque rural locations—featuring Mexican ranchos, native villages, and remote mountain hideaways—provide romantic backdrops against which the action plays out. But the landscape does more than merely function as scenery. It forms the basis of a dispute between the United States and Mexico over control of the region. For in order to lay claim to Mexican territory, as Jackson points out, the United States must conquer California itself, not just its residents.[2] In *Ramona*, natural landscapes are cultivated, tamed, and subdued, just as the Indians are.

---

[2] Helen Hunt Jackson, *Ramona* (1884; reprint, New York: Signet, 1988), 12. Subsequent citations refer to this edition.

The novel begins prior to U.S. invasion, when Mexico dominated California and its native inhabitants. In this pre-Anglo era, California appears as a leisurely, civilized paradise. But Jackson suggests that the romantic world of the Mexican landowning gentry is a carefully constructed façade. Señora Moreno, Ramona's Mexican stepmother, runs a feudal estate that at first appears picturesque. On the front veranda, the Señora grows potted plants and keeps flowers in water jars (15), and from the porch roof she hangs cages of songbirds (16). But her domestication of nature extends to human nature as well. Behind the hacienda, in the inner courtyard, the servants prepare food and sew (14). In this natural setting the labor seems unforced and festive. But the courtyard—outside, yet enclosed—permits the Señora to supervise her servants without standing over them. From any window inside the house, the mistress can look outdoors to see whether her servants are performing their duties.

The rectangular courtyard contains and frames nature, including gardens, orange groves, and orchards, which end at the banks of a brook. Here the maids do the washing, under the Señora's strict supervision, in a controlled rustic setting that cultivates nature while it tames native women. "No long dawdling, and no running away from work on the part of the maids, thus close to the eye of the Señora at the upper end of the garden," writes Jackson, who ironically adds, "if [the women] had known how picturesque they looked," beating laundry against stones in the brook, "they would have been content to stay at the washing day in and day out" (16).

The wicked stepmother, Señora Moreno, treats the Cinderella half-breed, Ramona, like one of the servants. When she goes to the brook to cleanse the Catholic altar cloth (47), Jackson suggests, Ramona is not only subject to a domestic system of slavery within a Mexican household but implicated in a process of religious indoctrination as well. Considering the Catholic Church's history of enslaving the Indians, in part by preaching a doctrine based on meek subjugation, Ramona's association with the soiled altar cloth becomes doubly meaningful. Ramona seems suited to domestic subservience, from the point of view of the Church and the Mexican upper class, because of her racial impurity. Like the altar cloth, she is sullied—in her case because of her mixed European and Indian ancestry.

Ultimately, Ramona rebels against Mexican maternal and religious authority. While pretending to launder "a bit of lace or a handkerchief," she lingers by the brook in hopes of meeting the shepherd boy. When Alessandro sees her there, wearing "a white reboso [draped] coquettishly over her head" (82), he begins to view her as a woman, not as the Señora's meek handmaiden (111). Ramona transgresses class boundaries, using her performance of a domestic task as an excuse to elude her stepmother's authority and to consort with an Indian servant who is beneath her in rank. At the same time, her romance with Alessandro and their subsequent marriage, an act of miscegenation, are portrayed as a fall from grace, from the point of view of Christian morality. The white reboso suggests Ramona's virginal innocence, although she wears it while she flirts with Alessandro "coquettishly." The dirty laundry that she washes at the brook symbolizes the sacrilegious nature of Ramona's indiscreet enterprise. As Margarita, a rival for Alessandro's affection, says: "A nice place it is for a lady to meet her lover, at the washing-stones! It will take swifter water than any in that brook, Señorita Ramona, to wash you white in the Señora's eyes" (111). Ramona's disobedience, as the Senora's stepdaughter-servant, is equated in this speech with her sexual and religious impurity.

Nestled within the heart of the Moreno estate, the garden where the two lovers meet is a post-Edenic paradise. The flowering vines, singing birds, and picturesque workers, although they appear in seemingly natural settings, are all closely supervised. Ramona and Alessandro, like the landscape itself, are subjects of Mexican feudalism and mission-style slavery: a half-breed and a full-blooded Indian whom the ruling class dominates. The lovers elope, escaping from a constructed false Eden, where the Señora shelters but also controls her dependents. Eventually, however, they will be dispossessed of their true Eden, by Anglo invaders who claim the native village and farmland that Ramona and Alessandro call home.

Whereas *Ramona* concentrates on the victimization of Native Americans, *The Squatter and the Don* dwells on the displacement of Mexicans, who, like the Spaniards before them, subjugated the Indians, only to be removed from the land by later white immigrants. After the Mexican-American War, U.S. citizens ventured into California, contested Mexican land grants, and staked their claims to the region by instigating lawsuits, boundary disputes, property surveys, and political schemes designed to invalidate Mexican land titles. In the novel, Don Mariano, one of the Mexican gentry, explains why white settlers who squat on his land wish to prolong litigation, "since it is 'the natives' who must bear the burden of taxation, while the titles are in the courts, and thus the pre-emptors hold the land free."[3]

The don asserts his prior claim to the land by describing himself, and the rest of the Mexican gentry, as natives. But the ruling elite bear little resemblance to the poor indigenous tribes that once lived on the land, and the fact that the don puts the term in quotation marks means

---

[3] María Amparo Ruiz de Burton, *The Squatter and the Don*, Rosaura Sánchez and Beatrice Pita, eds. (1885; reprint, Houston: Arte Público Press, 1997), 74. Subsequent references to this edition appear in the text.

that rancheros are natives, not in the true sense, but only compared to more recent arrivals. While the plight of the gentry is dramatized, the fate of the Indians, California's first natives, is minimized.[4] In the novel, Indian vaqueros are among the few indigenous peoples who have survived colonization by Spain and then Mexico. Banished to the margins of the text, they appear in one or two scenes as dependents who herd the don's cattle. In one scene, which takes place at a cow camp in winter, the men are "seen through the falling snow as if behind a thick, mysterious veil." Like shadowy reminders of a long-vanished past, the "enchanted" and "ghostly" vaqueros seem to exist in a magical valley, one "which must disappear with the first rays of day" (279).

Jackson and Ruiz de Burton both write about the disruption of "native" California societies and the loss of a region that is rightfully theirs. But whereas the land plays a central role in *Ramona*, as do Jackson's Indian characters, the land in *The Squatter and the Don* seems to have already vanished, like the vaqueros and their soon-to-be-displaced Mexican overlords. Writing about U.S. invasion in historical retrospect, nearly forty years after Mexico lost California in the Mexican-American War, Ruiz de Burton treats the loss of the land as a fait accompli. Her focus on racist U.S. government policies and dishonest capitalist practices—by corporate oligarchies and railroad monopolies that vie with white settlers for control of the region—transforms the land into the subject of an abstract debate. Every attempt to make California seem palpably real soon evaporates. In one chapter, in which several of her characters visit Yosemite, the author begins by describing their leave-taking. The natural wonders, like the beautiful ranchos or man-made estates, must be "left behind." Looking backwards, the men and women cast a "last lingering look towards the glorious rainbows" cast by a waterfall. They take with them a "memory of the mirror lakes," as well as a final impression that all joys are fleeting (153).

Helen Hunt Jackson, a white woman who visited California in the late nineteenth century, and María Amparo Ruiz de Burton, a Mexican citizen born and raised on the West Coast, were separated by race and were familiar with the region to different degrees. In addition, they

15

---

[4] Anne E. Goldman prefers Ruiz de Burton's "deglamorized" portrayal of the injustice to Mexicans over Jackson's nostalgic lament for indigenous Indians. See " 'I Think Our Romance Is Spoiled,' or, Crossing Genres: California History in Helen Hunt Jackson's *Ramona* and María Amparo Ruiz de Burton's *The Squatter and the Don*," in Valerie J. Matsumoto and Blake Allmendinger, eds., *Over the Edge: Remapping the American West* (Berkeley and Los Angeles: University of California Press, 1998), 65–85. David Luis-Brown disagrees, believing that Jackson takes Indian issues seriously, while Ruiz de Burton dismisses them. See " 'White Slaves' and the 'Arrogant *Mestiza*': Reconfiguring Whiteness in *The Squatter and the Don* and *Ramona*," *American Literature* 69 (Dec. 1997): 813–39.

focused on different cultures in California and different historical periods. But the two writers produced similar dystopic narratives. In *Ramona*, a false Mexican Eden ensnares the two native lovers. In *The Squatter and the Don*, the "rainbows" that arch over Yosemite and, by extension, over the region, represent broken or unfulfilled promises. The men and women, who look back regretfully as they exit the beautiful area, symbolize the Mexican gentry who will shortly be dispossessed of their gracious estates.

UNDERSTANDING THE TEXT

1. What does Allmendinger mean by saying that "California has been objectified" (para. 1), and how do his examples in paragraph 1 illustrate that concept?

2. What thematic roles does the California landscape play in *Ramona* and *The Squatter and the Don*, according to Allmendinger?

3. How, in Allmendinger's view, does the California dream serve as a "trope" (para. 5) in both fiction and nonfiction?

4. Summarize in your own words the thematic message conveyed in María Amparo Ruiz de Burton's *The Squatter and the Don*.

5. What does Allmendinger mean by "dystopic narratives" (para. 15), and why does he use that term to describe *Ramona* and *The Squatter and the Don*?

EXPLORING AND DEBATING THE ISSUES

1. Read *Ramona*, and write an essay in which you analyze how the California dream serves as a trope in the novel. Is the dream achieved, deferred, or defeated?

2. Read *Ramona* and *The Squatter and the Don*, and compare and contrast the role that ethnic conflicts and tensions play in each novel.

3. Read Raymond Chandler's *The Big Sleep* or Chester Himes's *If He Hollers Let Him Go*, and write your own analysis of the way in which the novel depicts California's symbolic landscape.

4. Compare Deborah Miranda's ("Indian Cartography," p. 72) depiction of the Native American experience in California with its portrayal in *Ramona* and *The Squatter and the Don*, according to Allmendinger. How do you account for any similarities or differences you may observe?

5. Read or reread David Mas Masumoto's "As If the Farmer Died" (p. 248), an essay that appeared in *Epitaph for a Peach*. Write an essay in which you assess the validity of Allmendinger's claim that in this book Masumoto faced the challenge "to reconcile some version of the California Dream with the actual or imagined reality" (para. 5).

Endings and Beginnings

Surviving Apocalypse

DAVID FINE

The entire world, as **David Fine** quotes Mike Davis in this selection, "seems to be rooting for L.A. to slide into the Pacific or to be swallowed up by the San Andreas Fault." Or so it would appear from the "138 novels and films since 1909" that have depicted the destruction of the City of the Angels. Why this should be the case is a complicated matter, Fine argues, but it amounts to the fact that "the destruction of Los Angeles by bomb, earthquake, fire, riot, or tsunami operates as a recurring metaphor for anxieties about the fate and future of the nation." With such a symbolic burden to bear, it's a wonder that Angelenos have not yet surpassed New Yorkers as poster children for psychiatric overindulgence. A professor emeritus of English at California State University, Long Beach, Fine has published numerous books, including *The City, The Immigrant, and American Fiction, 1880–1920* (1977) and *Imagining Los Angeles: A City in Fiction* (2000), in which this selection first appeared.

Whatever else California was, good or bad, it was charged with human hope. It was linked imaginatively with the most compelling of American myths, the pursuit of happiness. When the intensity of expectation was thwarted or only partially fulfilled . . . it could backfire into restlessness and bitterness. . . . As a hope in defiance of facts, as a longing which could ennoble and encourage but which could turn and devour itself, the symbolic value of California endured . . . a legacy of the Gold Rush.

—*Kevin Starr,* Americans and the California Dream, 1860–1915

Finally, it was the city that held us, the city they said had no center, that all of us had come to from all over America because this was the place to find dreams and pleasure and love.

—*Carolyn See,* Golden Days

L.A.'s fine in the long run. . . . you get to choose who you want to be and how you want to live.

—*Ann Goode in Alan Rudolph's film,* Welcome to L.A.

In *The Ecology of Fear,* Mike Davis reports that "at least 138 novels and films since 1909" deal with the destruction of [Los Angeles]. The destroying agents have been both natural and man-made (or the two in conjunction): earthquake, fire, and flood, atomic attack, extraterrestrial or other-race invasion (the former often as metonymic displacement of the latter). The destruction of Los Angeles by atomic or nuclear explosion dominates Davis's taxonomy (forty-nine times), followed by earthquake (twenty-eight), and then alien hordes and monsters. What is more significant than the frequency of the city's imagined destruction, though, according to Davis, is "the pleasure such apocalypses provide to readers and movie audiences." The entire world, he says, "seems to be rooting for L.A. to slide into the Pacific or to be swallowed up by the San Andreas Fault." In citing dozens of novels and films over the past ninety years that "celebrate" the city's destruction, he reminds us of how long the template for urban disaster has been in place in fiction and film about Los Angeles; apocalyptic renderings have been there almost as long as there have been novels about Los Angeles.

Many of these literary acts of destruction, he claims persuasively, have been generated by racial anxieties in California: white fear of darker-skinned people. His initiating example is Homer Lea's hysterical racist novel about the Japanese invasion and occupation of California, *The Valor of Ignorance* (1909). Lea's work, he indicates, is the beginning of a long line of xenophobic fictions, couched often enough in Bible Belt fundamentalist, kooky religious, or Aryan supremacist terms. Outside the realm of fiction, Los Angeles has had a long xenophobic prophet-of-doom tradition. An early twentieth-century exemplar was the Reverend "Fighting" Bob Schuler, the target of whose rantings was Los Angeles as city of sin (leveled largely at the predominantly Jewish film industry but also at Catholics and at big business) that would suffer the Almighty's wrath in apocalyptic destruction. More recently, there has been the American Nazi, Andrew Macdonald, who wrote *The Turner Diaries* (1978), an ugly futuristic fantasy based on a purportedly "real" diary kept by a martyr to the white cause, about Aryan soldiers, survivalists, fighting a guerrilla war in Los Angeles to rid the city of Jews and blacks.

While Anglo-Saxon racism has been a significant presence in doomsday renderings of Los Angeles, xenophobic literature is far from a local phenomenon. Davis documents the national strain, but he may be overstating his case by locating the racial ground so prominently in Los Angeles. Contemporary racism may well be linked to local fears about the surge of immigrants into the city in the last few decades, but xenophobia has been a common enough response in all immigrant cities. American literature from the middle of the nineteenth to the early twentieth century—a period coinciding with massive waves of European immigration; the first from northern and western Europe, the second from southern and eastern Europe—is replete with sometimes hysterical expressions of literary nativism. Anti-Semitic, anti-Catholic, and anti–"yellow horde" fiction has a long national history. Los Angeles is not exceptional here, although alien/other-race invasion renderings take on an added dimension when applied to a booster city, promoted in the early days to prospective migrants both as a white Protestant enclave (the future home, as Lummis put it, of the "Saxon homemaker") and as the place of the miraculous cure—a marketing strategy that drew a considerable number of sick and infirm migrants and encouraged as well a local susceptibility to healers, psychics, medical quacks, and doomsday prophets.

Disaster fiction in Los Angeles goes beyond the invasion mode, though, and there are a number of reasons—and not all of them racial— for apocalyptic fiction's taking sturdy root in Los Angeles. For one thing, although doomsday literature was not invented in Los Angeles but migrated west (in stages, as an urban form, from London through New York and Chicago), it established itself in a city that was positioned literally at the edge of the continent, a place where an unstable physical geography collided with an unstable human geography of displaced migrants and inflated expectation. Since the 1920s Los Angeles offered itself to novelists as the locus of uprooted Midwesterners looking for the quick fix. Among them were religious fundamentalists, desperate health seekers, and movieland castoffs adrift in a place where, their own dreams betrayed, they read the daily headlines of violent crime, municipal and corporate corruption, and Hollywood scandal, all of which fed a loathing for the city that deceived them. "Corn-belt fundamentalism," Davis writes, "with its traditional yeoman antipathy to the 'evil city,' collided head-on with the libertine culture of the Hollywood movie colony in an urban *kulturkamph*. Each side would resort to doomsday imagery to damn and excoriate the other."

Hollywood movies have been complicit with fiction in these disaster imaginings. The old booster city was the site of Armageddon in films ranging from the 1953 *War of the Worlds* (where the space invaders migrate to Los Angeles) to *Earthquake* (1974, inspired by the 1971 quake and featuring some theater seats that vibrated), *Blade Runner* (1982, with its replicants running wild among the vaguely Asian proletarian hordes), and *Escape from L.A.* (1997, with its largely Hispanic island-city concentration camp of misfits, loonies, and subversives). In Ridley Scott's dystopian *Blade Runner*, the twenty-first-century city is run by genetic engineers operating from the top of a towering pyramid (analog to Fritz Lang's mise-en-scène for *Metropolis*) while the masses crowd the derelict streets below under a persistent mist of acid rain. In Scott's scenario (based on a Philip Dick story set in San Francisco, not Los Angeles) even the violated or disfigured woman, so prominent in noir fiction and film, shows up: the beautiful heroine Rachel is not human at all but a replicant, a genetically engineered project. Joel Coen and Ethan Coen's Nathanael West send-up, *Barton Fink*, similarly, fuses the victimized woman theme with a Hollywood disaster scenario. Fink, a New York playwright who wants only to write "the theater of the common man" (an Arthur Miller or perhaps Clifford Odets stand-in?) is shanghaied, like Carl Van Vechten's Spider Boy, in a Hollywood inhabited by the usual Jewish producer and publicity man stereotypes. But also in residence is a William Faulkner look-alike named Bill Maher, an alcoholic, cynical self-destructive screenwriter who refuses to stay sober in Hollywood. When Maher's beautiful mistress turns up with a slashed throat in Fink's hotel room bed next to a typewriter with blank pages in its roller, the point seems to be that the beautiful, violated woman is metaphor, or metonymy, for Fink's creative impotence in Hollywood. What follows is the surrealistic blitz (with its Salvador Dali-like images of dripping wallpaper and melting walls), a hotel fire (echo of the "Burning of Los Angeles" canvas in West's novel), and the demonic laughter of Fink's neighbor, the good-natured Ben Meadows, a closeted serial killer (played with manic charm by John Goodman). The Coen brothers are playing here with a number of themes that have been around for a long time in local fiction.

As Los Angeles emerged as America's most conspicuous city—film, media, and pop music capital; nerve center of its war and space industries; and troublesome zone of so many unassimilated, ghettoized immigrants (legal and illegal) who constitute cities within the city—it became the most conspicuous national site for disaster scenarios on screen and in print. The metropolitan city that Davis claims has "500 gated subdivisions, 2,000 street gangs, 4,000 mini-malls, 20,000 sweatshops, and 10,000 homeless residents" (354) has become target, repository, and scapegoat for national foreboding; the place where the worst fears about the future could be placed. The destruction of Los Angeles by bomb, earthquake, fire, riot, or tsunami operates as a recurring metaphor for anxieties about the fate and future of the nation.

Geographic determinism, which Davis acknowledges but downplays, makes the city both an obvious and inevitable choice for doomsday renderings. The land itself, lying on a major fault line, given to periodic quakes as well as annual cycles of fire, flood and mudslide, offers itself to such dark visions. The hot, dry Santa Ana winds, meanwhile, product of the confluence of desert, mountain, and coastal basin, not only contribute to the annual (fall) fires in the hills and mountains, but inflame the nerves of local residents as well, intensifying the dark imaginings.

The ecodisaster in Los Angeles fiction characteristically works in conjunction with human failure, serving in some of the novels as a kind of cosmic wake-up call to man's destructive interventions on the fragile landscape. This theme of nature's response to man's greed is prominent in Ross Macdonald's crime fiction. Even earlier, in Myron Brinig's

The Flutter of an Eyelid (1933), the "Big One" comes as the answer of an angry God to Southern California Babylon, dumping the whole coast, "swiftly, relentlessly, into the Pacific Ocean," a prophesy that anticipates Curt Gentry's 1986 scenario in *The Last Days of the Late Great State of California* and John Carpenter's 1996 film *Escape from L.A.*

Even when not envisioned as the site of apocalypse, the constructed Los Angeles has been the recurring locus of the violent ending. That hard-boiled, brutal fiction has taken so strong a hold in a region so given to hyperinflated dreaming should be no surprise, even if we omit geographic determinism from the equation. From the 1920s to the present, the dominant theme in Los Angeles fiction has been the betrayal of hope and the collapse of dreams. Writing against the optimistic booster literature produced just before and after the turn of the century, the city's novelists constructed a counter-fable about loss. The principal local genres—the hard-boiled crime story, the tough-guy detective tale, and the Hollywood novel, as well as recent ethnic fiction—each in its way, envisioned the city as the place where dreams come from earthquake, nuclear bomb, or fiery conflagration; comes most often, as I have indicated in earlier chapters, as fatal automobile accident, murder, or suicide.

If, though, the major body of Los Angeles fiction has pointed to violent endings, there has been in the last few decades (since the 1960s) something of a countertrend in several recent survivor's tale novels, which take for their subjects not only disaster but also the coping with disaster—the living through, surviving and enduring disaster. The city might offer the prospect of doom, but in some contemporary works, urban disaster has provided the occasion for reaffirmation of self in the capacity to endure. The place of endings thus can become the place of beginnings—at least as some recent writers have asserted. Over against the ironic pseudo-affirmation of Alison Lurie's *The Nowhere City* or the dark, nihilistic vision of Joan Didion's *Play It as It Lays*, there have been novels, a significant number of them written by women, about people who find as they come to the end of the line and continent reasons for going on, mandates to affirm the demands of self, community, and spirit. Novels like Christopher Isherwood's *A Single Man* (1964), Kate Braverman's *Palm Latitudes* (1998), Cynthia Kadohata's *In the Heart of the Valley of Love* (1992), and, most strikingly, Carolyn See's *Golden Days* (1987) and *Making History* (1991) are such works. They do not represent a cyclic return to the old booster optimism, the pendulum swung back. Far from it. But they do offer affirmations of the strength of the human spirit in the face of millennial doom-saying and ecological and man-made disaster.

10

UNDERSTANDING THE TEXT

1. What, according to Mike Davis, are the reasons behind the many apocalyptic visions of Los Angeles in literature?

2. How, in Fine's view, does xenophobic literature focused on Los Angeles compare with the same sort of literature nationally?

3. What relationship does Fine see between Los Angeles disaster fiction and its cinematic counterparts?

4. In your own words, what does the term "geographic determinism" (para. 7) mean?

5. What themes does Fine believe counter the tradition of apocalyptic literature?

EXPLORING AND DEBATING THE ISSUES

1. Literature and film have disproportionately used Los Angeles as a setting for disaster stories. Using Fine's article for background, write an essay in which you present an argument for why Los Angeles has been so chosen. To support your position, refer both to literary and cinematic representations of L.A. and to real-life political, social, and environmental conditions that the city has faced in the past and in the present.

2. Rent a video or DVD of *Barton Fink*, and read Nathanael West's *The Day of the Locust*. Write an essay in which you evaluate Fine's claim that the film is a "Nathanael West send-up" (para. 5).

3. Rent a video or DVD of *Blade Runner* or *Escape from L.A.*, and write an essay in which you analyze the use of Los Angeles as a setting for the film. To what extent does the film reflect the dominant theme that Fine believes characterizes Los Angeles fiction: "the betrayal of hope and the collapse of dreams" (para. 9)?

4. Read one of the reaffirmation novels that Fine mentions in paragraph 10, and write an essay in which you assess whether that novel does "offer affirmations of the strength of the human spirit in the face of millennial doom-saying and ecological and man-made disaster."

5. Read or reread Blake Allmendinger's "All about Eden" (p. 319), and write an essay in which you argue that the two novels he discusses, *Ramona* and *The Squatter and the Don*, are or are not instances of nondoomsday novels that exhibit the xenophobia that Mike Davis finds at the heart of so much California literature.

The Day of the Locust

NATHANAEL WEST

Nathanael West (1903–1940) was on his way to becoming one of America's most daring and influential writers when his life was cut short suddenly in a car accident near El Centro, California. Beginning as an East Coast novelist, West (born Nathan Weinstein) reinvented himself as a Hollywood screenwriter in the 1930s. West's own experiences enabled him to write with scathing insight into the dreams and desires of the men and women who came to Hollywood during the golden age of the movies, as can be seen in this excerpt from what is probably the first great Hollywood novel, *The Day of the Locust* (1939). West's other novels include *The Dream Life of Balso Snell* (1931), *Miss Lonelyhearts* (1933), and *A Cool Million* (1934).

Around quitting time, Tod Hackett heard a great din on the road outside his office. The groan of leather mingled with the jangle of iron and over all beat the tattoo of a thousand hooves. He hurried to the window.

An army of cavalry and foot was passing. It moved like a mob; its lines broken, as though fleeing from some terrible defeat. The dolmans of the hussars, the heavy shakos of the guards, Hanoverian light horse, with their flat leather caps and flowing red plumes, were all jumbled together in bobbing disorder. Behind the cavalry came the infantry, a wild sea of waving sabretaches, sloped muskets, crossed shoulder belts and swinging cartridge boxes. Tod recognized the scarlet infantry of England with their white shoulder pads, the black infantry of the Duke of Brunswick, the French grenadiers with their enormous white gaiters, the Scotch with bare knees under plaid skirts.

While he watched, a little fat man, wearing a cork sun-helmet, polo shirt and knickers, darted around the corner of the building in pursuit of the army.

"Stage Nine—you bastards—Stage Nine!" he screamed through a small megaphone.

The cavalry put spur to their horses and the infantry broke into a dogtrot. The little man in the cork hat ran after them, shaking his fist and cursing.

Tod watched until they had disappeared, behind half a Mississippi steamboat, then put away his pencils and drawing board, and left the office. On the sidewalk outside the studio he stood for a moment trying to decide whether to walk home or take a streetcar. He had been in Hollywood less than three months and still found it a very exciting place, but

5

he was lazy and didn't like to walk. He decided to take the streetcar as far as Vine Street and walk the rest of the way.

A talent scout for National Films had brought Tod to the Coast after seeing some of his drawings in an exhibit of undergraduate work at the Yale School of Fine Arts. He had been hired by telegram. If the scout had met Tod, he probably wouldn't have sent him to Hollywood to learn set and costume designing. His large sprawling body, his slow blue eyes and sloppy grin made him seem completely without talent, almost doltish in fact.

Yes, despite his appearance, he was really a very complicated young man with a whole set of personalities, one inside the other like a nest of Chinese boxes. And *The Burning of Los Angeles*, a picture he was soon to paint, definitely proved he had talent.

He left the car at Vine Street. As he walked along, he examined the evening crowd. A great many of the people wore sports clothes which were not really sports clothes. Their sweaters, knickers, slacks, blue flannel jackets with brass buttons were fancy dress. The fat lady in the yachting cap was going shopping, not boating; the man in the Norfolk jacket and Tyrolean hat was returning, not from a mountain, but an insurance office; and the girl in slacks and sneaks with a bandanna around her head had just left a switchboard, not a tennis court.

Scattered among these masquerades were people of a different type.   10 Their clothing was somber and badly cut, brought from mail-order houses. While the others moved rapidly, darting into stores and cocktail bars, they loitered on the corners or stood with their backs to the shop windows and stared at everyone who passed. When their stare was returned, their eyes filled with hatred. At this time Tod knew very little about them except that they had come to California to die.

He was determined to learn much more. They were the people he felt he must paint. He would never again do a fat red barn, old stone wall or sturdy Nantucket fisherman. From the moment he had seen them, he had known that, despite his race, training and heritage, neither Winslow Homer nor Thomas Ryder could be his masters and he turned to Goya and Daumier.

He had learned this just in time. During his last year in art school, he had begun to think that he might give up painting completely. The pleasures he received from the problems of composition and color had decreased as his facility had increased and he had realized that he was going the way of all his classmates, toward illustration or mere handsomeness. When the Hollywood job had come along, he had grabbed it despite the arguments of his friends who were certain that he was selling out and would never paint again.

He reached the end of Vine Street and began the climb into Pinyon Canyon. Night had started to fall.

The edges of the trees burned with a pale violet light and their centers gradually turned from deep purple to black. The same violet piping, like a Neon tube, outlined the tops of the ugly, hump-backed hills and they were almost beautiful.

But not even the soft wash of dusk could help the houses. Only dynamite would be of any use against the Mexican ranch houses, Samoan huts, Mediterranean villas, Egyptian and Japanese temples, Swiss chalets, Tudor cottages, and every possible combination of these styles that lined the slopes of the canyon.   15

When he noticed that they were all of plaster, lath and paper, he was charitable and blamed their shape on the materials used. Steel, stone and brick curb a builder's fancy a little, forcing him to distribute his stresses and weights and to keep his corners plumb, but plaster and paper know no law, not even that of gravity.

On the corner of La Huerta Road was a miniature Rhine castle with tarpaper turrets pierced for archers. Next to it was a highly colored shack with domes and minarets out of the *Arabian Nights*. Again he was charitable. Both houses were comic, but he didn't laugh. Their desire to startle was so eager and guileless.

It is hard to laugh at the need for beauty and romance, no matter how tasteless, even horrible, the results of that are. But it is easy to sigh. Few things are sadder than the truly monstrous.

UNDERSTANDING THE TEXT

1. What are the images that West uses to present Hollywood as a place of make-believe?

2. What is West's attitude toward Hollywood culture, and how do his tone and diction convey that attitude?

3. Why might Tod's friends have felt that his leaving art school to work in Hollywood was "selling out" (para. 12)?

EXPLORING AND DEBATING THE ISSUES

1. The architecture that West describes represents a desire to invent an exotic and romantic personal environment. Write an essay in which you analyze contemporary architecture in California. To what extent do Californians still use architecture to express their desire for romance and adventure? Be sure to focus your comments on specific buildings or neighborhoods.

2. James J. Rawls claims that West explored the "failure of the myth" of the California dream in his writings (see "California: A Place, a People, a Dream," p. 22). Write an essay in which you explain whether this passage from *The Day of the Locust* demonstrates Rawls's claim.

3. West's description of the make-believe army marching through the streets exemplifies Hollywood's ability to invent fantasies for millions of Americans throughout this century. Referring to specific films and television programs, argue whether Hollywood today does more to spin fantasies, as West believed, or to depict reality.

4. Rent a videotape of the film *The Day of the Locust*, and write an analysis of the image of Hollywood and, more broadly, of California.

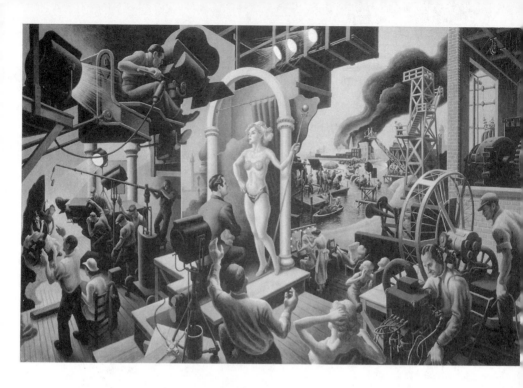

Hollywood (1937)

THOMAS HART BENTON

1. Assume the role of Tod Hackett, the main character in *The Day of the Locust*, and write an analysis of Thomas Hart Benton's depiction of Hollywood. To what extent do you think Tod would share Benton's artistic vision?

2. In this 1937 painting, Benton includes imagery in the foreground and background that highlights the kinds of fantasies that the movie industry creates. What fantasies are created by the background image of a burning town surrounded by water? How do you interpret the focus on the model standing in the center, who is being filmed while holding a scepter?

California through the Lens of Hollywood

DANA POLAN

As the universally acknowledged epicenter of the California dream machine, Hollywood would seem to be the quintessence of all things Californian. But as **Dana Polan** asks in this overview of the images of California that the Hollywood film industry has been sending to the rest of the world since its beginnings in the early twentieth century, "Are Hollywood films Californian?" The irony is that Hollywood has been especially good at constructing myths and images about other places, like New York, Paris, and the Old West. Equally ironic is the fact that Hollywood, which has disseminated the most gaudy mythologies of the California dream, has also been a center for film noir—a genre that "chronicles the misadventures of losers and loners who try to follow their dreams and desires . . . and frequently end up either dead or ruined." It's as if the Hollywood sign should contain a yin-yang symbol. Polan is professor of critical studies in the School of Cinema-Television at the University of Southern California. His books include *The Political Language of Film and the Avant-Garde* (1985), *Power and Paranoia: History, Narrative and the American Cinema, 1940–1950* (1986), *In a Lonely Place* (1993), and *Pulp Fiction* (2001).

From the cartoons that I watched on television in my East Coast childhood, I remember what was for me a primary image of California. Several cartoon characters were on their way to California and passed through torrential rain—a terrible downpour complemented by intensely dark skies and ear-shattering thunder. When they reached the border (literally a line on the terrain), the California side was instantly revealed as pure sunshine, a land of beautiful and resplendent weather (all of this no doubt to the accompaniment of a celebratory anthem like "California, Here I Come").

My first awareness of an idea of California may have come, however, from yet another vastly influential televisual source—*The Wonderful World of Disney*, hosted by Walt Disney. In its early astuteness about the synergy required of modern media enterprises, this popular TV show promoted Disney movies and, most especially, the relatively new Disneyland theme park. For many children of the 1950s and 1960s, California *was* Disneyland, the goal of a quest for ultimate ludic happiness (a quest parodied in *National Lampoon's Vacation*, in which a middle-American family will endure anything to visit Wally World, only to find the amusement park closed for the season).

It is a trivial question, perhaps, but I sometimes wonder which cartoon was the source of my memory of an abruptly sunny California. My suspicion, based on other recollections, is that there were similar scenes in any number of cartoons. This is just one example of a process that has gone on, to far more profound global effect, throughout the entire history of the cinema in California. Images of California circulate; modified, critiqued, or replaced, they float from film to film, often reinvigorated or reinvested with earlier mythic associations.

In a country in which one of the establishing myths is the pioneer quest, the move "out West," it has been easy in the realm of film to associate the journey into the frontier in general with a journey toward Los Angeles and Hollywood in particular. Indeed, one of the most famous movies about Hollywood filmmaking, the 1937 version of *A Star Is Born*, directly maps pioneer mythology onto the birthing of the star: wilting in the Midwest, Esther Blodgett (Janet Gaynor) takes inspiration from her granny, an old frontier woman who reminds Esther about the wagon trains and implores her to fulfill her Manifest Destiny. She must go west and realize her acting dreams in Hollywood. Esther takes Granny's advice and becomes a big star. But she falters in her devotion to the myth of success after the suicide of her husband, and the elderly granny must make her own heroic journey to the West Coast to inspire her granddaughter and to triumph with her at the film's finale at Grauman's Chinese Theatre, where the gleaming spotlights evoke the glittering gold that impelled earlier adventurers to California. . . .

The pioneer mythology that imagines California to be a site central or even inevitable and necessary to American self-realization has been tenacious in American cinema. A recent striking and somewhat surprising example of this is *Clockers* (1995), directed by inveterate New Yorker Spike Lee. The young hero of the story finally escapes the ills of East Coast ghetto life by hopping a train to California. In the film's final images, the golden gleam of a radiant sunset plays across the young man's face, investing him with well-deserved hope and expectation. It seems that even an ostensible independent like Lee cannot resist the seduction of California. 5

Are Hollywood Films Californian?

We might begin our investigation with a question that will at first seem paradoxical: Are Hollywood films Californian? We could raise this question on several levels: style (is there a particular look to some films that we might characterize as "Californian"?); content (is there a specifically Californian subject matter?); and even artistic material (are there materials that we might refer to as Californian, as we could in the case of certain building elements in California Arts and Crafts?). Such questions can seem curious given the extent to which California and Hollywood blur in the popular imagination. In a state that has few widely shared urban or geographic icons (the Golden Gate Bridge? the pointy spire of San Francisco's Transamerica Pyramid? the beach?), there is no doubt that for many, the Hollywood sign sums up the California experience. (It is one of the many ironies of Hollywood cinema that the sign originally had nothing to do with the film industry but instead had to do with real estate promotion; in the shortening of the original "Hollywoodland" to "Hollywood," an entire art and culture of cinematic imagination sprang up.)

To be sure, Hollywood may easily seem to have been the movies' destiny. In a 1927 lecture to business students at Harvard, Joseph Kennedy (then the owner of a film company) noted, "I suppose one of the things that may strike you as odd is that the distribution offices of all the companies are in New York City, while all the production is on the West Coast . . . The truth is that nature has given to California certain advantages which make it the ideal center for motion picture production. It has sunlight, a good climate, with little rain. Within a short radius of Hollywood there are mountains, plains, deserts, rivers, ruins, city streets, the sea, picturesque old Mexico. New York, on the other hand, remains the financial center."[1] To Kennedy's list of advantages, we could add more politicized ones, such as Los Angeles's long history of open-shop or even antiunion labor practices, which made it a company town with a labor pool that was easy to hire and to exploit.

And yet the geographical advantages of Los Angeles do not necessarily lead to the notion of a uniquely Californian cinematic style. Indeed, other locales possessed many of the same qualities that Kennedy outlined. The earliest years in the consolidation of the American film industry coincided with the industry's far-flung search for places in which to situate large-scale productions, from woody New Jersey, which was the site for a number of early Westerns (including Edwin S. Porter's breakthrough 1903 film, *The Great Train Robbery*) and remained a major locale for outdoor filming, to upstate New York (where D. W. Griffith filmed many adventure tales before heading west), Florida, and Cuba (sites of many productions and attempts at establishing permanent studios). American cinema was in transit, trying out many options before it settled on the Los Angeles region.[2] Moreover, as Kevin Starr notes, even if

---

[1] "General Introduction" to Joseph P. Kennedy, ed., *The Story of the Films; as Told by Leaders of the Industry to the Students of the Graduate School of Business Administration, George F. Baker Foundation, Harvard University* (Chicago and New York: A. W. Shaw Co., 1927), 21–22.

[2] For an excellent discussion of alternative sites on the way to Hollywood, see Richard Koszarski's *An Evening's Entertainment: The Age of the Silent Feature Picture, 1915–1928* (New York: Scribner, 1990).

California were one logical destination for filmmaking, there was a moment in which Northern California might have become the dominant locale for West Coast cinematic production. As Starr recounts in *Inventing the Dream: California through the Progressive Era,*

> In 1908 Essanay of Chicago established its studio outside of Southern California altogether, in Niles Canyon outside of Oakland in the San Francisco Bay area. Three years later Essanay was joined in the Niles by the Flying A Company, which produced Westerns. Had this Niles venture taken hold, [screenwriter] Anita Loos later speculated, the film industry would have developed—to everyone's benefit—in close contact with San Francisco's flourishing theatrical, literary, and artistic communities. A San Francisco–based film industry, Miss Loos believed, would have enjoyed California's excellent weather along with an urban sophistication lost when films migrated from the East.[3]

Elsewhere in the same volume, Starr repeats the legendary anecdote in which Cecil B. DeMille is said to have come to the city by accident: According to an often-told story, he decided to break into the lucrative business of filmmaking with a Western tale—*The Squaw Man*—which he had every intention of filming in Flagstaff, Arizona. A storm forced him further west to California, which he ending up making his long-term base of operations.

From the start, filmmakers extolled the environments around Los Angeles for their potential to represent so many places. The move into massive indoor sound stages on the vast studio lots provided even greater power to construct realities far removed from California. To take just one example, much of the cinematic image of New York in the 1930s—those magical scenes in which someone steps out onto the balcony of an apartment, beyond which a joyous image of the Big Apple rises up as so many tiny lights and foreshortened skyscrapers—was created in the magical world of the West Coast studios. Hence the perception in 1949 that the Gene Kelly film *On the Town* had revolutionized musicals, and escapist cinematic entertainment in general, by actually filming in the outdoor spaces of New York, starting with its docks.

Of course, if California can be enlisted in the representation of other   10
geographies, it is also true that an imagination of California can be constructed elsewhere. Billy Wilder's *Double Indemnity* (1944), a film in which Los Angeles seems so central that critic Richard Schickel declares, in a nice phrase, "You could charge L.A. as a co-conspirator in the crimes this movie relates,"[4] was partly shot in Phoenix, Arizona, due to wartime

---

[3] Kevin Starr, *Inventing the Dream: California through the Progressive Era* (New York: Oxford University Press, 1985), 288.

[4] Richard Schickel, *Double Indemnity* (London: British Film Institute, 1992), 10.

blackout restrictions on the coast.[5] Nevertheless, what is perhaps most Californian about Hollywood films is not necessarily the specific representation of California locales or experiences but the very ability of the place, indoors or outdoors, to represent any experience whatsoever. Moreover, the fabricated environments of the studio system frequently share an imaginary quality that we readily associate with Hollywood style, no matter which locale is supposedly represented. Filmed "entirely in Hollywood, USA," the end title of *An American in Paris* proudly announces. Whether Paris or New York, these re-created locales are now part of our mental image of the real places, yet they also seem to have something to do with qualities we attribute to California: a gleam, an ethereal artificiality, a magic that captivates by rendering its subject unreal yet imbued with a golden luster. Indeed, in one of the major attempts to argue that there is a definable uniqueness to California—what he calls its exceptionalism—the classic California writer Carey McWilliams finds one form of California specificity to lie in a sparkling luminosity, a certain glow (although he also points to the social and political ills only partially concealed by the magic). "There is a golden haze over the land," McWilliams writes, "the dust of gold is in the air—and the atmosphere is magical and mirrors many tricks, visions, and wondrous deceptions."[6] As such, and as part of its deception, California-based film appears as the culmination, the end point, of worldly mythologies and an inevitable force that absorbs all other experiences and realizes their implicit mythological import, gives them their ultimate meaning.

The movie industry may have settled in California only after a number of detours that seem to render the final location of its capital somewhat arbitrary, but early in its history, in film as well as in its publicity and self-promotion, the industry worked to build a theme of destiny, of Hollywood as the natural apotheosis of the American Dream. Clearly, by accident or design, the unique qualities of California and the advent of the film industry there have long had a powerfully causal relationship. Note, for instance, the way in which the language used by historian Kevin Starr to describe the history of Southern California suggests a sort of natural coming together of California and its movie industry:

> Southern California—meaning Los Angeles, meaning Hollywood— possessed an affinity between medium and place that would soon attract the entire industry to it like a powerful magnet.... In a very real sense the entire society [of Southern California] was a stage set, a visualization

[5] *Hollywood Reporter*, Sept. 14, 1943, 2.

[6] Carey McWilliams, *California: The Great Exception* (1949; reprint, Berkeley: University of California Press, 1999), 4.

of dream and illusion which was, like film, at once true and not true. New York City, upstate New York, suburban and rural New Jersey . . . offered locations and scenery aplenty, but Southern California offered certain energizing affinities between art and location. . . . Within a few short years this interaction between the medium of film and the society of Southern California would develop a symbiosis called Hollywood that would be of major importance to both the region and the film industry.[7]

To use a language of "affinity" and thereby to imply a necessary connection between Californian meanings and the look and subject of the Hollywood film requires a number of assumptions. For example, this implies that there is an overall identity to Hollywood cinema and that there is a pool of stable meanings that can be attributed to the idea of California (and beyond this, that the meaning of Hollywood and the meaning of California are always buoyantly about magic and mythology). At the same time, we find that escapism into a world of magic is not always the dominant representation in Hollywood; indeed, there is a Hollywood tradition of California films that allow little escape and tie their fatalism to specifically Californian themes.

California Noir

There is of course a standard model of the Hollywood film that includes narratives and styles of diverting luminosity and vitality—qualities, perhaps not incidentally, that Carey McWilliams and others have also attributed to the state of California. However, the history of California cinema makes it clear that this standard was never as monolithic as it seemed. Importantly, for our purposes, increased attention by scholars to the tough-minded film noir of the 1940s and 1950s—one of the pivotal genres of California-based filmmaking—has been key to a reevaluation of the meaning of California. In opposition to the cliché of California optimism, film noir offers an alternate tradition of Hollywood filmmaking that is not always about happy endings, lightness, or magical realizations of a pioneer American Dream.

Flourishing in the postwar period and into the early 1950s, film noir chronicles the misadventures of losers and loners who try to follow their dreams and desires—often to the point of criminality—and frequently end up either ruined or dead. Where earlier writings on film noir read the bleakness of the genre as somehow metaphysical or existential, it is now apparent that much of the pessimistic tone of noir comes from perceptions of the American experience that are fully sociological in nature,

[7] Starr, *Inventing the Dream*, 293.

positing that there are flaws in the perfection and realization of the American Dream. Such films offer up a fatalism that has less to do with the terrors of the general human condition than with the grimness of the options available to many Americans in contemporary society.

Given that the state was so crucial to the imagining of the American Dream in the 1940s and 1950s, California became central to film noir. As the focus of westward expansion, the state had long been a symbol for the realization of the American Dream, so it is not surprising that a cinema of cynicism of the sort we find in film noir would center so many of its shattering narratives on a California experience that implies the impossibility of grand dreams. "There are no second acts in American lives," wrote F. Scott Fitzgerald in the notes for his Hollywood novel, *The Last Tycoon*, and it is appropriate that he wrote this about Hollywood in Hollywood, where he failed at a career as a screenwriter. Defeat here is endemic to the American quest narrative, and failure at the California experience is seen as the summation of all other American(ist) failures.

Indeed, the effort to understand the tough films of the 1930s, 1940s, and 1950s as about American conditions rather than some abstract and generalized human condition has led at least two analysts of the films of this period, Noel Burch and Thom Anderson, to posit a subgenre they call *film gris* (gray film). Such films eschew the exoticism often characteristic of film noir, which tended to feature rarefied subjects like the private detective and femme fatale, to concentrate instead on ordinary figures caught up in criminality when mainstream options in American life fail them.[8] Here, too, California is a place where average citizens try to pull ahead of the rat race. For example, *Double Indemnity*—often classified as a tough-guy film for its style (trenchcoats in the night, snappy dialogue, harder than nails femmes fatales)—is in many ways not about special ways of life, the exoticism of the hard-boiled milieu, but quite directly concerned with ordinary experience and the desperate attempt by a regular Joe to beat the system. Insurance salesman Walter Neff (Fred MacMurray) and bored suburban housewife Phyllis Dietrich (Barbara Stanwyck) are both recognizable American figures rooted in a stifled version of the American Dream that they try to manipulate to their own ends.

In film gris (and this is what "grayness" alludes to), plain Americans caught in dreary lives try to break through the dead end imposed on them by resorting to desperate means. Symptomatic in this respect is a 1950 film, *The Prowler*, directed by Joseph Losey, who would soon after

[8] Noel Burch and Thom Anderson, *Les Communistes d'Hollywood: Autre chose que des martyres?* (Paris: Presses Universitaires de la Nouvelle Sorbonne, 1995).

leave Los Angeles to escape the blacklist. For our purposes, *The Prowler* is significant for its revision of the California myth of westward progress, the myth that by going to California one can achieve a pioneer dream of self-realization. In this film, an ordinary Los Angeles cop named Webb Garwood (Van Heflin) dreams of a better life (crystallized in a scene in his seedy apartment in which he reads muscle magazines that offer an image of enviable masculinity). He thinks he's found his chance when he begins an affair with the bored wife of a rich media figure and decides to kill the husband (played, in a deliberately ironic cameo, by blacklisted writer Dalton Trumbo, who wrote the film's script under a pseudonym). Garwood's ultimate desire is both ambitious and meager, as if a man of limited means could only have limited dreams: By killing the husband and marrying the wife with her inheritance, Garwood plans to buy a motel on the route to Las Vegas and benefit thereby from the money-hungry dreams of others not so different from himself. In this way, Garwood inverts the California pioneer dream by moving away from Los Angeles, east toward a new city that incarnates the magic luster of money but that also reveals the emptiness of its promise. In the barrenness of the Nevada desert, Garwood is trapped and shot down by the police, his body now just a dead weight that rolls unceremoniously down a hill.

The 1992 film *Bugsy*, directed by and starring Warren Beatty, also plays on the tensions between California and Las Vegas variants of the American Dream and the pioneer quest. Gangster Bugsy Siegel comes to California from New York and immediately is entranced by the glamour of the film world. After failing in his attempt to become an actor, Bugsy shifts the focus of his dreams from Hollywood to Las Vegas, where he envisions the first large-scale casino. Like a producer or director fighting the front office, Bugsy has to struggle with his bosses as the budget goes out of control and his project threatens to unravel. The dream fails, and Bugsy returns to the West Coast, where, alone with his movie audition reel unraveling in his private screening room, he is shot dead.

Even as it maintains the westerly direction of the pioneer narrative, another classic of film noir, the 1945 film *Detour* directed by the German emigré director Edgar G. Ulmer, goes even further in dismantling standard booster images of the California Dream. *Detour* is one of the most savage interpretations of California experience in the ways it specifically rewrites positive Los Angeles images to turn the California Dream into a nightmare. In this film, pianist Al Roberts (Tom Neal) works in sleazy New York bars, dreaming of a better life and believing that his musical talents are unappreciated and going to waste. When his girlfriend Sue understands that she too cannot realize her dreams in such a place, she announces to Al that she is going to Los Angeles to try to break into the movies. But neither Sue nor Al are destined to succeed. When Sue informs Al by phone that she has failed at becoming an actress and has ended up a waitress slinging hash, he sets out to hitchhike to her and pool their efforts. Soon, however, Al gets caught up in the tragic narrative of the deaths he causes along the way and that now prevent him from ever innocently realizing his dream (hence, the "detour" of the film's title). One of these deaths occurs in the claustrophobic space of a sleazy Los Angeles hotel room, an occurrence that, though accidental, Al knows he will not be able to explain to the police. (In a strange but not unprecedented confirmation of the ways in which cinema and life can blur in Hollywood, actor Tom Neal himself became a has-been and was eventually convicted of a death he claimed was accidental. While working as a gardener for the rich and famous of Palm Springs, Neal shot his wife to death but argued in court that the gun had gone off accidentally during a marital spat.

In virtually every way, *Detour* is a dismantling of optimistic myths   20
about California. The film's process of deconstruction starts even before Al leaves for the West Coast. As Alex Barris notes in his *Hollywood according to Hollywood*, one strand of the affirmative tradition often recounts the story of people discovered elsewhere and brought to Hollywood to realize their talents (the pioneer allegory of *A Star Is Born* is in keeping with this tradition).[9] *Detour* very clearly establishes Al and Sue as losers in the game from the start. They will never get a break, never be discovered for their talent. Their ill-fated destiny is established at the outset. There is here no way to claw oneself to the top, and California does not serve as the culmination of an American success story. Indeed, if the notion of California exceptionalism imagines the state—for better or worse—as somehow set apart from the meanings and values of the rest of the country, *Detour* falls into a tradition that imagines California to be the place where the fatalism that one carries within, through the simple fact of trying unsuccessfully to live the American Dream, reaches its logical and inevitable conclusion. *Detour*'s characters—Al, Sue, and Vera, the femme fatale hitchhiker whom Al picks up and who is already dying of consumption before he accidentally strangles her in Los Angeles—are all like the Middle Americans in Nathanael West's *The Day of the Locust*, who mill around Hollywood because, as the novelist's narrator declares, "they had come here to die."

This fatalism accounts for the particularly bleak image of westward travel and arrival in Los Angeles that *Detour* depicts. Throughout the journey, *Detour*'s desert is no romantic space of discovery (as opposed,

---

[9] Alex Barris, *Hollywood according to Hollywood* (New Brunswick, N.J.: A. S. Barnes, 1978).

for example, to *A Star Is Born*, in which radiant Technicolor makes the transition to the West glow with the delight of discovery) but an empty, immaterial wasteland (not unlike the desert of nothingness and mute alienation from which the antihero emerges at the beginning of *Paris, Texas*, a film by another German director, Wim Wenders). If anything, the transition into California is at best a move from the natural inhumanity of the desert into the human-produced inhumanity of a social world ruled by commerce and exploitative human relations: *Detour's* Los Angeles is not a place of wonder—of sandy beaches or movie studios or elegant night spots—but endless commercial streets filled with ratty businesses. Los Angeles here is a universe of used-car lots (where Al and Vera have to try to get rid of their hot car) and fleabag hotels (where Al and Vera hole up and spend their time lashing out at each other until their verbal and physical spats end in death).

But if it is common to think of film noir—as well as film gris, with its even more social-realist concern for ordinary schnooks in average walks of life—as a cinematic form about the difficulty of *urban* existence (with Los Angeles as one of its primary locales, along with a few other choice cities such as New York and San Francisco), it must be noted that film noir is also important in the history of California representation for its suggestion that the experience of the state is more than just increasing urbanization and the compacting of destinies into the oppressive site of the city. If film noir matters first of all because it reminds us of a different Hollywood cinema than the magical buoyant one, the genre is also of interest in its depiction of a California that has no single identity and cannot be reduced to Los Angeles (and to a very specific Los Angeles at that). Central to film noir as it evolves through the 1940s and 1950s is the fact that its subject matter—the modernity of postwar America—is evolving, and not just in urban directions.

In this respect, the 1949 film *Thieves' Highway*, normally classified as film noir but closer to film gris in its emphasis on ordinary workers who just want to make a buck, is key to the history of cinematic representations of California life for its recognition of a world beyond the urban experience of Los Angeles. The film narrates the bleak and often fatal experiences of fruit and vegetable truckers who go from the state's valleys to the wholesale markets of the Bay Area, where they encounter all sorts of hucksters and harlots out to plunder their meager gains even by means of violence. From its opening shot in which we see a tractor plowing farmlands up above a city, *Thieves' Highway* suggests that urban experience is inextricably linked to other geographies—the life of the farm, the transition from country to city—and presents the source of this linkage as the certainty of toil, the pressures of the system on the dreams and desires of the individual. *Thieves' Highway* chronicles the stages of capitalist production—from the harvesting of produce to its consumption in the restaurants of the state—and implies that at every point in the chain of production, the worker's dream of success is vulnerable to weakness, to accident, to systematic exploitation. California here is not the golden achievement of a dream (as the hero discovers when even his radiantly blond girlfriend deserts him) but the blunt realization of the fact that dreams matter less than inescapable entrapment in oppression and exploitation (this, despite the fact that *Thieves' Highway* has a happy ending, since even the cheerfully hokey, tacked-on conclusion—*Thieves' Market*, the book on which the film is based was much bleaker—seems to imply that an optimistic outcome can only be artificial, a forced magical solution).[10]

Hard-Boiled Mobility and the California Image

From the start, both film noir and film gris, as well as a major part of the pulp and detective fiction that fed into them, avoided a univocal representation of urban California experience. For example, San Francisco, with its sense of old-world mystery, became just as logical a locale for film noir as the more modern city of Los Angeles. Indeed, one of the works frequently cited as initiating the film noir cycle, John Huston's 1941 *The Maltese Falcon*, is very pointedly a *San Francisco* film, playing on alternative myths of that northern city as a space of flux (a port city with all sorts of curious personages in transition) and as a site of exoticism. San Francisco here is not a place where dreams are realized but where all projects and hopes are betrayed and subverted. The progression from *The Maltese Falcon* to later San Francisco–based film noir like *Out of the Past* (1947) is a logical one. In the latter film, Jeff Bailey (Robert Mitchum) is a former San Francisco private eye who is drawn back into intrigue in the big city but also forced to wander endlessly between city and country, as if to suggest that there is no longer any fixed space for the experience of self and that California's function is not so much to fix or free identity as to turn it into something errant (and Bailey himself will have several identities as he tries to hide out from a destiny that, in the film's title, will come "out of the past" to haunt and pursue him).

Indeed, if California can serve in boosterist mythology as the final desired place of stability and of self-realization in the American pioneer dream, a city like San Francisco, with its connotations of exoticism, can

25

---

[10] A. I. Bezzerides, *Thieves' Market* (1949; reprint, Berkeley and Los Angeles: University of California Press, 1997).

increasingly come to figure as a marker of difference and of the dismantling of a confident image of the California experience. Granny's pioneer lesson in *A Star Is Born* is unambiguous in the clarity of its optimism about Los Angeles as the place where American Dreams come true. In contrast, San Francisco comes to represent a geography beyond understanding, a site so given over to the transitory (as for the crooks just passing through in *The Maltese Falcon*) that the possibility for clear and fixed meanings is rendered difficult. Take, for instance, the 1986 film, *Big Trouble in Little China*, directed by John Carpenter, a director trained in a film school (USC) and who is quite aware of the history of American film, its perfection in the classic studio system, and eventual deconstruction in a postclassic period. A kung-fu science-fiction horror film, *Big Trouble in Little China* is an unstable hybrid work. What is intriguing for our purposes is the way in which the film's eclecticism has also to do with its subject: macho Caucasian truck driver Jack Burton (Kurt Russell) discovers that for all his boldly overexpressed confidence, San Francisco represents an experience beyond his understanding, one that endlessly comes to challenge his confident self-image of assured masculinity. To be sure, like the Los Angeles film *Chinatown*, with its suggestion that what undoes the quest for white male truth comes in large degree from impenetrable "Asian" mystery ("forget it, Jake, it's Chinatown"), *Big Trouble in Little China* is not free of its own reifying exoticism in its image of an inscrutable Chinatown that will teach Jack his own relative place in the world. (In this respect, in passing, we might note how important has been the attempt in Californian independent filmmaking to construct nonexoticizing representations of the Asian American experience. For filmmakers as varied as Wayne Wang and Rea Tajiri, an investigation of what it means to be Asian in California becomes a way of interrogating just what California as a privileged site for the American Dream means as well.)

But for all its own vulnerability to clichés of the exotic, *Big Trouble in Little China* is important for the ways it does dismantle sustaining myths of pioneer masculinity. Kurt Russell plays Jack Burton as a near parody of John Wayne and, in its depiction of the clashes and confusions that arise when this swaggering masculinity finds out how limited its sway and power really are, the film becomes an allegory of the fate of all optimistic and affirmative myths when they bump up against universes of meaning too complex to be held within the boundaries of simple mythologies. To come to California is not to realize the pioneer mythology but to lose hold of it.

It is significant to *Big Trouble in Little China*'s allegory that Jack Burton be a truck driver. Through this, the film suggests first of all that for all his swaggering attempt to play out male conquest fantasies, Jack is an ersatz, even fallen, version of the frontiersman. As with *Thieves' Highway*, with its theme of the inevitable exploitation of wildcat truckers (as its very title suggests), *Big Trouble in Little China* offers no romance of the road, no uplifting mythology of the trucker as modern-day frontier hero. Just as he cannot be John Wayne, Jack Burton cannot be a cowboy but only a derivative clichéd rendition of the now-faded romantic image of the Westerner. California is not (or is no longer) a place that sustains pioneer ambition but, quite the contrary, a force of modernization and multiculturalism that shows up boosterist machismo as an anachronism (just as Jack's big truck seems a clumsy intrusion as it gets stuck in the fog in the tight and narrow streets of Chinatown).

The trucker image is important too for its emphasis on movement, on an experience of identity that is itself transitory (the film begins and ends with Jack in his truck, unable to settle down, forced to be always on the move, not able to make California his end-point home). If pioneer mythology figures California as the site of destiny and destination—the place where one comes into identity and builds up a future—the flip side of this mythology is that no place can be stable. California is then not so much the site of assured values as the extreme rendition of the instability of all value systems, of a geography so much in flux that it can never be settled. One of the ultimate Los Angeles films, Ridley Scott's *Blade Runner*, represents the city precisely in opposition to booster mythology that would see it as the culmination or realization of the pioneer quest. Los Angeles here is not a place one would willingly voyage to in hopes of realizing a dream. On the one hand, those who stay in *Blade Runner*'s Los Angeles are portrayed as the flotsam and jetsam of a society that has gone beyond them; the city has become a backwater filled with scavengers, the ill, and the ill-fated (as in *The Day of the Locust*, so many of the city's people are "here to die"). On the other hand, the aerial ships that glide over the darkened city and speak of a better life elsewhere, "offworld," indicate that for privileged pioneers, Los Angeles can only be an ephemeral point of transit, no longer a destiny or a destination but one more memory to be cast off as one continues the quest elsewhere.

The Paradox of the Pioneer

In this respect, it is important to note that from its very founding, there is something contradictory and even self-destructive or self-defeating about the pioneer myth as a defining structure of the American experience. If it succeeds, the pioneer mission fails: to be precise, if the point of pioneering is to quest after a site of settlement, the achievement of that quest implies that there is no longer any place for pioneering. The pioneer cannot settle down without becoming something other than a pioneer. Numerous works in the history of American culture play on this paradox—for example, James Fenimore Cooper's Natty Bumppo enables others to go on to settlement even as he knows the new America he is helping to build can have no place for him. The Hollywood epic *How the West Was Won* (1962) no doubt intends to celebrate the western spirit, but its euphoria is undercut by an irony specifically linked to the film's depiction of the West Coast as an inevitable and unsurpassable end point. As the past tense of the title suggests, *How the West Was Won* is a film of nostalgia, of fixation on the past (the past of a golden age of Hollywood in the process of fading away as much as the past of the pioneer quest). Winning the West means the termination of the ongoing vitality of the mythology of western conquest. The film's triumphalist depiction of the American spirit is tinged with sadness and even regret as it dissolves from the fictional story of one-time pioneers at the end of their narrative to documentary footage of a Southern California freeway alongside the ocean.

It is not accidental that many films after the decline of the old Holly- 30 wood studio system make central reference to another Western, John Ford's *The Searchers*. That film's image of the errant frontiersman Ethan Edwards (John Wayne), who can know no sustaining home life, is also a metaphor for a cinema that admits the limitations of optimistic myths and can do no more than narrate them with sad nostalgia. Characters like Ethan Edwards and Jack Burton can rescue kidnapped or strayed figures and return them to the fold of community, but these men themselves can belong to no community and must always, like Huck Finn, light out ahead of civilization. Wim Wenders's *The State of Things* (1982) strikingly captures the paradox of quest narratives like *The Searchers*—if you stop moving, you're out of business—and maps it specifically into a bleak representation of the California experience. In this film, the searching hero (a filmmaker who has run out of funds for a pet project) tracks down and stays with a Hollywood producer on the run from gangsters he owes money to and who hides out in a mobile home that endlessly winds its way through the streets of Los Angeles (passing, at one point, a movie theater showing *The Searchers*). Such endless transit sustains a barren and desperate survival, and it is only when the "caravan" comes to rest for just a moment that the pursuers are able to catch up and the nomads are gunned down. To settle down is to die. (But to be on the move is to live in a constant state of paranoia.)

For all its sadness at the errancy of the loner hero, *The Searchers* also appeals no doubt for the optimism of its belief that errant heroes can indeed be heroic—helping to build civilization by restoring its lost children to it—even as they can find no place in the civilization they have aided. And yet, as things become more desperate and constrained for would-be heroes in a nonheroic age, heroism itself can turn into an irrational fixation on quirky acts of violence that supposedly give one's life meaning but are really signs of meaninglessness. Stuck on the West Coast, with no place to go, no new frontier to conquer, ersatz frontiersmen turn inward, confronting inner demons and manifesting their fatalism as inevitable violence.

Emblematic in its sense that the old mythologies of salvation no longer work in a new California is the controversial ending of Robert Altman's *The Long Goodbye* (1973) in which L.A. detective Philip Marlowe's discovery that he has been a patsy all along for a get-rich scheme by his supposed buddy, Terry Malloy, leads Marlowe to ungloriously shoot Malloy down and walk off. Many viewers found this conclusion to be a betrayal of novelist Raymond Chandler's insistence on Marlowe as a man of honor ("Down these mean streets a man must go . . ."), but Altman's point seems to be that the 1970s version is more in touch with the demythologizing impulses of the age. There is no longer any honor in heroism, and the new antiheroes have internalized the ugliness of the mean streets that they used to wander down. In *The Long Goodbye*, as Marlowe walks away from his act of violence, the melody of "Hooray for Hollywood" comes up on the sound track. If boosterist films like *A Star Is Born* celebrate Hollywood as an ostensibly natural conclusion to the pioneer quest, cinema since the breakup of the classic studio system looks back on Hollywood with pessimistic and ironic attitudes ranging from bittersweet nostalgia to hard-edged and relentless cynicism.

UNDERSTANDING THE TEXT

1. What was Polan's image of California when he was a child, and why do you think he begins his essay by recounting his childhood memories?

2. What were the various reasons that the film industry eventually chose Hollywood as its primary home, according to Polan?

3. What, in Polan's view, is the significance of the American pioneer myth for the growth of the film industry and its settling in California?

4. Define in your own words the two film genres that Polan emphasizes — film noir and film gris. In what ways is a California location central to these genres?

EXPLORING AND DEBATING THE ISSUES

1. In class, brainstorm recent films that depict California locations. Then categorize them according to whether they promote a boosterist, idealist

view of the state or a dark, pessimistic perspective. Use your results as the basis for an essay in which you analyze the vision of California as depicted in current movies. Is it an accurate vision of California realities?

2. Write an essay in which you propose your own response to Polan's question "Are Hollywood films Californian?" (para. 6). Be sure you support your position with references to specific films.

3. Write an essay in which you compare and contrast the film noir depictions of California and the apocalyptic films discussed in David Fine's "Endings and Beginnings: Surviving Apocalypse" (p. 326). Which genre do you believe offers a more balanced representation of California dreams and realities? Be sure to base your discussion on an analysis of specific films.

4. Rent a videotape or DVD of *How the West Was Won*, and write your own analysis of the role that the pioneer myth plays in this film. What is the ultimate message that the film sends about the mythology of western conquest?

5. Rent a video or DVD of *The Maltese Falcon*, and write an essay in which you support, refute, or modify Polan's assertion that "San Francisco comes to represent a geography beyond understanding, a site so given over to the transitory . . . that the possibility for clear and fixed meanings is rendered difficult" (para. 25).

The Automobile Age in California

JAMES J. FLINK

Although the American automobile industry was born in Detroit, California is the center of America's car culture. In this selection from his book *The Automobile Age* (1988), **James J. Flink** (b. 1932) shows how Los Angeles, the epicenter of American car culture, came to be shaped by the automobile. Already beginning to sprawl out along train and tram lines at the turn of the century, L.A. was destined to become a city without a center once the automobile arrived. A long-time student of American car culture, Flink is also the author of *America Adopts the Automobile, 1895–1910* (1970) and *The Car Culture* (1975).

California led the nation in 1929 as it had in 1910 in ratio of population to motor vehicle registrations. It remained true as well that the leading regions in motor vehicles per capita were still the Pacific and the West North Central states and that the South continued to lag behind the rest of the country in adopting the automobile. But the gaps among the various regions of the United States already had closed appreciably by 1920. During the decade 1910 to 1920 automobile registrations increased more rapidly in the Rocky Mountain states and in the South, the early laggards in adopting the automobile, than in the East North Central, Middle Atlantic, and New England states. Although the agricultural states of the trans-Mississippi West continued to be the largest market for new cars, and California remained known as a bottomless pit for automobile sales, regional differences in the diffusion of the motorcar were becoming less significant. With a United States average of 10.1 persons for every motor vehicle registered in 1921, California ranked first with a ratio of 5.2:1 and Mississippi last with 27.5:1. By 1929 the United States average was 4.5:1. California still led the states with 2.3:1, and Alabama ranked last with 9:1. Long-distance trucking and a new mobility of people were beginning to open up the Pacific Coast and the Southwest to commercial development, make specialized regional economies more interdependent, and lessen the distinctiveness of regional lifeways.

A lifestyle based on personal automobility first developed in Southern California, and nowhere in the world has mass motorization been more pervasive in its impact. "Mass motorization of the region was largely accomplished during the . . . span of the single decade following World War I," Ashleigh Brilliant relates. "Since the earliest days of motoring, Southern California, with its benevolent climate, attractive scenery, and relatively good roads, had been regarded as a 'motorist's paradise.' Until the postwar decade, however, the automobile was considered primarily as a means of recreation. For more practical purposes there was the Pacific Electric Railway, world famous for the efficiency of its service."[1]

Los Angeles has been called "a city built on transport." Its first population boom followed the completion of the Santa Fe Railroad line in 1885. Competition with the Southern Pacific reduced the railroad fare from Kansas City, Missouri, to only one dollar, bringing a flood of tourists and fortune seekers. Invalids and retired couples in particular sought the region's dry air and sunshine. Many came for a winter vacation and stayed on as permanent residents. Midwestern farmers relocated to become citrus growers.

In contrast with the immigrants to Eastern and Midwestern cities in the late nineteenth century, the immigrants to Southern California were older, overwhelmingly native-born and white, and relatively affluent. The largest proportion came from the rural Middle West, where a highly decentralized residential pattern was the norm. "Americans came to Los Angeles with a conception of the good community which was embodied in single-family houses, located on large lots, surrounded by landscaped

[1] Ashleigh E. Brilliant, "Some Aspects of Mass Motorization in Southern California, 1919–1929," *Southern California Quarterly* 47 (Oct. 1965): 191.

lawns, and isolated from business activities," Robert Fogelson points out. "Their vision was epitomized by the residential suburb—spacious, affluent, clean, decent, permanent, predictable, and homogeneous. . . . Here then was the basis for the extraordinary dispersal of Los Angeles."[2]

A decade prior to this first population boom, the Southern Pacific had built five lines radiating out from Los Angeles to San Fernando, San Bernardino, Anaheim, Wilmington (near the San Pedro port), and Santa Monica. Reyner Banham observes that this rail system "constitutes the bones of the skeleton on which Greater Los Angeles was to be built, the fundamentals of the present city where each of these old lines is now duplicated by a freeway." He goes on to note that "subdivision of adjoining land proceeded as fast as the laying of rails" and that "commuting began almost as soon as the rails were down. . . . Before 1880 then, the railways had outlined the form of the city and sketched in the pattern of movement that was to characterize its peculiar pattern of life."[3]

Horse-drawn streetcars began to connect the Los Angeles business district with fashionable residential areas in 1876, then suburban development began in 1887 when an electric trolley line began to operate from downtown out Pico Street to serve the Electric Railway Homestead Association Tract. This was the first of a number of trolley lines built by real estate developers out to large tracts of land in outlying areas that they subdivided into homesites. Easy access to downtown by trolley was emphasized in advertising the lots. "Often mechanically unreliable, and even more often on unsound financial footings, the street railways rarely turned profits as transportation businesses, though they often contributed to huge speculative profits in real estate," Martin Wachs writes. Building street railways out to low-density population areas was feasible because of these huge profits and because "Los Angeles . . . was just growing to maturity as a city when street railways were introduced and it had never developed a significant commercial and industrial core."[4]

Between 1901 and 1911 some seventy-two separate street railways were merged, reorganized, consolidated, and extended into the Pacific Electric Railway by Henry Edmunds Huntington, the heir of Southern Pacific magnate Collis P. Huntington. By 1911 this constituted the largest electric interurban system in the United States. Pacific Electric served fifty-six communities within a one hundred-mile radius over 1,164 miles

[2] Robert M. Fogelson, *The Fragmented Metropolis: Los Angeles, 1850–1930* (Cambridge: Harvard UP, 1967), 144–45.

[3] Reyner Banham, *Los Angeles: The Architecture of Four Ecologies* (New York: Harper, 1971), 77–78.

[4] Martin Wachs, "Autos, Transit, and the Sprawl of Los Angeles," *American Planning Association Journal* 50 (Summer 1984): 298, 300.

of standard-gauge track with its "Big Red Cars." The associated Los Angeles Railway Company operated streetcars over an additional 316 miles on narrow-gauge track within the city of Los Angeles. Proximity to streetcar lines, observes Mark Foster, "continued to be an important prerequisite for successful development until the 1920s. City maps drawn in 1902 and as late as 1919 show few streets more than five or six blocks from streetcar lines."[5]

Critics of urban sprawl have erroneously blamed the Southern California freeway system for making Los Angeles not a city but a collection of suburbs in search of a city. The unchecked horizontal growth of Greater Los Angeles in fact preceded rather than followed from mass motorization in the 1920s. Wachs notes that by 1910, "largely because of the Pacific Electric System, Los Angeles was functionally integrated with Long Beach, Santa Monica, and San Bernardino. The extent of the metropolitan region has not grown substantially since then, and most of the recent growth has consisted instead of filling in the spaces between outlying areas associated with important stations on the Pacific Electric." The Southern California freeway system closely parallels the 1923 Pacific Electric route map, which, as Banham says, "pretty well defines Greater Los Angeles as it is today." The socioeconomic impact of the Big Red Cars has been most thoroughly examined by Spencer Crump. "Unquestionably," he writes, "it was the electric interurbans which distributed the population over the countryside during the century's first decade and patterned Southern California as a horizontal city rather than one of skyscrapers and slums."[6]

Southern California's second great population boom occurred during the 1920s, when the population of Los Angeles County grew from 1.2 million to 2.2 million. By 1930 only 20 percent of Angelinos had been born in California. At the time, C. Warren Thornwaite characterized this mass movement as "the greatest internal migration in the history of the American people." "Like earlier booms, it was fostered by speculators, bankers, and businessmen," Wachs relates. "In 1921, the 'All Weather Club' was formed to advertise the wonders of Southern California in the East and especially to promote tourism, in the belief that a substantial proportion of those who vacationed in Southern California would be 'sold' on the idea of staying permanently."[7]

[5] Mark S. Foster, "The Model T, the Hard Sell, and Los Angeles's Urban Growth: the Decentralization of Los Angeles during the 1920s," *Pacific Historical Review* 4 (Nov. 1975): 476.

[6] Wachs, "Autos, Transit" 300; Banham, *Los Angeles* 82; Spencer Crump, *Ride the Big Red Cars: How Trolleys Helped Build Southern California* (Corona del Mar: Trans-Anglo, 1962), 100.

[7] C. Warren Thornwaite, *Internal Migration in the United States* (Philadelphia: U of Pennsylvania P, 1934), 18; Wachs, "Autos, Transit" 302.

Whereas earlier affluent vacationers generally had shipped their 10 open touring cars out from the East by rail, the combined effect in the 1920s of improved roads, better tourist services, and the closed car was that increasingly people came to Southern California in their motorcars. Motorization proliferated much faster than population. Between 1919 and 1929, while the population of Los Angeles roughly doubled, automobile registrations increased 550 percent, from about 141,000 to 777,000. Remarked city planner Gordon Whitnall in 1930, "So prevalent is the use of the motor vehicle that it might be said that Southern Californians have added wheels to their anatomy."[8] Although ridership on the Pacific Electric System increased into the 1930s, it failed to expand proportionately with population growth as more and more riders switched to motorcars. Significantly, the level of mass motorization, as measured by the ratio of motor vehicles to people, has not greatly increased in over half a century. Los Angeles County had one motor vehicle for every 2.85 persons in 1929 and one motor vehicle for every 1.7 persons in 1979, to lead the nation in automobiles per capita at both dates.

Despite Southern California's highly decentralized settlement pattern, a 1931 traffic study showed that over twice as many motor vehicles entered the Los Angeles central business district (CBD) as entered the CBDs of other large American cities. During identical twelve-hour periods, some 277,000 motor vehicles entered the Los Angeles CBD, while among cities with roughly equal-sized CBDs 113,000 entered in Chicago, 66,000 in Boston, and only 49,000 in St. Louis. Moreover, despite the fact that Los Angeles developed as a post-automobile city, its streets were the narrowest and most disconnected and it devoted the least land area to streets in its CBD of any large city in the United States. For example, in 1924 only 21.4 percent of the Los Angeles CBD was devoted to streets, compared with a range of 29 to 44 percent for other large American cities. This gave Los Angeles the most severe automobile traffic congestion in the world in the pre–World War II period. Downtown traffic snarls were already so bad during the 1919 Christmas shopping season that the city put into effect on April 10, 1920, a ban on street parking during business hours. Business dropped off so sharply that the ban was revised on April 26 to apply only during the evening rush hours.

Mass motorization fit hand in glove with a Southern California economy that necessitated the dispersion of business locations. For good reasons, a commercial-industrial core never developed in Los Angeles. To begin with, fear of earthquake damage led after 1906 to a 150-foot limitation on the height of downtown buildings, which remained in effect until

[8] Quoted in Foster, "The Model T, the Hard Sell," 470.

the mid-1950s. Citrus growing, the movie industry, and later the aircraft industry required large tracts of land available only in the suburbs. The petroleum industry, central to the local economy, located facilities where oil was found or near the port from which it was shipped. As petroleum exports mounted, by 1930 the port of Los Angeles had come to rank third in total commerce and second in tonnage in the United States. The port facilities and related commercial activity were located along forty miles of waterfront in the Long Beach, San Pedro, and Wilmington areas, whose northern edge was about twenty miles distant from the traditional commercial core of the city. New residential communities sprang up between downtown Los Angeles and the port area. Wachs notes that although manufacturing industries grew, the segment of the workforce engaged in manufacturing declined from 28 percent in 1920 to 22 percent in 1930. "Los Angeles was increasingly described as a 'white-collar' town; real estate, finance, and tourism expanded most prominently."[9]

Thus, mass motorization neither caused the dispersion of economic activities nor changed the form of residential patterns in Southern California. However, the motor vehicle permitted decentralization that went well beyond what had been possible with electric traction. And this created a new urban lifestyle in Southern California that uniquely combined big-city amenities with low population density, single-family housing, and unparalleled individual mobility and access to outdoor recreation.

In areas close to the central business district that were served well by streetcars—such as Hawthorne, Inglewood, and Gardena in the South Bay area—mass motorization had little impact. There was a substantial increase, however, in the number of new subdivisions opened as mass motorization enabled real estate promoters to develop tracts of land remote from streetcar lines. The development of the San Fernando Valley was the prime example. The number of new subdivision maps recorded soared from 346 in 1920 to peak of 1,434 in 1923. With this new suburban construction, the amount of land converted to urban use in the Los Angeles area increased from 14.2 percent in 1924 to 24.4 percent a decade later. Construction of single-family residential dwellings accounted for 75 percent of this urban land use in the area between 8.6 and 10.3 miles from downtown Los Angeles.

The 1930 United States census revealed that 93.7 percent of the dwelling units in Los Angeles were single-family homes—the highest proportion of any American city—and that population density in the Greater Los Angeles area was only 2,812 persons per square mile. This contrasted with densities of over 23,000 persons per square mile in New

15

9 Wachs, "Autos, Transit," 302–03.

York City, nearly 18,000 persons per square mile in Boston, and nearly 17,000 in Chicago. Single-family residences accounted for less than 53 percent of the dwelling units in all three of these cities.

The movement of population outward plus traffic congestion led to the rapid decline of downtown Los Angeles, as businesses and professional offices located outside the central business district. Between 1920 and 1930 the proportion of banks located outside the CBD increased from 45 percent to 89 percent, theaters from 26 percent to 80 percent, dentists' offices from 16 percent to 55 percent, and physicians' offices from 21 percent to 67 percent. The proportion of residents living within a ten-mile radius of the CBD who entered it daily declined from 68 percent in 1924 to 52 percent in 1931.

"The impact of the automobile upon Los Angeles's urbanization process compared to that in other cities is distinguished chiefly by its magnitude," Foster concludes. "Both critics and defenders of Los Angeles's decentralization generally concede that by 1930 the city was in many respects the prototype of the mid-twentieth-century metropolis."[10] This is most forcefully demonstrated by an examination of the parallel impact of the automobile on southern cities during the 1920s.

UNDERSTANDING THE TEXT

1. According to Flink, how did California lead the nation in the early development of America's car culture?

2. How, in Flink's view, did the characteristic suburban sprawl of Los Angeles develop prior to the automobile age?

3. How did the automobile contribute to the decline of downtown Los Angeles?

4. What effects did mass motorization have on Southern California communities in general?

EXPLORING AND DEBATING THE ISSUES

1. In your journal, reflect on your own attitudes toward automobiles. Do cars mean more than transportation to you? If so, in what ways?

2. In an essay, analyze how the image of Southern California car culture has been portrayed in popular culture. In addition to film and television depictions, you might review such pop tunes as The Beach Boys' "Little Deuce Coupe" and Jan and Dean's "Little Old Lady from Pasadena."

3. Flink claims that "[a] lifestyle based on personal automobility first developed in Southern California" (para. 2). In an essay, explain to what extent this observation applies to your region of the state.

[10] Foster, "The Model T, the Hard Sell," 483.

4. Denise S. Spooner ("A New Perspective on the Dream," p. 40) suggests that one reason Midwesterners came to California was to escape the tightly knit communities in their home states. How, in your opinion, has California car culture contributed to dispersed communities, both socially and geographically? Be sure to base your discussion on specific communities.

5. Compare and contrast Flink's attitudes toward California automotive culture with those of David Carle ("Sprawling Gridlock," p. 403). Which discussion do you find more persuasive, and why?

Berkeley Explained

ALICE KAHN

In the 1960s, California stood at the center of a cultural revolution in which masses of middle-class youth rejected what they saw as the materialistic values of their parents, and leading the way was Berkeley, which has been called Berserkley and the People's Republic of Berkeley as a result. But now, as **Alice Kahn** reports in this affectionate sendup of the place where Allen Ginsberg wrote the poem ("Howl") that helped start it all, a good deal has changed. Now that "things have come full circle as a new generation desperately wants a crack at a good job, a home, some status," Berkeley is the center of a consumerist cultural revolution. Where rampaging students once battled tear-gas-dropping helicopters and heavily armed police, YUPS and What's Lefts now hang out, argue about rent control, and eat themselves silly while property values skyrocket and the "necessities of life" include "built-in redwood buffets, . . . window seats, and . . . French doors"—at least as Kahn sees things. Kahn is a former high school teacher and current humorist whose collections of essays include the book from which this essay is excerpted, *Multiple Sarcasm* (1985), *My Life as a Gal* (1987), and *Luncheon at the Cafe Ridiculous* (1990).

I am walking north on Shattuck Avenue—Main Street—Berkeley, California. In my head I hear Elvis, the late King, singing "In the ghet-*toe*. . . ." I improvise his back-up, the Mighty Clouds of Joy, adding, "the gourmet ghetto. . . ."

A young man comes up to me on the corner of Cedar and Shattuck and asks, "Do you know where I can get any food around here? I'm new in town." I brace myself against a lamppost because the question is staggering. Can I answer him in three thousand words or less? Doesn't he know he's in the heart of what realtors call "the most dynamic and innovative retail shopping area in the United States"? Is he unaware that he has entered—da-da da-da da-da—the Gluttony Zone?

Before I lead him down the gustatory garden path I attempt to assess his level of knowledge. He arrived in town yesterday from SUNY

Binghamton and has come to do graduate work in microbiology. No, he has never heard of the gourmet ghetto. He has missed the articles about it in the *New York Times, Newsweek,* and *The Nation.* He doesn't know that the East Coast press loves to do a dance on how the Berkeley Left has become the food establishment, how "the counterculture has become the counter culture," how the radicals now eat radicchio, how the barricades have been replaced by the wheels of brie. No, he is just a new kid in town asking what appears to be a perfectly simple question. For him, and for all the other new recruits, the young men and women who are even now arriving from the provinces, I'd like to offer this modest guide to Berkeley.

If you dare to wander beyond the campus, beyond the dorms, beyond your "pig runs" and "animal houses," you will find a place that gets curiouser and curiouser. The first rule is that Berkeley, like Tina Turner, never does anything nice and easy. If you keep this in mind, you won't be surprised when what would seem to be the simplest of civic acts—from tree trimming to garbage disposal—become issues of heated debate, protest, emotion, and political intrigue.

But let's start with that innocent question: where to get food around here. I answer the young man by pointing out that we have just passed Poulet, the gourmet chicken deli, the Virginia Bakery, Borrelli's, an Italian deli, the Griffon, a new Scandinavian restaurant, and Warszawa, a place that proves that Polish cuisine is more than a Spam upsidedown cake. 5

Across the intersection is Smokey Joe's Cafe, a monument to the mellow hippie. Next to it, on the site of a former funeral home, there is a complex of shops including Sweet Temptations, a chocolate and yogurt heaven, a Japanese place where you can achieve yakitori, a place that actually serves hamburgers, and one of the innumerable croissant and cappuccino filling stations that have become the McDonald's of Berkeley. (Surely over ten billion served by now.) Never mind that this mortuary mall once inspired angry protests in the community. That and the ability to park nearby are now history.

On the next corner is the Co-op, the Shattuck branch of a chain of cooperative supermarkets. This particular store is one of the largest volume supermarkets in the country. It too has experienced constant political infighting: should it sell the cheapest food, the wholesomest food, or those products untainted by the human or labor rights violations of the companies who make them? Newcomers can join, or they can shop here without joining. If the clerk asks for your number, you can say "Farmworkers" or "Free Clinic" and nobody will know you're a stranger.

You will also want to check out the upstairs bulletin board where you might find a room to rent, a sofa, or your own true love.

My newfound friend and I proceed up Shattuck past the world-famous Chez Panisse and turn the corner to see the natives gather for coffee at a place called Peet's, which sells the sinsemilla of coffee beans as well as a variety of beans ordinaire. I tell him how on mornings here he'll find what my friend Sharon calls "independently wealthy mothers." These are the ones with working husbands and one perfect babe in an Aprica stroller. We listen as the men nearby bitch about how they're "not gettin' much."

You can even stop in at the Juice Bar for something as mundane as a turkey sandwich, I tell him. Just be sure you have a styrofoam cup in your hands at all times. This is your passport. Anyone caught wandering around the area without a styrofoam cup is immediately suspect. We have little gestapo type officers who approach you and ask to see "ze cup, pleeze!"

You'll probably want to stop in at Vivoli's for an Italian ice cream. I 10 keep hoping they'll add some truly local flavors like Walnut Square or Nuclear Freeze, but so far it's just plain old amaretto and fresh strawberry and stuff like that. Vivoli's represents a success story from one of Berkeley's unique minorities, the lesbian community. Unlike San Francisco, where the gay male community is ghettoized in the Castro district, the lesbian community is mostly mainstreamed into Berkeley life. It is speculated that there is one feminist therapist for every fifty people in Berkeley. A good thing too because you can't live here for very long without needing one of your own.

Nearby is Cocolat (Parlez-vous Berklaise?), recently the scene of a labor strike that forced chocolate decadence lovers to temporarily satisfy themselves with sex. Next door is a pathetic Northern California attempt at a Jewish deli redeemed by its Yiddishkeit live performances including, believe it or not, terrible Jewish comedians. Further up the street is Lenny's, a butcher shop where they'll "sell no swine before its time," and—what else?—another Italian bakery and restaurant. Then there's the Produce Center (always a bridesmaid to the formidable Monterey Market), where you can get five kinds of berries and four kinds of mushrooms and have a friendly conversation with the only normal person in Berkeley. You'll know her when you see her.

Completing the food mania is a sushi dealer, the Berkeley Fish Market, and Pig by the Tail, or as one neighborhood wag has dubbed it, Pig by the Balls. And last, but not least, we come to the Cheese Board.

Ah, blame it on the Cheese Board; they started it all. And is their face and politics red. This is one of the oldest and most successful food businesses in town. The collective that runs it seems quite uncomfortable with their newfound fame. Not only did they introduce us to the wonders of brie and their mock Boursin and a myriad of goat cheeses, but they perfected that ultimate symbol of the new Berkeley—the baguette. If you play your cards right and have a lot of time to kill, you may be able to score one. In a form of torture, they pollute the neighborhood with the smell of this delicacy baking.

I imagine someday the Cheese Board will organize a mass community therapy-in. The whole of Berkeley will be invited to engage in a huge swashbuckler scene. Some therapist-cum-facilitator will be perched on a lifeguard platform on the grassy road-divider strip and sound the *en garde*. Then we will all pull our baguettes out of their long white sheaths and begin nonviolently battering one another. "Have a nice day. Pow! Take that, you knave!"

I have another theory on the Cheese Board and their diabolically delicious baguettes. No, they don't just want to constipate us. I think the plan is to get the whole community hooked and then baguette tease us. First it'll be "Sorry, no baguettes tonight, honey, the collective has a headache." From there it'll progress to "Baguettes for activists only." Before long nobody will get a baguette unless she submits to working for world peace and against nuclear weapons research. They'll franchise out branches to strategic locales: The Cheese Board, Livermore; The Cheese Board, Los Alamos; The Cheese Board, Port Chicago. Believe me, if J. Edgar Hoover were alive today, we'd have a five-hundred-page report on this small band of ragtag slicers and bakers, and its potential to wreak havoc by baguette denial.

Now that I've told you all about my neighborhood, I want you to get out, leave, scram. I saw it first, and it's mine. If you must move beyond Larry Blake's or La Val's, go to somebody else's neighborhood. Wend your way through the maze of traffic diverters to another one of those islands in the Berkeley archipelago. Go to the Elmwood or Westbrae or Shattuck and Woolsey or College and Alcatraz or West Berkeley. There is actually better food to be had in these places than the ghetto. Some neighborhoods you can actually park in.

"But," protests the young man from the provinces, "all I wanted was to buy some bread and milk. That's all. If you really want to explain something, explain why it's so hard to find a place to live around here." (Phew! Couldn't he have asked me something simple like, "How can Reagan be removed from office?")

As I contemplate an explanation of the great Berkeley housing shortage, I hear Gene Pitney singing, "No, it isn't very pretty what a town without pity can do."

I walk him over to Henry Street behind the Safeway store (in North

Berkeley, even Safeways have gourmet counters; I hear McDonald's is contemplating the introduction of Quail McNuggets). I point out a three-story cellblock-like building which extends back a full block to Milvia Street and bears the name Luxor Apts. This, I explain, is a classic Berkeley ticky-tacky circa 1966. Now look at the place next door. Note the porch columns, the stained glass, the elegant entrance. If you really want to know the story of Berkeley, it's told in windows, eaves, and brown shingles. Berkeley is basically a museum of houses, few of them all *that* grand but each magnificent in its details.

The ticky-tackies threatened this character and charm. Speculation in rental housing made tearing down two old elegant houses and putting up a twenty-six-unit Luxor on the same lots a wise investment. Not three blocks from here is a row of ticky-tackies, one of them built on the site of a cottage where Allen Ginsberg reportedly wrote "Howl." Would the English tear down Shakespeare's house and put up units?

Two forces conspired to stop the ticky-tackification of Berkeley. One was the riots of the Vietnam and People's Park era. Much anger was focused then on the concept that property was more valued than life. People showed their contempt for property by stoning, bombing, and placing graffiti on it. This didn't look so good when the developers brought the investors through for a looksee. The other force was rent control—for years a threat and finally a reality. Some feel rent control was necessary for neighborhood preservation and to maintain low-cost housing. Others feel it represents an unfair limitation on the supply of housing caused by mealy-mouthed no-growthers and argue that it ultimately contributes to gentrification.

"But," the young man inevitably asks, "what about the new building over there with the greenhouse windows, the skylights, and the wood shingles?" Sorry, pal, you can't afford it. Those are for the YUPs, the young urban professionals. They've been lured to Berkeley, in part, by bargains in condos and single-family homes—bargains, that is, relative to Marin, San Francisco, and the Peninsula. BART, a public transportation system convenient to Montgomery Street and few other places, is also a plus. The influx of these commuters has encouraged a new phase of speculation in commercial real estate, as creative capitalists and tax shelter artists sense a rising demand among the disposable income types for sophisticated shops selling unique items.

I give him an example. For days I passed a sign in the window of La Cuisine that proclaimed: "SALE! INGRID PARTY BALLS, $19.95." Curious, I went inside and asked, "What are Ingrid Party Balls?" "I don't know," the clerk answered.

"But you've had them on special all week."

She went and called another clerk. "Are you the one asking about the   25
Ingrid Party Balls?" this one asked.

"Yes."

"I'm sorry," she said, "they're all sold out."

I considered calling up later and saying: this is Ingrid. Any messages?

I ask the young man if he understands now why he can't find a place
to live.

"Sort of. But say, do you think there are any vacancies at the Luxor?"   30

"Don't tell me you want to live there. There are no fireplaces, no
built-in redwood buffets, no window seats, no French doors—in short,
none of the necessities of life."

"I think I could learn to survive without French doors. You ever try
riding your bike from Pinole?"

I am about to suggest Oakland—"just over the rent control border,"
as they say in the real estate ads—but I can see something else is on his
mind. He has one more question: "Do you know where . . . this is kind of
hard to ask . . ."

Let's see. He said he was twenty-three. (Was I ovulating in 1960?)
"Look, I'm old enough to be your mother, boy. Ask me anything."

"Do you have any ideas on where I could meet girls?"   35

"Hey! Call us women," I retort—although, as I think about it,
"girl" has had a slightly different ring to it since I've turned thirty-five.
(What really enrages me is when twenty-three-year-old guys call me
"ma'am.")

I try to break it to him gently how hazardous looking for love in
Berkeley can be. I suggest he might want to join a men's group just to get
the old Yin and Yang into balance before he comes on too strong or too
weak to one of these young, assertive, hot-tub-on-the first-date types.
Next I suggest he make the necessary $25 investment in a haircut—one
of those no-sideburn, parted-on-the-side specials. The long hair, I tell
him, has got to go. I quote my friend Nina, who recently observed, "In
the '60s I saw a guy with long hair and thought: brother. Now I see one
and I think: mass murderer."

To meet women, he could try the clubs—Ruthie's, the Berkeley
Square, Ashkenaz, etc., but I warn him that most of Berkeley closes at
9:00 p.m. Only the nocturnal creatures venture out after that, so he'd
better be wary on the streets. Another approach would be to try the
bookstores. (You probably think that there are so many bookstores because this is a town of intellectuals, but guess again—Cody's, Moe's,
and their ilk have other uses.) I suggest he might be able to impress the

right woman with, "Excuse me. Do you know where I can find a copy of Barbara Ehrenreich's book about men and the flight from commitment?" A more aggressive try would be "Have you seen a copy of *(How to Satisfy Your Lover with) Extended Sexual Orgasm*? I've already read about ESO myself, but I need a copy for a friend." This will surely impress the red stiletto heels type. But what if he wants to meet a "Humboldt honey," an unshaven, Birkenstocked, Botticellian beauty? Here he might try, "I'm looking for a copy of *Death Begins in the Colon*. Do you know the book?"

While this bookish approach may work for recent East Coast arrivals, Californians generally prefer to get physical. A visit to the jogging track at Martin Luther King school may allow for a clever opener, such as "I couldn't help noticing how you never pronate." Or perhaps on a visit to Strawberry Canyon pool he could manage a quick "You swim laps often?" between strokes. I tell him the odds are even more favorable (one male: twenty females) at an aerobics class. While his head is between his legs, he can look to his right and say, "Good workout, huh?" He could also try hiking in Tilden Park—if he can find it.

Finally, if all else fails, there is Berkeley's favorite sport: hanging out, eating, and waiting for something to happen. So I hand the young man a step-by-step plan: "BERKELEY ON 5,000 CALORIES A DAY."

8:00 a.m.—Cappuccino at Caffe Mediterraneum. Walk up to a What's Left type (you know, Old Left, New Left, What's Left), and ask for an explanation of the mural at Telegraph and Haste. Jog up Dwight to College. Note woman in wheelchair helping blind man cross street.

9:00 a.m.—Vanilla malt at Elmwood Soda Fountain. Discover soda jerk is local sage. Grab a bag of watermelon Jelly Bellies from Sweet Dreams and a cruller from Dream Fluff Donuts. Check out the Ivy Shoppe. (This place, I predict, will be torn down soon, then reconstructed in fifteen years at considerable expense.)

10:00 a.m.—Bear claw and coffee at the Buttercup (the IRS willing). Too bloated to jog or walk. Call Taxi Unlimited and go down to Shattuck. Wander around Hink's—"a great store at home." Look at Berkeley Public Library.

11:00 a.m.—Optional snack at Edy's or Trumpetvine Court.

Noon—Szechwan Hot Sauce Noodles at the Taiwan Restaurant. Revitalized. Run down Hearst Street past Ohlone Park (who the hell was Ohlone?), noting St. Procopius Church and the Church of the Good Shepherd. Stop at grocery store at 7th and Hearst for homemade tortillas.

1:00 p.m.—Aerobics class at Goldies.

2:00 p.m.—Piece of pie at Bette's Diner. Meet beautiful woman with Mercedes who takes you to see her villa on San Luis Road.

4:00 p.m.—Stagger down to Fatapple's for a blueberry muffin and four cups of coffee with real cream and real sugar.

5:00 p.m.—Pick up ribs at Flint's Bar-B-Q.

6:00 p.m.—Pick up ribs at KC Bar-B-Q.   50

7:00 p.m.—Irish coffee at Brennan's. Get in argument over best barbecue place in Berkeley.

7:30 p.m.—Phone Herrick and Alta Bates Hospitals. Comparison shop for stomach pumping. Ask when Alta Bates cafeteria is open.

8:00 p.m.—Attend Berkeley City Council meeting. See our two political parties, the BCA and the ABC, in a ten-round exhibition match. (Tuesdays only.)

9:00 p.m.—Stroll Solano Avenue for Mu Shu Pork. Get a marble fudge cone at McCallums.

10:00 p.m.—Tune into KPFA for "Fat Is No Longer a Feminist Issue: 55
A Look at Manorexics."

11:00 p.m.—Fries and Merlot at the Santa Fe Bar and Grill.

Midnight—*Rocky Horror Picture Show* at the UC Theatre (Saturdays only). See the children of Berkeley disguised as perverts.

As I hand him the list, I add a personal note. I came to Berkeley in the era of Dustin Hoffman's *The Graduate*. We wanted to get out of the rat race, out of the plastic, out of boredom and mediocrity just as Benjamin did. Now the movie is dated. Things have come full circle as a new generation desperately wants a crack at a good job, a home, some status. We, the class of '65, could reject those things when they seemed so readily available.

"*The Graduate*, . . ." he ponders. "I saw that on the late show. Isn't that the one where Dustin Hoffman has an affair with an older woman?"

"Yeah."   60

"Well, do you think maybe I could buy you a drink, ma'am?"

"What? Pollute my body with alcohol and other toxic chemicals? You've got to be kidding, Babycakes. Now beat it. And welcome to Berkeley."

UNDERSTANDING THE TEXT

1. How does consumer culture serve as an organizing principle for this selection?

2. What does Kahn mean by calling Berkeley a "gourmet ghetto" (para. 1)?

3. What role does the young man play in this selection? Why do you think Kahn includes him?

4. Characterize Kahn's tone in this selection. How does it contribute to your understanding of Berkeley?

EXPLORING AND DEBATING THE ISSUES

1. Write an essay in which you support, refute, or complicate the proposition that the plethora of gourmet eateries and specialty food shops that Kahn describes has made Berkeley overly commercial.

2. Compare the food businesses that Kahn describes with the Asian markets and malls that Patricia Leigh Brown describes in "The New Chinatown? Try the Asian Mall" (p. 368). To what extent is each representative of California consumer culture?

3. Write an essay in which you assess the effectiveness of Kahn's humor in this selection. Does it work to express her image of Berkeley, or do you find it exaggerated?

4. Write an analysis of the restaurants and eateries in your community or at your college campus. To what extent has your community or campus become, like Berkeley, a "gourmet ghetto" (para. 1)?

5. Assume the role of one or more proprietors of the eateries Kahn mentions, and write a response to her selection.

The New Chinatown?
Try the Asian Mall

PATRICIA LEIGH BROWN

Thanks to such early Hollywood movies as those in the Charlie Chan series, generations of Americans have envisioned Chinatown, especially San Francisco's Chinatown, as an exotic labyrinth of incense- and lacquered-furniture-filled dens where
sinister intrigue might suddenly appear. But that image is alien to the contemporary clientele of 99 Ranch Market, a modern Asian American supermarket chain
where one can find "Fudgsicles next to the taro root ice bars in the frozen food
section" and "shelves of Skippy peanut butter and Gatorade across from the
frozen rice balls." Indeed, as **Patricia Leigh Brown**'s newspaper feature on California's new Asian shopping culture, which appeared first in the *New York Times* on
March 24, 2003, reveals, Rudyard Kipling's old refrain that "East is East, and West
is West, and never the twain shall meet" was dead wrong. Brown is a writer for
The New Yorker.

To Angela Huang, a thirty-one-year-old Taiwanese-born landscape
planner, nothing symbolizes California's Asian American culture
more than a kitchen cabinet overflowing with empty plastic grocery bags
from 99 Ranch Market. For it is among the wide, gleaming aisles of 99
Ranch supermarkets—with the mushroom and fungus buns, the mari-
nated pigs' ears, the 100 percent natural white gourd juice, and vast
tanks of live fish—that Ms. Huang and her friends feel most at home. "In
Chinatown you see mostly older people, walking slowly with pink plastic
bags full of vegetables, walking and stopping, stopping and walking," said
Ms. Huang, a consummate shopper who occasionally pauses midaisle to
call her aunt for recipes on a cellphone. "Here, the aisles are bright and
you can target what you want. You bump into your aunts, uncles, and
friends from school. It's a very important social space."

To Ms. Huang and her friends, 99 Ranch is an umbrella term not only
for the 99 Ranch chain, the giant of Asian supermarkets, with twenty-one
stores in California alone, but also the suburban-style, pan-Asian shopping malls they anchor. With Fudgsicles next to the taro root ice bars in the
frozen food section, with shelves of Skippy peanut butter and Gatorade
across from the frozen rice balls, these malls represent a classically California blending of old and new, exotic and ordinary—the Far East turned
American under the glow of fluorescent bulbs and the gentle strains of
Muzak. Even the supermarket's name reflects the blend. The 99 implies
eternity in Chinese numerology and "ranch" was added for an American
image.

Shoppers come from as far as Sacramento, seventy-two miles away, to the five-year-old Pacific East mall here, just north of Oakland and on the border of El Cerrito, long nicknamed "little Taipei," with a population that is 24 percent Asian. They can sip tapioca pearl tea, sing karaoke, have an eye examination, buy a sand-filled Taiwanese Hula Hoop or Chinese Harry Potter figures, sample Chinese gummi octopi candy, eat Filipino sweet bread filled with ham, cheese and sugar, or hang out at Cybergame, a cybercafe that attracts young men who stay glued to the video game Counter-Strike until the wee hours.

At the J&S Tea Shop, a popular tapioca pearl tea spot, Sho Kang, a thirty-five-year-old electrical engineer, was perusing Taiwanese entertainment magazines with his friend Eddie Pang, twenty-two, a University of California graduate. Mr. Kang was a "parachute kid," a nickname for Asian teenagers who are "dropped off" in the United States by their parents to go to school.

"The American mall is rigid because you can find the Gap anywhere," Mr. Kang said. "Chinatown is for the old immigrant; 99 Ranch is for the new. You can pretty much tell if a girl is single by what she buys at 99 Ranch."   5

The growth of Asian malls and supermarkets mirrors the growing prosperity of Asian Americans who have left urban enclaves for mainstream suburbs. Although there are no precise statistics on Asian malls, California is home to an estimated fifty to sixty of them, mostly in southern California. The state also has nine of the country's ten cities with the highest proportions of Asians. Honolulu is the other. Wan Loo, owner of Asiamall.com, an online directory and importing company, said there were roughly 140 such complexes around the country. For new Asian immigrants, many of them young professionals, the fifteen or so Asian malls around San Francisco—eight with 99 Ranches—encircle the Bay area like a necklace of familiarity.

"It's amazing how much like Singapore or Hong Kong these malls are," said Aihwa Ong, a professor of anthropology and Southeast Asian studies at the University of California at Berkeley. "There is a sense of the mall integrating different waves of ethnic Chinese immigrants from all over Asia. They may come from different classes, but the mall represents common ground." Professor Ong added, "It's the place where different streams of Asians become Asian American."

The 99 Ranch Market chain, a privately held company, does not release sales figures. The age of the typical shopper is thirty-five, said Tony Chen, chief operating officer for 99 Ranch in Northern California. Among diehard customers like Ms. Huang, the store is beloved for its wide variety of snacks, including pea pod crisps, dried mango, and fresh fish, which can be deep-fried on the spot for no extra charge. A sign above the pollock fish balls, squid balls, lobster balls, and lady fish balls outlines the choices for preparation: "1) Clean only, 2) Clean & tail off, 3) Clean & head off, 4) Steak, 5) Regular fry, 6) Deep fry." "In Safeway, it's fillet," said Frank Chang, a thirty-five-year-old engineer from Fremont. "Chinese people feel more comfortable when they see the fish's head."

Unlike traditional Chinatowns in Oakland and San Francisco, where the language is predominantly Cantonese, both the mall and 99 Ranch are linguistically inclusive, with English, Spanish, Vietnamese, Cantonese, Mandarin, and Filipino as common languages. The items on shelves and in towers of cardboard boxes reflect local demographics: the San Jose store is heavy on Coco Rico Soda and fish sauce, catering to the city's large Vietnamese population, while the one at Daly City with its large Filipino community has more Lauriat soy sauce and Datu Puti vinegar.

The ethnic food market is flourishing nationally, from the Asian   10
Square shopping center (with a 99 Ranch) in Doraville, Georgia, to Yaohan, an all-Japanese mall and food court in Arlington Heights, Illinois. A distinguishing characteristic of Asian malls as opposed to the Wal-Mart variety is the emphasis on eating and shopping as a family activity, said Roger Blackwell, a professor of marketing at the Fischer College of Business at Ohio State University. "These are family places, symbolic of a culture that is able to take commercial and cultural interests and blend them," Professor Blackwell said. "Asian consumers take their vacation every weekend at the mall."

Chiao Ku, twenty-two, a student at San Jose State University, frequents a cafe near a 99 Ranch on class breaks, shopping for books, comics, and videos. "This is the place to meet each other and have a comfortable conversation, just like traditional bowling alleys and movie theaters," Mr. Ku said. "It's basically the life we had back in Hong Kong or Taiwan."

Terry Kwong, president of the Pacific Infinity Company, developers of the Pacific East mall, said that a typical family would spend three or four hours there, "then buy some cakes, go home, and play mah-jongg together." (Mah-jongg mats are $4 at 99 Ranch.) Mr. Kwong, who was born in Hong Kong, appreciates such consumer loyalty. But he also knows that change is the California way.

"The Asian market is saturated," he said. "I'm planning to open a Latino mall."

UNDERSTANDING THE TEXT

1. Why, according to this article, does 99 Ranch Market symbolize the essence of California's Asian American culture?

2. What is the significance of the name "99 Ranch Market"?

3. In what ways are ethnic food markets family places?

4. Why does customer Sho Kang say that "Chinatown is for the old immigrant; 99 Ranch is for the new" (para. 5)?

EXPLORING AND DEBATING THE ISSUES

1. Visit a 99 Ranch Market or, if a 99 Ranch is not located in your town, a similar Asian market. Conduct your own analysis of the store, and use your observations to support, refute, or complicate Aihwa Ong's assertion that such stores are "where different streams of Asians become Asian Americans" (para. 7).

2. Write an essay in which you argue whether the 99 Ranch Market represents a community's genuine ethnic origins or, instead, is an Americanization of those origins.

3. Visit an American mall and an ethnic mall or retail area. Write an essay in which you compare and contrast the two retail districts. Is either mall "rigid" (para. 5), as customer Sho Kang puts it? Could either be characterized as a family place?

4. Developer Terry Kwong says that he is "planning to open a Latino mall" (para. 13). In class, brainstorm the features that a Latino mall might have. In what ways might it resemble the Asian malls, and how might it differ? How might it compare with typical American malls? Use your class discussion as the basis for an essay in which you advise Kwong on how he should plan his Latino mall.

Arcadia and Utopia

WILLIAM MCCLUNG

So all right, Florida has a citrus industry too, but it is the World War I–era California orange crate label that is most evocative of dreams and desires—a dream of
an Arcadian, or pastoral, paradise where nature and civilization come together in
perfect harmony. Look at the orange-crate labels that **William McClung** analyzes
in this selection from his book *Landscapes of Desire: Anglo Mythologies of Los Angeles* (2000). In such dream landscapes, the wilderness and the highway, commerce and human habitation, blend together seamlessly in a vision of the Southern
California good life that helped to lure thousands of Midwesterners to California in
the years between the world wars. McClung is a professor of English at Mississippi
State University and the author of *The Country House in English Renaissance Poetry* (1977) and *The Architecture of Paradise* (1983).

As a body of material culture as well as a text of meanings and messages, Los Angeles, since the latter half of the nineteenth century,
has been shaped by several traditions of imagined, ideal societies. At a
crucial period in its growth, these traditions spoke to a dominant Anglo
culture, some of whose visions have been literal and serious, even deadly
serious, while others have been playful or ironic. Some have subscribed
heavily to the physical properties of ancient myths of the good place and
the good life, like a golden climate and trees in perpetual fruit; others
have been figurative and abstracted, finding essences of myth and popular fantasy translated into suitable equivalents. An 1899 real estate
brochure, for example, covers its products in an envelope of allusion to
ancient dreams of Arcadia, a found natural paradise. The premise of its
imagery is that the built environment defers to the unbuilt, at most completing or fulfilling its implicit structure. . . .

The opposite of Arcadia is Utopia. In its purest form it would be a
spaceship, where the environment is as much a construction as the society itself. A Utopian designer customarily treats the landscape as raw
material to be shaped for human purposes and is never shy about asserting the dominance of the built over the unbuilt. Los Angeles, which has
developed on so many different scales and at so many different places,
offered plenty of blank canvasses upon which futures could be built. . . .

Representing or advertising Los Angeles has depended for the most
part on a blending and balancing of Arcadian and Utopian elements.
One of the hardiest of Southern California's industrial arts, the citrus-box
label, often strives for such a synthesis; the Questa lemon-box label of
the World War I period, for example, is virtually a diagram of a Southern

California of idealized juxtapositions. There are four approximately equal zones, starting at the mountains, which are wilderness (the land as it was and can, without damage to profits, be allowed to remain), and progressing to the citrus groves, an orderly and proper exploitation of nature. A boulevard next announces a modern city and its technological panache, displaying the imagery not of mass (i.e., rail) but of leisured transportation—open cars, a horseman, and a carriage or pony cart. Finally a lady appears on foot, hatted and handbagged, as if going to pay a call. The sidewalk and planting unite the smooth curves and bright surfaces of the impeccably engineered avenue to the lushness of the watered San Gabriel Valley suburbs; the lady's presence redoubles the basic dualism of the entire picture, which implicitly asserts that nature and civilization are perfectly in scale, and that the pace of the planted Arcadian city is simultaneously that of the motorist and of the pedestrian.

If we erase oily machinery and migrant laborers from the picture, we might find the Questa daydream within the bounds of possibility, at least for the eastern valleys of Los Angeles County in the heyday both of the citrus industry and of the sunny winter resort and health capitals: Riverside, Pasadena, and (for the local establishment only) San Marino. Something similar was in the works from the 1880s on, when much of

Citrus label showing zones of the San Gabriel Valley (c. 1915).

View of the San Gabriel Mountains, Pasadena, and the Raymond Hotel.

the region seemed to unite leisure and labor in a way that dissolved the distinction between them. Viewed from the wishfully named town of Ramona, Pasadena, as it is identified in the picture's original caption, appears to be completely contained in the great resort hotel, the Raymond, here fronted by vast citrus groves that look like part of the garden enjoyed by the woman and child in the foreground. The reality of the climate and the mystique of the orange combine in a reverie of existence that satisfies the biblical command to labor while reaping the rewards of an irrigated Eden.

UNDERSTANDING THE TEXT

1. Summarize in your own words what McClung means by "Arcadia" (para. 1) and "Utopia" (para. 2).

2. In what ways does the Questa citrus box label juxtapose Arcadian and Utopian elements?

3. What is the significance of the four equal zones in the Questa box label?

4. How are "nature and civilization" (para. 3) in scale in the Questa and Raymond Hotel box labels?

EXPLORING AND DEBATING THE ISSUES

1. Study contemporary images of California in tourist magazines such as *San Diego* or in publications such as *Sunset*. Write an essay in which you analyze the depiction of the state, using McClung's terms. To what extent is California characterized by arcadian and utopian elements?

2. Visit http://www.citrusbox.htm, a website devoted to California citrus-box labels, and select several crate labels that depict identifiable regions in California. Analyze the labels according to McClung's dichotomy between Arcadian and Utopian elements. Which element, if either, dominates your chosen labels? How might you account for your observations?

3. Visit the website for the California Department of Tourism (http://www .gocalif.ca.gov/state/tourism/tour_homepage.jsp), and study the images that present different regions of California. Write an essay in which you analyze the images used to market California to potential tourists. Do they present Arcadian and Utopian elements? If so, in what proportions? Or do they lack the dualism that so often is typical of the crate labels?

4. Read or reread Gary Nabhan's "The Palms in Our Hands" (p. 308), and write an essay in which you use McClung's dichotomy between Arcadian and Utopian to analyze Palm Springs.

Researching the Issues

1. Research the origins of the Hollywood movie industry. Who were the pioneers of the studio system, and why did they migrate to Southern California to found their industry? Use your research as the basis of your own argument about why this region was particularly appealing as a site for filmmaking.

2. Long before films such as *American Graffiti* celebrated California's car culture, this state was viewed as instrumental in transforming the automobile from functional convenience to an essential component of personal image. Research the evolution of California's car culture and its influence on American attitudes toward the automobile, with the goal of devising an essay that assesses California's influence on the rest of the country. You might start your research by surveying a museum exhibit now accessible online, "Rear View Mirror: Automobile Image and American Identity" (http://www.cmp.ucr.edu/photography/ mirror).

3. One of the state's unofficial exports in the last two decades has been what is called California cuisine, a style of cooking made popular by chefs such as Wolfgang Puck. Research the origins of California cuisine and how it has evolved. To what extent does its emergence as one of

the state's most popular food choices reflect the concomitant demographic changes in the state?

4. Brainstorm in class a list of television shows or movies that feature California as a setting (e.g., *Falling Down*, *Mulholland Drive*, *Blade Runner*, *L.A. Story*, *L.A. Confidential*, *Orange County*), and then pick one to analyze, showing the ways in which it reflects California mythology.

5. California has figured prominently in many popular songs, including "Hotel California," "California Dreamin'," "L.A. Woman," "California Girls," "Do You Know the Way to San Jose?" and "Californication." Choose several songs that feature California, and write an analysis of the image that they project.

6. One of California's most famous cultural exports is the theme park. Research the history of Disneyland and its many offspring, including those in other states and countries. To what extent has this theme park redefined one segment of American (and international) family entertainment?

7. California's cultural landscape has been strongly influenced by immigrants from around the world. Choose one immigrant group — such as Iranians or Vietnamese — and research that group's influence on aspects of California's culture, including fashion, cuisine, and music.

8. Throughout the state's history, California has produced icons — larger-than-life figures such as John Muir, Aimee Semple McPherson, John Steinbeck, Ronald Reagan, and Clint Eastwood. Select one such figure, and research the forces that led to his or her status as an icon.

9. Research the evolution of Chicano poster art in California's urban areas such as East Los Angeles. Use your findings as the basis for an essay in which you outline the cultural trends of such art and its influences on the broader culture.

6

(Mis)Managing California

POLITICS, ENVIRONMENT, AND
THE STATE OF THE STATE

Recall Madness

On October 7, 2003, the voters of California gave new meaning to the words "participatory democracy."

Or should we say, "acting governor"?

But, then, they already had done that in 1966, when they elected Ronald Reagan to the governorship.

Oh well, whatever. Many of the ramifications of the Great Recall of 2003 will not be known until well after the writing of these words, for the pace of history is not nicely calibrated to the tighter schedules of textbook publishing. But some things are already clear: once again California has proven to be a political trendsetter for the rest of the nation. For just as the passage of Proposition 13 in the 1970s eventually led to a national tax revolt and the election of Ronald Reagan as governor eventually led to the first Hollywood president of the United States, so too did the recall of Gray Davis in 2003 presage a new era of recall politics conducted not in the face of elected official misconduct but only because voters were fed up with and bored by someone.

However one feels about the recall of Davis and the election of Arnold Schwarzenegger, the whole matter points to a peculiar paradox in California politics. Most of the time, California voters have one of the

---

◀ *Monarch, California's last wild grizzly and symbol for state flag, California Academy of Sciences display.*

lowest voting rates in the country and are quite apathetic about politics. But when they are riled, they join in quasi-populist uprisings in which they take the management of the state into their own hands. Usually this is through the ballot initiative process, by which the voters can, and often do, directly rewrite the state constitution to create law when the legislature does not respond to the voters' desires. Such occasions of direct democracy have their advantages insofar as they enable the citizens of California to take direct charge of the political life of the state.

But such direct democracy also tends to be a rather haphazard affair, with each issue coming to a vote without an overarching vision or sense of direction. The ramifications, for example, of Proposition 13—the ballot initiative that set limits on property taxes and requires a two-thirds vote of the legislature for any tax increase—are still being felt in annual state budget crises and rising college and university fees. A number of other initiatives have resulted in restricting the flexibility of the state budgeting process by locking in funding guarantees to various state programs (such as prisons) at the expense of others (such as higher education). Racially charged initiatives—such as Propositions 187 (which attempted to prevent the provision of public services, including education, to illegal immigrants), 209 (which effectively ended state-sponsored affirmative action in California), and 227 (which placed strict restrictions on bilingual education in California schools)—have proven to be divisive and continue to reverberate through the political and cultural landscape.

You, your classmates, and your instructors probably have differing opinions on the various issues that California voters have taken into their own hands in their moments of voter revolt. But many people feel that the management of the state of California has become somewhat chaotic. Indeed, most voters who supported Arnold Schwarzenegger believed that he would "clean up the mess in Sacramento." The point of this chapter is to look at the mess and how it got that way.

Developing the Dream

The explosive growth of California, both economically and demographically, has challenged sound management policies. For here, too, there is something different about California. Throughout most of American history, the shape of the land has largely determined the patterns of its growth. The stony uplands of New England, for example, fostered an economy of small homesteads and river-driven mills, while the coastal plain of the Southeast allowed the development of vast plantations. Cities like Detroit and Chicago grew up along navigable rivers and lakes, which led to their becoming major transportation centers, while ranching became a way of life in states like Texas and Montana, where the climate was too arid for most agriculture. But in California, the pattern has been reversed: here the shape of human desire has led to a vast transformation of the land, and the results have been mixed.

Consider the question of water. Virtually all of Southern California is arid land, and yet Los Angeles has become the second-largest city in the nation and its largest greater metropolitan area. Vast water projects have diverted water from Northern California to L.A., while the Imperial Valley, a virtual desert in its natural state, has become one of the nation's most productive agricultural regions through enormous imports of water from the Colorado River. But as the arid states of Arizona and Nevada experience their own population booms and the coastal regions of California find themselves in competition with interior valley farmers for ever scarcer water supplies, the result has been a battle for water. Conducted largely behind the scenes, this battle has pitted California against the rest of the Southwest, and the populated coast against the agricultural valleys.

Then there is the matter of geology. The land of California was created by geotectonic forces that express themselves periodically in minor or massive earthquakes. This susceptibility to earth movement at first did limit architectural expression in California, restricting the height of office buildings in such urban centers as San Francisco and Los Angeles. But with the advent of seismic engineering, the skylines of Los Angeles and San Francisco have leaped upward, so that they now resemble the skylines of cities not threatened by earthquakes—an evolution skyward that the earth has yet to fully test.

Meanwhile, hillside dwellers from the Oakland Hills to Santa Barbara, from Malibu to the Laguna Hills, and, most recently, from San Diego to San Bernardino, Simi Valley, Santa Clarita, and the Rim of the World, have learned, time and again, that natural ecologies that have evolved to burn will, in fact, burn, while what doesn't burn may well slide. Resilient though we are in the face of such disasters—fire, landslide, and earthquake—we have had to face, time and again, the painful consequences of disregarding the natural conditions of the land.

It has not always been this way. Before the arrival of the Europeans, California's Indian populations largely adapted their lifestyles to the lands in which they dwelled, living in small hunter-gatherer groups that took what the land had to offer without radically modifying it. Later, the Spanish developed a rancho culture that conformed to the aridity of Southern California, scattering cattle and a sparse human population over thousands of square miles of land. But the story of California since the Mexican-American War has been one of transformation—of massive development projects that have diverted rivers for water and irrigation, blasted transportation routes through solid rock, filled in bays for housing tracts, and covered hillsides with subdivisions. In little more than a century and a half, the land of California has been virtually transfigured.

The Price of Progress

The physical transformation of California has, until recently, taken place in the name of progress and growth, hitherto sacred words in a history of explosive expansion. This expansiveness, itself a major component of California's promise of endless opportunity, has not been without its cost, however. Was providing San Francisco with a secure water supply, for example, worth the cost of damming the Tuolumne River and thereby flooding the Hetch Hetchy Valley, a place, John Muir believed, that was second in beauty only to Yosemite Valley? Should the farmers of the Owens Valley have been forced to pay the price for the diversion of their water southward so that the San Fernando Valley could blossom with housing tracts? Should the Colorado River be emptied before it can reach the sea so that the corporate farms of the Imperial Valley can be irrigated? As we experience the consequences of unchecked growth—pollution, overcrowding, water and power shortages, just to name a few—we must ask: was it worth it, after all?

"Dam Hetch Hetchy!" John Muir exclaimed. "As well dam for water tanks the people's cathedrals and churches, for no holier temple has ever been consecrated by the heart of man." But the Hetch Hetchy Valley was dammed, and we can never again know what the Central Valley looked like before its vast, elk-populated prairies were plowed under to grow strawberries and just about everything else. For better or for worse, the California land has been transformed. The critical question now is just how that transformation can be managed.

The Readings

The readings begin with Andrew Murr and Jennifer Ordonez's *Newsweek* feature article "Tarnished Gold," which takes a journalistic look at the economic downturn that led to the pernicious budget crises in the years before the recall election of 2003. Mark Baldassare follows with a statistical survey of what he sees as the four major geographic and demographic regions of the state, while David Carle looks at California's notorious traffic problems that, in one way or another, affect most Californians. Gerald W. Haslam's overview of the effects of the massive water projects that transformed the arid plains of the Central Valley into an agricultural cornucopia weighs the costs as well as the rewards of this transformation. Marc Reisner then tells the sorry story of the Kesterson reservoir in the San Joaquin Valley, one of the darker episodes in the history of California irrigation. Richard Steven Street's narrative shows how the politically marginalized Latino residents of Kettleman City organized to fight the construction of a toxic-waste incinerator in their community, demonstrating along the way that they were not as marginal as the incinerator company thought. Gary Soto follows with an elegiac poetic reflection on the dispossession of the first Californians. Victor Davis Hanson's essay "Paradise Lost" then offers a more contemporary view on what Californians have been losing, especially in the wake of the electricity crisis of 2001. And the chapter concludes with a pair of essays related to the recall election of 2003, with Anita Creamer taking a comic stance on the matter as she contemplates how it looked to the rest of the country, and Glen Browder offering a more serious analysis of the implications of California's recall for American politics as a whole.

Tarnished Gold

ANDREW MURR AND JENNIFER ORDONEZ

When dot-com went to dot-bomb in California, everything unraveled, with once high-flying Silicon Valley experiencing a leap in unemployment to over 8 percent, its "gleaming office parks once stuffed with start-ups" becoming "see-through ghost towns." With the tech crash came a state budget deficit of such monumental proportions that angry voters, as **Andrew Murr** and **Jennifer Ordonez** predict in this July 24, 2003, *Newsweek* report written over two months before the recall election of 2003, would toss out one governor and elect another. Seemingly stuck in a boom-and-bust pattern, California can hope for another boom, even as the movie, biotech, and real estate industries keep the state from a complete crash. But as Murr and Ordonez's "unemployed hopefuls" wait impatiently for something to turn up, one could ask whether there isn't a better way to run an economy. Murr is a correspondent in *Newsweek*'s Los Angeles bureau, and Ordonez is a staff writer for *Newsweek*.

The job fair ends in five minutes, but scores of unemployed hopefuls wait steadfastly, sweating in line under the Orange County sun. "They won't get in and yet they're still all standing there," says an incredulous Leo Delgadillo, manager of the California Employment Development office that is hosting the event.

More than seven hundred people started lining up at 6:30 a.m. to interview for a scant eighteen tech jobs with the City of Huntington Beach. Joseph Brown is among those still waiting. He hasn't been able to land full-time work since losing his $50,000 computer-programming job two years ago, and now he's kicking himself for not arriving earlier. The fifty-four-year-old father of four came to the fair after spending the morning reading gas meters, a part-time gig he landed a few months ago ahead of three hundred other applicants. "I stopped at home because I didn't want to show up in my gas uniform," he says. "But you can't get here late. Young, old, and in between, there are so many people out of work."

That's life in California these days. Pessimism and outright anger blanket the state like the smog, thanks to a noxious combination of a stalled economy and fiscal disaster in Sacramento. The state's $38 billion deficit—cited as reason No. 1 to oust Governor Gray Davis by those who are calling for his head—is so gigantic that it tops the entire *budgets* of forty-two other states. Rather than fix the mess, legislators missed a July 1 budget deadline, leaving the state to kite along entirely on IOUs. If Republicans and Democrats don't come to terms soon, as many as 30,000 state workers may be furloughed. Wall Street could cut the state's bond rating—already the nation's lowest—to "junk" status. Government employees across the state are bracing for the worst: fire departments aren't replacing trucks, school districts aren't buying new textbooks, police departments aren't hiring new cops, and some staffers at state unemployment offices are anticipating joining the ranks of the jobless. Last week two of the six employment-assistance offices in Orange County got notices they would be shut down, and some services at the remaining offices may be pared back at a time when demand is increasing.

The state's unemployment remains stubbornly high at 6.7 percent, above the national average of 6.4 percent, thanks in large part to continuing aftershocks in Silicon Valley (unemployment in Santa Clara County runs at a painful 8.5 percent). There, gleaming office parks once stuffed with start-ups are see-through ghost towns. Office vacancies in Silicon Valley remain near 30 percent; in the once trendy dot-com gulches of San Francisco, the rate is almost 40 percent. The NASDAQ has streaked up in the past few months, and bottom lines are improving at some of the larger companies, but the tech jobs haven't returned yet. Technical writer Kristina Hacke, thirty-four, moved to the Bay Area last September after losing her job in L.A., and has spent the better part of the year going from one fruitless interview to another. In two days last week she had three, including a seven-hour marathon that went nowhere. "It's worse than dating," says a frustrated Hacke. "If I don't hit it off with a potential date, I'm just lonely, but if I don't hit it off with a hiring manager, I don't eat."

However bleak things seem, the current joblessness doesn't touch the 9.7 percent high of the early 1990s recession, when California's defense and aerospace jobs vanished along with the cold-war threat. Excluding northern California, the state's economy is faring better than the nation as a whole. In Los Angeles, the movie industry is nearly recession-proof as fans continue to buy tickets in tough times, and sales of computer games are skyrocketing. Biotech is thriving, and increased defense spending for the conflict on Iraq and the war on terror has brought new jobs. Residential real estate continues to boom: median home prices in the state jumped by 15.6 percent in the past year, and banks are getting fat off mortgage refinancing. Citing the first slight rise in quarterly tax revenues in nine quarters, State Controller Steve Westly told *Newsweek*, "That's the first leading indicator of a turnaround."

But if the private sector is showing signs of life, the public sector is in near cardiac arrest. The state government's financial woes began with the tech recession, but Davis and legislators continued to spend money on popular programs long after tax revenues dropped. During the boom, state coffers were filled with taxes on capital gains and stock options from all those tech execs and dot-com millionaires. In the 2000–2001 fiscal year, these revenues leapt to $17 billion, representing 25 percent of all state income taxes collected. But by last year, that tax revenue had sunk to just $4.7 billion. The energy crisis of two years ago multiplied the damage, with California spending billions on high-priced electricity contracts after Enron and others manipulated the newly deregulated energy market on Davis's watch. But consumers, still fuming over rates that temporarily doubled and tripled, say the governor was asleep at the switch. Steve Hunyar, forty-two, a San Diego County software CEO, has near-photographic recall of an electric bill that spiked from $200 to $586. "I don't think anyone could have mismanaged the energy situation worse than Davis has," says Hunyar.

The day of reckoning in Sacramento can't be put off much longer. Democrats and Republicans continue to argue over whether to raise taxes, but whatever budget deal they reach, cuts will be deep and ugly. "It's not going to be a pretty sight," says Tom Lieser, a senior economist with UCLA's Anderson Forecasting unit. Among the hardest hit: education. The state has already cut $2.5 billion from the K–12 schools budget, with more to come.

The budget mess petrifies Cindy Kauffman, who directs a state-funded Adult Day Health Center in San Francisco's Richmond District. Kauffman's center provides nursing, physical therapy, counseling, and meals for 170 elderly clients, many suffering from strokes, dementia, or Alzheimer's. These facilities aren't cheap, but they save taxpayers millions of dollars by keeping poor, elderly folks like stroke victim Dorothy Shaw out of costlier nursing homes. Shaw, sixty-seven, comes here every week-day to improve her speech and movement. "I don't want to go to a nurs-ing home," Shaw says. Earlier this year Governor Davis proposed cutting funds by 15 percent, and Republicans recently called for even deeper cuts. Kauffman believes that cuts anywhere near that large would spell the death of the center. "If we closed, within six months 50 percent of our clients would be in a . . . nursing home," she says.

Even if the pols agree on a budget, don't expect happy times soon. Tax revenues aren't likely to approach the frothy levels of the bubble days, which means smaller budgets are here to stay. Forecasters say unemploy-ment will remain high for another year, partly because companies are afraid to add jobs despite having regained profitability, and many of the positions lost during the dot-bomb era will never return. All of which could keep unemployed folks like Joe Brown on the job-fair circuit. But after two years of looking, Brown is ready to lower his sights. With house-hold funds dwindling fast, he says he'll take the first full-time job offer he receives—even if that means trading his white-collar past for a blue-collar future. He says he'd even be happy if he can parlay his part-time work as a gas-meter reader into a new career as a gas-meter repairman. That job would pay $20,000 less than the $50,000 he once made, but the staunch Republican has warmed to the idea of union security. "At least," he says, "I know that the gas company is not going to be going away." In California, even that small measure of stability is comforting.

UNDERSTANDING THE TEXT

1. According to Murr and Ordonez, what are the consequences of Califor-nia's budget problems?
2. What are the regional differences in California's economy, and what ac-counts for those differences?
3. How do the economies of the public and private sectors differ, according to Murr and Ordonez, and what are the reasons for those differences?

EXPLORING AND DEBATING THE ISSUES

1. In a journal entry, reflect on your own expectations for economic stabil-ity after you graduate from college, taking into account both your future career goals and the region of California in which you live.
2. Interview students from different parts of the state, and write an assess-ment of Murr and Ordonez's position that California's economy is marked by regional differences. To develop your ideas, consult Mark Bal-dassare's "Regional Diversity" (p. 387).

3. In class, brainstorm strategies for resuscitating the public sector. Use your class discussion as the basis for an essay in which you recommend solutions to the state's economic crisis.

4. Write an essay in which you analyze the implications of the state's economic problems for the California dream. To develop your ideas, read or reread James J. Rawls's "California: A Place, a People, a Dream" (p. 22).

Regional Diversity

MARK BALDASSARE

One reason that California is difficult to manage effectively is that there really isn't a single California to manage: there are many Californias, highly diverse regions that fight each other over everything from water rights to air pollution. And as **Mark Baldassare** observes in this statistical survey of California's four major regional enclaves—Los Angeles County, the San Francisco Bay area, the Central Valley, and the Orange County/Inland Empire "mega-suburbs"—each region has its own "political, social, and economic" profile, with its own ideas on how the state can be best managed. With so many cooks stirring the pot, is it any wonder that the soup can get spoiled? Baldassare holds the Arjay and Francis Fearing Miller Chair in Public Policy at the Public Policy Institute of California and is president of Mark Baldassare and Associates, a public polling firm. This selection is from his book *California in the New Millennium: The Changing Social and Political Landscape* (2000).

Many states have distinct regions and tensions among those regions, but in California the distinctions and tensions are intensified by the state's unique geography. The distance between the northern and southern borders, and the imposing internal boundaries of mountains and deserts, have made it difficult for Californians to develop a sense of oneness. The history of the state has exacerbated the regionalism. In the mid-nineteenth century, San Francisco became the political and economic powerhouse as banking and trade during the Gold Rush turned the city into an international port. Los Angeles came on strong a half-century later, when oil was discovered, and stronger still when the movie and television studios and then the defense industry took root in Southern California. The vast suburbs surrounding Los Angeles eventually upstaged the city, as Orange County and the Inland Empire became the new destination for Americans seeking the California dream. At the same time, the rich earth and vast expanses of the Central Valley were developing into farms that became the major producers of the nation's food.

As the north, south, and central regions grew in size and economic importance, they found themselves in a nasty political battle over the water flowing out of the Sierras into the nearby rivers. This bitter rivalry over water continues today. It serves as a constant reminder of the testy political, cultural, and social relationships between the state's regions. California is a large state where both the politicians and the people have a history of forming internal competitions and losing track of the common interests that link their destinies.

Californians have trouble considering the state as a whole but are quick to offer negative judgments about regions other than their own. Regional stereotypes largely go unchecked in a state that lacks statewide newspapers and television stations. In the focus groups, some said they would prefer to have the state just split up so that the regions would not have to deal with one another. "The problems in California are so different they should just go to San Luis Obispo and draw a line straight through to Fresno and separate the state," said a San Francisco resident. "California is basically two states, Northern California and Southern California," remarked a San Diego resident. "I always thought if they took the state of California and cut it in half maybe two states would be easier to govern than one state," said a Los Angeles resident. There is a tendency to blame other regions for problems. "I've heard we get Bay Area pollution and it gets stuck in our Valley," said a Fresno resident. Growth problems are the result of people "coming from the Bay Area and Southern California," according to a Sacramento resident. The desire to be distinct from other regions was summed up by a San Diego resident who said, "We definitely don't want to be Los Angeles."

Although these regional perceptions are largely based on historical rivalries and stereotypes, there is, in reality, considerable regional diversity in California. Regions are distinct in their populations, growth, economy, geography, politics, and public concerns. Yet there is no general agreement about the exact configuration of regions and where the dividing lines are. Some people simply divide the state into Northern and Southern California. Others talk about coastal California versus inland California, although the merging of the San Francisco and Los Angeles areas has more critics than supporters. Philip Fradkin (1995) divides the state into seven regions: Deserts (southeast), Sierra (east), Land of Fire (northeast), Land of Water (northwest), the Great Valley (central inland), the Fractured Province (central coast), and the Profligate Province (southern coast). This amounts to an environmental tour guide that gives equal weight to vast empty regions and densely populated areas. Dan Walters (1992) divides the state into fourteen regions, including several within the San Francisco, Central Valley, and Los Angeles metropolises. The state government at one time divided California into a dozen regions for economic and planning purposes, also splitting up some of the contiguous urban regions (Baldassare et al., 1996). California has also been divided into about a dozen media markets for the purpose of buying and selling television advertising.

This essay focuses on . . . four regions . . . : Los Angeles County, the   5
San Francisco Bay area, the Central Valley, and Orange County and the Inland Empire.[1] These four large, highly populated regions reflect both the historical regional conflicts in the state and the important regional trends that are currently under way. Today Los Angeles and the San Francisco Bay area are the dominant regions. But in due time, as a result of . . . uneven regional growth . . . , the Central Valley and the Inland Empire and Orange County will be equals in population and political importance. . . .

Growth Patterns, Demographics, and Voting Trends

About 80 percent of Californians live in the four regions. Los Angeles County is the most populous and racially and ethnically diverse county in the state. The San Francisco Bay area is growing and changing as a result of immigration and the high-technology revolution. The Central Valley is one of the fastest-growing areas of the state, as farmlands give way to urban development. Orange County and the Inland Empire constitute the "mega-suburbs," where a huge and rapidly growing population has created a region distinct from nearby Los Angeles. These four regions have unique political, social, and economic profiles. They are all extremely important to elections and to the formation of public policy in the state. They each attract the separate attention of statewide candidates because of their size and distinctiveness.

Distinct Growth Patterns   Los Angeles County, the San Francisco Bay area, the Central Valley, and Orange County and the Inland Empire are

---

[1] I have separated Orange County and the Inland Empire of Riverside and San Bernardino Counties from Los Angeles County because the former three counties form a contiguous suburban region. The three-county area is defined as a suburban region because there is no dominant central city, and it is economically and politically separate from Los Angeles. See Baldassare (1986, 1992, 1998) and others (Fischer, 1984; Fishman, 1987; Garreau, 1991; Jackson, 1985; Kling, Olin, and Poster, 1991; Lewis, 1996; Logan and Molotch, 1987; Palen, 1995; Schneider, 1991; Teaford, 1997) for definitions of suburban regions and their political and economic importance. San Diego County is not considered to be part of this suburban region because it contains a city of over 1 million in population. The samples from the statewide surveys were not large enough to support a separate analysis of San Diego.

home to almost 28 million of the state's 33.5 million residents. Each has experienced a phenomenal increase in population over a fifty-year period. Los Angeles County, with about 10 million residents, is the most populous county in the nation. In the nine-county San Francisco Bay area, the population will reach 7 million residents in the not-too-distant future, with the Silicon Valley in Santa Clara County propelling the region's growth.[2] The Central Valley, defined as the eighteen-county area stretching from north to the south through the middle of the state, will soon contain 6 million residents, making it comparable to Los Angeles in the 1960s and the San Francisco Bay area in 1990s.[3] . . .

Regional States of Mind

The region of residence has a dramatic effect on how residents perceive the state of the state. To some extent, the differences in perceptions throughout the state can be explained by the composition of the populations—that is, by variations in their social, economic, and political profiles. To some degree, these differences can also be traced to the context of each region—that is, to its unique geography, land use, history, and culture. Whatever the causes, this phenomenon has profound implications for both public policy and elections in California. The fact that Los Angeles, the San Francisco Bay area, the Central Valley, and Orange County and the Inland Empire can see the same state so differently presents enormous challenges for political campaigns and state lawmakers seeking consensus.

Diverse Perceptions of the State's Direction   Most Californians felt upbeat about California during 1998, but at times substantial differences surfaced across the state's four major regions. When asked, "Do you think things in California are generally going in the right direction or the wrong direction?" 54 percent overall thought that things were going in the right direction and 34 percent in the wrong direction, with 9 percent unsure. However, Table 1 shows how different the state can look from different regions. In Los Angeles and in Orange County and the Inland Empire, optimists outnumbered pessimists by a wide margin. In the San Francisco Bay area, those who thought things were going in the right direction led by a fifteen-point margin. In the Central Valley, almost equal

[2] This region includes the counties of Alameda, Contra Costa, Marin, Napa, San Francisco, San Mateo, Santa Clara, Solano, and Sonoma.

[3] This area includes the counties of Butte, Colusa, Fresno, Glenn, Kern, Kings, Madera, Merced, Placer, Sacramento, San Joaquin, Shasta, Stanislaus, Sutter, Tehama, Tulare, Yolo, and Yuba.

TABLE 1. State Perceptions by Region

	Los Angeles	San Francisco Bay	Central Valley	Orange/ Inland
State Conditions				
Right track	64%	53%	48%	62%
Wrong track	29	38	43	32
Don't know	7	9	9	6
California Economy				
Excellent or good	52%	70%	48%	59%
Fair	38	23	38	33
Poor	10	7	14	8
Crime in California				
Big problem	69%	53%	78%	74%
Somewhat of a problem	26	42	20	24
Not a problem	5	5	2	2

Source: PPIC Statewide Survey, April, May, and September 1998, all adults.

numbers said the state was on the right track or the wrong track. This is intuitively consistent with the fact that economic conditions are not as robust in the Central Valley as in the other regions.

That connection is clarified in residents' perceptions of the state's economic conditions. In 1998, 57 percent of California residents believed that the state's economy was in excellent or good condition, one-third said it was in fair shape, and 10 percent considered it to be in poor condition. But regional responses were quite different. In the San Francisco Bay area, 70 percent thought that the state's economy was in excellent or good shape, and 60 percent in the Southern California mega-suburbs echoed that perception. In contrast, 52 percent in Los Angeles rated the state's economy as excellent or good. Fewer than half of those in the Central Valley gave the state economy a high rating, and more in this region than elsewhere rated it as poor. Evidently, the same, booming economy can look very different depending on where you are standing in the state.

Californians' perceptions of economic threats to the state also differ on a regional basis. In the fall of 1998, we asked residents if they thought the current financial situation in Asia would hurt the California economy in the next year or so. Statewide, two in three residents said they thought the Asian financial crisis would hurt California either a great deal (22 percent) or somewhat (44 percent). San Francisco residents (75 percent) were the most convinced that the Asian financial crisis would have at least some impact on the state's economy. Sixty-five percent of residents in both Los Angeles and Orange County and the Inland Empire were worried about the Asian crisis. Only 59 percent of residents in the Central Valley thought that the Asian problems would affect California. Here the varying views about the state's economy appear to be a result of regional dependence on technology exports.

We saw more evidence that the structure of the regional economy can affect the outlook on the state. Late in 1998, we asked residents if they thought that economic conditions in California would get better, get worse, or stay the same in the next twelve months. Recall that people in the San Francisco Bay area have higher incomes and are more likely than people in other regions to give high ratings to the state's economy. Yet people in that same area were more likely to say that economic conditions would get worse rather than better (30 percent to 22 percent). This is another indication of the fears generated in that region by the Asian financial crisis. Those in the Los Angeles area (31 percent to 21 percent) and in Orange County and the Inland Empire (27 percent to 21 percent) were more likely to say that the economy would get better than worse. Central Valley residents were evenly divided between optimism and pessimism (24 percent to 23 percent).

Residents' views about noneconomic conditions in the state can also vary dramatically from region to region. Crime perceptions offer a good example. As Table 1 shows, when asked how much of a problem crime was in California, two-thirds of the respondents answered that crime was a big problem. However, three in four residents in the Central Valley and in Orange County and the Inland Empire believed that crime was a big problem, compared with about two in three residents in Los Angeles and about half of the residents in the San Francisco Bay area. What makes people see the state's crime conditions differently may have more to do with the local media and demographic trends than actual crime statistics. Los Angeles and the San Francisco Bay area have, respectively, the highest and lowest overall crime rates of the four regions. The Central Valley and the Inland Empire and Orange County have similar crime rates, falling between those two extremes (U.S. Census, 1994), and yet people in the Central Valley are more worried than Los Angeles residents about crime. Another question in the same survey also revealed an elevated concern about crime in the Central Valley. The question asked residents if they thought that the crime rate in California had increased, had decreased, or had stayed about the same in the past few years. Government statistics reported rather frequently by the media indicate that the state's crime rate has gone down in recent years. Nevertheless, nearly half of Californians (46 percent) believed that the crime rate had increased, 28 percent said that it had stayed the same, and only 24 percent thought that it had actually declined. Central Valley residents were the most likely to say that the state's crime rate had increased (53 percent), followed by those living in Orange County and the Inland Empire (49 percent), the San Francisco Bay area (45 percent), and the Los Angeles area (40 percent).

We also observed differences in the perceptions of the state's public school system. We asked in one survey, "How much of a problem is the quality of education in kindergarten through twelfth-grade public schools?" Altogether, 46 percent of Californians thought it was a big problem. In the San Francisco Bay area, 53 percent thought that the quality of the state's schools was a big problem, compared with a little under half of the residents in Los Angeles (49 percent) and in Orange County and the Inland Empire (46 percent). On the other hand, only 39 percent of those living in the Central Valley thought that the public school system represented a "big problem" for the state.

Clearly, differing state perceptions can result in varying priorities for   15
state action. Many Central Valley residents were concerned about the direction of the state, while in the Southern California regions there was a sunny optimism about the way things were going. San Francisco Bay area residents were worried about the economic implications of a financial meltdown in Asia, while many other state residents saw it as a distant news story that did not affect them. Central Valley residents and those living in the mega-suburbs see crime as a big and escalating problem in the state, while those in the more urban coastal regions feel less threatened. The issue of public schools also registered different levels of concern across the major regions of the state. It seems to be difficult for Californians to reach basic agreement on what is taking place in the state.

Diverse Conditions in the Regions   It seems reasonable to assume that the differing views of the state result largely from different conditions in the regions where the respondents live. Certainly, the economic conditions were different in the four regions during the 1990s. High wages were the rule in the booming high-technology industries of the San Francisco Bay area. Jobless rates were low in Orange County and the Inland Empire. The economy improved markedly in Los Angeles after tanking in the early 1990s. Some observers have referred to the Central Valley as the place the recovery has left behind. In the late 1990s, housing prices were escalating in Los Angeles and the mega-suburbs, and homes for sale in the San Francisco Bay area were routinely receiving multiple offers. At the same time, home prices were declining in some parts of the

Central Valley. The coastal regions are among the most expensive areas in the nation in which to live; Orange County and the Inland Empire have many new areas that are more affordable, but the cost of living is considerably lower in the Central Valley. To what extent are these economic conditions reflected in residents' perceptions of their regions?

In the focus groups, respondents offered different views about jobs and housing. Their perceptions were highly dependent on their region. Coastal residents were predictably worried about housing and the cost of living, while this was less of a concern elsewhere. "With rents as high as they are, a lot of people can't afford to live here," said a San Francisco resident. "If you want to get into a decent area, you almost have to work two jobs to survive," complained a Los Angeles resident. "Housing is very affordable," said a Sacramento resident. "There's plenty of housing," observed a Fresno resident.

Table 2 shows the regional differences in satisfaction with jobs and housing. Seventy-six percent of Californians are satisfied with the job opportunities in their region, with 26 percent saying they are very satisfied. About half of the San Francisco Bay area residents are very satisfied with the job opportunities, compared with one-fourth in the Southern California regions and even fewer in the Central Valley. As for the availability of affordable housing, the regional trends are again very strong. Throughout the state, about one-third are not satisfied with the housing choices in their region. More than half in the San Francisco Bay area are not satisfied with the selection of affordable housing available to them in their region, compared with one-third in Los Angeles, and one-fifth in the Central Valley and in Orange County and the Inland Empire region.

When asked about the most pressing issues facing the state, Californians put education and crime at the top of the list in the statewide surveys. However, traffic, growth, and sprawl emerged in the focus groups when we asked people about the issues that are creating big problems for the regions they live in. These issues were more prominent in the coastal areas. The salient issue for the Central Valley was rural-to-urban change generated by recent growth. "Since I moved here five years ago, my commute has doubled," said a San Francisco resident. "We have too many people in too small an area," lamented a Los Angeles resident. "Growth . . . it's going to get worse," predicted an Orange County resident. "This is the San Joaquin Valley and a lot of our trees are being cut down . . . and we are supposed to feed the world," said a Fresno resident of the changes under way. "We probably will have lovely freeways to get from one end of the sprawl to another," a Fresno resident predicted for the region's future.

One in three Californians in the statewide survey considered traffic congestion a big problem in their region. As Table 2 shows, San Francisco 20

TABLE 2. Regional Perceptions by Region

	Los Angeles	San Francisco Bay	Central Valley	Orange/ Inland
Job Opportunities				
Very satisfied	22%	46%	18%	23%
Somewhat satisfied	54	42	45	51
Not satisfied	24	12	37	26
Housing Availability				
Very satisfied	23%	11%	31%	29%
Somewhat satisfied	44	31	49	49
Not satisfied	33	58	20	22
Traffic Conditions				
Big problem	36%	54%	15%	31%
Somewhat of a problem	38	29	34	41
Not a problem	26	17	51	28
Population Growth				
Big problem	27%	38%	15%	28%
Somewhat of a problem	38	40	42	37
Not a problem	35	22	43	35

Source: PPIC Statewide Survey, April and May, 1998, all adults.

Bay area residents were the most likely to complain about this issue, with more than half seeing traffic congestion as a big problem. In Los Angeles and in Orange County and the Inland Empire, about one-third said that traffic congestion was a big problem. Central Valley residents were by far the least likely to complain about traffic.

Since traffic congestion and population growth usually go hand in hand, one would expect a correlation between people's concern about these phenomena. About 25 percent of Californians rate population growth and development as a big problem in their region. As Table 2 shows, San Francisco Bay area residents were, once again, the most likely to complain, with 38 percent saying that growth was a big problem in their region. Slightly more than one-quarter of Los Angeles and Orange County and Inland Empire residents saw growth as a major problem. The fewest complaints were, once again, voiced in the Central Valley, where 15 percent said growth was a big problem for their region. . . .

Diverse Opinions on Race and Immigration   The four regions have all experienced a substantial amount of immigration and undergone a significant degree of racial and ethnic change. These demographic changes have been very dramatic in Los Angeles, significant in the San Francisco Bay area and in Orange County and the Inland Empire, and least evident in the Central Valley. The regions have also had varied experiences with racial problems. In 1992, Los Angeles suffered the most destructive outburst of racial violence in the United States in the twentieth century, with the participants including Latinos, blacks, Koreans, and whites. Next we examine the ways in which residents of these regions differ in their feelings about race and immigration issues.[4]

Our survey shows surprisingly little variation across regions in perceptions of immigration and of racial change. Three in four residents in all four regions think that California has been experiencing an increase in the immigrant population. Across all regions, at least two in three residents believe that the racial and ethnic makeup of their region has been changing.

In the focus groups, participants also said that they were highly aware of immigration and racial change. However, in both the focus groups and the surveys we found regional variations in opinions about the effects of these changes. "Demographics are changing. A lot of businesses are catering to different ethnic groups," said a San Francisco resident. "There's a lot of new arrivals from out of the country into our area and it's impacting things," remarked a Los Angeles resident. "Most of the communities are multimixed, and people seem to be getting along pretty good," said a Sacramento resident. "It seems like we've got our pockets where everyone keeps themselves segregated and separated," observed an Orange County resident. "Fresno is such a culturally diverse community. There are so many misunderstandings and misconceptions about each other's races," said a Fresno resident. "No matter where you are, there's that racial tension, discrimination," said another Fresno resident.

Perceptions about the effects of immigration differ markedly between the more liberal coastal regions and the more conservative Central Valley and the Orange County and Inland Empire regions. As Table 3 shows, San Francisco Bay area residents by a twenty-point margin (53 percent to 33 percent), and Los Angeles residents by a twelve-point margin (50 percent to 38 percent) believe immigration is a benefit rather   25

---

[4] Many have written about racial and ethnic tensions in Los Angeles (see Baldassare, 1994; Dear, Schockman, and Hise, 1996; Fulton, 1997; Keil, 1998; Rieff, 1991; Scott and Sonja, 1998; Sonenshein, 1993; and Steinberg, Lyon, and Vaiana, 1996). See Neiman (1997), Fernandez and Neiman (1997), and Neiman and Fernandez (1998) for findings and analysis of anti-immigrant attitudes in the Inland Empire.

TABLE 3. Immigration and Racial Attitudes by Region

	Los Angeles	San Francisco Bay	Central Valley	Orange/ Inland
Effect of Immigrants				
Benefit	50%	53%	45%	37%
Burden	38	33	42	52
Neither	12	14	13	11
Effect of Racial Change				
Good	27%	26%	20%	19%
Bad	21	18	22	25
No difference	52	56	58	56

Source: PPIC Statewide Survey, April and October 1998, all adults.

than a burden to the state. By contrast, Central Valley residents are divided in perceiving immigration as a benefit versus a burden (45 percent to 42 percent), while a majority in Orange County and the Inland Empire see immigration as more of a burden than a benefit (52 percent to 37 percent).[5] San Francisco Bay area residents by an eight-point margin (26 percent to 18 percent) and Los Angeles residents by a six-point margin (27 percent to 21 percent) say that racial and ethnic change has had a good effect rather than a bad effect on their region. By contrast, Central Valley residents are as likely to say that racial and ethnic change has had a bad effect as a good effect (22 percent to 20 percent), while in Orange County and the Inland Empire more residents say that racial and ethnic change has been bad rather than good for their region (25 percent to 19 percent).

A more conservative outlook of Central Valley and of Orange County and Inland Empire residents is clearly evident in other attitudes toward immigration. The residents of Orange County and the Inland Empire (55 percent) and the Central Valley (49 percent) are more likely than San Francisco Bay area (41 percent) and Los Angeles (40 percent) residents to say that illegal immigration from Mexico to California has been a big

---

[5] In the December 1998 survey, we asked if Mexican immigrants were a benefit or a burden to California. The findings were consistent with responses to the general immigration questions, with "benefit" leading "burden" by a bigger margin in the San Francisco Bay area (53 percent to 31 percent) and Los Angeles (57 percent to 30 percent), than in the Central Valley (48 percent to 39 percent) and Orange County and the Inland Empire (47 percent to 43 percent).

problem in recent years. Residents in Orange County and the Inland Empire (27 percent) and the Central Valley (24 percent) are more likely than residents in the San Francisco Bay area (19 percent) and Los Angeles (17 percent) to say that children who are illegal immigrants should be prevented from attending public schools. Many people continue to be swayed by the arguments that led to the passage of Proposition 187, and the message is especially powerful in the more conservative regions, where the initiative passed overwhelmingly.

The coastal region's more liberal politics is most evident in attitudes toward affirmative action and other policies aimed at improving the economic opportunities for racial and ethnic groups. The higher proportion of Latinos and nonwhites in Los Angeles also contributes to support for affirmative action. Many residents of Los Angeles (47 percent) and the San Francisco Bay area (40 percent) want affirmative action programs to continue, with fewer in the Central Valley (33 percent) and Orange County and the Inland Empire (35 percent) in favor. Two in three people in Los Angeles (66 percent) and the San Francisco Bay area (65 percent) favor having employers and colleges use outreach programs to hire minority workers and attract minority students, compared with about half of the people in the Central Valley (51 percent) and Orange County and the Inland Empire (55 percent). Similarly, residents in Los Angeles (72 percent) and the San Francisco Bay area (66 percent) are strongly in favor of high schools and colleges providing special educational programs to assist minorities in competing for college admissions. Once again, public support is weaker in the Central Valley and Orange County and the Inland Empire.

In sum, there is a very high level of public recognition that the state and its major regions are undergoing racial and ethnic change as a result of immigration. The attitudinal differences seem to be largely explained by the conservative politics in the Central Valley and in Orange County and the Inland Empire versus the more liberal political orientations in the coastal regions. The more conservative views in the most rapidly growing regions of the state—the Central Valley and the mega-suburbs of Southern California—will have an increasing effect on elections and public policy. There is already evidence of this in the success of the three race and immigration initiatives.

References

Baldassare, Mark. 1986. *Trouble in Paradise: The Suburban Transformation in America.* New York: Columbia University Press.

Baldassare, Mark. 1992. "Suburban Communities." *Annual Review of Sociology* 18: 475–494.

Baldassare, Mark. 1994. *The Los Angeles Riots: Lessons for the Urban Future.* Edited volume. Boulder, CO: Westview Press.

Baldassare, Mark. 1998. *When Government Fails: The Orange County Bankruptcy.* Berkeley: University of California Press and Public Policy Institute of California.

Baldassare, Mark, Joshua Hassol, William Hoffman, and Abby Kanarek. 1996. "Possible Planning Roles for Regional Government: A Survey of City Planning Directors in California." *Journal of the American Planning Association* 62:17–29.

Baldassare, Mark, and Cheryl Katz. 1997. *Orange County Annual Survey: 1997 Report.* Irvine: University of California.

Baldassare, Mark, and Cheryl Katz. 1998. *Orange County Annual Survey: 1998 Report.* Irvine: University of California.

Dear, Michael, H. Eric Schockman, and Greg Hise. 1996. *Rethinking Los Angeles.* Edited volume. Thousand Oaks, CA: Sage Publications.

Fernandez, Kenneth, and Max Neiman. 1997. "Models of Anti-Immigration Sentiment and Other Speculations Regarding the Rise of Contemporary Xenophobia." Paper presented at the 1997 Annual Meeting of the Southwest Political Science Association, New Orleans.

Fischer, Claude S. 1984. *The Urban Experience.* New York: Harcourt Brace Jovanovich.

Fishman, Robert. 1987. *Bourgeois Utopia: The Rise and Fall of Suburbs.* New York: Basic Books.

Fradkin, Philip L. 1995. *The Seven States of California: A Natural and Human History.* New York: Henry Holt.

Fulton, William. 1997. *The Reluctant Metropolis: The Politics of Urban Growth in Los Angeles.* Point Arene, CA: Solano Press.

Garreau, Joel. 1991. *Edge Cities.* New York: Doubleday.

Jackson, Kenneth. 1985. *Crabgrass Frontier: The Suburbanization of the United States.* New York: Oxford University Press.

Keil, Roger. 1998. *Los Angeles: Globalization, Urbanization and Social Struggles.* New York: John Wiley.

Kling, Rob, Spencer Olin, and Mark Poster. 1991. *Postsuburban California: The Transformation of Orange County since World War II.* Berkeley: University of California Press.

Lewis, Paul, 1996. *Shaping Suburbia: How Political Institutions Organize Urban Development.* Pittsburgh: University of Pittsburgh Press.

Logan, John, and Harvey Molotch. 1987. *Urban Fortunes: The Political Economy of Place.* Berkeley: University of California Press.

Neiman, Max. 1997. *Inland Empire Annual Survey: 1997.* Riverside: University of California.

Neiman, Max, and Kenneth Fernandez. 1998. "Dimensions and Models of Anti-Immigrant Sentiments: Causes and Policy Relevance." Paper presented at the Annual Meeting of the American Political Science Association, Boston.

Palen, John. 1995. *The Suburbs.* New York: McGraw-Hill.

Rieff, David. 1991. *Los Angeles: Capital of the Third World.* New York: Touchstone.

Schneider, William. 1991. "Rule Suburbia: America in the 1990s." *National Journal* 39:2335–2336.

Scott, Allen J., and Edward Soja. 1998. *The City: Los Angeles and Urban Theory at the End of the Twentieth Century.* Edited volume. Berkeley: University of California Press.

Sonenshein, Raphael. 1993. *Politics in Black and White: Race and Power in Los Angeles.* Princeton, NJ: Princeton University Press.

Steinberg, James David Lyon, and Mary Vaiana. 1996. *Urban America: Policy Choices for Los Angeles and the Nation*. Santa Monica, CA: RAND.

Teaford, Jon C. 1997. *Post-Suburbia: Government and Politics in the Edge Cities*. Baltimore: Johns Hopkins University Press.

U.S. Census. 1994. *County and City Data Book: 1994*. Washington, DC: Department of Commerce.

Walters, Dan. 1992. *The New California: Facing the Twenty-First Century*. 2nd ed. Sacramento: California Journal Press.

UNDERSTANDING THE TEXT

1. Summarize in your own words the causes of California's regional differences in political and economic views, as Baldassare explains them.

2. What rationale does Baldassare provide for viewing California as distinct regions, as opposed to as a unified state?

3. What explanations does Baldassare provide for the different attitudes that are held by Californians from the four regions toward California's economy and immigration?

4. What sort of evidence does Baldassare provide for his analysis, and how does it contribute to the persuasiveness of his selection?

5. Answer in your own words a question that Baldassare asks: "To what extent are . . . economic conditions reflected in residents' perceptions of their regions?" (para. 16).

EXPLORING AND DEBATING THE ISSUES

1. Select one of the four regions that Baldassare describes, and write a profile of it that synthesizes his information. You may want to consult current news reports about the region's economic and political conditions, to keep your profile up to date, and consult Chapter 4, "The Geography of Desire: California and the Sense of Place."

2. Does the California dream have the same meaning for all Californians, despite regional differences? To develop an argument in response to this question, you might interview students or acquaintances from different regions of the state. You could also read James J. Rawls's "California: A Place, a People, a Dream" (p. 22).

3. In "In Search of Oildorado" (p. 274), James D. Houston provides a rich description of the political and social attitudes of Kern County residents, who are part of Baldassare's Central Valley quadrant. Write an essay in which you assess the extent to which Houston's description reflects Baldassare's characterization of the region, keeping in mind that Houston wrote his essay twenty years before Baldassare wrote his. Alternatively, select another author who discusses a region of California in Chapter 4, "The Geography of Desire: California and the Sense of Place," and base your assessment on that location.

4. Write an argumentative essay responding to the Southern Californians' comments that "California is basically two states, Northern California and Southern California" and "I always thought if they took the state of California and cut it in half maybe two states would be easier to govern than one state" (para. 3).

5. In what ways does your hometown reflect the regional identity that Baldassare assigns to your community? Write an essay in which you explore this question, keeping in mind the various concerns that Baldassare raises: employment opportunities, housing costs, crime, schools, and the effect of immigration, among others.

Life's Best Mixture: Sun and Air and Gasoline (December 1912)

SUNSET MAGAZINE

1. Imagine that this illustration is making an argument. To whom is it addressed? What claims does it make? What assumptions does it make about the place of the automobile in our culture?

2. Read or reread David Carle's "Sprawling Gridlock" (p. 403), and assume his perspective to write a critique of this illustration. Alternately, read or reread Michael J. O'Brien's "Orange County Historian" (p. 75), and write a poetic response.

Sprawling Gridlock

DAVID CARLE

The California dream has long included the automobility that a vast network of freeways was built to facilitate, but with unchecked suburban tract development and the number of registered cars, trucks, and motorcycles nearly equal to the number of residents, that dream has become a gridlocked nightmare. **David Carle** describes how the situation has gotten as bad as it is—looking at the history of California transit, beginning with the trolley lines that brought L.A.'s first commuters to work in the early twentieth century, and at the stories of families who are under pressure to sell some of the state's last remaining undeveloped land in the exploding exurbs. Virtually imprisoned within their cars, Californians have, on occasion, attempted to strike back with "slow-growth" and "smart-growth" initiatives, but the California Building Industry Association is ever ready to fight them every step of the way. Road rage anyone? Carle was a state parks ranger for twenty-seven years and has taught biology and natural history courses at Cerro Coso Community College. He is the author of *Drowning the Dream: California's Water Choices at the Millennium* (2000), from which this selection is taken.

Traffic Supplants Crime Atop Bay Poll, Packed Freeways Are No. 1 Concern. (*San Francisco Chronicle*, January 3, 1997)

I grieve the loss of the dirt. (Nicole Warne-McGraw, June 27, 1999)

Of all of the changes that Californians experienced through the 1990s, traffic congestion—creeping, gridlocked freeways and surface roads—became perhaps the most widely shared manifestation of the deteriorating California dream. The freedom that the automobile represented, including the opportunity to live in suburbs and commute to work, changed into a daily ordeal of wasted time and pressure on raw nerves; "road rage" joined the societal vocabulary. The media relished stories of brandished guns, shots fired, vehicles used as weapons, and periodic tragedies whenever the various weapons became deadly. The phenomenon was so widespread that the Automobile Association of America published grin-and-bear-it advice for avoiding road rage incidents: allow more time for trips (accept the delays and slow pace), be patient not aggressive (yield the road, nicely, when confronted by obscenities, gestures, or threats).

Commuters creeping along the freeways had plenty of time to read billboards designed for legibility at much higher speeds, advertising new subdivisions under construction nearby. Each time another hundred houses were completed and sold, a couple hundred more cars joined the daily stop-and-go masses, worsening the gridlock. But few objected to the construction itself. How could they object? The dogma pervading the

403

region was that home construction equated with a healthy economy; growth was good.

In 1996, drivers in the San Bernardino–Riverside area spent more time in gridlock than commuters anywhere else in the country, according to a study of urban roadway congestion by the Texas Transportation Institute. In that region, inland from Los Angeles and once famous for navel oranges, commuters averaged seventy-six hours a year in congested traffic. The Texas think tank's calculations of costs to drivers and their employers from time wasted and fuel consumed approximated $1,000 per person per year (Schrank and Lomax, 1996). Californians, as a whole, wasted a half-million hours each day in traffic congestion, at a cumulative cost of $2 billion a year, according to the California Department of Transportation.

"Inland Empire Leads in Fatal Road Rage" was the *Los Angeles Times* headline on March 9, 1999, when another study summarized road rage statistics. "The sprawl of suburbs and the relative lack of mass transit in the Riverside–San Bernardino area trigger deadly speeding, tailgating and red-light jumping at a rate more than double that in the region consisting of Los Angeles and Orange counties." The average speed of a San Bernardino–Riverside commute was thirty-five miles per hour. Speeds were slower in Los Angeles and Orange Counties—about twenty-eight miles per hour—ironically making for safer commutes. An Orange County transportation specialist explained, in the story, that "The only reason we aren't ranked higher is because no one can get moving fast enough."

In 1996 there were 24 million cars, trucks, and motorcycles and another 3 million trailers registered in the state. While that total was close to one vehicle for every single resident, the total number of miles traveled on the state's highways accounted for much of the congestion. The *average* commute for "inland empire" residents was twenty-two miles long, taking thirty-six minutes each way. The range of commute times included many thousands of drivers whose daily trips were measured in hours, rather than minutes, each morning and night.

The link between transport systems and urban sprawl had roots back in the early twentieth century, when citizens of Los Angeles were encouraged by the Pacific Electric trolley company to "Live in the Country and Work in the City." Pacific Electric "Big Red" trolley cars carried 110 million passengers in 1924 on a thousand miles of track running as far south as Balboa and north to San Fernando. Automobiles did not have to follow tracks or stick to timetables, though, and the convenience and freedom they represented doomed the region's mass-transit trolley system. The transformation was quickened by aggressive competition

5

from the automobile industry and government-funded highway construction projects. On December 30, 1940, the first freeway opened in California; the six-mile Arroyo Seco Parkway (later known as the Pasadena Freeway) connected Pasadena with downtown Los Angeles. In the 1960s alone, 450 miles of freeways were constructed in California. A phrase from Ian McEwan's novel *Amsterdam* (though concerning a different time and place) captured that decade's construction frenzy of "new roads probing endlessly, shamelessly, as though all that mattered was to be elsewhere" (McEwan, 1999, 68). By 1996, the state was crisscrossed by 170,500 miles of streets, roads, and highways. Yet California could not build roads fast enough to keep up. Not only was the "Red Queen" of highway construction running as fast as she could just to stay in one place, she constantly lost ground. The pattern repeated, over and over: gridlock conditions led to a highway-widening "solution"; construction slowdowns produced several years of increased frustration; after two years of improved traffic flow on the wider highway, daily gridlock was back.

Ironically, the freedom from timetables and the mobile convenience that cars represented were replaced by incarceration in traffic gridlock "prisons." Cars became cells, where major portions of life wasted away. Yet commuters showed the amazing adaptability of human beings: frustration turned to resignation, acceptance, and, finally, a loss of real understanding that there were alternatives to such a lifestyle. "If motorway driving anywhere calls for a high level of attentiveness, the extreme concentration required in Los Angeles seems to bring on a state of heightened awareness that some locals find mystical. . . . Yet what seems to be hardly noticed or commented on is that the price of rapid door-to-door transport on demand is the almost total surrender of personal freedom for most of the journey" (Banham, 1971, 214, 217). Banham's use of the word "rapid" is the part of his observation that became less accurate by the 1990s. More and more often, road rage burst forth while society's behavior modification experiment—the daily rush hour—uncovered a fuming, frustrated subconscious in many drivers.

There was a strong connection between growing gridlock and urban sprawl. Between 1970 and 1990, Los Angeles' population grew by 45 percent, but its developed land area increased 300 percent. From 1990 to 1998, the fastest-growing California cities were on the fringes of the major metropolitan areas—in many cases, areas with true desert climates. Palmdale, on the far side of the mountains from the coastal basin—the Mojave Desert side—grew by 36 percent during the 1990s. Its neighboring community, Lancaster, increased 21 percent; both cities had more than 100,000 residents by 1998, according to the California Department of Finance. Air conditioning, the State Water Project, and the region's freeway system helped explain the development pattern. During the same period, the city of Los Angeles increased by a more modest 3.2 percent (to 3.6 million people), while Long Beach, the state's fifth largest city (just south of Los Angeles), remained essentially stable, with only a 0.4 percent increase.

The fastest-growing city in California from 1990 to 1998 was Corona, located next-door to "road-rage Riverside." Corona's population jumped up 48 percent in that span of years. Some of the last orange groves in that "Inland Empire" region were being yanked from the ground by bulldozers in the 1990s. One of the Riverside orchards that still remained at the end of the decade was owned by the Warne family, who had moved their operations out of Orange County during the 1960s. Henry and Ellen Warne's son, Jim, lived and worked on Lake Ranch—named for a small reservoir on one part of the 130-acre farm. The orange groves were Jim's portion of the family agricultural business (most of which was concentrated, by then, south of the Salton Sea).

Ellen Warne died within a year of Henry's passing in 1998. Their descendants faced pressures to sell the family's remaining farm parcels in Orange and Riverside Counties—pressures that followed what became a classic pattern in the conversion of agricultural land to urban sprawl. A "planned residential community" was being built adjacent to Lake Ranch, and the development company pushed hard for sale of the orchard land. At the same time, taxes were coming due on Ellen and Henry's estate. The federal tax system required payment of 55 percent of its value. Such estate tax bills, due within a year of the death of land-rich farmers, led directly to the sale and paving over of many agricultural parcels.

Despite such pressures, Ellen and Henry's descendants decided that the Riverside orange groves would remain; Jim's home and livelihood would continue at Lake Ranch. In Westminster, however, where the Warnes had originally settled, nine acres of strawberry fields—the remnants of their original farm—would finally be liquidated. In densely populated Orange County, nine acres of strawberries might have special value as rare open space—a psychic benefit to hundreds of neighboring residents and thousands creeping past in the daily gridlock traffic of the nearby freeway. But the parcel was zoned by the city of Westminster for medium density, single-family homes, and, as such, was worth millions of dollars—enough to cover the estate taxes coming due. "I am grieving now not only the loss of my grandparents," Henry and Ellen's granddaughter told me, "but the impending loss of some of the last open farmland in

Westminster. Unfortunately, something *must* be sold. I grieve the loss of the dirt" (Warne-McGraw, June 27, 1999).

In 1990, California was the most urbanized state in the Union, according to the U.S. Census. More than 80 percent of Californians lived in metropolitan areas with over 1 million people. The consequences of sprawl, including traffic congestion, air pollution, endangered species, and permanent loss of open space and farmland, prompted the publication of *Beyond Sprawl: New Patterns of Growth to Fit the New California* in 1995 (Bank of America et al., 1995). It was published by an unusual coalition of business, government, and private interests: the State Resources Agency, the Greenbelt Alliance, the Low Income Housing Fund and, most surprisingly (considering its stake in development financing) the Bank of America. The report called for "smarter growth," for filling in open space within already developed areas, for redevelopment of older neighborhoods and business districts, and for encouraging higher-density living. It verified some facts that growth promoters hated the public to hear—that the costs of public services and infrastructure are seldom covered by development fees and taxes charged to new businesses and residents. Development that sprawled into the fringes of metropolitan areas, the report suggested, should finally start paying the full marginal costs inflicted on the region.

How much should they pay? Eben Fodor, author of *Better NOT Bigger* (1999), calculated infrastructure costs totaling $24,500 for each new single-family house in Oregon. That total considered schools, sewage systems, transportation facilities, water systems, parks and recreation facilities, stormwater drainage, and fire and emergency services. *Not* included in those calculations were the capital costs of police facilities, open space, libraries, general government facilities, electric power generation and distribution, natural gas distribution systems, and solid waste disposal facilities. Also not included were environmental and quality-of-life costs (decreased air and water quality, noise, traffic congestion, crime, and so forth)—which are real costs to the community or region but difficult to quantify.

Contrary to the myth that growth brought wide prosperity to communities and regions, most often the burden of new expenses fell on current residents, whose individually small tax and fee increases subsidized a relatively few profit takers. Like a pyramid scheme, adding additional taxpayers to the "subsidy pool" was the only way the growth machine could stay ahead of the true costs of growth. While the list of costs applied particularly to local governments, in a similar manner the Metropolitan Water District subsidized sprawl by spreading costs of new pipeline and infrastructure among all its customers, charging the same water rates to everyone in the region, new and old alike. The growth cartel dominating the political process, against only weak opposition from the general population, was yet another example of "The Tragedy of the Commons" (Hardin, 1968). Costs spread among many individuals in a community (the "commons," in this case) meant less motivation to participate in government planning and decision-making processes. Direct benefits to developers, real estate agents, and construction companies, on the other hand, ensured that they would be enthusiastic lobbyists for growth-inducing policies.

Predictably, *Beyond Sprawl* (Bank of America et al., 1995) was criti- 15 cized as serving "no-growthers" and NIMBYs. The acronym NIMBY—"Not in My Back Yard"—became a particular favorite of development interests. The critical label made the most sense when applied to "selfish" residents who would share benefits of essential developments (such as schools and fire stations) yet were adamant that such facilities be located in someone else's "backyard." The term was often applied, however, to opponents of strip malls and housing tracts. Whoever questioned growth, in general, was liable to be called a NIMBY. The label, like many derogatory terms, substituted emotion for fact. Carried to a logical extreme, its message was that it was *wrong* to cherish one's backyard—to be concerned with the environment and quality of life where one lived. Actually, NIMBYs tended to be those who truly cared about communities and were willing to get involved in shaping their best future. Yet the label remained a powerful tool for developers confronting opposition.

In 1987, citizens (who would be labeled NIMBYs) placed a growth control initiative on the Orange County ballot. "It had become painfully apparent to many that if regional limits on growth were not promoted and constructed from the bottom up, then such growth would most certainly be imposed by powerful interests from the top down" (Olin, 1991, 239). Organized opposition to the initiative came from the "ranches" controlling the only remaining undeveloped lands in the county—the 1980s corporate manifestations of the Stearns and Irvine families, who had acquired the area's Mexican ranchos a hundred years earlier. They were joined by some of Orange County's multinational corporations. As *Beyond Sprawl* noted: "the complex of office centers around John Wayne Airport in Orange County—built on land that was, until a generation ago, cultivated for lima beans—recently surpassed downtown San Francisco as the second-largest employment center in the state" (Bank of America et al., 1995, 5). International corporations had little motivation to consider "backyard" quality-of-life concerns. "In *Your* Back Yard"—IYBYism—might be the appropriate label for such developers. The well-financed opposition to the growth control measure spent $2.5 million during an intense five-week saturation campaign. They defeated the initiative, 56 percent to 44 percent, in June 1988.

The measure had not actually been designed as a "*no*-growth" initiative. "Slow-growth" and "smart-growth" became the slogans for many organized efforts to redirect the state's future throughout California. "Slow" and "smart" sounded less negative than "no growth," and they seemed easier to sell to Californians, whose long history and culture had been built around a dogma of growth. In an essay about the connections between water and "smart growth," the editor of *Western Water* pointed to a poll (in *Time* magazine, March 22, 1999), in which 57 percent of respondents favored greenbelts between their communities and new development. "Of course, Cliff Moriyama of the California Building Industry Association noted that poll and others do not include the opinions of the new Californians who are not here yet. Therefore, he said, the newcomers cannot participate in the debate" (Sudman, 1999, 2). That rather amazing concept in community planning suggested that the citizens the California Building Industry Association cared most about were theoretical, future customers. If these customers required land where greenbelt buffers might otherwise exist, they should be served. It was a logic that only made sense if one widely held belief remained unquestioned—the idea that growth in California was inevitable and would be never-ending.

The same article added comments from a water agency spokesman offering both frustration and hope for Californians who might prefer that their government show concern for actual, living citizens. Randy Kanouse, of the Easy Bay Municipal Utility District, said districts like his "can't stop growth by constricting water supplies but first priority must be for utilities to protect existing water users" (Sudman, 1999, 2). If they actually followed that first priority, limits of the water supply *would*, ultimately, limit growth.

Conspicuously lacking in many of the growth control discussions had been consideration of the fact that, whether slow or fast, smart or dumb, growth remained growth. Higher-density concentrations—one way to reduce sprawl as numbers increased—had never been attractive to Californians. Quality-of-life choices led to the suburban lifestyle—with a yard to landscape, personalize, and call one's own. Telling people to embrace high-density urban living—the late 1990s message from many "smart-growth" advocates, was telling people something they did not want to hear. The other point that was conspicuously absent from such discussions was a realistic approach toward a long-term stabilization of California's population.

The key to *today's* choices, those that will shape California in the twenty-first century, continues to be water to facilitate population growth. Agriculture, with its major share of the developed water in California, is now a prime target for thirsty urban interests. Water "wasted" to the

20

environment remains another source that may be tapped, should Californians make that choice. There remains another alternative that receives very little attention. Considering the lessons to be learned from the state's environmental history, Californians might adopt a radically different path for the coming century. They might choose to stabilize their state's population as soon as possible.

References

Banham, Reyner. 1971. *Los Angeles: The Architecture of Four Ecologies.* New York: Harper and Row.

Bank of America, California Resources Agency, Greenbelt Alliance, and Low Income Housing Fund. 1995. *Beyond Sprawl: New Patterns of Growth to Fit the New California.* San Francisco: Bank of America Corp.

Fodor, Eben. 1999. *Better NOT Bigger: How to Take Control of Urban Growth and Improve Your Community.* Gabriola Island, B.C., Canada: New Society Publishers.

Hardin, Garrett. 1968. "The Tragedy of the Commons." *Science* 162, 1243–48.

McEwan, Ian. 1999. *Amsterdam.* New York: Nan A. Talese imprint, Doubleday, Anchor Books edition.

Olin, Spencer. 1991. "Intraclass Conflict." In *Postsuburban California: The Transformation of Orange County since World War II,* edited by Rob Kling, Spencer Olin, and Mark Poster. Berkeley: University of California Press.

Schrank, David L., and Timothy J. Lomax. 1996. *Urban Roadway Congestion: 1982–1993.* Vol. 1, *Annual Report.* Texas Transportation Institute. Texas A&M University, College Station, Texas.

Sudman, Rita Schmidt. 1999. "Editor's Desk" column. *Western Water.* (Water Education Foundation, Sacramento) (March/April): p. 2.

Warne-McGraw, Nicole. 1999. Personal correspondence. La Habra, Calif.

UNDERSTANDING THE TEXT

1. According to Carle, what were the historical conditions that led to the current "gridlock" (para. 3)?

2. In your own words, what are the human and political consequences of urban and suburban sprawl and the resulting traffic problems?

3. Summarize in your own words what Carle means when he refers to the "smart-growth" movement (para. 17).

4. Articulate the logic behind Carle's comparison between housing growth and a pyramid scheme. To what extent does he provide evidence to support this comparison, and do you find it persuasive?

5. Why does Carle believe that the term "NIMBY . . . substituted emotion for fact" (para. 15)?

EXPLORING AND DEBATING THE ISSUES

1. Write an essay in which you demonstrate, challenge, or complicate Carle's opening assertion: "Of all the changes that Californians experienced through the 1990s, traffic congestion—creeping, gridlocked freeways

and surface roads—became perhaps the most widely shared manifestation of the deteriorating California dream" (para. 1).

2. Throughout the essay, Carle describes the concept behind "smart
   growth" (para. 17). In an argumentative essay, set forth your position on
   whether such a vision would improve the quality of life in California. To
   develop your ideas, consult Joel Garreau, "Edge City: Irvine" (p. 298), and
   Gary Paul Nabhan, "The Palms in Our Hands" (p. 308).

3. Carle advocates that water availability be a criterion in permitting future
   development in California. Write an essay in which you support, challenge, or complicate his position. As you develop your ideas on this
   question, you might consult Gerald W. Haslam, "The Water Game"
   (p. 411), or Victor Davis Hanson, "Paradise Lost" (p. 428).

4. To what extent does the traditional vision of the California dream (see
   James J. Rawls, "California: A Place, a People, a Dream," p. 22) create the
   gridlock and the quality-of-life problems that Carle describes?

5. Write an argumentative essay that defends, opposes, or modifies Carle's
   concluding recommendation that Californians "might choose to stabilize their state's population as soon as possible" (para. 20). Keep in mind
   that Carle is not necessarily referring to immigration from foreign nations in this remark.

The Water Game

GERALD W. HASLAM

Though now one of the most productive agricultural regions in the world, the Central Valley was not always a promising place to grow crops. In this overview of the
development of Central Valley agriculture, **Gerald W. Haslam** (b. 1937) explores
both the rewards and the costs of the vast irrigation projects that transformed the
Valley from an arid savannah to an agricultural cornucopia. A native of the Central
Valley and an emeritus professor of English at Sonoma State University, Haslam
has written and edited numerous collections of short stories and essays focused
on the Valley, including *California Heartland: Writing from the Great Central Valley*
(1978), *That Constant Coyote: California Stories* (1990), *Condor Dreams and Other
Fictions* (1994), *The Other California: The Great Central Valley in Life and Letters*
(1990), from which this selection is taken, *The Great Tejon Club Jubilee* (1996),
and *Workin' Man Blues: Country Music in California* (1999).

John Phoenix is acknowledged to have been one of the West's first great
humorists. Phoenix was actually the *nom de plume* of a mischievous
and talented graduate of West Point, George Horatio Derby. A topograph-
ical engineer for the United States Army, Derby wrote hilarious sketches
even while on military assignments. In 1849, however, when he was

dispatched to survey the Great Central Valley's farming potential, the wag turned grim.

The area north of Fresno—now the richest agricultural county in America—he reported, was "Exceedingly barren, and singularly destitute of resources, except for a narrow strip on the borders of the stream; it was without timber and grass, and can never, in my estimation, be brought into requisition for agricultural purposes." Near present-day Bakersfield in Kern County (the nation's second-most productive), he found "the most miserable country that I ever beheld."

That same parched vale is now the most abundant agricultural cornucopia in the history of the world. Last year it produced over fifteen billion dollars in agriculture. How was that transformation possible? Distinguished historian W. H. Hutchinson says there were three principal reasons: "Water, water, and *more* water."

The control and manipulation of water in the arid West have been the key to everything from economics to politics here. Without water projects, there would be few Idaho potatoes; without water projects, little Arizona cotton, no Utah alfalfa. There would also be no Phoenix, no Las Vegas, and no Los Angeles—not as we know them, anyway. There would be no Reno or El Paso or Albuquerque, either, because they too have grown in desiccated areas.

The American West is, in the main, arid to semiarid land. But the   5
natural beauty and value of arid lands has rarely been apparent to people whose ancestors migrated from green Europe, so enormous amounts of money have been spent and rapacious bureaucracies created in an effort to "make the desert bloom." Nonetheless, only a tiny portion of the land has so far been "developed," but that has bloomed abundantly.

Unfortunately, these efforts have also produced the seeds of their own doom: problems such as soil salinization, compaction, and subsidence; the leaching and concentrating of natural toxins from previously dry earth; the overuse of agricultural chemicals, which in turn concentrate in the environment; and the devastation of once-huge aquifers in order to flood-irrigate crops better suited to other climates in other places. These developments now seem to have placed Westerners on a path trod by Assyrians, Mesopotamians, and Aztecs, desert peoples who also once challenged nature—and failed.

In the past year, ten photographers have embarked on a project to dramatize this long-ignored environmental crisis. "We've been managing water as an abstract legal right or a commodity," points out Robert Dawson, the Californian who initiated the endeavor, "rather than the most basic physical source of life. We believe that water is misused nationwide. We're focusing on the arid West because development here stands in high relief against the vast, open landscape. It's here that the impact of technology, government, and human ambition is most visible." Many major water-policy decisions remain to be made, and only an informed public can do that.

Nowhere are the gains and losses associated with water manipulation more obvious than in Dawson's home region, the Great Central Valley of California, the physical and economic core of our richest state. All significant cities here, the state's heartland, grew near watercourses; it is an oasis civilization.

But it isn't the existence of cities that makes this area vital. It is the fact that 25 percent of all table food produced in the United States is grown in this single valley.

The climate here seems close to perfect for farming: following a   10 short, splendid spring, an extended summer develops. Sun prevails and the horizon seems to expand. Thanks to water pumped or imported, the list of crops grown in this natural hothouse is continually expanding as new varieties are planted: exotic herbs and condiments this year, kiwi fruit and frost-free berries the next. Meanwhile, native plants are rare and native animals—pronghorns, grizzlies, and condors—stand stuffed in local museums.

Here, too, a largely Hispanic workforce toils on great farms owned by corporations because this remains a place where poor of any background can at least try to escape the cycle of poverty, one generation laboring that another might take advantage of the region's rich promise. But it isn't an easy climb; there has tended to be a direct link between centralized irrigation systems and centralized political and economic power, and that in turn has created a paternalistic, class-ridden society with nonwhites on the bottom.

Modern agribusiness is competitive, and Valley farmers and ranchers have been notable, inventing such agricultural devices as special adaptations of the clamshell dredge, peach defuzzers, olive pitters, wind machines to fight frost, hydraulic platforms for pruning, pneumatic tree-shakers for bringing down the fruit and nuts—a technological nascence of amazing creativity. But none of them would mean much without im- ✳ ported or pumped water.

Many farmers date their entry into Valley agriculture to the period just after World War I when the unregulated pumping of ground water allowed fields to burgeon. Eventually farmers were pumping more and more from wells that had to be drilled deeper and deeper into unreplenishable aquifers. When the Central Valley Project and the California State Water Project—the two largest and most complex irrigation systems on earth—were completed, it seemed that at last the tapping of irreplaceable ground water in the Valley could cease.

Today, more than twelve hundred dams have been built and thousands of miles of canals cross this one-time desert. Even that hasn't stopped subsurface pumping; it has actually expanded since those huge stores of surface water became available. Pumping now exceeds replenishment by more than a half-*trillion* gallons annually, while ecosystems hundreds of miles to the north are threatened by the diversion of their rivers and creeks.

Writer Wallace Stegner has suggested that this area's—and by analogy, the West's—agriculture may have "to shrink back to something like the old, original scale, and maybe less than the original scale because there isn't the ground water there anymore. It's actually more desert than it was when people first began to move in." Hutchinson adds, "We have to stop pretending we're frontiersmen dealing with unlimited water. There's too damn many of *us* and too damned little of *it*." 15

Giant agribusinesses in the Valley can buy that water for less than ten dollars per acre foot, while northern California householders have paid well over one thousand dollars for the same acre foot—with the difference subsidized by taxpayers. It seems to critics that such water is too cheap to use wisely and that both hubris and ignorance are manifest in the illusion that moisture unused by humans is somehow squandered, the natural world be damned—and dammed. Ironically, most people—including most Westerners—seem to prefer not to be aware of all this, lest salads and beef suddenly become more expensive.

Irrigation is big business, and both the vast water projects in California were justified, in part at least, as measures that would save existing family farms and perhaps increase the number of acres cultivated by small farmers. In fact, both have led to more and more acres coming under cultivation by huge corporations—Chevron U.S.A., Prudential Insurance Company, Shell Oil Company, Southern Pacific Railroad, J. G. Boswell Company, Getty Oil, among others.

How has the quest for water changed the West? Last year, driving in the southwest corner of Central Valley, I decided to investigate Buena Vista Lake, where I'd fished when I was a boy. I crossed the California Aqueduct, then drove west and finally stopped the car. An immense agricultural panorama opened before me, cultivated fields of various hues extending in all directions.

All its tributary streams have been diverted and its bed is now dry so, ironically, Buena Vista Lake must be irrigated. As I gazed at this scene, a red-tailed hawk wheeled overhead, riding a thermal. Far to the east a yellow tractor shimmered through heat waves like a crawdad creeping across the old lake's floor. I saw no dwellings, few trees.

That hawk swung far over a green field where tiny fingers of water   20
from elsewhere glistened through rows and where a lone brown man, an
irrigator, leaned on a shovel.

Welcome to the real West, where agribusiness executives in corporate boardrooms, not cowboys or Indians or even irrigators, are the principal players.

UNDERSTANDING THE TEXT

1. What does Haslam mean when he says that water projects "have placed
   Westerners on a path trod by Assyrians, Mesopotamians, and Aztecs"
   (para. 6)?

2. What gains and losses does Haslam find in the history of Central Valley
   irrigation?

3. How has irrigation shaped the social-class system of the Central Valley,
   according to Haslam?

4. What does Haslam learn when he returns to his childhood recreation
   area, Buena Vista Lake?

EXPLORING AND DEBATING THE ISSUES

1. In class, brainstorm the pros and cons of heavy irrigation in the Central
   Valley. Then form teams, and debate Wallace Stegner's proposition that
   farming should "shrink back to something like the old, original scale"
   (para. 15) in this region. Be sure to offer solutions to the groundwater
   problem if you oppose Stegner. If you support his position, suggest alternative means of livelihood for displaced farmers.

2. Haslam notes that agribusiness customers in the Central Valley pay ten
   dollars for an acre foot of water while urban consumers pay as much a
   thousand dollars for the same amount. Write an essay arguing for or
   against the taxpayer subsidization of agricultural production through
   this differential price structure for water.

3. In your journal, describe how you would plan the future of the Central
   Valley if you had the power to dictate water policy there. Share your
   entry with your classmates.

4. Write an essay in which you analyze the role that water has played in
   making the California dream possible. To develop your ideas, read or
   reread James J. Rawls's "California: A Place, a People, a Dream" (p. 22)
   and Victor Davis Hanson's "Paradise Lost" (p. 428).

5. Haslam criticizes large agribusiness in his essay. Write an argument that
   supports, challenges, or modifies his position. To develop your ideas,
   you might want to consult Joan Didion's "Notes from a Native Daughter"
   (p. 54), David Mas Masumoto's "As If the Farmer Died" (p. 248), or Marc
   Reisner's "Things Fall Apart" (p. 416).

Things Fall Apart

MARC REISNER

The story **Marc Reisner** (1948–2000) tells in this selection is a nightmare that began with good intentions. The vast irrigation projects of the San Joaquin Valley needed a place where all that water could drain; the migrating fowl that fly over the Valley needed a place to rest and feed. So the creation of the Kesterson Reservoir seemed to be a good solution to both problems—until the birds began to die of selenium poisoning from the irrigation runoff. A former staff writer for the Natural Resources Defense Council, Reisner tells this tale and others like it in *Cadillac Desert* (1986), an environmentalist history of western water policy. Reisner was also the author of *Overtapped Oasis: Reform or Revolution for Western Water* (1990) and *Game Wars: The Undercover Pursuit of Wildlife Poachers* (1991).

In the Colorado Basin, the effects of wastefully irrigating saline lands are not, for the most part, being felt by those doing the irrigating. Thanks mainly to the taxpayers, the farmers who are contributing the lion's share of the salts to the river have had drainage facilities built which flush the problem down to someone else. In the San Joaquin Valley, it is a different story. The San Joaquin's problem is unique—an ingenious revenge by nature, in the minds of some, on a valley whose transformation into the richest agricultural region in the world was wrought at awesome cost to rivers, fish, and wildlife. Several times in the relatively recent geologic past—within the last couple of million years—the valley was a great inland sea, thick with diatomaceous life and tiny suspended sediments which settled near the middle of the gently sloping valley floor. Compressed and compacted, the stuff formed an almost impervious layer of clay that now underlies close to two million acres of fabulously productive irrigated land. In the middle of the valley, the clay membrane is quite shallow, sometimes just a few feet beneath the surface soil. When irrigation water percolates down, it collects on the clay like bathwater in a tub. In hydrologists' argot, it has become "perched" water. Since the perched water does not have a chance to mingle with the relatively pure aquifer beneath the clay, it may become highly saline, as in Iraq. The more the farmers irrigate, the higher it rises. In places, it has reached the surface, killing everything around. There are already thousands of acres near the southern end of the valley that look as if they had been dusted with snow; not even weeds can grow there. An identical fate will ultimately befall more than a million acres in the valley unless something is done.

For years, the planners in the state and federal water bureaucracies have talked about the need for a "master drain" to carry the perched water out of the San Joaquin Valley. It is more accurate to say that their *reports* have talked about it, while the officials, whose main concern was building more dams to satisfy the demands of the irrigators, ignored the need for drainage because neither they nor (they guessed) the public and the farmers could face the cost. "In the early and mid-1970s," says van Schilfgaarde,[1] "the state's position was that no drainage problem exists. The early reports all said that the State Water Project makes no sense without a drain because it would add inevitably to the perched water problem. But the public doesn't read reports, so no one mentioned them. Then, a few years ago, when the problem began threatening to become critical, there was suddenly an awful drainage problem that threatened the future of agriculture in California."

Today, three decades after the first reports spoke of the need for a huge, valleywide drainage system, no such system exists. A modest-sized spur, called the San Luis Drain, is being completed as a part of the Westlands Water District, which, by introducing a prodigious amount of new surface water into a relatively small area, threatened to waterlog the lands downslope. But the water carried off by the San Luis Drain has nowhere to go until a master drain is built. For the time being, it is being dumped into a manmade swamp called Kesterson Reservoir, near the town of Los Banos, which slowly fills and evaporates according to the intensity of the valley heat and the irrigation cycle. From the air, the reservoir, when it is full, is an attractive sight to migrating waterfowl, which descend on it by the tens of thousands as their ancestors once descended by the many millions on the valley's primordial marshes and shallow lakes. The presence of all of those coots, geese, and ducks at Kesterson Reservoir gave the Bureau an idea about how to solve one of the most daunting problems associated with the master drain: its enormous cost. By the time the San Luis Drain, a modest portion of the proposed master drain, is completed, its price tag will be more than $500 million. In 1984, Interior Secretary William Clark made an offhand projection that solving the drainage problem valleywide could end up costing $4 to $5 billion. That comes to about $5,000 an acre to rescue the affected lands, which is more than most of the land itself is worth. The farmers, a number of whom are corporations or millionaires, are understandably loath to pay the bill. If one wrote off a third of the cost as a wildlife and recreational benefit, however, it would be easier to swallow. That is exactly what the Bureau and California's Department of Water Resources, in a 1979 interagency study entitled "Agricultural Drainage and

---

[1] Jan van Schilfgaarde, director of the U.S. Department of Agriculture's Salinity Control Laboratory in Riverside, California. [Eds.]

Salt Management in the San Joaquin Valley," proposed to do in the case of the master drain, which, in that report, was projected to cost $1.26 billion in 1979 dollars. Ascribing annual benefits of $92 million to the master drain, the Bureau and the state's Department of Water Resources elected to write off about a third of that total, or $31.7 million, as a non-reimbursable benefit, payable by the taxpayers, for the creation of artificial marshes. If one were to divide the number of ducks which might reasonably be expected to use those manmade wetlands into $31.7 million, they would become very expensive ducks indeed. When the Bureau's dams went up, regulating the rivers and allowing the marshlands to be dried up—about 93 percent of the Central Valley's original wetlands are gone—it virtually ignored the economic value of the millions of ducks it was about to displace. Now, suddenly, they have become almost priceless.

Due to a distressing twist of fate, however, the Bureau of California may consider themselves lucky if they succeed in writing off *any* part of the master drain to wildlife benefits. Sometime in 1982, hunters and biologists around Kesterson Reservoir began to observe that many over-wintering birds seemed lethargic and sick—so ravaged by some strange malady that they could not even float on the water, and often drowned. At first, duck hunters and conservationists put forth an explanation that the farm lobby had always pooh-poohed—that pesticides and other chemical wastes in the sumpwater were making the birds die. By 1984, however, biologists were quite certain that the main cause of the ducks' awful fate was selenium, a rare mineral, toxic in small doses, that occurs in high concentrations in southern Coast Range soils—exactly those soils which, washing down from the mountains over aeons, formed the Westlands Water District. The *San Francisco Chronicle*, which has carried on a long, bitter battle against water exports to the valley and southern California, has played the story for all it is worth. But none of its news stories and editorials had quite the impact of a poignant front-page photograph of a gorgeous dying male pintail duck at Kesterson Reservoir, a duck about to sink like a doomed boat to the bottom of the poisoned manmade marsh its presence is to subsidize.

Since there can be only one ultimate destination for the wastewater carried by the master drain—San Francisco Bay—the spectacle at Kesterson has infuriated many of the five million people who reside in the Bay Area. They may pollute the bay badly enough themselves, even if they do not admit it; but to have a bunch of farmers grown wealthy on "their" water, and subsidized by their taxes, sending it back to the bay full of toxic wastes, selenium, boron, and salt—that is intolerable. The farmers, the Bureau, and the Department of Water Resources might reject such reasoning as simplistic and emotional. But the fact is that the people of the Bay Area appear to have the political clout to prevent the drain from ever reaching there, and they seem determined to use it. It matters little that the salts in the wastewater (the selenium and boron and pesticides are another matter) would hardly affect the salinity of a great bay into which the ocean rushes every day. What matters is that the San Joaquin Valley farmers asked for water and got it, asked for subsidies and got them, and now want to use the bay as a toilet. To their urban brethren by the ocean, living a world apart, all of this smacks of a system gone mad.

UNDERSTANDING THE TEXT

1. What are the geological conditions that led to the appearance of " 'perched' water" (para. 1) in the San Joaquin Valley?
2. Why is a drainage system so vital to the San Joaquin Valley?
3. What miscalculations were made by the California Department of Water Resources in the creation of the Kesterson Reservoir?
4. What were the reasons for the death of wildlife at Kesterson Reservoir?

EXPLORING AND DEBATING THE ISSUES

1. Assuming the role of a farmer, write a letter to Reisner in which you respond to his comment, "What matters is that the San Joaquin Valley farmers asked for water and got it, asked for subsidies and got them, and now want to use the bay as a toilet" (para. 5).
2. In class, form two teams that represent San Joaquin Valley farmers and San Francisco Bay environmentalists, and debate the construction of a master drain from the Valley to the Bay.
3. Reisner points out that irrigating land can also destroy it with salt pollution. Write an essay arguing whether the development of Central Valley agriculture—a major part of the California economy—is worth the price.
4. In class, discuss the tone of Reisner's essay. What assumptions about the various groups that he discusses—farmers, state bureaucrats, biologists, urbanites—are revealed through his tone?
5. Write an essay in which you argue whether the cost of protecting wildlife from human-caused disasters such as the Kesterson Reservoir should be borne by all state citizens.

Warning Sign, Almaden Quicksilver
County Park, San Jose (1996)

1. Write an essay in which you outline the attitudes toward nature that are implicit in this sign posted by the Santa Clara Health Department.

2. In class, discuss the design of the sign, including the use of many languages and the iconic image. What does the design suggest about California culture?

3. The sign is a passive response to environmental degradation. Assume the perspective of Richard Steven Street ("Battling Toxic Racism," p. 421), and propose a solution to the contamination that prompted the posting of this sign. You might consult as well Gerald W. Haslam, "The Water Game" (p. 411), and Marc Reisner, "Things Fall Apart" (p. 416).

Battling Toxic Racism

RICHARD STEVEN STREET

The popular image of an environmental activist is that of a white, middle-class sub-urbanite, but as the saga of Kettleman City reveals, this image is both false and mis-leading. For the tale of Kettleman City, as told here by **Richard Steven Street**, is a story of how a community of Central Valley Latinos, in alliance with environmental activists from around the state, successfully blocked the construction of a toxic-waste incinerator near their homes. In so doing, they demonstrated that environmentalism knows no racial or social boundaries. An award-winning photographer and essayist, Richard Steven Street is the author of *A Kern County Diary* (1983), *Breadbasket of the World: California's Great Wheat-Growing Era 1860–1890* (1984), and *Beasts of the Field: A Narrative History of California Farm Workers, 1769–1913* (2004), as well as the coauthor, with Samuel Orozco, of *Organizing for Our Lives* (1992), from which this selection is taken.

Every day hundreds of semitrailers rumble in and out of Kettleman City, an isolated farming town just off Interstate 5, midway between Los Angeles and Sacramento. Many of those trucks are packed full of fruit and vegetables, the bounty of the San Joaquin Valley on its way to people around the world. However, other trucks contain a different cargo—a deadly cargo. These trucks deliver toxic waste bound for burial three miles outside of Kettleman City at the largest landfill west of Louisiana.

The residents of Kettleman City detest this dangerous traffic. Nevertheless, Chemical Waste Management, the owner of the landfill, is targeting the town for the site of a new toxic waste incinerator. The residents are calling it "a landfill in the sky" and have banded together to stop Chem Waste from building any more toxic facilities in their town. "Do you think we'd have this toxic mess here if we were a community of rich white people?" asks Mary Lou Mares, a lettuce cutter who has lived in Kettleman City for fifteen years. "Our rights have never been taken seriously."

Led by poor farm workers, hundreds of citizens of Kettleman City have formed *El Pueblo para El Aire y Agua Limpio* (People for Clean Air and Water), a multiethnic coalition whose aim is to stop the proposed incinerator. Many people are comparing the David-and-Goliath struggle of *El Pueblo* to the United Farm Workers (UFW) organizing campaigns of the 1960s. Similar to the UFW campaigns, the anti-incinerator coalition in Kettleman City must confront multimillion-dollar corporations, law enforcement, and hostile government agencies.

El Pueblo's most effective tactic to date has been a lawsuit filed on their behalf by California Rural Legal Assistance, a poverty law program that has been operating in rural California since 1965. This lawsuit is the first in the nation to charge that "environmental racism" played a role in a corporation's decision to build a toxic waste facility in a low-income community. The lawsuit accuses Chem Waste of targeting Kettleman City because it is largely a community of poor, monolingual, Spanish-speaking Mexican field hands. Kettleman's thirteen hundred residents are 95 percent Latino. The suit also discloses a nationwide pattern of building toxic facilities in low-income communities. All of Chem Waste's incinerator facilities are located in communities that are more than 75 percent poor people of color—communities such as Sauget, Illinois, Port Arthur, Texas, and the south side of Chicago.

When Chem Waste built its toxic landfill in Kettleman City in 1979, the corporation did not have to obtain approval from the local community because Kettleman City is unincorporated. There is no mayor, city council, planning commission, or newspaper. All Chem Waste had to do was buy an existing oil disposal company and apply for permits with the state and federal governments. Within a year it was not only operating a full-scale toxic landfill in Kettleman City, but it was using Interstate 5 as a kind of toxic runway for fleets of top loaders heaped with contaminated solids, tankers full of toxic liquids, and flatbeds stacked high with fifty-five-gallon drums of cyanide, benzene, asbestos, cleaning solvents, heavy metals, and hundreds of other chemicals.

"We noticed all the trucks rolling through and assumed they were going to some kind of construction project," explains Adela Aguilera, a teacher's aide and mother of three. "We didn't know what was going on." Strange, oily-garlic odors drifting into town with the evening winds first signaled that something nasty was brewing out in the Kettleman hills. Unexplained, nagging health problems ranging from nosebleeds to fainting spells led a small group of citizens to uncover the frightening truth— a truth that no government official had bothered to tell the largely Latino population who were being affected by it. With more than 200,000 tons of poisons rolling in every year, Kettleman City had been transformed overnight, with no public notice, from a rural backwater into the toxic capital of the western United States.

In 1988, Chem Waste applied for permits from Kings County to build an incinerator near the existing landfill. The corporation held its public hearings on the incinerator in Hanford, thirty-five miles from Kettleman City and the proposed site. Residents of Kettleman City were not told about the hearings. "We found out through Greenpeace," explains Ramon Mares. "They asked us if we knew that an incinerator was going to be built. We said no. We didn't know anything. Greenpeace began to educate us so we could fight it."

Although they were unfamiliar with the concept of environmental social justice, several Kettleman City residents had read about the community coalitions blocking hazardous dumping or incinerators in Emelle, Alabama, and in East Los Angeles. With the help of Greenpeace, residents learned the basics of grassroots activism—phone trees, meetings, and door-to-door organizing. "We began to understand our rights," recalls Bertha Martinez, who has lived in Kettleman for twenty-four years. "We saw we weren't alone."

After forming *El Pueblo,* Kettleman City's residents launched a campaign that has become a model for community organizations across the nation. They have created a unique coalition that cuts across racial and economic boundaries, pulling together Latino farm managers, migrant farm workers, and Anglo residents who own larger farms in the area. By linking up with civil rights organizations and environmental activists, *El Pueblo* publicized its cause, lobbied, marched, and gained the attention of activists and politicians nationwide.

"Chem Waste never imagined we'd fight," says Espy Maya, a mother   10
of four who is a leader in *El Pueblo*. "The company just thought we were a bunch of dumb little hicks and illegals, so hard up for work that we'd be tickled to death to get some menial jobs burning their poisons or burying them at their dump."

Some of the group's most surprising allies turned out to be former opponents. Downwind from the proposed incinerator, farmers like Jose Maya and Dick Newton, who usually had little patience for environmental causes supported by Greenpeace or the Sierra Club, found their interests to be in alignment. "If just one head of lettuce is contaminated, I'll lose the entire crop, and I'll be ruined," explains Maya, who grows 3,000 acres of lettuce, tomatoes, and cantaloupes. "All the farmers in this area will be ruined." As for Chem Waste's claims that its incinerator would be 99.99 effective in burning 100,000 tons of toxic material a year, *El Pueblo* notes that even if they accepted that, which they don't, the incinerator would still put ten tons of deadly ash into the air annually. "Chem Waste says that's acceptable," protests farmer Dick Newton, a resident of the town of Stratford. "What right does it have to force me to breathe highly toxic dust?"

El Pueblo has hammered away at local authorities who have denied the mostly Spanish-speaking members their rights. In addition to charging Chem Waste with discriminatory siting of the incinerator, *El Pueblo's* suit also charged the Kings County Board of Supervisors with running a discriminatory public participation process. "The Kings County Board of Supervisors likes to hold public hearings in Hanford, thirty-five miles away from Kettleman City because they know that field hands can't get off work and make the long drive to attend the daytime meetings," says Espy Maya. "And when they did attend in the evenings, the farm workers couldn't understand anything because the meetings were always conducted in English, and the critical documents, some 3,000 pages of them, were never translated into Spanish."

El Pueblo protested these undemocratic hearings in a mass rally last fall when more than 1,000 people packed into Kettleman City. The Reverend Jesse Jackson and Congresswoman Maxine Waters led the community in a march on Chem Waste and shut down the landfill for a day. Officials from Kings County claimed that Greenpeace and other "outside agitators" orchestrated the march, manipulating residents for their radical goals.

This accusation infuriates Apolonia Jacobo, a farm worker and member of *El Pueblo*. "Chem Waste is the outsider. Nobody from Chem Waste lives in Kettleman City. Their lawyers and representatives all drive in from Fresno and Hanford. The only reason why supervisors bow to them is money. Chem Waste's taxes pay for about 8 percent of the Kings County budget."

In December 1991, Kettleman residents scored a major victory in court. State Superior Court Judge Jeffrey Gunther ruled that Chem Waste and Kings County had failed to provide adequate information on the air pollution effects of the toxic burner. The judge also ordered county officials to prepare and translate an extended summary of the environmental impact report into Spanish so that Kettleman residents could study it. In 1992 bids by Chem Waste to begin construction have twice been rejected by the judge. Construction on the incinerator is already years behind schedule. Now it may never be built. The people celebrated their victory with a mariachi party. "We Mexican people have made a difference," says Mary Lou Mares. "We have changed. Five years ago you would never have seen us challenging a big company like Chem Waste. Now we're not afraid. We know how to fight. We're in this for the long haul."

15

The campaign organized by *El Pueblo* to stop the toxic incinerator signals an important change in the nation's controversy over hazardous waste disposal. The group's actions have garnered coverage in numerous national magazines and newspapers, as well as on national television news programs.

In other countries, such as India and Brazil, poor people have long spearheaded movements to stop harmful development and environmental destruction. Now, in the United States, the contribution of poor people to environmental social justice, once seen by the public as the exclusive province of white middle-class activists, is no longer invisible.

Mares explains, "We're in a country where we can be heard if we speak up. Many of us still believe that we can't talk, that we have to stay quiet, that we can't beat the government. But we can win. If we speak as a group, we can be heard."

UNDERSTANDING THE TEXT

1. In your own words, define the term "environmental racism" (para. 4).

2. How, in the view of Kettleman City activists involved in the controversy over toxic-waste disposal in their community, did the political process obstruct rather than invite their participation?

3. How did Chem Waste's proposal to build a toxic-waste incinerator in Kettleman City unite a number of traditionally divided and sometimes hostile interests?

EXPLORING AND DEBATING THE ISSUES

1. This essay was originally published in 1992. Conduct a research project to learn what has happened since Chem Waste first planned to build a toxic-waste incinerator in Kettleman City.

2. While the residents of Kettleman City oppose the location of a toxic-waste incinerator in their community, America annually produces vast quantities of toxic waste that requires disposal. In class, form teams and debate whether Kettleman City is an appropriate location for this purpose.

3. Read or reread Glen Browder's "Guiding the Great Experiment: California's Recall and America's Democratic Destiny" (p. 435), and write an essay in which you assess the extent to which the opposition to Chem Waste is an example of "direct democracy."

4. Read or reread Gary Snyder's "Cultivating Wildness" (p. 256), then analyze whether the experience of Kettleman City verifies, negates, or complicates Snyder's vision of a public policy that meets the needs of both the environment and economic development.

The First

GARY SOTO

Gary Soto (b. 1952) has emerged as one of California's leading voices in contemporary poetry and short-story writing. Having grown up in Fresno, Soto offers a Central Valley view of California literature, one that he often injects with his Latino background and heritage. In this poem, Soto sadly reflects on the first Californians, the Native Americans whose world was swept away by the European conquest, never, this poem concludes, to return. The author of numerous collections of poetry and short stories, Soto's recent works include *Baseball in April and Other Short Stories* (1990), *Chato's Kitchen* (1995), *New and Selected Poems* (1995), *Buried Onions* (1997), and *Petty Crimes* (1998). This poem is from *New and Selected Poems*.

After the river
Gloved its fingers
With leaves
And the autumn sunlight
Spoked the earth   5
Into two parts,
The villagers undid
Their houses,
Thatch by thatch,
And unplucked   10
The stick fences
That held grief
And leaned from the wind
That swung their way.
What the sun raised—   15
Squash and pumpkin,
Maize collared
In a white fungus—
They left, for the earth
Was not as it was   20
Remembered, the iguana
Being stretched
Into belts
The beaver curling
Into handbags;   25
Their lakes bruised
Gray with smoke

That unraveled from cities.
Clearing a path
Through the forest,   30
A path that closed
Behind them
As the day opened
A smudge of its blue,
They were the first   35
To leave, unnoticed,
Without words,
For it no longer
Mattered to say
The world was once blue.   40

UNDERSTANDING THE TEXT

1. In a prose paragraph, summarize the sequence of events that Soto poetically describes.
2. What does Soto mean in lines 21–25: "the iguana / Being stretched / Into belts / The beaver curling / Into handbags"?
3. What is the effect of the short line structure of this poem?

EXPLORING AND DEBATING THE ISSUES

1. Write a poem of your own about the effects that human beings have had on California's natural environment. Share your poem with your class.
2. Soto concludes his poem by saying "For it no longer / Mattered to say / The world was once blue" (ll. 38–40). In an essay, agree, disagree, or expand on this statement. To develop your ideas, you can consult any of the readings in this chapter.
3. In class, discuss the use of color and imagery in this poem. How do they contribute to Soto's message?
4. The people whom Soto calls "the first" (l. 35) are not all gone. California Indians continue to live in modern society, seeking to preserve what is left of their sacred territories. Conduct a research project to determine how particular California Indians, such as the Chumash, are involved in current land-use issues.

Paradise Lost

VICTOR DAVIS HANSON

Like many Californians, **Victor Davis Hanson** is alarmed by the current state of the state: electricity shortages, overpopulation, water wars, traffic gridlock, over-crowded state colleges and universities. His indictment is comprehensive. But un-like many Californians, Hanson believes that the solution to our problems is to do what our Californian forefathers did—to build more dams, universities, electric power plants, and freeways: "you must build and get dirty," Hanson warns not only his fellow Californians but his fellow Americans as well, who, he fears, may be lured to destruction by California's "sirens of the affluent society." A professor of classics at California State University, Fresno, Hanson's books include *The Land Was Everything* (2000), *An Autumn of War: What America Learned from September 11 and the War on Terrorism* (2002), *Carnage and Culture: Landmark Battles in the Rise to Western Power* (2002), and *Mexifornia: A State of Becoming* (2003).

L ike that of many Third World countries, California's electrical grid can now fail with little notice. Rolling blackouts leave households in the dark, university classes canceled, and families without essential appli-ances. The most elemental responsibility of a humane and liberal society—the ability to shield its citizenry from the age-old banes of dark-ness and cold—we in California cannot always meet. We sue in the most ingenious ways over the environmental and aesthetic consequences of power production. We are eloquent in our endless debates in the state legislature over the wisdom of regulatory oversight. And we show moving public concern about the effects of outages on our poor and aged.

But for all that rhetoric, we still cannot guarantee accessible and rea-sonably priced heat, light, and power to our citizens. Not since the robed philosophers of Rome and Greece bickered and harangued each other by lamplight has history seen such a sophisticated preindustrial society as our own.

California is no longer a public of 20 million or even 25 million souls, but will soon exceed 35 million. For all our self-inflicted calamities, immi-grants, both foreign and domestic, are still pouring into the state. Some-thing must soon give in a sea of vast conflicting agendas. Our apparent birthright of sprawling suburbs with rye lawns, pools, residential lakes, and golf courses cannot exist alongside millions of acres of irrigated agriculture—at least not in the Mediterranean climate and deserts of Cali-fornia. We can either water 30 million Californians to surfeit or continue to be the greatest food producer in the nation; we can no longer do both.

Our underground aquifers are tapped and our mountain runoff long ago claimed. Very soon, water shortages, rationing, and astronomical price spikes will make our current electricity calamity pale in comparison. Water, even more so than power, is necessary for life—and for the good life it must flow in great abundance. Meanwhile, Californians talk of restoring uninterrupted rivers and streams for their rafts, fish, scenic hikes, and bays. But they would do better first to ensure that there will be enough water in their taps and toilets.

The effects of the impending crisis in education are not as obvious as darkened streets and empty taps, but they reveal our state's same inability to act—as well as the growing paradox between the lifestyle we demand and the honesty and sacrifices we shun. California's institutions of higher education—the marvelous tripartite system of junior colleges, state universities, and elite universities that was once the envy of the nation—are in paralysis. At some California state university campuses, 30 percent to 40 percent of the course offerings are now remedial in nature. In response, we advocate ending the SAT as a criterion for admission. Classes taught by part-time faculty nearly approach the number of those offered by professors.

Since we will not, or cannot, open new campuses—our faculties are more concerned over ethnic diversity and therapeutic curricula—there is no guarantee that we can educate and train a new generation to maintain the next link in the chain of an increasingly strained civilization. Just as we suck power from other states for our insatiable electrical appetite, so perhaps we will soon export our burgeoning youth to be educated by the rest of you.

Our transportation woes mirror the sorry state of our universities. That our two great airports, San Francisco and Los Angeles, are habitually backlogged and in dire need of expansion is no surprise, given the dysfunctional nature of American air travel these days. But our highways may be even in worse shape. Quite literally we have no continuous north-south freeway of three lanes in the entire state.

The older State Route 99 and U.S. 101 freeways are in places not free at all, little more than highways laced with cross traffic—one potted and patched right lane clogged by a caravan of trucks, the left a nightmarish obstacle course as cars dodge trucks passing other trucks. Our third artery, Interstate 5, is more a collapsed vein, in most places no wider than when it served 20 million Californians two decades ago. Perhaps Californians can make movies and boutique wines, but we apparently cannot guarantee safe and expeditious travel.

What has happened to our beloved state? We were not always so impotent and confused in the face of problems with power, water, and education. A drive along the central coast of California reveals massive though aged electrical generators at Moss Landing, Morro Bay, and

Diablo Canyon, impressive workhorses our forefathers built to ensure long ago that we might have power today. In contrast, we have not constructed a sizable generator in over a decade. For us, such factories are either too dirty, dangerous, costly, or unsightly—or perhaps in comparison to movies, wine, and computers, merely boring enterprises better left to the less sophisticated in Utah, Nevada, and Oregon.

Our network of Sierra dams and canals was once the most sophisticated in the world, as our forefathers sought to ensure a California of 10 million people plentiful irrigation, hydroelectric power, and recreational lakes. In contrast, our generation not only builds no more dams but fantasizes instead of tearing down those that were bequeathed so that more Sierra runoff might reach the ocean. Very soon we Californians shall learn that summers can be dark, dry, and hot all at once.

Over thirty years ago, we founded almost simultaneously three university campuses at Irvine, San Diego, and Santa Cruz; today, after years of delay and concerns over strange species of crustaceans and rare grasses, we cannot even start construction on a single proposed new campus at Merced. True, California State University at Monterey recently opened—but only because the federal government gave the state the free land and infrastructure of the old military base at Fort Ord. It remains to be seen whether its trendy curriculum of new-age technologies, "human communication," and multicultural studies will attract students in desperate need of a traditional liberal education.

Californians today are not like those of old who matched the state's natural beauty and bounty—timber, oil, farmland, temperate weather—with their own courage, genius, and strength to create an oasis. Now we dream and enjoy rather than build. Yet our comfortable lifestyle and romantic ideology are claiming the wages of our inaction and sloth.

We took for granted instantaneous, cheap electricity, but not dams, generators, or nuclear plants—to do so would have suggested that we were unkind to the environment or did not enjoy the natural beauty of white water and alpine air. We became infatuated with large sport utility vehicles and luxury pickup trucks, but not equally so with either freeways to accommodate such monstrosities or the oil wells to fuel them.

In one sense, we were parasites who lived off the work of our forefathers and the gifts of nature. And our unearned affluence spawned a smugness of the worst kind: Given water, power, universities, and roads by others, we dawdled, pontificated, and nuanced about the particulars of our own utopia. The result of this California disease is that we can save a newt but not always guarantee power in the library.

We are told that California is moving away from its traditional main-   15
stays of agriculture, construction, and manufacturing to an economy of
tourism, entertainment, and service. No doubt. But what is forgotten in
such a shift is that we are losing a type of Californian and a credo that
once made us what we were. Before you enjoy the new age of dot-coms,
drive in all-terrain cars, and equip your suburban house with new-age
gadgets—and feel guilty in the abstract about the cultural, environmental, and social consequences of such splendor—you must build and get
dirty, and, yes, battle an unforgiving nature that can bring cold, darkness, and thirst in its wake.

Beware, America, of the new Californians, sirens of the affluent society who would lure you onto our shoals.

UNDERSTANDING THE TEXT

1. What does Hanson mean by calling California a "sophisticated preindustrial society" (para. 2)?
2. Summarize the problems that Hanson believes are afflicting California.
3. Hanson is explicit in describing California's problems, but his discussion
   of the underlying causes is more implicit. In your own words, what are
   these underlying causes?
4. Define in your own words the "type of Californian" and the "credo that once
   made us what we were" (para. 15) that Hanson sees as having vanished.
5. Characterize Hanson's tone here. Does his style make you more or less
   sympathetic to his position?

EXPLORING AND DEBATING THE ISSUES

1. Hanson focuses primarily on the problems affecting power, water, transportation, and education in California. Select one of these categories,
   and write an essay in which you argue whether you believe that his dire
   description of the problems is accurate. To develop your ideas, you
   might consult Chapter 3 on education or this chapter.
2. In class, debate Hanson's supposition that overly zealous environmentalism is at the root of many of the problems he describes. Use the debate as
   a collective brainstorming session for writing your own argumentative
   essay on the topic.
3. Both Hanson and James J. Rawls ("California: A Place, a People, a
   Dream," p. 22) offer a broad overview of California's attractions and its
   problems. Compare and contrast the two essays, addressing not only the
   authors' positions but also their tone and argumentative strategies.
4. In class, discuss what specific cultural and social habits are behind Hanson's claim that "Now we dream and enjoy rather than build" and his

attack on "our comfortable lifestyle and romantic ideology" (para. 12). Use the discussion as preparation for writing an essay that evaluates the validity of Hanson's characterization of Californians today.

5. Assuming the perspective of Joan Didion ("Notes from a Native Daughter," p. 54), write a response to Hanson's claim that "we were parasites who lived off the work of our forefathers and the gifts of nature" (para. 14).

We're Only Confirming California's Flaky Image

ANITA CREAMER

At first, few commentators could believe it: an obscure California law that was written to remove from office corrupt or criminal governors was going to be used to ditch a governor who had broken no laws and who had been reelected only a year before. Then came the stampede of candidates, which seemed to include everyone in the state from former child star Gary Coleman to a no-longer-so-obscure porn star, from 1984 Olympics coordinator Peter Ueberroth to a former body builder turned actor named Arnold Schwarzenegger. For **Anita Creamer**, this was all craziness, but, somehow, business as usual in the flaky state where "politics has to be fun for people to pay attention." Anita Creamer is a staff writer for the *Sacramento Bee*, where this piece appeared on August 13, 2003.

Embrace the insanity, California.

Traditionally speaking, August—a slow news month—brings us fabulously weird news of the celebrity variety. Past stars of August's madness have included, in no particular order, Woody Allen, Michael Jackson, O. J. Simpson, Bill Clinton, and Gary Condit.

This year, we've outdone ourselves.

California's the star of the show, now that we've launched into a quickie election to determine whether to recall a governor reelected to office less than a year ago. This has served to confirm to the rest of the nation that Californians at best have a pitifully short attention span—and at worst are utter flakes. And the slate of gubernatorial wannabes only seals the deal: California, fruitcake central.

Why fight the stereotype?   5

We're long on entertainment and short on substance in this state. Let's not deny that reality; let's revel in it.

For example, so what if you cared so little about the future of the state that you didn't even bother to vote in last fall's election?

Millions of Californians don't get to the polls with any regularity, including, according to reports, Arnold Schwarzenegger, who'd like to be governor now. (No word yet on the voter participation record of porn king Larry Flynt, former child star Gary Coleman, L.A. billboard personality Angelyne, and the 200-plus other candidates huddled under the circus tent, vying for the state's highest office.)

Politics has to be fun for people to pay attention. Faced with ordinary, noncelebrity slates of candidates and less-than-thrilling issues to decide, people don't bother. They blame attack ads for alienating them and the candidates themselves for offending them. The truth is, they're simply not interested because they're not entertained. The ordinary day-to-day developments of politics and current events bore them senseless.

But every dozen years or so, Californians arise from their apathy,   10
look around at the state, get really upset—oh, no!—and decide the people in charge are to blame.

Popular uprisings ensue. It's a California tradition.

This, despite the years of voter lethargy that helped create the crisis of the moment—and despite the fact that regardless of who's in office, it's the lobbyists and consultants who really run the show. Too bad we can't vote them out.

The nation always watches and worries that the madness will spread.

At last, we're having fun. Woo-hoo, citizens! To the barricades, guys! It's party time in California!

So the rest of the country thinks we're shallow and immature. So   15
what? Let's go with it.

A word on the simmering frustration fueling the recall:

Sure, Californians are fed up—and frankly, not just with Gray Davis, the megabillion-dollar state budget deficit and politics as usual, but also with the country's sluggish economy, widespread corporate corruption and an array of troubling national and international issues. And you know what? If Davis is recalled, a large portion of these people will still be fed up, alienated and angry. It's who they are, regardless of bubble or bust.

Postrecall, they'll drift back into apathy for another dozen years, until it's time for the next great California citizen revolt, when they'll continue refusing to take the smallest shred of responsibility for having helped to create the complicated mess they suddenly and desperately want easy answers to fix.

California, a state frantically in need of a caring and patient therapist.

Instead, we have Arnold. And, of course, Arianna Huffington, Peter   20
Ueberroth, and the rest of the stars of our entertaining summer carnival.
Who knows what any of them stands for? Hey, who cares?

Party on, dudes.

UNDERSTANDING THE TEXT

1. Describe Creamer's tone. How does it affect the persuasiveness of her argument about California's image?
2. Why does Creamer say that Californians should "revel" in being "short on substance" (para. 6)?
3. According to Creamer, where does political power in California really exist?
4. Why does Creamer say that California is "a state frantically in need of a caring and patient therapist" (para. 19)?

EXPLORING AND DEBATING THE ISSUES

1. Write an argument supporting, refuting, or modifying Creamer's contention that California voters are "simply not interested [in politics] because they're not entertained" (para. 9). To develop your argument, consult the other articles in this chapter.
2. Assume the perspective of Mark Baldassare ("Regional Diversity," p. 387), and write a response to Creamer's argument that California voters respond more to entertainment than to serious issues.
3. College students typically vote less often than other age groups (this pattern was true even in the recall election). Conduct a survey of students at your school, asking them about their voting habits. Use your results as evidence in an essay that assesses the extent to which students share the interest in politics as entertainment that Creamer describes.
4. Read or reread Andrew Murr and Jennifer Ordonez's "Tarnished Gold" (p. 383), and write an essay in which you assess the validity of Creamer's assertion that Californians are "long on entertainment and short on substance" (para. 6).

Guiding the Great Experiment

California's Recall and America's
Democratic Destiny

GLEN BROWDER

Here it is: proof that what happens in California is bound to affect the rest of the nation. Writing for the *Anniston Star*, an Alabama newspaper, shortly after the 2003 gubernatorial election, **Glen Browder**, himself a former Alabaman Congressman, analyzes the election of Arnold Schwarzenegger and recall of Gray Davis and cautiously likes what he sees. For Browder, the great recall election of 2003 represents the response of an increasingly diverse polity to the pressures of change, signaling the emergence of a "centrifugal democracy" through which a neopopulist insistence for direct democracy is challenging traditional representative governmental institutions. While legitimate, in Browder's opinion, such a movement can also "wreak havoc," making it all the more important that Californians and non-Californians pay thoughtful attention to what is happening. Eminent Scholar in American Democracy at Jacksonville State University and Distinguished Visiting Professor of National Security Affairs at the Naval Postgraduate School in California, Glen Browder served in the U.S. Congress from 1989 to 1997 and is the author of *The Future of American Democracy: A Former Congressman's Unconventional Analysis* (2002).

Now that the dust has settled, maybe it's time we ask what's the real meaning of California's recall experience?

Is it simply voter anger? The energy/economy/budget/immigration crisis? Vengeance against an unpopular politician? The star power of a celebrity antipolitician?

Is there anything worthwhile to be learned from a state that unceremoniously dumps a sitting governor that it just reelected within the past year? Could anybody else among the hundred-plus official wannabees—including the unflashy second-in-command, the muscular movie star, a porno queen, a smut peddler, a former child star—govern California successfully? Is it possible to think seriously about California democracy while snickering about "Conan the Governor," "Governor Terminator," and "Honorable Gropinator"?

Does the recall of Gray Davis (D) and the anointing of Arnold Schwarzenegger (R) help or hurt President George Bush's reelection prospects?

(Closer to home, should Alabama Governor Bob Riley start worrying   5
about being kicked out of office?)

Actually, amid all the questions, conjecture, and snickering, there's a valuable civics lesson here that the American people can learn about themselves and their historic democratic experiment.

435

First, however, we should admit that there's no one, true, simple explanation for the California recall earthquake; it's a very complicated situation involving a variety of causes and symptoms. Second, maybe it's time to cease snickering; the recall is a legitimate part of the California constitutional system and Governor-Elect Schwarzenegger deserves a chance to show what he can do. Third, we can ignore partisan spin about Bush and Election 2004; in terms of political life, the presidential election is a long, long way off, and there's no telling what will take place between now and then. (Finally, forget about recalling Governor Riley; there's no constitutional option in Alabama.)

Most important, we should recognize that the Golden State recall movement is a legitimate, progressive phenomenon of state and national interest and perhaps long-term, systemic consequence for the Great Experiment of American democracy. While California is not perfectly analogous to broader America, its trending society, politics, and government are worth noting as we assess similar, more slowly developing pressures on our national democratic experiment. In other words, America (just like California) is changing fundamentally; and we all can learn from this West Coast experience in direct democracy.

The California Analogy   The essence of my California analysis is that this state is an unfolding precedent for America in its cultural, political, and governmental transformation. Specifically, a very large, diverse, dynamic California is experiencing increased confrontation between popular movements (such as public recall, initiative, and referendum) and traditional governance (embodied in elected politicians and institutions in Sacramento). The Golden State is going through inevitable systemic challenges slightly ahead of the rest of us; and Californians seem to be struggling—pretty distemperately—in that process.

Growing Forces of Centrifugal Democracy   In transformational termi-   10
nology, the California system evidences the cumulating forces and disruptive pressures of centrifugal democracy. Power, influence, and energy are spinning outward (away from traditional, centralized, governmental leaders and political institutions) to "the people" wherever and however they choose to aggregate and conduct their daily lives. This centrifugal phenomenon generally exerts itself in two prominent patterns—subculturalism (in the form of societal diversity, divergence, dissentience) and neopopulism (in the form of aggressive direct democracy initiatives newly enhanced through modern technology). Actually, California has been experiencing these forces for some time, having escaped crisis thus far through vibrant social and economic growth. But now the state's

republican experiment seems gridlocked, pressed democratically beyond its governing capacity.

Tendency toward Democratic Dysfunction   Particularly in a large, diverse system such as California, the centrifugal forces of subculturalism and neopopulism can wreak havoc; and much of the state's contemporary distemper—not just the recall movement—can be traced to raw conflict between an established system of representational government and the public's penchant for direct democracy initiatives. A representational republic is a time-proven albeit imperfect brand of democracy, and direct popular mechanisms can be useful adaptations; however, combined in uncoordinated, confounding manner, these dueling approaches tend toward democratic dysfunction. If a large, diverse society wants to augment historic republican government with self-governing plebiscites, then that process must be attempted in deliberative fashion rather than a series of rogue democratic attacks—with differing societal factions employing competitive assaults—on stubborn, resistant, professional politicians.

A Choice for California   Perhaps the most immediate item atop Governor Schwarzenegger's agenda thus should be statewide discussion about "what California means" culturally and "how California democracy should work" politically and governmentally. California's leaders, parties, media, and citizens need to consider redesigning their democratic experiment to more effectively incorporate diverse, popular participation in the traditional policy process; and the next few months present prime opportunity to debate a choice between two very different versions of that experiment—contentious feudalism or collaborative deliberation—in the twenty-first century.

A Lesson for America?   As for the rest of us (including Alabama in that "us"), the West Coast situation certainly merits close attention. The Golden State is a developing vision of our democratic destiny; and the lesson thus far is that the historical experiment fares poorly when direct democracy raucously confronts and confounds representational government.

Considering important demographic changes and the surge of centrifugal democracy throughout the American system, it is possible that, in the next few decades, the American people will rethink various substantive concepts of their public life (maybe debating anew the ideas of national community and universal, fundamental freedoms) and representational aspects of their national experiment (for example, reforming the electoral college and maybe experimenting with a national referendum). Therefore, it is critical that America learn something positive from the California experience about reconciling confrontations and contradictions in our transforming Great Experiment.

The recall movement has trumped traditional politics in California; 15
and we now await—some eagerly, some anxiously—the hybridized governance of direct/representative democracy in that contentious land. Perhaps, over the next few years, the West Coast vanguard will provide a transformational model for national society. In the meantime, the analogous dynamics of the contemporary California political system provide some useful points of caution and guidance about important developments—the interplay among cultural diversity, representational governance, and direct democracy—in the American political system.

Most Americans, leaders and citizens alike, recognize the unsettling possibilities of recall, initiative, and referendum; but direct democracy (to some degree and in some form) is, inevitably and increasingly, part of our future. Maybe it's time to consider expanding our Great Experiment— within a constructive, deliberative framework—to include greater public participation in our democratic destiny.

UNDERSTANDING THE TEXT

1. In this selection, Browder shifts his tone several times. Study his tone throughout the essay. What is the effect of the tonal shifts?

2. Why does Browder see California as a microcosm of the United States?

3. In your own words, what does Browder mean by "centrifugal democracy" (para. 10) and "representational government" (para. 11)?

4. What message does Browder believe that the recall election should send to the nation?

EXPLORING AND DEBATING THE ISSUES

1. Compare and contrast Browder's postrecall perspective with Anita Creamer's prerecall discussion ("We're Only Confirming California's Flaky Image," p. 432). To what extent does Browder, an Alabaman, confirm Creamer's belief that the recall "has served to confirm to the rest of the nation that Californians at best have a pitifully short attention span— and at worst are utter flakes" (p. 432, para. 4)?

2. In class, brainstorm specific examples of "subculturalism" and "neopopulism" that Browder says constitute "centrifugal democracy" (para. 10). Then, in your own essay, write an argument supporting, refuting, or modifying Browder's contention that those two patterns of political action lead to "democratic dysfunction" (para. 11).

3. Browder suggests that the state should engage in a "discussion about 'what California means' culturally and 'how California should work' politically and governmentally" (para. 12). Select one of these topics, and write your argument about "what California means" or "how California should work."

4. In an essay, analyze whether you find Browder's characterization of California's impact on America's political system to be realistic or exaggerated.

Researching the Issues

1. Rent a videotape or DVD of the movie *Chinatown*, and write a critique of the film's accuracy in presenting California's water politics. Support your critique with additional library research on the history of California water development.

2. Research a local land-use controversy (such as a proposed housing development in an environmentally sensitive area, a freeway expansion project, or a landfill near a residential zone). As part of your research, interview both opponents and proponents, and use your results to formulate an argument supporting or opposing the proposal you choose.

3. Marc Reisner's report on the history of the Kesterson Reservoir was published in 1986. Research the current status of the reservoir, and report on the changes, if any, that have occurred since Reisner's book appeared.

4. Because there are no new sources of water for California, conservation will have to be part of future water planning in the state. Form a research team, and investigate the state's plans for water conservation. To assist your research, visit the websites of the California Urban Water Conservation Council (http://www.cuwcc.com), the California Department of Water Resources (http://www.dwr.water.ca.gov), and your local municipal water district.

5. Managing California includes managing the threats caused by the state's vulnerability to natural disasters, such as earthquake and wildfires, that have become an explicit feature of land-use policy in California. Research the ways in which the land-use policies in your town or region respond proactively to these dangers, and use your findings as a basis of an essay in which you evaluate the adequacy of these policies.

6. In 2001 and 2002, California faced a cataclysmic energy crisis brought on by deregulation of the industry. Form teams, and research different aspects of this crisis (such as the effect of deregulation and its economic and political consequences). Use the class's collective research as

the basis of your own assessment of the long-term consequences of this crisis.

7. Research the origins of the 2003 gubernatorial recall election campaign. What were the motivations and goals of the recall's sponsors? And then research the outcome and the political and economic changes effected by the recall. Use your research as the basis of an essay in which you compare the goals with the results: to what extent was the outcome what was intended by the recall's inaugurators?

8. In the aftermath of the 2003 gubernatorial recall election, the news was filled with proposals for additional recall elections, including a recall of newly elected Governor Schwarzenegger. Research the status of such proposals, any new ones, and the state laws governing recall elections. Use your findings as the basis for an argument demonstrating, refuting, or complicating the proposition that the recall provisions in the state constitution are being used inappropriately.

9. A supermajority, or two-thirds vote, is required for all bond measures that would raise taxes (these typically are intended to raise funds for such services as education, libraries, police, or public parks). The state legislature must pass the annual state budget with the same percentage. Research the pattern of success for such bond measures in the last few years and the legislature's annual budget negotiations, which typically last months after the mandated deadline of June 30. Use your findings to support your argument about whether the supermajority stipulation should be altered. (You should keep in mind that in March 2004, Ballot Measure 56, which would have allowed the state budget to pass the legislature with a 55 percent majority, lost at the polls.)

ACKNOWLEDGMENTS (*continued from p. ii*)

Anonymous, "Notes of a California Expedition" from *To the Golden Shore,* edited by Peter Browning. Lafayette, CA: Great West Books, 1995. Reprinted by permission of Great West Books.

Mark Baldassare, "Regional Diversity" from *California in the New Millennium: The Changing Social and Political Landscape.* Copyright © 2000 The Regents of the University of California. Reprinted by permission of the University of California Press.

Glen Browder, "Guiding the Great Experiment: California's Recall and America's Democratic Destiny," Special to *The Anniston (AL) Star,* October 26, 2003. Reprinted by permission of the author. www.futureofamericandemocracy.org.

Patricia Leigh Brown, "The New Chinatown? Try the Asian Mall" from *The New York Times,* March 24, 2003. Copyright © 2003 by The New York Times Co. Reprinted with permission.

David Carle, "Sprawling Gridlock" from *Water and the California Dream: Choices for the New Millennium.* Copyright © 2000 by David Carle. Reprinted by permission of Sierra Club Books.

Contra Costa Times editors, "Revamp Immigration," from *Contra Costa Times,* June 4, 2003. Reprinted with permission of Ed Diokno/Contra Costa Newspapers, Inc.

Anita Creamer, "We're only confirming flaky image" from *The Sacramento Bee,* August 13, 2003. Copyright © 2004 by The Sacramento Bee. Reprinted by permission of The Sacramento Bee.

Joan Didion, "Notes from a Native Daughter" from *Slouching Toward Bethlehem.* Copyright © 1965, 1968 by Joan Didion. Reprinted with the permission of Farrar, Straus, & Giroux, Inc.

Chitra Banerjee Divakaruni, "Yuba City School" from *Black Candle: Poems about Women from India, Pakistan, Bangladesh.* Copyright © 1991 by Chitra Banerjee Divakaruni. Reprinted with the permission of CALYX Books.

J. A. English-Lueck, "Identified by Technology" from *cultures@siliconvalley.* Copyright © 2002 by the Board of Trustees of the Leland Stanford Jr. University. All rights reserved. Used with the permission of Stanford University Press, www.sup.org.

David Fine, "Endings and Beginnings: Surviving Apocalypse" from *Imagining Los Angeles: A City in Fiction,* University of New Mexico Press, 2000. Reprinted by permission of the University of New Mexico Press.

James J. Flink, "The Automobile Age in California" from *The Automobile Age.* Copyright © 1988 by The Massachusetts Institute of Technology. Reprinted with the permission of The MIT Press.

Sylvia S. Fox, "Testing, Anyone?" from *California Journal,* March 1998. Copyright © 1998. Reprinted with the permission of the author and Information for Public Affairs, Inc.

Ernesto Galarza, excerpt from *Barrio Boy.* Copyright © 1971 by University of Notre Dame Press, Notre Dame, Indiana, 46556. Reprinted by permission of the University of Notre Dame Press.

Mario Garcia, "My Latino Heart." Reprinted with the permission of the author.

Ramon Garcia, "Suburbia" from *Quarry West,* annual literary journal of the University of California, Santa Cruz. Reprinted by permission of the author.

Joel Garreau, "Edge City: Irvine" from *Edge City.* Copyright © 1991 by Joel Garreau. Used by permission of Doubleday, a division of Random House, Inc.

Jewelle Taylor Gibbs and Teiahsha Bankhead, "Coming to California: Chasing the Dream" from *Preserving Privilege.* Copyright © 2001 by Jewelle Taylor Gibbs and Teiahsha Bankhead. Reproduced with permission of Greenwood Publishing Group, Inc., Westport, CT.

Dana Gioia, "California Hills in August" from *Daily Horoscope*. Copyright © 1986 by Dana Gioia. Reprinted with the permission of Graywolf Press, Saint Paul, Minnesota.

Victor Davis Hanson, "Paradise Lost" from *The Wall Street Journal.* Copyright © 2001 Dow Jones & Company, Inc. All rights reserved. Reprinted by permission of Dow Jones & Company, Inc.

Gerald W. Haslam, "The Water Game" from *The Other California: The Great Central Valley in Life and Letters.* Copyright © 1990 by Gerald W. Haslam. Reprinted with the permission of the University of Nevada Press.

Pierrette Hondagneu-Sotelo, "Maid in L.A." from *Doméstica: Immigrant Workers Cleaning and Caring in the Shadows of Affluence.* Copyright © 2001 The Regents of the University of California. Reprinted by permission of the University of California Press.

James D. Houston, "In Search of Oildorado" from *Californians: Searching for the Golden State* (New York: Alfred A. Knopf, 1982). Copyright © 1982 by James D. Houston. Reprinted with the permission of the author.

Jeanne Wakatsuki Houston and James D. Houston, "Manzanar, U.S.A." from *Farewell to Manzanar.* Copyright © 1973 by James D. Houston. Reprinted by permission of Houghton Mifflin Company. All rights reserved.

Carol Jago, "Something There Is That Doesn't Love a List" from the *American Educator,* Winter 2001. Reprinted with permission from the author and the *American Educator,* the quarterly journal of the American Federation of Teachers, AFL-CIO.

Alice Kahn, "Berkeley Explained" from *Multiple Sarcasm.* Copyright © 1985 by Alice Kahn. Reprinted with permission of Ten Speed Press, Berkeley, CA. www.tenspeed.com.

KQED, "Feature Q&A on The Castro" with Peter Stein, KQED Public Television (http://www.kqed.org/w/hood/castro/castroqa.html), courtesy of KQED, Inc. (1998).

William Langewiesche, "Invisible Men" from *The New Yorker,* February 23 and March 2, 1998. Copyright © 1998 by William Langewiesche. Reprinted with the permission of Darhansoff & Verrill Literary Agency.

Judith Lewis, "Interesting Times" from *Another City: Writing from Los Angeles* by David L. Ulin. Copyright © 2001 by Judith Lewis. Reprinted by permission of City Lights Books.

Jack Lopez, "Of *Cholos* and Surfers" from *Cholos & Surfers: A Latino Family Album.* Reprinted with the permission of Capra Press, P.O. Box 2068, Santa Barbara, CA 93120.

David Mas Masumoto, "As If the Farmer Died" from *Epitaph for a Peach: Four Seasons on My Family Farm.* Copyright © 1995 by David Mas Masumoto. Reprinted with the permission of HarperCollins Publishers Inc.

Lesli A. Maxwell, "Cuts Crush College Promise" from *The Sacramento Bee,* August 11, 2003. Copyright © 2004 The Sacramento Bee. Reprinted with permission of The Sacramento Bee.

William McClung, "Arcadia and Utopia" from *Landscapes of Desire: The Los Angeles of Anglo Imagination.* Copyright © 2000. Reprinted by permission of the University of California Press.

John McWhorter, "It Shouldn't Be Good to Have It Bad." Copyright © 2002 The Washington Post Company. Reprinted by permission of the author.

Donald E. Miller, Jon Miller, and Grace Dyrness, "Religious Dimensions of the Immigrant Experience" from *Southern California and the World,* edited by Eric J. Heikkila and Rafael Pizarro. Copyright © Eric J. Heikkila and Rafael Pizarro. Reproduced with permission of Greenwood Publishing Group, Inc., Westport, CT.

Deborah Miranda, "Indian Cartography" from *Indian Cartography*, Greenfield Review Press, 1999. Reprinted by permission of Greenfield Review Press.

Andrew Murr and Jennifer Ordonez, "Tarnished Gold" from *Newsweek*, July 28, 2003. © 2003 Newsweek, Inc. All rights reserved. Reprinted with permission.

Gary Paul Nabhan, "The Palms in Our Hands" from *Gathering the Desert*. Copyright © 1985 The Arizona Board of Regents. Reprinted by permission of the University of Arizona Press.

Ruben Navarrette Jr., "'Well, I Guess They Need Their Minority'" from *A Darker Shade of Crimson*. Copyright © 1993 by Ruben Navarrette Jr. Used by permission of Bantam Books, a division of Random House, Inc.

Sandra Nichols, "A Win-Win for the High School Exit Exam" from *Education Matters: Essays on California Education — and Beyond*, May 17, 2003. Reprinted with permission of Sandra Nichols, MA, Speech and Language Pathology.

Frank Norris, "The 'English Courses' at the University of California" from *Frank Norris: Novels and Essays*, edited by Donald Pixer. Published by the Library of America, New York. First published in "The Wave," November 28, 1896. This material is in the public domain.

Michael J. O'Brien, "Orange County Historian" from *Gridlock: An Anthology of Poetry about Southern California*, edited by Elliot Fried, Applezaba, 1990.

Dana Polan, "California through the Lens of Hollywood" from *Reading California: Art, Image, and Identity 1900–2000*. Copyright © 2000 by Museum Associates, Los Angeles County Museum of Art and the Regents of the University of California. Reprinted by permission of the Los Angeles County Museum of Art.

James J. Rawls, "California: A Place, a People, a Dream" from Claudia K. Jurmain and James J. Rawls (eds.), *California: A Place, a People, a Dream* (San Francisco: Chronicle Books/The Oakland Museum, 1986). Reprinted with the permission of The Oakland Museum.

Marc Reisner, "Things Fall Apart" from *Cadillac Desert, Revised and Updated*. Copyright © 1986, 1993 by Marc P. Reisner. Reprinted with the permission of Viking Penguin, a division of Penguin Putnam, Inc.

Richard Rodriguez, "Proofs" from *To the Promised Land*. Copyright © 1988 by Richard Rodriguez. Reprinted by permission of Georges Borchardt, Inc., for the author.

Mike Rose, "A Visit to Edwin Markham Intermediate School" from *Possible Lives: The Promise of Public Education in America*. Copyright © 1995 by Mike Rose. Reprinted by permission of Houghton Mifflin Company. All rights reserved.

Gary Snyder, "Kitkitdizze, A Node in the Net," pp. 252-263 from *A Place in Space* by Gary Snyder. Copyright © 1995 by Gary Snyder. Reprinted by permission of Counterpoint Press, a member of Perseus Books, LLC.

Gary Soto, "The First" from *New and Selected Poems*. Copyright © 1995 by Gary Soto. Reprinted with the permission of Chronicle Books, San Francisco.

Denise S. Spooner, "A New Perspective on the Dream: Midwestern Images of Southern California in the Post–World War II Decades" from *California History,* Spring 1997. Copyright © 1997. Reprinted with the permission of the California Historical Society.

Richard Steven Street, "Battling Toxic Racism" from *Organizing for Our Lives: New Voices from Rural Communities* by Richard Steven Street and Samuel Orozco (NewSage Press, 1992). Reprinted by permission of NewSage Press.

Nayereh Tohidi, "Iranian Women and Gender Relations in Los Angeles" from *Irangeles.* Copyright © 1993 The Regents of the University of California. Reprinted by permission of the University of California Press.

Nathanael West, "The Day of the Locust: Chapter 1" from *Miss Lonelyhearts & The Day of the Locust*. Copyright © 1939 by Estate of Nathanael West. Reprinted by permission of New Directions Publishing Corp.

Nancy Wride, "Vietnamese Youths No Longer Look Homeward" from the *Los Angeles Times*, April 4, 1994. Copyright © 1994 by the *Los Angeles Times*. Reprinted with permission from TMS Reprints.

Yeh Ling-Ling, "State Needs a 'Time-Out' from Mass Immigration" from *The Mercury News*, September 5, 2002. Copyright © Yeh Ling-Ling, www.diversityalliance.org. Reprinted with the permission of the author.

Connie Young Yu, "The World of Our Grandmothers" from Asian Women United of California (ed.), *Making Waves: An Anthology of Writings by and about Asian American Women* (Boston: Beacon Press, 1998). Copyright © 1989 by Asian Women United of California. Reprinted by permission.

Art

"California Dream" orange crate label. Permission courtesy Villa Park Orchards Association, Fillmore, CA. Photo: John Walcek, courtesy Placentia Library, Placentia, CA.

"California Quarter," 2003. Photo: AP/Wide World Photos.

"Group of young Japanese girls arriving at Long Beach, CA, railroad station, April 4, 1942." Gift of Dr. and Mrs. Charles K. Ferguson, Japanese American National Museum, Los Angeles. (19.116.1).

"Hollywood" by Thomas Hart Benton, 1937. Tempera with oil on canvas mounted on panel. The Nelson-Atkins Museum of Art, Kansas City Missouri. (Bequest of the artist) F75-21/12. Photo by Jamison Miller. Art © T. H. Benton and R. P. Benton Testamentary Trusts/UMB Bank Trustee/Licensed by VAGA, New York, NY.

Hollywood sign. Rufus F. Folkks/Corbis.

"Life's Best Mixture: Sun and Air and Gasoline" from *Sunset Magazine*, December 12, 1912, p. 76. Permission courtesy Sunset Magazine/photo courtesy California Historical Society, San Francisco.

"Map of North America Showing California as an Island" by William Grent, 1625. Courtesy of the Syndics of Cambridge University Library.

"Monarch, California's last wild grizzly and model for state flag." © California Academy of Sciences, San Francisco/Photo: Caroline Kopp.

"The New Order" by Ricardo Duffy, 1996. Screenprint. Los Angeles County Museum of Art, Art Museum Council Fund/photo © 2004 Museum Associates/LACMA. Permission courtesy Ricardo Duffy.

"Oildorado Day World Champion Well Pullers," Courtesy Kern County Library, Bakersfield, CA.

"Petaluma Fields" by Willard Dixon, 1987. Oil on Canvas. Collection of California State Teachers Retirement System, Sacramento. Permission courtesy Willard Dixon, San Rafael, CA.

"Questa" orange crate label. This item reproduced by permission of The Huntington Library, San Marino, CA.

"Roadkill Warrior: Last of His Tribe" by Judith Lowry, 2001. Acrylic on canvas. Photo: Rob Wilke. Permission courtesy Judith Lowry.

"Strip Mall, Los Angeles, 1996" by Dennis Keeley. Permission courtesy Dennis Keeley.

"Time for Another Tuition Increase, Sir?" by Paul Fell. From *National Crosstalk*, Fall 2000. Permission courtesy Paul Fell.

"View of the San Gabriel Mountains, Pasadena, and the Raymond Hotel" from *Southern California: Its Climate, Trails, Mountains, Canyons, Watering Places, Fruits, Flowers, and Game. A Guidebook* by C. F. Holder, 1888. Courtesy of The Bancroft Library, University of California.

"Warning Sign, Almaden Quicksilver County Park, San Jose, CA." Photograph by Robert Dawson © 1996. Permission courtesy Robert Dawson.

Index of Authors and Titles